ENCYCLOPEDIA OF EDUCATION

SECOND EDITION

EDITORIAL BOARD

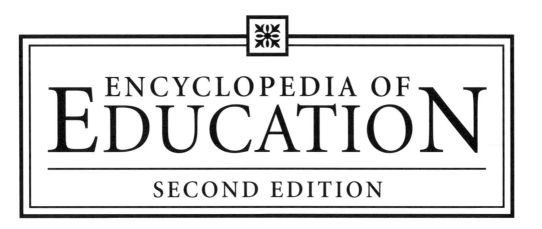

ENCYCLOPEDIA OF EDUCATION

SECOND EDITION

James W. Guthrie, Editor in Chief

VOLUME

3

Faculty–Hutchins

MACMILLAN
REFERENCE
USA™

THOMSON
————————
GALE

New York • Detroit • San Diego • San Francisco • Cleveland • New Haven, Conn. • Waterville, Maine • London • Munich

Encyclopedia of Education, Second Edition

James W. Guthrie, Editor in Chief

©2003 by Macmillan Reference USA. Macmillan Reference USA is an imprint of The Gale Group, Inc., a division of Thomson Learning, Inc.

Macmillan Reference USA™ and Thomson Learning™ are trademarks used herein under license.

For more information, contact
Macmillan Reference USA
300 Park Avenue South, 9th Floor
New York, NY 10010
Or you can visit our Internet site at
http://www.gale.com

For permission to use material from this product, submit your request via Web at http://www.gale-edit.com/permissions, or you may download our Permissions Request form and submit your request by fax or mail to:

Permissions Department
The Gale Group, Inc.
27500 Drake Road
Farmington Hills, MI 48331-3535
Permissions Hotline: 248-699-8006 or
800-877-4253 ext. 8006
Fax: 248-699-8074 or 800-762-4058

While every effort has been made to ensure the reliability of the information presented in this publication, The Gale Group, Inc. does not guarantee the accuracy of the data contained herein. The Gale Group, Inc. accepts no payment for listing; and inclusion in the publication of any organization, agency, institution, publication, service, or individual does not imply endorsement of the editors or publisher. Errors brought to the attention of the publisher and verified to the satisfaction of the publisher will be corrected in future editions.

LIBRARY OF CONGRESS CATALOGING-IN-PUBLICATION DATA

Encyclopedia of education / edited by James W. Guthrie.—2nd ed.
  p. cm.
Includes bibliographical references and index.
  ISBN 0-02-865594-X (hardcover : set : alk. paper)
1. Education—Encyclopedias. I. Guthrie, James W.
  LB15 .E47 2003
  370'.3—dc21   2002008205

ISBNs
Volume 1: 0-02-865595-8
Volume 2: 0-02-865596-6
Volume 3: 0-02-865597-4
Volume 4: 0-02-865598-2
Volume 5: 0-02-865599-0
Volume 6: 0-02-865600-8
Volume 7: 0-02-865601-6
Volume 8: 0-02-865602-4

Printed in the United States of America
10 9 8 7 6 5 4 3 2

F

FACULTY AS ENTREPRENEURS

Although entrepreneurship is a term seldom associated with educational institutions, faculty entrepreneurial activities are not a recent development. Known as consulting, sponsored research, knowledge commercialization, academic capitalism, or moonlighting, the multifaceted phenomenon of faculty entrepreneurship has existed for some time on campuses. Nevertheless, little research has been undertaken on this topic. In part, this reflects the lack of consensus on what constitutes faculty entrepreneurship as well as the secrecy that often surrounds outside activities of faculty members. The objectives of this chapter are threefold. First, the reasons underlying the growth of faculty entrepreneurship are addressed. Second, a definition of what constitutes faculty entrepreneurship is provided. Finally, advantages and disadvantages of faculty entrepreneurship are discussed.

Growth of Faculty Entrepreneurship

Traditionally, faculty members have provided industry, communities, governments, and other entities with their professional expertise and research findings. Faculty entrepreneurial activities date back to the medieval period when members of law and medical faculties engaged in professional practice to supplement their university salaries. Later, in the seventeenth century, university faculty played an important role in the formation of the pharmaceutical industry in Germany. In the initial decades of the twentieth century, the growth of the service element in the university mission, coupled with technological advancement, provided a strong impetus for faculty entrepreneurship by linking research to the needs of businesses. The railroad industry, petroleum refining, and polymer industries are just a few examples of commercial endeavors that benefited from these linkages. In the second half of the twentieth century, entrepreneurial activities of university faculty played an instrumental role in the development of the computer industry and also contributed to the emergence and rapid growth of biotechnology.

What is new at the start of the twenty-first century is the rapid increase in the scope and intensity of faculty entrepreneurial activities as well as the normative shift towards an emerging academic culture that values equally the intellectual and commercial potential of faculty expertise and research. The growth of faculty entrepreneurship is spurred by the synergetic interaction of pull and push factors. The pull factors include the rise of the knowledge-based economy, technological advancement, and globalization, which generate demands for faculty expertise, thus creating new opportunities for scholars and scientists to engage in commercial activities. The push factors, such as waning public support for higher education, increasing research costs, institutional reward systems that tend to encourage faculty to generate external revenues, and state pressures on institutions to become more active actors in economic development, motivate faculty to engage in paid outside activities, thus augmenting the supply of academic entrepreneurship. Widely publicized successes of university entrepreneurs in biotechnology and new legislations permitting the commercialization of knowledge further encourage faculty entrepreneurship.

What Is Faculty Entrepreneurship?

Faculty entrepreneurship involves efforts to transform individual academic expertise and research results into intellectual property, marketable commodities, and economic development, thereby enhancing faculty remuneration and professional status. An essential characteristic of a faculty entrepreneur is entrepreneurial expertise, which is described by Sheila Slaughter and Larry L. Leslie as the ability to recognize the market potential of faculty research and other intellectual property, to cultivate commercial partnerships, and to negotiate contracts.

Historically, faculty entrepreneurship has followed two basic patterns. The first represented the application of specialized expertise to solve specific industrial problems by chemical and electrical engineering faculty in the late nineteenth century. Contractual research, consulting, and external teaching generally followed this pattern. The second pattern, which originated at the Massachusetts Institute of Technology in the 1920s, involved the patenting, development, and commercialization of faculty discoveries. In many instances, this involved the formation of firms by researchers—especially in the engineering and life sciences.

Magnus Klofsten and Dylan Jones-Evans suggest the following typology of contemporary faculty entrepreneurial activities: (1) large-scale science projects funded through public grants or industrial sources; (2) research contracted to solve specific problems; (3) consulting or the sale of personal expertise directed towards the resolution of identifiable problems; (4) patenting/licensing; (5) the formation of new firms or organizations to exploit the results of academic research; (6) external teaching; (7) commercial selling of research products; and (8) provision of testing and calibration services to external entities.

The most common types of entrepreneurial activities undertaken by faculty members appear to be consulting, contractual research, large-scale science projects, and external teaching. Although types and levels of entrepreneurial activities vary by academic fields, faculty in the disciplines of engineering, computer science, medicine, agriculture, chemistry, and biotechnology are the most likely to be engaged in entrepreneurial activities, followed by social scientists, natural scientists, and humanists. Traditional activities such as consulting appear to be distributed evenly across the disciplines while activities such as the formation of private firms, including those involved in the patenting or commercialization of new products and processes, are dominated most often by the life sciences and engineering.

Advantages of Faculty Entrepreneurship

Individual faculty members, their institutional employers, clients, and the society at large share in the benefits of faculty entrepreneurship. The obvious benefit for the individual faculty member is supplemental income, which improves faculty economic status and sometimes contributes to additional research funding. Furthermore, outside activities often enhance the continuing education of faculty, help to ensure currency of teaching and research, and provide faculty with external affirmation of their expertise and greater peer recognition.

The primary benefit of faculty entrepreneurship for clients is efficient access to sources of specialized expertise. Moreover, sponsors often have first access to research findings and privileged positions with respect to exclusive patent licenses. Involving faculty researchers in product commercialization also enables clients to gain a competitive edge in the marketplace by accelerating new product development and launching. Another important benefit is the cross-fertilization of ideas between industry and institutions of higher education. Synergies with respect to the training and development of staff may be significant as well.

Faculty entrepreneurial activities also benefit institutions. External funds secured by faculty entrepreneurs may supplement monies available to institutions for conducting basic research and offering improved grants or assistantships to graduate students. Permissive policies regarding faculty entrepreneurship enable institutions to recruit professors who otherwise would be inclined to opt for employment in private industry or government. Additionally, successful faculty entrepreneurs improve institutional visibility and reputation.

Faculty entrepreneurs take an active part in solving various social or community problems by providing their expertise to non-profit organizations and governmental agencies. Furthermore, academic entrepreneurship, especially efforts that involve start-up companies, plays an increasingly important role in regional and national economic development. On the whole, faculty entrepreneurial activities promote technological advancement and accelerate the transfer of knowledge from discovery to utilization, thus contributing to social progress.

Disadvantages of Faculty Entrepreneurship

On the negative side, faculty entrepreneurial activities may lead to situations involving conflicts of interest, commitment, or internal equity. Conflicts of interest are usually of a financial nature and may lead to biases in the design of research, the interpretation of results, publication delays and/or secrecy, as well as conflicts with student interests.

Conflicts of interest may arise when faculty entrepreneurs engage in activities to advance their own financial interests that might harm their institutional employer. The potential for conflicts of interest exists, for example, when faculty entrepreneurs use institutional resources for their outside activities or have financial interests in entities that do business with the institution.

A faculty entrepreneur may manipulate research design or fail to present accurate research results if the findings do not yield a profit or desired result for the sponsoring entity, and the dissemination of research findings may be unduly delayed or prevented on the grounds that proprietary information has to be protected in order to secure the competitive edge of the client. Another important, but often overlooked, conflict of interest involves student interests. Potential exists for faculty entrepreneurs to abuse their positions by using students as inexpensive labor or to exploit students' ideas without giving them credit. More subtle conflicts that also represent significant risks include steering student research toward topics that reflect the priorities of a faculty entrepreneur or corporate sponsor, or delaying student publications because of proprietary interests.

Conflicts of commitment between the role of the faculty entrepreneur and the role of teacher, researcher, or public servant merit attention. The central issue to consider when assessing possible conflicts of commitment is whether particular entrepreneurial activities negatively influence faculty teaching, research, and service productivity. Existing research provides mixed results and suggests that the relationships between entrepreneurial activities and faculty productivity are nonlinear, may vary across academic disciplines, and depend on the time spent on outside activities.

Conflicts of internal equity involve conflicts between the values of faculty as entrepreneur and faculty as collegian. Internal institutional practices increasingly favor academics engaged in entrepreneurial activities. These individuals tend to receive higher salaries and benefits as well as lower workloads than their nonentrepreneurial peers. These considerations, coupled with the unequal positioning of disciplines and institutions relative to the market, are potentially detrimental to collegiality and may exacerbate existing stratification between faculty, disciplines, and institutions.

Conclusion

Faculty members are increasingly pushed, encouraged, and provided with opportunities to take on new entrepreneurial roles. At a time when "entrepreneurship is the key to present and future institutional and cultural preference, approval, and legitimacy" (Slaughter and Leslie, p. 200), the ignorance of faculty entrepreneurship or attempts to hinder its development may contribute to intellectual stagnation or a loss of talent and knowledge from academia. Faculty entrepreneurial activities should be studied carefully and managed cautiously in order to maximize their benefits and minimize disadvantages.

See also: UNIVERSITY-INDUSTRIAL RESEARCH COLLABORATION.

BIBLIOGRAPHY

ALLEN, DAVID N., and NORLING, FREDERICK. 1991. "Exploring Perceived Threats in Faculty Commercialization of Research." In *University Spin-off Companies: Economic Development, Faculty Entrepreneurs, and Technology Transfer,* ed. Alistair M. Brett, David V. Gibson, and Raymond W. Smilor. Savage, MD: Rowman and Littlefield.

BIRD, BARBARA J., and ALLEN, DAVID N. 1989. "Faculty Entrepreneurship in Research University Environments." *Journal of Higher Education* 60(5):583–596.

BOYER, CAROL M., and LEWIS, DARREL R. 1985. *And on the Seventh Day: Faculty Consulting and Supplemental Income.* ASHE-ERIC Higher Education Report No. 3. Washington, DC: GWU, ERIC Clearinghouse on Higher Education/ASHE.

CAMPBELL, TERESA I. D., and SLAUGHTER, SHEILA. 1999. "Faculty and Administrators' Attitudes

Toward Potential Conflicts of Interest, Commitment, and Equity in University-Industry Relationships." *Journal of Higher Education* 70(3):309–352.

ETZKOWITZ, HENRY. 1983. "Entrepreneurial Scientists and Entrepreneurial Universities in American Academic Settings." *Minerva* 21(2–3):198–233.

ETZKOWITZ, HENRY; WEBSTER, ANDREW; and HEALEY, PETER., eds. 1998. *Capitalizing Knowledge: New Intersections of Industry and Academia.* Albany: State University of New York Press.

FAIRWEATHER, JAMES S. 1996. *Faculty Work and Public Trust: Restoring the Value of Teaching and Public Service in American Academic Life.* Boston, MA: Allyn and Bacon.

KLOFSTEN, MAGNUS, and JONES-EVANS, DYLAN. 2000. "Comparing Academic Entrepreneurship in Europe—The Case of Sweden and Ireland." *Small Business Economics* 14:29–309.

LINNEL, ROBERT H., ed. 1982. *Dollars and Scholars: An Inquiry into the Impact of Faculty Income upon the Function and Future of the Academy.* Los Angeles: University of Southern California Press.

LOUIS, KAREN S.; BLUMENTHAL, D.; GLUCK, MICHAEL E.; and SOTO, MICHAEL A. 1989. "Entrepreneurs in Academe: An Exploration of Behaviors Among Life Scientists." *Administrative Science Quarterly* 34(1):110–132.

MITCHELL, JOHN E., and REBNE, DOUGLAS S. 1995. "Non-Linear Effects of Teaching and Consulting on Academic Research Productivity." *Socio-Economic Planning Sciences* 29(1):47–57.

SLAUGHTER, SHEILA, and LESLIE, LARRY L. 1997. *Academic Capitalism: Politics, Policies, and the Entrepreneurial University.* Baltimore, MD: Johns Hopkins University Press.

ALEXEI G. MATVEEV

FACULTY CONSULTING

The central issue concerning faculty who consult with outside clients is the relationship of the faculty to the college or university that employs them. This relationship is evolving rapidly. The institutions first opposed faculty consulting, then tolerated it, next encouraged it, and then some even began to sponsor faculty consulting through organized programs of technical assistance to industry.

Three aspects of faculty consulting will be discussed in this entry: major issues associated with the practice; typical policies drawn up by institutions to guide relationships with faculty who consult; and characteristics of faculty who consult compared to those who do not, taking into consideration differences due to academic discipline. Also reported are findings about the amount of outside income faculty earn from consulting.

Issues

A continuing concern of employing institutions is the extent to which faculty who consult may be shortchanging their teaching responsibilities and restricting their opportunities to interact with students. Institutions may also be concerned that faculty who do outside consulting may have less time for curriculum development or departmental committee work.

In addition, the product of paid consulting work is generally the property of the clients who may keep the results proprietary and not make them available in the public domain. This is considered by many as contrary to the spirit of free inquiry which they believe should characterize the academic world.

From an institutional perspective, management issues may also arise about the extent to which college or university resources, such as office space or equipment, are used by faculty inappropriately for outside consulting projects. Further, involvement of students in outside consulting projects may need to be monitored to determine whether it constitutes a legitimate learning experience, a valuable internship with a potential future employer, or exploitation.

Faculty consulting contracts are considered by institutions to be personal agreements, but these contracts may create conflicts of interest with employing institutions or subject the institutions to risks. Consequently, some institutions provide reviews of the consulting contracts to ensure that the provisions recognize the preexisting obligations of the faculty to their primary employing institution, including the obligations to disclose new inventions and assign patent rights.

On the other hand, companies hiring faculty consultants may require that their company's proprietary information be kept confidential, and restrict disclosure and use of the information. This practice may not contribute to the free and open inquiry promoted in the academic world.

Thus, the ultimate issue with respect to faculty consulting is who benefits? Faculty benefit from consulting if they derive opportunities to strengthen their research, especially in fields where the leading edge of scientific inquiry is migrating to industry from academic institutions—because industry has more money. Faculty also benefit from consulting if they collaborate in meeting real-world challenges that may make their teaching more relevant and lively, which in turn benefits students. Consulting also gives faculty opportunities to supplement their income, which may be especially important in fields where there is a great, and growing, disparity between salaries earned in business and in the academic world. Consulting projects may also provide learning opportunities for students, and possibly employment opportunities working on practical projects. Institutions may benefit by building stronger business, community, and governmental relationships, which may lead in the long run to greater financial support. Indeed there is likely a complementary relationship between the reputation of faculty and that of their employing institutions: the better the reputation of the institution, the greater the recognition of the faculty they can attract; the greater the recognition of the faculty, the wider the range of consulting opportunities and the greater the amount of outside support faculty can garner for their institutions.

Financial and academic costs and other negative outcomes are also issues in assessing the value of faculty consulting to an academic institution. An institution has an interest in protecting itself from charges of abuse of the employment relationship by a faculty member consulting and inappropriately invoking the reputation of the institution. Apparent, and real, conflicts of interest sometimes arise that might affect faculty judgments about educational matters. Faculty otherwise engaged may become inaccessible to students or to other faculty. Outside agendas may distort academic priorities, leading to active student opposition, as in the 1960s when students objected to what they considered to be too great involvement of the faculty with defense contractors.

Policies

Faculty handbooks generally set forth the policies and procedures defining and governing consulting by their faculty with outside clients. These conditions are then incorporated into faculty employment contracts. Typically, these provisions apply only to full-time faculty, not part-time faculty, and apply during the nine-month academic year, including the summer months only if the faculty member is teaching during the summer session. The institution may not limit the amount of consulting done during periods when the faculty is not on the payroll (during the summer or on leave), but the institution's policies with respect to conflict of interest and restrictions on the use of institutional resources still apply. Faculty employment contracts typically allow faculty up to one day, or ten hours, a week—or four days a month—for outside consulting. More than that is considered to jeopardize the commitment to teaching, research, and service at the employing institutions.

Faculty consulting is subject to varying reporting requirements and oversight by the colleges and universities. Some boards of trustees require periodic reporting by the institution of the policies and procedures that cover faculty consulting and how they are enforced. They may consider the following:

- how faculty consulting is defined
- the types of clients served
- the nature of the services performed
- the amount of time that is spent consulting on a particular project
- the total amount of time spent consulting cumulated over the academic year
- the amount and sources of outside remuneration
- reimbursement of the institution for the use of institutional resources, facilities, or services

The board of trustees may also require an evaluation of the value of faculty consulting to their institution.

Some institutions require that faculty make annual reports of their outside consulting, but only of consulting that relates to their academic specialty, which consequently may raise a question about how broadly the specialty is defined. Some institutions have made a distinction between consulting for a single occasion that is reported annually after the fact, and consulting that is of a longer duration and

TABLE 1

Percentage of faculty who earn income from consulting by academic discipline, 1998	
Engineering	32.7
Business	26.2
Agriculture and home economics	25.4
Education	23.4
Social sciences	23.3
Fine arts	22.6
Natural sciences	18.6
Health sciences	17.9
Humanities	15.4
All other programs	22.2

SOURCE: Based on data from National Center for Education Statistics, National Survey of Postsecondary Faculty: 1999, Data Analysis System.

requires specific prior approval. Public institutions may take into consideration whether the consulting is for another state agency or for an outside client.

Institutions actively reaching out to their local business community have more recently begun to actually sponsor faculty consulting through formal technical assistance programs. The programs are characterized as community service programs which help local businesses and contribute more broadly to regional economic development.

Characteristics of Faculty Who Consult

At the start of the twenty-first century about one out of every five faculty members at American colleges and universities earns income from consulting or freelance work. Based on estimates derived from the 1999 National Survey of Postsecondary Faculty (NSOPF99) using the data analysis system of the National Center for Education Statistics, the percentage ranges by type of primary employing institution from 30 percent of faculty at private research institutions to only about half that, or 14 percent, at public two-year colleges. In general, a higher percentage of the faculty at all types of private institutions consult than do the faculty at counterpart public institutions.

The percentage of faculty who earn income from consulting also varies significantly by academic discipline. As shown in Table 1, the percentage ranges from 33 percent for engineering faculty to only 15 percent of faculty in the humanities.

The percentage of faculty who consult varies significantly by gender, age, and race. Considering gender, a much higher percentage of faculty men (23 percent) earn consulting income than do faculty women (17 percent). Considering age, a much higher percentage of faculty aged 35 and over (19 to 23 percent) earn consulting income than did those under the age of 35 (only 14 percent). Faculty aged 55 to 59 report the highest percentage earning consulting income (23 percent). Even 21 percent of the faculty aged 70 and over report consulting income. Consulting also varies by race/ethnicity, with only 13 percent of the faculty who are Asian reporting consulting income compared with 18 percent of the African Americans, 19 percent of the Hispanics, and 21 percent of the whites.

It might be expected that lower-income faculty would be using consulting to supplement their income. They do, but an even higher percentage of the higher-income faculty report earning consulting income. About 15 percent of those faculty with base salaries of $25,000 to $40,000 report earning consulting income compared with 34 percent of those with base salaries of $85,000 to $100,000. The opportunities to consult are much greater for those who are older, tenured, and have well-established reputations in their field.

The higher-income faculty also report earning much higher amounts of consulting income. Of those faculty who do earn consulting income, the amounts range from an average of about $4,000 for those who earn $25,000 to $40,000, rising progressively to about $19,000 for those faculty who earn $130,000 or more. Although the dollar amounts of consulting income rise steeply, the percentage of the base salary from the institution increases only from about 12 percent at the $25,000 to $40,000 range to about 14 percent at the higher income ranges. Faculty with the lowest base salaries from the institution, under $25,000, appear to be an exception, reporting about $8,500 in consulting income, which represents a considerably higher percentage of the base salary.

A slightly higher percentage of faculty (24 percent) who have had previous employment outside of higher education earn consulting income than those who do not (20 percent), a smaller difference than might be expected to result from prior connections with industry or government. Though consulting is likely to be covered by collective bargaining agreements, the consulting practices of union and nonunion members do not significantly differ. Seventeen percent of union members report earning consulting income, compared to 21 percent of those who are not members.

Impact of Consulting on the Faculty Commitment to Teaching and Research

The most heated debate over the extent of faculty consulting concerns the impact of consulting on teaching and research. The NSOPF99 survey data suggest that there is a positive relationship. Generally speaking, the higher the number of student contact hours per week, the higher the percentage of faculty who earn income from consulting. There is, however, a great difference depending on the level of students instructed. Eighteen percent of those instructing only undergraduate students reported consulting income, compared with 27 to 30 percent for those instructing graduate students.

Opportunities to consult are directly connected with faculty research. In general, the higher the amounts of research grants and contracts awarded to faculty, the higher the percentage of faculty who earn income from consulting. The percentage of faculty who earn income from consulting ranges from under 20 percent for those faculty with less than $10,000 in outside research grants and contracts to almost 40 percent for those with $100,000 or more.

Faculty with consulting income also reported comparatively higher rates of participation in unpaid activities at the institutions, including administrative duties, curriculum development, meeting with students, mentoring, and community service. On the other hand, these faculty reported comparatively lower rates of attending faculty meetings, holding office hours, grading papers, or attending athletic events. Thus, it appears that, in general, faculty who consult value their time and are less willing to spend hours on the bureaucratic aspects of academic work. They also appear to have less leisure time, indicating that faculty who consult are not shortchanging their students, but are simply busier.

The opportunities to consult appear to affect somewhat positively overall faculty satisfaction with their work. Of those faculty who are very satisfied with their salary and with their job security, a higher percentage earn consulting income than do those faculty who are very dissatisfied. The opposite is true considering satisfaction with the work load: a higher percentage of those who are dissatisfied report earning consulting income than do those who are satisfied.

Faculty who earn consulting income respond differently from those who do not when asked to contemplate the factors most important to them if they were to leave their institution. Among those faculty who reported the factors of more opportunities for advancement, greater opportunities to do research, and good research facilities and equipment, a higher percentage earned income from consulting than did those reporting the factors of salary level, benefits, or job security. Interestingly, faculty consulting apparently has little or no effect on interest in taking early retirement.

With faculty salaries slipping further below salaries of comparable professionals, it might be expected that the percentage of faculty who consult to supplement their income would be increasing. This is not the case, however. As cited earlier, about 20 percent of all faculty reported earning income from consulting in 1998, which is almost exactly the same percent as reported in 1992, and slightly lower than the 24 percent reported in 1987. While the extent of consulting is not increasing, the percent of faculty reporting income from self-owned businesses is increasing. Thus, faculty are not only consulting but also becoming more entrepreneurial. Indeed, one of the most important new phenomena in the academic world may be the transformation of the faculty consultant into the faculty entrepreneur.

See also: FACULTY AS ENTREPRENEURS; UNIVERSITY-INDUSTRIAL RESEARCH COLLABORATION.

INTERNET RESOURCES

BOYER, CAROL M., and LEWIS, DARRELL R. 1986. "Faculty Consulting and Supplemental Income." <www.ed.gov/databases/ERIC_Digests/ed284521.html>.

UNIVERSITY OF MASSACHUSETTS. 1997. "Policy on Conflicts of Interest Relating to Intellecual Property and Commercial Ventures." <www.umass.edu/research/ora/confl.html>.

UNIVERSITY OF MICHIGAN, SCHOOL OF ENGINEERING, OFFICE OF THE ASSOCIATE DEAN FOR ACADEMIC AFFAIRS. 2002. "Consulting Days Policies." <www.engin.umich.edu/academic affairs/consulting.html>.

CAROL FRANCES

FACULTY DIVERSITY

Race, ethnicity, and gender are the most common characteristics that institutions observe in order to measure faculty diversity. Individuals from various minority or racial/ethnic groups (e.g., American Indian/Alaskan Native, Asian/Pacific Islander, African American, and Hispanic) comprise nearly 30 percent of the population but account for only 15 percent of the professoriate. While females constitute 51 percent of the population; their representation in academe is 45 percent. An even broader approach to faculty diversity involves age, socioeconomic background, national origin, sexual orientation, and diverse learning styles and opinions.

Higher education institutions are generally concerned with structural diversity, which is the numerical representation of women and people of different racial and ethnic groups. Research confirms that institutions desiring to improve the campus climate for diversity must first increase the structural diversity of the institution. Increasing the structural diversity provides a "critical mass" of individuals from diverse social and cultural backgrounds who interact across racial/ethnic and gender groups. However, improving structural diversity alone will not enhance the environment that faculty encounter. Institutions must take steps to transform the psychological and behavioral climate if faculty diversity and all that it encompasses is to be achieved. For example, the diversity of thought and scholarship includes building a group of faculty with different opinions who work within competing paradigms and whose differences serve to foster intellectual growth.

The Growth of Faculty Diversity as an Ideal

In order to understand why diversity has become a worthy goal, one must first understand that, until the latter part of the twentieth century, the professoriate in the western world was composed almost exclusively of wealthy, heterosexual males of Caucasian descent. Prominent studies in 1969 and 1975 include data on changes in faculty background characteristics, but a 20-year lag in the observation of some of these variables left a critical void in the literature pertaining to the changing professoriate. Additionally, all of the previous studies discussed the social origins of faculty across both age and gender. However, none of these studies reported differences in socioeconomic background relative to race.

Although the face of America began to evolve dramatically in the late 1800s with the introduction of newly-freed slaves into society and, later, with the tremendous infusion of immigrants, the representation of various racial/ethnic groups in the ranks of the professoriate remained at insignificant levels throughout much of the twentieth century. It was not until the 1973 court decision of *Adams v. Richardson*, which mandated an increase in minority faculty at public institutions, that noticeable numbers of minority faculty were hired at predominantly white institutions (PWIs). However, historically black colleges and universities (HBCUs), hispanic serving institutions (HSIs) and tribal colleges (TCs) have employed faculty from diverse racial and ethnic groups since their inceptions. Moreover, at least one-third of minority faculty members are employed at HBCUs, HSIs, and TCs, further minimizing their presence at PWIs. For example, 48 percent of full-time African-American faculty work at HBCUs.

The passage of equal employment legislation and the momentum of the civil rights movement in the 1960s stimulated greater participation of women in the workforce. By 1970, 23 percent of all faculty members were females. The next three decades saw female faculty increase to 39 percent in 1993, of which 33 percent were full-time. While encouraging, these gains have been mitigated by the disproportionate representation of women at two-year institutions in non-tenured and part-time positions.

Prompted by affirmative action and encouraged by influential idealists in academe, most colleges and universities continue to espouse the notion that having a diverse faculty can be a positive force in the attempt to increase the breadth of scholarship and the pursuit of knowledge in general. Though some institutions have committed themselves to this ideal in varying degrees and with differing interpretations, the goal of fostering a more diverse faculty seems to have widespread appeal in mainstream postsecondary institutions, though the move from idea to praxis is an arduous one.

Barriers in the Academic Workplace

Some studies reveal that this paucity of diversity may simply be related to a problem of supply and demand. For example, African Americans, Native Americans, and Hispanics are underrepresented in graduate schools, resulting in the fact that there are relatively few people from these groups available for faculty positions. Therefore, it would seem that an obvious solution would be to increase the supply by encouraging persons of color to attain doctoral degrees, especially in those fields where their numbers are the smallest (e.g., engineering). Opponents of the

FIGURE 1

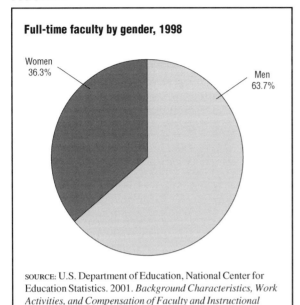

Full-time faculty by gender, 1998

Women 36.3%

Men 63.7%

SOURCE: U.S. Department of Education, National Center for Education Statistics. 2001. *Background Characteristics, Work Activities, and Compensation of Faculty and Instructional Staff in Postsecondary Institutions: Fall 1998.* Washington, DC: U.S. Department of Education.

FIGURE 2

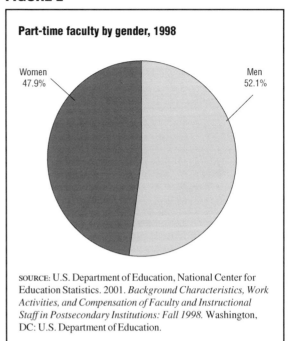

Part-time faculty by gender, 1998

Women 47.9%

Men 52.1%

SOURCE: U.S. Department of Education, National Center for Education Statistics. 2001. *Background Characteristics, Work Activities, and Compensation of Faculty and Instructional Staff in Postsecondary Institutions: Fall 1998.* Washington, DC: U.S. Department of Education.

educational pipeline approach maintain that a greater supply will not remove the other barriers within academia that hinder institutional and individual efforts at promoting growth in faculty diversity across gender and racial/ethnic groups.

A review of the literature reveals several common barriers that women and minority faculty encounter across all institutional types: (1) Isolation: Faculty members are often excluded—intentionally or otherwise—from the informal social networks that exist in academia; (2) Tokenism: In some departments, senior faculty believe that they have fulfilled their obligation to diversify once they have hired one minority or female faculty member; (3) Lack of Professional Respect: Senior faculty members often assume that women and minority faculty members are less capable of scholarly pursuits; thus women and minority faculty members are often denied opportunities for research and other scholarly pursuits; (4) Occupational Stress: Minority and female faculty members are often expected to serve on various committees related to diversity as well as to serve as "token" representatives on departmental and institutional committees. They are further burdened when students seeking role models seek them out for mentoring and support; and (5) Institutional Racism: Tenured, mainstream faculty often denigrate research relative to female and minority issues

by viewing such work as less than scholarly, especially if the research is published in periodicals outside of the mainstream. Often the expression "brown on brown research" is used to describe the work of minority faculty members who research issues related to their own minority group. In a related manner, obstacles encountered by women and minority faculty can be likened to many other underrepresented groups if the concept of diversity is broadened to encompass attributes such as age, national origin, and sexual orientation.

Research reveals that an overwhelming majority of post-secondary institutions emphasize structural diversity by recruiting faculty across gender and racial/ethnic groups. However, the fact remains that many of these same institutions provide little—if any—organized support to attain the goal of faculty diversity.

Demographics

In 1998, the National Center for Education Statistics (NCES) reported that 57 percent of faculty were full-time, of which 64 percent were men and 36 percent were women (see Figure 1). However, males and females were almost evenly divided among part-time faculty with women and men accounting for 48 and 52 percent, respectively (see Figure 2). Also, NCES reported that racial/ethnic faculty members repre-

FIGURE 3

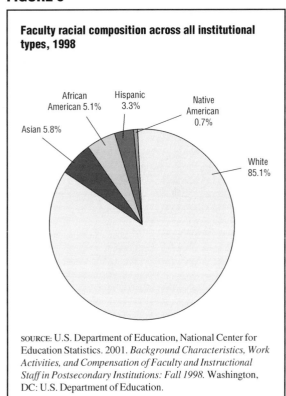

Faculty racial composition across all institutional types, 1998

African American 5.1%
Hispanic 3.3%
Native American 0.7%
Asian 5.8%
White 85.1%

SOURCE: U.S. Department of Education, National Center for Education Statistics. 2001. *Background Characteristics, Work Activities, and Compensation of Faculty and Instructional Staff in Postsecondary Institutions: Fall 1998.* Washington, DC: U.S. Department of Education.

sented 15 percent (Asians, 6%; African Americans, 5%; Hispanics, 3%; Native Americans, 1%) of all faculty across all institutional types (see Figure 3). Nonetheless, minority faculty are still disproportionately underrepresented in higher education since they constitute 29 percent of the general population. In contrast, Caucasians comprise 69 percent of the general population but account for 85 percent of the teaching force.

Even though findings from the Martin Finkelstein, Robert Seal, and Jack Schuster (1998) analysis of the National Study of Postsecondary Faculty database confirm the professoriate is becoming more diverse with representation across gender, race and ethnicity, the findings also reveal that there is still a disproportionate number of faculty who are from moderate to high socioeconomic backgrounds. With regard to educational background, research reveals that new career entrants' fathers are better educated (40%) than the fathers of senior faculty (32%). Likewise, as senior faculty increased in age, the educational level of both parents decreased. For example, only 11 percent of fathers of new faculty in the youngest age category (less than 35 years old) held less

than a high school diploma, compared to 24 percent of faculty in the same age range who had already attained the status of senior faculty. This held true for mothers of faculty as well, with 22 percent of senior faculty having mothers with less than a high school diploma versus 12 percent of new career entrants. However, this division across age could be indicative of the increased educational aspirations of society after World War II.

When gender is considered, women of the new academic generation make up 49 percent of all faculty members, while in the senior generation females comprise only 29 percent of the faculty population. Despite the increasing number of women entering the profession, the higher socioeconomic status of the new academic generation continues to be attributed to males. Among new career entrants, both female and male faculty are equal (40% and 41%, respectively) relative to their fathers' possession of bachelor's degrees. Additionally, race is also better-represented in the new generation, with minority faculty members comprising 17 percent of the faculty compared to 12 percent in the senior generation.

See also: ACADEMIC LABOR MARKETS; AFFIRMATIVE ACTION COMPLIANCE IN HIGHER EDUCATION; AMERICAN ASSOCIATION OF UNIVERSITY PROFESSORS; MULTICULTURALISM IN HIGHER EDUCATION.

BIBLIOGRAPHY

AGUIRRE, ADALBERTO, JR. 2000. *Women and Minority Faculty in the Academic Workplace: Recruitment, Retention, and Academic Culture.* San Francisco: Jossey-Bass.

FINKELSTEIN, MARTIN J.; SEAL, ROBERT K.; and SCHUSTER, JACK H. 1998. *The New Academic Generation: A Profession in Transformation.* Baltimore: Johns Hopkins University Press.

GAINEN, JOANNE, and BOICE, ROBERT, eds. 1993. *Building a Diverse Faculty.* San Francisco: Jossey-Bass.

GARCIA, MILDRED. 1997. *Affirmative Action's Testament of Hope: Strategies for a New Era in Higher Education.* New York: State University of New York Press.

GLAZER-RAYMO, JUDITH. 1999. *Shattering the Myths: Women in Academe.* Baltimore: Johns Hopkins University Press.

SCHRECKER, ELLEN. 2000. "Diversity on Campus." *Academe* 86(5).

TURNER, CAROLINE; GARCIA, MILDRED; NORA, AMAURY; and RENDON, LAURA, I. 1996. *ASHE Reader: Racial and Ethnic Diversity in Higher Education.* Needham Heights, MA: Simon and Schuster.

TURNER, CAROLINE; SOTELLO, VIERNES; and MYERS, SAMUEL L., JR. 2000. *Faculty of Color in Academe: Bittersweet Success.* Needham Heights, MA: Allyn and Bacon.

U.S. DEPARTMENT OF EDUCATION, NATIONAL CENTER FOR EDUCATION STATISTICS. 2001. *Background Characteristics, Work Activities, and Compensation of Faculty and Instructional Staff in Postsecondary Institutions: Fall 1998.* Washington, DC: U.S. Department of Education.

INTERNET RESOURCE

U.S. CENSUS BUREAU. 2002. "Profile of General Demographic Characteristics: 2000." <www.census.gov/prod/cen2000/dp1/2kh00.pdf>.

BARBARA J. JOHNSON
KYLE J. SCAFIDE

FACULTY MEMBERS, PART TIME

Part-time faculty are employed by colleges and universities to work on some basis that is less than a full-time contract. Some part-time faculty teach a single course, while others teach more than one course per academic term. Some part-timers have only a brief relationship with their employing institution and are used to fill a specific short-term instructional need, while others teach on a part-time basis for many years in order to meet ongoing educational needs. Part-time faculty provide a variety of educational services and represent an important part of the instructional work force in American higher education.

In the fall of 1998, 43 percent of college and university faculty worked part time—a proportion that grew steadily during the preceding three decades. In 1987, for example, 33 percent of all faculty worked part time, while in 1970 only 22 percent of college and university professors worked part time.

Although part-time faculty play important roles throughout higher education, their numbers vary by type of institution and academic field. Community colleges employ the highest percentage of part-time faculty. In 1997, 65 percent of the faculty in community colleges worked part time. In contrast, only about 33 percent of the faculty in four-year institutions worked on a part-time basis. The use of part-time faculty also varies across different academic fields. According to the U.S. Department of Education, in the fall of 1998 well over one-third of the faculty worked part time in such academic areas as fine arts (49%), education (40%), and the humanities (38%). In contrast, less than one-fourth of the faculty worked part time in areas such as the natural sciences (23%), engineering (20%), and agriculture and home economics (14%). In U.S. colleges and universities, women hold a proportionately greater number of part-time than full-time faculty positions. In 1997 women accounted for 36 percent of full-time faculty positions and 47 percent of part-time faculty posts.

The growth of part-time faculty positions appeared to have leveled off in the 1990s. Between 1992 and 1998 the percentage of part-time faculty in American higher education grew only 1 percent, from 42 percent to 43 percent. This decline in the part-time faculty growth rate may represent an attempt by institutions to achieve balance in their use of part-time and full-time faculty appointments. Even though the rate of growth of part-time positions had moderated, in the early twenty-first century part-time faculty represented a larger component of the instructional work force in colleges and universities than ever before.

Reasons for the Growth of Part-Time Faculty

Several reasons account for the increased employment of part-time faculty, including a leveling off of public subsidies of higher education, the aging and *tenuring in* of the full-time faculty, and an oversupply of qualified potential instructors in many fields. The overriding reasons for the heavy reliance on part-time faculty, however, appear to be the expansion of community colleges, and particularly the financial hard times and increased competition that have made many institutions reluctant to make long-term financial commitments to full-time tenure-eligible faculty positions. Hiring an instructor on a part-time basis usually costs substantially less than a full-time appointment, and also provides the flexibility institutions wish to preserve in a time of rapid change.

Who Are the Part-Time Faculty?

Most part-time faculty have full-time jobs in primary occupations outside of higher education—or they are partially or fully retired from another career. In addition, some part-time faculty are freelancers who have built a career around several part-time teaching positions, often at more than one institution. Another segment of the part-time teaching force includes aspiring professors who hope to achieve full-time, permanent academic employment eventually. In research done in the 1990s, Judith Gappa and David Leslie found that part-time faculty are far less likely than full-time faculty to have doctoral degrees. They also found, however, that while only 16 percent of part-time faculty had doctorates at the time of the study, 10 percent had terminal professional degrees (degrees that indicate that the recipient has reached the end of formal education in his/her field) and 52 percent had one or more master's degrees. Gappa and Leslie concluded from their analysis that "part-time faculty are well qualified by reason of preparation and experience to teach the courses they are assigned—principally undergraduate courses" (1996, p. 9).

What Do Part-Time Faculty Do?

Typically, part-time faculty have a more limited range of responsibilities than their full-time colleagues. Although part-time faculty roles vary somewhat by discipline and type of institution, most teach primarily lower division, introductory level, or skill building courses (e.g., elementary modern languages, English composition, science laboratories). Often, advanced courses for majors and graduate students are reserved for regular full-time faculty. Many part-time faculty whose primary employment is outside of higher education teach courses directly related to their careers in professional fields such as accounting, journalism, allied health, or education. In addition, part-time faculty typically play no role, or a very restricted role, in curriculum development and institutional governance. Due to the limited nature of their appointments, many are not available to assist students outside of class or to provide long-term career guidance. Furthermore, the American Association of University Professors (AAUP) reports that part-time faculty spend less time on class preparation and have lower publication rates than do full-time faculty. These findings suggest that part-time faculty fill more limited roles involving fewer responsibilities than their full-time faculty counterparts.

Benefits of Employing Part-Time Faculty

Part-time faculty bring valuable expertise and experience to their institutions at relatively low cost. Those who come from primary careers outside of higher education bring to the classroom the added benefit of a practitioner's perspective and direct contact with their employment sector. Gappa and Leslie (1993) cite evidence that part-time faculty, in general, perform just as well in the classroom as their full-time colleagues. By hiring temporary faculty on a per-course basis, institutions avoid the added costs of fringe benefits, professional development, and office and laboratory facilities that usually accompany full-time faculty appointments. By hiring part-time instructional staff members, institutions also maintain the flexibility to respond quickly to changing student interests and community needs.

Disadvantages of Employing Part-Time Faculty

Opponents of heavy reliance on part-time faculty cite numerous reservations about this academic employment practice. While recognizing the financial benefits of using part-time academic staff, critics cite the "hidden costs" of substituting part-time faculty for more involved and accessible full-time faculty. Essentially, critics are concerned about the impact of part-time faculty employment on: (1) students and educational program quality, (2) full-time faculty and institutional governance, and (3) the careers of the part-time faculty themselves. Critics fear that using part-time faculty to teach many introductory level courses disadvantages students who may need extra assistance as they make the transition to college. Because part-time faculty are usually compensated only for the courses they teach, and often do not have offices, they can be quite inaccessible to students needing out-of-class assistance. When large numbers of part-time faculty work at an institution, the responsibility for advising students, developing and monitoring academic programs, and institutional policymaking falls more heavily on the full-time faculty. Reduced program coherence is a potential negative consequence when a large segment of those providing instruction are not involved in governance, program planning, and student advising. Extensive use of part-time instructors thus increases the workload and limits the flexibility of the full-time permanent faculty.

Finally, those opposed to heavy use of part-time faculty argue that part-time faculty themselves are disadvantaged by their temporary employment status. They contend that the "payment-per-course system" inadequately rewards part-time teaching and provides little incentive for scholarship or continued professional development. Likewise, the uncertainty associated with short-term contracts makes it extremely difficult for many part-time faculty to plan a stable career and advance professionally. The result of dual academic-employment tracks is a two-class faculty in which members of the upper class have opportunities, resources, and benefits unavailable to their second-class (part-time) counterparts. Gappa and Leslie concluded from their national study of part-time faculty that, for the most part, part-timers "do not feel 'connected to' or 'integrated into' campus life. Instead, they feel powerless, alienated, and invisible" (1996, p. 19).

Contemporary Issues

Full-time employment with a long-term commitment to the faculty role is the standard model of academic life. Most policies and practices in higher education are based on this conception of faculty work. Part-time faculty do not fit this model, and they are disadvantaged to some extent by their aberrant status. At many institutions they are treated as exceptions to the norm rather than as key members of the academic work force who perform essential services and make important contributions to their institutions' missions.

Trends in the academic profession suggest that colleges and universities can no longer afford to possess such a narrow and unrealistic view of the roles part-time faculty play in the higher education system of the twenty-first century. Experts on part-time faculty recommend that colleges and universities fully integrate part-time faculty into their academic community in order to maintain a seamless academic work force committed to the same mission and striving to achieve shared goals. The literature on part-time faculty suggests that several important issues must be addressed before a diverse but unified faculty becomes reality.

Compensation. The per-course pay system commonly used to compensate part-time faculty takes a narrow view of the faculty role. It rewards the formal teaching process, but fails to encourage or compensate important faculty functions such as out-of-class contact with students, professional development activity, or curriculum development work. One alternative strategy is to compensate part-time faculty according to the percentage of full-time work they are hired to perform. This alternative can provide part-time faculty with compensation for student advising, governance involvement, or other important faculty functions. A more generous approach to part-time faculty compensation may be a key element of efforts to strengthen the diverse faculty work force common on campuses today.

Working conditions. Typically, part-time faculty have access only to whatever support services, office space, and supplies are available after the needs of regular full-time faculty are met. Rarely do part-timers receive offices, computers, or consistent secretarial support. Such difficult working conditions can hamper their job performance, and some institutions that acknowledge the important roles part-time faculty perform are taking steps to enhance their working conditions.

Professional growth and job security. Gappa and Leslie found that part-timers typically receive far less support for their professional development than do full-time faculty. Institutions that rely heavily on part-time faculty in a time of rapid changes in knowledge and educational technology cannot afford to neglect their professional development. Faculty advocates argue that colleges and universities should make provisions to support the professional development of part-time faculty who serve important functions, especially over the long term. Job security is also an ongoing concern for many part-time faculty, who often work on an unpredictable "as needed" basis. In cases where part-time faculty meet ongoing instructional needs, the opportunity for an extended contract that recognizes long service and successful performance would benefit both the individual instructor and institution that depends on the part-timer's services.

Academic freedom. Academic freedom is a core value of higher education. For many professors this freedom is protected by tenure status, which prevents the termination of a faculty contract without due process. Most part-time faculty are not eligible for tenure, however, and lack this basic academic freedom protection. To maintain the vitality of the academic enterprise when part-timers play an increasingly important role, the AAUP believes that appeal and grievance procedures should be in place to prevent violations of part-timers' rights as academic professionals.

Professional status. Most literature on part-time faculty acknowledges their second-class status. Labels such as *invisible faculty* and *subfaculty* clearly give the impression that part-timers are lower forms of academic life. These status distinctions are harmful to the academic community and belie the valuable contributions part-time faculty make to higher education. Advocates for part-time faculty have recommended a variety of initiatives, such as those listed above, to raise the status of part-timers and strengthen the academic profession as a whole.

The Future

In 2000 contingent faculty working part-time or in temporary full-time positions made up the majority of the American academic profession, and there is no evidence suggesting that colleges and universities will reduce their use of part-time faculty in the foreseeable future. Researchers who have studied the part-time faculty issue in depth, as well as faculty interest groups, have called for reforms in personnel policies and practices to move part-time faculty from their marginal status to the center of the academic profession. They argue that enhancing the work lives of part-time faculty will, in the long run, strengthen the quality of the educational system and better serve the needs of a society increasingly dependent on lifelong learning.

See also: COLLEGE TEACHING; FACULTY ROLES AND RESPONSIBILITIES.

BIBLIOGRAPHY

AMERICAN ASSOCIATION FOR UNIVERSITY PROFESSORS. 1998. "Statement from the Conference on the Growing Use of Part-Time and Adjunct Faculty." *Academe* 84(1):54–60.

BALDWIN, ROGER G., and CHRONISTER, JAY L. 2001. *Teaching Without Tenure: Policies and Practices for a New Era.* Baltimore: Johns Hopkins University Press.

GAPPA, JUDITH M., and LESLIE, DAVID W. 1993. *The Invisible Faculty.* San Francisco: Jossey-Bass.

GAPPA, JUDITH M., and LESLIE, DAVID W. 1996. "Two Faculties or One? The Conundrum of Part-Timers in a Bifurcated Work Force." Inquiry No. 6. Washington, DC: American Association for Higher Education Forum on Faculty Roles and Rewards.

LEATHERMAN, COURTNEY. 2000. "Part-Timers Continue to Replace Full-Timers on College Faculties." *Chronicle of Higher Education* 46(21).

LESLIE, DAVID W. 1998. "Part-Time, Adjunct, and Temporary Faculty: The New Majority?" Report of the Alfred P. Sloan Conference on Part-Time and Adjunct Faculty. Williamsburg, VA: College of William and Mary, School of Education.

LESLIE, DAVID W., ed. 1998. *The Growing Use of Part-Time Faculty: Understanding Causes and Effects.* San Francisco: Jossey-Bass.

WILSON, ROBIN. 2001. "Proportion of Part-Time Faculty Members Leveled Off From 1992 to 1998, Data Show." *Chronicle of Higher Education* 47(34).

ZIMBLER, LINDA. 2001. *Background Characteristics, Work Activities, and Compensation of Faculty and Instructional Staff in Postsecondary Institutions: Fall 1998.* Washington, DC: U.S. Department of Education, National Center for Education Statistics.

ROGER G. BALDWIN

FACULTY PERFORMANCE OF RESEARCH AND SCHOLARSHIP

The scholarly performance of faculty is of interest to many groups, including the general public; university faculty, students, and administrators; makers of public policy; and higher-education scholars. A brief history of how the emphasis on research has emerged within American higher education can help one to understand the factors that have intensified pressures on faculty to publish. An appreciation for the nature of scholarship in several fields of study, institutional variations in the priority given to research, and faculty characteristics that can affect their work provides insights into the complexity of defining and documenting scholarly performance and drawing generalizations about professors as a single group.

Historical Background

The colonial colleges in America were established to prepare citizens to become religious and civic leaders. Faculty members were selected for their religious commitment, not their scholarly accomplishments, and they were held responsible for the civic, moral, and intellectual development of their students.

However, by the mid-nineteenth century, a discernable emphasis on scholarship could be found in

American colleges and universities. A research tradition was emerging in Germany that emphasized scientific rationality and the pursuit of knowledge through experimentation. Growing numbers of American faculty completed their doctoral studies in Germany and sought to replicate these learning environments at home. Established private universities such as Yale and Princeton began to offer programs of study leading to the Ph.D. degree and, in 1876, Johns Hopkins University, a prototype of the modern American research university, was founded. By the late nineteenth century, the University of Chicago had implemented a formal system of faculty review in which research productivity was the primary criterion for promotion in rank and salary. At the same time, the missions of public land-grant institutions were expanding to include service to their states through the application of faculty research to local problems. The idea was that scholarship has utilitarian value, and that research findings could be used to improve production (e.g., agricultural, manufacturing) and the well-being of citizens.

In the twentieth century, particularly during the Great Depression and World War II, the contributions of academic scholars to government efforts and to scientific advancement were widely recognized. The status of professors as an occupational group was enhanced as the value of their expertise, built through research, was publicly acknowledged. Increasing numbers of doctorally prepared scholars moved from research universities to faculty posts on other types of campuses carrying with them a desire to recreate the intellectual climates in which they had studied. Federal monies to support faculty research grew, as did the number of academic presses, disciplinary associations, and professional journals that provided avenues for the dissemination of knowledge. In one decade alone, 1978–1988, more than 29,000 new scientific journals were launched.

By the mid-twentieth century, faculty in general—not just at research universities—understood that they were evaluated primarily as researchers, even though they were hired to teach. At the end of the twentieth century, the issue for many faculty was how to both keep up with and contribute to the ever-expanding body of knowledge in their fields.

Factors Affecting Scholarly Performance

Although the knowledge explosion has occurred across all subject-matter areas, it is a mistake to assume that the amount of time given to research and the volume of scholarly contributions are uniform across college and university professors. Faculty work is influenced by the cultures of both their institutions and the scholarly fields in which they work. Differences in the norms and rewards lead to variations in scholarly performance.

Institutional cultures serve to bring together people who work in diverse fields around a shared understanding of how they ought to behave as faculty members. One widely used taxonomy of colleges, the Carnegie Classification system, highlights some key differences among campuses, dividing them into several types based on the degrees offered, the comprehensiveness of their mission, and the level of federal support for research achieved by their faculty. Research universities offer baccalaureate and graduate degrees and place a high priority on faculty scholarship. They have the highest level of federal funding for research and award the largest number of doctoral degrees. Doctorate-granting universities share with the research universities a commitment to graduate education, but award fewer doctoral degrees and have fewer research grants. Comprehensive universities and colleges prepare students at the baccalaureate and master's degree levels and tend to emphasize undergraduate education. Liberal arts colleges focus primarily, if not exclusively, on undergraduate education. Two-year community, junior, and technical colleges emphasize instruction and typically offer certificates and associate of arts degrees. The responsibilities and expectations for faculty research, teaching, and service vary across these institutional contexts and in relation to campus priorities.

Disciplinary cultures link people on different campuses who work in the same field through a shared understanding of what constitutes knowledge and how it ought to be communicated. Consider the scholarly lives of chemists and English literature specialists and some key distinctions become clear. Each group has distinctly different sets of research issues on which they focus, as well as assumptions about what constitutes evidence and appropriate methods for collecting and analyzing data. Ultimately, the forms in which they communicate their findings vary—one group employs numeric representations and figures, the other uses words. Whereas teamwork is common among chemists, solitary scholarship is more the prototype in English literature. Funding for chemistry research typically exceeds that available for literary studies. Factors such as these greatly affect the time and resources available for scholarship and, together with the ways knowledge is customarily reported, affect the rates of publication within a given time period. Teams of chemists simultaneously produce and publish several journal articles, each with multiple authors, while English literature specialists are typically sole authors, more often of books than articles.

Individual characteristics, in addition to the normative pressures exerted by institutions and fields, also affect scholarly performance. Part-time faculty have less time and resources for research than full-time professors, doctorally prepared faculty are more likely to engage in research, individuals with stronger research interests give more time to their scholarship, and professors nearing promotion decisions tend to increase their publication productivity. Tenure often allows faculty more freedom in how they divide their time among teaching, research, and service, resulting in scholarly performance differences within institutions and fields.

Defining Scholarship

Of course, the preceding discussion begs the question of what scholarship is—by assuming it is inquiries that result in publications. Several writers believe that this perspective is shortsighted and argue for a more expansive definition. In his seminal work, *Scholarship Reconsidered* (1990), Ernest Boyer differentiates among four types of faculty scholarship: (1) *discovery,* consisting of original studies and creative works (e.g., discovering a new planet, composing a symphony); (2) *integration,* consisting of interdisciplinary inquiries, synthetic writing that connects information from multiple sources, and interpretive work that critiques existing research and suggests alternative explanations; (3) *application,* consisting of creative uses of theoretical knowledge to solve problems (e.g., applications of genetic research in the design of medical treatments); and (4) *teaching,* which is what research faculty do to instruct their classes, as well as inquiries into the effectiveness of their instruction. From Boyer's perspective, scholarship culminates in many products, including original ideas, works of art, critiques of other scholars' ideas, books and conference papers, solutions to practical problems developed through the application of abstract theories and principles to real life situations, new computer hardware and programs, and innovative teaching.

Measurement

Various organizations, as well as individual researchers, gather information about faculty. Government offices, such as the National Center for Educational Statistics (NCES) and the U.S. Department of Education, collect data to monitor the demographic characteristics (e.g., professorial ranks, race, income) and activities (e.g., distribution of effort to different professional activities) of faculty in the United States. Nongovernmental organizations, such as the American Council on Education and the Carnegie Foundation for the Advancement of Teaching, gather similar data, but also conduct international surveys of faculty for comparative purposes. Colleges and universities collect faculty information on a regular basis for annual reports to their governing boards and for decision making (e.g., merit salary increases). Individual investigators conduct studies to answer theoretical and practical questions of interest to their academic communities. Most often, these studies involve faculty self-reports of their activities and publications. Critics note the subjective nature of such estimates, but comparisons of professors' estimates with other independent measures of their workloads and publication rates have found the self-reports to be reliable.

Scholarly Activities and Products

Given that professors' fields, institutional affiliations, and individual attributes can affect their work, writers must exercise caution when generalizing about the American professoriate as a single group. Furthermore, answers to questions such as who is conducting research, or whether faculty scholarship has positive or negative effects on their teaching, depend on how one defines scholarship. With these caveats in mind, national data on the distribution of faculty across institutional types and fields of study are presented along with findings regarding their scholarship.

In 1992 about 4,000 institutions employed approximately 528,000 full-time faculty in the United States. They were distributed as follows: 26 percent were in research universities, 15 percent in doctoral universities, 25 percent in comprehensive universities, 7 percent in liberal arts colleges, and 21 percent in two-year colleges. In the same year, these institutions employed about 340,000 part-time faculty, the greatest percentages of which were found in two-year colleges (44.2%) and comprehensive universities (22%), with the smallest percentage in liberal arts colleges (6%). The proportion of full-time faculty with doctorates ranged from about 71 percent in the research universities to about 16 percent in the two-year colleges. The distribution is skewed so that in the early twenty-first century, as in the past, greater proportions of faculty employed in research universities have completed programs of graduate study designed to prepare them as specialized scholars.

In the research, doctoral, and comprehensive universities, the greatest proportion of full time faculty held the rank of professor (between 30 and 40%) whereas in the liberal arts colleges the percentages were quite evenly distributed across the ranks of professor, associate professor, and assistant professor (between 25 and 29% in each category). Research universities had the largest group of tenured faculty (about 60%) and two-year colleges had the smallest (about 31%). Around half the faculty in the other institutional types were tenured. Nationally, the largest group of full-time faculty was in the natural sciences (19.5%), followed by health (15.3%), humanities (14.2%) and social sciences (11.2%).

Existing studies of scholarly productivity do not provide data on some forms of scholarship identified by Boyer. However, there are data regarding the pressures on faculty to do research—and on how they respond in terms of time given to scholarship and teaching, the number of courses taught, and publications written.

Studies of professors consistently show that, regardless of field, faculty in research universities experience more pressure to conduct research and publish than their counterparts in other types of institutions. Given their graduate preparation, it is not surprising that faculty in these universities also report the most interest in doing research and the greatest sense of competence as researchers.

However, writers have noted a tendency within all institutions, beginning in the 1970s, to increase the emphasis on faculty scholarship in both recruitment and promotion practices. This phenomenon is taken to be a reflection of the importance accorded faculty research in national rankings of universities and colleges. Administrators know that the stature of their faculty as scholars significantly affects the reputations of their campuses. Faculty, too, understand that their tenure and mobility within the faculty labor market is affected by their scholarly accomplishments. Hence, the overall trend has been a heightened emphasis of scholarship, and there has

been a burgeoning of publications across campuses and subject-matter areas. In one year (1989–1990) 300,000 monographs, books, and chapters and a million journal articles were published.

Generally, studies show that faculty in research universities give the most time to research, and faculty in liberal arts and two-year colleges devote the most time to teaching. In 1992 faculty reported an average of fifty-three hours worked per week, with individuals in research universities reporting the highest average (about fifty-seven hours) and two-year colleges the lowest (about forty-seven hours). Faculty in the research universities allocated the greatest portion of this time to research (about 34%), with doctoral and comprehensive universities following in rank order with about 22 percent and 13 percent, respectively. The percentage of time given to teaching was highest in two-year colleges and liberal arts colleges (69% and 64%, respectively), and lowest in research universities (about 38%). Faculty in research universities and doctoral universities, on average, taught two to three courses per year, whereas their counterparts in comprehensive universities and liberal arts colleges typically taught three and four courses, respectively.

Another finding that seems to hold across studies of faculty in all but the two-year colleges is that faculty in the natural sciences (e.g., chemistry, biology, physics) report the greatest portion of their time is given to research, with faculty in the health sciences (e.g., medicine, biochemistry), social sciences (e.g., psychology, sociology), and humanities (e.g., history, languages) following in rank order. The trend is different when one focuses on teaching. Humanities professors give the most time, followed by those in the social sciences, natural sciences, and health sciences.

When the measure of scholarly performance is the number of books, articles, chapters, monographs, and other written products produced within a set time period (e.g., a year) or over the professional life of a faculty member, research university professors consistently publish more than their counterparts in other types of institutions. Similar comparisons across fields of study show that faculty in the natural sciences report the greatest number of publications per year and over their careers. To illustrate the volume produced, consider that, in 1988, faculty in research universities reported they had each authored about thirty-nine publications over their careers, while professors in doctoral universities authored about twenty-four. Faculty in comprehensive universities and liberal arts colleges, however, had written about twelve and nine publications, respectively. Data for the same year showed that professors in the natural sciences averaged thirty-five publications over their careers, compared with thirty among health scientists, twenty-five among social scientists, and twenty-one among humanities professors.

Questions abound regarding what motivates faculty to do research, teach, and provide service—and empirical studies provide multiple answers. Researchers continue to grapple with questions about how to measure scholarly performance (particularly the outcomes suggested by Boyer) and how to assess the quality of faculty research. Nonetheless, the results of more than forty years of research on faculty consistently document that professors in research universities experience the most pressure to be engaged in research, give more time to their scholarship, and publish most often. Furthermore, natural science faculty tend to write more publications over their careers than their counterparts in other fields. Finally, individuals vary in their research interests, scholarly competence, and tenure status, and these differences contribute to disparities in the scholarly performance of faculty within the same institution and/or within the same field.

See also: ACADEMIC DISCIPLINES; ACADEMIC FREEDOM AND TENURE; ACADEMIC LABOR MARKETS; FACULTY RESEARCH AND SCHOLARSHIP, ASSESSMENT OF; FACULTY ROLES AND RESPONSIBILITIES.

BIBLIOGRAPHY

BLACKBURN, ROBERT T., and LAWRENCE, JANET H. 1995. *Faculty at Work.* Baltimore: Johns Hopkins University Press.

BOYER, ERNEST L. 1990. *Scholarship Reconsidered: Priorities of the Professoriate.* Princeton, NJ: The Carnegie Foundation for the Advancement of Teaching.

CARNEGIE FOUNDATION FOR THE ADVANCEMENT OF TEACHING. 1987. *The Carnegie Classification of Institutions of Higher Education,* revised edition. Princeton, NJ: Carnegie Foundation for the Advancement of Teaching.

CLARK, BURTON R. 1987. *The Academic Life: Small Worlds, Different Worlds.* Princeton, NJ: The Carnegie Foundation for the Advancement of Teaching.

FAIRWEATHER, JAMES S. 1996. *Faculty Work and Public Trust.* Needham Heights, MA: Allyn and Bacon.

U.S. DEPARTMENT OF EDUCATION, NATIONAL CENTER FOR EDUCATIONAL STATISTICS. 2001. *Digest of Educational Statistics, 2000.* Washington, DC: National Center for Education Statistics.

JANET H. LAWRENCE

FACULTY RESEARCH AND SCHOLARSHIP, ASSESSMENT OF

Traditional definitions of faculty work frame contemporary views of its assessment. Faculty work generally falls into three categories: (1) research, which is the discovery or creation of knowledge through systematic inquiry; (2) teaching, which is the transmission of knowledge through class instruction and other learning-focused activities; and (3) service, meaning service to others through application of one's special field of knowledge. Assessment protocols have considered, to a varied extent, scholarly activities performed in each of these areas. Faculty assessment is conducted for purposes of reappointment, promotion, the awarding of tenure, and professional development.

During the last decades of the twentieth century, a societal focus on the work of college and university faculty as a measure of return on the public's investment in higher education stimulated a reevaluation of how faculty performance ought to be measured and assessed. The work of Charles Glassick and his colleagues (1997) has significantly influenced scholarship focused on developing workable evaluation systems. Their work is rooted in the broadened definitions of scholarship proposed by Ernest Boyer in 1990, and on how these definitions impact assessment systems. As scholarship is being conceived more broadly, traditional assessment systems are being reexamined to include all work conducted by faculty.

The development of workable assessment systems is difficult largely due to the fact that the value of assessment is often controversial. The controversy stems from several factors, according to Larry Braskamp and John Ory's 1994 study. First of all, faculty are not used to fully describing or judging their work. Secondly, systems that have been developed are often criticized by faculty as inadequate, particularly as assessment applies to teaching and service work. Lastly, a preoccupation with *how* to assess has resulted in a lack of attention to *what* is to be assessed. Successful assessment systems are based on clearly specified performance assessment criteria and standards for faculty performance in relevant areas of work. Each of these will be covered in turn.

Performance Assessment Criteria

While faculty are typically assessed based on their performance in their teaching, research, and service roles, the weight assigned to each of these areas varies depending on the type of institution and its associated expectations for faculty involvements in each area. For example, the assessment process for tenure-track faculty in research-focused institutions may place relatively more emphasis on the performance of the research role. An exception is for faculty whose appointments are not tenure-eligible, such as adjunct faculty or those in full-time appointments with a specified term. In these cases, assessment is typically weighted according to the specified terms of each individual's contract, or according to expectations for performance as determined by institutional policy or tradition. For faculty in teaching-oriented liberal arts colleges or community colleges, evaluation processes may focus more on teaching.

Assessment criteria also vary by academic discipline to accommodate the sometimes disparate intellectual products. The intellectual work of faculty in management and education, as applied disciplines, may be best evidenced by corporate or institutional testimonial of improved organizational effectiveness as a result of faculty involvement. The intellectual products of the so-called pure disciplines, such as history, are more appropriately characterized by written articles, reviews, and monographs.

Performance Standards and Quality

Standards for performance quality and assessment protocols are to a large extent determined by the governing bodies of each institution. Weighting of performance in teaching, research, and service is variable as well. Largely due to the disproportionate value placed on the research role of faculty, promotion and tenure guidelines have been clearer in articulating standards for research performance. Relative to assessment of teaching and service, the standards for judging research performance are clear and sys-

tematically linked to guidelines for promotion and the awarding of tenure. Performance is typically measured in terms of productivity, relying largely on the use of quantitative measures such as the number of publications or other creative works produced over a specified period of time.

Standards for teaching performance on the other hand, particularly in research-focused institutions, are less clear. The inherent difficulty in judging teaching performance lies in the fact that effectiveness is best measured by how much students learn. Because evidence of learning is often subjective or qualitative, it is more complicated to measure. This leads to questions of what measures are most appropriate for purposes of faculty evaluation, particularly when faculty compensation, if not entire careers, may rest on reliable assessment processes. This dilemma continues to fuel debates around the best way to assess teaching performance and contributes to faculty mistrust of evaluation systems. In many cases, efforts to develop workable measurement systems have stalled.

Evaluation of service remains illusive. Consequently, when it comes to tenure and promotion, service is often forgotten. This has led, unwittingly, to a devaluing of service work, and "virtually no institution has yet figured out how to quantify such work" (Glassick et al., p. 20). Reliable assessment of the service work of faculty must therefore rely on qualitative judgments rooted in institutionally developed standards for performance. Assessing service work across the professoriate is seen as a formidable challenge, yet, unlike the challenge of teaching evaluation, it has yet to benefit from a significant body of research and experimentation.

As the notion of what constitutes legitimate scholarship is broadened, and as increased attention is being paid to the outcomes of faculty teaching, academe is pressed to redefine measures of quality. Institutions, and the profession as a whole, are facing new questions, such as: How is student learning, as evidence of quality teaching, best documented? What processes associated with the transmission of knowledge are to be considered legitimate evidence of faculty performance? What constitutes appropriate evidence of application of a disciplinary knowledge base into service activities? How is integration of one's area of expertise into a multidisciplinary intellectual context best evidenced?

In 1997 Glassick and colleagues offered a solid framework for institutions considering modifications of faculty assessment systems. This work has received considerable attention by scholars of higher education and, as of the beginning of the twenty-first century, it has presented the most well-defined approach to assessing faculty work. In this book, the authors examined methods for judging scholarly performance by colleges and universities, granting agencies, journal editors, and university presses. Applying Boyer's four domains of scholarship (discovery, teaching, application, and integration) to define faculty work, they identified six standards commonly associated with high-quality scholarly work: clear goals, adequate preparation, appropriate methods, significant results, effective presentation, and reflective critique. These criteria for determining quality are noteworthy in that they offer not only a framework for evaluation, but also aid in understanding the kinds of intellectual activities and outputs that are legitimate components of the work that faculty perform.

Assessment Tools

There are numerous tools used for collecting evidence of faculty performance quality. Braskamp and Ory cite the following assessment tools: evaluations by students and peers, as well as self-evaluations, of teaching; the evaluative conference; evaluative letters from colleagues and experts in the field; and portfolios that explicate professional accomplishments. Evaluators may vary depending on institution type. For faculty in research-oriented institutions, considerable weight is placed on the judgments of peers, including scholars from other institutions. In many liberal arts colleges and community colleges, where the faculty role is more oriented toward teaching, there may be greater reliance on the judgments of local faculty who are most familiar with institutional teaching and learning philosophies and standards for teaching performance.

Teaching performance has historically been accomplished by student evaluations at the end of each course, with the weight afforded such evaluations varying from institution to institution and, often, from department to department. In liberal arts colleges and other teaching-focused institutions, a combination of student evaluations and peer review is often used. Peer review involves a review of one's pedagogical skills by his or her faculty colleagues. Toward the end of the twentieth century, peer review of teaching became more popular in research-focused institutions, with a goal of providing a simi-

lar level of support, consultation, and evaluation typically provided for research. Some institutions have begun to enhance rewards for teaching performance, largely in response to societal concerns about the quality of undergraduate education. Such rewards have been in the form of cash awards, special stipends for teaching improvement, and endowed chairs devoted to teaching excellence.

While research performance is commonly measured in terms of the number of published articles, books, and other research products, there is a qualitative aspect to such measures. The type of publication, and whether or not selection for publication involved peer review, also determines research quality. Publications subjected to a peer-review process are typically considered to be of higher quality in that they are thought to have undergone a more rigorous critique than published work that is not reviewed.

The Portfolio as an Assessment Tool

As definitions of faculty work are broadened, ideas about what constitutes adequate evidence of such work must be broadened as well. The notion of the professional portfolio has received wide attention as a comprehensive way to represent the work of a faculty member. The professional portfolio is a collection of artifacts and materials gathered and presented by each faculty member. It represents the requirements for one's work, as defined by expectations specified at the time of appointment or at the start of the review period. Building on Peter Seldin's notion of the teaching portfolio, Robert Froh and his associates in 1993 specified a set of principles to guide the development of portfolios and their evaluation. While the concept of the portfolio does incorporate elements of the traditional dossier compiled by faculty to document their performance, the portfolio takes a broader view of scholarship by integrating the values of the faculty member with those of the departmental and institutional community. This might be accomplished through a reflective essay and work samples that uniquely represent such an integration of values. Thus, the more standardized representation of work that is characteristic of the traditional dossier must be transformed to reflect the work of each individual and the unique contributions he or she has made in relevant areas of scholarship.

Assessment Challenges

Assessment of faculty work has become an important consideration for both faculty and administrators, particularly as the pressure for measuring outcomes of faculty work over and above the easily quantifiable numbers of publications has escalated. Policymakers are calling for increased accountability of faculty members' time, and for evidence that the time spent produces acceptable outcomes, specifically with respect to undergraduate education. State governing bodies and Congress have become more involved with academic issues associated with student access, equality, and research integrity, all of which influence how faculty conduct their work and how institutions monitor and assess it. Such external pressures, combined with increasing trends that emphasize the importance of faculty professional development have led to increased attention on faculty assessment systems. Reevaluation of these systems is not without its challenges, however.

First, definitions of scholarship vary from discipline to discipline, and these differences have significant implications for how assessment systems are structured and implemented. Also, the importance of communication of discipline-specific performance factors across disciplines must be addressed if faculty on promotion and tenure review committees are to effectively and reliably judge the work of their colleagues. Second, effective evaluation systems depend on the communication of standards upon which judgments of quality will be based and acceptable mechanisms for documenting faculty work. Third, any changes to traditional assessment systems must maintain the historic autonomy of faculty as sole judges of quality scholarship. As members of a profession, faculty reserve the right to be the sole judges of the quality of the work performance of those claiming membership among their ranks.

Judgments of quality are based on standards set by the profession as a whole, the specific mission of the institution within which a faculty member's work is conducted, and standards circumscribed by the discipline and the institution. As definitions of scholarship are broadened, indicators of quality must be well considered in order to preserve the status of the profession and simultaneously satisfy new calls for accountability. Lastly, assessment systems must be flexible enough to consider the unique work profiles and needs of a growing segment of the professoriate—the full-time, non-tenure-track faculty. This is the environment within which effective evaluation systems must be developed so as to serve the changing roles of faculty in higher education.

See also: ACADEMIC FREEDOM AND TENURE; FACULTY PERFORMANCE OF RESEARCH AND SCHOLARSHIP; FACULTY ROLES AND RESPONSIBILITIES.

BIBLIOGRAPHY

BALDWIN, ROGER E., and CHRONISTER, JAY. 2001. *Teaching Without Tenure.* Baltimore: Johns Hopkins University Press.

BOYER, ERNEST L. 1990. *Scholarship Reconsidered: Priorities of the Professoriate.* Princeton, NJ: The Carnegie Foundation for the Advancement of Teaching.

BRASKAMP, LARRY, and ORY, JOHN. 1994. *Assessing Faculty Work: Enhancing Individual and Institutional Performance.* San Francisco: Jossey-Bass.

DIAMOND, ROBERT M. 1993. "Changing Priorities and the Faculty Reward System." In *Recognizing Faculty Work: Reward Systems for the Year 2000,* ed. Robert M. Diamond and Bronwyn E. Adam. *New Directions for Higher Education* 81:5–12.

FROH, ROBERT C.; GRAY, PETER J.; and LAMBERT, LEO M. 1993. "Representing Faculty Work: The Professional Portfolio." In *Recognizing Faculty Work: Reward Systems for the Year 2000,* ed. Robert M. Diamond and Bronwyn E. Adam. *New Directions for Higher Education* 81:97–110.

GLASSICK, CHARLES E.; HUBER, MARY T.; and MAEROFF, GENE I. 1997. *Scholarship Assessed: Evaluation of the Professoriate.* San Francisco: Jossey-Bass.

SELDIN, PETER. 1991. *The Teaching Portfolio.* Boston: Anker.

MARIETTA DEL FAVERO

FACULTY ROLES AND RESPONSIBILITIES

The roles and responsibilities of college and university faculty members are closely tied to the central functions of higher education. One primary formal description of these functions was contained in the 1915 "Declaration of Principles" formulated by a representative committee of faculty members including members of the American Association of

University Professors (AAUP). According to the Declaration, the functions of colleges and universities are "to promote inquiry and advance the sum of human knowledge, to provide general instruction to the students, and to develop experts for various branches of the public service" (Joughin, pp. 163–164). Correspondingly, college and university faculty members undertake research, teaching, and service roles to carry out the academic work of their respective institutions. Each of these roles enables faculty members to generate and disseminate knowledge to peers, students, and external audiences. The balance among teaching, research, and service, however, differs widely across institution types and by terms of the faculty member's appointment. The major portion of this article will deal with these kinds of differences while latter sections will focus on the faculty as collective entities and related trends within higher education.

The Teaching Role

The teaching role of faculty members reflects their centrality in addressing the primary educational mission among colleges and universities. As faculty members teach, they disseminate and impart basic or applied knowledge to students and assist students with the learning process and applying the knowledge. In this construction of the teaching role, the teacher is the content expert, and students are regarded as learners or novices to the academic discipline or field of study. Faculty members are expected to follow developments in the field so their expertise and knowledge base remain current. At many universities, faculty members are also expected to participate in creating the new developments that are taught, which sometimes leads to tensions about appropriate priorities for research and teaching roles.

In the 1980s and 1990s the teaching role came under increased scrutiny as studies such as the Wingspread Report (1993) appeared, outlining the shortcomings of undergraduate education and the failure of higher education to prioritize appropriately its educational mission. New approaches to revitalizing teaching effectiveness include placing an emphasis on effective pedagogy and paying increased attention to the learning needs of students. Consequently, an emphasis on faculty members as facilitators of students' learning has emerged. This focus on learning incorporates a broad set of goals for learners, such as students' mastery of content, their abilities to consider and critique, and particu-

larly in professional fields, the development of skill sets that enable students to undertake career positions.

Faculty members employ a variety of teaching strategies based on the institutions where they work. In a large undergraduate lecture section, a faculty member may deliver lectures that are complemented by regular and smaller recitation sections led by graduate teaching assistants. At a community college, faculty members may work side by side with students diagnosing and addressing a mechanical problem in a piece of machinery. At a liberal arts college, faculty members from different disciplines may team teach a small first-year survey course on human civilization.

In a natural sciences class, students may conduct experiments or field work in regular laboratory sessions to complement their growing conceptual knowledge and hone their inquiry skills. Students in a theater class may work alongside faculty members, fellow students, professional actors, and house staff to produce a stage performance. In a graduate seminar, students may lead selected discussions supplemented by a faculty member's input and appraisal. Students enrolled in a distance-learning class may attend class using technological real-time hookups or may independently complete learning modules and communicate with the instructor through e-mail only as needed or stipulated. The teacher is also responsible for assessing students' learning, and a wide range of strategies may be used, such as tests, papers, and project-oriented demonstrations of knowledge.

Of the three roles of teaching, research, and service, the teaching role is the most widely shared among faculty members across institutional types. At liberal arts colleges, regional universities, and community colleges, the teaching role takes precedence for most faculty members. Faculty members spend the majority of their time in teaching-related work, and effective teaching is rewarded. At research universities, some faculty members may hold research-only appointments, but the vast majority of faculty members teach courses in addition to maintaining a research agenda. Although effective teaching is rewarded, teaching may be seen as less prestigious and less well rewarded than success in conducting research and securing external funding. At virtual universities, faculty members may not teach so much as participate in creating instructional modules and provide feedback to students on their degrees of success in mastering specified knowledge.

Depending on the history of an institution, imparting knowledge and developing students' learning abilities may not be the sole purpose for teaching. In religiously affiliated colleges, institutions may expect a faculty member's teaching to be consistent with and complemented by tenets of the sponsoring religious organization. In these institutions, faculty members may be expected to support the college's ministerial or evangelical objectives. In historically black colleges and universities, women's colleges, and tribal colleges, a complementary teaching focus may be on issues of social justice and empowerment of students from these underrepresented and less empowered groups.

Other institutional personnel increasingly have positioned themselves as educators to complement or enhance the traditional teaching role of faculty members. Student affairs professionals, for example, have placed greater focus on out-of-classroom learning opportunities, learning communities, and community service learning as mutually-reinforcing learning opportunities to create a more complete campus learning environment.

The Research Role

Many university faculty members engage in research, thereby contributing to the knowledge base of the discipline or academic field. Research commonly is associated with conducting empirical studies, whether confirmatory or exploratory, but in some academic disciplines research also encompasses highly theoretical work. The extent to which faculty members have a research role as part of their work responsibilities depends largely on the mission of the employing institution, with larger universities more likely to have research and knowledge creation as a significant part of their missions. Although higher education institutions are most often the sites for and sponsors of faculty members' research, the primary audience for most academic researchers is their national and international community of disciplinary colleagues. Faculty members with active research agendas and involvement in their disciplinary communities have been regarded as more cosmopolitan in orientation, with stronger allegiances and loyalties to their disciplines than to their home institutions.

More emphasis is placed on the faculty research role in large universities in part because large univer-

sities also house the majority of graduate programs and provide resources to support the pursuit of research agendas. Additionally, research-oriented faculty members often participate actively in generating internal and external monetary support to underwrite their laboratories or specific research projects. Faculty rewards often are based on the extent to which faculty members contribute to their disciplines through publishing articles and books, presenting research findings, giving performances and exhibits, or disseminating their work to external audiences in other ways. Additionally, rewards may also be based on the faculty member's success in securing funding from external public agencies or companies.

With the growth of externally funded research, concerns have been raised about the potential conflicts of interest between academic freedom to research and disseminate findings and the proprietary ownership of data and findings from externally financed research. This issue is reminiscent of post–World War I concerns, as articulated in Upton Sinclair's study of American education in 1923, about an "interlocking directorate" of higher education and business representatives that disproportionately served the needs of private companies. However, concerns surrounding this trend have increased as support from traditional funding sources for large public universities, including research support, has declined. Faced with this situation, faculty members have become more entrepreneurial and in some cases more reliant on alternate funding streams such as those accompanying research contracts and grants.

Research is seldom, if ever, a significant part of a community college's or virtual university's mission, and participation in research by faculty members at these institutions is not especially common. Although these institutions may employ part-time and adjunct faculty members who work in the research and development divisions of their companies and agencies, their primary work at the community college is to teach. However, the research role is not restricted to faculty members at research-oriented universities. Faculty members at institutions other than research-oriented universities conduct research as part of their faculty role, partly because faculty members who have earned terminal degrees from large universities likely were socialized to conduct research and seek funding for such pursuits. Also, colleges and universities increasingly have focused on faculty research as a way to increase their institutional profiles and prestige. Over the last quarter of the twentieth century, many higher education institutions saw their missions expand to encompass graduate education and research endeavors.

The Service Role

Institutional service performed by faculty members includes serving on internal committees and advisory boards, mentoring and advising students, and assuming part-time administrative appointments as program or unit leaders. In some cases, faculty members also assume term appointments in full-time roles as mid-level or senior level institutional administrators. Some level of faculty members' service to the institution is expected, although tenure-track faculty members may be discouraged or exempted from heavy service commitments to permit greater focus on their research and teaching. Some institutional service roles may carry some prestige, and appointments may include a salary supplement. However, institutional service is not as highly regarded as research and teaching with respect to advancement within faculty ranks.

The public service role for faculty is associated with colonial colleges' preparation of ministers and teachers to serve the citizenry. A local, outreach-oriented faculty service role was codified through land-grant institutions, with their instruction in agricultural, mechanical, and practical subjects. In addition to incorporating these subjects within the curriculum, land-grant institutions also disseminate scientific knowledge and best practices to residents of the state. These universities utilize extension services, often with satellite offices, to provide information in areas such as agricultural innovations, economic and community development, child development and nutrition, and environmental conservation. Faculty members' extension and service roles tend to be less highly valued and rewarded than the research and teaching roles at universities. However, revitalizing the service role has also been offered as an important way to recapture public trust in higher education and demonstrate institutional responsiveness to society and its concerns.

Faculty service is a more central role in community colleges and regional institutions, both of which are characterized by relatively closer ties to the surrounding area. In these institutions, although teaching is the primary faculty role, faculty are also expected to address local needs. Many community colleges develop educational programs that are tailored to the needs of local industries, thus assuming partial responsibility for employee training or retraining. The service role and faculty members' outreach and demonstrations of responsiveness to local needs are valued and rewarded more highly at these institutions.

Integration of Faculty Roles and Responsibilities

The teaching, research, and service roles of faculty members overlap conceptually and practically. For example, instruction in a particular discipline or skill yields a service in the form of educated or appropriately trained persons, and outreach to a farmer or small business owner may lead to an applied research project undertaken by the faculty member. Some attempts have been made to validate the various forms of faculty work and unify them conceptually. Perhaps the most famous recent model has been the American educator and government official Ernest Boyer's 1990 stipulation of discovery, application, integration, and teaching as separate but related forms of scholarship. Among other outcomes, these models address concerns regarding the implicit hierarchy that grants the most prestige to research and the least to service.

Variable career emphasis programs can also help to integrate these faculty roles by offering opportunities for faculty members to stipulate their role emphases at various points in their work lives. Institutions with such programs acknowledge changes and evolutions in faculty members' professional interests and commitments. In some cases negotiations about role emphasis are part of a developmental post-tenure review program. Post-tenure reviews are considered to be responsive to concerns about faculty members' continued vitality and contributions in their later years, particularly since the abolishment of most mandatory retirement age provisions. However, concerns remain about the potential for post-tenure review and variable role emphasis negotiations to be used for punitive rather than developmental purposes.

The Collective Faculty

Although the faculty of an institution is traditionally considered to refer to full-time faculty members, part-time and adjunct faculty members at many institutions have assumed a larger proportion of teaching responsibilities. Although the proportions of women and minority group members in the full-time faculty ranks grew slowly in the last quarter of the twentieth century, women and minority group members also are concentrated in the lower faculty ranks such as instructors and part-time and adjunct faculty positions. Some blame this slow progress on inadequate numbers of diverse students in graduate programs, market factors that make other career choices more attractive or lucrative, or individual lifestyle choices. However, focus also has been shifted to institutional structures and norms, professional socialization experiences, and tacit assumptions that serve as barriers to progress within faculty ranks. For example, William G. Tierney and Estela M. Bensimon suggest that faculty members from underrepresented groups are found to pay a cultural tax in the form of increased service loads and disproportionate expectations for student advising and mentoring—service roles that often are not valued or rewarded.

The identity, authority, and functions of an institution's collective faculty are largely dependent on institutional type, history, and traditions, as well as on formal codifications of faculty authority and role. The faculty traditionally is responsible for planning and delivering curricula and instruction consistent with the educational goals of the institution and selecting and evaluating probationary faculty members within their colleges, departments, or units. Individual faculty members also may serve term appointments as administrative officers responsible for various functions of the institution, and faculty members may participate in representative assemblies like faculty senates. These bodies provide arenas for faculty deliberations and decision-making where representative faculty members articulate, endorse, or dissent from positions and draft and pass senate resolutions.

While resolutions or legislated outcomes from faculty senates often do not ultimately become university policy on the targeted issues, at institutions with traditions of strong faculty senates, senate actions represent steps in ongoing negotiated processes with administrators in determining institutional policies, especially but not only with respect to academic matters. Faculty senates also provide a regular, representative forum for administrators to meet with the faculty about proposed or enacted institutional decisions and policies.

Faculty members often are less routinely involved in institution-level budget processes, including retrenchment decisions and strategic planning—with the exception of academic planning, curriculum planning, and degree program implications. In general, faculties at older institutions and larger institutions have tended to play a more significant role in shaping or influencing institutional governance decisions.

By contrast, many institutions are now more likely to vest a majority of institutional governance functions with professional administrators. In the last two decades of the twentieth century, the number of administrative personnel at universities expanded concurrently with faculty members' becoming more oriented toward their disciplines and less toward the institution. Because of their academic, curriculum, personnel, and shared or dual governance functions, a university's faculty or the faculty at an established liberal arts college may hold a more central and influential position within the organization. In other institutions, faculties are less likely to have such collective identities and influential statuses, perhaps with the exception of unionized faculties.

Faculty collective bargaining units provide faculty members with a formal voice in institutional deliberations and decision-making, and many faculty members regard collective bargaining as a check against the growing degree of professional administrators' authority. A wave of faculty labor organization in the 1960s and 1970s has been followed by a period of less organizing activity by non-unionized faculties. However, more recent participants in academic labor organizing have been graduate students, particularly teaching assistants, in the 1980s and 1990s at relatively prestigious, research-oriented universities. This turn to collective bargaining measures by graduate teaching assistants may presage a resurgence of academic unionization as these teaching assistants become future faculty members at colleges and universities.

See also: COLLEGE TEACHING; FACULTY PERFORMANCE OF RESEARCH AND SCHOLARSHIP; FACULTY RESEARCH AND SCHOLARSHIP, ASSESSMENT OF; FACULTY SERVICE ROLE, THE.

BIBLIOGRAPHY

AMERICAN COLLEGE PERSONNEL ASSOCIATION. 1994. *The Student Learning Imperative: Implications for Student Affairs.* Washington, DC: American College Personnel Association.

BIRNBAUM, ROBERT. 1988. *How Colleges Work: The Cybernetics of Academic Organization and Leadership.* San Francisco: Jossey-Bass.

BLAU, PETER M. 1973. *The Organization of Academic Work.* New York: Wiley.

BOYER, ERNEST L. 1990. *Scholarship Reconsidered: Priorities of the Professoriate.* Princeton, NJ: Carnegie Foundation for the Advancement of Teaching.

FAIRWEATHER, JAMES S. 1996. *Faculty Work and Public Trust: Restoring the Value of Teaching and Public Service in American Academic Life.* Boston: Allyn and Bacon.

FLOYD, CAROL. 1984. *Faculty Participation in Decision Making* (ASHE–ERIC Higher Education Report No. 8). Washington, DC: Association for the Study of Higher Education.

GOULDNER, ALVIN W. 1957. "Cosmopolitans and Locals: Toward an Analysis of Latent Social Roles." *Administrative Science Quarterly* 2:281–307.

JOUGHIN, LOUIS, ed. 1969. *Academic Freedom and Tenure: A Handbook of the American Association of University Professors.* Madison: University of Wisconsin Press.

PARK, SHELLEY M. 1996. "Research, Teaching, and Service: Why Shouldn't Women's Work Count?" *The Journal of Higher Education* 67(1):46–84.

PEW HIGHER EDUCATION RESEARCH PROGRAM. 1990. *The Lattice and the Ratchet.* Philadelphia: University of Pennsylvania, Pew Higher Education Research Program.

SINCLAIR, UPTON. 1923. *The Goose-Step: A Study in American Education,* Vols. 1–4. Girard, KS: Haldeman-Julius.

TIERNEY, WILLIAM G., and BENSIMON, ESTELA M. 1996. *Promotion and Tenure: Community and Socialization in Academe.* Albany: State University of New York Press.

WINGSPREAD GROUP ON HIGHER EDUCATION. 1993. *An American Imperative: Higher Expectations for Higher Education.* Racine, WI: Johnson Foundation.

FLORENCE A. HAMRICK

FACULTY SENATES, COLLEGE AND UNIVERSITY

Since the 1960s the concept of shared governance has both blossomed and withered. Founded on the principals of western European worker-participation models, the practice of instituting faculty senates at universities and colleges throughout America was intended to alleviate the growing pains of the higher education system brought about by the influx of baby boomers (persons who were born between the years of 1946 and 1964, and who enrolled as traditional college students between the years of 1964 and 1987). The American Association of University Professors (AAUP) first suggested formalized shared governance schemes in the 1966 *Statement on Government of Colleges and Universities.* As a result, many institutions began to experiment with various shared governance arrangements, primarily in the form of faculty senates.

According to Barbara Lee, the ebb and flow of shared governance has been guided by two driving forces: politics and economics. Valerie Collins, however, contends that during the 1960s and 1970s a unique set of political factors, including the civil rights movement and the Vietnam War, converged on American campuses. In response to the unrest and mistrust this politically ripe time instilled in students, faculties began using senates to ensure their influence over decisions that would affect an increasingly large portion of campus life for both students and faculty. A third interpretation, as expressed in William Tierney and Richard Rhodes's work on faculty socialization, addresses the effect of culture: the culture of the discipline, of the institution, and of the profession. They argue that the culture of the profession engendered a need for faculty service roles in the institution and that this need created a condition that allowed for the inception of faculty senates.

Faculty senates have shared responsibilities, ranging from a limited role in program approval and review of tenure decisions to a more comprehensive role that includes budget review and allocation, senior administrative recruitment, and strategic planning. Faculty senates have been studied to show their effect on participation and influence of faculty members and to critique their inabilities to meet with campus financial constraints. As a result, they have met with both praise and criticism.

The majority of faculty senates operate under a mission statement. These mission statements give the senates guidelines and provide them with an outline of their areas of authority. Jack Blendiger and colleagues list six strengths of academic senates, stating that they provide the means for: (1) determining short- and long-range interests and needs of faculty; (2) articulating expectations of faculty, staff, and students; (3) developing goals and planning strategies; (4) establishing standards and procedures for the review and evaluation of proposed administrative action dealing with curricula offerings, budgetary practices, and faculty recruitment and retention; (5) increasing knowledge and understanding of issues in departments and units; and (6) allocating resources equitably.

The debate about the worth and ultimate viability of faculty senates lies in these senates' missions. In cases where so-called corporate mentalities have infiltrated campuses, the fault has often been in the shortsightedness of the faculty senates' missions. Sheila Slaughter and Larry Leslie describe a case at San Diego State University when the administration attempted to lay off more than 130 tenured faculty members (the layoff ultimately did not go through); the faculty senate was up in arms yet was powerless to act because their mission had left them devoid of power in financial situations. Conversely, in some situations the university administration may have no ability to adjust faculty levels and program existence due to lack of authority or shared authority and may be perceived as weak by the public and by its board of trust.

As the baby-boomer enrollment gave way to the baby bust (individuals who were born between 1970 and 1985, and who have been enrolled in colleges as traditional students since 1988 and will continue to be enrolled through 2007), many colleges and universities began to feel the economic effects of declining enrollment. The shortages of students brought about an era in which *streamline, retrench,* and *economize* were common words spoken at most campuses, and in which all aspects of campus governance began to come into question.

Faculty senates and the institution of shared governance remain a vital part of academia. While it is true that universities must maintain financial solvency, they exist in their own microcosm that allows for adherence to cultural artifacts, regardless of their economic efficiency. As Robert Birnbaum has suggested, academic senates may not always work, but they will not go away.

See also: ACADEMIC DEAN, THE; BOARD OF TRUSTEES, COLLEGE AND UNIVERSITY; CHIEF ACADEMIC AFFAIRS OFFICERS, COLLEGE AND UNIVERSITY; COLLEGES AND UNIVERSITIES, ORGANIZATIONAL STRUCTURE OF; GOVERNANCE AND DECISION-MAKING IN COLLEGES AND UNIVERSITIES; PRESIDENCY, COLLEGE AND UNIVERSITY.

BIBLIOGRAPHY

BENDIGER, JACK; CORNELIOUS, LINDA; and MCGRATH, VINCENT. 1998. "Faculty Governance: The Key to Actualizing Professionalism." Paper presented at the Annual Meeting of the American Association of Colleges for Teacher Education, New Orleans, Louisiana, February.

BENJAMIN, ROGER. 1994. *The Redesign of Governance in Higher Education.* Santa Monica, CA: RAND Corporation.

BESS, JAMES L. 1982. *University Organization: A Matrix Analysis of the Academic Profession.* New York: Human Sciences Press.

BESS, JAMES L. 1988. *Collegiality and Bureaucracy in the Modern University: The Influence of Information and Power in Decision Making Structures.* New York: Teachers College Press.

BIRNBAUM, ROBERT. 1989. "The Latent Organizational Functions of the Academic Senate: Why Senates Do Not Work but Will Not Go Away." *Journal of Higher Education* 60(4):423–442.

COLLINGS, VALERIE H. 1996. *The Faculty Role in Governance: A Historical Analysis of the Influence of the American Association of University Professors and the Middle States Association on Academic Decision Making.* Paper presented at the Annual Meeting of the Association for the Study of Higher Education, Memphis, Tennessee.

DOUGLAS, JOEL M. 1995. "An Investigation of Employee Involvement Schemes and Governance Structures in Professional Employment." *National Center for the Study of Collective Bargaining in Higher Education and the Professions Newsletter* 23(4).

LEE, BARBARA A. 1979. "Governance at the Unionized Four-Year College: Effects on Decision Making Structures." *Journal of Higher Education* 50(5):565–585.

MILLETT, JOHN D. 1978. *New Structures of Campus Power.* San Francisco: Jossey-Bass.

RIDGELY, JULIA. 1983. "Faculty Senates and the Fiscal Crisis." *Academe* 79(6):7–11.

SLAUGHTER, SHEILA, and LESLIE, LARRY L. 1997. *Academic Capitalism: Politics, Policies, and the Entrepreneurial University.* Baltimore: Johns Hopkins University Press.

TIERNEY, WILLIAM G., and RHOADS, RICHARD A. 1993. "Enhancing Promotion, Tenure, and Beyond: Faculty Socialization as a Cultural Process." *AHSE-ERIC Education Report* 93(6).

WILLIAMS, DON; OLSWANG, GARY; and HARGETT, GARY. 1986. "A Matter of Degree: Faculty Morale as a Function of the Involvement in Institutional Decisions during Times of Financial Distress." *Review of Higher Education* 9(3):287–301.

STEVEN P. YOUNG

FACULTY SERVICE ROLE, THE

The faculty service role includes a variety of activities: from providing the most advanced knowledge to serve global markets and priorities to performing the most humble committee work designed to assist in the routine functioning of campuses and community groups. Through faculty service activity, colleges and universities maintain shared governance, faculty promote disciplinary networks, and partnerships are sustained between the university and community organizations, governmental agencies, businesses, and industries.

Nature of the Faculty Service Role

In the United States the mission of colleges and universities has long been described as tripartite, including teaching, research, and service. Historic roots of the American faculty service role can be seen in the founding of land-grant, city, metropolitan, and state universities and community colleges, all of which were provided public lands and funds, and nonprofit tax status, with an expectation that faculty members provide not only teaching and research but also service in return. Both the amount and the kinds of faculty service activities have increased over time.

Outside of the United States, the tradition of service activity is not as long. However, developments in many countries during the last two decades of the twentieth century, which have tied universities more closely to national priorities that support economic development, have made the issues surrounding the faculty service role no longer a uniquely United States concern.

Distinctions among Types of Service

Ernest A. Lynton suggested in 1995 that faculty engage in four types of activities that tend to be described by their institutions as "service": committee work, program building, and other administrative work related to the promotion of a university's institutional service. When faculty make contributions to their disciplinary associations and edit disciplinary journals they partake in disciplinary service. Faculty provide community service through civic contributions in the form of speeches, board or committee membership, or volunteer work with religious, philanthropic, or other nonprofit organizations. When faculty fulfill their department, college, or university's outreach mission by using their professional expertise to assist communities in responding to real-world problems, they engage in professional service. Examples of professional service activity include agricultural extension, continuing education, social problem solving, policy analysis, program evaluation, assistance with economic development, technology transfer, and entrepreneurial activity. In many institutional mission statements and some of the literature, community service and professional service are combined under the more general rubric of public service.

Importance in the Academic Reward Structure

Through the twentieth century the importance of faculty service in the academic reward structure varied depending on institutional type and priorities, discipline, and status of the profession. In the first colonial colleges, teaching, community service, and institutional service were the primary responsibilities of faculty, and they were rewarded accordingly. As American higher education shifted from colonial colleges to land-grant universities, however, a gradual shift occurred in which faculty became more influenced by networks of colleagues at other institutions than by local, institutional, or community priorities. Although to different degrees depending on institutional type, the reward system followed faculty priorities. By the late 1980s and early 1990s, most colleges and universities favored scholarship, understood as traditional research, over teaching and service in tenure, promotion, merit pay, and contract renewal decisions.

Ironically, at the same time reward systems were evolving to favor research, faculty were being called upon to engage in more and more service. Land-grant universities, urban and metropolitan universities, and community colleges were all created with explicit outreach missions. These institutions expected all of their faculty, and especially those in professional schools, to link their expertise to real-world problems. As time went on even faculty in liberal arts and private institutions were called upon by the public to engage in community service and professional service.

The tradition of shared governance has always meant a significant proportion of faculty time is spent on maintaining and improving the institution. Typically senior faculty take on more institutional service responsibilities than junior faculty. However, within the last quarter of the twentieth century, women and faculty of color reported increased demands on their time to serve on university committees, advise women and students of color, and serve their respective communities. Also, as the number of disciplinary associations, journals, and professional awards has grown so have the demands on faculty to supervise them.

Despite an increase in activity and demands for service, service is not, and has never been, rewarded comparably to teaching and research within academic communities. In most institutions it occupies a distant and somewhat ambiguous third place behind teaching and research. Service is not easy to evaluate for purposes of reward because it is often difficult to assess the quality of service activities, and to quantify and document service activity that results from ongoing partnerships or ad hoc projects. It is not clear what, if anything, should be evaluated when faculty participate in committees, editorial review boards, or mentoring groups.

During the last decade of the twentieth century, however, significant progress was made in elevating professional service in the academic reward system. In the early 1990s a national movement to reexamine faculty roles and rewards led by the American Association for Higher Education and the 1990 seminal work of Ernest Boyer, *Scholarship Reconsidered,* offered colleges and universities an attractive framework for assessing and rewarding a diversity of faculty work. Hundreds of campuses around the country began to redefine scholarship—the primary activity faculty were rewarded for—to include the teaching, discovery, integration, and application of knowledge. Lynton (1995) and Amy Driscoll (1999) extended this framework by advocating ways in which

faculty could document their professional service as scholarship. Some campuses have written this framework into faculty evaluation policies, offering an opportunity for faculty professional service to be assessed and rewarded with a similar currency to traditional research in the academic reward system.

Debates about the Faculty Service Role

There is a lively debate about the nature and extent of faculty and institutional service obligations. It is often framed by such questions as the following:

- Do colleges and universities serve best through basic research and the preparation of future generations or through social problem solving, social activism, and social criticism?

- Among the many external demands for the professional expertise of faculty members, whose should have the greatest priority?

- Do colleges and universities have stronger obligations to state and national governments, their primary sources of financial support, than to community groups, the disadvantaged, or the disenfranchised?

- Should faculty consulting work count as service for purposes of the reward system?

The inclusion of economic development and entrepreneurial activities under the banner of service has inspired much controversy, in the United States and elsewhere, about the extent to which such activity is in the public interest or whether it serves the more private financial ambitions of colleges and universities and individual faculty members. Sheila Slaughter and Larry Leslie argue that such activity, which they term *academic capitalism,* changes the nature of the faculty role and the relationship between faculty members and their employing institutions. As institutions come to rely on faculty entrepreneurial activity as part of their financial base, they come to value this activity over other faculty work with negative consequences for teaching and research in areas not close to the market. Slaughter and Leslie anticipate increasing controversies between faculty members and their employing institutions over matters of the ownership of intellectual property, workload, and governance.

From close examination of selected universities in four countries, Burton R. Clark describes a new breed of entrepreneurial university that aggressively seeks to bring in new financial resources to augment and offset the support traditionally provided by national and state governments. Governmental support, he argues, is no longer sufficient to the ever-increasing demands on universities for new knowledge with marketplace applications. Entrepreneurial universities must rely on their faculty members to turn their knowledge capital into new revenue streams for the institution. Clark describes the "expanded periphery" within entrepreneurial universities—vastly increased numbers of research and outreach centers and institutes as well as multidisciplinary and externally oriented academic units growing up alongside traditional academic departments to engage in applied or policy research and technology transfer. New administrative structures are established to further economic development, manage intellectual property, and profit from the work of the faculty. These institutional changes have important implications for the nature of faculty work and the faculty service role.

Whether as a result of the natural expansion of traditional and generally accepted forms of faculty service or the newer forms propelled by globalization, technology transfer, economic development, academic capitalism, and entrepreneurial behavior, it seems clear that debates about the faculty service role will continue long into the future. There is no doubt that these will be matters of continuing controversy in higher education.

See also: COLLEGES AND UNIVERSITIES, ORGANIZATIONAL STRUCTURE OF; FACULTY ROLES AND RESPONSIBILITIES.

BIBLIOGRAPHY

BOYER, ERNEST. 1990. *Scholarship Reconsidered: Priorities of the Professoriate.* Princeton, NJ: Carnegie Foundation for the Advancement of Teaching.

CLARK, BURTON R. 1998. *Creating Entrepreneurial Universities: Organizational Pathways of Transformation.* Oxford and New York: International Association of Universities and Pergamon.

CROSSON, PATRICIA H. 1983. *Public Service in Higher Education: Practices and Priorities.* ASHE-ERIC Higher Education Report No. 7. Washington, DC: Association for the Study of Higher Education.

DRISCOLL, AMY, and LYNTON, ERNEST A. 1999. *Making Outreach Visible: A Guide to Documenting Professional Service and Outreach.* Washington, DC: American Association for Higher Education.

EDGERTON, RUSSELL. 1995. "Foreword." In *Making the Case for Professional Service,* by Ernest. A. Lynton. Washington, DC: American Association for Higher Education.

LYNTON, ERNEST A. 1995. *Making the Case for Professional Service.* Washington, DC: American Association for Higher Education.

RICE, EUGENE. 1996. *Making a Place for the New American Scholar.* Washington, DC: American Association for Higher Education.

SLAUGHTER, SHEILA, and LESLIE, LARRY. 1997. *Academic Capitalism: Politics, Policies, and the Entrepreneurial University.* Baltimore: Johns Hopkins University Press.

PATRICIA CROSSON
KERRYANN O'MEARA

FACULTY TEACHING

See: COLLEGE TEACHING.

FACULTY TEACHING, ASSESSMENT OF

A comprehensive model of evaluating teaching advocates the use of multiple sources of information to confirm decisions. Each source—students, self-reports, colleagues and chairs, and evidence of learning—has particular strengths and limitations. The weight of the accumulated results leads to the most valid personnel decisions. Using a mixture of evaluation sources can also lead to greater improvement in teaching because different sources are helpful to different teachers and can help identify weaknesses in different areas of instruction.

Four major sources of information are used to determine the effectiveness of an individual teacher: student evaluations, teacher self-reports, colleague/department chair evaluations, and evidence of student learning. Each of these approaches can be useful in making personnel decisions (salary, promotion, and tenure) or in improving teaching. Each approach has strengths and weaknesses that must be kept in mind and that make it imperative to combine evidence for the best judgments.

Student Evaluations

Evaluations of teaching by students have become important and a frequently used method of assessment, the rationale being that students, and only students, are constant observers of what happens in the classroom. Moreover, only students can answer questions about the effects of instruction on them. Research over the past forty-five years has generally demonstrated their validity, reliability, and utility in improving instruction; this same body of research has shown that systematic course evaluations by students can provide useful information in assessing teachers for salary, promotion, and tenure decisions.

Although typically administered during the last week or two of the semester (but prior to final exams and grades), rating forms are on occasion given at midsemester so the instructors may make immediate adjustments for a particular course. Machine-scored forms are frequently used in order to process the large amounts of college and department data, but the open-ended comments solicited by most rating forms often provide teachers with more specific suggestions for improvement. The questions asked about teaching or the course commonly fall into these categories: organization or planning, teacher–student interaction or rapport, clarity or communication skill, workload and course difficulty, grading and assignments, and student self-reported learning. In addition there are always questions asking students to provide a global or overall rating of the course, the instructor, or the instruction received.

Many colleges have assembled their own student rating forms and some allow students to make their ratings by computer. Commercial forms published by the Educational Testing Service (SIR II) and Kansas State University (IDEA) have for many years provided colleges with score summaries, comparison information, and research reports.

Any use of student evaluations should take into account the vast amount of evidence from research (more than two thousand studies in the Educational Resource Information Center (ERIC) system since 1971). This evidence provides the foundation for guidelines for the proper use of student evaluations. Some of the guidelines that institutions should keep in mind follow.

1. Use several sets of evaluation results. Because an individual course may not accurately reflect a teacher's performance, a set of results based on several classes should be used for personnel decisions. Some research suggests using at least five classes.

2. Have a sufficient number of students evaluate each course. Averaging responses from enough students will minimize the effects of a few divergent opinions. Generally, fifteen students is a sufficient number, assuming they represent at least half of the enrolled students in a class. Research also has shown that student evaluations are consistent over short periods of time.

3. Consider some course characteristic in interpreting ratings. Although any single characteristic does not have a great effect, a combination could effect a teacher's evaluation. Research shows, for example, that small classes receive slightly higher ratings and that subject areas such as natural sciences and mathematics receive somewhat lower ratings. Courses that are college required, but not to satisfy the requirements of a major or minor, are also rated lower.

4. For personnel decisions, emphasize global ratings and estimates of learning. Research has shown that an overall or global rating correlated best with measured student achievement—more highly than ratings dealing with different teaching styles and presentation methods. Likewise, student estimates of their learning in a course are good reflections of instructional effectiveness.

5. Student evaluations can improve instruction, depending on how instructors use the results. Good evaluation forms help teachers diagnose their strengths and weaknesses. Studies indicate that some teachers can use the results directly, while others may need to discuss the results with a colleague or a professional consultant.

6. Give those being evaluated an opportunity to respond to evaluation results and to describe their teaching in writing. Teachers being evaluated for personnel purposes should have a chance to describe what they were trying to accomplish in the course and how their teaching methods fit those objectives. The self-report of teaching, which can be part of a teaching portfolio, gives teachers an opportunity to make their own best case.

Teacher Self-Reports

Teacher self-reports are descriptive information about teaching, which generally becomes part of a teacher's annual report. Self-ratings or self-evaluations can be included in self-reports but they should not be given much emphasis in personnel decisions because they lack validity and objectivity. In studies in which self-ratings were compared to ratings of the teacher made by students or colleagues, there was little agreement between teacher's view of themselves and others view of them. For personnel decisions, self-reports are important because they give the teacher the opportunity to make their own best case. Annual reports, sometimes called "brag sheets," are the most common type of self-report. The reports usually include information about the following activities.

- **Teaching:** teaching load, advising load, honors received, evaluations by students or others.

- **Scholarship and creative endeavors:** publications completed or in press, works in progress, grants, awards, presentations at conferences, performances, exhibitions.

- **Service:** service to the institution (e.g. committee work), service to the government or local community, service to the profession.

The Teaching Portfolio

The teaching portfolio has been heralded as an important new contribution to teaching evaluation because it allows teachers to provide continuous documentation of their performance. Borrowed from such fields as art and architecture, where the practice is for professionals to display samples of their work to perspective clients or employers, the teaching portfolio (or teaching dossier) contains three kinds of information:

- Products of good teaching (e.g. student workbooks or logs, student pre- and postexamination results).

- Materials developed by the teacher (course materials, syllabi, descriptions of how materials were used in teaching and in innovations attempted, and curriculum development materials).

- Assessments or comments by others (students, colleagues, alumni).

Most writers, including Russell Edgerton and colleagues, believe that a portfolio should include not only those items that present the teachers' views about their teaching but also examples and artifacts that they or others contribute. They also argue that the portfolio should be reflective and explain the teachers' thoughts and hopes as they made instructional decisions. During the 1990s many colleges have used teaching portfolios for both instructional improvement and personnel decisions. Some institutions also encourage graduate students to use teaching portfolios to document their experience and to demonstrate their potential for prospective employers.

Colleague and Department Chair Evaluations

Colleagues and department chairs can provide information that is not available from any other source. Neither students, who lack the background and perspective, nor deans, who lack the time, can contribute the kind of information that colleagues and chairs can. Colleagues and chairs can make judgments about the following areas:

- Organization of the subject matter and course. (Does the content appear to be appropriate and relevant?)

- Effective communication. (Are student assignments well defined?)

- Knowledge of subject matter and teaching.

- Fairness in examinations and grading (Do exams test course objectives?)

- Appropriateness of teaching methodology (Do instructional approaches suggest creativity and flexibility?)

- Appropriate student learning outcomes (Are student-produced documents and examinations consistent with course goals and objectives?)

Colleagues can make their judgments about the effectiveness of the teacher by examining course syllabi, assignments, and other documentary evidence. Colleagues in the same subject field as the person being evaluated can best judge several of the areas. In small institutions or in small departments, however, it is virtually impossible to limit evaluators to those in the same departments. In fact, given possible friendships or rivalries within departments, a more balanced evaluation may be achieved by including colleagues from other departments.

For tenure or promotion decisions, colleagues and chairs usually prepare formal written recommendations for candidates from their departments.

Although tenure and promotion committees include faculty representatives, these committee members usually do not have the time to obtain their own information on a candidate's teaching, scholarship, or service performance. Instead, they must rely on other sources. For teaching an ad hoc faculty subcommittee could review each candidate's dossier or teaching portfolio and collect supplementary evidence of teaching effectiveness. Their report and recommendation then is made to the tenure and promotion committee. At institutions in which teaching is of primary importance, this approach provides a way for colleagues to have greater influences in personnel decisions. At least one study by Lewis S. Root in 1987 has shown that a small group of colleagues relying on a variety of evidence on teaching performance, such as that suggested for the ad hoc committees on teaching, do make reliable and valid assessments.

Colleagues can also play an important role in improving teaching through their evaluations and collaboration. One example is a faculty-mentoring program, in which senior faculty members provide intellectual, emotional, and career guidance for young, untenured colleagues. Another example is the so-called buddy system, in which two or three colleagues agree to collaborate on a teaching improvement program. Activities include mutual classroom visitations, student interviews, and discussions among colleagues. Although faculty members vary in their ability to offer useful suggestions to each other, colleagues can still provide a perspective that students or others cannot.

The department chair should meet annually with any faculty member whose teaching is substantially below the department's expectations. Such meetings should be made well before final personnel decisions are to be made so that the candidate has ample opportunity to develop a plan to improve his or her teaching.

Evidence of Student Learning

Assessing student learning as a way of evaluating teaching performance has always been an important faculty responsibility. Teachers ask students questions in class, administer examinations, and evaluate projects and performance in laboratories and field settings. Some faculty members feel that student scores on final examinations in their courses provide a valid measure of student learning and that this measure should be used to assess their effectiveness as a teacher. Yet many factors other than the faculty member's teaching competence can affect examination results. Prior knowledge and their ability, interest, and skills in the subject area can also contribute greatly to how students score on examinations.

Another way to assess student learning is to test students at the beginning and then again at the end of a course and inspect the "gain scores." This procedure also is valuable to improve instruction: if significant numbers of students do not understand an important concept, instructional changes are needed. But because gain scores are easily misinterpreted, manipulated and may not be statistically reliable, they should not be used for examining student learning for tenure, promotion or salary decisions.

The Importance of Evaluation

Tenure decisions have important financial as well as educational implications for a college. Because a faculty member may spend thirty to thirty-five years at an institution, granting tenure amounts to more than a two million-dollar commitment at early twenty-first century salary and fringe benefits rates. When an institution makes this decision, they must consider their own goals and the faculty member's performance related to those goals. At community colleges and at many four-year colleges, teaching is the primary activity; so faculty members are evaluated largely as teachers, although their service and scholarly activities can also receive emphasis. At universities and certain four-year colleges, evidence of research and scholarship is primary, though teaching and to some extent service are also considered. In fact some doctoral-granting universities have made concerted efforts to evaluate and improve teaching performance.

See also: COLLEGE TEACHING; FACULTY ROLES AND RESPONSIBILITIES.

BIBLIOGRAPHY

CENTRA, JOHN A. 1973. "Self-Ratings of College Teachers: A Comparison with Student Ratings." *Journal of Education Measurement* 10(4):287–295.

CENTRA, JOHN A. 1993. *Reflective Faculty Evaluation, Enhancing Teaching and Determining Faculty Effectiveness.* San Francisco: Jossey-Bass.

EDGERTON, RUSSELL; HUTCHINGS, PATRICIA; and QUINLAN, KATHERINE. 1991. *The Teaching Port-*

folio: Capturing the Scholarship of Teaching. Washington DC: The American Association of Higher Education.

FELDMAN, KENNETH A. 1989. "Instructional Effectiveness of College Teachers as Judged by Teachers Themselves, Current and Former Students, Colleagues, Administrators and External (Neutral) Observers." *Research in Higher Education* 30:137–189.

MARSH, HERBERT W. 1987. "Student Evaluations of University Teaching: Research Findings, Methodological Issues, and Directions for Future Research." *International Journal of Educational Research* 11:253–388.

MCKEACHIE, WILBUR J. 1979. "Student Ratings of Teaching: A Reprise." *Academe* 65:384–397.

ROOT, LEWIS S. 1987. "A Faculty Evaluation: Reliability of Peer Assessments of Research, Teaching, and Service." *Research in Higher Education* 26:71–84.

JOHN A. CENTRA

FAMILY AND CONSUMER SCIENCES EDUCATION

Family and consumer sciences education is a field of study that focuses on families and work—and on their interrelationships. Family and consumer sciences education tries to empower individuals and families to identify and create alternative solutions to significant everyday challenges and to take responsibility for the consequences of their actions in a diverse global society. These challenges are experienced by people of all ages in their families, workplaces, and communities. Consequently, the central concern of the field is the physical, economic, and sociopsychological well-being of individuals and families within that diverse society. From its inception in the nineteenth century, the field has used knowledge to improve people's quality of life.

Goals and Purposes

Family and consumer sciences education contributes to a broad range of intellectual, moral, and workforce development goals. Its mission is to prepare students for family life, work life, and careers in family and consumer sciences. Nine specific goals, developed in 1994 by the Family and Consumer Sciences Division of the American Vocational Association (now the Association for Career and Technical Education [ACTE]) provide the direction for curriculum:

1. Strengthen the well-being of individuals and families across the life span

2. Become responsible citizens and leaders for family, community, and work settings

3. Promote optimal nutrition and wellness across the life span

4. Manage resources to meet the material needs of individuals and families

5. Balance personal, home, family, and work lives

6. Use critical and creative thinking skills to address problems in diverse family, community, and work environments

7. Foster successful life management, employment, and career development

8. Function as providers and consumers of goods and services for families

9. Appreciate human worth and accept responsibility for one's actions and success in family and work life

These goals guided the development of national family and consumer sciences content standards during the 1990s. Recommended content includes reasoning for action; career, community, and family connections; consumer and family resources; family development; human development; interpersonal relationships; nutrition and wellness; and parenting. In addition, standards were recommended for the knowledge, skills, and practices required for careers in consumer service; early childhood education and services; facilities management and maintenance; family and consumer services; food production and services; food science, dietetics, and nutrition; hospitality, tourism, and recreation; and housing, interiors, and furnishings.

Family and consumer sciences education is an interdisciplinary field. Teachers integrate knowledge and processes from empirical, interpretive, and critical sciences to help students identify, understand, and solve continuing human concerns or problems that individuals and families experience. To address these concerns, the field draws on social sciences, physical and biological sciences, arts, humanities, and mathematics. Core processes are integrated in most courses and programs. Scientific and practical reasoning processes are integrated to learn about and solve *what-to-do* problems. Communication processes, including the use of information technology, are integrated to sensitively identify and meet the needs of self and others through caregiving and education. Shared democratic leadership processes are integrated in classroom and community service learning experiences. Management and other processes, such as mathematics, are also incorporated, as needed, into concrete learning activities like those experienced in homes, families, and communities. Academic partnerships between family and consumer sciences and colleagues in science, language arts, and social studies result in team-taught courses in food and nutrition and family issues and relationships.

Family and consumer sciences education is an action-oriented field. It is concerned with the work of the family through everyday life-enhancing, caregiving activities and interactions carried out privately within the family and publicly in the community. Private caregiving focuses on the optimum development of family members. Public caregiving is provided through public service and service careers, such as child-care and food service careers. These personal service careers provide the caregiving that was provided only in homes before the twentieth century.

Educational experiences focus on developing three interrelated and interdependent kinds of reasoned action or processes needed for the work of the family in the home and community: communicative, reflective, and technical action. Communicative action involves developing learning and interpersonal skills needed for sharing meanings and understanding the needs, intentions, and values of family and community members. Reflective action involves developing the critical and ethical thinking skills needed for evaluating and changing social conditions, norms, and power relationships that may be accepted without question, but may be harmful to families, their members, and, ultimately, to society. This critical reflective action focuses on enhancing human capabilities and the physical, psychosocial, and economic well-being of the family and its members in a rapidly changing society. Finally, technical action involves developing the care-giving skills needed for using a variety of methods and technology to meet family needs for food, clothing, shelter,

protection, and the development of family members. Such technical action varies historically and from culture to culture.

Action-oriented classrooms develop and extend these skills into homes and communities. For example, students in a high school parenting education course take communicative, reflective, and technical actions as they analyze, discuss, and evaluate the effects that violence in Saturday morning cartoons has on children. These kinds of actions can then be integrated and used when students or family members plan and work together to effect change in this type of programming—which has become a cultural norm for many children—such as through community education activities for parents and legislators and for companies who sponsor violent programming.

History of Family and Consumer Sciences Education

From its inception, the field has been concerned with using knowledge to improve the quality of life. Family and consumer sciences education began in the mid-nineteenth century as *domestic economy* for girls. During this time—and into the early twentieth century—women were relegated to the private life of the family and separated from the public life of the community. The educational reformer Catharine Beecher (1800–1878) envisioned a field to help students develop the critical thinking skills needed in their homes and in the wider community. Initially, this new field of study was an integral part of a general science-based liberal arts education that prepared females for their "professions" as wives and mothers. By the late 1800s, land-grant colleges offered *domestic science* courses for young women, thus making it acceptable for women to attend coeducational institutions. Two prevailing cultural assumptions supported this new field: (1) domestic tasks are women's work; and (2) women need specific formal training for their home-centered duties.

During the twentieth century, the family and consumer sciences field evolved along with cultural, political, legislative, and pedagogical change to meet the needs of diverse populations. In the early 1900s, concern for the deterioration of the family and its members in a rapidly changing society motivated Ellen H. Richards (1842–1911) to found the American Home Economics Association (now the American Association of Family and Consumer Sciences). She envisioned this professional organization as one that would emphasize cultural, ethical, and social ideals, and the scientific management of household work.

Soon after the establishment of this organization, changing political circumstances culminated in federal legislation that extended the field into communities and schools throughout the country. First, the Smith-Lever Act of 1914 established the Cooperative Extension system to provide community educational programs in every county throughout the United States. Home economics education was established as part of this community-based educational system, which continues to provide links between the U.S. Department of Agriculture and land-grant universities for family and consumer education programming in an effort to improve lives and communities.

The Smith-Hughes Act of 1917 established vocational education for paid employment and vocational home economics education in most public schools. By providing funding for teachers and equipment, this legislation transformed the field of study from a female version of general liberal arts and science education for a few women in colleges to *vocational home economics education* for girls in secondary schools throughout the country. Even though this act defined vocational education as technical education for paid employment, home economics education was meant for useful employment and merged two diverse curricular goals: (1) a general liberal arts and science education for family and community members, and (2) preparation for their assumed life work as homemakers. This educational and social reform played a liberating role for girls, since they were encouraged to stay in school at a time when girls tended to drop out after the eighth grade. It also prepared them to participate in their communities. Community leadership was developed through a cocurricular high school student organization, the Future Homemakers of America (FHA), which was established in 1945. Gradually, home economics education prepared girls for every area of home life in the first half of the twentieth century; namely, clothing construction, food preparation and preservation, sanitation, home furnishings, child care, health care, and family relations. Social benefits centered on the country having wise, prepared mothers; responsible family members and citizens; healthy and moral households; and productive and confident homemakers.

By the 1950s the country and the field had begun a transformation as a result of changing cultural assumptions that had limited women's work to the home—and men to work outside the home. Production of food, clothing, and home furnishings—and home care of children and sick, elderly, and handicapped family members—began to occur outside the home. Most families were becoming consumers rather than producers of these goods and services, and career choices expanded for males and females. More women entered wage-earning careers outside the home—including, but not limited to, home- and family-related service careers. Some men's work expanded to homemaking and parenting roles within the home. Consequently, both males and females needed help with recognizing and meeting new challenges of families and consumers, including deciding the direction of their careers and preparing for and managing family, career, and community responsibilities. To meet these needs, many schools offered at least one home economics course for young men, and when Title IX of the Education Amendments Act of 1972 prohibited sex discrimination in education, all courses were suddenly open to males and females. Consequently, male enrollment increased in middle school and high school career and family-related programs, and especially in food and interpersonal relationships courses, to approximately 40 percent in the 1990s. By 1994 the field changed its name and emphasis to *family and consumer sciences* to reflect these and other cultural and educational developments. Subsequently, the Future Homemakers of America student organization was renamed the Family, Career and Community Leaders of America (FCCLA).

Major Trends, Issues, and Controversies

These name changes reflect major trends and issues within the field. Over the years the field has shifted between technical and critical-science approaches. In the early twenty-first century the trend is toward a critical science approach, as educators focus on perennial and evolving issues concerning families and communities. Problem solving occurs within the context of real-world issues, and this approach integrates academic and workforce preparation. Skill development continues, but rather than emphasizing the development of homemaking skills, the thinking and interpersonal skills needed in families, workplaces, and communities are emphasized. In addition to scientific reasoning, practical or ethical reasoning is being added to the curriculum. While economic values such as efficiency and productivity continue to be reflected in the curriculum, moral and ethical values, such as personal and social responsibility and respect for all people, and all other types of values are openly discussed (rather than assumed) when discussing and solving problems affecting family and community members.

Grounded in the concrete and abstract experiences of the home, family, and community, family and consumer sciences education provides meaningful ways of knowing and learning for young people and adults with varying abilities and needs. Courses are being designed to help all students (including students at risk for dropping out of school) meet high academic expectations and stay in school. Authentic experiences help students make connections with other academic disciplines and the world beyond the classroom.

With this approach, family and consumer sciences education has become an integral part of the current educational reform movement. Yearlong, comprehensive courses and programs are being redesigned to meet high academic standards and student needs. National and state academic and family and consumer sciences content standards are used to strengthen programs and plans, and courses are becoming more specialized. However, academics, technology, and workforce-development skills are now integrated into the way students learn. These transferable skills are core learnings in process-centered family and consumer sciences classrooms. Real-world, problem-based instruction often includes service learning and other ways of extending learning beyond the classroom. Teachers are designing courses to fit flexible scheduling options, including semester, nine-week, and block-scheduling courses, to replace comprehensive yearlong courses.

Professionals continue to debate the role of family and consumer sciences in schools, as well as teacher preparation needs, teacher certification/licensure requirements, and ways to recruit teachers. These are interrelated issues, since inadequate numbers of teachers are being prepared to replace and expand the family and consumer sciences teaching force.

School and Community Curriculum Offerings

Family and consumer sciences educational programs are provided for youth and adults in schools and communities throughout the world. School programs for elementary age children are more likely to be offered in other countries, such as Japan and Malaysia, than in the United States. However, middle schools, high schools, and colleges around the world offer elective and required courses in family and consumer sciences education. Such programs have varying names, such as family and consumer sciences, human development and family science, family studies, work and family life, human ecology, or home economics.

High school curriculum offerings include comprehensive home and family life-skills courses and specialized personal, family, career, or community-focused courses. Comprehensive courses are more likely to be offered in the elementary and middle school levels, and specialized courses tend to be at the high school and college levels. Personal development courses are designed to help adolescents and adults learn about themselves, careers, and family responsibilities so they can make reasoned life choices. Course titles reflect these comprehensive emphases: Building Life Skills, Orientation to Life and Careers, Independent Living, Adult Roles and Responsibilities, Leadership in the Workplace, Career Connections, and Career Choices.

More specialized family-oriented courses include titles such as Family Relationships, Interpersonal Relationships, Human Behavior, Parenting and Child Development, Family and Technology, Families in Society Today, Dynamics of Relationships, Families of Many Cultures, and Families in Crisis. Food, nutrition, and wellness courses may be designed to meet personal, family, and career needs—as well as science requirements. Courses offered include Nutrition and Wellness; Family, Food and Society; Sports Nutrition; Modern Meals; Global Cuisine; Food Science; Chemistry of Food and Nutrition; and Experimental Foods. Consumer and family resource management courses, such as Consumer Economics, Life Management, Financial Management, and Life Planning, tend to be more comprehensive in that they are designed to prepare students for their adult roles and responsibilities.

Career-oriented courses in high schools, colleges, and universities prepare students for their family work and an array of personal service careers. High school courses range from exploring career options and developing core processes in a nine-week or semester course to a one- or two-year workforce development course focused on developing the knowledge and skills necessary for careers in food service, child care, hospitality and tourism, facilities care and management, housing and interiors, or apparel and textiles related careers. Two-year and four-year college programs include combinations of specialized courses to prepare for professional careers in early childhood education; consumer services; financial planning; dietetics; food science; hospitality and food management; interior design; fashion design and merchandising; and product research and development. Baccalaureate and master's degree programs prepare family and consumer sciences educators for schools and Cooperative Extension. Master's and Ph.D. programs prepare researchers, specialists, and university educators.

Family and consumer sciences content may be combined in a variety of ways to meet the special needs of students and communities. School-based programs and courses are offered for pregnant and parenting students, dropout-prone students, and developmentally handicapped students. Graduation rates for pregnant and parenting students from these programs is more than 85 percent, while the national retention rate for these teenagers is 40 percent. Rates of subsequent pregnancies and low birth weights are also lower than state and national averages. School-based and community-based entrepreneurship courses help students, especially in small communities and developing countries, create their own businesses, often providing family and consumer sciences–related services.

Community-based family and consumer sciences community programs are offered by Cooperative Extension and other community agencies and organizations. These family and consumer sciences programs address a variety of individual, family, and community needs and issues. Cooperative Extension is a non-formal educational system concerned with issues faced throughout the life cycle, including child care, parenting, family life, nutrition and food safety, money management, and adult development and aging. Cooperative Extension family and consumer sciences educators collaborate with other county and state Cooperative Extension educators to provide community programming. Basic programming includes 4-H (a non-formal educational program for five- to nineteen-year olds focused on developing their "head, heart, hands, and health") youth and adult leadership development and adult education; agriculture; community resources and economic development; family development and resource management; leadership and volunteer development; natural resources and environment management; and nutrition, diet, and health. National initiative programming focuses on nationally important issues, such as financial security, caring for children and youth, food safety and quality, healthy people and communities, and workforce preparation.

Current Status

Family and consumer sciences education is an integral component of the U.S. educational system, and of some other countries' systems. Some countries, such as Japan, require home economics at all levels of their public schools. Most U.S. secondary schools offer family and consumer sciences courses, and some require middle school life-skills courses and/or high school career connections, parenting and child development, and interpersonal relationships courses for all their students. State and local school funding has replaced most federal funding for these programs. Many family and consumer sciences programs strengthened their place in the middle and high school curriculum during the 1990s, especially when curriculum was revised to contribute to academic, technological, workplace, and family and consumer sciences standards and local and state needs. For example, enrollment more than doubled in Ohio's Work and Family Life program during this period. While family and consumer sciences programs have maintained or expanded enrollment in many middle schools and high schools, some schools have eliminated their programs due to the unavailability of teachers.

Cooperative Extension family and consumer sciences programs have maintained their community educational role in rural and small towns and expanded their urban programs. Websites connect families to sources of information and resources such as fact sheets, educational events, self-directed studies, and research findings. All states provide educational programming with varying emphases to meet local needs.

See also: CURRICULUM, SCHOOL; SECONDARY EDUCATION, *subentries on* CURRENT TRENDS, HISTORY OF; VOCATIONAL AND TECHNICAL EDUCATION, *subentries on* HISTORY OF, TRENDS.

BIBLIOGRAPHY

AMERICAN VOCATIONAL ASSOCIATION. 1994. *Home Economics Vision and Mission Statement.* Alexandria, VA: American Vocational Association.

ARCUS, MARGARET; SCHVANEVELDT, JAY D.; and MOSS, J. JOEL, eds. 1993. *Handbook of Family Life Education,* Vols. 1 and 2. Newbury Park, CA: Sage.

BROWN, MARJORIE M. 1978. *A Conceptual Scheme and Decision-Rules for the Selection and Organization of Home Economics Curriculum Content.* Bulletin No. 0033. Madison: Wisconsin Department of Education.

BROWN, MARJORIE M. 1980. *What Is Home Economics Education?* Minneapolis: University of Minnesota, Minnesota Research and Development Center for Vocational Education.

BROWN, MARJORIE M. 1993. *Philosophical Studies of Home Economics in the United States: Basic Ideas by which Home Economists Understand Themselves.* East Lansing: Michigan State University.

JOHNSON, JULIE, and FEDJE, CHERYL, eds. 1999. *Family and Consumer Sciences Curriculum: Toward a Critical Science Approach.* Family and Consumer Sciences Teacher Education Yearbook 19. Peoria, IL: Glencoe/McGraw-Hill.

LASTER, JANET, and JOHNSON, JULIE. 2001. "Family and Consumer Sciences." In *Curriculum Handbook.* Alexandria, VA: Association for Supervision and Curriculum Development.

LASTER, JANET F., and THOMAS, RUTH G., eds. 1997. *Thinking for Ethical Action in Families and Communities.* Family and Consumer Sciences Teacher Education Yearbook 17. Peoria, IL: Glencoe/McGraw-Hill.

NATIONAL ASSOCIATION OF STATE ADMINISTRATORS OF FAMILY AND CONSUMER SCIENCES. 1998. *National Standards for Family and Consumer Sciences.* Decatur, GA: V-TECS Southern Association of Colleges and Schools.

NATIONAL COUNCIL ON FAMILY RELATIONS. 1997. *Framework for Life-Span Family Life Education,* Revised Edition. Minneapolis, MN: NCES.

REDICK, SHARON S. 1995. "Home Economics: The Family and Consumer Sciences Curriculum." In *Content of the Curriculum,* 2nd edition, ed. Allan A. Glatthorn. Alexandria, VA: Association of Supervision and Curriculum Development.

REDICK, SHARON S., ed. 1996. *Review and Synthesis of Family and Consumer Sciences Education Research 1985–1995.* Family and Consumer Sciences Teacher Education Yearbook 16. Peoria, IL: Glencoe/McGraw-Hill.

SEEVERS, BRENDA; GRAHAM, DONNA; GAMON, JULIE; and CONKLIN, NIKKI. 1997. *Education through Cooperative Extension.* Albany, NY: Delmar Publishers.

SMITH, FRANCES M., and HAUSAFUS, CHERYL O., eds. 1994. *The Education of Early Adolescents: Home Economics in the Middle School.* Home Economics Teacher Education Yearbook 14. Peoria, IL: Glencoe Division, Macmillan/McGraw-Hill.

STAGE, SARAH, and VINCENTI, VIRGINIA B., eds. 1997. *Rethinking Home Economics: Women and the History of a Profession.* Ithaca, NY: Cornell University Press.

VAIL, ANN; FOX, WANDA S.; and WILD, PEGGY, eds. 2000. *Leadership for Change: National Standards for Family and Consumer Sciences.* Family and Consumer Sciences Teacher Education Yearbook 20. Peoria, IL: Glencoe/McGraw-Hill.

JANET FENTRESS LASTER

FAMILY COMPOSITION AND CIRCUMSTANCE

OVERVIEW

Much research has been conducted on what children need to grow up healthy, ready to learn, and to succeed in school. Many aspects of a child's growth and development, family circumstance, and school success have been studied, analyzed, and reported on in an effort to help parents, educators, health care professionals, and policymakers better understand what they can do to assure a child's success. A review of this research reveals two significant circumstances that seem to have the most impact on a child's growth, development, and ultimate educational success: poverty and family interactions. Barring significant birth defects or injury, these two circumstances hold the key to virtually every aspect of a child's life that affects his or her ability to grow up healthy and to learn. However, it must be noted that these two factors overlap in many respects and cannot be viewed in isolation. In addition, while it is recognized that a child's behavior is what is sometimes most disruptive to the family, due to the child's drug abuse, mental illness, disability, or other factors, the focus here is on the effects of outside factors on the growth and development of the otherwise normal, healthy child.

Effects of Poverty on Children

All other things being equal, children living in extreme poverty or below the poverty line for many years have the worst outcomes for health and school success. (The most chronically poor counties in the United States are in rural areas of Appalachia and in the South.) The effects of poverty are multiple and profound. Children who are born into families living in poverty generally do not receive adequate prenatal care. Lack of good nutrition for a pregnant woman can result in a baby that has a low birthweight, is more vulnerable to illness, is underdeveloped, and is likely to require more care, compared to the child of a well-nourished mother. Healthy brain development in children from birth to three years of age is critical in the development of speech and language, coordination, and reasoning. Children who suffer from poor brain development are at high risk for delayed speech and motor skills, neurological disorders, learning disabilities, and behavior problems.

Children living in poverty do not usually receive proper and timely health care, which can lead to chronic illness, such as asthma, or chronic infections, such as ear infections that can lead to hearing loss. They often do not receive required immunizations, which can delay school entry and lead to serious childhood illnesses. They are also more prone to complications from minor injuries or illnesses. Many mothers living in poverty suffer from depression, making them less able to properly nurture, stimulate, and interact with their children. As a result, their children suffer from neglect, failure to thrive, and decreased brain development.

Poverty frequently means that a family lives in a neighborhood that has a high rate of violence. Housing in these neighborhoods often exposes children to unsafe living conditions, including environmental toxins, poor ventilation, and infestations of rodents and insects. Low-income children have more than triple the risk of lead poisoning, which causes neurological damage and has been linked to lower IQ and long-term behavior problems such as impaired concentration and violence.

Poor families are more likely to be single-parent families with a parent who is young with unstable employment and low earning potential. These parents suffer stress associated with the constant strain of trying to provide adequate food, housing, clothing, and health care for their children. Parents under stress have a more difficult time providing the nurture and support necessary to establish positive bonding, enable speech acquisition, teach problem-solving skills, and promote early learning activities that affect school readiness. Parents living in poverty are more likely to have low educational attainment and less knowledge about early childhood education and brain development in infants. There are generally fewer books, educational toys and games, and outside opportunities for learning, such as family vacations and trips to a museum.

Children living below the poverty line are 1.3 times more likely to experience learning disabilities and developmental delays than are children who are not poor. Children with learning disabilities and developmental delays are more likely to experience school difficulties, and school failure at an early age is a leading indicator in school drop-out rates.

Families living in poverty also experience housing instability. Children who move frequently tend to have fewer friends, experience social isolation, and have higher truancy rates than those who grow up in more stable homes. In addition, social and educational services designed to support families in poverty are disrupted when the family moves frequently. Many families in poverty experience periods of homelessness, which exposes children to communicable diseases and the chaos found in shelters. Homeless children suffer increased rates of illnesses such as diarrhea, asthma, anemia, and infection. Simply being born into poverty affects a child's ability to grow up healthy, to be nurtured in a safe and stable home, to enter school ready to learn, and to remain in school and complete a high school education.

Family Interactions

Researchers have studied the effects on school success of single-parent families, blended families, extended families, divorce, death of a parent, foster care, adoption, and gay families. Within each of these family compositions, examples of children who thrive and children who fail can be found. But more important than family composition is family interaction—how family members relate to each other. Can a child who lives in a two-parent home where there is poor family interaction due to drug abuse, domestic violence, or mental illness be said to be at less risk of school failure than a child born into a single-parent family living in extreme poverty?

Family interaction significantly impacts the development of the children in the home, regardless of income level. However, research does show that certain types of family interactions are more common in low-income homes. For example, drug abuse and poverty are the two most common factors cited in domestic violence and child abuse cases.

In families where one or both parents abuse drugs or alcohol, children are frequently neglected, and sometimes injured or abused. In addition, much of the family income is spent on supporting the drug habit, and the family suffers from the diminished resources available for food, clothes, housing, and medical care. Children growing up in homes where drug abuse is present are frequently exposed to violence, unpredictable behavior, overt displays of sexual behavior, absence of one or both parents, poverty, homelessness, and a lack of consistent supervision. Children are often truant from school and may lack school supplies and appropriate seasonal clothing. Nonrelatives are frequently present in the home and prevent the child from maintaining a close relationship with one or both parents. Children may also be expected to perform most household chores, such as cooking and cleaning, and to care for younger siblings or elderly grandparents. Children living in these circumstances may appear tired, lonely, sad, angry, afraid, malnourished, dirty, withdrawn, aggressive, anxious, or defensive, and they may exhibit a wide array of physical symptoms including complaints of stomachaches and headaches, hair loss from stress, nervous tics, stuttering, and thumb/finger/hand sucking when not age appropriate.

Children who live in homes where neglect, abuse, and/or domestic violence are present suffer many of the same effects as those mentioned above. The interactions between adults, and between adult and child, significantly impact the child's growth and development. Children who are abused or ne-

glected suffer from low self-esteem, anger, depression, fear, anxiety, and feelings of abandonment. They manifest these feelings through physical symptoms such as headaches, stomachaches, vomiting, diarrhea, and sometimes sleeping or eating disorders. Very young children are particularly vulnerable to neglect and abuse in homes where domestic violence is present. The victim of domestic violence, which is most often the mother/woman present in the home, may ignore her children to appease the offender. Very young children are particularly at risk of injury or abuse from shaken baby syndrome or battered child syndrome.

Effects of Government Intervention

When the government intervenes to protect children living in homes with drug abuse, domestic violence, or child abuse, the family interactions are again affected. Once a determination is made that a child's safety is at risk, one of two approaches are generally taken: either the child is removed from the home and placed in a home with relatives or in foster care, or the family is provided with in-home counseling and support services. In-home services are considered less intrusive and disruptive to the child and the parent-child relationship. In an ideal situation, the in-home service provider visits with the family members at home and conducts counseling sessions with all family members to help the family interact in more positive ways. However, family members frequently resent the intrusion of an outsider and the child is blamed for the intrusion.

The focus of Child Protective Services, an array of agencies and collaborations designed to assure the safety of children, is specifically on the safety and well-being of the child. As a result, the adults in the home may view the child as the reason for the intervention, causing additional stress on the child. The child may feel guilty that his parents are required to attend counseling sessions, court hearings, or to pay for services. The parents may talk openly around the child about the intrusion and inconvenience of such services, and about their resentment. If the services are not effective, then additional court hearings are held and there may be additional finger pointing and blame directed at the child. Ultimately, the child may be removed from the home, again causing the child to feel that he or she is being punished.

When a child is removed from home, family interactions are very much affected. The child may be in a safer environment, but there is stress associated with the change in living circumstances. In general, the parent may not be happy with the removal of the child from the home. The parent may call or visit the child and accuse the new caretaker (either a relative or foster parent) of not caring for the child properly, and again the parent may cast blame on the child for causing the disruption.

The parents may also be required to make child-support payments while the child is out of the home, and they may have to receive some type of treatment or counseling as a condition for the child to return home. If the parent fails to complete the court-ordered treatment, the child may view that failure as an indication that the parent has abandoned or does not love him or her. It is reasonable to believe that any period of time in which the child is out of the home is a time of stress and confusion. Even when the child feels more physically safe when not at home, there are emotional attachments that bind the child to the home and make the removal difficult.

Effects of Mental Illness

The term *mental illness* describes a broad range of mental and emotional conditions that disturb a person's behavior, mood, thought processes and/or social interpersonal relationships. Children who live with a family member who is mentally ill must deal not only with the stigma of mental illness in their family, but also with the stress caused by that illness. While the extreme circumstances of mental illness are widely reported in the news (such as mothers who, while suffering from depression, kill their children), the much more common situations of a parent who suffers from some type of mental disorder or a parent who is caring for a relative with mental illness are found in millions of homes in the United States. Some of the most common types of mental illness are:

- Depression, which is characterized by extreme or prolonged periods of sadness.
- Schizophrenia, a very severe illness characterized by disordered thought processes that can lead to hallucinations and delusions.
- Bipolar disorder, which is a brain disorder involving periods of mania and depression.
- Dementia, which is a loss of mental function usually associated with advanced age and characterized by memory loss, personality change, confusion or disorientation, impairment of judgment, and deteriorating intellectual capaci-

ty. There are many types of dementia, including Alzheimer's disease.

Mental illness can occur in any family. When it first occurs, the family members may at first deny that something different has happened. During an acute episode, family members may react with surprise, fear, and alarm, and once the episode is over there may follow a period of relief and calm. But, as symptoms persist, it becomes clear that life will never again be normal.

Children are particularly affected by the strange behavior of a parent or older sibling. They may have little knowledge about mental illness and blame themselves for what is happening to their relationship with a loved one. They are frequently afraid to discuss their feelings with others, particularly their friends or people outside their families, and they therefore become isolated and withdrawn. How other family members handle the situation is critically important to the child. If other family members, particularly the other parent, become distraught and helpless, then the child will become even more distressed.

A child will receive less attention at this time, because other family members are attending to the member with the illness. The child may begin to exhibit behavior problems at home and at school, become depressed or withdrawn, and exhibit sleeping or eating disturbances. Every episode becomes more difficult to handle, and the child may try to escape by running away from home. Even though the child is not being abused, the effects appear similar, with anger, aggression, fear, depression, anxiety, withdrawal, and sadness all being possible outcomes.

Similar circumstances exist when a family is faced with caring for an extended family member who develops dementia or any other mental illness. If the family member moves into the home, the child is sometimes displaced from his or her room, daily routines may change, and finances may be strained. All of this is very disruptive to children, particularly school-aged children. It is difficult for a child to see a change in the behavior of a beloved relative (grandparent, aunt, uncle, etc.), which might frighten the child. The presence of this person in the household affects the parent-child relationship, as parental responsibility is shifted and there is less time to spend with the child. The resultant stress and concern can create serious family problems. Family life is disrupted and often unpredictable, and the needs of the ill family member often become the priority.

What Do Children Need to Be Successful?

Although much research has focused on issues that negatively affect the outcomes for children, little research has focused on what characteristics make children successful. In the mid-1990s the Search Institute, led by Dr. Peter Benson, conducted a nationwide survey of 100,000 young people in more than 200 communities to learn about the assets of successful teens. This research specifically targeted teenagers, but the implications of how the assets were developed are applicable to children of all ages.

The survey identified forty developmental assets that help young people make better decisions, choose positive pathways, and grow up to be competent, caring, and responsible. These assets are grouped into eight categories: support, empowerment, boundaries and expectations, constructive use of time, commitment to learning, positive values, social competencies, and positive identification.

Support. Children need to feel loved and supported by their family. Teens reported that spending time with parents, being hugged, being told that they are loved and doing things as a family are important to them. Children learn to love by example. Eating at least one meal per day together as a family, spending time with each child individually, listening and valuing their opinions, respecting their concerns, attending school events, and going to worship together are all examples of how families can show support and love to their children.

Empowerment. Young people need to feel that they are valued by their community and that they have the opportunity to contribute to the welfare of others. They need to feel safe at home, at school, and in the neighborhood. Those surveyed reported that they need and want to feel useful in their communities, and that they need to have opportunities to give service back to the community.

Boundaries and expectations. Young people need to know what is expected of them and whether their activities and behaviors are acceptable, or "inbounds." Boundaries are important not only within the family, but in the school and neighborhood as well. Families need clear rules and consequences for behavior, as well as ways of monitoring behavior. When the rules are clearly communicated and the consequences are fairly and consistently enforced,

children are more comfortable controlling their own behavior, and they make better choices. Teenagers report that positive adult role models are helpful and desirable. Adult role models can be teachers, scout leaders, coaches, parents of friends, or adults they meet and know through community activities such as worship, community service, and sports.

Constructive use of time. Young people need opportunities for constructive and creative activities. These opportunities can occur through participation in faith-based organizations and youth programs; through lessons in art, dance, music, drama, and sports; or through learning skills at home, such as cooking, decorating, sewing, building, or designing. Parents can encourage their children to explore arts, sports, or other creative outlets by volunteering to help with a sports team or youth group, or by taking the child to local museums, dance performances, or plays. Activities such as these encourage physical activity, promote problem-solving skills, stimulate creativity, and help young people meet others with similar interests. As an interest in such activities develops, there is less opportunity or interest in watching TV, hanging out on the street with undesirable companions, or experimenting with drugs and sex. As children grow older, parents can encourage them to obtain part-time employment to earn money and teach them how to manage their money.

Commitment to learning. Young people need to develop a lifelong commitment to education and learning. Children need to experience at a very young age that learning is fun and that parents value education. Every effort should be made to assure that the child is successful in school. Parents should also model lifelong learning by engaging in new learning experiences, taking part in community and government life, and helping their children apply their knowledge to real life activities. Parents should visit their child's school, talk with the teacher, and help with homework. Parents can help their children bond with their school by encouraging participation in school activities, showing school spirit, inviting school friends home to work on projects, and participating in school cleanup and work days.

Children who are good readers are better learners, so children should learn to read for pleasure as well as for schoolwork. Parents should start reading to children when they are very young, and they should teach children that books have wonderful stories and interesting information. It is helpful to take children to the public library as soon as they are able to look at picture books. As children grow older, books can be read together and discussed. Parents can start a young-reader book club with their child and their child's friends to encourage them to read together.

Positive values. Young people need to develop strong values that guide their choices. These values include caring, equality and social justice, integrity, honesty, responsibility, and restraint (believing that it is important not to use drugs or alcohol and not to be sexually active). These values help young people make good decisions and it is important for parents to help their children develop these values. It is not enough just to tell children what their values should be; parents must demonstrate that they have these values and how these values translate into everyday life. Children learn by example, so if parents are caring, honest, responsible, and demonstrate restraint in the use of drugs and alcohol, then children will learn these things. As a child grows older, parents can label the values and show how they and others incorporate these values into their lives.

Social competencies. Young people need skills and competencies that equip them to make positive choices and to build relationships. Life is full of choices, and how young people make those choices will affect how they spend their time, who their friends are, what work ethics they have, who they choose as a mate, and how they raise their own children. The ability to make choices, and to see how those choices impact the future, is critical in becoming a successful adult. Very young children have a very short sense of time, and they make choices based on what is immediately available to them and what they need or want in that moment. But as children grow older they can learn that choosing to watch TV now means that there is not enough time later to read a story or play a game. Parents can begin to help children understand how a decision will affect their goals. Goal-oriented decision making is a skill that must be learned and practiced successfully.

Another social competency is learning to make friends. Friendships will not last long if a child is self-centered and insensitive to the feelings of others. Parents can help children learn to be empathetic and sensitive by discussing with them how other people feel when they are treated unkindly or when they are hurt. Children learn to respond with empathy and kindness when they see their parents respond to them with these same feelings.

Children must also learn to be comfortable with people of different cultures, races, and ethnic backgrounds. This is sometimes more difficult if the family lives in a very homogenous neighborhood, but through books, films, television programs, and newspapers parents can make children aware of the different people and cultures in the world, and teach them that just because something is different it is not to be feared or disliked. In communities where people of different cultures live, it is important for parents to treat everyone with respect and to introduce their child to experiences of different cultures. Parents can take the child to markets and stores that sell products of different countries, listen to music from other cultures, or invite people of different cultures to speak to a class about their customs, dress, and food.

Children need to learn to resist negative influences and peer pressure. Parents can help by engaging in role-playing situations with them and talking with them about choices that their friends are making. Children need to learn active resistance and about the dangers of being "in the wrong place at the wrong time." Children also need to learn how to resolve conflict peacefully. Parents can start teaching children at a very young age that hitting is not acceptable behavior, and how to resolve conflicts without violence. Parents must also model this behavior in their choice of discipline and in their own behavior.

Positive identification. Young people need a strong sense of their own power, purpose, worth, and promise. Teenagers reported in the Search Institute survey that it was important for them to feel that they have control over things that happen to them. Parents can reinforce their children's sense of power and worth in many ways. Helping children learn to make good choices and praising them when those choices are made, helping children identify their strengths and showing them how to use those talents, and giving children time for recognition are all ways of building self-esteem. It is important for young people to feel positive about their future, and to feel that their life has purpose.

Teenagers easily fall into periods of depression due to hormonal changes that occur during different stages of development, and due to the peaks and valleys that occur in friendships and relationships. One day they are on top of the world and the next day everything seems pointless. Some of this is quite normal in the life of a teenager, but parents can help them view their lives with some perspective and minimize the negative feelings that occur.

Parents should not always shield younger children from failure and disappointment. It is important for children to experience failure along with success, as these experiences help cushion hard times later in life. Children who have learned to cope with disappointment and felt the pride of having overcome adversity become much more resilient teenagers and adults.

While much of what has been learned from research on family composition and circumstance seems quite logical, the impact of this research is profound. It helps explain why some children rise above seemingly overwhelming odds of poverty and family composition to succeed, and why others struggle.

See also: CHILD PROTECTIVE SERVICES; FAMILY, SCHOOL, AND COMMUNITY CONNECTIONS; FAMILY SUPPORT SERVICES; PARENTING; POVERTY AND EDUCATION.

BIBLIOGRAPHY

BENSON, PETER L.; GALBRAITH, JUDY; and ESPELAND, PAMELA. 1998. *What Kids Need to Succeed.* Minneapolis, MN: Free Spirit.

BROOKS-GUNN, JEANNE, and DUNCAN, GREG J. 1977. "The Effects of Poverty on Children." *The Future of Children* 7(2):55–71.

DEYOUNG, ALAN J., and LAWRENCE, BARBARA. 1995. "On Hoosiers, Yankees, and Mountaineers." *Phi Delta Kappan* 77(2):104–112.

NATIONAL CENTER FOR CHILDREN IN POVERTY. 1997. *Poverty and Brain Development in Early Childhood.* New York: National Center for Children in Poverty, Columbia School of Public Health.

SHERMAN, ARLOC. 1997. *Poverty Matters: The Cost of Child Poverty in America.* Washington, DC: Children's Defense Fund.

INTERNET RESOURCES

NATIONAL ALLIANCE FOR THE MENTALLY ILL. 2001. <www.nami.org/>.

PATHWAYS TO PROMISE: MINISTRY AND MENTAL ILLNESS. 2001. "Impact of Mental Illness on Families." <www.pathways2promise.org/families/impact/htm>.

PSYCHIATRY24X7. 2001. <www.psychiatry24x7.com>.

DEBBIE MILLER

ADOPTION

In the 1990s an average of 120,000 children were adopted yearly in the United States. Adoption involves the legal transfer of parental rights and responsibilities from birth parents to adoptive parents. The adopted child, adoptive parents, and birth parents form what is known as the *adoptive triad*—three entities profoundly affected by this process. According to the Evan B. Donaldson Adoption Institute, 60 percent of Americans are touched by adoption—either as a relative, friend, or member of the adoption triad.

Most children are placed with their adoptive families through public child-welfare agencies or licensed private adoption agencies. These agencies typically place children after obtaining legal custody of children due to the voluntary or involuntary termination of birth parents' rights. Children are also placed with adoptive parents directly by birth parents; attorneys typically facilitate this process of *independent adoptions.*

Although the legal exchange of rights and responsibilities of parenthood is common to all adoptions, there are different types of adoption. *Infant adoptions* involve the placement of infants; *older-child adoptions* typically involve the placement of children over age three. In *transracial adoptions* children of one race are placed with a family of a different race, while in *international adoptions* children from one country are placed with a family in another country.

Adoptions vary in how much contact or information is shared between adoptive parent and birth parent. Harold Grotevant and Ruth McRoy offer the following definitions: *confidential* adoptions involve no contact at all; *mediated* adoptions involve the exchange of nonidentifying information through a third party; and fully *disclosed* adoptions involve the exchange of at least some identifying information and often include face-to-face meetings.

Adoption and Children's Development

Two questions typically get asked about adopted children. First, are they better off in adoptive families than they would have been in foster care, institutions, or with their birth families? Coping with the loss of the birth parent is often an important theme for adopted children. However, research on their adjustment clearly shows that they have more positive emotional and behavioral adjustment than children who are raised in foster care, in institutions, or with birth families who continue to have serious problems that impair parenting. Furthermore, Richard Barth and his colleagues have shown that adoption in infancy can greatly minimize the vast problems in learning, social relationships, and emotional development among children who were prenatally exposed to drugs. So, adoption can be an appropriate solution for children whose birth parents cannot, or will not, provide adequate safety and nurturance.

Second, how do adopted children fare in comparison with children in families that more closely resemble their adoptive families? Adopted children tend to receive more mental health services—which some professionals view as a sign that adopted children have many more problems than do their peers. However, adoptive parents also are more likely to seek professional help—for various reasons—than are biological parents. In general, many studies suggest that most adopted children tend to have more adjustment problems than nonadopted children. These problems include school adjustment and learning problems; impulsive, hyperactive, or rule-breaking behavior; and drug use. However, it is important to note that for most adopted children, these problems fall within what is considered a normal range.

Given the slightly higher risk for adopted children to have adjustment difficulties, what are important issues that adoptive families face as children develop? In infancy and toddlerhood, the critical challenge is for adoptive parents to form healthy relationships with the child. Known as a *secure attachment,* this relationship can enable the child to have success in later years forming friendships, learning in school, and learning about the world.

In the preschool years the important step for parents is to begin the process of telling about adoption. David Brodzinsky's work indicates that teaching children about adoption is an ongoing process throughout childhood that should start with words that the child can understand. He and his colleagues have shown that children's understanding of adoption evolves over years—from an ability in the preschool years to make a simple distinction between adoption and birth as paths into a family, to an abili-

ty in adolescence to understand the abstract themes associated with termination of parental rights and adoption.

During the elementary years, as adopted children become able to understand that in order to be adopted someone had to give them up, they become vulnerable to having difficulties with their sense of self. During these years, it is especially important for parents and adopted children to talk openly about adoption.

In the adolescent years, when youth rework their identity, the meaning of being adopted may have little or great significance, depending on how adoption has been handled by family, peers, and the larger community. As adopted adolescents work on their identity, they may explore questions of searching for information about one's birth parents. Marshall Schechter and Doris Bertocci note that although young people vary in their need for information about, or contact with, birth parents, their curiosity about their origins is quite normal. Although little is known about the outcome of searching during adolescence, adults who have searched for birth families have generally been satisfied with the outcome.

Unique Issues with Different Types of Adoption

Placements of children from foster care are somewhat risky: 10 to 15 percent disrupt or fail, sending children back to foster care. Children who are older, or have severe behavior problems (e.g., fire setting, sexual acting-out, suicidal behavior) are most likely to experience disruption. The adopted child comes with his or her own experiences with previous families and expectations for how families function, and these do not always fit with the expectations that adoptive families have. Flexible parenting styles, maintaining realistic expectations about the adoptee and the placement, and a clear commitment to the placement are important qualities that can enable families to be successful.

In international adoptions challenges for families include medical problems and cultural differences. Children who come from countries lacking in adequate medical care often have physical problems, including infectious disease, growth delay, and neurological diagnoses as a result of their preadoptive experiences. In addition, language and other cultural differences between the adopted child's home country and the adoptive family's country may further complicate adoptive family life.

Transracial adoptions have been very controversial, largely because they often involve European-American parents and adopted children of color. Research generally shows that transracially adopted children can adjust as well as children adopted by families of the same race. The success of such placements are determined, at least in part, by how well adoptive parents promote a sense of ethnic pride, how well they raise their children to be prepared for the discrimination they face, and how well they function as a family of color in the world.

Summary

Adoption provides children and families with an alternate path to family life that can be both similar to and different from biological family life. Usually, the differences pose unique challenges and complications for family life and children's development; however most adopted children tend to adjust as normally as do nonadopted children. An understanding of the complications and similarities by all—not just the 60 percent of persons touched by adoption—can facilitate more appropriate support for adoptive families and adopted children.

See also: FAMILY COMPOSITION AND CIRCUMSTANCE, *subentry on* FOSTER CARE; OUT-OF-SCHOOL INFLUENCES AND ACADEMIC SUCCESS; PARENTING.

BIBLIOGRAPHY

BARTH, RICHARD P.; FREUNDLICH, MADELYN; and BRODZINSKY, DAVID M. 2000. *Adoption and Prenatal Alcohol and Drug Exposure: Research, Policy and Practice.* Washington, DC: Child Welfare League of America.

BRODZINSKY, DAVID M., and PINDERHUGHES, ELLEN E. 2002. "Parenting and Child Development in Adoptive Families." In *Handbook of Parenting,* 2nd edition, ed. Marc H. Bornstein. Mahwah, NJ: Erlbaum.

BRODZINSKY, DAVID M.; SINGER, LESLIE M.; and BRAFF, ANNE M. 1984. "Children's Understanding of Adoption." *Child Development* 55:869–878.

EVAN B. DONALDSON ADOPTION INSTITUTE. 1997. *Benchmark Adoption Survey: Report on the Findings.* New York: Evan B. Donaldson Institute.

GROTEVANT, HAROLD D., and McROY, RUTH G. 1998. *Openness in Adoption: Exploring Family Connections.* Thousand Oaks, CA: Sage.

GROZA, VICTOR, and ROSENBERG, KAREN F. 2001. *Clinical and Practice Issues in Adoption: Bridging the Gap Between Adoptees Placed as Infants and as Older Children.* Westport, CT: Bergen and Garvey.

SCHECTER, MARSHALL D., and BERTOCCI, DORIS. 1990. "The Meaning of the Search." In *The Psychology of Adoption,* ed. David M. Brodzinsky and Marshall D. Schechter. New York: Oxford University Press.

INTERNET RESOURCES

EVAN B. DONALDSON ADOPTION INSTITUTE 2002. "Overview of Adoption in the Unites States." <www.adoptioninstitute.org/FactOverview.html#head>.

NATIONAL ADOPTION INFORMATION CLEARINGHOUSE. 2000. "Adoption: Numbers and Trends." <www.calib.com/naic/pubs/s_number.htm>.

ELLEN E. PINDERHUGHES

ALCOHOL, TOBACCO, AND OTHER DRUGS

Substance abuse is a family disease, one that can be transmitted both genetically and through the family environment. Children in families are affected by substance abuse in several ways, as illustrated in Figure 1. This chart shows that legal and illegal use of alcohol, tobacco, and other drugs (ATOD) can affect children through a number of avenues, including prenatal exposure *in utero.* This has very powerful policy implications, including its message that prenatal drug exposure, while very important in its effects on younger children, is only one of the several ways that children can be affected by these substances. Children are also exposed through their parents' and caretakers' use and abuse, through commercial media messages advertising alcohol and tobacco, and through community norms and regulations regarding substance use. The legality of a substance, as well as the way in which children are exposed to its use, plays a significant role in its effect on a child. Often, an emphasis is placed on the effects of illicit drugs, rather than on the harmful effects of tobacco and alcohol. At the federal level, for example, there is an annual "National Drug Policy Strategy" document; no such documents exist for alcohol or tobacco.

FIGURE 1

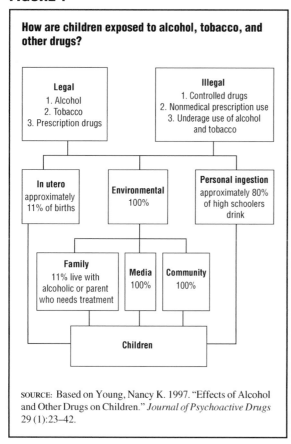

How are children exposed to alcohol, tobacco, and other drugs?

SOURCE: Based on Young, Nancy K. 1997. "Effects of Alcohol and Other Drugs on Children." *Journal of Psychoactive Drugs* 29 (1):23–42.

Both prenatal and postnatal exposure to alcohol, tobacco, and other drugs can affect children in lasting ways. Children who fail to form secure attachments to their parents or caregivers because of their parents' or caregivers' inability to give them sustained attention, children who live in a home where violence and substance abuse are frequent, children who grow up in neighborhoods where there are ten times as many liquor outlets and ads as in the rest of the community, adolescents who receive daily messages that to use alcohol is to be surrounded by attractive people having fun—all of these situations can have a lasting effect on the children involved.

According to the California State Commission on Children and Families, "prenatal exposure to tobacco, alcohol, and illicit drugs increases a child's risk of mental retardation, neurodevelopmental deficits, attention deficit disorders with hyperactivity, fine-motor impairment, as well as more subtle delays in motor performance and speech. Maternal smoking and infant exposure to environmental tobacco smoke has been linked to asthma, low birth weight and an increased risk of sudden infant death syndrome" (p. 56).

As important as these effects are, however, a 1999 report of the U.S. Department of Health and Human Services cited data showing that 11 percent of all children in the nation live with a parent who is either alcoholic or in need of treatment for their abuse of illicit drugs. According to this report, "children prenatally exposed to drugs and alcohol represent only a small proportion of the children affected and potentially endangered by parental substance abuse" (p. ix).

Thus, as important as prenatal exposure is, a much larger number of children are exposed to milder effects of substance abuse than those exposed to its extreme effects *in utero* such as fetal alcohol syndrome, which has definite facial and other characteristics. The policy and practice questions this raises include whether measurable results will be more readily achieved by targeting severe or milder risk cases; and for which children, and at which points in their development, intervention should be attempted. It may be more appropriate to think of *treatment funds* being allocated to the most affected children and families, *early intervention funds* being allocated to those that are at risk of becoming seriously involved, and *prevention funds* being allocated to a much wider group of children whose needs are not as severe.

How Are Schools Affected?

For schools, the issues of substance abuse in families arise at many levels of the preschool and school experience. These include:

- The mandated responsibility of schools to identify younger preschool-age children with disabilities, some of whom have been affected by exposure to alcohol and drugs.

- The effects of parental substance abuse on early learning, such as parents' willingness and ability to read to their children regularly.

- The effects of parental substance abuse on the home learning environment, such as whether there is a quiet place to study and a predictable schedule for homework.

- The effects of parental substance abuse on the development of peer-resistance skills that address the learned techniques of responding to negative pressure from peers.

• The effects of adolescent substance experimentation, use, and abuse on learning and social skills.

A 2001 analysis of the impact of substance abuse on schools conducted by researchers at Columbia University found that "substance abuse and addiction will add at least $41 billion—10 percent—to the costs of elementary and secondary education this year, due to class disruption and violence, special education and tutoring, teacher turnover, truancy, children left behind, student assistance programs, property damage, injury and counseling" (Center for Addiction and Substance Abuse, p. 6).

Schools' Responses

Schools have responded with a variety of practices and policies, ranging from *zero-tolerance zones* to drug resistance education and individual counseling. Recent assessments of "what works" have emphasized the following ingredients in successful school-based and school-linked programs:

• They are developmentally appropriate.

• They are culturally sensitive.

• They include the perspectives of young people.

• They have sufficient *dosage* (and when needed, *booster* features) to make a difference. In this context dosage refers to the intensity of the program; some models of prevention programs provide as little as 17 hours of instruction during the fifth grade year, which has been shown to be an inadequate dosage to achieve any lasting impact.

• They are multifaceted, reflecting the dimensions of peers, parents, and the larger community.

• They are evaluated in enough depth to make midcourse corrections possible.

The U.S. Department of Education has rated several programs "exemplary" and "promising," based on seven criteria developed by the department.

It should also be pointed out that from birth to age eighteen children spend only 9 percent of their lives physically at school, suggesting that one of the most important things schools can also do to respond to the problems of substance abuse is to support effective family- and community-focused prevention and intervention programs.

Conclusions

The effects of family substance abuse on schools and learning are pervasive. However, as concerns about adolescent tobacco, drug, and alcohol use have grown, so have the tools available to respond with both preventive and intervention activities. Schools should not venture into these arenas alone, but need to understand the available approaches and the literature on what works.

See also: DRUG AND ALCOHOL ABUSE, *subentry on* SCHOOL; RISK BEHAVIORS, *subentry on* DRUG USE AMONG TEENS.

BIBLIOGRAPHY

CALIFORNIA STATE COMMISSION ON CHILDREN AND FAMILIES. 2000. *Guidelines.* Sacramento, CA: State Commission on Children and Families.

CENTER FOR ADDICTION AND SUBSTANCE ABUSE AT COLUMBIA UNIVERSITY. 2001. *Malignant Neglect: Substance Abuse and America's Schools.* New York: Center for Addiction and Substance Abuse.

DRUG STRATEGIES, INC. 2000. *Making the Grade: A Guide to School Drug Prevention Programs.* Washington, DC: Drug Strategies.

U.S. DEPARTMENT OF HEALTH AND HUMAN SERVICES. 1999. *Blending Perspectives and Building Common Ground.* Washington, DC: Department of Health and Human Services.

YOUNG, NANCY K. 1997. "Effects of Alcohol and Other Drugs on Children." *Journal of Psychoactive Drugs* 29(1):23–42.

INTERNET RESOURCE

U.S. DEPARTMENT OF EDUCATION. 2001. "Safe, Disciplined, and Drug-Free Schools: Expert Panel for Exemplary and Promising Programs." <www.ed.gov/offices/OERI/ORAD/KAD/expert_panel/>.

NANCY K. YOUNG

FOSTER CARE

According to data from the U.S. Department of Health and Human Services's Children's Bureau, the number of children in foster care nationwide increased 93 percent between 1986 and 1999, from approximately 280,000 children to 581,000 children. Approximately 70 percent of the children in foster care in 1999 (405,000) were school-age children. The following paragraphs provide a definition of foster care before discussing the influence of foster care on students' academic growth and development.

Foster Care

Foster care is a substitute arrangement for children whose families are not able to provide basic social, emotional, and physical care, and who therefore require a substitute caregiver to assume the parental role to provide care, supervision, and support, on a short- or long-term basis. According to the Child Welfare League of America, "children should be removed from their parents and placed in out-of-home care only when it is necessary to ensure their safety and well-being" (p. 7).

Foster care (i.e., out-of-home care) is part of an array of child-welfare services that includes family support programs, family preservation programs, and permanency planning. The array can be described as a continuum, with out-of-home care viewed as a third line defense, following family preservation programs. Family support efforts focus on the prevention of child abuse and neglect, working to educate parents and alleviate a multitude of stressors that may increase the likelihood of maltreatment. Family preservation programs, foster care, and permanency planning efforts occur after a charge of child abuse or neglect has been substantiated by the public child-welfare agency. Family preservation programs, though not instituted in all abuse and neglect cases, provide intensive, in-home services in an effort to avoid out-of-home placement. Permanency planning—efforts to establish a permanent home for the child, either with his or her biological family, through adoption, or in legal guardianship—begins immediately, and permanency is the final goal for a child involved with the child-welfare system. Foster care is defined as a temporary arrangement for children while their families work to resolve the issues that resulted in an out-of-home placement for the child. However, foster care may also be a long-term option when other permanency efforts (i.e., family reunification, adoption, legal guardianship) are not successful.

Children may live in a variety of foster-care settings, depending on the characteristics of their case. Children with urgent substitute care needs may be placed in receiving or shelter homes for a short period of time. Like the array of child-welfare services, the remaining foster-care placement settings can be viewed as a continuum from the least restrictive environment and level of service intensity to the most restrictive environment and level of service intensity. In kinship foster care, children are placed with a relative; licensing requirements and eligibility for a foster-care payment for costs associated with raising the child depend on policies set by individual states. Family foster care is provided by foster parents who are licensed by a state or county after completing minimal training and meeting health and safety standards, and they receive a federal or state foster-care payment for each child residing in their home. Foster family agencies are private agencies contracted and licensed by the state or county to provide substitute care similar to family foster care but often with a greater level of service intensity. Group homes and residential treatment centers serve children with more specialized needs (i.e., emotional and behavioral difficulties) than other placement settings, are generally operated by private agencies contracted and licensed by the state or county, are more restrictive in their environment and therapeutic in their focus, and are staffed by individuals with more specific skills.

Vulnerability of Children in Child Welfare

School-age children in foster care have any number of life experiences that make them vulnerable to bad outcomes, particularly if those experiences occurred at a young age. Judith A. Silver provides an overview of the risk factors frequently experienced by children who become involved with the child-welfare system and are placed in foster care. Citing Arnold Sameroff, Silver notes that the link between risk factors and outcomes is not deterministic, but the risk factors increase the likelihood of having a negative outcome, such as low test scores. Poverty, the principal risk factor, is a condition faced by the majority of families known to the child-welfare system. Poverty's impact ranges beyond low-socioeconomic status, influencing the effect of other risk factors. A second risk factor, maternal substance abuse, is associated with negative outcomes for children (i.e., low birth weight, premature birth) that influence neurodevelopmental functioning. Exposure to violence, whether during pregnancy or in the home as a child, is another important risk factor that affects a child's mental health as well as his or her cognitive development and ability to learn. Attachment (the stable, emotional connection with a caregiver) is an important consideration for children in foster care, given that the natural parenting structure has collapsed, children have been removed from their biological families, and face placement within a new and unfamiliar home with new and unfamiliar people. Finally, a substantial proportion of children in foster care are there due to the maltreatment inflicted upon them by a caregiver. Maltreatment can vary (physical abuse, sexual abuse, neglect), but "all forms have predictable outcomes: devastating effects on sense of self, and emotional, social, and cognitive capabilities" (Silver, p. 15).

The Impact of Foster Care on Student Learning

The impact of foster care on student learning is difficult to assess. The difficulty is due to what Gilles Tremblay calls a "constellation of factors" that determines the influence of foster care on a child (p. 87). Tremblay has organized the factors into five categories: (1) factors relating to the child; (2) familial factors; (3) placement factors; (4) factors related to professional assistance; and (5) external factors. Parsing out the influence of these additional variables to gauge the unique effect of being in care on student learning is problematic.

The educational standing of school-age foster children while in foster care and when leaving foster care is less ambiguous. Researchers using cognitive assessments, academic achievement outcomes, school completion outcomes, and school behavior outcomes as a measure of scholastic achievement have found that children are not faring well while in foster care, or when they leave the foster-care system at the point of their eighteenth birthday.

School-age children in foster care have not faired well in general IQ assessments or on more specific assessments of cognitive functioning. According to reports by Annick Dumaret (1985), Mary Fox and Kathleen Arcuri (1980), and Theresa McNichol and Constance Tash (2001), average IQ scores were 100 or below, and a high number of those studied (up to 46%) were rated as doing poorly on assessments of cognitive functioning.

Performance at the age-appropriate grade level, grade retention, course grades, test scores, and graduation are common indicators of academic performance. A number of studies have found that large percentages (up to 47%) of children in foster care were performing below grade level and that children in foster care were behind in their progress or performing below average across a range of academic subjects. In addition, a high percentage (up to 90%)

of children in foster care repeated at least one grade over their academic career. Researchers also reported that low percentages of students in foster care achieved passing grades, and many had low grade point averages. Children in foster care did not make gains in standardized test scores over time while in care, and scores were below the fiftieth percentile. School completion percentages were low for children discharged from foster care on their eighteenth birthday and a high percentage of children in foster care reported dropping out of school.

School behavior outcomes are important components of educational progress. Attendance appeared to be problematic for some children in foster care, as did general classroom behavior. Study findings for suspension and expulsions were less definitive.

Conclusion

Assessing the impact of foster care on student learning is difficult due to the influence of various factors. However, research indicates that school-age children in foster care face difficulties in the learning process. Additional research, as well as policies and interventions, are required to assist children in achieving educational goals to ensure a lasting quality of life.

See also: CHILD PROTECTIVE SERVICES; FAMILY COMPOSITION AND CIRCUMSTANCE, *subentry on* ADOPTION; OUT-OF-SCHOOL INFLUENCES AND ACADEMIC SUCCESS.

BIBLIOGRAPHY

BARTH, RICHARD P. 1990. "On Their Own: the Experience of Youth after Foster Care." *Child and Adolescent Social Work* 7:419–440.

BENEDICT, MARY I.; ZURAVIN, SUSAN; and STALLINGS, REBECCA. 1996. "Adult Functioning of Children Who Lived in Kin Versus Nonrelative Family Foster Homes." *Child Welfare* 75:529–549.

BERRICK, JILL D. 1998. "When Children Cannot Remain Home: Foster Family Care and Kinship Care." *The Future of Children* 8(1):72–87.

BERRICK, JILL D.; BARTH, RICHARD P.; and NEEDELL, BARBARA. 1994. "A Comparison of Kinship Foster Homes and Foster Family Homes: Implications for Kinship Foster Care as Family Preservation." *Children and Youth Services Review* 16(1/2):33–63.

BLOME, WENDY W. 1997. "What Happens to Foster Kids: Educational Experiences of a Random Sample of Foster Care Youth and a Matched Group of Non-Foster Care Youth." *Child and Adolescent Social Work Journal* 14:41–53.

CHILD WELFARE LEAGUE OF AMERICA. 1995. *Standards of Excellence for Family Foster Care Services.* Washington, DC: Child Welfare League of America.

COOK, RONNA J. 1994. "Are We Helping Foster Care Youth Prepare for Their Future?" *Children and Youth Services Review* 16:213–229.

DUBOWITZ, HOWARD, and SAWYER, RICHARD J. 1994. "School Behavior of Children in Kinship Care." *Child Abuse and Neglect* 18:899–911.

DUMARET, ANNICK. 1985. "IQ, Scholastic Performance and Behaviour of Sibs Raised in Contrasting Environments." *Journal of Child Psychology and Psychiatry* 26:553–580.

ENGLISH, DIANA J.; KOUIDOU-GILES, SOPHIA; and PLOCKE, MARTIN. 1994. "Readiness for Independence: A Study of Youth in Foster Care." *Children and Youth Services Review* 16:147–158.

FANSHEL, DAVID, and SHINN, EUGENE B. 1978. *Children in Foster Care: A Longitudinal Investigation.* New York: Columbia University Press.

FESTINGER, TRUDY. 1983. *No One Ever Asked Us: A Postscript to Foster Care.* New York: Columbia University Press.

FOX, MARY, and ARCURI, KATHLEEN. 1980. "Cognitive and Academic Functioning in Foster Children." *Child Welfare* 59:491–496.

HEATH, ANTHONY F.; COLTON, MATTHEW J.; and ALDGATE, JANE. 1994. "Failure to Escape: A Longitudinal Study of Foster Children's Educational Attainment." *British Journal of Social Work* 24:241–260.

IGLEHART, ALFREDA P. 1994. "Kinship Foster Care: Placement, Service, and Outcome Issues." *Children and Youth Services Review* 16:107–122.

KADUSHIN, ALFRED, and MARTIN, JUDITH A. 1988. *Child Welfare Services.* New York: Macmillan.

MCNICHOL, THERESA, and TASH, CONSTANCE. 2001. "Parental Substance Abuse and the Development of Children in Family Foster Care." *Child Welfare* 80:239–256.

RUNYAN, DESMOND K., and GOULD, CAROLYN L. 1985. "Foster Care for Child Maltreatment. II. Impact on School Performance." *Pediatrics* 76:841–847.

SAMEROFF, ARNOLD J. 1995. "General Systems Theories and Developmental Psychopathology." In *Developmental Psychopathology,* Vol. 1: *Theory and Methods,* eds. Dante Cicchetti and Donald J. Cohen. New York: Wiley.

SAWYER, RICHARD J., and DUBOWITZ, HOWARD. 1994. "School Performance of Children in Kinship Care." *Child Abuse and Neglect* 18:587–597.

SEYFRIED, SHERRI; PECORA, PETER J.; DOWNS, A. CHRIS; LEVINE, PHYLLIS; and EMERSON, JOHN. 2000. "Assessing the Educational Outcomes of Children in Long-Term Foster Care: First Findings." *School Social Work Journal* 24:68–88.

SILVER, JUDITH A. 1999. "Starting Young: Improving Children's Outcomes." In *Young Children and Foster Care,* eds. Judith A. Silver, Barbara J. Amster, and Trude Haecker. Baltimore: Brookes.

SMUCKER, KAREN S.; KAUFFMAN, JAMES M.; and BALL, DONALD W. 1996. "School-Related Problems of Special Education Foster Care Students with Emotional or Behavioral Disorders: A Comparison to Other Groups." *Journal of Emotional and Behavioral Disorders* 4:30–39.

STEIN, ELEANOR. 1997. "Teachers' Assessments of Children in Foster Care." *Developmental Disabilities Bulletin* 25(2):1–17.

TREMBLAY, GILLES. 1999. "Impact of Child Placement: A Review of Literature." *Canadian Social Work* 1:82–90.

WALD, MICHAEL S.; CARLSMITH, JAMES M.; and LEIDERMAN, HERBERT. 1988. *Protecting Abused and Neglected Children.* Stanford, CA: Stanford University Press.

INTERNET RESOURCE

U.S. DEPARTMENT OF HEALTH AND HUMAN SERVICES, ADMINISTRATION FOR CHILDREN AND FAMILIES, ADMINISTRATION ON CHILDREN, YOUTH, AND FAMILIES, CHILDREN'S BUREAU. 2001. "The AFCARS Report No. 6: Interim FY 1999 Estimates as of June 2001." <www.acf.dhhs.gov/programs/cb/publications>.

CHARLIE FERGUSON

FAMILY, SCHOOL, AND COMMUNITY CONNECTIONS

The goal of positive and productive family and community involvement is on every school improvement list, but few schools have implemented comprehensive programs of partnership. Research suggests that this goal is an important one to reach because families and communities contribute to children's learning, development, and school success at every grade level.

Studies are accumulating that show that well-designed programs of partnership are important for helping all families support their children's education in elementary, middle, and high schools. That is, *if* schools plan and implement comprehensive programs of partnership, *then* many more families respond, including those who would not become involved on their own.

Three questions need to be addressed to help educators move from believing in the importance of family and community involvement to conducting effective programs of partnership:

1. What is a comprehensive program of school, family, and community partnerships?
2. How do family and community partnerships link to other aspects of successful schools?
3. How can all schools develop and sustain productive programs of partnerships?

Components of a Comprehensive Program of Partnerships

A framework of six types of involvement guides schools in establishing full and productive programs of school-family-community partnerships. This section summarizes the six types of involvement and discusses a few *sample practices* that are being implemented in schools across the country that are working to improve and increase family and community connections. Also noted are some of the *challenges* that all schools must overcome to create successful partnerships, along with examples of *results* that can be expected from each type of involvement for students, families, and educators.

Comprehensive programs of partnerships include activities for all six types of involvement. Because there are many activities to choose from, elementary, middle, and high schools can tailor their programs of partnerships by selecting activities that match specific school goals and the interests and needs of students and families.

Type 1—Parenting. Type 1 activities are conducted to help families strengthen parenting skills, understand child and adolescent development, and set home conditions to support learning at each school level. Type 1 activities also enable families to provide information to schools so that educators understand families' backgrounds, cultures, and goals for their children.

Sample practices. Among Type 1 activities, elementary, middle, and high schools may conduct workshops for parents; provide short, clear summaries of important information on parenting; and organize opportunities for parents to exchange ideas with other parents, educators, and community experts on topics of child and adolescent development. Topics may include health, nutrition, discipline, guidance, peer pressure, preventing drug abuse, and planning for the future. Type 1 activities also provide families with information on what to expect and how to prepare for students' transitions from preschool to elementary school, elementary to middle school, and middle to high school. Additional topics for successful parenting may concern family roles and responsibilities in student attendance, college planning, and other topics that are important for student success in school. Schools also may offer parents General Educational Development (GED) programs, family support sessions, family computer classes, and other learning and social opportunities for parents and for students. To ensure that families provide valuable information to the schools, teachers may ask parents at the start of each school year or periodically to share insights about their children's strengths, talents, interests, needs, and goals.

Challenges. One challenge for successful Type 1 activities is to get information from workshops to parents who cannot come to meetings and workshops at the school building. This may be done with videos, tape recordings, summaries, newsletters, cable broadcasts, phone calls, and other print and nonprint communications. Another Type 1 challenge is to design procedures that enable all families to share information easily and as needed about their children with teachers, counselors, and others.

Results expected. If useful information flows to and from families about child and adolescent development, parents will increase their confidence about parenting, students will be more aware of parents' continuing guidance, and teachers will better understand their students' families. For example, if practices are targeted to help families send their children to school every day and on time, then student attendance will improve and lateness will decrease. If families are part of their children's transitions to elementary, middle, and high school, then more students will adjust well to their new schools, and more parents will remain involved across the grades.

Type 2—Communicating. Type 2 activities increase school-to-home and home-to-school communications about school programs and student progress through notices, memos, conferences, report cards, newsletters, telephone calls, e-mail and computerized messages, the Internet, open houses, and other traditional and innovative communications.

Sample practices. Among many Type 2 activities, elementary, middle, and high schools may provide parents with clear information on each teacher's criteria for report card grades; how to interpret interim progress reports; and, as necessary, how to work with students to improve grades or behavior. Type 2 activities include parent-teacher conferences; parent-teacher-student conferences; or student-led conferences with parents and teachers. Student involvement in conferences helps youngsters take personal responsibility for learning. Activities may be designed to improve school and student newsletters by including student work, a feature column for parents' questions, calendars of important events, and parent response forms. Many schools are beginning to use e-mail, voice mail, and websites to encourage two-way communication between families and teachers, counselors, and administrators.

Challenges. One challenge for successful Type 2 activities is to make communications clear and understandable for all families, including parents who have less formal education or who do not read English well, so that all families can understand and respond to the information they receive. Other Type 2 challenges are to know which families are and are not receiving and understanding the communications in order to design ways to reach all families; develop effective two-way channels of communication so that families can easily contact and respond to educators; and make sure that students understand their roles as couriers and interpreters in facilitating school and family connections.

Results expected. If communications are clear and useful, and if two-way channels are easily accessed, then school-to-home and home-to-school interactions will increase; more families will understand school programs, follow their children's progress, guide students to maintain or improve their grades, and attend parent-teacher conferences. Specifically, if computerized phone lines are used to communicate information about homework, more families will know more about their children's daily assignments. If newsletters include respond-and-reply forms, more families will send ideas, questions, and comments to teachers and administrators about school programs and activities.

Type 3—Volunteering. Type 3 activities are designed to improve recruitment, training, and schedules to involve parents and others as volunteers and as audiences at the school or in other locations to support students and school programs.

Sample practices. Among many Type 3 activities, schools may collect information on family members' talents, occupations, interests, and availability to serve as volunteers. These important human resources may help enrich students' subject classes; improve career explorations; serve as language translators; monitor attendance and call parents of absent students; conduct "parent patrols" and "morning greeters" to increase school safety; and organize and improve activities such as clothing and uniform exchanges, school stores, and fairs. Schools may organize volunteers to serve as homeroom parents, neighborhood representatives, and sports and club contacts and may establish telephone trees to help parents communicate with each other about school programs and events. Schools may establish a corps of volunteers to offer a "welcome wagon" of information about the school to students and families who enroll during the school year. Schools also may create opportunities for mentors, coaches, tutors, and leaders of after-school programs to ensure that students have experiences that build and expand their skills and talents and that keep them safe and supervised after school. Some Type 3 activities may be conducted in a parent room or family center at the school where parents obtain information, conduct volunteer work, and meet with other parents.

Challenges. Challenges for successful Type 3 activities are to recruit volunteers widely so that parents and other family members feel welcome; make hours flexible for parents and other volunteers who work during the school day; provide needed training; and enable volunteers to contribute productively to the school, classroom, and after-school programs. Volunteers will be better integrated in school programs if there is a coordinator who is responsible for matching volunteers' available times and skills with the needs of teachers, administrators, and students. Another Type 3 challenge is to change the definition of "volunteer" to mean anyone who supports school goals or students' learning at any time and in any place. This includes parents and family members who voluntarily come to school as audiences for students' sports events, assemblies, and musical or drama presentations, and for other events that support students' work. It also includes volunteers who work for the school at home, through their businesses, or in the community. A related challenge is to help students understand how volunteers help their school and to encourage students to interact with volunteers who can assist them with their work and activities.

Results expected. If tasks are well designed, and if schedules and locations for volunteers are varied, more parents, family members, and others in the community will assist elementary, middle, and high schools and support students as members of audiences. More families will feel comfortable with the school and staff; more students will talk and interact with varied adults; and more teachers will be aware of and use the time, talents, and resources of parents and others in the community to improve school programs and activities. Specifically, if volunteers serve as attendance monitors, more families will assist students to improve attendance. If volunteers conduct a "hall patrol" or are active in other locations, school safety will increase and student behavior problems will decrease because of a better student–adult ratio. If volunteers are well-trained as tutors in particular subjects, student tutees will improve their skills in those subjects; and if volunteers discuss careers, students will be more aware of their options for the future.

Type 4—Learning at home. Type 4 activities involve families with their children in academic learning activities at home that are coordinated with students' classwork and that contribute to student success in school. These include interactive homework, goal-setting for academic subjects, and other curricular-linked activities and decisions about courses and programs.

Sample practices. Among many Type 4 activities, elementary, middle, and high schools may provide information to students and to parents about the skills needed to pass each class, course, or grade level and about each teacher's homework policies. Schools also may implement activities that can help families encourage, praise, guide, and monitor their children's work by using interactive homework strategies; student-teacher-family contracts for long-term projects; summer home-learning packets; student-led at-home conferences with parents on portfolios or folders of writing samples or work in other subjects; goal-setting activities for improving or maintaining good report card grades in all subjects; and other approaches that keep students and families talking about schoolwork at home. Family fun and learning nights are often used as a starting point to help parents and students focus on curricular-related topics and family interactions. These meetings require parents to come to the school building. A systematic approach to increasing academic conversations at home is found in the Teachers Involve Parents in Schoolwork (TIPS) interactive homework for the elementary and middle grades.

Challenges. One challenge for successful Type 4 activities is to implement a regular schedule of interactive homework that requires students to take responsibility for discussing important things they are learning, interviewing family members, recording reactions, and sharing their work and ideas at home. Another Type 4 challenge is to create a schedule of activities that involve families regularly and systematically with students on short-term and long-term goal-setting for attendance, achievement, behavior, talent development, and plans for college or careers.

Results expected. If Type 4 activities are well designed and implemented, student homework completion, report card grades, and test scores in specific subjects will improve; and more families will know what their children are learning in class and how to monitor, support, and discuss homework. More students should complete required course credits, select advanced courses, and take college entrance tests. Students and teachers will be more aware of families' interest in students' work.

Type 5—Decision-making. Type 5 activities include families in developing schools' mission statements and in designing, reviewing, and improving school policies that affect children and families. Family members become active participants on school improvement teams, committees, PTA/PTO or other parent organizations, Title I and other councils, and advocacy groups.

Sample practices. Among Type 5 activities, elementary, middle, and high schools may organize and maintain an active parent association and include family representatives on all committees for school improvement (e.g., curriculum, safety, supplies and equipment, partnerships, fund-raising, postsecondary college planning, career development). In particular, along with teachers, administrators, students, and others from the community, parents must be members of the "Action Team for Partnerships," which plans and conducts family and community involvement activities linked to school improvement goals. Schools may offer parents and teachers training in leadership, decision-making, policy advocacy, and collaboration. Type 5 activities help to identify and provide information desired by families about school policies, course offerings, student placements and groups, special services, tests and assessments, annual test results for students, and annual evaluations of school programs.

Challenges. One challenge for successful Type 5 activities in all schools is to ensure that leadership roles are filled by parent representatives from all of the major race and ethnic groups, socioeconomic groups, and neighborhoods that are present in the school. A related challenge is to help parent leaders serve as effective representatives by obtaining information from and providing information to all parents about school issues and decisions. At the high school level, a particular challenge is to include student representatives along with parents in decision-making groups and in leadership positions. An ongoing challenge is to help parents, teachers, and students who serve on an Action Team for Partnerships or other committees learn to trust, respect, and listen to each other as they collaborate to reach common goals for school improvement.

Results expected. If Type 5 activities are well implemented in elementary, middle, and high schools, more families will have input into decisions that affect the quality of their children's education; students will increase their awareness that families and students have a say in school policies; and teachers will increase their understanding of family perspectives on policies and programs for improving the school.

Type 6—Collaborating with the community. Type 6 activities draw upon and coordinate the work and resources of community businesses; cultural, civic, and religious organizations; senior citizen groups; colleges and universities; governmental agencies; and other associations in order to strengthen school programs, family practices, and student learning and development. Other Type 6 activities enable students, staff, and families to contribute their services to the community.

Sample practices. Among many Type 6 activities, elementary, middle, and high schools may inform students and families about the availability of community programs and resources, such as after-school recreation, tutorial programs, health services, cultural events, service opportunities, and summer programs. This includes the need to assist students and families to gain access to community resources and programs. Some schools work with local businesses to organize "gold card" discounts as incentives for students to improve attendance and report card grades. Collaborations with community businesses, groups, and agencies also strengthen the other five types of involvement. Examples include enhancing Type 1 activities by conducting parent education workshops for families at community or business locations; increasing Type 2 activities by communicating about school events on the local radio or television stations, and at churches, clinics, and supermarkets; soliciting volunteers from businesses and the community to strengthen Type 3 activities; enriching Type 4 activities by offering students learning opportunities with artists, scientists, writers, mathematicians, and others whose careers link to the school curriculum; and including community members on Type 5 decision-making councils and committees.

Challenges. One challenge for successful Type 6 activities is to solve problems associated with community-school collaborations, such as "turf" problems of who is responsible for funding, leading, and supervising cooperative activities. The initial enthusiasm and decisions for school-community partnerships must be followed by actions that sustain productive collaborations over the long term. Another Type 6 challenge is to recognize and link students' valuable learning experiences in the community to the school curricula, including lessons that build on students' nonschool skills and talents, their club and volunteer work, and, in high school, their part-time jobs. A major challenge is to inform and involve families in community-related activities that students conduct. Related challenges are to help students understand how community partners help their school and to engage students, themselves, as volunteers and in service-learning in their own schools, in other schools, and in the community.

Results expected. Well-implemented Type 6 activities will increase the knowledge that families, students, and schools have about the resources and programs in their community that could help them reach important goals. Well-designed community connections will increase student access to and participation in community programs. Coordinated community services could help many students and their families prevent health, social, and educational problems or solve problems before they become too serious. Type 6 activities also should support and enrich school curricular and extracurricular programs.

Summary. The six types of involvement create a comprehensive program of partnerships in elementary, middle, and high schools, but the implementation challenges for each type of involvement must be met in order for programs to be effective. The quality of the design and content of the involvement activities directly affect the expected results. Not every practice that involves families will result in higher student achievement test scores. Rather, practices for each type of involvement can be selected to help students, families, and teachers reach specific goals and results. The examples above include only a few of hundreds of suggestions that can help elementary, middle, and high schools develop strong programs of partnerships.

How Partnerships Link to Other Aspects of Successful Schools

Good schools have qualified and talented teachers and administrators, high expectations that all students will succeed, rigorous curricula, engaging instruction, responsive and useful tests and assessments, strong guidance for every student, *and* effective school, family, and community partnerships. In good schools, these elements combine to promote students' learning and to create a school climate that is welcoming, safe, caring, stimulating, and joyful for all students, educators, and families.

All of the elements of successful schools are interconnected. It is particularly important for educators to understand that partnerships are not extra, separate, or different from the "real work" of a school, but that they contribute to the quality of a school's program and to student success. Two examples help clarify the links of family and community involvement to the success students experience in schools' academic and guidance programs.

Family and community involvement may contribute to the quality of schools' academic programs and student learning. National and local surveys indicate that students and their families have very high aspirations for success in school and in life. Fully 98 percent of a national sample of eighth-grade students planned to graduate from high school, and 82 percent planned at least some postsecondary schooling, with over 70 percent aiming to complete college. Tenth- and twelfth-grade students had similar high ambitions. In order to help students reach their aspirations, educators and families must work better together to help students: succeed at every grade level, pass the courses they need to complete high school, and initiate actions to attend college. Schools, with families' support, also must provide some students with extra help and more time to learn in coaching classes, extra-help courses, summer school, and tutoring, mentoring, and other responsive programs.

Families need good information about their children's curriculum each year; the teachers' instructional approaches; extra help available to students; and the nature of tests and assessments in order to be able to discuss important academic topics with their children at home. Families also need to understand how their children are progressing in each subject, how to help students set and meet learning goals, and how to work with students to solve major problems that threaten course or grade-level failure. Some elementary, middle, and high schools create individual student educational plans and conferences with all students and parents.

Many schools use new and varied teaching strategies that are unfamiliar to most families. These may include group activities, problem-solving processes, prewriting techniques, student-as-historian methods, interactive homework, and other innovative approaches to promote learning. Families and others in the community also need to know about major tests, report card criteria, and other state and local standards that schools use to determine students' progress and pathways through school. Some schools' Action Teams for Partnerships design daytime or evening workshops for parents to learn about and try items on new performance-based assessments.

With clear information about all aspects of schools' academic programs, more families could guide their children's decisions about courses, homework completion, studying for tests, and taking steps toward college or work. If classroom teachers, students, and parents communicate clearly and frequently about students' academic programs, progress, and needs, more students will succeed at high levels and fulfill their own and their families' high expectations.

Family and community involvement may contribute to the quality of schools' guidance programs and students' attitudes and behavior. School guidance and support services are stronger and serve students better if educators, students, and families are well connected. Students need to know that their guidance counselors and teachers understand and appreciate their families' cultures, hopes, and dreams. As students proceed through the grades, they struggle to balance their love for their family, need for guidance, and need for greater independence. Educators and parents can help students see that these seemingly contradictory pressures can co-exist.

Guidance counselors, school social workers, and school psychologists in elementary, middle, and high schools should meet with students' families and serve as key contacts for parents to call if questions arise about students' academic progress, behavior, peer relations, or interactions with teachers. In some middle and high schools, guidance counselors are members of interdisciplinary teams of teachers who meet with parents and students on a regular schedule. In all schools, guidance counselors could contact parents *before* students are at serious risk of failing courses because of absence, attitudes, classwork, or homework in order to devise collaborative approaches to help students succeed in school.

Families need to know about the formal and informal guidance programs at their children's schools. This includes knowing the names, phone or voice-mail numbers, and e-mail addresses of their children's teachers, counselors, advocates, and administrators in order to reach them with questions about their children's progress or problems. This is particularly important at times of transition when students move into elementary school, or from elementary to middle or middle to high school. With good information, parents and other family partners become and remain more involved in their children's education, and more of them can assist students to adjust successfully to their new schools.

When students, guidance counselors, teachers, and parents communicate well about students' social and emotional development and special needs, more students are likely to succeed each year and stay in school.

How Schools Can Develop and Sustain a Productive Partnership Program

Many schools are demonstrating how to design, implement, and sustain strong programs of school, family, and community partnerships. These schools are using the framework of six types of involvement to ensure that families are well informed about and engaged in their children's education at school and at home. They are using the research base summarized above, and they are being supported and assisted by school principals, district administrators and key staff, state leaders, and others.

In well-designed partnership programs, each school forms an Action Team for Partnerships consisting of teachers, parents, administrators, and others. Each team writes an annual action plan for partnerships, implements and oversees activities, maintains an adequate budget, evaluates the quality of partnerships, and improves plans and activities from year to year. In excellent programs, activities to involve families and community partners are linked to school improvement goals to produce the kinds of results described above. For example, family and community involvement activities may be selected to increase the support that all students receive at home, at school, and in the community to help students improve reading skills, math scores, attendance, behavior, and other indicators of school success. To aid this process, the National Network of Partnership Schools at Johns Hopkins University provides research-based guidelines, training, and ongoing assistance and professional development to schools, districts, and states that want to establish and sustain effective partnership programs.

Many research studies have helped answer the three questions posed at the beginning of this entry. By drawing on the growing research base, educators, parents, and community leaders can work together, think about, talk about, and take action to develop comprehensive programs of school, family, and community partnerships in their schools. Annual plans should include family and community involvement activities that support school improvement goals and that contribute to the success of elementary, middle, and high school academic programs and guidance services for all students. This can be done with new and useful research-based tools, materials, and networks to establish and continually improve programs and practices of partnerships.

Despite important advances since the 1980s in research and in practice on school, family, and community partnerships, there still are many questions that must be addressed to inform and productively involve all families in their children's education. Studies are needed at all grade levels to identify which family and community involvement activities significantly improve students' reading, math, and other skills and attitudes; and which involvement activities are particularly helpful to families and students at times of transitions to new schools. There are important questions to address on how to reach families with diverse cultural and language backgrounds, and how to integrate all families to create a strong, supportive school community. Also needed is more knowledge about how to involve fathers more effectively in their children's education; how community resources can be tapped to assist students, families, and school programs; and how to increase students' understanding of their roles and responsibilities in facilitating partnership activities that link home, school, and community.

Notably, this field of study has successfully linked research results to the development of educational policy and school practice. As new questions about school, family, and community partnerships are systematically addressed, knowledge will accumulate that should continue to improve the connections of home, school, and community to benefit students.

See also: COMMUNITY-BASED ORGANIZATIONS, AGENCIES, AND GROUPS; COMMUNITY EDUCATION; FAMILY COMPOSITION AND CIRCUMSTANCE; PARENTAL INVOLVEMENT IN EDUCATION; PARENTING.

BIBLIOGRAPHY

BALFANZ, ROBERT, and MAC IVER, DOUGLAS J. 2000. "Transforming High-Poverty Urban Middle Schools into Strong Learning Institutions." *Journal of Education for Students Placed at Risk* 5(1/2):137–158.

BOOTH, ALAN, and DUNN, JUDITH F., eds. 1996. *Family-School Links: How Do They Affect Educational Outcomes?* Mahwah, NJ: Erlbaum.

CATSAMBIS, SOPHIA. 1998. *Expanding Knowledge of Parental Involvement in Secondary Education: Social Determinants and Effects on High School Academic Success.* Baltimore: Johns Hopkins University, Center for Research on the Education of Students Placed at Risk.

CHRISTENSON, SANDRA L., and CONOLEY, JANE C., eds. 1992. *Home-School Collaboration: Enhancing Children's Academic and Social Competence.* Silver Spring, MD: National Association of School Psychologists.

COMER, JAMES; HAYNES, NORRIS; JOYNER, EDWARD; and BEN-AVIE, MICHAEL. 1996. *Rallying the Whole Village: The Comer Process for Reforming Education.* New York: Teachers College Press.

DORNBUSCH, SANFORD M., and RITTER, PHILLIP L. 1988. "Parents of High School Students: A Neglected Resource." *Educational Horizons* 66:75–77.

ECCLES, JACQUELYNNE S., and HAROLD, RENA D. 1996. "Family Involvement in Children's and Adolescents' Schooling." In *Family-School Links: How Do They Affect Educational Outcomes?*, ed. Alan Booth and Judith F. Dunn. Mahwah, NJ: Erlbaum.

EPSTEIN, JOYCE L. 1995. "School/Family/Community Partnerships: Caring for the Children We Share." *Phi Delta Kappan* 76:701–712.

EPSTEIN, JOYCE L. 2001. *School, Family, and Community Partnerships: Preparing Educators and Improving Schools.* Boulder, CO: Westview.

EPSTEIN, JOYCE L., and LEE, SEYONG. 1995. "National Patterns of School and Family Connections in the Middle Grades." In *The Family-School Connection: Theory, Research, and Practice*, ed. Bruce A. Ryan, Gerald R. Adams, Thomas P. Gullotta, Roger P. Weissberg, and Robert L. Hampton. Thousand Oaks, CA: Sage.

EPSTEIN, JOYCE L.; SALINAS, KAREN C.; and JACKSON, VIVIAN. 1995. *Teachers Involve Parents in Schoolwork (TIPS) in the Elementary and Middle Grades.* Baltimore: Johns Hopkins University, Center on School, Family, and Community Partnerships.

EPSTEIN, JOYCE L.; SANDERS, MAVIS G.; SALINAS, KAREN C.; SIMON, BETH S.; JANSORN, NATALIE; and VAN VOORHIS, FRANCES L. 2002. *School, Family, and Community Partnerships: Your Handbook for Action,* 2nd edition. Thousand Oaks, CA: Corwin Press.

ERB, THOMAS O. 2001. *This We Believe . . . and Now We Must Act.* Westerville, OH: National Middle School Association.

GROLNICK, WENDY S., and SLOWIAZEK, MARIA L. 1994. "Parents' Involvement in Children's

Schooling: A Multi-dimensional Conceptualization and Motivational Model." *Child Development* 65:237–252.

HO, ESTHER S., and WILLMS, J. DOUGLAS. 1996. "Effects of Parental Involvement on Eighth-Grade Achievement." *Sociology of Education* 69:126–141.

HOOVER-DEMPSEY, KATHLEEN V., and SANDLER, HOWARD M. 1997. "Why Do Parents Become Involved in Their Children's Education?" *Review of Educational Research* 67:3–42.

JOHNSON, VIVIAN R. 1996. *Family Center Guidebook.* Baltimore: Johns Hopkins University, Center on Families, Communities, Schools, and Children's Learning.

LEE, SEYONG. 1994. "Family-School Connections and Students' Education: Continuity and Change of Family Involvement from the Middle Grades to High School." Ph.D. diss., Johns Hopkins University.

LLOYD, GARY M. 1996. "Research and Practical Applications for School, Family, and Community Partnerships." In *Family-School Links: How Do They Affect Educational Outcomes?*, ed. Alan Booth and Judith F. Dunn. Mahwah, NJ: Erlbaum.

MCPARTLAND, JAMES; BALFANZ, ROBERT; JORDAN, WILL; and LEGTERS, NETTIE. 1998. "Improving Climate and Achievement in a Troubled Urban High School through the Talent Development Model." *Journal of Education for Students Placed At Risk* 3:337–361.

MULHALL, PETER F.; MERTENS, STEVEN B.; and FLOWERS, NANCY. 2001. "How Familiar Are Parents with Middle Level Practices?" *Middle School Journal* 33(2):57–61.

NATIONAL ASSOCIATION OF SECONDARY SCHOOL PRINCIPALS. 1996. *Breaking Ranks: Changing an American Institution.* Reston, VA: National Association of Secondary School Principals.

RUTHERFORD, BRUCE, ed. 1995. *Creating Family/ School Partnerships.* Columbus, OH: National Middle School Association.

SALINAS, KAREN C., and JANSORN, NATALIE. 2001. *Promising Partnership Practices, 2001.* Baltimore: Johns Hopkins University, Center on School, Family, and Community Partnerships.

SANDERS, MAVIS G. 1998. "School-Family-Community Partnerships: An Action Team Approach." *High School Magazine* 5(3):38–49.

SANDERS, MAVIS G. 1999. "Improving School, Family, and Community Partnerships in Urban Middle Schools." *Middle School Journal* 31(2):35–41.

SANDERS, MAVIS G. 2001. "Schools, Families, and Communities Partnering for Middle Level Students' Success." *NASSP Bulletin* 85(627):53–61.

SANDERS, MAVIS G.; EPSTEIN, JOYCE L.; and CONNORS-TADROS, LORI. 1999. *Family Partnerships with High Schools: The Parents' Perspective.* Baltimore: Johns Hopkins University, Center for Research on the Education of Students Placed at Risk.

SIMON, BETH S. 2001. "Family Involvement in High School: Predictors and Effects." *NASSP Bulletin* 85(627):8–19.

SLAVIN, ROBERT, and MADDEN, NANCY. 2000. "Roots and Wings: Effects of Whole School Reform on Student Achievement." *Journal of Education for Students Placed at Risk* 5(1/2):109–136.

VAN VOORHIS, FRANCES L. 2001. "Interactive Science Homework: An Experiment in Home and School Connections." *NASSP Bulletin* 85(627):20–32.

INTERNET RESOURCE

NATIONAL NETWORK OF PARTNERSHIP SCHOOLS. 2002. "Teachers Involve Parents in Schoolwork." <www.partnershipschools.org>.

JOYCE L. EPSTEIN

FAMILY SUPPORT SERVICES

OVERVIEW
Jacquelyn McCroskey
INCOME SUPPORT SERVICES FOR CHILDREN AND
FAMILIES
Susan E. Smith

OVERVIEW

Most schools encourage parents to become involved in their children's education, and some may even require parent participation in school activities. Most teachers and educational administrators, however, realize that parents who are working several jobs to make ends meet or struggling with complicated health or family problems may not be able to help their children learn. Those who are recent immigrants or who did not do well in school themselves may not know how to help or may feel intimidated by school. The challenges of daily life can be so overwhelming—especially for poor families living in dangerous or decrepit inner-city neighborhoods or those living in far-flung rural areas with few resources—that educational success for children may not seem to be a realistic family priority.

In response, many schools are increasing their efforts to support families and to assure that both parents and children get the social and health services they need. Theories and models of how to do this effectively vary widely, and experts have suggested a number of different approaches. Some schools focus on assuring referral to outside agencies providing services for families and children, others on partnering with these allied agencies to bring services on or near school campuses, and still others on increasing support services offered by the school itself. These programs are designed to increase access to needed services, to improve academic performance, and to help parents prevent or resolve problems, develop new skills, and learn how to participate more effectively in their children's education.

Such programs draw from a century of reform efforts on two parallel, but often interrelated, tracks—education reform and neighborhood-based social services. In 1995 David Tyack and Larry Cuban described some of the ways that these ideas have overlapped:

> Prodded by a variety of lay reformers to expand social and health services, educational administrators added programs of physical education and recreation and gave instruction in health. Hundreds of cities added vacation schools (later called summer schools), school lunch programs, and medical and dental care, especially for the children of working-class immigrant families. States and urban districts began creating special schools or classes for physically or emotionally handicapped students—the number of separate state or district schools for such children increased from 180 in 1900 to 551 in 1930. Cities also created new categories of classes for "misfits"—children who were too "backward" to proceed at the normal rate in graded classrooms or too

unruly for the teachers to handle. (pp. 20–21)

Late-nineteenth-century settlement houses offer one of the earliest examples of how neighborhood-based services for families can supplement the work of overcrowded inner-city schools. For example, the first Hull-House (established in Chicago in 1889 by Jane Addams and her associates) developed programs such as a day nursery and kindergarten for the children of "hard-driven mothers who went out to work all day, sometimes leaving the little things in the casual care of a neighbor, but often locking them into their tenement rooms" (Addams, p. 127). Hull-House also sponsored "clubs" for the "large number of children who leave school the very week they are fourteen years old, only too eager to close the school-room door forever on a tiresome task that is at last well over" (Addams, p. 86).

While settlement houses offered many ideas about how to support families, another approach was taken in the late nineteenth century by Charity Organization Societies, which developed case-by-case methods of aiding poor and troubled families. During the last century, ideas about how to help poor families and children swung back and forth between these twin poles of casework and neighborhood-based social services. One end of the continuum suggests that problems are primarily within the individual or family (requiring individualized casework) and the other that they are social, structural, or economic (requiring neighborhood and community solutions). Recent interest in orienting family support services around neighborhood schools can be seen, at least in part, as another generation's "reinvention" of neighborhood-based support services for families and their children.

Conflicting Values about How Schools Should Support Families

Some argue that schools need to focus on educational issues, leaving social issues to families, religious, civic, and community institutions. Others believe that children who come to school hungry, sick, or frightened cannot learn, no matter how thoughtful the curriculum or how accomplished the teacher. Opinions on how schools should interact with families are varied and deeply felt, based on individual experiences, values, and perceptions.

While questions about whether and how schools should be involved in supporting families are debated in forums across the country, however, most schools already provide a broad range of nonclassroom "support services" designed to promote academic achievement. Because each school district or local educational authority sets its own policies in response to local expectations and conditions, there is a very wide range in the nonclassroom-based supports and services offered across school districts or even between schools in the same district. Some schools have many such services whereas others have very few—and some do a better job than others of tracking and organizing the resources they do have. For example, distress over there being "no services" for the children in one inner-city school in Los Angeles in the mid-1990s led to a count of the different kinds of programs already in place to provide support services to students. When the counters found that seventeen different kinds of "school support services personnel" were already working in the school, everyone agreed that the first priority was a "resource coordinating council." Coordinating the support services that were already available was an essential first step, but the next steps included assessing the other needs of teachers, students, and parents and developing partnerships with local allied agencies to provide some of the services most needed in the community.

What Are Family Support Services?

All families need help and support in raising their children. Some can get by with the informal support of family and friends, employment-related benefits such as health insurance, and fee-for-service arrangements to purchase child care or other needed services. Many families, however, will also need help from public, nonprofit, and community-based agencies that provide services to children and families on a free or low-cost basis. The service delivery systems that provide these services are organized somewhat differently in each community, but the services needed by families generally include child care, parent education, income support, and health and mental health services. Some families also need help in dealing with dependent (abused or neglected) or delinquent youth.

In some communities (often suburbs or relatively homogenous smaller urban areas), the established public and private human service systems work reasonably well, information about and referral to different kinds of services is available, and families find the help they need. In too many other communities, however, families face serious barriers to accessing and using services. In rural areas, the services may be far away or not available at all. In dense urban areas—especially poor inner-city neighborhoods with large numbers of immigrants and families with multiple needs—human service delivery systems tend to be chaotic, overwhelmed, and confusing. Sometimes even the most knowledgeable people do not know where to find key child and family agencies, much less how families get access to different kinds of specialized services.

Schools are the most visible neighborhood institutions serving families and children, but many school personnel do not know about many community resources so they cannot guide parents who need help. Some school employees are reluctant to get involved in family troubles or to try to bridge complex institutions, and others are frustrated when their efforts to help do not work. Despite these difficulties, however, in many rural areas and inner-city communities where the needs of children and families are most visible and urgent, partnerships between schools, allied public and private agencies, and community-based groups are flourishing.

In some places, reform efforts have led schools to better define and mobilize their internal resources or to develop connections with services offered by allied agencies. In others, schools have opened their buildings and playgrounds after the school day ends to external organizations that provide after-school activities, parent education, and many other family support services. In some jurisdictions, school leaders have actively engaged in partnerships to change local policies to assure that the services families need are available through allied agencies. Assuring that these allied agencies are ready and able to help families can free schools to attend to their primary purpose, as Lisbeth B. Schorr suggested in a 1997 description of Missouri's Caring Communities program:

> teachers who had once been kept at arm's length by human service professionals, were trained to spot signs of trouble in their pupils—from slumps in classroom performance to depression—and to convey their concerns to Caring Communities coordinators. "The greatest accomplishment of Caring Communities is that I feel relieved of responsibility for social problems," said one teacher. "I can really teach." (p. 288)

Because conditions are so different in each community, there are many ways to approach the question of what schools can and should do to support families and assure that children are not so hungry, sick, or troubled that they cannot pay attention to learning. The answers are being invented (and sometimes reinvented) in communities across the country. The solutions devised are as varied and numerous as the communities served, but the following critical issues have received special attention from professionals in the field:

1. How to prevent family problems from developing in the first place

2. How to assure that young children are ready for school

3. How schools can more effectively connect families to specialized treatment services

4. How to improve training for and the evaluation of family support services

Preventing Family Problems

While the idea of supporting families is not new, discussions took on a different tone in the early 1980s with the establishment of the Family Resource Coalition, later called Family Support America. This national organization serves as a catalyst to assure that families have access to the support they need in welcoming surroundings in their own communities, where knowledgeable and respectful staff speak the family's language and understand its cultural traditions. These services are designed to recognize and build on family strengths, increase family stability, prevent problems, improve parenting skills, and enhance child development.

Whether they are based in schools, child-care centers, social agencies, or medical clinics, preventively oriented family support programs should be guided by shared principles, which include: (1) staff and families work together in relationships based on equality and respect; (2) families are resources to their own members, to other families, to programs, and to communities; (3) programs affirm and strengthen families' cultural, racial, and linguistic identities and enhance their ability to function in a multicultural society; (4) programs advocate with family members for services and systems that are fair, responsive, and accountable; and (5) programs are flexible and responsive to emerging family and community issues. Guided by such principles, the "family support movement" is working to change

professional attitudes and practices, encouraging more egalitarian, flexible, respectful, and responsive interactions with families.

School Readiness

Guided by the family support movement, many people have focused on providing effective early childhood intervention programs to enhance child development and help children and parents get ready for school. After analyzing results from a number of the most rigorously evaluated early intervention programs, RAND researchers in 1998 concluded that these programs can provide significant benefits, especially for disadvantaged children and their families.

The significance of early childhood experiences in later learning was reaffirmed by the National Research Council and the National Institute of Medicine in a 2000 analysis of the extensive scientific evidence:

> A fundamental paradox exists and is unavoidable: development in the early years is both highly robust and highly vulnerable. Although there have been long-standing debates about how much the early years really matter in the larger scheme of lifelong development, our conclusion is unequivocal: What happens during the first months and years of life matters a lot, not because this period of development provides an indelible blueprint for adult well-being, but because it sets either a sturdy or fragile stage for what follows. (Shonkoff and Phillips, pp. 4–5)

Their summary of the evidence affirms the positive effects of high-quality early childhood programs on school performance, and suggests that a number of different kinds of preschool programs can be effective: "Taken together, the follow-up literature provides abundant evidence of intervention-control group differences in academic achievement during middle childhood, but no consistent or distinctive pattern of preschool curriculum or program format" (Shonkoff and Phillips, p. 351).

Recognizing the salience of early development, more programs are being developed to help both preschool children and their parents—assuring that children and parents are ready to get the most from school. For example, school-linked family support services can help parents find affordable, high-quality child care, improve parenting skills through parent education information and experiences, and help ease the transition between child care and school. At the same time, leaders in communities around the country have also realized that significant changes may be needed to help schools get ready for the changing population of children and families.

Connecting Families to Specialized Treatment Services

Many schools have focused on identifying children with problems so that they can be referred for testing, special education, or treatment. Even with more access to early childhood development and prevention services, specialized treatment for children and youth with behavior and health problems will still be needed. In this area too, there are enormous local differences in the availability, cost, and quality of specialized treatment services. Not surprisingly, problems are most likely to be found in poor rural districts where families have little access to services and in large inner-city districts where there are not enough resources to go around.

Partnerships between schools and allied public agencies responsible for providing health and mental health services, intervening in cases of child abuse and neglect, and responding to juvenile violence and delinquency are working effectively in some communities. For example, evaluation of California's Healthy Start Initiative, a statewide effort designed to help schools build bridges to allied public and community-based agencies that serve the same families and children, has demonstrated significant improvements in child and family outcomes. The long-term goal of many such reform efforts is to restructure existing child and family services systems so that they are less fragmented and more integrated, less intimidating and more accessible, and less confusing and more understandable to families. Unfortunately, that goal remains a dream in most places.

The Challenges of Training and Evaluation

Efforts to develop and sustain school-community partnerships present a number of challenges. Two questions require immediate attention.

First, how can education and training be improved to build connections? The possibilities of training different kinds of professionals to form effective interprofessional teams, and to collaborate more effectively with families, are being explored in

university-community pilot projects throughout the country. Most university-based training for teachers and health and human services professionals, however, is still based in separate specialties that do not prepare professionals for work across disciplinary and organizational boundaries. Most of the people who work in school-community partnerships must learn on the job, and only a few have the time, energy, or resources to share the important lessons they are learning.

Second, how can the effectiveness of all kinds of school-community partnerships be continuously evaluated? The people involved in such partnerships should be able to document the costs and benefits of different approaches to family support services. Targeted evaluation research can help to refine and improve programs, to improve planning, and to document results for participants, school boards, principals, teachers, and taxpayers. While some data is available on the outcomes of these efforts, a great deal more information is needed to guide further development of the field.

See also: FAMILY, SCHOOL, AND COMMUNITY CONNECTIONS; FAMILY SUPPORT SERVICES, *subentry on* INCOME SUPPORT SERVICES FOR CHILDREN AND FAMILIES; WELFARE REFORM.

BIBLIOGRAPHY

ADAMS, PAUL, and NELSON, KRISTINE, eds. 1995. *Reinventing Human Services: Community- and Family-Centered Practice.* Hawthorne, NY: Aldine de Gruyter.

ADDAMS, JANE. 1999. *Twenty Years at Hull-House, with Autobiographical Notes* (1910). New York: Signet Classic.

ADELMAN, HOWARD S., and TAYLOR, LINDA. 2000. "Looking at School Health and School Reform Policy through the Lens of Addressing Barriers to Learning." *Children's Services: Social Policy, Research, and Practice* 3(2):117–132.

BRIAR-LAWSON, KATHARINE, and LAWSON, HAL. 1997. *Connecting the Dots: Progress towards the Integration of School Reform, School-Linked Services, Parent Involvement, and Community Schools.* St Louis, MO: Danforth Foundation.

CIBULKA, JAMES G., and KRITEK, WILLIAM J., eds. 1996. *Coordination among Schools, Families, and Communities: Prospects for Education Reform.* Albany, NY: State University of New York Press.

DRYFOOS, JOY G. 1994. *Full Service Schools: A Revolution in Health and Social Services for Children, Youth, and Families.* San Francisco: Jossey-Bass.

DRYFOOS, JOY G. 1998. *Safe Passage: Making It through Adolescence in a Risky Society.* New York: Oxford University Press.

HALPERN, ROBERT. 1999. *Fragile Families, Fragile Solutions: A History of Supportive Services for Families in Poverty.* New York: Columbia University Press.

KAGAN, SHARON L.; POWELL, DOUGLAS R.; WEISSBOURD, BERNICE; and ZIGLER, EDWARD F., eds. 1987. *America's Family Support Programs.* New Haven, CT: Yale University Press.

KAROLY, LYNN A.; GREENWOOD, PETER W.; EVERINGHAM, SUSAN S.; HOUBE, JILL; KILBURN, M. REBECCA; RYDELL, C. PETER; SANDERS, MATTHEW; and CHIESA, JAMES. 1998. *Investing in Our Children: What We Know and Don't Know about the Costs and Benefits of Early Childhood Interventions.* Santa Monica, CA: RAND.

KNAPP, MICHAEL S. 1995. "How Shall We Study Comprehensive, Collaborative Services for Children and Families?" *Educational Researcher* 24(4):5–16.

MCCROSKEY, JACQUELYN, and EINBINDER, SUSAN. 1998. *Universities and Communities: Remaking Professional and Interprofessional Education for the Next Century.* Westport, CT: Praeger.

MCCROSKEY, JACQUELYN, and MEEZAN, WILLIAM. 1998. "Family-Centered Services: Approaches and Effectiveness." *Future of Children* 8(1):54–71.

SCHORR, LISBETH B. 1997. *Common Purpose: Strengthening Families and Neighborhoods to Rebuild America.* New York: Doubleday, Anchor Books.

SHONKOFF, JACK P., and PHILLIPS, DEBORAH A., eds. 2000. *From Neurons to Neighborhoods: The Science of Early Childhood Development.* Washington, DC: National Academy Press.

TYACK, DAVID, and CUBAN, LARRY. 1995. *Tinkering toward Utopia: A Century of Public School Reform.* Cambridge, MA: Harvard University Press.

WAGNER, MARY; GOLAN, SHARI; SHAVER, DEBRA; NEWMAN, LYNN; WECHSLER, MARJORIE; and KELLEY, FIONA. 1994. *A Healthy Start for California's Children and Families: Early Findings from a Statewide Evaluation of School-Linked Services.* Menlo Park, CA: SRI International.

WALBERG, HERBERT J.; REYES, OLGA; and WEISSBERG, ROGER P., eds. 1997. *Children and Youth: Interdisciplinary Perspectives.* Thousand Oaks, CA: Sage.

INTERNET RESOURCE

FAMILY SUPPORT AMERICA. 2002. <www.familysupportamerica.org>.

JACQUELYN MCCROSKEY

INCOME SUPPORT SERVICES FOR CHILDREN AND FAMILIES

Because of a combination of demographic trends and inadequate income supports, children comprise the demographic group at greatest poverty risk in the United States. In the mid-1970s, there was grave concern about elderly poverty, as nearly one in three elderly adults lived in poor households. Since then, the indexing of social security benefits to inflation has allowed benefits to better keep up with living costs. As a consequence, the elderly are now less likely to be poor than most other Americans. Alongside this success story of social policy ameliorating poverty, however, is the unfortunate fact that children have replaced the elderly at the low end of the U.S. economic ladder.

While the percent of children living in single-parent homes increased from 10 percent in 1960 to 31 percent in 1998, in 2000 more than half of poor families were headed by unmarried mothers. A minority of children will experience a childhood in which both parents are present, and, though mothers are more likely than ever to be employed, many are the only earner in their household. Mother-only families not only rely on lower wages than those typically earned by males but also must manage childcare and other parenting responsibilities alone. Income supports become increasingly important in these instances.

As more middle-class mothers become employed, income support for parents has increasingly required work participation. This trend culminated in the passage in 1996 of the Personal Responsibility and Work Opportunity Reconciliation Act, which created the principal program for poor families,

Temporary Assistance to Needy Families. Cash support for families is limited. In response to concerns over work disincentives and fraud, in-kind benefits have become more common than cash. These in-kind benefits, particularly food stamps, health insurance, and health care, are available to more families than are income supports.

Specific Income Support Programs

There are six family income support programs, divided into cash supports and tax benefits. The Earned Income Tax Credit (EITC) blurs the line between the two categories. No program alone raises families from poverty, but the EITC, coupled with full-time work, can raise a small family just above the poverty line. To make ends meet, low-earning, single-parent families must often supplement income supports with child-care and housing subsidies, medical assistance, and food stamps.

Temporary Assistance to Needy Families (TANF). The TANF program, which is the best-known income support program, is often generically referred to as "welfare." This program replaced Aid to Families with Dependent Children (AFDC) as part of the Personal Responsibility and Work Opportunity Reconciliation Act of 1996. TANF provides time-limited cash support to families with minor children. While states have discretion in defining program details, particularly benefit levels, states may not use federal money to offer families cash grants for more than two consecutive years or for more than five years over their lifetime. Adult recipients are also mandated to participate in work, or work-related activities, for at least thirty-two hours per week. Certain provisions exempt a small number of parents, such as those with newborns or those caring for children or relatives with disabilities.

Supplemental Security Income (SSI). SSI provides cash assistance to elderly persons or persons with disabilities whose income falls below the federal poverty line. Originating as Aid to the Blind and Aid to the Aged, part of the Social Security Act of 1935, then as Aid to the Disabled in 1950, SSI was created in 1972 from the consolidation of existing programs for the disabled and indigent elderly. Eighty-nine percent of SSI recipients also receive Social Security. Children with disabilities are also eligible for SSI.

SSI funding comes solely from the federal government, and it is administered by the Social Security Administration. As a result, benefits and eligibility

are uniform across states. The maximum allowable annual federal SSI benefit in 1999 was $6,000. Overall, SSI income support is about 75 percent of the poverty level.

General Assistance (GA). While no federal program exists to aid able-bodied adults under sixty-five years of age, most states and localities offer minimal cash grants. Most recipients are single adults, but others receiving benefits may include parents with children in public custody, parents previously convicted of a felony (making them ineligible for TANF), and parents who have timed off of TANF. GA grants are generally intended to offset minimal living expenses, not as a substitute for work, and offer support well below the poverty level. In 1992, forty-one states offered GA programs. Since then, there have been severe cutbacks in GA programs, with some states, such as Michigan, eliminating the programs altogether.

Earned Income Tax Credit (EITC). The EITC program was originally established in 1975 to address a major criticism of AFDC—that it encouraged single parenting and discouraged work by limiting eligibility to nonworking single parents. The EITC, which is administered by the Internal Revenue Service, functions like a negative income tax, supplementing the earnings of low-income workers who have children. While tax policy is more often used to assist middle-class families, in the form of mortgage deductions and business credits, the EITC uses tax policy for a program targeting low-income families.

In 1996 a family with one child with earnings of up to $25,000 per year would be eligible for a tax refund under the EITC program. The tax credit has survived several important revisions over the years. Eligibility has expanded to include nearly all low-income families with children. The credit can be paid in installments throughout the year, instead of as a year-end refund. The maximum grant is paid to minimum-wage, full-time workers, with the consequence of lifting their wage up to poverty level. Proponents argue that the credit must be sufficient to ensure that full-time workers, even at minimum wage, do not have to raise their families in poverty.

Tax deductions and credits. Nearly all families benefit from tax code provisions, most often from the $600 per child tax credit and the $2,900 per person tax exemption. Tax code also allows for the deduction of certain child-care expenses. Unlike most benefits to families and children, these are universal supports to families regardless of income. Other tax policies, such as mortgage interest deductions, disproportionately assist middle- and upper-income families.

See also: POVERTY AND EDUCATION; WELFARE REFORM.

BIBLIOGRAPHY

CENTER ON BUDGET AND POLICY PRIORITIES. 1995. *General Assistance Programs: Gaps in the Safety Net.* Washington, DC: Center on Budget and Policy Priorities.

DOBELSTEIN, ANDREW W. 1996. *Social Welfare Policy and Analysis.* Chicago: Nelson-Hall.

LEVY, FRANK. 1998. *The New Dollars and Dreams: American Incomes and Economic Change.* New York: Russell Sage Foundation.

SEGAL, ELIZABETH A., and BRZUZY, STEPHANIE. 1998. *Social Welfare Policy, Programs, and Practice.* Itasca, IL: F. E. Peacock.

U.S. HOUSE COMMITTEE ON WAYS AND MEANS. 1992. *Background Material and Data on Programs within the Jurisdiction of the Committee on Ways and Means—Green Book.* Washington, DC: U.S. Government Printing Office.

SUSAN E. SMITH

FAWCETT, HAROLD P. (1894–1976)

Professor of mathematics education at Ohio State University, Harold P. Fawcett was best known for his work on pedagogy in geometry, particularly the teaching of reasoning and proof. Fawcett was born in Upper Sackville, New Brunswick, Canada. In 1914 he received an A.B. from Mount Allison University and obtained a high school teaching position in a New England village. After World War I service with the United States Army in France, Fawcett taught in the home study division of the New York Young Men's Christian Association (YMCA) schools (1919–1924). He was awarded an A.M. in 1924 by Columbia University and continued doctoral work while teaching in Columbia's extension division. In 1937 he received a Ph.D. in mathematics education from Teachers College, Columbia University. Faw-

cett joined the faculty at Ohio State University in 1932, where he rose to full professor (1943), served as chair of the Department of Education (1948–1956), and retired with emeritus rank (1964). During his early years at Ohio State, Fawcett also taught at the affiliated University School, where he served three years as associate director. In 1958 he was elected to a two-year term as president of the National Council of Teachers of Mathematics (NCTM).

The most enduring contribution by Fawcett to the field of mathematics education was the thirteenth yearbook of the National Council of Teachers of Mathematics, *The Nature of Proof* (1938). The publication was, essentially, his doctoral thesis, which drew upon his experiences and experiments in teaching high school geometry at the University School. Fawcett believed that, with respect to geometry, contemporary classroom practice was incongruous with the new emphasis on the development of critical and reflective thought advocated by national committees and influential mathematicians. If asked, Fawcett asserted, many teachers would express agreement with the new emphases for demonstrative (proof-oriented) geometry to introduce students to the nature of deductive reasoning and to develop in them an understanding of what proving something really means. Fawcett's experience, however, suggested to him that, rather than emphasizing the role of logical processes in developing and establishing a geometrical system, most teachers taught geometry as a given set of definitions and theorems to be memorized.

Fawcett's approach was based upon four assumptions: (1) high school students enter a geometry course with practical experience in reasoning accurately; (2) students should be permitted to use their own approaches to reasoning in geometry; (3) the students' logical processes, not those of the teacher, should guide development of the subject; and (4) students need opportunities to apply the deductive method to situations that have clear relevance to their own lives. These assumptions reflect the influence of broader educational trends of the 1930s, including student-centered pedagogy, an investigation–discovery orientation, the incorporation of experiences external to school, and a concern for transfer of skills to areas outside mathematics.

Classroom implementation of Fawcett's pedagogical approach was unique at the time. Virtually nothing was given to the students. Rather than receiving a published textbook, students developed their own notebooks, with individuality welcomed. Students decided which terms should be undefined and which needed definition. The definitions were developed and refined by the students after discussion, and then entered into their notebooks. If a proposition appeared obvious to the students, it was taken as an assumption. Instead of being given a statement to prove, students were presented with a figure and encouraged to identify properties of the figure that might be assumed. Following this, they were to discover the implications of these properties. With guidance from the teacher, important implications were generalized into theorems, resulting in a limited, but richly understood, structure. In effect the students developed the geometry curriculum themselves, through a process of questions, discussion, and reasoned reflection.

Criteria of success for Fawcett's program was based on its effect on students' behaviors in approaching problem tasks. For example, did students first seek to clarify definitions or conditions of the problem situation? Fawcett's own investigation suggested that his approach, emphasizing reasoning processes rather than skills, improved reflective thinking more than did the traditional course, without significant loss of competence in subject matter knowledge. In light of his ideas on the pedagogy of geometry, Fawcett was invited to join the Committee on the Function of Mathematics in General Education, appointed by the Progressive Education Association's Commission on the Secondary School Curriculum. His work influenced the sections of the committee report that dealt with logic and proof. Renewed interest in Fawcett's pedagogical approach to geometry and his emphasis on helping students to develop critical, reflective thinking processes led the National Council of Teachers of Mathematics to reissue the *Nature of Proof* in 1995.

Although Fawcett championed the role of the student in developing deductive mathematical systems, he viewed the teacher as an indispensable guide to move students toward self-directed, independent learning. He believed that a geometry course could provide opportunities to gain knowledge and develop understanding of deductive reasoning; however, only the teacher could provide the classroom environment in which original and creative thinking could flourish. From his early days as a student in a small Canadian school with an enrollment of just two dozen, Fawcett never forgot the im-

pact of the new mathematics teacher who arrived at the school when he was fourteen years old. He credited her with taming his rebelliousness and inspiring him to pursue a career in education by engaging his intellect in adventurous pursuit of geometric understanding. It became for Fawcett a lifelong quest.

See also: MATHEMATICS EDUCATION, PREPARATION OF TEACHERS; MATHEMATICS LEARNING.

BIBLIOGRAPHY

CATTEL, JAQUES, and ROSS, E. D. 1948. *Leaders in Education: A Biographical Dictionary*, 3rd edition. Lancaster, PA: Science Press.

FAWCETT, HAROLD P. 1964. "Reflections of a Retiring Teacher of Mathematics." *Mathematics Teacher* 57(7):450–456.

FAWCETT, HAROLD P. 1970. "The Geometric Continuum." *Mathematics Teacher* 63(5):411–420.

FAWCETT, HAROLD P. 1995. *The Nature of Proof.* Thirteenth Yearbook of the National Council of Teachers of Mathematics (1938). Reston, VA: National Council of Teachers of Mathematics.

EILEEN F. DONOGHUE

FEDERAL EDUCATIONAL ACTIVITIES

HISTORY
  Elizabeth H. DeBray
SUMMARY BY AGENCY
  Jason L. Walton

HISTORY

The roots of federal participation in education lie deep in American history, beginning in the days of the Confederation. When it became clear in 1777 that the soldiers of the Continental Army lacked necessary competence in mathematics and military regimen, instruction was provided in these areas. Soon thereafter it became evident that the nation's safety required a corps of trained military officers. Despite the general fear of a standing army, the national leaders united to establish the U.S. Military Academy at West Point in 1802. These actions in the interest of national defense were the first in which the federal government set up and operated its own educational programs. Support of education in the individual states began in 1785 when the Congress of the Confederation adopted an ordinance concerning public lands in the Western Territory. This ordinance provided that one section of land owned by the national government be set aside in each township for the endowment of schools.

In the Northwest, the Ordinance of 1787 granted Ohio two townships as an endowment for a university—the first instance of federal support for higher education. Beginning with the admission of Ohio to the Union in 1802, Congress established the policy of granting federally owned lands to new states at the time of admission for the endowment of public education. In addition, as new states were created, Congress granted them 15 percent of the receipts from sales of federal lands within their areas. Of the twenty-nine states receiving such funds, sixteen were required to turn them to the support of education, and after 1889 all new states were required to do so.

Aid to Higher Education

With the passage of the Morrill Act of 1862, higher education became the first major beneficiary of federal educational assistance, and it remained the major beneficiary for more than fifty years. The Morrill Act was passed to provide support and endowment for colleges established, as the act states, "to teach such branches of learning as are related to agriculture and the mechanics arts, in such manner as the legislatures of the States may respectively prescribe." Perhaps the wartime influence accounted for the requirement that the beneficiary schools, later called land-grant colleges, teach military science. The Morrill Act granted 30,000 acres of federal lands to each state for each senator and representative in Congress from that state. This land was to be sold to provide an endowment for at least one college. When federal lands were insufficient to meet this obligation, the states were granted scrip. The Second Morrill Act of 1890, as amended in 1907, established a new pattern of money grants for the support of instruction in a wide variety of subjects, and none of the money was to go for buildings or land.

The first major support for higher education through student-aid programs came with the passage of the Servicemen's Readjustment Act of 1944. This act provided stipends and tuition assistance to practically all veterans. Under its provisions, close to 8 million servicemen were able to attend college be-

fore the educational provisions of the act terminated in 1956.

Pell Grants are the major source of grants for college for economically disadvantaged students. Other grant and loan programs include the College Work-Study program, Supplemental Educational Opportunity Grants, and Stafford and Perkins Loans. The Leveraging Educational Assistance Partnerships program matches each dollar that states commit to need-based aid. Other key federal higher education programs such as GEAR UP (Gaining Early Awareness and Readiness for Undergraduate Programs) help prepare middle school students from low-income families for college.

Title IX of the Higher Education Act of 1972 stated that "no person in the United States shall, on the basis of sex, be excluded from participation in, be denied the benefits of, or be subjected to discrimination under any education program or activity receiving Federal financial assistance." Exempted were single-sex undergraduate institutions, religious institutions, and military academies. Title IX's enforcement has brought federal regulation onto every public and private campus in the nation.

Impact aid. In 1941 the federal government began a program of assistance to local school districts whose local tax bases are adversely affected by the presence of defense installations and by other federal activities such as public-housing projects and Indian reservations. The program was set up under the Lanham Act of 1940. Although the full-scale operation of this program to meet the needs of wartime activity ceased in 1946, the expansion of federal activities in the postwar period made it necessary to continue appropriations. The annual appropriation for Impact Aid is approximately $864 million.

Aid to elementary and secondary education. In 1917 the passage of the Federal Vocational Education Act (also known as the Smith-Hughes Act) launched the federal government into a new educational policy arena: for the first time, federal funds were to be used in a specific area of precollege education. The act provided funds both for vocational courses in public schools and for the training of teachers for these courses.

The largest single program is Title I of the Elementary and Secondary Education Act (ESEA), signed into law by President Lyndon B. Johnson in 1965 with the goal of providing compensatory education to economically disadvantaged students. The proposed budget appropriation for 2003 for Title I is $11.4 billion, a substantial increase over its prior level of $8.2 billion. The 1994 reauthorization of the ESEA was an important one in policy terms, as it required states to develop and adopt systems of academic standards, assessments, and accountability. The ESEA was reauthorized by the Congress and signed into law by President George W. Bush in 2002 as the No Child Left Behind Education Act. The law contains provisions for identifying schools that fail to narrow the racial achievement gap, and calls for every state to test all students annually in grades three through eight. Thus Title I is still evolving from a funding stream to a program with specified performance targets for schools.

The standards movement. In 1983 Ronald Reagan's Secretary of Education, Terrell Bell, released a commission report entitled *A Nation at Risk,* which asserted that the U.S. elementary and secondary educational system was failing gravely. In the aftermath of the report's release, many states strengthened their graduation course-taking requirements. The report began a movement that was a high federal priority in the 1990s: the educational standards movement. President George Bush, in 1990 following the Charlottesville, Virginia governors' summit on education, proposed an initiative called America 2000. The bipartisan National Education Goals Panel was created to monitor the country's progress toward the six goals by the year 2000. It was not until President Bill Clinton's term, however, that the National Education Goals were enacted into law in 1994 as part of the Goals 2000: Educate America Act. As one of the national goals was that all students demonstrate proficiency in math, science, history, and English/language arts, a variety of federal activities to encourage the development of standards and assessments in those content areas were initiated. The Office of Educational Research and Improvement in the early 1990s made grants to various universities and professional associations to develop standards that states and localities could adopt. In 2002 the National Education Goals Panel was shut down, as its function of monitoring goals was considered obsolete.

Department of Defense Education Activity (DoDEA) Schools. Founded after World War II, the overseas elementary and secondary school system created to educate children of military personnel is the Department of Defense Dependent Schools (DoDDS). The Department of Defense Domestic Dependent Elementary and Secondary Schools (DDESS) serve children of personnel stationed in the United States. In 2001 both parts of the DoDEA system served approximately 112,000 students.

Students with disabilities. The Individuals with Disabilities Education Act (IDEA) was funded at $9.7 billion in the 2002 budget. The federal government provides approximately nine percent of the total funding on special education in the United States. In 1975, the Education for All Handicapped Children Act was created to ensure equal access to education for students with disabilities. The law required that each such child receive an "Individualized Education Program," which encompassed instructional goals and evaluation procedures for determining whether the goals had been reached. The 1997 reauthorization of the IDEA strengthened the requirement for children with disabilities to have access to schools' general education curriculum.

Vocational Education

The Vocational Rehabilitation Act of 1918 was the first educational program for veterans, providing vocational rehabilitation to any honorably discharged veteran of World War I. The program terminated in 1928. The Vocational Rehabilitation Act of 1943 provided a similar program for World War II veterans; rehabilitation of disabled veterans was separately provided for in the Servicemen's Readjustment Act of 1944. The Carl D. Perkins Vocational-Technical Education Act of 1998 provides basic grants to states for career and technical education for secondary school students. The School-to-Work Opportunities Act of 1994 provided grants for states to build high school learning systems for further education and careers through "work-based learning." A new office was created to administer the program, combining staff from the Departments of Education and Labor. The act expired in 2001.

U.S. Office of Education

For several years prior to the Civil War, associations of educators had recommended that an agency be established in the federal government for the promotion of education throughout the United States. In 1867 Congress responded by creating an independent department of education under direction of a commissioner. The department began with an authorized staff of four and an appropriation of $25,000; its stated objectives were the dissemination of educational statistics and promotion of the cause of education. From 1869 to 1939 the agency was located in the Department of the Interior. In 1939, the Office of Education became part of the new Federal Security Agency, which in turn became the Department of Health, Education, and Welfare (HEW) in 1953. The U.S. Office of Education was reorganized within HEW in 1965.

U.S. Department of Education

In 1979 the Carter administration created the U.S. Department of Education. While President Ronald Reagan initially sought to dismantle the agency in 1981, it remained intact. Its programmatic offices include the Office for Civil Rights, the Office of Elementary and Secondary Education, and the Office of Indian Education. The federal budget for discretionary education programs, including postsecondary education, was $48.9 billion in fiscal year 2002.

Research remains one of the primary activities of the federal role in education. The National Institute of Education was created in 1972 during the Nixon administration to oversee a program of studies and data collection. Total funding for the Office of Educational Research and Improvement grew tenfold between 1980 and 2000, but the percentage of those dollars supporting studies fell sharply in the 1980s and by 2002 was approximately just 15 percent. Federally funded educational development activities such as the National Diffusion Network have effectively ceased to exist. The National Center for Education Statistics is the bureau that collects and disseminates data and statistics.

National Science Foundation (NSF)

The National Science Foundation (NSF) was established by Congress as an independent agency in 1950. Its original programs were concerned with supporting basic research and awarding graduate and postdoctoral fellowships in the sciences. By 1968 approximately 90 percent of NSF's expenditures were directly or indirectly in support of research and education. During the 1990's, NSF's precollegiate strategy was "systemic initiative grants" to states and school districts to help them overhaul their science and mathematics programs.

International Activities

Under terms of a treaty signed at Buenos Aires in 1936, the United States began a continuous exchange of two graduate students per year with each of the sixteen signatory nations among the Latin American republics. Later the program was expanded to include exchange of trainees in government and industry as well as exchanges of teachers, professors, and specialists with all the Latin American republics. The Department of Education participates in several international activities. In 2001 these included data collection activities, such as those with the Asia-Pacific Economic Cooperation, and the Organisation for Economic Co-operation and Development's study of school performance and school system characteristics.

See also: COLLEGE FINANCIAL AID; FEDERAL FUNDING FOR ACADEMIC RESEARCH; FEDERAL FUNDS FOR HIGHER EDUCATION; IMPACT AID, PUBLIC LAWS 815 AND 874; GOVERNMENT AND EDUCATION, THE CHANGING ROLE OF; U.S. DEPARTMENT OF EDUCATION.

BIBLIOGRAPHY

BAILEY, STEPHEN, and MOSHER, EDITH. 1968. *ESEA: The Office of Education Administers a Law.* Syracuse, NY: Syracuse University Press.

ELMORE, RICHARD, and McLAUGHLIN, MILBREY. 1988. *Steady Work: Policy, Practice, and the Reform of American Education.* Santa Monica, CA: Rand.

JENNINGS, JOHN. 1998. *Why National Standards and Tests? Politics and the Quest for Better Schools.* Thousand Oaks, CA: Sage.

KING, JACQUELINE E., ed. 1999. *Financing a College Education: How It Works, How It's Changing.* Phoenix, AZ: Oryx.

NATIONAL COMMISSION ON EXCELLENCE IN EDUCATION. 1983. *A Nation at Risk: The Imperative for Educational Reform.* Washington, DC: Government Printing Office.

NATRIELLO, GARY, and McDILL, EDWARD. 1999. "Title I: From Funding Mechanism to Educational Program." In *Hard Work for Good Schools: Facts Not Fads in Title I Reform,* ed. Gary Orfield and Elizabeth DeBray. Cambridge, MA: The Civil Rights Project, Harvard University.

QUATTLEBAUM, CHARLES A. 1968. *Federal Educational Policies, Programs and Proposals, Parts 1–3.* Washington, DC, Government Printing Office.

RAVITCH, DIANE. 1983. *The Troubled Crusade: American Education 1945–1980.* New York: Basic Books.

RAVITCH, DIANE. 1995. *National Standards in American Education: A Citizen's Guide.* Washington, DC: Brookings Institution.

SMITH, MARSHALL; LEVIN, JESSICA; and CIANCI, JOANNE. 1997. "Beyond a Legislative Agenda: Education Policy Approaches of the Clinton Administration." *Educational Policy* 11(2):209–226.

SMREKAR, CLAIRE; GUTHRIE, JAMES W.; OWENS, DEBRA E.; and SIMS, PEARL G. 2001. *March Toward Excellence: School Success and Minority Student Achievement in Department of Defense Schools.* Nashville, TN: Peabody Center for Education Policy, Vanderbilt University.

ELIZABETH H. DeBRAY

SUMMARY BY AGENCY

An extensive network of departments and agencies has developed over the course of American history in response to the needs of the government and the nation. In 2001 the executive departments numbered fourteen. The most recent addition was in 1989 when the Veterans Administration was elevated to department-level status and renamed the Department of Veterans Affairs. The president shares the burden of implementing the policies and laws of the nation with these departments and a vast array of other agencies that deal with specific areas of national and international affairs. All departments are headed by a secretary, with the exception of the Department of Justice, which is headed by the attorney general. These department heads, who make up the president's cabinet, must first be nominated by the president and then confirmed by the Senate. These departments can be broken down into divisions, bureaus, offices, and services operating in thousands of locations both in the United States and abroad. The educational activities of these departments and other major agencies can be divided into two categories: those that serve employees of the government and those that serve people outside the government.

Legal Foundations of Government Employee Training

Government departments and agencies have always had the authority to deliver their own training programs. There are, however, a number of legal references that make up the foundation for government employee training and education. The Government Employee Training Act of 1958 (GETA) first outlined how departments and agencies would plan, develop, establish, implement, evaluate and fund these activities, which were designed to improve the quality and performance of the government workforce. This act has been amended many times since 1958. Legislative acts that prescribe action by federal departments and agencies are codified and published shortly after passage. Title 5 of the U.S. Code is dedicated to human resource issues, with chapter 41 being devoted to training.

In 1967 Executive Order No. 11348 provided agency and department heads information on how GETA should be carried out. This was amended in 1978 by Executive Order No. 12107, which provided further direction and clarification.

The Code of Federal Regulations (C.F.R.) is the collected general and permanent rules published in the Federal Register by executive departments and agencies. Part 410 of Title 5 of the C.F.R. details the general and specific policies and requirements for training in government agencies. Part 412 of the same title addresses the development of supervisors, managers, and executives. Parts 410 and 412 were both substantially restructured in 1996 to reflect changes to chapter 41 of Title 5 of the U.S. Code.

Department of Agriculture

The Department of Agriculture assists American farmers and ranchers while providing a number of other services to the general public. The Farm and Foreign Agricultural Services (FFAS) Mission Area comprises three entities, which are designed to protect the interests of American farmers and ranchers amid market and weather uncertainty: the Farm Service Agency, the Foreign Agricultural Service, and the Risk Management Agency. These organizations attempt to strengthen the agricultural economy through delivery of commodity, credit, conservation, disaster, and emergency assistance. FFAS also promotes expansion of export sales to foreign markets. Wide-ranging crop insurance programs and risk management tools are also offered.

The Food, Nutrition, and Consumer Service (FNCS) administers the federal food assistance programs while coordinating policy and research on nutrition. The FNCS comprises two organizations: the Food and Nutrition Service (FNS) and the Center for Nutrition Policy and Promotion (CNPP). Under the FNS umbrella are the following programs:

• Food Stamps Program

- School Breakfast Program
- School Lunch Program
- After-School Snacks Program
- Special Milk Program
- Summer Food Service Program
- Child and Adult Care Food Program
- Special Supplemental Nutrition Program for Women, Infants, and Children (popularly known as WIC)
- Farmer's Market Nutrition Program, Food Distribution, and Team Nutrition

The CNPP was created in 1994 to link research with the nutritional needs of the public.

The Food Safety and Inspection Service (FSIS) works to ensure that meat, poultry, and egg products are safe, wholesome, and accurately labeled. FSIS also works to provide resources on food safety for consumers, educators and health professionals.

The Natural Resources and Environment (NRE) Mission Area is responsible for ensuring the health of the land through sustainable management. The NRE is composed of the Forest Service (FS) and the Natural Resources Conservation Service (NRCS). Each of the agencies assists with rural development and renders aid relative to natural resource concerns like erosion control, watershed protection, and forestry.

The Research, Education, and Economics (REE) Mission area disseminates information resources. The REE includes four services: the Agricultural Research Service, the Cooperative State Research, Education, and Extension Service, the Economic Research Service, and the National Agricultural Statistics Service.

Department of Commerce

The Department of Commerce and Labor was created on February 14, 1903. Ten years later, separate department designations for labor and commerce were established. Through its numerous and diverse bureaus the modern Department of Commerce (DOC) has evolved to perform an widely varied range of education-related foreign and domestic services.

The Bureau of Export Administration (BXA) is involved in many areas of national security and high technology. Among other activities, the BXA provides technical assistance to Russia and other newly emerging countries to develop effective export control systems and to help convert their defense industries. Assisting foreign supplier countries establish export control systems helps ensure that U.S. industries will not be undercut.

The Economic and Statistics Administration (ESA) is responsible not only for producing and analyzing some of the nation's most important demographic and economic data, but also for the dissemination of that data to the American public. Major offices under the ESA are the Bureau of the Census, the Bureau of Economic Analysis, and STAT-USA. The Bureau of Census conducts the decennial census of population and is a world leader in statistical research and methodology. The Bureau of Census makes its statistics available in a variety of media and offers assistance to data users from its headquarters in Suitland, Maryland, as well as through the twelve other regional offices. The Bureau of Economic Analysis (BEA) generates a number of important economic reports including a monthly "Survey of Current Business," a quarterly report on Gross Domestic Product, and regional, domestic, and international economic accounts. The BEA also generates occasional reports on travel, tourism, and international transactions.

The Economic Development Administration (EDA) targets economically distressed communities to generate new employment, industry, and commerce. A portion of these efforts involves skill training as well as job retraining.

The International Trade Administration (ITA) is the lead unit for trade in the DOC. The Trade Development area of ITA is organized by industry and provides analysis and advice on trade and investment issues to U.S. businesses, counseling U.S. exporters and service providers about marketing their products globally, and provides literature centers and seminars. The U.S. Foreign and Commercial Service employs trade specialists that assist companies wishing to enter into new markets. These specialists also lend support through alerting businesses to distribution channels, pricing, relevant trade shows, and available trade finance programs.

The Minority Business Development Agency (MBDA) promotes growth and competitiveness of the nation's minority and Native American–owned businesses. The agency has counseling centers located in areas with large concentrations of minority populations and businesses, offering management and technical assistance in all areas of establishing and operating a business.

The National Oceanic and Atmospheric Administration (NOAA) is dedicated to predicting and protecting the environment. NOAA has five divisions: the National Weather Service (NWS), the Office of Oceanic and Atmospheric Research (OAR), the National Environmental Satellite, Data and Information Service (NESDIS), the National Ocean Service (NOS), and the National Marine Fisheries Service (NMFS). The National Weather Service (NWS) works with federal, state, and local agencies to protect life and property as the official source of all watches and warnings of severe weather for the United States. The NWS also provides data, products, and services to private meteorologists. NOAA funds scientists and university researchers through the National Sea Grant College Program and the National Undersea Research Program to solve critical weather-related environmental problems such as tornadoes, hurricanes, El Niño-driven storms, solar storms, and other severe weather. The National Ocean Service conducts research on the health of the U.S. coasts and provides expertise during oil and hazardous chemical spill cleanup operations, as well as other duties.

The National Telecommunications and Information Administration (NTIA) assists the administration, Congress, and other regulatory agencies by addressing diverse technical and policy questions relative to telecommunications. The agency comprises six offices: the Office of Policy Coordination and Management (OPCM), the Office of Policy Analysis and Development (OPAD), the Office of International Affairs (OIA), the Office of Spectrum Management (OSM), the Institute for Telecommunication Sciences (ITS), as well as the Telecommunications Information Infrastructure Assistance Program (TIIAP). Employees of this agency include policy analysts, computer scientists, electronic engineers, attorneys, economists, mathematicians, and other specialists. The ITS office serves as the federal government's primary research laboratory for telecommunications science and engineering.

The Office of the Inspector General (OIG) was established in 1978 to protect the American public's interests and investments in the Department of Commerce. The office is authorized to conduct audits, investigations, and an array of inspections, systems evaluations, and other reviews of the Department of Commerce. The OIG provides timely, useful, and reliable information and advice to department officials.

The Patent and Trademark Office (PTO) is the federal mechanism that protects new ideas and investments. The PTO encourages innovation in American industry through providing patent and trademark protection. A substantial portion of this protection results from the clerical functions of the office, which includes preservation, classification, and distribution of information. Since its establishment in 1790, the PTO has accumulated the largest collection of applied technical information in the world. The Patent Office Search Room and the Trademark Office Search Room are both located in Arlington, Virginia, and are open to the public. In addition, the PTO publishes *Basic Facts About Patents, Basic Facts About Trademarks,* along with weekly publications describing registered patents and trademarks.

The Technology Administration (TA) was established in 1988 and consists of the National Institute for Standards and Technology (NIST), the National Technical Information Service (NTIS), and the Office of Technology Policy (OTP). NIST laboratories specialize in electronics and electrical engineering, manufacturing engineering, chemical science and technology, physics, materials science and engineering, building and fire research, and information technology. NTIS is the repository for all U.S. government research and development results. The NTIS collection is in excess of 3 million titles. These titles are organized, maintained, and disseminated in a variety of media formats. NTIS has also developed an online information dissemination system called FedWorld, which is recognized as a comprehensive electronic source for government information.

Department of Defense

The Department of Defense (DoD), so named in 1949, evolved from the Department of War, which was established by the first Congress. The mission of the DoD is to "provide military forces needed to deter war and to protect the security of our country." The DoD consists of three military departments, fourteen defense agencies, nine unified combatant commands, and seven field activities. The three military departments are the army, the navy, and the air force (the Marine Corps is a second armed service in the Department of the Navy).

The National Defense University (NDU) is the nation's premier joint professional military educational institution. Its component colleges and centers include the following: the Joint Forces Staff College, the Industrial College of the Armed Forces, the Information Resources Management College, the Institute for National Strategic Studies, the National War College, and the Center for Hemispheric Defense Studies. The NDU also offers a variety of other educational programs separate from these colleges and centers.

Military service academies provide officer education through precommission and reserve training. These academies include the U.S. Military Academy, the U.S. Naval Academy, the U.S. Air Force Academy, the U.S. Coast Guard Academy, and the U.S. Merchant Marine Academy.

Ongoing education and training opportunities for individuals are available immediately upon enlistment in any of the armed services. Military education typically begins with eight to thirteen weeks, depending upon the service, of basic training and continues afterwards with individual job training, which continues throughout enlistment. As men and women are promoted within their job specialty, training becomes more sophisticated. In 2001 there were more than 300 military training centers offering more than 10,000 courses (of which 68 percent were certified for college credit) to train men and women in some 4,100 separate job specialties (of which 88 percent had civilian counterparts).

The military also offers a wide variety of programs that help recruits earn college credit, attend college while in the service, and/or provide cash for college tuition. Department of Defense statistics indicate that in 1999 more than 26,000 military members participated in Servicemember Opportunity Colleges (SOC), which is a group of approximately 1,400 colleges and universities that agree to transfer credits among themselves for military members and their families. In addition, most Base Education Centers will grant course credit to enlisted men and women who can pass available examinations and tests on subjects ranging from mathematics to Western civilization.

The Community College of the Air Force (CCAF) allows its enlisted personnel to earn an associate degree in a job-related field. Beyond one's job specialty, each CCAF degree requires coursework in leadership, management, military studies, general education, and physical education.

Programs of educational financial support include tuition assistance, Montgomery G.I. Bill, college fund programs, and loan repayment programs. The terms and amounts of financial assistance from theses programs differ slightly depending on one's branch of service and military status.

The DoD also offers pre-kindergarten through twelfth-grade education through a system of schools in the United States and abroad for dependents of military personnel and civilian employees of the military. This activity is divided between two programs: the Domestic Dependent Elementary and Secondary Schools (DDESS) and the Department of Defense Dependents Schools (DoDDS). The DDESS serves an estimated 36,000 students in seventy schools across seven states, Guam, and Puerto Rico. The DoDDS serves an estimated 76,000 students in 154 schools in thirteen countries.

Department of Education

One of the Department of Education's earliest historical roles that has remained prominent involves collecting and sharing information on education. Since 1966 the department has operated the Educational Resources Information Center (ERIC), which is the world's largest education database. ERIC is accessible through the Department of Education website. Prominent annual publications include the *Digest of Education Statistics* and the *Condition of Education*. The department funds the National Assessment of Educational Progress (NAEP), which serves as "the nation's report card." The department also funds ten regional educational laboratories aimed at assisting state and local decision makers by providing the most recent teaching and learning knowledge.

Federal financial assistance for postsecondary education is a significant area of department activity. The department prints and processes the Free Application for Federal Student Aid (FAFSA), which students use to apply for financial assistance. Federal aid comes in a variety of formats and is administered through a assortment of programs including the Federal Pell Grant Program, the William D. Ford Direct Loan Program, the Federal Family Education Loan Program, the Federal Perkins Loan Program, the Federal Supplemental Educational Opportunity Grant Program, and the Federal Work-Study Program.

The department manages the distribution of many formula-based grants that target districts and students with special educational needs. Most federal funding of education is authorized under either the Elementary and Secondary Education Act (ESEA) of 1965 or Part B of the Individuals with Disabilities Education Act Amendments of 1997. Funding for advancement and innovation in elementary, secondary, and postsecondary education are made available through competitive grant programs.

The department provides vocational and lifelong learning opportunities through an assortment of programs developed to maintain American competitiveness in an emerging global economy. These program activities range from providing localities with School-to-Work Opportunities Act seed money designed to prepare students for a first job, to awarding state grants to fund vocational training and rehabilitation. Additional grant programs target literacy, high-school equivalency certification, and English language proficiency.

Department of Energy

The educational activities of the Department of Energy (DOE) are aligned with its longstanding goals of dissemination of energy-related information and increasing the American science and technology base. Department of Energy partnerships with schools such as the Energy Smart Schools Program focus on increasing awareness of energy-related issues, reducing energy consumption, and reinvesting energy cost savings.

The department's website serves as the chief portal for energy-related education resources. The DOE website offers teachers and students from elementary to postsecondary levels links to topics such as energy efficiency, alternative fuels, atmospheric research, and the Human Genome Project. The department serves as an information clearinghouse on internships and fellowships in all areas of endeavor in science and technology. The DOE also sponsors energy-related contests and competitions.

Department of Health and Human Services

The Department of Health and Human Services (HHS) is the primary healthcare and social service agency of the federal government. The department is divided among twelve major operating divisions, which administer more than 300 programs covering a wide range of activities. In fiscal year 2001 the agency employed more than 63,000 employees, provided in excess of 60,000 grants, and had a budget in exceeding $429 billion.

The Administration for Children and Families (ACF) is the division responsible for the economic and social well being of children, individuals, families, and communities. Programs in the ACF target welfare, refugee assistance, repatriation, foster care, adoption assistance, independent living assistance, low-income energy needs, mental retardation, family preservation, family support, child abuse, childcare, child support enforcement, developmental disabilities, and Native Americans. The most prominent ACF education-related activity is the national Head Start program. Grants are awarded to public or private nonprofit entities at the local level to provide comprehensive developmental services to children between the ages of three and five from low-income families. Legislation in 1994 created the Early Head Start program, expanding the benefits to include children under three and pregnant women. American Indian Head Start and Migrant Head Start offer identical services, but modify delivery of services to better meet the needs of these special populations.

The Administration on Aging (AOA) is the division charged with administering various programs mandated by the Older Americans Act of 2000. In keeping with the many titles of this act, the division is the primary federal advocate for older Americans and their concerns. The educational activities of this division include making resources available on the following: caregiver support, antifraud initiatives, elder abuse prevention, long-term care, retirement information, finance counseling, job vacancies, disaster assistance, and legal advice. The AOA also compiles, storehouses, and disseminates information and statistics on aging.

The Health Care Financing Administration (HCFA) is the division responsible for administering Medicare, Medicaid, and the State Children's Health Insurance Program. The HCFA offers a number of learning resources on its Internet site relative to health insurance. These resources inform interested parties of changes and progress in the range of coverage offered through HCFA. One such resource is the Medicare Learning Network, which provides health care professionals and others appropriate information on topics such as proper submission of Medicare claims and appropriate payment to Medicare beneficiaries for services rendered. Medicare Learning Network users may also subscribe to an array of electronic mailing lists that provide emerging information on specific areas of health coverage.

Two of the more prominent public health divisions are the Food and Drug Administration (FDA), which protects the public's health by screening consumer products before they reach the market using a blend of law and science, and the National Institutes of Health (NIH), which attempts to uncover new knowledge through the research and training conducted at its multiple centers and institutes. The National Library of Medicine is also under the NIH umbrella.

Six of the seven remaining divisions are also considered public health divisions designed to meet the physical and mental health needs of the population. They include the Centers for Disease Control and Prevention (CDC), the Substance Abuse and Mental Health Service Administration (SAMHSA), the Health Resources and Services Administration (HRSA), the Indian Health Service (IHS), the Agency for Healthcare Research and Quality (AHRQ), and the Agency for Toxic Substances and Disease Registry (ATSDR).

The twelfth working division of HHS is the Program Support Center (PSC); it serves the various administrative functions of the department.

Department of Housing and Urban Development (HUD)

While HUD was created as a cabinet-level position within the executive branch of the federal government in 1965, its history extends all the way back to the passage of the National Housing Act of 1935. Aside from orientation of department personnel, education and training activities conducted by HUD are products of its awarding of grants whose scope of activity fulfills the mission of the department. Several examples of such activities during the decade of the 1990s follow.

Youthbuild was authorized as the "Hope for Youth" program as a part of the Housing and Community Development Act of 1992. The program provides HUD grants on a competitive basis to nonprofit organizations assisting high-risk youth between the ages of sixteen to twenty-four to learn housing construction skills. The program also helps participating youth complete their high school education. Skills development takes places as participants assist in the construction of housing for low-to-moderate-income persons.

HUD provided the Philadelphia Housing Authority with an Apprenticeship Demonstration Grant to provide hands-on training in the removal of asbestos, in lead abatement, and for driver's education training. Participants were eighteen to twenty-four years old and high school dropouts. This grant was coordinated with the welfare-to-work initiatives of the Department of Labor. That same housing authority received additional funding to conduct nurse's assistant training and adult basic education.

HUD has also provided training in the K–12 arena. An education advocacy project was funded through Wright State University in Dayton, Ohio. Tutors were trained to provide academic remedial and enrichment services in the critical areas of reading, mathematics, and science to improve the academic performance of students from low-income groups and ethnic minority groups who have consistently experienced low academic achievement. Tutors were taught techniques for supporting students in their grasp of procedural, declarative, and conditional knowledge.

Department of the Interior

The Department of Interior is composed of eight bureaus and more than twenty-five offices and committees. Education initiatives generated within the department range from the operation of support of local tribal school systems to support for minority higher education institutions to K–12 programs.

The Office of Educational Partnerships was established in 1994 to advance support of minority higher education institutions and the Goals 2000: Educate America Act and other related activities that support K–12 education.

The most extensive education initiative undertaken by Department of the Interior is through the Bureau of Indian Affairs (BIA). Present statutory law allows the BIA to either support local tribal school systems or to actually operate the education enterprise for the local tribal government.

The Department of the Interior also conducts management development programs to provide upgrade training to bureau personnel in a variety of occupational specialties who have limited field experience. Orientation programs are also conducted within the various bureaus and departments. Several of the bureaus provide training for foreign personnel in such diverse fields as irrigation project operation and topographic mapping.

Department of Justice

The Department of Justice represents the citizens of the United States in enforcing the federal laws that have been passed in the public interest. There are thirty-eight components within the department, and a number of those components have specialized education and training responsibilities. Such programs include employee training, programs for inmates of penal and correctional institutions, and training of law enforcement officers. Many of the training and technical assistance initiatives are designed to bring about changes in the law enforcement profession and to enhance the effectiveness of the criminal justice system.

One of the major training activities undertaken by the Department of Justice is the operation of the FBI National Academy through the Federal Bureau of Investigation. The FBI carries the charge of providing leadership and law enforcement assistance to federal, state, local, and international agencies. The academy provides initial training of all new special agents as well as refresher training for all agents. It also provides specialized, needs-based training for full-time law enforcement officials from local, county, and state levels. Officials from the District of Columbia and Puerto Rico are also provided opportunities for training.

Like the FBI, the Immigration and Naturalization Service operates training programs for its border patrol law enforcement personnel. These law officers are charged with maintaining the integrity of the borders of the United States from illegal immigration. The U.S. Federal Marshals Service conducts training of U.S. marshals and provides other training opportunities through regional meetings and conferences.

The Federal Bureau of Prisons is charged with the responsibility of developing and operating correctional programs that are balanced between punishment, deterrence, incapacitation, and rehabilitation. Inmate programs range from high school equivalency to college level courses to help provide for successful reintegration of inmates into society. Vocational training in semiskilled to skilled trades is coordinated by the Federal Prison Industries, Inc., a wholly owned government corporation founded in 1934. Additionally, the National Institute of Corrections is charged with the responsibility of providing training to state and local correctional agency personnel to advance a broad agenda of correctional practices.

The Community Relations Service is the single federal agency with the responsibility to help state and local government agencies, public and private organizations, and community groups resolve and prevent community racial conflicts. Technical assistance is provided to help communities address conflicts arising out of actions, policies, and practices perceived to be discriminatory.

The Office of Justice Programs, created in 1984, is responsible for providing training and technical assistance to state, local, and tribal governments and community groups. Assistance is designed to reduce crime, enforce drug laws, and improve the function of the criminal justice system.

The Office of Community Oriented Policing Services (COPS) is charged with creating change in the police profession. The Training and Technical Assistance Division operates through Regional Community Policing Institutes, the Community Policing Consortium, targeted training initiatives, and training conferences and workshops.

Department of Labor

In addition to the Office of the Secretary, the Department of Labor includes more than twenty additional agencies, one independent corporation, and related committees and commissions. A variety of education and training programs are made available to both federal employees and private sector workers and employers.

The Occupational Safety and Health Administration (OSHA) was created to advise and assist the Secretary of Labor on all matters related to the policies and programs that are designed to assure safe and healthful working conditions for the working men and women of the nation, and to provide executive direction to the occupational safety and health program. OSHA education and training services include federal agency personnel, programs and assistance for small businesses, and training of workers in nonprofit organizations. The primary scope of all such training is to train individuals to recognize, avoid, and prevent safety and health hazards. Programs in the nonprofit sector are conducted under Susan Harwood Training Grants. Grantees develop pertinent training and educational programs that address OSHA-selected topics. Federal agency training is conducted through a number of educational centers that include the Naval Safety Training Center, the Air Force Safety School, and NASA sites nationwide. The OSHA Outreach Training Program authorizes individuals completing the training to teach courses in general industry or construction safety and health standards. The primary arm within OSHA for coordinating education and training programs is the Office of Education and Training.

The Bureau of Labor Statistics provides a fellowship program in conjunction with the American Statistical Association (ASA), under a grant from the National Science Foundation (NSF). The Senior Research Fellow Program's objective is to bridge the gap between academic scholars and government social science research.

The Office of the Assistant Secretary for Administration and Management conducts the Senior Executive Service (SES) Forum Series. The Senior Executive Service provides convenient, cost-effective learning opportunities for top-level government officials. Forums cover a wide range of topics relevant to the major missions and programs of federal departments and agencies.

The Employment and Training Administration operates programs for both adults and youth. Adult programs include training programs for Native American populations. Programs are also provided for migrant and seasonal workers. Apprenticeship training for industry is designed to assist industry in developing and improving apprenticeship programs. Welfare-to-work services are also provided to assist the hard-to-employ and noncustodial parents to get and keep jobs. Training is provided for workers affected by shutdowns and downsizing and for workers over fifty-five years of age. Youth programs include school-to-work, Job Corps, and apprenticeship programs authorized under the Workforce Investment Act of 1998.

The Women's Bureau sponsors workshops and joint initiatives with other governmental agencies on gender discrimination. Other programs are marked by collaborative efforts that encourage girls to study and pursue careers in information technology, engineering, math, and science. Trade conferences are conducted to highlight the contributions of women in the trades.

The Mine Safety and Health Administration's (MHSA) Directorate of Educational Policy and Development implements MHSA's education and training programs that are designed to promote safety and health in the mining industry.

Department of State

The Department of State is the nation's lead foreign affairs agency. The Bureau of Educational and Cultural Affairs and the Foreign Service Institute carry out the Department of State's educational activities.

The Bureau of Educational and Cultural Affairs (ECA) offers an array of international educational and training programs aimed at promoting understanding between the United States and other countries. The bureau promotes personal, professional, and institutional ties among individuals and organizations, and presents overseas audiences with U.S. history, society, art, and culture.

The Fulbright Program, which is sponsored by ECA, was introduced in 1946 under legislation sponsored by Senator J. William Fulbright of Arkansas. The Fulbright Program offers cultural exchange opportunities to individuals from the United States and abroad who have demonstrated leadership potential. The Fulbright program operates in 141 countries and awards approximately 4,500 grants annually.

The Office of Global Education Programs is charged with the administration of three major Fulbright exchange activities. They include the Teacher Exchange Program, the Humphrey Fellowship Program, and various university linkage programs.

The Fulbright Teacher Exchange program arranges exchange opportunities for U.S. and foreign college faculty members, teacher trainers, secondary-level teachers, and school administrators. Many teachers elect to teach their native languages at host institutions. A limited number of semester and shorter-term initiatives are also available.

The Hubert H. Humphrey Fellowship Program is a Fulbright exchange activity. Established in 1978 to honor the late senator and vice president, the program brings accomplished midlevel professionals from foreign countries for one year of study and professional experience.

The university linkage programs enables U.S. colleges and universities to partner with institutions overseas to pursue specific mutually beneficial goals. Projects typically last three years and consist of exchange of teachers, administrators, and graduate students.

The Educational Information and Resources Branch of the ECA offers U.S. educational opportunities to foreign students and scholars and serves as a resource to U.S. institutions wanting to strengthen international educational exchange. Overseas, the branch provides international students and scholars information on the U.S. educational system through a worldwide network of approximately 450 educational advising centers. Domestically, the branch administers a study abroad scholarship program for U.S. students and connects educational advisers overseas with counterparts at U.S. educational institutions.

ECA also administers a variety of degree and nondegree academic exchange programs for Russia and the new independent states, which include the following:

- Freedom Support Act Undergraduate Program
- Bosnia and Herzegovina Undergraduate Development Program
- Edmund S. Muskie Graduate Fellowship Program
- Ron Brown Fellowship Program
- Community Connection Program
- Russia–U.S. Young Leadership Fellows for Public Services Program
- Regional Scholar Exchange Program
- Freedom Support Act in Contemporary Issues
- Junior Faculty Development Program
- Internet Access and Training Program

The Office of English Language Programs is responsible for U.S. government English teaching activities outside the United States. The office offers a number of products and services primarily in the capital cities of host countries through American embassies.

The Study of the U.S. Branch of ECA promotes better understanding of the United States by offering summer institutes to foreign university faculty. One of the projects of primary importance offered by this branch is the maintenance and dissemination of the American Studies Collection. The collection was established by a congressional endowment to promote a better understanding of the United States abroad. This collection is designed expressly for university libraries outside the United States. The core of the collection consists of 1,000 titles selected by leading American scholars on a wide variety of disciplines germane to the study of American culture.

The ECA International Visitor Program operates under the authority of the Mutual Educational and Cultural Exchange Act of 1961. This program brings foreign professionals with potential for leadership in the areas of government, politics, media, education, and other fields to meet and confer with their professional counterparts and to experience the United States.

The ECA Office of Citizen Exchanges makes grants available to nonprofit American organizations to develop professional, cultural, and youth programs. The objective is for foreign participants to see how Americans deal with issues of professional interest and for American participants to receive a similarly cross-cultural perspective. The office has three geographic divisions, which include Europe/Asia, the Middle East, and South Asia/Africa.

The ECA International Cultural Property Protection program was established as a result of the 1970 United Nations Educational, Scientific and Cultural Organization (UNESCO) Convention on the Means of Prohibiting and Preventing the Illicit Import, Export, and Transfer of Ownership of Cultural Property. In accordance with the convention's precepts, the requests of foreign countries are accepted for import restrictions on archaeological or ethnological artifacts, whose removal or display might jeopardize the national cultural history of those countries.

The ECA Au Pair Program is a one-year educational and cultural exchange program with a strong emphasis on childcare. Au pairs are put through a screening and selection process and then matched with American families. The au pair provides forty-five hours of childcare per week. Au pairs are also required to attend an institution of higher learning during their stay to earn at least six hours of credit. Host families are required to pay the au pair minimum wage for child care and $500 for education-related costs.

The Foreign Service Institute is responsible for training all officers and support personnel of the U.S. foreign affairs community. The National Foreign Affairs Training Center in Arlington, Virginia, offers approximately 500 courses, including classes in 60 foreign languages to members of the foreign affairs community from the Department of State, the military service branches, and other government agencies. Course range in length from one day to two years and designed to promote success within professional assignments, ease transitions, enhance leadership and management, and prepare families for a mobile lifestyle and living abroad. Training and professional development are also available specific to professional assignment.

Department of Transportation

The Department of Transportation (DOT) was created in 1967 when a number of transportation-related agencies, services, and functions that were dispersed throughout the government were combined into one department. In the early twenty-first century the department works to further the vital national transportation interests through promotion of the following broad strategic goals: safety, mobility, economic growth and trade, human and natural environment protection, and national security. The components of the department include the Office of the Secretary, the Transportation Administrative Service Center, the Surface Transportation Board, and eleven major operating divisions.

The U.S. Coast Guard (USCG) is responsible for ensuring safe transportation on American waterways and protection of the marine environment. During times of war and conflict the USCG comes under the control of the Department of Defense. Traditional education-related functions of this division have included marine safety, boating safety, oil spill response, and emergency training.

The most prominent educational component of the division is the U.S. Coast Guard Academy, which is located in New London, Connecticut. The Coast Guard Academy is unique among federal service academies because admission is based on a competitive nationwide application process rather than congressional nomination. Applicants who are accepted to the program are given full four-year scholarships. Founded in 1876, the academy provides cadets a four-year bachelor of science program in eight majors including naval architecture and marine engineering, civil engineering, mechanical engineering, electrical engineering, operations research, marine and environment science, government, and management. Cadets who demonstrate a high level of academic performance can qualify to participate in the academy's honors program or take elective course work at nearby Connecticut College. A range of student government and athletic opportunities are also made available to cadets. Summers are spent in military and professional training, except for three weeks of vacation. Each academy graduate receives a commission as an ensign in the U.S. Coast Guard and is required to serve a minimum of five years of active duty.

Leadership training for both cadets and civilian employees of the USCG is provided through the Leadership Development Center (LDC). Schools which form the LDC include the Chief Petty Officer Academy, the Leadership and Quality Institute, the Chief Warrant Officer Indoctrination, Officer Candidate School, Officer-in-Charge School, Command and Operations School, and the Unit Leadership Training Program.

The Federal Aviation Administration (FAA) was established in 1958 by the Federal Aviation Act, which combined the Civil Aeronautics Administration and the Airways Modernization Board. Although the FAA predates the DOT, it became one of the major operating divisions when the DOT was established in 1967. The FAA is responsible for administering the federal aviation system, which includes activities such as certifying pilots and aircraft, promoting all aspects of aviation safety, enhancing airport security, maintaining the federal air traffic control system, and assisting in the development of commercial and space transportation.

The FAA Aviation Education Program is maintained in fulfillment of the Congressional Mandates of the Airport and Airway Development Act of 1970. The congressional intent of the Aviation Education Program is to maintain America's preeminence in the world of aviation by supporting the growth of aviation through education. This includes increasing the public's knowledge of the dynamics of aviation and its key role in improving America's economic and social well being. The FAA is also congressionally mandated to acquaint young people with the full potential of a career in aviation. An information distribution program in each of the nine FAA regions provides expertise and informational materials on civil aviation, aeronautics, and air commerce safety to state and local administrators, college and university officials, and officers of civil and other interested organizations.

The FAA also hosts a number of educational outreach resources and initiatives including curriculum, activities, summer camps, scholarships, grants, aviation career guides, an online resource library, and a listing of aviation schools and universities.

The Federal Highway Administration (FHWA) is responsible for coordinating highway transportation programs among states and other partners. The FWHA organization comprises the Washington Headquarters, four resource centers, fifty-two operating federal aid division offices, and three federal lands highway divisions.

The education-related activities include offering training and technical expertise to transportation agency managers at the state and local level, partner agency employees, and to FHWA staff. Training topics cover a range of highway transportation concerns such as snow and ice technology, seismic bridge design, and civil rights contract compliance. Technical expertise is offered in the following areas: roadway and bridge design, construction methods, highway planning and policy, safety, maintenance, environmental protection, innovative financing, and land acquisition.

Nationwide public service announcements are produced in print, audio, and video to educate and inform the public concerning FHWA safety initiatives. Seed money is provided through grants to state and local transportation agencies to promote FHWA safety programs.

FHWA also supports highway-related research, development, and technology transfer through promotion of initiatives such as the Intelligent Transportation Systems. The Intelligent Transportation Systems program partners FHWA with government, industry, and research community partners to develop, test, and implement the latest technological advancements in the transportation system. These technology-infused transportation applications seek to move people and goods more smoothly, safely, and efficiently.

The Federal Railroad Administration (FRA) promotes safe and environmentally sound rail transportation. Much of the educational activity of the FRA revolves around its longstanding responsibility of ensuring railroad safety throughout the nation. The FRA Office of Safety provides the public with safety data on rail incidents, accidents, and inspections. The FRA conducts research, development, tests, evaluations, and projects to support its safety mission and enhance the railroad system as a national transportation resource. The FRA also makes railroading curriculum, presentation aids, and safety resources available to teachers online. Students are offered links rail transportation-related career development links as well as links to an online railroad library.

The National Highway Traffic Safety Administration (NHTSA) is responsible for promoting and implementing effective educational, engineering, and enforcement programs to end preventable tragedies and reduce economic costs associated with vehicle use and highway travel. NHTSA provides the public with information on motor vehicle safety recalls, child safety seat recalls, seat belts, air bags, antilock breaks, highway safety statistics, federal motor vehicle safety standards, vehicle crash test reports, vehicle safety ratings, vehicle theft ratings, and traffic safety educational materials.

The Federal Transit Administration (FTA) is responsible for providing financial and technical assistance to local transit systems and their forms of mass transportation including buses, rail vehicles, commuter ferryboats, trolleys, inclined railways, and subways.

The National Transit Library is the FTA repository of reports, documents and data generated by professionals and laypersons. The intent of the library is to facilitate document sharing within the transit community.

The FTA Office of Safety and Security offers a range of programs to achieve the highest practical level of safety and security among all modes of mass transit. This office assists in the development of guidelines and best practices, and performs system safety analysis and review. Training is provided through regularly offered courses, conferences, and seminars.

Transit City, U.S.A., is a mythical American city accessible through the FTA homepage, which serves as an online resource for students of all ages, to assist in the development and enhancement of knowledge, skills, and abilities through use of the transit medium.

The University Transportation Center Program, enacted in 1998 under the Transportation Equity Act for the 21st Century, established thirty-three university transportation centers. Of the thirty-three centers, ten were designated as regional centers. The intent of the program is to offer a multidisciplinary program of course work to advance transportation technology and expertise through the mechanisms of education, research, and technology.

The St. Lawrence Seaway Development Corporation (SLSDC) is a corporation wholly owned by the federal government and created by statute in 1954 to construct, operate, and maintain that part of the St. Lawrence Seaway between Montreal and Lake Erie, within the limits of the United States. Education-related services of the SLSDC include publication of transit regulations for vessels, trade reports, traffic reports, special information newsletters, seminars, workshops, and marketing advice for entities importing to or exporting from the Great Lakes region.

The Maritime Administration (MARAD) promotes the development and maintenance of an adequate, well-balanced, U.S. merchant marine, sufficient to carry the nation's domestic waterborne commerce and a substantial portion of its waterborne foreign commerce, and capable of serving as a naval and military auxiliary in time of war or national emergency.

MARAD administers the U.S. Merchant Marine Academy (USMMA), which is located in Kings Point, New York. The purpose of the academy is to educate young men and women to become officers in the American merchant marine. Cadets are offered a range of professional degree and credential options including: a bachelor of science degree, a U.S. Coast Guard (USCG) license as deck or engineering officers, a commission in the U.S. Naval Reserve, or another uniformed service. USMMA graduates must meet service obligations upon graduation.

MARAD provides financial assistance to six state maritime academies to train merchant marine officers pursuant to the Maritime Education and Training Act of 1980. State maritime academy cadets who participate in the Student Incentive Payment (SIP) Program receive an annual stipend to offset school costs. State Maritime Academy students are obligated to meet service requirements upon successful completion of their program.

MARAD provides supplemental training for seafarers in basic marine firefighting, advanced marine firefighting, defense readiness, hostage threat prevention, piracy, and Chemical Biological and Radiological Defense (CBRD).

The Adopt-a-Ship plan is sponsored through the Propeller Club of the United States. The plan provides the opportunity for a school classroom (fifth through eight grade) to adopt a ship of the American Merchant Marine and exchange correspondence with it. MARAD also compiles and makes available through both print and electronic sources a comprehensive repository of maritime publications and statistics.

The Research and Special Programs Administration (RSPA) is unique among the major operating divisions of the DOT because of its multimodal mandate. It was established in 1977 to administer those programs that did not fit within the mandates of the other operating divisions. The educational activities of the RSPA include advancing intermodal transportation and technology, conducting transportation research, and delivering training and technical assistance in transportation safety.

The RSPA's Volpe National Transportation Systems Center in Cambridge, Massachusetts, works on a broad range of transportation projects to enhance the nation's transportation capabilities and meet future requirements. The center serves as a federal bridge between industry, academia, and other government agencies. The Volpe Center receives no appropriation from Congress. It is completely funded through a fee-for-service structure.

The Transportation Safety Institute of the RSPA is located in Oklahoma City, Oklahoma. The institute provides training in aviation safety, hazardous materials, pipeline safety, transit safety and security, highway traffic safety, Coast Guard container inspection, automotive sampling, and other specialized programs.

The Bureau of Transportation Statistics (BTS) is the lead division of the DOT charged with developing and coordinating intermodal transportation statistics. The Bureau of Transportation Statistics compiles and makes available highly detailed national-level data on the all aspects of the U.S. transportation system including economic performance, safety records, energy use, and environmental impacts.

The Federal Motor Carrier Safety Administration (FMCSA) was established as a working division of the DOT on January 1, 2000, pursuant to the Motor Carrier Safety Improvement Act of 1999. Formerly a component of the FHA, the new division's primary mission is to prevent commercial motor vehicle-related fatalities and injuries. The Motor Carrier Research and Development (MCR&D) program is organized into eight focus areas designed to support the commercial carrier industry: crash causation and profiling, regulatory evaluation and reform, compliance and enforcement, hazardous material and cargo tank integrity, commercial driver training and performance management, driver alertness and fatigue, driver physical qualifications, and car-truck proximity. The FMCSA also maintains publications on commercial carrier safety regulations, rules, compliance issues, and notices.

Department of Treasury

The Department of Treasury is organized into two major components. Departmental offices are primarily responsible for the formulation of policy and overall management of the department. Operating bureaus carry out the specific operations assigned to the department. Including the Office of the Secretary, there are thirty offices and bureaus within the treasury department.

Education and training activities are provided by the Federal Law Enforcement Center. Established in 1970, FLETC instructs agents and officers from various governmental law enforcement agencies. Within the treasury department itself, the center trains agents for the U.S. Secret Service, the U.S. Custom Service, and the Bureau of Alcohol, Tobacco, and Firearms. Nondepartmental agencies whose personnel receive training include the Immigration and Naturalization Service and the U. S. Park Police.

One other departmental component has a training responsibility for non–law enforcement personnel. The Office of the Assistant Secretary (Management) Chief Financial Officer is charged with the responsibility of conducting training necessary to meet the demands of the department's overall mission.

Department of Veterans Affairs

The Department of Veterans Affairs oversees two areas of program services that provide education and training benefits to veterans. The benefits program for which VA is best known comes under the umbrella of its Education Service. The Education Service administers the Montgomery G.I. Bill for active duty personnel. The MGIB program provides up to thirty-six months of education benefits for degree and certification programs, flight training, apprenticeship and on-the-job training, and correspondence courses. Remedial, deficiency, and refresher courses may be approved under limited circumstances. General MGIB benefits are payable for up to ten years following release from active duty.

Tuition assistance is provided by an amendment to the Montgomery G.I. Bill–Active Duty education program. This amendment permits VA to pay a tuition assistance top-up benefit that is equal to the difference between the total cost of a college course and the amount of the tuition assistance that is paid by the military for the course.

In addition to the MGIB–Active Duty program, there is a program under the Montgomery G.I. Bill for selected reserve personnel, including the Army Reserve, Navy Reserve, Air Force Reserve, Marine Corps Reserve, and Coast Guard Reserve. It also includes the Army National Guard and the Air National Guard. MGIB–Selected Reserve benefits are similar to active duty benefits.

The Vocational Educational Assistance Program may be used by those veterans who contributed a portion of their military pay to participate in the program. Benefits are similar to those for MGIB–active duty personnel.

Survivors' and Dependents' Educational Assistance provides education and training opportunities to eligible dependents of veterans, if the veteran is permanently or totally disabled due to a service-related condition, or to the surviving dependents of veterans who died on active duty as a result of a service-related condition. Benefits are similar to MGIB–active duty personnel.

Education benefits are also provided under the Educational Assistance Test Program. This program was created by the Defense Authorization Act of 1981 to encourage enlistment and reenlistment in the armed forces.

The Work-Study Program is available to any student receiving VA education benefits who is attending school three-quarter time or more. Work-study students are employed in VA offices and facilities or at approved state employment agencies. Students are paid either the state or federal minimum wage, whichever is greater. The Department of Veterans Affairs also provides tutorial assistance for students receiving VA benefits who are enrolled at least half-time and have a deficiency in a subject, making tutorial necessary.

The Office of Vocational Rehabilitation and Employment, for those veterans who have service-connected disabilities, provides a number of vocational counseling and planning services, coupled with on-the-job training and nonpaid work experience. If needed, the disabled veteran may also quality for education training leading to a certificate or to a two-year or four-year degree.

See also: FEDERAL FUNDS FOR HIGHER EDUCATION; FEDERAL SCHOOLS AND COLLEGES; GOVERNMENT AND EDUCATION, THE CHANGING ROLE OF; LIFELONG LEARNING; MILITARY TRAINING DOCTRINE, PHILOSOPHY AND PRACTICE; U.S. DEPARTMENT OF EDUCATION.

INTERNET RESOURCES

NATIONAL TECHNICAL INFORMATION SERVICE. 2002. "FedWorld." <www.fedworld.gov>.

U.S. DEPARTMENT OF AGRICULTURE. 2002. <www.usda.gov>.

U.S. DEPARTMENT OF COMMERCE. 2002. <www.osec.doc.gov>.

U.S. DEPARTMENT OF DEFENSE. 2002. <www.defenselink.mil>.

U.S. DEPARTMENT OF EDUCATION. 2002. <www.ed.gov>.

U.S. DEPARTMENT OF ENERGY. 2002. <www.energy.gov>.

U.S. DEPARTMENT OF HEALTH AND HUMAN SERVICES. 2002. <www.hhs.gov>.

U.S. DEPARTMENT OF HOUSING AND URBAN DEVELOPMENT. 2002. <www.hud.gov>.

U.S. DEPARTMENT OF INTERIOR. 2002. <www.doi.gov>.

U.S. DEPARTMENT OF JUSTICE. 2002. <www.usdoj.gov>.

U.S. DEPARTMENT OF LABOR. 2002. <www.dol.gov>.

U.S. DEPARTMENT OF STATE. 2002. "Outline of U.S. Government." <www.usinfo.state.gov/products/pubs/outusgov/ch3.htm>.

U.S. DEPARTMENT OF STATE. 2002. <www.state.gov>.

U.S. DEPARTMENT OF TRANSPORTATION. 2002. <www.dot.gov>.

U.S. DEPARTMENT OF TREASURY. 2002. <www.treasury.gov>.

U.S. DEPARTMENT OF VETERANS AFFAIRS. 2002. <www.va.gov>.

JASON L. WALTON

FEDERAL FUNDING FOR ACADEMIC RESEARCH

The federal government's role in supporting research and development (R&D) in the United States has grown from a very minor one for much of the nation's history to one that was dominant during much of the twentieth century, and finally to one that at the beginning of the twenty-first century is still significant and essential but has been eclipsed in scale by industry-supported R&D. Federal support for R&D in colleges and universities paralleled this pattern in the first half of the twentieth century but has remained the primary source of R&D funding for these institutions.

Why does the federal government support R&D at all, especially if the private sector invests so much in it? First, the federal government supports R&D that clearly serves important national needs, for example, in areas such as national defense, health, energy, the environment, natural resources, and agriculture. Second, the federal government supports most of the nation's basic or fundamental research—research that is not directed toward any practical problem but is focused on gaining knowledge or understanding phenomena irrespective of any specific application. History is full of examples of such apparently abstract, undirected research providing the basis for applications that prove to be extremely important—for example, disease-fighting medicines, weapons for national defense, and the growth of information technology. According to Albert H. Teich, basic research is "the primary source of the new knowledge that ultimately drives the innovation process" (p. 6). Historically, however, such fundamental research has not been supported on a significant scale by the private sector. Private firms anticipate that they will not be able to appropriate sufficient benefits from basic research to make sizable investments in it cost-effective. Nevertheless, such research is acknowledged by all to be vital to long-term national interests, and so its support is undertaken by the federal government.

Industry and federal research laboratories rank ahead of colleges and universities in terms of federal R&D funding received (see Figure 1). Yet despite their relatively small share of federal R&D support, colleges and universities historically have played an essential role in the nation's overall R&D efforts, for several reasons. First, much of the nation's greatest scientific and technical talent is in these institutions. Second, colleges and universities are particularly well-suited for performing basic research, although they perform a great deal of applied research as well. In 2000 basic research accounted for 69 percent of all college and university R&D. Third, federally funded research at colleges and universities (whether basic or applied) plays a crucial role in educating the next generation of scientists and engineers. It is an investment in the nation's most highly skilled work-

FIGURE 1

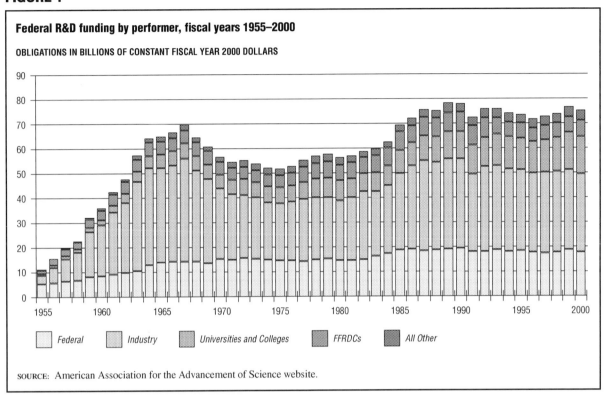

Federal R&D funding by performer, fiscal years 1955–2000

OBLIGATIONS IN BILLIONS OF CONSTANT FISCAL YEAR 2000 DOLLARS

Legend: Federal | Industry | Universities and Colleges | FFRDCs | All Other

SOURCE: American Association for the Advancement of Science website.

force, which in turn will be the backbone of an innovative, growing national economy.

A Brief History of Federal Involvement in University-Based Research

The development of federal involvement in university-based R&D is intertwined with the broader issue of federal involvement in science and technology (S&T) in the United States. Federal involvement in scientific or technical matters was explicitly provided for in the U.S. Constitution only in the provisions for a system of patents and for a census to be held every ten years. For decades in the early history of the country, the doctrine of states' rights (preventing a concentration of authority in the federal government) together with a strain of populist antielitism and a faith in the indigenous development of pragmatic technologies kept the nation from realizing either Thomas Jefferson's vision of strong federal support for science, largely through agriculture, or Alexander Hamilton's advocacy of government subsidies for the advancement of technologies to the benefit of industry. From time to time, the U.S. Congress would deviate from this stance and invest in limited operations in support of exploratory or commercial interests, such as the Lewis and Clark expedition or the establishment of the Coast Survey, both in the early 1800s.

In the 1840s, two events—the establishment of the Smithsonian Institution under federal auspices and the creation of the American Association for the Advancement of Science—highlighted the growing visibility of S&T and foreshadowed the later development of a more significant federal involvement in science and technology. These events, together with what William G. Wells Jr. called a "tide of technological developments . . . in industry, in agriculture, in communications, and in transportation" (p. 8) in the 1850s, set the stage for a qualitative change in the federal role in these areas; this change came in the 1860s as a result of several events. First, the Civil War provided the first of several recurring examples of war focusing the government's attention and resources not just on technology but on the science underlying the technology. Second, the creation of the National Academy of Sciences in 1862 put the elite of American scientists, most of them in universities, at the service of governmental needs. Third, the passage of the Morrill Act and the creation of the U.S. Department of Agriculture, both of which occurred in 1862, established the land-grant college system, heavily focused on agriculture and the mechanical arts, and developed government bureaus related to agricultural research, in a symbiotic relationship that, by the end of the nineteenth century, approached the Jeffersonian vision of a century earlier.

Meanwhile, in the late nineteenth and early twentieth centuries, the forerunner of the National Institutes of Health was established and undertook programs of research aimed at public-health problems, although much of this work took place in government rather than in university laboratories. Additional initiatives putting governmental resources in the service of S&T-based activities in the areas of conservation, industry, and (to a limited extent) aviation took place in the first two decades of the twentieth century. These did not yet involve significant amounts of university-based R&D, but their importance was that, with the curious exception of military applications, the essential infrastructure of federal government involvement in S&T was firmly in place by the 1920s, and, according to A. Hunter Dupree, "a government without science was already unthinkable" (p. 288). Belief in the importance of research had become infused throughout much of the U.S. economy, and industrially based R&D was becoming established in certain industries.

Science, like nearly all other programs, was significantly affected by government cutbacks during the Great Depression. But it was World War II (1939–1945) that was to provide the major turning point in the relationship between the federal government and S&T in the twentieth century. With the establishment by executive order of the National Defense Research Committee in June 1940 and its expansion into the Office of Scientific Research and Development (OSRD) in July 1941—both prior to the attack on Pearl Harbor and the formal entry of the United States into the war—the groundwork was laid for a historically incomparable system for mobilizing science for a war effort. The OSRD, headed by Vannevar Bush, was responsible for developing "a wide range of militarily decisive marvels" (Wells, p. 23), such as radar, medical drugs, and, of course, atomic weapons. This performance demonstrated beyond any doubt the power and effectiveness of federal support for R&D on a large scale, a lesson that carried over into the postwar era and that continued into the twenty-first century. Much of this research took place in university settings, and the massive expansion of federal R&D in the period fol-

lowing World War II included large increases in the amount of federal funds flowing to academically based R&D (see Figure 1).

Vannevar Bush's report, *Science—the Endless Frontier: A Report to the President on a Program for Postwar Scientific Research,* produced at the close of World War II, set the framework for the "social contract" between science and government that would last for decades, whereby government would provide funds for science but, wherever feasible, leave to scientists the decisions about what projects would be supported and how the research would be conducted. This, it was argued, was the surest path not only to breakthroughs in basic science but also indirectly to the development of products for more direct societal benefit. Bush, in writing it, had clearly in mind the idea that much of that research would be conducted in colleges and universities. In the period immediately following the war, a number of major new S&T agencies were created in the federal government, including the National Science Foundation (NSF), the Atomic Energy Commission, and the Office of Naval Research (ONR); in addition, the National Institutes of Health (NIH) was reformulated and significantly expanded. These agencies—particularly ONR, NIH, and NSF—were soon to become mainstays of federal support for academically based R&D.

Much of the rapid growth in federal R&D in the decades following World War II was driven by cold war concerns and was militarily oriented. The launch of the *Sputnik* satellite by the Soviet Union in 1957 shook U.S. assumptions of technical superiority and fueled an even greater increase in defense- and space-related R&D. In the 1950s and 1960s the federal government was clearly the dominant source for national R&D, although by the early 1970s industrial R&D had caught up and was to move clearly ahead in total investments in R&D over the next three decades (see Figure 2).

Figure 3 illustrates the remarkable growth of R&D support received by colleges and universities over the latter half of the twentieth century. (The figures have been adjusted for inflation, using fiscal year 2002 as the standard, and so represent actual growth in "purchasing power" of those R&D dollars.) The figure dramatically shows not only the overall growth in academic R&D support from all sources but also that this growth was fueled primarily by the growth in federal support. The federal government has been the primary source of support for

FIGURE 2

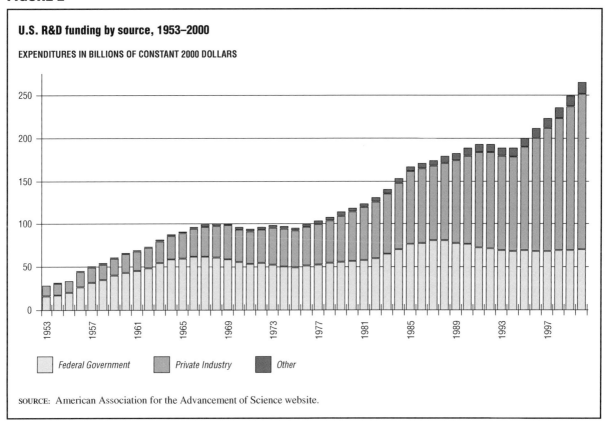

U.S. R&D funding by source, 1953–2000

EXPENDITURES IN BILLIONS OF CONSTANT 2000 DOLLARS

Federal Government Private Industry Other

SOURCE: American Association for the Advancement of Science website.

R&D in colleges and universities since the post–World War II days, and it continues to be so.

The 1980s saw an important step in federal government–university relations, with the passage (in 1980) and subsequent amendment (in 1984) of the Bayh-Dole Act. This act revised federal patent policy to give recipients of federal funds who invented or developed a product or process with that funding the opportunity to hold title to the item and to realize gains from transferring it into commercial channels. Previously, the federal government had reserved for itself the title to products developed with federal funds, but that policy was seen as bottling up potentially useful and commercializable inventions. Opinions differ about the act's full impact, but it clearly facilitated the growth of activities within universities for retaining intellectual property in items developed under university-based research and for trying to realize income from outside commercial use of those items.

The last two decades of the twentieth century saw the clear movement of research universities into a prominent place in the "knowledge-based econo-

my." Research support from all sources, not simply federal agencies, became much more aggressively sought, and university R&D portfolios were much more carefully managed with revenue and even commercial goals in mind. It became common knowledge that one of the key elements to commercial development of a region through technology-driven change was the presence of an active, high-quality research university. Consequently, more than ever before, a university's neighbors feel that they have an important stake in that institution's success in securing research funds. Furthermore, according to Teich, "policymakers regard universities as catalysts for high-tech economic development both through entrepreneurial activity that spins off from their research and through the concentrations of highly trained human resources they attract and generate" (p. 5).

Table 1 helps to place federal funding for academic R&D in an overall national context at the beginning of the twenty-first century. Federal R&D funding accounted for $69.6 billion (roughly 26%) of the national total of $264.6 billion for R&D in 2000. Colleges and universities received $30.2 billion

FIGURE 3

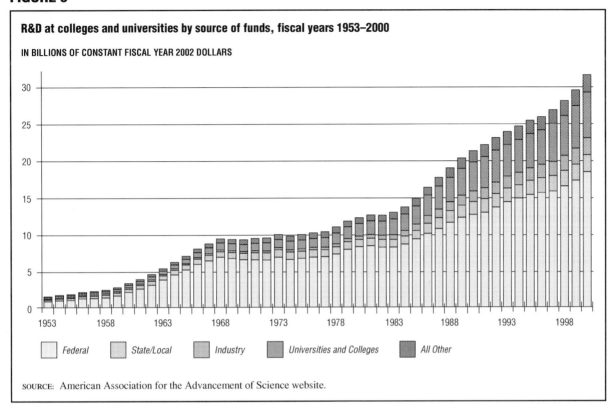

R&D at colleges and universities by source of funds, fiscal years 1953–2000

IN BILLIONS OF CONSTANT FISCAL YEAR 2002 DOLLARS

Legend: Federal   State/Local   Industry   Universities and Colleges   All Other

SOURCE: American Association for the Advancement of Science website.

from all sources in 2000, which accounted for just over 11 percent of the national totals. The intersection of these two patterns—the federal level of support for R&D in colleges and universities—was $17.5 billion, a figure that represented 58 percent of all academic R&D support. (It also represented just over 25 percent of total federal R&D support to all R&D performers.) The next section provides further detail about particular agencies and their levels of academic R&D support.

Key Federal Agencies

Federal support for R&D in colleges and universities in the United States is concentrated in six agencies, which together accounted for 95 percent of the totals in 1999. These six are summarized briefly below, in decreasing order of support. The first three agencies listed—NIH, NSF, and the Department of Defense—alone accounted for 83 percent of college and university R&D from federal sources in 1999. (See Figure 4 for historical trends in support from these agencies.)

The National Institutes of Health, within the Department of Health and Human Services, is by far the largest source of federal support for academic

R&D, providing $8.2 billion to colleges and universities in 1999—58 percent of federal support to these institutions. The NIH's mission is to advance knowledge promoting improvements in human health, and it does this by supporting biomedical and other fundamental research related to health and disease. The major fields supported by NIH are overwhelmingly in the life sciences (89% of its academic support in 1997), principally microbiology and medical sciences. Other fields that receive NIH support are psychology (4%), the physical sciences (1.5%), and the social sciences (1%). NIH's domination of academic R&D support has shifted the balance among the disciplines in universities' R&D portfolios, with engineering and the physical sciences accounting for smaller shares than in previous years.

The National Science Foundation ranks second in R&D support to colleges and universities, furnishing $2.2 billion in 1999, or 15 percent of federal totals. NSF is unique among federal agencies, being the only one whose mission is fundamental research and education in all major scientific and engineering fields. Thus, NSF's support is more evenly balanced among the disciplines than most of the mission agencies. The distribution in 1997 was: physical sci-

TABLE 1

National Patterns of R&D, 2000

	Sources of Funds				
	Federal Government	Industry	Colleges and Universities[2]	Non-Profit Institutions	Total
Preliminary expenditures, in thousands, 2000					
Performers:					
Federal	19,143	–	–	–	19,143
Industry	19,635	177,645	–	–	197,280
Colleges and Universities	17,475	2,310	8,166	2,203	30,154
FFRDCs[1]	9,294	–	–	–	9,294
Nonprofits	4,079	1,085	–	3,586	8,750
TOTAL	69,627	181,040	8,166	5,789	264,622
Percent change in constant dollars (1999 to 2000)					
Performers:					
Federal	2.3%	–	–	–	2.3%
Industry	-4.6%	8.6%	–	–	7.1%
Colleges and Universities	3.7%	6.1%	4.7%	4.5%	4.2%
FFRDCs[1]	1.4%	–	–	–	1.4%
Nonprofits	7.5%	8.9%	–	5.8%	7.0%
TOTAL	0.8%	8.6%	4.7%	5.3%	6.2%

[1] Federally funded research and development centers. Includes all FFRDCs (administered by industry, nonprofits, and universities).
[2] Includes an estimated $2.2 billion in state and local government funds provided to university and college performers.

SOURCE: American Association for the Advancement of Science website.

ences, 22 percent of NSF academic support; engineering, 21 percent; environmental sciences, 17 percent; life sciences, 16 percent; computer sciences and mathematics, 15 percent; and the social and behavioral sciences, 4 percent.

The Department of Defense (DoD) is the third-largest federal agency in terms of support for academic R&D, providing $1.4 billion in 1999, or 10 percent of federal totals to colleges and universities. DoD is the mission agency par excellence, being responsible for providing the military forces needed to deter or win wars and to protect the security of the country. DoD is by far the largest supporter of R&D among the federal agencies. Most of its R&D, however, is devoted to the development, testing, and evaluation of weapons systems, and only about 12 percent of its R&D has gone for actual research (both basic and applied) in recent years. The major fields supported by DoD academic R&D funds are engineering (40% of DoD academic support in 1997), computer sciences (23%), physical sciences (11%), and life sciences and environmental sciences (at about 10% each).

After the above three, the levels of support by other agencies drop off noticeably. The National Aeronautics and Space Administration (NASA) provided $719 million in support to colleges and uni-

versities in 1999, which was about 5 percent of federal totals to these institutions. NASA's mission is to undertake aeronautic and space research and activities for the benefit of all humankind. The major fields receiving NASA academic R&D support were physical sciences (37%—principally astronomy), environmental sciences (29%—mostly atmospheric science), engineering (15%), and life sciences (9%).

The Department of Energy contributed $598 million toward R&D in colleges and universities in 1999, about 4 percent of federal support for them. The Energy Department's mission is much broader than simply energy, and even its R&D programs have several components, including energy research, support for fundamental physical science research, and research involving nuclear security in support of the nation's defense function. The physical sciences (dominated by physics) received 59 percent of Department of Energy support to academic institutions, followed by life sciences, engineering, and environmental sciences, each with about 13 percent.

The U.S. Department of Agriculture (USDA) supported R&D in colleges and universities with $400 million in 1999, nearly 3 percent of federal totals to such institutions. The USDA's mission is also broad but centers on its responsibility for the ade-

FIGURE 4

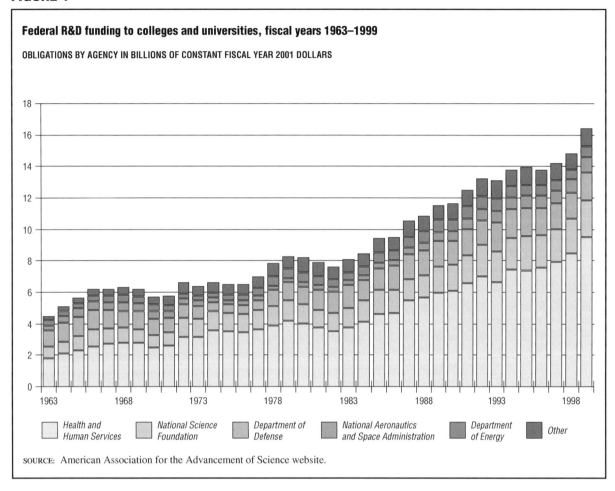

Federal R&D funding to colleges and universities, fiscal years 1963–1999

OBLIGATIONS BY AGENCY IN BILLIONS OF CONSTANT FISCAL YEAR 2001 DOLLARS

☐ Health and Human Services   ☐ National Science Foundation   ☐ Department of Defense   ☐ National Aeronautics and Space Administration   ☐ Department of Energy   ☐ Other

SOURCE: American Association for the Advancement of Science website.

quacy and safety of the nation's food supply and for developing and expanding markets, both domestically and abroad, for agricultural products. Its academic R&D support, not surprisingly, went overwhelmingly (77%) to the life sciences, comprised largely of agricultural sciences (39%), nonenvironmental biology (21%), and environmental biology (15%). The next highest supported fields were the social sciences (12%), primarily economics.

All other federal agencies combined accounted for $739 million of support to academic institutions in 1999, or about 5 percent of the federal totals. This is not to diminish their importance, however. The Departments of Commerce, Transportation, Interior, and Education and such agencies as the Environmental Protection Agency support appreciable amounts of research in colleges and universities, and they rely upon those institutions to provide important research and expertise relevant to their respective missions.

Advantages and Disadvantages of Federal Research Support

Not surprisingly, research support from federal sources has both advantages and disadvantages. The chief advantage is the sheer scale of support—for most fields, there is simply more money potentially available from federal agencies than from any other source. The decentralized nature of federal R&D support sometimes makes it possible for principal investigators (those submitting proposals) to have more than one potential sponsor to which to submit their ideas. Another advantage is that the researcher usually has greater autonomy with federal support in comparison with support from industry. For most grants (as opposed to private contracts), federal agencies have a relatively hands-off stance regarding the researchers and their work.

Because both the scale of support and the relative autonomy afforded researchers attract large numbers of proposals from researchers, most agencies are quite selective in what they support and pride themselves on supporting only the highest quality work. To ensure this level of excellence, many agencies rely upon "peer review" or "merit review" (review of proposals by those most knowledgeable in the relevant areas of research). In addition, the managers of particular research programs within the agencies are often highly accomplished and knowledgeable researchers in their own right. Thus, there is a certain prestige attached to researchers whose work is supported by certain federal agencies, particularly NSF and NIH. This prestige can carry over not only to the researchers' own careers generally but also to their home institutions.

On the other hand, federal support has disadvantages as well. The forces that make winning support from the "better" agencies more prestigious—because of the sheer number of applicants relative to the available resources—also make it less likely. Success rates for proposals to NSF and NIH since 1990 and perhaps earlier have been in the 20 and 30 percent range. Eventual success often comes only through resubmitting proposals after revising them based on feedback from the first round of reviews. The high number of applicants also means that grants, even if obtained, may be inadequately funded to complete the proposed research.

In addition to these daunting considerations, the paperwork requirements for submitting proposals to federal agencies are formidable. Researchers spend inordinate amounts of time and effort writing proposals, often with unfavorable chances of success. (As some agencies have shifted to electronic submission of proposals, "paperwork" may no longer be the operative word, but the burden of documentation in proposals remains very high.) Apart from the paperwork burden, the task of dealing, over the several months required for decisions on proposals, with inherently cautious, often ponderous federal bureaucracies can be draining for researchers. Finally there is often a lack of stability in funding levels for some areas of research, resulting from the vagaries of the annual budget process and from changes in policymakers' enthusiasm for particular areas.

The cumulative effect of these difficulties can extend to the point of discouraging some students from pursuing scientific careers. For many, if they could simply do their science, they would be happy. But when they see that they will also have to expend so much effort in trying to obtain funding, with so little chance of success, some may turn to other career options.

There is no question that both the nature and the scale of federal funding for R&D has transformed colleges and universities over the past century, especially in the last several decades. The relationship has always been, and continues to be, a dynamic one, filled with both rewards and tensions. A central question for the future is whether that relationship can continue to be a productive one, in which each partner can grow and adapt while also retaining the core of its purpose and identity, in ways that clearly benefit the public.

See also: FACULTY PERFORMANCE OF RESEARCH AND SCHOLARSHIP; FACULTY RESEARCH AND SCHOLARSHIP, ASSESSMENT OF; FACULTY ROLES AND RESPONSIBILITIES; RESEARCH UNIVERSITIES.

BIBLIOGRAPHY

DUPREE, A. HUNTER. 1957. *Science in the Federal Government: A History of Policies and Activities to 1940.* Cambridge, MA: Harvard University Press, Belknap Press.

GILMAN, WILLIAM. 1965. *Science: U.S.A.* New York: Viking.

KOIZUMI, KEI. 2002. "R&D Trends and Special Analyses." In *AAAS Report XXVII: Research and Development, FY 2003,* by Intersociety Working Group. Washington, DC: American Association for the Advancement of Science.

NATIONAL SCIENCE BOARD. 2000. *Science and Engineering Indicators, 2000.* Arlington, VA: National Science Foundation.

NATIONAL SCIENCE FOUNDATION. 2001. *Survey of Research and Development Expenditures at Universities and Colleges, Fiscal Year 2000.* Washington, DC: National Science Foundation.

NELSON, STEPHEN D. 1984. "A Brief History of the Development of the National Institutes of Health." Unpublished background paper for the Institute of Medicine report, *Responding to Health Needs and Scientific Opportunity: The Organizational Structure of the National Institutes of Health.* Washington, DC: National Academy Press.

PRICE, DON K. 1965. *The Scientific Estate.* Cambridge, MA: Harvard University Press, Belknap Press.

Teich, Albert H. 2002. "R&D in the Federal Budget: Frequently Asked Questions." In *AAAS Report XXVII: Research and Development, FY 2003,* by Intersociety Working Group. Washington, DC: American Association for the Advancement of Science.

Wells, William G., Jr. 1994. *Science, Technology, and the Congress: The First 200 Years.* Washington, DC: American Association for the Advancement of Science.

Stephen D. Nelson

FEDERAL FUNDS FOR HIGHER EDUCATION

The federal government plays a critical role in providing financial support for higher education. In fiscal year 1996 approximately $40 billion, or one-fifth of the total revenue received by degree-granting institutions of higher education, originated from the federal government (National Center for Education Statistics). These funds generally are provided in two forms: through direct support to colleges and universities, generally for research or facilities; and through grants and loans made to students enrolled in postsecondary institutions.

This support inevitably comes with political strings attached. The federal government, as does any political entity, establishes program and policy priorities, and expends funds in support of those priorities. The provision of federal funds generally brings along with it rules and regulations that govern how the funds can be used. Recipients of these funds, whether higher education institutions or their students, must agree to comply with these regulations as a condition of their receipt. Throughout history, the relationship between the federal government and higher education has changed, and along with it has been a change in the priorities and regulations with which federal funds are provided to higher education.

History

Throughout U.S. history, overriding federal polices on higher education have been noteworthy chiefly by their absence. Federal policies have usually been implemented through appropriations rather than general rules and regulations and have thus affected only selected kinds of institutions, programs, students, and faculty. Even the unrestricted grants of four million acres of federal land, which helped to support universities in seventeen of the twenty-one new states established before the Civil War, were confined to public institutions.

The Morrill Act of 1862 strengthened the budding network of state universities by granting public lands (or the equivalent in scrip) to every state for "the endowment . . . and maintenance of at least one college where the leading object shall be . . . to teach such branches of learning as are related to agriculture and the mechanic arts . . . in order to promote the . . . education of the industrial classes." By 1890 at least twenty new public institutions had been established under the act, and another twenty institutions had expanded or had been placed under public control. The Second Morrill Act of 1890 provided additional annual grants to certain fields of practical instruction but not to the other scientific and classical studies that the 1862 act had embraced.

Gradually, between the Civil War and World War I the principles that continue to govern many federal programs developed: (1) the annual subvention of designated kinds of education and research; (2) the retention by the federal government of the authority to review proposed plans before committing funds, to place conditions on their use, and to audit expenditures; and (3) the encouragement of practical studies and public service activities.

The next major expansion in federal programs came during the Great Depression, when federal outlays rose from $21 million in 1930 to $43 million in 1936. This represented an increase of from 4 to 9 percent of institutions' total annual income. In 1937 federal aid to students reached its peak during this era, when 139,000 students (11% of all students) received an average of $12 per month for undergraduates and $20 per month for graduate students as part of the National Youth Administration's work-study program.

Federal support for higher education expanded greatly during World War II, increasing to over $300 million in 1944. The bulk of this expansion was due to research spending in support of the war effort, though colleges and universities also supported the military by providing training courses to over 315,000 army and navy trainees.

Although military research slowed down with the close of World War II, the Servicemen's Readjustment Act of 1944 (more commonly known as the G.I. Bill) provided a new revenue stream for colleges and universities. In 1948 the federal government supported more than 1 million veterans in college, with payments for tuition totaling approximately $365 million, and another $1.3 billion provided to the veterans themselves for subsistence costs. As returning G.I.'s completed their postsecondary education and reentered the workforce, federal support for higher education began to decline. After peaking at $1.9 billion in 1949 (including subsistence funds for veterans), federal support declined and did not reach this level again until 1963.

The late 1950s saw the creation of the first generally available student loan program through the passage of the National Defense Education Act in 1958. This legislation, passed in response to the launching of the *Sputnik* satellite by the Soviet Union, sought to promote access to higher education as a means toward increasing the technological capabilities of the United States. Now called Perkins Loans, these loans were funded by providing capital directly to colleges, which in turn lent the money to students at highly subsidized interest rates. This era also saw a resurgence in federal support for research, particularly military research to support the cold war efforts of the nation.

The next major milestone in federal support for higher education was the passage of the Higher Education Act of 1965. Title IV of this legislation created the student grant and loan programs that still provided the foundation of financial aid support for students at the beginning of the twenty-first century. Provision of this support was based on the financial need of the students and their families; the aid—both grants and loans—was targeted at the nation's neediest students. In addition to the broad-based student aid programs, the Higher Education Act also provided direct funding for college libraries, historically black colleges and universities, and a number of smaller, specialized programs. The Higher Education Act has undergone reauthorization approximately every five years since its initial passage. With every reauthorization has come changes to how financial aid is provided to students and institutional support to colleges and universities.

Federal support for research has also grown since 1965. According to the National Center for Education Statistics, research support provided to educational institutions (the great majority of which goes to postsecondary institutions) has grown from $1.8 billion in 1965 to $21 billion in fiscal year 2000.

Federal Support for Students

Since the passage of the Higher Education Act of 1965, financial aid for students has been central to federal support for postsecondary education in the nation. In fiscal year 2000 the federal government provided $47.7 billion in financial aid to college students at both the undergraduate and graduate levels, a sum that represented 70 percent of all aid available that year. Just over half of this amount ($24.2 billion) was in the form of private loans guaranteed and subsidized by the federal government; the remaining amount was in the form of grants, work-study, and loan capital provided directly by the federal government. Federal funds for student aid more than doubled in constant dollars between 1975 and 2000, far outpacing the growth in enrollments of 28 percent during the same period.

The Higher Education Act has as one of its goals the equalization of educational opportunity for all students in the United States, seeking to remedy "the appalling frequency with which a student is presently forced to forego the opportunity of postsecondary education because of inability to meet the costs" (Mumper, p. 78). The provision of aid under Title IV of the act has been made almost exclusively based on the financial need of the student and his or her family. In the early years, the emphasis was on meeting the college access needs of poor students through the use of grants. When first fully funded in fiscal year 1975, Pell Grants, the foundation grant program, provided more than 80 percent of the cost of attendance (tuition, room, board, books, and other expenses) at a typical public, four-year institution. Loans were available for students who wanted to attend a more expensive institution.

Over the ensuing twenty-five years, the Pell Grant program did not keep pace with the rise in college costs. By fiscal year 2000 the maximum Pell Grant provided only 40 percent of the cost of attendance at a public four-year institution. While total Pell Grant spending had grown 691 percent over the preceding twenty-five years, federal loan volume had increased 2000 percent over the same period, thus shifting the foundation of the Title IV programs from grants to loans.

The loan programs, which like Pell Grants had initially been targeted at students from financially needy families, were opened up to all students in 1978. While Congress and the Reagan administration rescinded this change three years later, the income limits in the loan programs (and the limits on the amount of loans that could be taken out) were liberalized again in the 1992 amendments to the Higher Education Act.

Another important milestone in federal funding for higher education students was the passage of the Taxpayer Relief Act of 1997. This legislation, which created the Hope and Lifetime Learning tax credits for college tuition, was initially estimated to cost the government $40 billion in foregone tax revenue in its first five years, or slightly more than the estimate for Pell Grant spending during that period. Unlike Pell Grants, which are targeted at the nation's neediest students (those from families making less than $45,000 per year in 2000), the tax credits were made available to families with incomes of up to $100,000. The structure of the tax legislation helped shift even more federal resources away from the neediest college students and toward middle- and upper-income students.

The changes in the provision of federal support for college students since the passage of the Higher Education Act in 1965 can best be characterized as a shift away from meeting the college access needs of poor students to subsidizing college affordability for students from wealthier families. While the Pell Grant program continues to receive much attention in Congress and on college campuses, its position as the cornerstone of federal support for postsecondary education has been usurped by the emphasis on the use of loans and tax credits as alternative means for providing federal funding to students and their families.

Federal Support for Research

As noted earlier, federal support for research at educational institutions grew to reach a level of more than $21 billion in fiscal year 2000. These expenditures are generally tightly coupled with national priorities. For example, during the latter half of the 1970s, when the nation faced an energy crisis due primarily to the OPEC oil embargo, there was an expansion of funding for energy-related research. In the 1980s the focus turned back towards military research, as the Reagan administration and Congress created new defense initiatives. In the latter half of that decade, with the end of the cold war and the

aging of the American populace, funding for health-related research grew fastest.

These changing priorities can be demonstrated by examining the amount spent by individual departments and agencies as a percentage of total federal research. In 1965 the Department of Defense represented 24 percent of all federally sponsored research at educational institutions. It dropped to approximately 10 percent of the total in the 1970s, before recovering in the 1980s to 15 percent. In fiscal year 2000 it stood at less than 8 percent of the total (National Center for Education Statistics). In contrast, spending by the Department of Health, Education, and Welfare in 1965 represented approximately 26 percent of total federal research. This share grew steadily (represented by the successor Department of Health and Human Services), reaching 44 percent of the total in 2000.

University-based research tends to follow the priorities established by the federal government. Most federally sponsored research is highly targeted, so that academic researchers need to adjust their research programs to attract federal dollars. Federal research dollars also bring with them support for indirect costs, those expenses associated with operating a large, complex university that cannot be directly attributed to specific research projects. Included in indirect costs are such items as library operations, plant maintenance, repair and operations, administrator salaries, and the costs of managing sponsored research on the campus.

Federally sponsored research has the effect of influencing not just the research agendas of faculty members, but also the decisions of students to enroll in doctoral programs. Doctoral students in most large research universities, particularly those in the sciences and engineering, commonly receive fairly generous fellowships and stipends. Most institutions depend upon sponsored research to support these students. As research dollars flow from sponsors, particularly the federal government, into and out of particular fields, financial support for students also varies. These dollars have the effect of influencing the decisions of students to enroll in specific fields, as well as the ability of universities to support them.

Through its financial support of both students as well as colleges and universities, the federal government has played an influential role in shaping the growth of the higher education industry throughout history. Even though the political and management control of institutions remains in the hands of states and private boards of trustees, the influence of federal funds for higher education is strongly felt by almost all of the institutions and by most students throughout higher education.

See also: COLLEGE FINANCIAL AID; FEDERAL EDUCATIONAL ACTIVITIES, *subentries on* HISTORY, SUMMARY BY AGENCY; FEDERAL FUNDING FOR ACADEMIC RESEARCH; G.I. BILL OF RIGHTS.

BIBLIOGRAPHY

AXT, RICHARD G. 1952. *The Federal Government and Financing Higher Education.* New York: Columbia University Press, for the Commission on Financing Higher Education.

COLLEGE BOARD. 2000. *Trends in Student Aid, 2000.* Washington, DC: College Board.

MUMPER, MICHAEL. 1996. *Removing College Price Barriers: What Government Has Done and Why It Hasn't Worked.* Albany: State University of New York Press.

NATIONAL CENTER FOR EDUCATION STATISTICS. 2001. *Digest of Education Statistics, 2000.* Washington, DC: U.S. Department of Education.

U.S. NATIONAL ADVISORY COMMITTEE ON EDUCATION. 1931. *Federal Relations to Education.* 2 vols. Washington, DC: National Capital Press.

DONALD E. HELLER

FEDERAL INTERAGENCY COMMITTEE ON EDUCATION

The Federal Interagency Committee on Education (FICE) is mandated to ensure "effective coordination of Federal education programs." It was first established by Executive Order 11185, issued by President Lyndon B. Johnson on October 16, 1964, and subsequently amended by Executive Order 11260 (1965) and by Executive Order 11761, issued by President Richard M. Nixon in 1974.

FICE was included in section 214 of Public Law 96-88, the Department of Education Organization Act. The act designates the U.S. Secretary of Education as the chair of FICE. On January 12, 1982, President Reagan issued a memorandum to the Secretary of Education stating that "senior policy making officials from the following agencies, commissions and boards should be assigned to the committee: the U.S. Department of Education; National Endowment for the Arts; National Endowment for the Humanities; National Science Foundation; and the Departments of Agriculture, Defense, Interior, Labor, Health and Human Services, Housing and Urban Development, Transportation, Treasury, and Veterans Affairs."

Subsequently, FICE membership grew to include representatives from the Department of Justice, Federal Emergency Management Agency, Environmental Protection Agency, The GLOBE Program, Institute of Museum and Library Services, Library of Congress, National Aeronautics and Space Administration, Peace Corps, Smithsonian Institution, and U.S. Commission on Civil Rights.

In these acts of legislation, Congress recognized the importance of coordination of federal education programs. FICE assists the Secretary of Education in providing a mechanism to ensure coordination between the Department of Education and other federal agencies that administer education programs. The Department of Education's Office of Intergovernmental and Interagency Affairs is the office responsible for managing FICE.

In the late 1960s and 1970s FICE made recommendations on a variety of postsecondary issues including expanded federal support for graduate study, federal support of historically black colleges and universities, and consumer protection for postsecondary education. These activities led to better interagency cooperation in these areas. FICE's work in consumer protection for postsecondary education led to legislation to protect consumers from the questionable activities of some postsecondary institutions.

Other accomplishments have included planning for an International Conference on Environmental Education in 1987, and making recommendations for research on rural education. The latter were summarized in a 1991 article (later published as a pamphlet) entitled "An Agenda for Research and Development on Rural Education."

In 1999 FICE began an important project to catalog all federal education programs. The committee began with a pilot to test the feasibility of compiling an inventory of federal education programs. The Departments of Education, Treasury, Interior, and Agriculture combined with the National Science Foundation to form a subcommittee that developed a definition of an education program and inventoried programs meeting the definition within Interior, Agriculture, and the National Science Foundation. This resulted in a report entitled *Single Source: Towards an Inventory of Federal Education Programs.* Since the completion of the report, seven additional agencies have compiled inventories based on the definition.

The Department of Education's interagency team presented *Single Source* to the department in December 2000. After departmental review, several changes were made to the definition of an education program. These changes were presented to and adopted by FICE. All participating agencies were expected to utilize the definition to compile their inventories by the end of fiscal year 2001. FICE defined an education program as one that comprised activities backed by a congressional authorization and current appropriation, with the main purpose of providing support to, or strengthening education at, pre-K though graduate levels. Adult education is included in the definition, but activities such as employment training or public information efforts are excluded. Additional activities that fall under the definition of an education program are development of instructional methods and materials, professional enhancement and utilization of educational technology in schools, provision of assistance to students, upgrading of physical and educational school facilities, and research that has a goal of improving education.

FICE members participate in a number of Department of Education activities and initiatives. In the future, the inventory and list of education activities will provide a better understanding of the depth and breadth of the federal effort to improve education.

See also: FEDERAL EDUCATIONAL ACTIVITIES; U.S. DEPARTMENT OF EDUCATION.

BIBLIOGRAPHY

FEDERAL INTERAGENCY COMMITTEE ON EDUCATION. 1991. "An Agenda for Research and Development on Rural Education." *Journal of Research in Rural Education* 7(2):89–92.

FEDERAL INTERAGENCY COMMITTEE ON EDUCATION. OFFICE OF INTERGOVERNMENTAL AND INTERAGENCY AFFAIRS. 1996. *Achieving the Goals—Goal 5: First in the World in Math and Science, Technology Resources.* Washington, DC: U.S. Government Printing Office.

FEDERAL INTERAGENCY COMMITTEE ON EDUCATION. SUBCOMMITTEE ON EDUCATIONAL CONSUMER PROTECTION. 1975. *Toward a Federal Strategy for Protection of the Consumer of Education.* Washington, DC: U.S. Department of Health, Education, and Welfare.

TONY FOWLER

FEDERAL SCHOOLS AND COLLEGES

The U.S. federal government operates, financially supports, or has chartered a number of schools and colleges to meet a variety of specific educational needs thought to be best addressed at the national level. Traditionally, elementary and secondary schools in the United States are primarily the responsibility of local school districts. Two- and four-year institutions of higher education are supported by state and local governments and by private entities. Private nonprofit and religious schools also play an important role in providing K–12 education, and there is a more recent rise in the number of for-profit businesses delivering education and educational services. In several instances, however, based on historical and geographical circumstances, the federal government complements these more customary means of providing education.

Overview

In elementary and secondary education, the federal government directly operates school systems serving children of personnel living on military bases, and systems serving Native Americans and Native Alaskans living on reservations and in native villages. Within higher education, the federal government provides substantial assistance toward supporting schools for deaf, African-American, Native American, and other students. Several institutions of higher education are also directly operated by the federal government, including the U.S. Military Academy at West Point, the U.S. Naval Academy, and the U.S. Air Force Academy, among others. In addition to operating schools directly, the federal government also provides numerous financial and other incentives aimed at advancing elementary, secondary, and higher education outcomes.

Elementary and Secondary Schools

Because of the large, diverse, and mobile nature of military deployment, the Department of Defense Education Activity (DoDEA) program operates two elementary and secondary school systems for the children of military and civilian personnel. Children of department employees within the United States, Guam, Puerto Rico, and Cuba are served by the Domestic Dependent Elementary and Secondary Schools (DDESS) system, while dependents living abroad are served by the Dependents Schools (DoDDS) system. Together, these systems enrolled more than 100,000 students in more than 200 schools in the year 2000. If these DoDEA schools were classified as a single state school district, it would rank among the twenty-five largest school districts, based on enrollment, in the United States.

The Bureau of Indian Affairs, within the U.S. Department of Interior, also operates a sizable school system serving Native Americans. The federal responsibility for providing education for Native Americans has been established historically through a succession of laws, treaties, and court decisions. As a result, the Office of Indian Education Programs (OIEP) directly operates nearly 70 schools, and provides grants and contracts to tribes to operate 116 additional schools. These schools enroll more than 50,000 students.

These military and Native American schools maintain curricula, standards, and educational goals that correspond to those found in local public school districts nationally. In addition, they also address unique educational aspects facing the populations they serve. Because military service requires frequent movement, for example, DoDEA teachers and counselors on military bases must be especially aware of how these numerous changes in environment and classmates may affect students academically and personally. In addition, DoDEA schools maintain a consistency of curriculum, which facilitates students' continuum of study and learning despite frequent geographical transfers. At the same time, each locality where students attend school also presents unique opportunities for them to learn local culture and language, which is encouraged in DoDEA schools. Within schools on reservations, efforts are made to maintain native and tribal cultures and languages as aspects of the curriculum. In fact, over the past decades and with the encouragement of the U.S. Congress and the OIEP, more and more schools on reservations are being operated by tribes and tribal school boards, rather than directly by the federal government, supported through the federal grants and contracts administered by OIEP.

Students from military families living off-base, or on bases with insufficient numbers to support a federally operated school, generally attend local public schools, as do children living on other federal land. These students often comprise a substantial share of the local community's school population, however. To compensate for the financial impacts incurred as the result of this federal presence, the federal Impact Aid Program provides funds to affected local school districts. The basis for this aid is that the federal employees, especially those who live on federal land or military bases, diminish the tax base that traditionally supports local school districts. Local revenues are lost, for example, because personnel living on federal property pay no property taxes, and often shop in stores on bases that generate no local sales tax revenue. Impact Aid also is provided to some school districts enrolling students who live in low-rent housing, and additional students who live on Indian reservations.

In addition to operating schools directly, or providing funds to schools directly affected by its presence, the federal government supports many educational programs and activities geared toward serving populations that have been, or are likely to be, at risk or underserved by traditional educational mechanisms. Federal funds partially support, for example, such students through Title I, Part A of the Elementary and Secondary Education Act of 1965, the Individuals with Disabilities Education Act (formerly the Education for All Handicapped Children Act), and the Head Start programs. Federal assistance is also provided to school systems in the commonwealths of Puerto Rico and the Northern Mariana Islands, and the territories of American Samoa, Guam, and the U.S. Virgin Islands, both through their participation in programs funded partially by the federal government (including those for at-risk students), and through the Department of Defense schools and Impact Aid. Federal revenues for public elementary and secondary schools alone range from nearly 80 percent of all school funding in American Samoa, to 25–30 percent in the Northern Mariana Islands and Puerto Rico, and less in the Virgin Islands and Guam.

Institutions of Higher Education

Although the federal government does directly operate a number of educational institutions such as the military service academies, it more commonly facilitates the formation of, and provides significant funding support for, schools and colleges established under its auspices, while leaving their organization and management to the institutions themselves.

Two institutions of higher education directly chartered by Congress are Gallaudet University and Howard University, both in Washington, D.C. In 1864, at the height of the Civil War, President Abraham Lincoln signed the bill authorizing Gallaudet University to grant college degrees. Efforts by Amos Kendall, an influential Washington writer and politician, led to the formation in 1857 of a school to serve deaf and blind children, officially known as the Columbia Institution for the Instruction of the Deaf, Dumb, and Blind. Believing that the school should grant college degrees and open the opportunity for higher education to deaf students, Kendall and the school's first president, Edward Miner Gallaudet, presented their case to Congress. They noted that higher learning for deaf individuals was possible with sign language, and that sign language enabled such education to be on a par with that obtained through spoken language. The initial emphasis of this college was to train teachers to work in the growing number of state schools for the deaf, and since these schools were spread across the United States, the federal government was asked to support a postsecondary institution to provide this training. By 1865 the school served only deaf students in both a pre-college school and in the college (blind students were transferred to a state school for the blind). Gallaudet College became Gallaudet University in 1986, and maintains the Kendall Demonstration Elementary School and the Model Secondary School for the Deaf on its campus.

Only a few years after the Civil War ended, the need also became clear for the establishment of a comprehensive institution of higher education serving the four million freed slaves and several hundred thousand free African Americans in the United States. The initial plan was to establish a theology school—an effort led by members of the First Congregational Society, a prominent Washington, D.C., church. General Oliver O. Howard, at the time the Commissioner of the Freedmen's Bureau in the U.S. War Department, was a member of this group and supported the idea. Soon afterwards, the plan was expanded to create a school for both theological training and to train teachers. While not the first college for African Americans (there is some evidence that Cheyney University in Pennsylvania was the first), the comprehensive plan for the new university soon grew to include programs in the arts, sciences, medicine, and law. These efforts culminated in the signing of the charter for Howard University by President Andrew Johnson in 1867. Although the charter of Howard University indicated the institution was for all individuals, there was no doubt that the intent was to serve freed slaves and other African Americans.

Both Gallaudet University and Howard University were established in times when there was great debate about whether deaf individuals and freed slaves (and freemen) were capable of achieving higher education. At the start, both universities had an initial goal of training teachers for the growing number of deaf institutions and in schools where freed slaves were obtaining public education for the first time. Both universities, although chartered to grant degrees by the federal government and receiving substantial shares of their revenues from the federal government, are private, nonprofit institutions, governed by boards of trustees. While there is some federal review of their policies, they continue to maintain the independence to determine their own academic and strategic planning objectives. Both universities continue to be national in scope, are fully accredited, and enroll both undergraduate and graduate students from across the United States in unique educational, cultural, and social environments. The importance of these two federally chartered schools is similarly seen in their impact on the wider communities they serve.

Deaf education. Gallaudet University is the only institution of higher education for deaf and hard of hearing students in the world. As such, it is a center for the study of deaf culture, history, and language. It is also the only institution of higher education where all communication between students, faculty and staff is direct and in sign language. A great majority of deaf teachers for deaf children obtained their bachelor's degree at the university, as have leaders in business, science, the arts, and other endeavors. In 1988, spurred by a student movement, Dr. I. King Jordan was named the university's first deaf president, an event that further served to encourage deaf students around the world to raise their aspirations and expectations for their futures.

African-American education. Howard University sets a national standard for the education and aspirations of African-American students in the United States. Established nearly 100 years before the passage of the Civil Rights Act in 1964, it has provided unique and diverse opportunities for African Americans in an era of segregation and discrimination. Howard University's mission continues to emphasize the history, culture, education, and societal role of African Americans, as well as other historically disenfranchised groups. Dr. Mordecai Johnson was named as the university's first African-American president in 1926.

Howard University is one of more than one hundred historically black colleges and universities (HBCUs) in the United States. These colleges and universities were all established prior to 1965, at which time Congress agreed to provide increased financial support to them, compensating for past lapses in federal aid. Subsequent Presidential Executive Orders strengthened the federal role in providing financial and educational support for HBCUs. Among the diverse group of HBCUs are Clark Atlanta University, Florida A&M, Grambling State University, Hampton University, and Southern University. Similarly, the federal government continues its support for additional study by deaf students through funding for the National Technical Institute for the Deaf (NTID) at the Rochester Institute of Technology in New York.

Native American education. The first institution of higher education for Native Americans, Diné College (formerly Navajo Community College), opened on the Navajo Reservation in Arizona in 1968, more than one hundred years after the federal government's first impetus to assist the then educationally disenfranchised groups of deaf and African-American students. The founding of this first tribal college was supported by funds from the federal Office of Equal Opportunity, with federal funds continuing to play a crucial role in the ongoing success of this and more than thirty other tribal colleges in the United States. Most of these schools are two-year colleges, but a growing number are adding four-year and graduate degrees, with South Dakota's Oglala Lakota College and Sinte Gleska University being among the first to do so.

The educational environments and philosophies in these comparatively new tribal colleges are strikingly similar to those of their century-old counterparts serving deaf and African-American students.

Chartered by tribal governments, these institution's curricula highlight native culture, language, and traditions. Academic and developmental programs are geared towards the specific needs of the indigenous student populations. The colleges not only serve those on each reservation, but also are resources for the entire reservation and for members of tribal communities nationally. Most tribal college presidents are Native Americans, further encouraging aspirations of future generations in higher education.

Funding

In addition to direct support to institutions of higher education, the federal government provides many other types of funding for students and organizations as well. Aid to individuals, for example, is given through student financial assistance programs, loans to individuals and families, work-study grants, and other incentives. Colleges and universities also receive aid through research and development grants, and additional federal funds support education at a variety of research facilities. In addition, an institution affiliated with the federal government but receiving no direct U.S. government funding, the U.S. Department of Agriculture Graduate School, offers programs geared towards the needs of federal workers and managers. Although this institution operates on a self-supporting basis, much of its funding is derived through federal agency tuition payments. Further, the government provides training for its senior executives at the Federal Executive Institute and Management Development Centers, as well as training opportunities at various public and private colleges and within federal agencies.

Goals

A more direct federal role in supporting schools and colleges within the otherwise state, local, and private educational mandate in the United States is presented here; however, in a broader sense, the federal role in education encompasses an extensive range of programs established to promote a wide variety of goals. These goals include improving academic achievement, expanding knowledge, providing equality of educational opportunity, collecting and disseminating education data, encouraging research and development, fostering health, advancing national security, and maintaining international relations. Viewed this way, spending for all types of educational activities accounted for approximately 10 percent of all federal expenditures in fiscal year 2000.

See also: FEDERAL EDUCATIONAL ACTIVITIES, *subentry on* SUMMARY BY AGENCY; FEDERAL FUNDS FOR HIGHER EDUCATION; U.S. WAR COLLEGES.

BIBLIOGRAPHY

ATWOOD, ALBERT W. 1964. *Gallaudet College: Its First One Hundred Years.* Lancaster, PA: Intelligencer.

BOLT, CHRISTINE. 1987. *American Indian Policy and American Reform: Case Studies of the Campaign to Assimilate the American Indians.* London: Allen and Unwin.

BOYER, PAUL. 1997. *Native American Colleges: Progress and Prospects.* Princeton, NJ: The Carnegie Foundation for the Advancement of Teaching.

BUDDIN, RICHARD; GILL, BRIAN P.; and ZIMMER, RON W. 2001. *Impact Aid and the Education of Military Children.* Santa Monica, CA: Rand.

CARNEY, CARY MICHAEL. 1999. *Native American Higher Education in the United States.* New Brunswick, NJ: Transaction.

CHRISTIANSEN, JOHN B., and BARNARTT, SHARON N. 1995. *Deaf President Now!: The 1988 Revolution at Gallaudet University.* Washington, DC: Gallaudet University Press.

GALLAUDET, EDWARD MINER. 1983. *History of the College for the Deaf, 1857–1907,* ed. Lance J. Fischer and David de Lorenzo. Washington, DC: Gallaudet College Press.

GANNON, JACK R. 1989. *The Week the World Heard Gallaudet.* Washington, DC: Gallaudet University Press.

HOAG, RALPH L. 1989. *The Origin and Establishment of the National Technical Institute for the Deaf: A Report on the Development of NTID, a Special Federal Project, Sponsored and Authorized by the United States Congress.* Rochester, NY: National Technical Institute for the Deaf.

HOFFMAN, CHARLENE M. 2000. *Federal Support for Education: Fiscal Years 1980 to 2000.* Washington, DC: U.S. Department of Education, National Center for Education Statistics.

HOFFMAN, CHARLENE M.; SNYDER, THOMAS D.; and SONNENBERG, BILL. 1996. *Historically Black Colleges and Universities, 1976–1994.* Washington, DC: U.S. Department of Education, National Center for Education Statistics.

JANKOWSKI, KATHERINE A. 1997. *Deaf Empowerment: Emergence, Struggle, and Rhetoric.* Washington, DC: Gallaudet University Press.

LOGAN, RAYFORD W. 1968. *Howard University: The First Hundred Years, 1867–1967.* New York: New York University Press.

MOEN, PHYLLIS; DEMPSTER-MCCLAIN, DONNA; and WALKER, HENRY A. 1999. *A Nation Divided: Diversity, Inequality, and Community in American Society.* Ithaca, NY: Cornell University Press.

WRIGHT, DAVID E., III; HIRLINGER, MICHAEL W.; and ENGLAND, ROBERT E. 1998. *The Politics of Second Generation Discrimination in American Indian Education.* Westpost, CT: Bergen and Garvey.

VAN CLEVE, JOHN V., and CROUCH, BARRY A. 1989. *A Place of Their Own: Creating the Deaf Community in America.* Washington, DC: Gallaudet University Press.

U.S. DEPARTMENT OF EDUCATION, NATIONAL CENTER FOR EDUCATION STATISTICS. 2000. *Revenues and Expenditures for Public Elementary and Secondary Education: School Year 1997–1998.* Washington, DC: Superintendent of Documents, U.S. Government Printing Office.

INTERNET RESOURCES

AMERICAN INDIAN HIGHER EDUCATION CONSORTIUM. 1999. "Tribal Colleges: An Introduction." <www.aihec.org/intro.pdf>.

U.S. BUREAU OF INDIAN AFFAIRS, OFFICE OF INDIAN EDUCATION PROGRAMS. 2002. "Fingertip Facts." <www.oiep.bia.edu/>.

U.S. DEPARTMENT OF DEFENSE, DEPARTMENT OF DEFENSE EDUCATION ACTIVITY. 2001. "Department of Defense Education Activity Strategic Plan, 2001." <www.odedodea.edu/csp>.

STEPHEN CHAIKIND

FEMALE STUDENTS

See: AMERICAN ASSOCIATION OF UNIVERSITY WOMEN; GENDER ISSUES, INTERNATIONAL; INDIVIDUAL DIFFERENCES, *subentry on* GENDER EQUITY AND SCHOOLING; SINGLE-SEX INSTITUTIONS; TITLE IX; WOMEN'S STUDIES.

FINANCE, HIGHER EDUCATION

OVERVIEW
Scott L. Thomas

COMMUNITY AND JUNIOR COLLEGES
Richard L. Alfred

OVERVIEW

While many college-bound students and their families view higher education as a means to professional success and economic security, this end belies the myriad of contributions that America's colleges and universities make to the broader society. Although such social benefits often defy precise measurement they nonetheless establish the rationale for the public support of higher education. By any measure, public support of higher education is huge. In fiscal year 1996, federal, state, and local governments gave well in excess of $75 billion to degree-granting institutions of higher education (calculated from data generated by the National Center for Education Statistics). Tens of billions more dollars were provided indirectly through student financial assistance in the form of scholarships, grants, loans, and tax deductions.

Higher education is a massive enterprise with fiscal year 1996 expenditures of just more than $190.4 billion. Taking into account further expenditures of $20.9 billion in additions to physical plant value, combined expenditures on higher education comprised roughly 2.7 percent of the nation's gross domestic product during that year. By all accounts it is expected that higher education will continue to grow throughout the first part of the twenty-first century.

Expenditures

Higher education expenditures fall into two general categories: capital outlay (land, buildings, and equipment) and annual operating expenses. Annual operating expenses—or current-fund expenditures—occur in four distinct areas: educational and general expenses, auxiliary enterprises, hospitals, and independent operations.

In fiscal year 1996, colleges and universities devoted roughly $20.9 billion to capital outlays with the largest expenditure area (60.1% of total) being buildings, followed by expenditures on equipment (36.1%) and land (3.8%). Thus, capital expenditures made up roughly 10 percent of total higher education expenditures in this year. The percentage of all expenditures devoted to capital additions has fluctuated within 1.5 percentage points since the early 1980s.

The remaining 90 percent of higher education expenditures are devoted to education and general expenses—items such as instruction, research, libraries, administration, campus operations and maintenance, institutional scholarships and fellowships, auxiliary enterprises (e.g., residence halls, food services, intercollegiate athletics), independent operations (usually research and development centers), and university hospitals. Almost four-fifths of current-fund spending is accounted for by education and general expenditures. Costs associated with instruction (including faculty salaries) constitute just under one-third of annual expenditures and represent the single largest expense category in the higher education budget. Research expenses and institutional support costs (for example, general administrative services, legal and fiscal operations, community relations) each account for just under 10 percent of current-fund expenditures.

Outside of the educational and general expenditure area, institutions of higher education may devote significant resources to auxiliary services, independent operations, or hospitals. Such expenditures are generally revenue generating (although not always revenue neutral) and therefore have some capacity to be self-supporting. Roughly 20 percent of current-fund expenditures are directed at such units.

While these numbers are helpful in providing a very general description of higher education expenditures, they will vary dramatically across different types of campuses, generally in accordance with size and institutional mission. Relatively few campuses, for example, support hospitals or independent research centers.

Revenues

Public investment in higher education is based on the belief that colleges and universities provide social benefits to society that individual students cannot capture. To the degree that this belief is correct, the demand for higher education by individual students would be less than the social demand and an underproduction of higher education would inevitably result. Public subsidies are therefore used to address this imbalance in demand. Historically colleges and universities have been controlled and financed by state as opposed to federal government. While the federal government and students themselves provide a substantial amount of revenue to institutions of higher education, state revenues are the single largest source of government support for public institutions.

Capital projects on U.S. campuses are supported by revenues from a variety of sources. These most often take the form of private gifts, grants, and loans from the federal government, appropriations by state or local legislative bodies, general obligation bond issues by states or localities, borrowing by state building authorities or similar public corporations, and institutional issues of revenue bonds by the institutions themselves.

Current-fund revenue for higher education—money received during any given fiscal year from revenue that can be used to pay current obligations due, and surpluses reappropriated for the current fiscal year—also comes from many different areas and in many different forms. The majority of current-fund revenue received by institutions of higher education comes from students (through tuition) and federal, state, and local governments. Almost 28 percent of revenues in fiscal year 1996 came from students and their families while federal, state, and local governments combined provided 38 percent during this year. State governments provide the largest share of public funds directed to institutions (comprising roughly 60% of public funds in 1996), followed by the federal government (32%), and local governments (8% of total government support). The remaining 34 percent of current-fund revenues was made up from private sources, endowment income, and sales and services during this fiscal year.

This pattern of support has changed significantly since the early 1990s, with tuition revenue surpassing the amount of state appropriations to higher education institutions. The proportion of current-fund revenues received from each of these sources varies dramatically by sector, with private colleges and universities much more reliant upon tuition revenues. Table 1 shows that most revenues for higher education come from one of four distinct sources: the federal government, state governments, students (through tuition), and the sales of goods and services that are incidental to the conduct of research, instruction, or public service.

Federal Support

Since the Northwest Ordinance legislation in 1787 authorized land grants for the establishment of educational institutions, the federal government has been a major player in the financing of higher education. The first Morrill Act (1862) set the stage for the development of the nationwide system of land-grant colleges and universities to which the United States owes much of its extraordinary agricultural productivity since the late nineteenth century. Subsequent federal legislation supporting higher education has helped ensure the nation's military and industrial dominance for most of the twentieth century.

The U.S. government provides funds directly to institutions as well as to students in the form of financial aid. Most federal support comes through categorical aid programs administered by various departments within the executive branch or through independent agencies of the federal government. Of those funds provided directly to institutions of higher education, the bulk of federal support comes through such categorical programs in the form of restricted or unrestricted grants and contracts. The remainder of federal institutional support is provided either as direct appropriation or through independent operations usually involving major federally funded research and development centers (see Table 2).

Federal grants and contracts have long played an important role the advancement of science and engineering in the country. The National Defense Education Act of 1958 and grants and contracts provided through the Higher Education Act of 1965 and subsequent reauthorizations are good examples of this historic commitment. Toward the end of the twentieth century attention has been drawn to the increasing tendency of federal lawmakers to provide generous earmarks directly to institutions in their respective states. Scientists and college officials across the country have voiced concerns that the purely political distribution of funds traditionally awarded on competitive bases tends to erode the efficient provision of federal support aimed at leveraging the largest advances in knowledge and access to higher education.

While substantial funds flow from the federal government directly to institutions of higher education, the major portion of federal support for higher education comes in the form of student financial aid. Dramatic shifts in the economics of higher education and in policies defining the composition and delivery of student aid occurred between 1972 and 2001.

Civil rights–era ideals of federal student aid programs (largely falling under Title IV of the Higher

TABLE 1

Percentage of current revenue fund for higher education institutions,1981 and 1996

	Public Institutions			Private Institutions		
	1980–1981	1995–1996	Percent change	1980–1981	1995–1996	Percent change
Tuition and fees	12.9	18.8	45.7	36.6	43.0	17.5
Federal government	12.8	11.1	-13.3	18.8	13.8	26.6
State government	45.6	35.8	-21.5	1.9	1.9	–
Local government	3.8	4.1	7.9	0.7	0.7	–
Private gifts, grants, and contracts	2.5	4.1	64.0	9.3	9.1	2.2
Endowment income	0.5	0.6	20.0	5.1	5.2	2.0
Sales and services	19.6	22.2	13.3	23.3	21.0	-9.9
Other sources	2.4	3.3	37.5	4.2	5.3	26.2

SOURCE: U.S. Department of Education, National Center for Education Statistics. 2001. *Digest of Education Statistics*. Washington, DC: U.S. Department of Education.

Education Act) focused on providing need-based grant aid to ensure that low-income youth would not face a greater economic burden than their peers from more affluent backgrounds. These progressive ideals were soon eroded by the economic and political realities of the mid- to late 1970s, realities that radically altered the funding environment for higher education programs across the country. Marked gains in lower-income student access and persistence associated with Title IV were diminished as the need-based grant aid ideal was nudged toward the margins by more cost-effective and politically palatable loan programs.

The trend away from the need-based ideals outlined in the early Title IV programs was followed by a series of federal policy actions across the 1980s that devolved federal responsibility for a wide variety of public programs down to the state level. This devolution effectively relieved an exploding federal budget from a large share of the funding burden associated with a number of traditionally federally sponsored programs, including numerous high cost health and welfare programs.

One consequence of shifting responsibility to the states was that many states began experiencing severe financial strains—strains associated with unfunded mandates concomitant with the reassignment of many of these high cost federal programs. Strains on state budgets throughout the 1980s and early 1990s, combined with a serious economic recession in the early part of the 1990s, ultimately led to cutbacks in state general fund expenditures directed at public higher education which in turn fueled a run-up in tuition prices in the public postse-

condary education sector. A slightly different but no less malignant set of forces undergirded an even more dramatic tuition escalation in the private sector across this period.

State Support

States serve as the locus of control for higher education and are the single largest government funding source for public institutions. Any effective consideration of state support for higher education requires the separate treatment of public and private institutions. While public institutions receive generous state appropriations designed to subsidize the real costs of instruction, private institutions are generally less likely to receive such subsidies and are therefore much more reliant on tuition revenues (see Table 3).

Public institutions. Appropriations to institutions of higher education were made largely on the basis of political decisions in the post–World War II expansion. This strictly politically driven mode of funding had largely given way to funding based on enrollment-driven formulas by the late 1970s. Throughout the 1970s and 1980s the formulas used by state officials became much more refined to better reflect the varied missions, structures, and histories of state institutions. Many states during the 1980s adopted various forms of budgeting based on performance measures that usually affected a small portion of the overall funding. By the 1990s the mixed results from adherence to these various forms of budgeting led many states to abandon formula-based allocations and attempts to distribute funds on the basis of performance. Those states turning away from these earlier budgeting schemes began to develop policies that take into account previous allocations then making adjustments for inflation and changes in enrollment.

Similar to the federal government, states provide revenue to institutions directly in the form of appropriations, unrestricted grants and contracts, and restricted grants and contracts. And like the federal government, states provide financial aid to students that is then redirected to the institutions at which they enroll to cover the price of attendance. State student aid has taken many forms over the last half of the twentieth century. Although most programs were initially merit-based, many states had developed need-based aid programs by the mid-1960s. Need-based state aid programs were widely adopted by the mid-1970s to take advantage of the federal State Student Incentive Grant program passed in the 1972 reauthorization of the federal Higher Education Act. In the early twenty-first century, contractions in federal and state spending and political sensitivity to the dismay of middle- and upper-middle class families over spiraling tuition costs are driving state aid programs back toward the merit-based (as opposed to need-based) model.

Private institutions. States have long recognized the contributions of private higher education to enhancing the quality of life of its citizens. In addition to providing a greater diversity of higher education opportunity and enhancing states' economic and cultural richness, state leaders realize that these institutions also absorb the subsidization costs of students who would have otherwise attended a public institution in the state. Moreover, private institutions play an important role in the expansion of higher education opportunity in many states that would otherwise be hard pressed to underwrite such growth. Consequently, many states make significant public investments in these institutions.

While some states have chosen to provide direct intuitional aid to private colleges and universities, others target their support at specific high need programs or at the development of research and technological capacity. Another important source of state revenue for private institutions comes through state student aid programs. Student aid programs in which students enrolling in private institutions can participate have become ubiquitous. In addition, many states have developed tuition equalization grant programs to encourage access to this sector.

TABLE 2

Current-fund federal revenue of degree granting institutions, fiscal year 1996

Type of federal revenue	1995–1996 amount (in thousands)	Percentage of federal funds
Appropriations	2,036,948	8.5
Unrestricted grants and contracts	3,652,186	15.3
Restricted grants and contracts	14,713,289	61.5
Independent operations	3,536,653	14.8
Total federal revenue	23,939,076	100.0

SOURCE: U.S. Department of Education, National Center for Education Statistics. 2001. *Digest of Education Statistics.* Washington, DC: U.S. Department of Education.

State allocations to private institutions remain relatively modest however when compared to state contributions to institutions in the public sector (roughly 3% of state institutional support goes to the private sector). Differences in the types of funds made available to private institutions are also noteworthy. While more than 90 percent of state funds provided to public institutions are in the form of straight appropriations, almost three-quarters of state support allocated for private institutions is provided in the form of restricted grants and contracts (see Table 3).

Tuition Support

Public and private institutions have become more reliant upon tuition revenues than on any other single source. Most institutions chose to raise tuition charges paid by students and their families as revenues from state and federal sources declined throughout the latter part of the twentieth century. Escalating tuition prices during this period resulted in intense political pressure and close scrutiny of college costs. Many, especially those from lower- and middle-class families, expressed fear that they were being rapidly priced out of higher education.

The resultant political pressure combined with a strong economic recovery by the mid-1990s in most states allowed an easing of tuition increases over the course of the last several years. This hiatus, however, appears to be short lived as states come to grips with long-term structural budget deficits that will erode their ability to continue to provide revenue at current levels, let alone fund the further expansion necessary to accommodate the growing

TABLE 3

Current-fund state revenue of degree granting institutions, public and private, fiscal year 1996

Type of state revenue	Public Institutions		Private Institutions	
	1995–1996 amount (in thousands)	Percentage of state funds	1995–1996 amount (in thousands)	Percentage of state funds
Appropriations	40,081,437	90.6	241,864	16.7
Unrestricted grants and contracts	924,837	2.1	166,095	11.4
Restricted grants and contracts	3,236,272	7.3	1,042,168	71.9
Total state revenue	44,242,546	100.0	1,450,127	100.0

SOURCE: U.S. Department of Education, National Center for Education Statistics. 2001. *Digest of Education Statistics.* Washington, DC: U.S. Department of Education.

demand for higher education across the country. Many experts have concluded that this is not a cyclical pattern and that state spending on higher education is being permanently altered.

With the continued escalation of public sector costs in areas such as K–12 education, health, welfare, and prisons, higher education's claim on public funds is becoming increasing tenuous. Most experts agree that as the federal and state governments struggle to meet the demands in areas outside of higher education, tuition revenues will continue to become an ever larger source of revenue for all institutions, public and private.

Sales of Services, Private Giving, Endowment, and Other Support

As competition for government funds increases, institutions of higher education are becoming increasingly reliant upon other sources of support. Throughout the early 1990s rapid increases in tuition charges highlighted one strategy for replacing funds traditionally provided by state and federal governments. Recognizing that sustained tuition increases such as those in the 1990s were eroding access and would eventually affect demand, higher education leaders began to more aggressively encourage the cultivation of less dominant revenue sources. Colleges and universities are resorting to selling goods and services that were historically provided at no or little cost; faculty and staff are increasingly and openly encouraged to be more entrepreneurial when thinking about their research and teaching; and few institutions, public and private alike, lack coordinated fund-raising mechanisms (despite the reality that only the most prestigious institutions realize much from this source). Such activities are likely to become more pronounced throughout the early part of this century as higher education leaders struggle to balance the burgeoning demand and dramatic declines in levels of public support.

See also: ACCOUNTING SYSTEMS IN HIGHER EDUCATION; COLLEGE FINANCIAL AID; FEDERAL FUNDING FOR ACADEMIC RESEARCH; FEDERAL FUNDS FOR HIGHER EDUCATION; STATES AND EDUCATION, *subentry on* STATE GOVERNMENTS IN HIGHER EDUCATION.

BIBLIOGRAPHY

BECKER, WILLIAM E., and LEWIS, DARRELL R., eds. 1992. *The Economics of American Higher Education.* Boston: Kluwer Academic.

BOWEN, HOWARD R. 1977. *Investment in Learning.* San Francisco: Jossey-Bass.

CALLAN, PATRICK M., and FINNEY, JONI E., eds. 1997. *Public and Private Financing of Higher Education.* Phoenix, AZ: American Council on Education/Oryx Press.

CLOTFELTER, CHARLES T.; EHRENBERG, RONALD G.; GETZ, MALCOLM; and SIEGFRIED, JOHN J. 1991. *Economic Challenges in Higher Education.* Chicago: University of Chicago Press.

COHN, ELCHANAN, and GESKE, TERRY G. 1990. "Financing Higher Education." In *Economics of Education,* ed. Elchanan Cohn and Terry Geske. New York: Pergamon.

EHRENBERG, RONALD E. 2000. *Tuition Rising.* Cambridge, MA: Harvard University Press.

HELLER, DONALD E. 2001. *The States and Public Higher Education Policy.* Baltimore: Johns Hopkins University Press.

NATIONAL CENTER FOR EDUCATION STATISTICS. 2002. *Digest of Education Statistics, 2001,* NCES 2002–130. Washington, DC: U.S. Department of Education.

PAULSEN, MICHAEL B., and SMART, JOHN C., eds. 2002. *The Finance of Higher Education: Theory, Research, Policy and Practice.* Edison, NJ: Agathon.

SLAUGHTER, SHEILA, and LESLIE, LARRY. 1997. *Academic Capitalism.* Baltimore: Johns Hopkins University Press.

SCOTT L. THOMAS

COMMUNITY AND JUNIOR COLLEGES

Comprehensive two-year colleges emerged at the beginning of the twentieth century during a period of experimentation in all sectors of American education. In keeping with the spirit of the time, the community college—initially known as the junior college—developed as a result of increasing demand by the American public for accessible and affordable education. This unique institution, in which the associate degree is most commonly the highest degree awarded, quickly became a bridge between work and further education for traditional and adult learner populations. Throughout this entry, the term *community college* will be used to refer to public comprehensive two-year colleges. Included in this designation will be publicly supported associate degree institutions, technical colleges, and branch campuses. Private two-year colleges, usually recognized as junior colleges, are not included in this designation.

Historical Background

Beginning with Joliet Junior College in 1901, community colleges evolved in three distinct ways: as an upward extension of public school systems, as a downward extension of the university, and through voter approval. In the first half-century, most community and junior colleges were influenced in structure and operation by the public school systems and boards of education of the states in which they were located. According to a 2000 report from the American Association of Community Colleges, growth was steady during the first half of the twentieth century, with 648 institutions enrolling 168,000 students in 1950. With the expansion of the economy following World War II and growing public need for access to postsecondary education, community college campuses and enrollments grew at an explosive pace. By 1975, the number of two-year colleges (known variously as community colleges, junior colleges, technical colleges, associate degree institutions, branch campuses, etc.) had grown to 1,230 institutions enrolling 3,836,000 students. In fall 1999, the latest year for which official statistics are available, two-year colleges numbered 1,600 institutions and enrolled 5,339,000 students—one out of every two students enrolling in college on a first-time basis and 44 percent of all undergraduate students enrolled in American colleges and universities.

Although much of this growth has been attributed to changing demographic and economic conditions, it was also a product of public sentiment that favored the development of community colleges as a distinct educational entity within a local service region. Citizens committed to the idea of an affordable college within easy reach approved bond and tax referenda that provided capital and operating support at a record pace between 1960 and 1990. Local support not only paved the way for large-scale growth, it also positioned community colleges as a different type of institution from other postsecondary institutions. Public community colleges in most states receive significantly more support from local tax funds than do for-profit and baccalaureate degree granting institutions. And, as a reflection of their status as community-based institutions emphasizing access and convenience, tuition and student fees are typically lower than student charges at other institutions.

Financing Community and Junior Colleges

In significant ways, the financing of community and junior colleges is similar to college and university finance. All two-year institutions charge tuition and fees. They generate support from gifts and grants and the proportion of support they get from state funds is more like that received by baccalaureate colleges than K–12 school systems. State funds are often distributed to public community colleges by formula rather than by direct appropriation from the state legislature, which is the typical procedure used for state financing of four-year colleges and universities. Private junior colleges, of course, rely much more heavily on tuition than do public community colleges. In this respect, they are more like privately controlled four-year colleges and universities.

By looking at the methods of financing community and junior colleges over the six-year period from academic year 1991–1992 through academic year 1996–1997, one can gain an understanding of both the sources of funding for these colleges and the shifts that have occurred over time. Inclusion of funding data for four-year colleges and universities in the analysis provides a framework for comparison of resources allocated to different institutions by source over a common reporting period.

Sources of revenue. The status and methods of financing current operations between 1991–1992 and 1996–1997 for community and junior colleges and four-year colleges are illustrated in Table 1. (In interpreting these data, it is important to note that Pell revenue is not included in tabulations of support from the federal government.) Several observations of note can be gleaned from this information. One is that public community colleges are holding steadily to the principle that funds from state appropriations, local tax, and student payments in the form of tuition should be the primary sources of revenue in support of operations. For independent junior colleges—smaller in number and enrollment—tuition and fees are the primary source of operating income. When public and private two-year colleges are considered together, state, local, and student sources of income constitute, in combined form, more than 80 percent of the operating income. It appears that tuition and local tax are providing a proportionally greater share of support for operations in 1996–1997 compared to their level in 1991–1992 and that state appropriations are declining as a source of support for operations. The percentage of revenue through state appropriations shows a shift from 45 percent in 1991–1992 to 42 percent in 1996–1997. Student tuition and fees accounted for 21 percent of operating revenue in 1991–1992 and 23 percent in 1996–1997. In 1991–1992, local tax constituted 17 percent of operating revenue; by 1996–1997, it had increased to 18 percent.

Support provided through the federal government remained stable at roughly five percent between 1991–1992 and 1996–1997 for community and junior colleges. Gifts, private grants, and contracts account for only one percent of the revenue received by community colleges. This income source has become increasingly important to two-year colleges, however, as indicated in the 24 percent gain registered between 1991–1992 and 1996–1997.

Finally, the table illustrates the great variation in proportion of funding from different sources for public community colleges and four-year colleges. Public and private four-year colleges show a markedly higher reliance on student tuition and fees to support operations in comparison to community colleges. Additionally, they rely more on the federal government, auxiliary enterprises, private gifts and grants, and other revenue to finance their operations. Public community colleges, in contrast, rely more on local tax support. The information in Table 2 shows the proportion of operating revenues from different funding sources on a state-by-state basis for two-year colleges in 1996–1997. Public community colleges in thirty-five states received local tax support for their operations ranging from $.02 per capita in Washington to $56.57 per capita in Arizona. Public community colleges in states like Arizona, Wisconsin, California, and Illinois received a healthy portion of their operating revenue—in excess of one-third—from local tax while colleges in states like Connecticut, Indiana, Massachusetts, and Utah relied exclusively on state appropriations and student charges for operating support.

An interesting sidebar to the data in Table 1 is the basic difference in the way public and private two-year colleges are financed. Detailed information showing the distribution of revenue by source and type of institution for 1996–1997 (Table 3) reveal that private junior colleges get about two-thirds of their operating revenue from student tuition and fees. The only other significant sources of operating funds are private gifts, grants, and contracts and revenue earned through auxiliary enterprises. This pattern is similar to that found in privately controlled four-year colleges and universities, but even here significant differences are noted. Private four-year colleges and universities receive only about 43 percent of their income from student tuition and fees and more than one-third of their total revenue from gifts, grants, and contracts and other sources such as endowment. Clearly, private junior colleges have much smaller endowments than private four-year colleges on which to draw to support their current operations.

Open access. Student charges are an important source of revenue for all postsecondary institutions. For public community colleges, however, the cost of education is an important part of their mission. Access to educational opportunity is a defining characteristic for them and keeping

TABLE 1

Distribution of revenue by type of institution, 1991–1992 to 1996–1997

	Community Colleges			Four-Year Colleges			Total All Colleges
	Public	Independent	Total	Public	Independent	Total	
1991–1992							
Federal (1)	4.7%	5.4%	4.7%	11.5%	9.6%	10.8%	10.1%
State	46.2%	5.2%	45.1%	36.7%	2.4%	23.0%	25.5%
Local	18.1%	0.1%	17.6%	0.6%	0.6%	2.6%	
Private grants, gifts, and contracts	0.9%	9.5%	1.1%	4.6%	8.3%	6.1%	5.5%
Tuition and fees	19.9%	59.6%	21.1%	16.4%	40.5%	26.0%	25.5%
Auxiliary enterprises	6.6%	14.2%	6.8%	10.0%	10.5%	10.2%	9.8%
Other Revenue	3.5%	6.0%	3.6%	20.1%	26.0%	23.3%	21.0%
1992–1993							
Federal (1)	4.7%	5.4%	4.7%	11.5%	9.6%	10.8%	10.1%
State	46.2%	5.2%	45.1%	36.7%	2.4%	23.0%	25.5%
Local	18.1%	0.1%	17.6%	0.6%	0.6%	2.6%	
Private grants, gifts, and contracts	0.9%	9.5%	1.1%	4.6%	8.3%	6.1%	5.5%
Tuition and fees	19.9%	59.6%	21.1%	16.4%	40.5%	26.0%	25.5%
Auxiliary enterprises	6.6%	14.2%	6.8%	10.0%	10.5%	10.2%	9.8%
Other Revenue	3.5%	6.0%	3.6%	20.1%	26.0%	23.3%	21.0%
1993–1994							
Federal (1)	4.7%	5.4%	4.7%	11.5%	9.6%	10.8%	10.1%
State	46.2%	5.2%	45.1%	36.7%	2.4%	23.0%	25.5%
Local	18.1%	0.1%	17.6%	0.6%	0.6%	2.6%	
Private grants, gifts, and contracts	0.9%	9.5%	1.1%	4.6%	8.3%	6.1%	5.5%
Tuition and fees	19.9%	59.6%	21.1%	16.4%	40.5%	26.0%	25.5%
Auxiliary enterprises	6.6%	14.2%	6.8%	10.0%	10.5%	10.2%	9.8%
Other Revenue	3.5%	6.0%	3.6%	20.1%	26.0%	23.3%	21.0%
1994–1995							
Federal (1)	4.7%	5.4%	4.7%	11.5%	9.6%	10.8%	10.1%
State	46.2%	5.2%	45.1%	36.7%	2.4%	23.0%	25.5%
Local	18.1%	0.1%	17.6%	0.6%	0.6%	2.6%	
Private grants, gifts, and contracts	0.9%	9.5%	1.1%	4.6%	8.3%	6.1%	5.5%
Tuition and fees	19.9%	59.6%	21.1%	16.4%	40.5%	26.0%	25.5%
Auxiliary enterprises	6.6%	14.2%	6.8%	10.0%	10.5%	10.2%	9.8%
Other Revenue	3.5%	6.0%	3.6%	20.1%	26.0%	23.3%	21.0%
1995–1996							
Federal (1)	4.7%	5.4%	4.7%	11.5%	9.6%	10.8%	10.1%
State	46.2%	5.2%	45.1%	36.7%	2.4%	23.0%	25.5%
Local	18.1%	0.1%	17.6%	0.6%	0.6%	2.6%	
Private grants, gifts, and contracts	0.9%	9.5%	1.1%	4.6%	8.3%	6.1%	5.5%
Tuition and fees	19.9%	59.6%	21.1%	16.4%	40.5%	26.0%	25.5%
Auxiliary enterprises	6.6%	14.2%	6.8%	10.0%	10.5%	10.2%	9.8%
Other revenue	3.5%	6.0%	3.6%	20.1%	26.0%	23.3%	21.0%
1996–1997							
Federal (1)	4.7%	5.4%	4.7%	11.5%	9.6%	10.8%	10.1%
State	46.2%	5.2%	45.1%	36.7%	2.4%	23.0%	25.5%
Local	18.1%	0.1%	17.6%	0.6%	0.6%	2.6%	
Private grants, gifts, and contracts	0.9%	9.5%	1.1%	4.6%	8.3%	6.1%	5.5%
Tuition and fees	19.9%	59.6%	21.1%	16.4%	40.5%	26.0%	25.5%
Auxiliary enterprises	6.6%	14.2%	6.8%	10.0%	10.5%	10.2%	9.8%
Other Revenue	3.5%	6.0%	3.6%	20.1%	26.0%	23.3%	21.0%
Percentage Change, 1991–1992 to 1996–1997							
Federal (1)	4.7%	5.4%	4.7%	11.5%	9.6%	10.8%	10.1%
State	46.2%	5.2%	45.1%	36.7%	2.4%	23.0%	25.5%
Local	18.1%	0.1%	17.6%	0.6%	0.6%	2.6%	
Private grants, gifts, and contracts	0.9%	9.5%	1.1%	4.6%	8.3%	6.1%	5.5%
Tuition and fees	19.9%	59.6%	21.1%	16.4%	40.5%	26.0%	25.5%
Auxiliary enterprises	6.6%	14.2%	6.8%	10.0%	10.5%	10.2%	9.8%
Other revenue	3.5%	6.0%	3.6%	20.1%	26.0%	23.3%	21.0%

(1) Excludes Pell revenue, which is included in other categories.

SOURCE: National Center for education Statistics, Integrated Postsecondary Education Data System data files.

TABLE 2

Total and per capita state and local appropriations estimates for community colleges by state, 1996–1997

State	Total Appropriations			Population Estimate (7/1/97)	Per Capita Appropriations		
	State Appropriations	Local Appropriations	State and Local Appropriations		State Appropriations	Local Appropriations	State and Local Appropriations
Alabama	$176,996,016	$1,784,242	$178,780,258	4,291,110	$41.25	$0.42	$41.66
Alaska	$1,582,472	$647,231	$2,229,703	605,212	$2.61	$1.07	$3.68
Arizona	$95,145,602	$237,165,054	$332,310,656	4,432,202	$21.47	$53.51	$74.98
Arkansas	$85,116,084	$3,567,117	$88,683,201	2,505,073	$33.98	$1.42	$35.40
California	$1,524,127,485	$1,355,032,602	$2,879,160,087	31,762,190	$47.99	$42.66	$90.65
Colorado	$103,276,470	$29,260,539	$132,537,009	3,813,778	$27.08	$7.67	$34.75
Connecticut	$126,515,164	$0	$126,515,164	3,263,910	$38.76	$0.00	$38.76
Delaware	$44,352,601	$0	$44,352,601	727,113	$61.00	$0.00	$61.00
Florida	$699,173,526	$51,521	$699,225,047	14,424,868	$48.47	$0.00	$48.47
Georgia	$206,401,221	$5,251,855	$211,653,076	7,334,183	$28.14	$0.72	$28.86
Hawaii	$59,028,596	$0	$59,028,596	1,187,283	$49.72	$0.00	$49.72
Idaho	$22,025,536	$10,519,868	$32,545,404	1,186,239	$18.57	$8.87	$27.44
Illinois	$191,134,665	$433,746,427	$624,881,092	11,933,597	$16.02	$36.35	$52.36
Indiana	$106,777,197	$0	$106,777,197	5,827,423	$18.32	$0.00	$18.32
Iowa	$131,266,683	$28,003,977	$159,270,660	2,848,603	$46.08	$9.83	$55.91
Kansas	$61,703,882	$109,985,553	$171,689,435	2,584,650	$23.87	$42.55	$66.43
Kentucky	$82,609,500	$0	$82,609,500	3,882,545	$21.28	$0.00	$21.28
Louisiana	$46,450,326	$2,909,491	$49,359,817	4,339,871	$10.70	$0.67	$11.37
Maine	$25,984,078	$0	$25,984,078	1,238,003	$20.99	$0.00	$20.99
Maryland	$112,606,413	$138,775,085	$251,381,498	5,057,839	$22.26	$27.44	$49.70
Massachusetts	$195,507,454	$0	$195,507,454	6,082,910	$32.14	$0.00	$32.14
Michigan	$259,563,437	$207,744,700	$467,308,137	9,733,774	$26.67	$21.34	$48.01
Minnesota	$292,916,312	$0	$292,916,312	4,648,081	$63.02	$0.00	$63.02
Mississippi	$147,198,512	$30,349,674	$177,548,186	2,710,022	$54.32	$11.20	$65.52
Missouri	$109,236,958	$76,950,691	$186,187,649	5,368,911	$20.35	$14.33	$34.68
Montana	$10,286,300	$3,554,319	$13,840,619	876,734	$11.73	$4.05	$15.79
Nebraska	$39,467,710	$56,416,306	$95,884,016	1,648,041	$23.95	$34.23	$58.18
Nevada	$61,329,000	$0	$61,329,000	1,600,345	$38.32	$0.00	$38.32
New Hampshire	$19,685,762	$0	$19,685,762	1,159,546	$16.98	$0.00	$16.98
New Jersey	$100,679,103	$160,277,905	$260,957,008	8,007,905	$12.57	$20.01	$32.59
New Mexico	$103,708,351	$42,603,450	$146,311,801	1,707,902	$60.72	$24.94	$85.67
New York	$398,551,177	$290,152,657	$688,703,834	18,142,162	$21.97	$15.99	$37.96
North Carolina	$492,626,079	$85,528,237	$578,154,316	7,308,656	$67.40	$11.70	$79.11
North Dakota	$20,414,848	$339,966	$20,754,814	642,805	$31.76	$0.53	$32.29
Ohio	$270,094,215	$71,481,654	$341,575,869	11,169,546	$24.18	$6.40	$30.58
Oklahoma	$115,575,836	$18,571,666	$134,147,502	3,295,928	$35.07	$5.63	$40.70
Oregon	$162,027,806	$85,297,437	$247,325,244	3,195,409	$50.71	$26.69	$77.40
Pennsylvania	$132,604,581	$84,822,173	$217,426,754	12,033,856	$11.02	$7.05	$18.07
Rhode Island	$29,068,571	$0	$29,068,571	988,130	$29.42	$0.00	$29.42
South Carolina	$137,506,927	$26,823,088	$164,330,015	3,736,947	$36.80	$7.18	$43.97
South Dakota	$3,435,029	$0	$3,435,029	737,227	$4.66	$0.00	$4.66
Tennessee	$162,328,911	$10,199	$162,339,110	5,307,222	$30.59	$0.00	$30.59
Texas	$739,000,412	$301,995,771	$1,040,996,183	19,032,987	$38.83	$15.87	$54.69
Utah	$73,851,839	$0	$73,851,839	2,022,234	$36.52	$0.00	$36.52
Vermont	$1,230,900	$0	$1,230,900	586,333	$2.10	$0.00	$2.10
Virginia	$191,595,631	$2,110,487	$193,706,118	6,667,373	$28.74	$0.32	$29.05
Washington	$377,742,094	$103,643	$377,845,737	5,518,801	$68.45	$0.02	$68.47
West Virginia	$14,503,249	$0	$14,503,249	1,820,261	$7.97	$0.00	$7.97
Wisconsin	$122,757,255	$293,208,039	$415,965,294	5,174,348	$23.72	$56.67	$80.39
Wyoming	$44,975,312	$14,013,010	$58,988,322	480,060	$93.69	$29.19	$122.88
Total	$8,736,958,254	$4,210,744,050	$12,947,702,304	264,650,148	$33.01	$15.91	$48.92

SOURCE: National Center for Education Statistics, Integrated Postsecondary Education Data System data files; and U.S. Bureau of the Census, Population Estimates files.

the door to opportunity open through low tuition is both a philosophical premise and a practical necessity.

Comparative student charges for two-year colleges and four-year colleges are shown in Table 4. Over the 22-year period from academic year 1976–

TABLE 3

Distribution of revenue by source and type of institution, 1996–1997
In thousands.

	Community Colleges			Four-Year Colleges			Total All Colleges
	Public	Independent	Total	Public	Independent	Total	
Federal appropriations	$110,987	$0	$110,987	$1,815,781	$204,721	$2,020,501	$2,131,488
Federal grants and contracts (1)	$1,125,283	$34,595	$1,159,878	$10,955,577	$5,900,043	$16,855,620	$18,015,498
Federal Total	**$1,236,270**	**$34,595**	**$1,270,865**	**$12,771,357**	**$6,104,764**	**$18,876,121**	**$20,146,986**
State appropriations	$8,740,787	$798	$8,741,585	$33,834,348	$248,366	$34,082,714	$42,824,299
State grants and contracts	$1,211,264	$42,848	$1,254,112	$2,913,510	$1,113,903	$4,027,413	$5,281,525
State Total	**$9,952,051**	**$43,646**	**$9,995,697**	**$36,747,858**	**$1,362,269**	**$38,110,127**	**$48,105,824**
Local appropriations	$4,209,056	$260	$4,209,316	$196,796	$3,171	$199,967	$4,409,283
Local grants and contracts	$169,382	$879	$170,261	$491,448	$307,618	$799,066	$969,327
Local Total	**$4,378,437**	**$1,140**	**$4,379,577**	**$688,244**	**$310,789**	**$999,033**	**$5,378,610**
Tuition and fees	$4,917,379	$519,595	$5,436,974	$19,784,053	$31,134,456	$50,918,509	$56,355,483
Private gifts, grants, and contracts	$241,385	$90,864	$332,249	$5,346,254	$6,856,636	$12,202,891	$12,535,139
Endowment income	$19,243	$18,605	$37,848	$775,243	$3,794,211	$4,569,454	$4,607,302
Sales and services of educational activities	$161,404	$6,799	$168,203	$3,726,429	$1,995,386	$5,721,815	$5,890,018
Auxiliary enterprises	$1,345,971	$90,055	$1,436,027	$10,942,491	$7,416,382	$18,358,873	$19,794,900
Hospital revenues	$0	$0	$0	$12,682,554	$6,564,759	$19,247,313	$19,247,313
Other sources	$710,446	$36,361	$746,807	$3,623,587	$3,728,850	$7,352,437	$8,099,244
Independent operations	$7,443	$795	$8,239	$265,359	$3,049,606	$3,314,965	$3,323,204
Total current fund revenue	**$22,970,030**	**$842,455**	**$23,812,485**	**$107,353,428**	**$72,318,110**	**$179,671,538**	**$203,484,023**

Percentage Distribution

	Community Colleges			Four-Year Colleges			Total All Colleges
	Public	Independent	Total	Public	Independent	Total	
Federal appropriations	0.5%	0.0%	0.5%	1.7%	0.3%	1.1%	1.0%
Federal grants and contracts (1)	4.9%	4.1%	4.9%	10.2%	8.2%	9.4%	8.9%
Federal Total	**5.4%**	**4.1%**	**5.3%**	**11.9%**	**8.4%**	**10.5%**	**9.9%**
State appropriations	38.1%	0.1%	36.7%	31.5%	0.3%	19.0%	21.0%
State grants and contracts	5.3%	5.1%	5.3%	2.7%	1.5%	2.2%	2.6%
State Total	**43.3%**	**5.2%**	**42.0%**	**34.2%**	**1.9%**	**21.2%**	**23.6%**
Local appropriations	18.3%	0.0%	17.7%	0.2%	0.0%	0.1%	2.2%
Local grants and contracts	0.7%	0.1%	0.7%	0.5%	0.4%	0.4%	0.5%
Local Total	**19.1%**	**0.1%**	**18.4%**	**0.6%**	**0.4%**	**0.6%**	**2.6%**
Tuition and fees	21.4%	61.7%	22.8%	18.4%	43.1%	28.3%	27.7%
Private gifts, grants, and contracts	1.1%	10.8%	1.4%	5.0%	9.5%	6.8%	6.2%
Endowment income	0.1%	2.2%	0.2%	0.7%	5.2%	2.5%	2.3%
Sales and services of educational activities	0.7%	0.8%	0.7%	3.5%	2.8%	3.2%	2.9%
Auxiliary enterprises	5.9%	10.7%	6.0%	10.2%	10.3%	10.2%	9.7%
Hospital revenues	0.0%	0.0%	0.0%	11.8%	9.1%	10.7%	9.5%
Other sources	3.1%	4.3%	3.1%	3.4%	5.2%	4.1%	4.0%
Independent operations	0.0%	0.1%	0.0%	0.2%	4.2%	1.8%	1.6%
Total current fund revenue	**100.0%**	**100.0%**	**100.0%**	**100.0%**	**100.0%**	**100.0%**	**100.0%**

(1) Excludes Pell revenue, which is included in other categories.

SOURCE: National Center for Education Statistics, Integrated Postsecondary Education Data System data files.

TABLE 4

Average tuition and fees by type of institution in constant 1997–1998 dollars, 1976–1977 to 1997–1998						
	Community Colleges			Four-Year Colleges		
Academic Year	Public	Independent	Total	Public	Independent	Total
1976–1977	$774	$4,352	$946	$1,687	$6,927	$3,329
1977–1978	$782	$4,362	$967	$1,675	$6,904	$3,301
1978–1979	$760	$4,256	$955	$1,599	$6,876	$3,248
1979–1980	$727	$4,221	$923	$1,511	$6,602	$3,097
1980–1981	$720	$4,441	$968	$1,480	$6,657	$3,090
1981–1982	$741	$4,445	$1,007	$1,551	$7,018	$3,254
1982–1983	$778	$4,950	$1,111	$1,697	$7,634	$3,520
1983–1984	$836	$4,904	$1,155	$1,817	$8,059	$3,709
1984–1985	$890	$5,314	$1,252	$1,872	$8,472	$3,914
1985–1986	$953	$5,459	$1,320	$1,959	$9,099	$4,139
1986–1987	$956	$5,335	$1,299	$2,048	$9,643	$4,406
1987–1988	$982	$5,787	$1,125	$2,138	$9,901	$4,452
1988–1989	$969	$6,396	$1,300	$2,185	$10,253	$4,610
1989–1990	$957	$6,581	$1,239	$2,254	$10,633	$4,813
1990–1991	$991	$6,701	$1,308	$2,271	$10,927	$4,823
1991–1992	$1,094	$6,715	$1,385	$2,474	$11,411	$5,135
1992–1993	$1,161	$6,863	$1,445	$2,661	$11,661	$5,383
1993–1994	$1,242	$7,033	$1,545	$2,801	$12,091	$5,652
1994–1995	$1,280	$7,422	$1,597	$2,878	$12,325	$5,787
1995–1996	$1,294	$7,411	$1,590	$2,975	$12,790	$6,045
1996–1997	$1,298	$7,358	$1,569	$3,037	$13,098	$6,221
1997–1998	$1,318	$7,536	$1,582	$3,110	$13,392	$6,329
			Percent Change			
1976–1977 to 1997–1998	70%	73%	67%	84%	93%	90%
1987–1988 to 1997–1998	34%	30%	41%	45%	35%	42%
1992–1993 to 1997–1998	14%	10%	9%	17%	15%	18%

SOURCE: National Center for Education Statistics, 1999.

1977 to academic year 1997–1998, tuition and fees in two-year colleges have, on the average, amounted to one-quarter of those for four-year colleges. This differential has widened over time as state appropriations to four-year colleges and universities have diminished in periods of economic fluctuation and tuition has increased to reduce the gap between income and expenditures. In 1976–1977, for example, the average cost of tuition and fees for a full-time student in two-year colleges ($946) approximated 28 percent of the average cost for students enrolled in four-year colleges ($3,329). By 1997–1998, the disparity had increased with the cost of tuition and fees in two-year colleges ($1,592) averaging 25 percent of those for four-year colleges ($6,329). When private two- and four-year colleges are removed from the analysis leaving only public institutions, the cost differential diminishes considerably with tuition and fees at public community colleges ($1,318) averaging 42 percent of those at public colleges and universities ($3,110).

Expenditures. Generally speaking, budgets and financial reports of colleges and universities are devel-

oped and analyzed according to categories of educational and general expenses. Subdivisions are commonly used to organize and report expenditures; the most common are instruction, research, public service, academic support, student services, institutional support, plant maintenance and operations, scholarships and fellowships, and transfers.

The information in Table 5 shows that public community colleges employ all nine expenditure subdivisions. As would be expected in any educational institution, the largest category of expenditure is instruction with 43 percent of all educational and general expenditures classified in this category in 1996–1997. When costs for academic support, student services, and institutional support are added to instructional cost, they account for more than three-quarters of all expenditures. These costs, for the most part, are attributable to personnel, which is why two-year colleges, and colleges and universities in general, are described as labor intensive organizations.

It is interesting to note that the categories of cost fluctuate as a percentage of expenditures as cost allo-

TABLE 5

Public community college expenditures in current and constant 1996–1997 dollars, 1991–1992 to 1996–1997

	Current Dollars		Constant, 1996–1997 Dollars		
	Total Expenditures (in millions)	Expenditures per FTE Student	Total Expenditures (in millions)	Expenditures per FTE Student	Percentage Distribution
1991–1992					
Instruction	7,977	2,565	$9,158	$2,945	45.8%
Salaries and wages for instruction	5,863	1,885	$6,731	$2,164	33.7%
Research	23	7	$26	$8	0.1%
Public service	358	115	$411	$132	2.1%
Academic support	1,292	415	$1,483	$477	7.4%
Student services	1,616	520	$1,855	$597	9.3%
Institutional support	2,408	774	$2,765	$889	13.8%
Operation and maintenance of plant	1,641	528	$1,884	$606	9.4%
Scholarships and fellowships	1,772	570	$2,034	$654	10.2%
Mandatory transfers	95	31	$109	$35	0.5%
Non-mandatory transfers	228	73	$261	$84	1.3%
Total educational and general expenditures	17,411	5,598	$19,988	$6,427	100.0%
1992–1993					
Instruction	8,449	2,686	$9,412	$2,992	45.5%
Salaries and wages for instruction	6,275	1,995	$6,991	$2,222	33.8%
Research	27	9	$30	$10	0.1%
Public service	391	124	$436	$138	2.1%
Academic support	1,371	436	$1,527	$485	7.4%
Student services	1,759	559	$1,960	$623	9.5%
Institutional support	2,528	803	$2,816	$895	13.6%
Operation and maintenance of plant	1,711	544	$1,906	$606	9.2%
Scholarships and fellowships	2,045	650	$2,279	$724	11.0%
Mandatory transfers	107	34	$120	$38	0.6%
Non-mandatory transfers	186	59	$207	$66	1.0%
Total educational and general expenditures	18,574	5,904	$20,691	$6,577	100.0%
1993–1994					
Instruction	8,855	2,858	$9,614	$3,103	44.8%
Salaries and wages for instruction	6,499	2,097	$7,057	$2,277	32.8%
Research	29	9	$32	$10	0.1%
Public service	425	137	$462	$149	2.2%
Academic support	1,478	477	$1,605	$518	7.5%
Student services	1,868	603	$2,028	$654	9.4%
Institutional support	2,709	874	$2,941	$949	13.7%
Operation and maintenance of plant	1,850	597	$2,008	$648	9.3%
Scholarships and fellowships	2,256	728	$2,449	$790	11.4%
Mandatory transfers	121	39	$132	$42	0.6%
Non-mandatory transfers	196	63	$213	$69	1.0%
Total educational and general expenditures	19,788	6,386	$21,484	$6,933	100.0%
1994–1995					
Instruction	9,145	2,968	$9,654	$3,133	44.5%
Salaries and wages for instruction	6,674	2,166	$7,046	$2,287	32.5%
Research	29	9	$31	$10	0.1%
Public service	433	140	$457	$148	2.1%
Academic support	1,502	487	$1,586	$515	7.3%
Student services	1,980	643	$2,091	$679	9.6%
Institutional support	2,866	930	$3,026	$982	13.9%
Operation and maintenance of plant	1,917	622	$2,024	$657	9.3%
Scholarships and fellowships	2,334	758	$2,464	$800	11.4%
Mandatory transfers	130	42	$137	$45	0.6%
Non-mandatory transfers	225	73	$238	$77	1.1%
Total educational and general expenditures	20,561	6,674	$21,707	$7,045	100.0%

[continued]

cations change over time. For example, total expenditures for instruction increased by 25 percent between 1991–1992 and 1996–1997 whereas expenditures for academic support increased by 40 percent, expenditures for student services by 38 percent, and expenditures for instructional support by 39

TABLE 5 [CONTINUED]

Public community college expenditures in current and constant 1996–1997 dollars, 1991–1992 to 1996–1997					
	Current Dollars		Constant, 1996–1997 Dollars		
	Total Expenditures (in millions)	Expenditures per FTE Student	Total Expenditures (in millions)	Expenditures per FTE Student	Percentage Distribution
1995–1996					
Instruction	9,622	3,165	$9,885	$3,252	43.9%
Salaries and wages for instruction	6,960	2,290	$7,150	$2,352	31.7%
Research	23	8	$24	$8	0.1%
Public service	471	155	$484	$159	2.1%
Academic support	1,675	551	$1,721	$566	7.6%
Student services	2,150	707	$2,209	$727	9.8%
Institutional support	3,090	1,016	$3,174	$1,044	14.1%
Operation and maintenance of plant	2,053	675	$2,109	$694	9.4%
Scholarships and fellowships	2,450	806	$2,517	$828	11.2%
Mandatory transfers	153	50	$157	$52	0.7%
Non-mandatory transfers	241	79	$248	$82	1.1%
Total educational and general expenditures	21,929	7,214	$22,529	$7,411	100.0%
1996–1997					
Instruction	9,970	3,251	$9,970	$3,251	43.1%
Salaries and wages for instruction	7,019	2,289	$7,019	$2,289	30.4%
Research	25	8	$25	$8	0.1%
Public service	511	167	$511	$167	2.2%
Academic support	1,811	590	$1,811	$590	7.8%
Student services	2,221	724	$2,221	$724	9.6%
Institutional support	3,335	1,088	$3,335	$1,088	14.4%
Operation and maintenance of plant	2,127	694	$2,127	$694	9.2%
Scholarships and fellowships	2,629	857	$2,629	$857	11.4%
Mandatory transfers	183	60	$183	$60	0.8%
Non-mandatory transfers	287	93	$287	$93	1.2%
Total educational and general expenditures	23,109	7,536	$23,109	$7,536	100.0%
Change 1991–1992 to 1996–1997					
Instruction	25.0%	26.8%	8.9%	10.4%	-5.8%
Salaries and wages for instruction	19.7%	21.4%	4.3%	5.7%	-9.8%
Research	8.9%	10.4%	-5.2%	-3.8%	-18.0%
Public service	42.6%	44.6%	24.2%	26.0%	7.5%
Academic support	40.2%	42.1%	22.1%	23.8%	5.6%
Student services	37.5%	39.4%	19.7%	21.4%	3.6%
Institutional support	38.5%	40.4%	20.6%	22.3%	4.3%
Operation and maintenance of plant	29.6%	31.4%	12.9%	14.5%	-2.3%
Scholarships and fellowships	48.4%	50.5%	29.3%	31.1%	11.8%
Mandatory transfers	92.2%	94.9%	67.4%	69.8%	44.8%
Non-mandatory transfers	25.9%	27.7%	9.7%	11.2%	-5.1%
Total educational and general expenditures	32.7%	34.6%	15.6%	17.2%	0.0%

SOURCE: National Center for Education Statistics, Integrated Postsecondary Education Data Systems data files.

percent. This could be a reflection of the tendency of community colleges to shift more of the instructional workload to part-time faculty as a method for decreasing fixed costs and increasing flexibility. Proportionally larger costs for academic support could indicate that more resources are needed to acquire advanced technology in support of classroom instruction and to provide tutorial assistance to students experiencing academic difficulty. Rising costs for student services and institutional support could be a result of more extensive efforts by community colleges to market programs and services to a wide array of audiences and to make more and better services available using technology and specialized support staff.

Out of these trends a greater focus is emerging on using resources more effectively through strategic planning. In this approach to allocating resources, priorities are determined through gathering and analyzing information about trends in the external environment and internal capabilities. Resources are allocated to these priorities in the operating budget and institutions measure their performance against achievement criteria established for each priority as a method for determining their progress in reaching stated goals. The fiscal impact that each priority has on expenditure categories in the operating budget is then analyzed to determine cost benefits and additional resource requirements. What are the costs of implementation associated with each priority? How much revenue did the priority generate? What additional resources need to be allocated to fully achieve the priority?

Critical Issues

A number of important finance and finance-related issues will challenge public community colleges, and to some extent private junior colleges, in the decade ahead. These issues can be organized and described in four categories: limits to institutional development, changing market conditions, new sources of support, and accountability.

Limits to institutional development. Public community colleges have been criticized in past years for having an unfocused mission—for being "all things to all people." As their mission has expanded to encompass new activities such as workforce development and corporate training, the requirement for resources to support these activities, in addition to a comprehensive battery of current programs and services, has stretched to a breaking point. Where will new and additional resources come from to support an expanding mission? Will contraction be necessary to free up resources for new activities? How will institutions support a comprehensive mission in a period when resources are drying up? Planning will become important to institutions in the future as a method to make better decisions with fewer resources.

Changing market conditions. Shifting economic conditions and resulting impacts on programs and services are a fact of life for community colleges. In forty-three states, state revenues lag behind projections; governors and legislatures in states including California, Florida, Virginia, and Washington are faced with filling budget holes of $1 billion. In most states, deep cuts in state expenditures once again mean higher education is facing a sharp-edged budget ax. Cuts in higher education will be used to balance overall state budgets in the short-term.

Demography will exert further pressure on states. By 2020, the retirement of baby boomers will cause an exodus from the workforce of 46 million workers with at least some postsecondary education.

Replacing these workers will be an estimated 49 million new adults with at least some college education—a net gain of 3 million. But this gain of 3 million will not be nearly enough. The Bureau of Labor Statistics projects a 22 percent increase in jobs that will require at least some college by 2008. If the trend holds through 2020, roughly 15 million new jobs that require postsecondary-educated workers will be created. In sum, the nation faces a deficit of approximately 12 million workers with at least some college education by 2020. Community colleges will be expected to address this shortage by providing new and additional programs and services. In a tight economy, however, where will the resources come from to develop and sustain new services?

New sources of support. As state spending for higher education declines in periods of economic recession, new sources of revenue will need to be found or community colleges will face the uncomfortable task of reducing their operating budgets. Many colleges are ill-prepared for budgetary reduction: systems for review of programs and services are not in place, performance information is not available, and the culture of most institutions is focused on growth, not decline. To avoid the trauma of reduction, many colleges will turn to new sources of revenue such as training dollars from the corporate sector and private gifts and grants. Resources in these arenas are historically tight, however, in periods of economic recession. What new sources of support will be available to community colleges to finance growth? When will colleges develop a capability to contract—to grow smaller through program and service reductions—as a method to allocate resources to new programs and services?

Accountability. Community colleges, and colleges and universities in general, have been criticized for performing quite poorly over time in reporting performance and cost information to the public. Legislators are reluctant to provide blank checks to institutions that are not accountable for what they do or how they spend public money. What is the effect of poor or weak reporting systems on institutional credibility? What new standards will elected officials put in place to improve accountability? What steps will institutions take to improve cost and performance reporting in a way that will help the public understand what they do?

The Future

What does the future hold for finance in two-year colleges? In the public sector, the long-standing reliance on state appropriations and local tax funds and on student tuition and fees as primary sources of operating income will change dramatically. As economic conditions fluctuate, private sources of revenue will become more important as part of the operating budget. Institutions will seek to establish partnerships as a method for acquiring new revenue and reducing costs.

Community colleges in the twenty-first century will be more complex than their predecessors. At the same time, they will have less mass; many of the functions now handled in-house will be performed through alliances and networks. Shifting market opportunities and continuously evolving external networks will make these organizations dynamic. The power of an institution's "brand" will become increasingly important and new approaches to planning and budgeting will develop around the idea of brand. Budgeting will take on strategic importance as a method for transforming institutions in a turbulent market.

See also: COLLEGE FINANCIAL AID; COMMUNITY COLLEGES; FEDERAL FUNDS FOR HIGHER EDUCATION; STATES AND EDUCATION, *subentry on* STATE GOVERNMENTS IN HIGHER EDUCATION.

BIBLIOGRAPHY

ALFRED, RICHARD L. 2000. "Assessment as a Strategic Weapon." *Community College Journal* 70(4):12–18.

AMERICAN ASSOCIATION OF COMMUNITY COLLEGES. 2000. *National Profile of Community Colleges: Trends and Statistics,* 3rd edition. Washington, DC: American Association of Community Colleges.

CONKLIN, KRISTIN. 2002. "After the Tipping Point." *Change* March/April: 24–29.

NATIONAL CENTER FOR EDUCATION STATISTICS. 1999. *College and University Finance Data.* Washington, DC: National Center for Education Statistics.

SCHMIDT, JAMES A. 1999. "Corporate Excellence in the New Millennium." *Journal of Business Strategy* 20(6):39–43.

RICHARD L. ALFRED

FINANCIAL AID
See: COLLEGE FINANCIAL AID.

FINANCIAL SUPPORT OF SCHOOLS

HISTORY
  Jason L. Walton
CAPITAL OUTLAY IN LOCAL SCHOOL SYSTEMS
  John G. Augenblick
  Anne K. Barkis
  Justin R. Silverstein
STATE SUPPORT
  Lawrence O. Picus

HISTORY

School finance history is characterized by varying degrees of local, state, and federal support. Throughout history, local support of schools has suffered from glaringly inequitable tax structures resulting in wide variations in funding. State intercession has reduced local control but increased equalization in funding through regulations based on conditions associated with state aid. Federal financial activity evolved rapidly in the latter half of the twentieth century with contributions reaching their highest levels in the 1970s and again in the late 1990s. Federal-level rhetoric about support of education reemerged at the beginning of the twenty-first century, but the levels of funding and programmatic efforts were fractured along political divisions. These trends may be viewed within a historical perspective that encompasses five periods, beginning in 1607.

The Colonial Period

The colonial period began with the establishment of the permanent settlement at Jamestown and ended with the conclusion of the Revolutionary War in 1783. During this period, support and control of schooling were exclusively a local matter. Local support, grounded in either the church or the home, grew from limited support of European investors. Monies that were earmarked for education were often redirected to other community needs, such as the building of hospitals. Schooling in the southern colonies was based on apprenticeships or the use of pauper schools. Wealthier areas in the Northeast supported community-financed grammar schools. The wide disparity in a revenue base for schooling mirrored similar disparities in quality of teaching, buildings, and curricula.

Once agreement had been reached to build and finance a school, local communities identified revenue sources that included subscriptions (specified amounts paid by townspeople), rents, donations, bequests, land grants from the British Crown, and other efforts made from the resources of the town. Puritan-Calvinist New England supported taxation to support an education system of common schools for all students, Latin schools for upper grades, and a college for ministerial preparation. A different system evolved in the mid-Atlantic colonies because these colonies did not have a church majority. Parochial schools dominated, despite their inevitable decline because of a lack of state regulation. State interference was resented and opposed. The state had no role or obligation to support such schools. The dominant trend emerging from the colonial period was that public education should not be limited to poor children or require tuition.

The National Period

The national period began with the close of the Revolutionary War and extended through the end of the Civil War. Publicly supported and controlled education was implemented slowly. Financing of schools suffered because of needs associated with national security, the economy, and a significantly rapid increase in population. Local schools became less accessible due to westward expansion. Greater dispersion of the general population resulted in town decentralization and the establishment of the school district. Creating districts extended the concept of local control but resulted in poorer financing and reduced quality. Despite such limitations, the idea of the common school prospered between 1830 and 1865. The idea of tax-supported schools for all children also prospered. The driving mechanism for the common school movement was an expanding national economy based on manufacturing, trade, and industry.

Tax support during this period took a tremendous step forward. The designation in the western territories of sixteenth section township revenue increased support to common schools. (Revenue from the sixteenth section of each township was earmarked for the support of the township's common school.) Revenue obtained from two other sections within each township was also set aside to endow a university. States from the original colonies that did not have township revenue looked to other methods of tax support including literary funds (New York,

Maryland, and New Jersey); liquor-license fees (Connecticut); and state lotteries (New York). Bank taxes were also used between 1825 and 1860. States that did not use direct taxation looked to the property tax, but widespread use of this form of taxation was hard-won. Critics of pauper schools argued that the segregation of the poor into special schools did not represent the American ideal of an egalitarian democracy. Free schools also came under attack, because many were not actually free. In many cases, these schools were supported by rate bills that required a family to pay a tuition based on the number of children attending the school.

One of the main outcomes of the national period was an increase in state supervision with accompanying state requirements. Both outcomes were based on conditional state aid, a tactic also followed by the federal government. Government aid through land endowments to church schools was effectively ended. An outcome of the increase of sectarian control (loss of church dominance) over education was a decrease in the quality of local education and school attendance. This condition continued until state supervision over local outcomes began to increase.

The Post–Civil War Period

The post–Civil War period began with the Reconstruction era and continued until 1905. The Civil War slowed educational expansion in the North, and completely stalled it in the South. Not until 1900 did southern educational standards come to meet the standards of 1860. In the South, education was in such a dilapidated state that the average value of a school building in 1900 was about $100. The South was the last region to establish tax support because of slow improvement in the southern economy and it took the South a much longer time to generate a sufficient revenue stream to meet the needs of a public education system. The North, on the other hand, benefited from rapid urbanization, a vigorous economy, and an increased demand for skilled workers. Taxation reflected earlier trends, with nontax revenues used when possible and the property tax serving as the foundation for securing local support. State funding, when available, was characterized by a wide disparity in levels of aid to wealthy and poor areas.

The Early Reform Period

Beginning in 1905, the early reform period witnessed increases in the general population, the number of students attending school, average daily attendance (ADA), the number of teachers, and programs for handicapped children. Greater revenue was available for maintenance, operations, capital outlay, and transportation. Competition for tax dollars increased due to the growing number of lobbyists for special interest groups. Taxes, while more acceptable, were no more popular, and tax dollars were not automatically available for school support. Of great concern during this time was the idea of finding a fair and equitable means of distributing school funds and of maintaining local control.

This was also the era that witnessed the birth of school finance theory. The evolution of school finance theory can be traced through the work of a handful of scholars. As early as 1905, Ellwood Cubberly argued that the states should be responsible for ensuring that local communities establish and maintain local schools, for requiring employment of qualified teachers for a minimum annual period of time, and for setting requirements for educational outcomes. In 1922 Harlen Updegraff promoted the idea of rewards for local effort, incentive grants, equalization aid, and a variable level foundation program of state assistance based on local tax effort. George Sturgis followed in 1923 with proposed penalties for noncompliance with minimum state standards. Sturgis used a minimum, uniform tax levied for each school district and a level of state aid based on the difference between revenue acquired by a wealthy and a poor district. In 1924 Paul Mort defined a satisfactory minimum program and developed a measure of financial need based on a weighted pupil-typical teacher method that used such factors as ADA, educational level, and size of district. Henry Morrison argued that earlier efforts had failed and proposed a full state support model based on the fact that under law education is a state responsibility. The practical foundation for establishing state support through various aid formulations was created through the work of such theorists.

The Modern Reform Period

The modern reform period began in 1965 when President Lyndon B. Johnson signed the Elementary and Secondary Education Act (ESEA) as part of his War on Poverty. Although this period is known for a diversity of finance-related reforms such as improved property assessment and inclusion of income in district wealth determination, ESEA was the signal event in the evolution of federal financial activity. ESEA enacted a wide range of programs such as Title I, which pushed states to do more to serve their most needy students. Separately, Head Start services were provided for underprivileged preschoolers. Many laws followed ESEA targeting special needs groups including the Bilingual Education Act, the Native American Education Act, and the Education for All Handicapped Children Act (later renamed the Individuals with Disabilities Education Act). Federal aid reached a twentieth-century zenith under the Carter administration (adjusting for inflation), dropped slightly during the Reagan administrations, and resurged again during the two Clinton administrations. Education funding remains a key political issue in the twenty-first century for both Republicans and Democrats, despite their parties' very different views on the funding priorities.

See also: FINANCIAL SUPPORT OF SCHOOLS, *subentries on* CAPITAL OUTLAY IN LOCAL SCHOOL SYSTEMS, STATE SUPPORT.

BIBLIOGRAPHY

ROBELEN, ERIK W. 2000. "The Evolving Federal Role." In *Lessons of a Century: A Nation's Schools Come of Age,* ed. Virginia B. Edwards. Bethesda, MD: Editorial Projects in Education.

VIADERO, DEBBIE. 2000. "Financial Burden Shifts." In *Lessons of a Century: A Nation's Schools Come of Age,* ed. Virginia B. Edwards. Bethesda, MD: Editorial Projects in Education.

WEBB, L. DEAN; MCCARTHY, MARTHA M.; and THOMAS, STEPHEN B. 1988. "History and Background of School Finance." In *Financing Elementary and Secondary Education.* Columbus, OH: Merrill Publishing Company.

JASON L. WALTON

CAPITAL OUTLAY IN LOCAL SCHOOL SYSTEMS

Construction of facilities, including major renovation, additions, and upgrades for technology, is a major expenditure for public schools. Historically these expenses were borne primarily by local school districts, through the issuance of municipal bonds. In the last decade of the twentieth century, states took on a greater role in paying for capital and debt service costs of school districts. The federal government, in a departure from its traditional role, has begun to consider providing a significant amount of support for facilities. This change is stimulated by growing enrollment, the deteriorating condition of buildings, litigation over state funding for facilities, and a desire by lawmakers to equalize funding for facilities as they have done for operating expenditures. States use a variety of approaches to distribute aid for capital, with some states providing a fixed amount per student, some reimbursing districts for a portion of their costs, and some providing support based on a review of the districts' needs. Few components of the school finance system are changing as rapidly as the one focused on facilities.

The Magnitude of Capital Costs

Public elementary and secondary education is provided in more than 91,000 schools nationwide. The majority are elementary schools with enrollments of less than 500 pupils. With the median cost of building a school between $12,500 and $17,000 per student, or $11 million to $26 million per building depending on the school's grade-span, the cost of constructing facilities is a significant component of public school expenditures. In 1997–1998, school districts spent nearly $36.2 billion in capital outlay and debt service, about 9 percent of all expenditures.

Growth in Student Population

Although enrollment in public schools declined in the 1970s and 1980s, from 45.6 million in 1969 to 40.5 million in 1989, enrollment rose in the 1990s and was expected to continue to rise for long into the future. By 1999, enrollment was 46.8 million and projected enrollment for 2009 is 47.1 million. This growth varies from state to state and, more importantly, within states, placing a dramatically different burden on different school districts.

The buildings constructed to accommodate the last wave of enrollment growth have reached the end of their useful lives. Because of the location of population growth and the cost of renovating existing facilities, many new buildings are needed while older buildings are likely to be torn down or used for other purposes.

The Condition of Buildings

Nationally, 76 percent of all public schools require work to bring all school features into good overall condition. Fifty percent have at least one building feature rated less than adequate, and 43 percent of the buildings rate at least one environmental feature less than adequate. Between 1999 and 2001, 51 percent of all U.S. public schools had at least one major repair, renovation or replacement planned. In 1999, 20 percent of public schools had life safety features that rated less than adequate.

More than $5.8 billion in renovations and an additional $5.5 billion in school building additions were scheduled to be completed in 2001. New projects started in 2001 decreased slightly, with $4.6 billion in renovations planned and $5.4 billion in additions. More than 50 percent of all building upgrades planned for 2001 involved electrical overhaul, accommodating new demands for educational technology needs. Of the new middle and high schools constructed in 2001, 100 percent included security equipment. Of all renovations undertaken, more than 89 percent were changes designed to put buildings in compliance with the Americans with Disabilities Act of 1990.

Many studies have been conducted regarding how the atmosphere and environment of buildings affect student learning. These studies examined furniture arrangement, classroom density, noise, and effect of renovation. Furniture arrangement and floor plan reportedly influences student behavior and attitudes toward school. Studies demonstrate that students in high-density classrooms tend to be more aggressive and less socially integrated. Continued exposure to high noise from external sources, such as airports or traffic, correlates with lower reading scores. Children in classrooms with external noise also exhibit greater distractibility, lack of task persistence, and have significantly higher blood pressure than children in quieter settings. Another study showed that elementary school children exposed to noise had lower reading scores and poorer language acquisition. A study comparing performance of children in newly remodeled facilities to those in facilities that had not been renovated reported a positive correlation between parental involvement and condition of school building, and between upgraded school facilities and math achievement.

Litigation

In some states, lawsuits have led to an increase in state funding for capital. A case in Colorado, *Giardino v. State Board of Education,* resulted in a settlement whereby the state agreed to increase assistance to local districts. This case argued that requiring students to attend less than adequate facilities violated their right to due process, and that the funding system in place created too much variation among public schools, denying a thorough and uniform educational opportunity required by the Colorado Constitution. *Roosevelt v. Bishop*, an Arizona case, led the state supreme court to require state funding of all facilities to a minimum standard. The court there determined that the state school facilities board must set "minimum adequacy requirements," which every school facility must meet. In response to this decision, three funds were established, providing approximately $1.3 billion in capital funding. The court also set a date by which facilities must achieve the standard. A 2001 Wyoming state supreme court decision, *State of Wyoming v. Campbell County School District*, found the entire school finance system unconstitutional, but spoke specifically of capital construction, stating that "all facilities must be safe and efficient." It went on to provide a specific definition of safe and efficient, and provided that "the legislature must fund the facilities deemed required by the state" for all students in Wyoming.

State Aid for Capital Purposes

Historically, states played a limited role in paying for school construction. Until the 1980s, the primary role of the state was facilitating the use of bonds by school districts to incur debt for construction; states placed limits on the extent of debt districts could have, typically a proportion of their property value, and required that a supermajority of voters approve the issuance of debt. Some states provide an amount per pupil for capital purposes, others provide loans to school districts, reimburse a fixed percentage of annual debt service, or attempt to pay all capital costs. Some states provide no state aid for school facilities. However, an increasing number of states have implemented new forms of state assistance to supplement local funds. In at least four states, lottery ticket sales are put toward capital expenditures. Florida school districts receive funds from a tax on automobile licensing. California taxes new development to help pay for school construction. Other states have loan, reimbursement, or grant programs that allow local districts to supplement or replace money from local budgets with funds from the state. The state of Arizona, in response to the court ruling, pays for nearly all capital construction in order to ensure a uniform, minimal standard of quality.

The Federal Role

The federal government has provided little support for the capital needs of school districts. During World War II the government provided support to school districts with military installations. This program has continued into the twenty-first century and expanded to include other districts impacted by federal interests. As federal aid for pupils with disabilities expanded after 1965, the government restricted most of its funds to assure that resources were focused on the instructional needs of students. Since the closing years of the twentieth century, attention has been devoted to developing new ways federal aid might be distributed to assist school districts in meeting facilities needs. These include the use of the tax system, through tax credits and tax waivers, to stimulate investment while avoiding direct expenditures. While the federal government is concerned about the condition of buildings and the need for new facilities, it may need to recognize that some of the other policies it promotes, from expanded use of technology to smaller class size, have implications for facilities.

Other Capital Issues

A variety of other issues have implications for capital funding in the future. One issue is class size. Many states are considering requiring smaller class sizes, particularly in early grades, in light of the literature that supports such a policy. If states do require smaller classes, not only would more teachers be needed but more classrooms would be required as well, creating a major impact on elementary schools. Another issue is the expanding use of schools for preschool as well as for learning opportunities for parents. As more states consider moving to full-day kindergarten or providing preschool activities, the demand for space will increase. Schools may respond to this demand in the same way that some have dealt with playgrounds, athletic facilities, and libraries: by sharing their use with municipalities, which allows costs to be shared.

Another issue is technology. As more schools invest in hardware and software, several issues emerge: (1) the capacity to handle the telecommunications wiring and space needs for technology; (2) sufficient equipment to assure access to technology for all students; and (3) the frequency of upgrading technology. This last issue raises the distinction between current operating expenditures—costs consumed in one year—and capital expenditures, which typically have a period of use over which costs may be depreciated. Many technological supplies and materials might be expected to last three to five years, creating a new category of expenditures.

A final issue is emerging from both the states' use of new accountability systems, and the expanding use of technology. As more students can fulfill graduation requirements without actually attending school, and more students use technology to take courses and do homework, the concept of a school may change. If schools serve as a place where students meet with teachers periodically, rather than a place they spend a specific amount of time each day, school buildings, particularly high schools, could take on a new look and become smaller than they are now. The cost of these buildings could decrease substantially. At a minimum, the internal organization of schools might change, reducing the need for libraries, laboratories, and auditoriums, which would lower their cost in communities that had those facilities available in other buildings.

See also: FINANCIAL SUPPORT OF SCHOOLS, *subentries on* HISTORY, STATE SUPPORT; SCHOOL FACILITIES.

BIBLIOGRAPHY

GERALD, DEBRA E., and HUSSAR, WILLIAM J. 2000. *Projections of Education Statistics to 2010.* Washington, DC: U.S. Department of Education, National Center for Education Statistics.

LEWIS, LAURIE, et al. 2000. *Condition of America's Public School Facilities: 1999.* Washington, DC: U.S. Department of Education, National Center for Education Statistics.

MAXWELL, LORRAINE E. 1999. *School Building Renovation and Student Performance: One District's Experience.* Scottsdale, AZ: The Council of Educational Facility Planners International.

SNYDER, THOMAS D., and HOFFMAN, CHARLENE M. 1993. *Digest of Education Statistics 1993.* Washington, DC: U.S. Department of Education, National Center for Education Statistics.

SNYDER, THOMAS D., and HOFFMAN, CHARLENE M. 2000. *Digest of Education Statistics 2000.* Washington, DC: U.S. Department of Education, National Center for Education Statistics.

INTERNET RESOURCES

ABRAMSON, PAUL. 2002. "2002 Construction Report." <www.peterli.com/spm/special/constrpt/2002/2000rpt.cfm>.

SIELKE, CATHERINE C., et al. 2001. "Public School Finance Programs of the U.S. and Canada: 1998–1999." <http://nces.ed.gov/pubsearch/pubsinfo.asp?pubid=2001309>.

JOHN G. AUGENBLICK
ANNE K. BARKIS
JUSTIN R. SILVERSTEIN

STATE SUPPORT

School finance involves the interrelated issues of raising, distributing, allocating, and using revenues for the purpose of educating children. Early in the twentieth century, local school districts were primarily responsible for providing funds—mostly through property taxes—for schools. Considerable disparities in the per pupil property wealth of school districts led to dramatic differences in both local property tax rates and in the amount of money available for schools. It was not uncommon to find districts with very low tax rates and high expenditures as well as districts with high tax rates and low expenditures.

In 1968 plaintiffs in California filed the first successful legal challenge, known as the *Serrano* case, to such school funding systems. The California state supreme court held that such inequities were unconstitutional and ordered the state to equalize spending differences based on property wealth. Challenges have been filed in most other states and have been successful in about half of these cases. In the late 1980s, plaintiffs began to challenge state funding systems by arguing that they do not provide adequate resources for education. These cases have been successful in a number of states, most notably in Kentucky, Ohio, and Wyoming.

Faced with such court rulings, or in many cases simply faced with a legal challenge, states have increased the level of support for schools. Whereas in 1920, local property taxes accounted for nearly 90 percent of school district revenues, by 2001, the federal government provided about 6 percent of school revenues with the remaining 94 percent shared approximately equally between states and local school districts. Although these percentages vary considerably from state to state, the general pattern of increased state involvement in the funding of schools is clear.

States rely on two major types of intergovernmental grants to school districts and use a variety of distribution formulas to actually allocate funds to each district. The two major types of grants are *general aid* and *categorical grants.*

General Aid

General—or unrestricted—aid represents the largest source of state revenue for local school districts in all of the states. General aid is money distributed to school districts with relatively few strings attached. This money, combined with local resources, usually represents between 70 and 90 percent of a district's budget and is spent for such things as teacher salaries, administrators, operations, and maintenance, instructional support, and the general operations of the schools. Much of this money is distributed to school districts in inverse relation to the local property wealth per pupil, with the intended consequence of equalizing differences in revenue capacity. States use the following mechanisms to allocate general aid to school districts.

Flat grants. A flat grant is a fixed amount of money given to each school district regardless of need. Popular in the early twentieth century, flat grants, if they are used at all, are relatively small today. Flat grants have lost favor because of their disequalizing impact and the fact that they provide assistance to districts regardless of local property wealth.

Foundation programs. Under a foundation program, the state establishes a base—or foundation—level of revenue that each district should maintain. It also establishes a required tax rate that each district must levy. The state then provides resources to each school district to make up the difference between the foundation level and how much is raised by that school district though the required property tax rate. If a district raises more than the required amount some states take those additional funds and use them to finance the state's share in other districts. This process is known as *recapture.* A foundation program works well in states where the court has ruled that some minimum level of funding is necessary to insure adequate educational opportunities.

Guaranteed yield. Another approach is to guarantee each district the ability to raise money as if it had a specified level of property wealth. The state estab-

lishes a guaranteed wealth level and as under the foundation program, districts with per pupil property wealth below that guarantee are given state aid so that at any tax rate they can raise as much revenue as the district whose wealth is equal to the guarantee. As before, wealthy districts are able to raise more than the guarantee. Some states recapture this difference and others do not.

The principle difference between foundation programs and guaranteed yield programs is that under a foundation program all districts are required to level a fixed tax rate and have the same revenue guarantee. This provides for considerable equity across districts, but limits local choices over how much to spend. Districts seeking to spend more than the foundation guarantee must do so with unequalized local property taxes. To the extent that the foundation level defined by the state does not grow as fast as school district revenue needs, larger portions of total revenue will become unequalized. This problem occurred in many states in the last half of the twentieth century.

Guaranteed yield programs specify a wealth guarantee. This gives districts more flexibility in determining how much they wish to spend, and insures that all districts (whose wealth is less than or equal to the guaranteed level) have access to the same level of per pupil revenue with equal tax rates. This approach allows for more local choice, but if the wealth guarantee does not keep up with growth in property values in the state, it too can lead to substantial portions of local revenue not being equalized.

A common solution to this problem is a two-tiered approach to distributing general aid to school districts. The first tier is a traditional foundation program requiring all districts to levy a minimum property tax and guaranteeing funding at a minimum level. The second tier relies on a guaranteed yield system, offering districts an equal amount of revenue per pupil for each increment in property tax rate above the foundation required tax rate. This guarantee often is capped at some level. Some states even allow districts an unequalized property tax above the second tier.

Categorical Grants

Not all students have the same needs. Some children have disabilities that require special assistance to help them learn. There is also considerable evidence that children from low-income homes are at a disadvantage in learning compared to children from higher-income families. Therefore, simply providing an equal level of revenue for each child may not offer equal educational opportunities. In addition, the characteristics of school districts may lead to differences in cost structures that must be compensated for if all children are to have equal access to educational services. Categorical grants are generally used by states to compensate for these differences in student and district characteristics. Among the categorical approaches most frequently in place are the following.

Pupil weighting. Something of a hybrid between general and categorical aid, the practice of pupil weighting counts students with special needs more than once before general state aid is distributed to school districts. For example, a child with a learning disability may receive an additional weight of one, meaning he or she is counted as two students for the purpose of state aid distribution. This has the effect of reducing the districts per pupil property wealth and hence increasing the state aid per pupil, and of providing that state aid for that child twice. It is assumed that the additional revenues will be used to meet the needs of the children who generate the funds, although not all states actually require that.

Program-specific grants. An alternative approach, program-specific grants give districts additional money based on child or district characteristics. For example, grants could be provided to help fund the special educational needs of children with disabilities. This can come in the form of direct reimbursements, or paying a fixed amount of money for each child so identified. In the case of compensatory education (money for children from low-income homes), additional revenue is often provided to enhance educational opportunities. Generally it is required that the funds be spent on the children who generated the funds in the first place.

States also provide categorical funds to assist districts with programs where costs may vary for reasons that are out of the control of the district. For example, geographically large but sparsely populated districts generally have higher transportation costs per pupil than do more densely populated urban districts. Many states provide separate transportation assistance to districts to compensate for these differences.

Geographic cost differences. In addition to the cost differences that school districts experience described above, across most states there are substantial differences in the costs of the personnel, supplies and materials that schools purchase. Some states have begun to make adjustments to state aid formulas to accommodate these differences. For example, the costs of housing may be higher in large urban areas of a state compared to rural areas. In addition, there may be more competition for individuals with high levels of education and training (such as teachers) in some areas of a state. As a result, it may cost a district more to provide exactly the same services different parts of any state. Therefore, a geographic cost adjustment could be included in the state aid formula to adjust for those differences. These adjustments are often controversial and frequently poorly understood by state policy makers. Their intent is to equalize differences in costs faced by school districts that are out of their control. But legislators faced with allocating more money to other parts of the state often have difficulty supporting such adjustments and as a result they are only infrequently used today.

It is likely that over time, as lawsuits focused on school funding adequacy grow in importance, the state share of support for public education will grow. How states elect to distribute funds to local school districts will not only continue to be an important policy issue, but its importance will grow over time.

See also: FINANCIAL SUPPORT OF SCHOOLS, *subentries on* HISTORY, CAPITAL OUTLAY IN LOCAL SCHOOL SYSTEMS; SCHOOL FACILITIES; STATES AND EDUCATION.

BIBLIOGRAPHY

ODDEN, ALLAN R., and PICUS, LAWRENCE O. 2000. *School Finance: A Policy Perspective,* 2nd edition. New York: McGraw Hill.

LADD, HELEN F.; CHALK, ROSEMARY; and HANSEN, JANET S. 1999. *Equity and Adequacy in Education Finance: Issues and Perspectives.* Washington, DC: National Academy Press.

LAWRENCE O. PICUS

FLEXNER, ABRAHAM (1866–1959)

Author of the monumental survey *Medical Education in the United States and Canada* (1910), Abraham Flexner contributed to a period of reform in

American medical education that hastened the closing of commercial medical schools and strengthened university-affiliated institutions adopting scientific approaches. A Louisville, Kentucky, native who earned his A.B. degree at Johns Hopkins University, Flexner established his own preparatory school in Louisville. However, he gained prominence as an educator through his critical essays, surveys, and reports about American educational institutions and practices. Throughout the early twentieth century, Flexner's ideas wielded influence through the sponsorship and largesse of powerful corporate foundations. Finally, from 1930 through 1939, Flexner designed and directed the Institute for Advanced Study at Princeton.

Early Learning and Teaching Experiences

Born into a poor but ambitious family, Flexner developed an appetite for reading and studying outside of school. The endorsement of a Johns Hopkins alumnus sent Flexner to Baltimore in 1884, and an older brother's modest business income provided funds for his college tuition and expenses. Although inexperienced in the prerequisite studies of Latin and Greek, Flexner exercised industry and gained mastery of the classical languages. Against the norm, Flexner earned his bachelor's degree in two years.

Flexner returned to Louisville and secured employment in the Louisville High School, where he taught primarily Greek and Latin for four years. Supplementing his salary through private tutoring after school proved challenging and lucrative, however, and in 1890 Flexner opened his own school. This endeavor allowed Flexner to practice a rigorous and progressive student-centered pedagogy without the customary rules, tests, and reports. "Mr. Flexner's School" earned the reputation for preparing wealthy and sometimes troublesome boys for college. Furthermore, Flexner's work caught the attention of college presidents in the Northeast, who noticed that Flexner's students outperformed graduates of eastern prep schools. Flexner's pedagogical authority increased through articles he authored about his work in *The Educational Review* and *The International Journal of Ethics*.

Attaining Status as Educational Expert

In 1904 Abraham Flexner closed his school and left Kentucky with his wife, Anne Crawford Flexner, to pursue advanced study at Harvard University. Despite Flexner's initial enthusiasm, he left the university after a year, disappointed in his professors and assistantship. Never to earn an advanced degree, Flexner embarked instead upon an extended period of observation of all types of schools and universities both in New York and Europe. In his study and travel, Flexner benefited from sponsors and social acquaintances, including those of his brother Dr. Simon Flexner of the Rockefeller Institute for Medical Research. Thus, Flexner enjoyed unequalled access to institutions and introductions to professors, researchers, and foreign ministers. Settling at the University of Berlin and later Heidelberg, Flexner penned his first book, *The American College: A Criticism,* an overall critique of Harvard, which was based upon his personal experiences, including a scathing indictment of the elective system. This book, published in 1908 upon Flexner's return to America, received little notice except by the president of the Carnegie Foundation for the Advancement of Teaching, Dr. Henry S. Pritchett. Pritchett soon offered Flexner the opportunity to conduct the survey of medical schools that elevated him to national prominence.

To Henry Pritchett, Abraham Flexner was a "layman educator" capable of completing a key assignment in the Carnegie Foundation's larger institutional classification scheme, (i.e., differentiating colleges from secondary schools; universities from colleges, and accounting for appropriate work at each level). A vanguard force in the early-twentieth-century movement to increase standardization, efficiency, effectiveness, and the use of scientific methods, Pritchett deemed the Carnegie Foundation a champion of the public good. Pritchett presumed that Flexner's exhaustive survey of medical schools would improve American medical care by exposing society's overabundance of poorly trained physicians and the inferiority of its commercial medical schools. In combination with other social trends, Flexner's observations and scathing critique nurtured the scientific and professional practice of medicine. Specifically, schools labeled inferior eventually closed, the competing practice of homeopathy lost momentum, the admissions standards for prospective medical students increased, and the professional authority and status of university-trained physicians soared. Flexner's report earned him accolades and afterward he conducted a complete study of medical education in Europe.

Flexner continued to be a part of the elite circles of foundation administrators and consulted often in matters of benefaction. In 1913 Flexner's foundation role became formalized through an appointment as assistant secretary to another Rockefeller-funded philanthropy, the General Education Board (GEB). Flexner worked for the GEB until 1929, having advanced to the position of executive secretary and member of the board. Importantly, Flexner's "expertise" as an educational reformer achieved new significance, with the philanthropy of the GEB behind him as a powerful incentive for institutional change. For example, from his studies of medical education Flexner advocated full-time appointments for clinical teachers in medical schools. Thus, those university medical schools first willing to require full-time clinical staffs (e.g. Johns Hopkins, Yale, Chicago, Cornell, Vanderbilt, and Iowa) received large foundation grants.

However, Flexner's GEB work was not limited to medical education. Flexner continued to practice sponsorship by offering financial support to promising scholars for research and travel. Also, Flexner directed extensive surveys and evaluations of public school systems. Maryland, Delaware, North Carolina, Indiana, and Kentucky, to name a few, contracted with the GEB for these services. Finally, Flexner created and established the Lincoln School at Teachers College, Columbia University, through a GEB endowment gift. Highly regarded for its experimental pedagogy, the Lincoln School eschewed the classical curriculum for modern languages, science, and social studies.

Retirement and the Institute for Advanced Study

Upon his retirement from the GEB, Flexner accepted the prestigious invitation for residence at Oxford for the Rhodes Trust Memorial Lectures, which later he published as *Universities: American, English, German* in 1930. Extolling the intellectual vigor of the German research tradition, this work became institutionalized as Flexner obtained a gift of $5 million to create and direct the Institute for Advanced Study at Princeton. Ironically, the intellectual life of Flexner's institute benefited from the increasing repression of German universities, as foreign scholars, most notably Albert Einstein, found a place for research in the United States. Flexner left the institute in 1939 to spend his final years producing his autobiography and several other books.

See also: EDUCATION REFORM, *subentries on* OVERVIEW, REPORTS OF HISTORICAL SIGNIFICANCE; GRADUATE SCHOOL TRAINING; MASTER'S DEGREE, THE; MEDICAL EDUCATION.

BIBLIOGRAPHY

BERLINER, HOWARD S. 1985. *A System of Scientific Medicine: Philanthropic Foundations in the Flexner Era.* New York: Tavistock.

FLEXNER, ABRAHAM. 1908. *The American College: A Criticism.* New York: Century.

FLEXNER, ABRAHAM. 1910. *Medical Education in the United States and Canada.* New York: Carnegie Foundation for the Advancement of Teaching.

FLEXNER, ABRAHAM. 1930. *Universities: American, English, German.* New York: Oxford University Press.

FLEXNER, ABRAHAM. 1940. *I Remember: The Autobiography of Abraham Flexner.* New York: Simon and Schuster.

WHEATLEY, STEVEN. 1988. *The Politics of Philanthropy: Abraham Flexner and Medical Education.* Madison: University of Wisconsin Press.

AMY E. WELLS

FOREIGN LANGUAGE EDUCATION

Foreign language education in the United States at the beginning of the twenty-first century is energized by some of the most dramatic developments in its modern history. Proficiency movement and standards initiatives have changed the focus of language instruction and assessment. Implications of emerging brain research have fueled renewed interest in early and intensive language learning for children in the first years of formal schooling, as well as programwide emphasis on meaningful use of language in authentic contexts. The resources of the Internet and other technology tools provide new opportunities for students to have direct experiences with the target language and its cultures, both within and beyond the school setting.

Proficiency

The American Council on the Teaching of Foreign Languages (ACTFL) Proficiency Guidelines, first published in 1986, shifted the emphasis in language instructional goals from what learners know *about* language to what they can *do with* the language they have learned, and at the same time they established a common metric for measuring student performance. The Proficiency Guidelines describe student performance in listening, speaking, reading, and writing at the novice, intermediate, advanced, and superior levels. They were adapted from guidelines developed in U.S. government language schools and have made "proficiency-oriented instruction" a part of the vocabulary of every language teacher. The 1986 guidelines were subsequently reevaluated and revised, beginning with the 1999 document "ACTFL Proficiency Guidelines—Speaking" and with the 2001 document "Preliminary Proficiency Guidelines—Writing."

Standards

The *Standards for Foreign Language Learning in the Twenty-First Century,* introduced in 1996 and revised in 1999, created the bold vision of a long sequence of language instruction for all learners, beginning in kindergarten and continuing through grade twelve and beyond. Eleven content standards were clustered within five major goals:

- Communication: Communicate in Languages Other than English

- Cultures: Gain Knowledge and Understanding of Other Cultures

- Connections: Connect with Other Disciplines and Acquire Information

- Comparisons: Develop Insight into the Nature of Language and Culture

- Communities: Participate in Multilingual Communities at Home and Around the World

Sample performance indicators were provided for grades four, eight, and twelve, and sample learning scenarios described classroom activities that reflect the standards. After introduction of the general standards in 1996, supporting documents were developed for nine languages and were included in the 1999 edition.

ACTFL Performance Guidelines for K–12 Learners, devised in 1998, support the content standards with descriptions of student performance. Based on both the Proficiency Guidelines and the *Standards* document, the Performance Guidelines reinforce the vision of the K–12 sequence and dramatize the idea that proficiency development requires time and intensity of language instruction.

Assessment

The Oral Proficiency Interview (OPI) is the tool by which trained interviewers place foreign language speakers on a proficiency continuum from novice to superior. By focusing on the ability to use the language to accomplish communicative tasks of increasing complexity, the OPI has influenced curriculum, teaching, and assessment, as well as standards for licensure of language teachers.

The application of the proficiency model to the other language skills of writing, reading, and comprehension created a new focus in assessment on performance tasks rather than linguistic manipulation. Teachers create contexts and rubrics for evaluating student performance and portfolios of student work, in addition to more traditional tests of accuracy and grammatical competence.

Because of the usefulness of performance assessments, adaptations of OPI-based assessments have been developed for use in K–8 settings and for articulation between high school and college programs. The Center for Applied Linguistics developed an oral interview for students in immersion and other elementary school language programs called the Student Oral Proficiency Assessment. Similar to the OPI, this test uses contexts and environments more appropriate to the child in grades three to five. Another test, the Early Language Listening and Oral Proficiency Assessment, was subsequently developed for language learners from pre-K to grade two. These tests are intended primarily for program evaluation, although they give teachers feedback on effectiveness of teaching and student progress, as well as tools for constructing their own classroom oral assessments.

Technology

The growing use of technology throughout society has had an impact on foreign language instruction as well, especially at the middle and high school level. The language labs of the 1960s and 1970s have become multimedia learning laboratories. Students and teachers supplement their textbooks with CD-ROMs, access foreign-language websites, hold online conversations with students in other countries, and interact regularly with their "key pals," often in the target language. Many students keep electronic portfolios and build culminating projects using Internet resources and multimedia software such as PowerPoint or HyperStudio. They may create individual or class web pages, and outstanding student work may appear on the school web page. Teachers use the web to post activities and information, to communicate with parents and the community, and to provide resources for students, parents, and other teachers. In many respects the Internet is the realization of a long-held dream: Students can be in regular contact with authentic foreign language resources, both at school and at home, and they can use the target language for meaningful, personal purposes.

Technology can also help teachers and school districts provide foreign language instruction even in remote and isolated settings. Interactive television has made it possible for one Spanish teacher in North Dakota, for example, to reach students in schools many miles away. Interactive television can bring a Russian or a Japanese class to one or two high school students who would otherwise have to wait until college to enroll in the language of their choice. Distance learning is the only option for language education for some rural and isolated school districts. Because of the popularity of distance learning and the special conditions necessary for its success, the National Council of State Supervisors of Foreign Language issued a position paper on the topic in 2002.

Support for Foreign Language Teachers

K–12 foreign language teachers of the early twenty-first century have unprecedented support and resources available to them. Each of the major languages has a national organization that provides guidelines, resources, and sometimes funding to assist teachers and programs. The American Council on the Teaching of Foreign Languages (ACTFL) serves as an umbrella organization for all languages, and in this role it has initiated major projects such as the ACTFL Proficiency Guidelines, the *Standards,* and the ACTFL Performance Guidelines for K–12 Learners. Teachers also have access to state and national conferences sponsored by these organizations, as well as regional conferences such as the Northeast Conference on the Teaching of Foreign Languages, the Southern Conference on Language Teaching, the Southwest Conference on Language Teaching, and the Central States Conference on Teaching Foreign Languages. Most sessions at these conferences focus on curriculum and pedagogy for the K–12 level.

The Center for Applied Linguistics provides research and information about K–12 language learning, and its Educational Resources Information Center (ERIC) Clearinghouse on Languages and Linguistics offers a wide range of resources in foreign language education. The language resource centers were established by Congress in 1989 to serve as resources to improve the nation's capacity to teach and learn foreign languages effectively. One of these, the K–12 Foreign Language Resource Center at Iowa State University, is focused specifically on issues of curriculum, assessment, and teacher development for K–12 programs.

Listservs provide teachers with the opportunity to post questions about programs, materials, or methodology and share their ideas with colleagues from all over the country. Two of the most popular are FLTeach, used especially by middle and high school teachers, and Nandu, the early language listserv for K–8 teachers. Many other listservs address the needs of specific languages and topic areas.

Elementary School Foreign Language Programs

Paul Garcia, then president of the ACTFL, was asked in a 2000 interview in *Curriculum Technology Quarterly* about new trends in foreign language education. He identified the continuing growth of foreign language programs for primary school learners as the most important trend and made special note of immersion education within that development. After a surge in the 1960s and a steep decline in the 1970s and early 1980s, interest in early language learning accelerated and sustained momentum through the turn of the century.

National reports played a strong role in this reawakening of interest. These reports included:

- *Strength through Wisdom,* a 1979 report of the President's Commission on Foreign Language and International Studies, which specifically recommended that language learning begin in the elementary school and continue throughout a student's schooling.

- *A Nation at Risk,* a 1983 report of the National Commission on Excellence in Education, which ranked foreign language education at the same level as the "basic academic fields."

Such reports emphasized the national and economic importance of attaining a level of proficiency in a foreign language that could only be accomplished over a long period of study.

Further impetus for early language learning came from results and interpretation of brain research, brought to popular awareness through reports in *Newsweek* in 1996 and *Time* in 1997. In the

Time article, J. Madeline Nash wrote, "The ability to learn a second language is highest between birth and the age of six, and then undergoes a steady and inexorable decline. . . . What lessons can be drawn from the new findings? Among other things, it is clear that foreign languages should be taught in elementary school, if not before" (p. 56).

A number of states responded with mandates for teaching languages at the elementary school level, in some cases without funding to support the new programs. By 2002 there were mandates for foreign languages in the elementary school curriculum in at least eight states: Arizona, Arkansas, Louisiana, Montana, New Jersey, North Carolina, Oklahoma, and Wyoming. Other states worked without a mandate to increase and promote elementary school foreign language offerings.

In 1997 there were foreign language programs in 31 percent of all public and private elementary schools surveyed by the Center for Applied Linguistics, up from 22 percent in 1987. Spanish was taught in 79 percent of the programs, followed by French at 27 percent. Programs in German, Latin, Japanese, and Spanish for Spanish speakers were also well represented.

Elementary school foreign language programs generally fit into three major categories: immersion, FLES (foreign languages in elementary schools), and FLEX (foreign language exploration or experience).

Immersion education. Foreign language immersion programs, in which the content of the school curriculum is taught in the foreign language, are among the most influential innovations of the final decades of the twentieth century. Immersion goals are twofold: fluency in the foreign language and mastery of the content of the school curriculum. Most immersion programs begin in kindergarten or grade one, and many continue through the middle and high school levels. The first North American public school immersion program began in 1965 with a kindergarten in St. Lambert, a suburb of Montreal, Canada. Supported and advised by researchers from McGill University in Montreal, this French program was shaped by sound professional advice and carefully researched as it progressed from one grade to the next. Longitudinal research validated the effectiveness of immersion in meeting both language and content goals and served to inspire new immersion programs across Canada and in the United States.

The first U.S. immersion program was established in Spanish in Culver City, California, in 1971.

In 1974 a total immersion program in French began in Montgomery County, Maryland, and partial immersion programs in French, Spanish, and German began in Cincinnati, Ohio. Other programs soon followed, and by 1993 approximately 28,200 students were enrolled in nine languages in 139 programs, in twenty-five states and Washington, DC. Spanish was the most frequently taught language, followed by French, Japanese, and German. By 1999 the total number of immersion schools had risen to 278, with approximate 46,000 students enrolled, in eleven languages. More than half the programs were in Spanish.

In *total immersion* programs all instruction during the school day is conducted in the target language, beginning with four- or five-year-olds in kindergarten, and children learn to read first in their new language. English language instruction is usually introduced in grade two or three, commonly for a half hour per day, and is gradually increased each year until by grade five or six, 20 to 40 percent of the day is taught in English.

Partial immersion programs deliver the curriculum in the English language for approximately half the school day and in the foreign language for the other half of the day. Children learn to read in both languages simultaneously or in English first and then in the new language. This balance of English and foreign language instruction continues from the beginning of schooling until grade five or six.

Both total immersion and partial immersion are designed primarily for native speakers of English, although native speakers of other languages are also successful immersion students. In most cases the teacher is the only fluent language model for the students in the classroom. *Two-way immersion*, or *bilingual immersion*, is a model that grew rapidly after its introduction in 1963. In this approach, native speakers of English and the target language learn together, half a day in one language and half a day in the other. Each group of students is learning in its new language during half the school day, and student native speakers serve as language models for one another. By 2000 there were 260 programs in twenty-three states, most of them in Spanish. This model depends on the presence of a stable population of native speakers of both languages, and the growing Spanish population in the United States creates ideal conditions for two-way Spanish immersion programs.

FLES (foreign languages in elementary schools) programs. FLES programs have a long history in the

United States, with a notable surge in popularity in the 1960s and a resurgence in the late 1980s. As generally defined, FLES programs are part of a long sequence of language study, beginning before middle school, that lead to continuing courses at the middle and high school levels. The programs of the late 1980s emphasized integrated, thematic planning and a close connection with the general elementary school curriculum. Some "content-based" or "content-related" programs make a special effort to reinforce student learning in other content areas. Class periods range from ten to forty minutes in length, from once to five times per week.

This variability of starting points, instructional time, and degree of content orientation has made it very difficult to evaluate the overall results of FLES programs. The task force that developed the "ACTFL Performance Guidelines for K–12 Learners" addressed this problem by recommending that "the accomplishment of such content standards (in the ACTFL *Standards* document) required students to be enrolled in elementary programs that meet from 3–5 days per week for no less than 30–40 minutes per class" (Swender and Duncan, p. 482).

The Georgia ESFL (elementary school foreign language) model programs, established in 1992 with state funding, provide a clear picture of what is possible in a FLES program. Georgia model programs were designed to provide optimum conditions for language learning and to serve as a case study for the amount of language proficiency children can attain after six years of language study. Program guidelines require participating schools to offer a foreign language for thirty minutes per day, five days per week, beginning in kindergarten and continuing at least through grade five. Instruction is delivered in the target language, and teachers are expected to teach no more than eight classes per day. Testing in 1996, 1998, and 2001 by the Center for Applied Linguistics affirmed the outstanding results of these programs in all the languages represented—French, German, Japanese, and Spanish—and the 2001 report commended the program as a model for the entire United States.

FLEX programs (foreign language exploration or experience). Some school districts that find it impossible to fund more intensive foreign language programs for all students offer short-term programs that give learners a sample of one or more languages over a limited period of time. In 1994 Helena Curtain and Carol Ann Bjornstad Pesola characterized

FLEX programs as "frequent and regular sessions over a short period of time or short and/or infrequent sessions over an extended period of time" (p. 30). These programs have limited goals, usually stated in terms of interest and awareness, and in some cases they are taught mostly in English. Sometimes FLEX programs are offered as a way of helping students choose which language they will later study in depth. When carefully designed and well taught, FLEX programs can serve to enhance cultural awareness and motivate future language study, but they do not claim measurable language skills as an outcome.

Middle School Programs

Middle school programs face several major challenges. The first is the learners themselves, who have developmental characteristics that require instructional materials and strategies that are different both from those appropriate for the elementary school and from those effective with high school students. These needs are not adequately met by simply extending textbook instruction over two years instead of one, a typical program format. Second, as elementary school programs continue to grow, the middle school is literally caught in the middle of the long sequence, with a responsibility to coordinate with both elementary school and high school programs. Experienced language learners need continuation courses in the same language learned in the elementary school, and they also benefit from the option to begin a third language in the middle school. Middle schools that receive students from immersion programs or K–5/6 FLES programs sometimes offer content courses taught in the target language, especially mathematics and social studies. Third, middle schools have very limited time available for electives, and so long as foreign language classes are viewed as electives, they are often in competition with such attractive options as music, art, and applied arts.

Exploratory programs, long a popular approach for the middle school, fit well with the philosophy of exploration that has been a hallmark of the middle school curriculum. While FLEX programs may equip students to make an experience-based choice of a language for further study, they do not fit well with the projected K–12 sequence of the *Standards* document, nor with the recommendations of the task force for the ACTFL Performance Guidelines, which call for "middle school programs that meet daily for no less than 40–50 minutes" (Schwender and Duncan, p. 482). These programs also do not meet the needs of learners who have spent four to seven years in an elementary school FLES or immersion program.

A typical middle school format before the advent of proficiency and the *Standards* document included one semester to one year of the language in grade seven, followed by one semester to one year in grade eight, both considered to be "Level One." Students entering grade nine would then be eligible to enroll in "Level Two" of the language. This format, often preceded by a one-semester or one-year exploratory program, continues to be typical at the beginning of the twenty-first century.

Clearly the variety of programs at the middle school level, ranging from nothing to a continuation of an effective elementary school program, made the *Standards* vision of a K–12 foreign language sequence difficult to attain. As Myriam Met pointed out in 1996, "Foreign language instruction in middle schools will be critical to the success of long sequences in the coming years" (p. 1).

High School Programs

The curriculum at the high school level has continued to be textbook-driven, although proficiency and the *Standards* have had a growing impact on textbooks, methodology, and student success. Teachers use partner and group work to help students develop strong communication skills. Influenced by the *Standards,* many teachers build units thematically, focus them on culminating projects, and integrate content from the general curriculum.

As with the middle school level, there is a vast variability across the country in terms of access to foreign language instruction at the high school level. Students in districts with well-developed K–12 programs emerge with impressive levels of proficiency from full five- to six-year programs spanning middle school and high school. At the same time there are other students, often in rural areas, who have virtually no access to foreign language instruction. Some schools have addressed the problem of access through the use of interactive television or by encouraging summer enrollment in various college or camp offerings.

Block scheduling in many schools has challenged teachers to rethink how they involve students with learning over class periods lasting ninety minutes and longer. Lack of continuity in language study, common in block scheduling, can create obstacles to the attainment of proficiency goals and place added stress on students and teachers.

In years three to five of the high school curriculum, a number of programs offer courses leading to the International Baccalaureate (IB), a schoolwide program that entitles graduates to enter universities around the world. Other programs offer Advanced Placement (AP) classes, which prepare students to take examinations that can result in college credit. Both IB and AP classes tend to focus on literature. Some states offer college-in-the-schools programs that allow advanced students to take college courses in their high school environment.

Many schools offer travel programs for foreign language students, often during spring or summer breaks, and in some cases a partner school in the target culture also sends students to the United States. These opportunities for authentic language practice are popular with students and teachers. Even short programs help to solidify language skills and motivate further language study. Other authentic language opportunities are found in popular weekend and summer language camps, such as the Concordia Language Villages in northern Minnesota.

Foreign Language Programs in Other Countries

A study of nineteen countries on six continents completed by the Center for Applied Linguistics in 2000 identified a number of contrasts between U.S. programs and those elsewhere. Most of the countries surveyed require the study of at least one foreign language, beginning in elementary grades. Some countries require two languages in the course of schooling, and Israel requires three languages—Hebrew plus two others. In countries of the European Union, foreign language study is moving earlier and earlier in the curriculum, and many countries begin in first grade.

Another contrast with the United States is the presence of strong language policy in many of the surveyed countries. Such policies include compulsory foreign language education, a national curriculum or curriculum framework, and designated amounts of time required for foreign language instruction. In many of the countries surveyed foreign languages are considered to be core subjects. In Germany, for example, languages command the same status and time commitment as mathematics, reading, and social studies. All of these policies stand in sharp contrast to the U.S. school setting.

The influence of immersion education and content-based instruction is notable in Europe and Australia, as increasing numbers of programs use the target language as a tool and not only a focus of instruction. Canada continues to show leadership in the development of and research into immersion programs, mainly for English-speaking learners of French. Two-way immersion programs are proliferating in Germany and Australia.

Communicative language teaching methods have been increasingly evident in Europe. As political and economic barriers among European countries have dropped away, the need to function in several languages has increased sharply, and priority has been placed on proficiency in written and spoken language. These priorities are reflected in both materials and teaching approaches. The Goethe Institute, a German government organization that provides German language instruction throughout the world, has been a leader in the development and dissemination of communicative teaching methodologies.

Challenges for K–12 Foreign Languages

As teachers work toward the vision of K–12 language programs and performance-based curriculum and instruction, several major challenges await them. First, developing smooth transitions from elementary to middle to high school, and then from high school to colleges and universities, will be a high priority. Making time for languages in the crowded middle school curriculum will be a major obstacle. Using the resources of technology to stretch the potential of the language classroom will be a constant challenge, especially as the technology continues to provide new opportunities. Teachers continue to be in short supply at all levels. Finally, there is the fundamental challenge: claiming a secure place in the school day and in the K–12 curriculum for foreign language instruction.

See also: CURRICULUM, SCHOOL; ELEMENTARY EDUCATION, *subentry on* CURRENT TRENDS; LANGUAGE ACQUISITION; SCHOOL REFORM; SECONDARY EDUCATION, *subentry on* CURRENT TRENDS.

BIBLIOGRAPHY

ACCESS ERIC. 1998. "K–12 Foreign Language Education." *ERIC Review* 6(1).

AMERICAN COUNCIL ON THE TEACHING OF FOREIGN LANGUAGES. 1986. *Proficiency Guidelines.* Hastings-on-Hudson, New York: American Council on the Teaching of Foreign Languages.

BEGLEY, SHARON. 1996. "Your Child's Brain." *Newsweek* 127(8):55–62.

BREINER-SANDERS, KAREN E.; LOWE, PARDEE, JR.; MILES, JOHN; and SWENDER, ELVIRA. 2000. "ACTFL Proficiency Guidelines—Speaking. Revised 1999." *Foreign Language Annals* 33:13–18.

BREINER-SANDERS, KAREN E.; SWENDER, ELVIRA; and TERRY, ROBERT M. 2002. "Preliminary Proficiency Guidelines—Writing. Revised 2001." *Foreign Language Annals* 35:9–15.

CURTAIN, HELENA, and PESOLA, CAROL ANN BJORNSTAD. 1994. *Languages and Children: Making the Match,* 2nd edition. White Plains, NY: Longman.

GILZOW, DOUGLAS F., and BRANAMAN, LUCINDA E. 2000. *Lessons Learned: Model Early Foreign Language Programs.* Washington, DC: Center for Applied Linguistics; McHenry, IL: Delta Systems.

HADLEY, ALICE OMAGGIO. 2001. *Teaching Language in Context,* 3rd edition. Boston: Heinle and Heinle-Thomson Learning.

MET, MYRIAM. 1996. "Middle Schools and Foreign Languages: A View for the Future." *ERIC Digest* ED392246:1.

MET, MYRIAM, ed. 1998. *Critical Issues in Early Second Language Learning.* Glenview, IL: Scott Foresman-Addison Wesley.

NASH, J. MADELEINE. 1997. "Fertile Minds." *Time* 149(5):49–56.

NATIONAL STANDARDS IN FOREIGN LANGUAGE EDUCATION PROJECT. 1999. *Standards for Foreign Language Learning in the Twenty-First Century.* Yonkers, NY: National Standards in Foreign Language Education Project.

PUFAHL, INGRID; RHODES, NANCY C.; and CHRISTIAN, DONNA. 2000. *Foreign Language Teaching: What the United States Can Learn from Other Countries.* Washington, DC: Center for Applied Linguistics.

RHODES, NANCY C., and BRANAMAN, LUCINDA E. 1999. *Foreign Language Instruction in the United States: A National Survey of Elementary and Secondary Schools.* Washington, DC: Center for Applied Linguistics; McHenry, IL: Delta Systems.

SWENDER, ELVIRA, and DUNCAN, GREG. 1998. "ACTFL Performance Guidelines for K–12 Learners." *Foreign Language Annals* 31:479–491.

INTERNET RESOURCES

CENTER FOR APPLIED LINGUISTICS. 2002. <www.cal.org>.

MET, MYRIAM. 1996. "Middle Schools and Foreign Languages: A View for the Future." *ERIC Digest.* <www.ed.gov/databases/ERIC_Digests/ ed392246.html>.

NATIONAL COUNCIL OF STATE SUPERVISORS OF FOREIGN LANGUAGE. 2002. "NCSSFL Position Statement on Distance Learning in Foreign Languages." <www.ncssfl.org/distance learning.htm>.

STATE UNIVERSITY OF NEW YORK COLLEGE AT CORTLAND. 2002. FLTeach. <www.cortland. edu/flteach>.

CAROL ANN DAHLBERG

FOSTER CARE

See: FAMILY COMPOSITION AND CIRCUMSTANCE, *subentry on* FOSTER CARE.

FRATERNITIES AND SORORITIES

See: SOCIAL FRATERNITIES AND SORORITIES.

FREIRE, PAULO (1921–1997)

Paulo Reglus Neves Freire was a Brazilian educator whose revolutionary pedagogical theory influenced educational and social movements throughout the world and whose philosophical writings influenced academic disciplines that include theology, sociology, anthropology, applied linguistics, pedagogy, and cultural studies. He was born to a middle-class family in Recife, in the state of Pernambuco in the northeast of Brazil. His early work in adult literacy—the most famous being his literacy experiments in the town of Angicos in Rio Grande do Norte—was terminated after the military coup in 1964. That year he went into exile, during which time he lived in Bolivia; then Chile where he worked for the United Nations Educational, Scientific and Cultural Organization (UNESCO) and the Chilean Institute for Agrarian Reform, and where he wrote his most important work, *Pedagogy of the Oppressed* (1970); Mexico; the United States where he held a brief appointment at Harvard University's Center for Studies in Development and Social Change; and Switzerland where he worked for the World Council of Churches as the director of their education program. He also served as an adviser for various governments, most notably the government of Guinea-Bissau. In 1980 he returned to Brazil to teach and later to serve as secretary of education for São Paulo. He worked as a consultant for revolutionary governments such as the New Jewel Movement in Grenada, the Sandinista government in Nicaragua, and the government of Julius K. Nyerere in Tanzania. From 1985 until his death in 1997, Freire served as the honorary president of the International Council for Adult Education. Freire's conception of education as a deeply political project oriented toward the transformation of society has been crucial to the education of revolutionary societies and societies undergoing civil war, as well as established Western democracies. Freire's work has exercised considerable influence among progressive educators in the West, especially in the context of emerging traditions of critical pedagogy, bilingual education, and multicultural education.

Freire's revolutionary pedagogy starts from a deep love for, and humility before, poor and oppressed people and a respect for their "common sense," which constitutes a knowledge no less important than the scientific knowledge of the professional. This humility makes possible a condition of reciprocal trust and communication between the educator, who also learns, and the student, who also teaches. Thus, education becomes a "communion" between participants in a dialogue characterized by a reflexive, reciprocal, and socially relevant exchange, rather than the unilateral action of one individual agent for the benefit of the other. Nevertheless, this does not amount to a celebration of the untrammeled core of consciousness of the oppressed, in which the educator recedes into the background as a mere facilitator. Freire conceived of authentic teaching as enacting a clear authority, rather than being authoritarian. The teacher, in his conception, is not neutral, but intervenes in the educational situation in order to help the student to overcome those aspects of his or her social constructs that are paralyzing, and to learn to think critically. In a similar fashion, Freire validated and affirmed the experiences of the oppressed without automatically legitimizing or validating their content. All experiences—including those of the teacher—had to be interrogated in order to lay bare their ideological assumptions and presuppositions. The benchmark that Freire used for evaluating experiences grew out of a Christianized Marxist humanism. From this position, Freire urged both students and teachers to unlearn their race, class, and gender privileges and to engage in a dialogue with those whose experiences are very different from their own. Thus, he did not uncritically affirm student or teacher experiences but provided the conceptual tools with which to critically interrogate them so as to minimize their politically domesticating influences.

Conceptual Tools

Banking education. Freire criticized prevailing forms of education as reducing students to the status of passive objects to be acted upon by the teacher. In this traditional form of education it is the job of the teacher to deposit in the minds of the students, considered to be empty in an absolute ignorance, the bits of information that constitute knowledge. Freire called this *banking education.* The goal of banking education is to immobilize the people within existing frameworks of power by conditioning them to accept that meaning and historical agency are the sole property of the oppressor. Educators within the dominant culture and class fractions often characterize the oppressed as marginal, pathological, and helpless. In the banking model, knowledge is taken to be a gift that is bestowed upon the student by the teacher. Freire viewed this false generosity on the part of the oppressor—which ostensibly aims to incorporate and improve the oppressed—as a crucial means of domination by the capitalist class. The indispensable soil of good teaching consists of creating the pedagogical conditions for genuine dialogue, which maintains that teachers should not impose their views on students, but neither should they camouflage them nor drain them of political and ethical import.

Problem-posing method. Against the banking model, Freire proposed a dialogical *problem-posing method* of education. In this model, the teacher and student become co-investigators of knowledge and of the world. Instead of suggesting to students that their situation in society has been transcendentally fixed by nature or reason, as the banking model does, Freire's problem-posing education invites the oppressed to explore their reality as a "problem" to be transformed. The content of this education cannot be determined necessarily in advance, through the expertise of the educator, but must instead arise

from the lived experiences or reality of the students. It is not the task of the educator to provide the answer to the problems that these situations present, but to help students to achieve a form of critical thinking (or *conscientization*) that will make possible an awareness of society as mutable and potentially open to transformation. Once they are able to see the world as a transformable situation, rather than an unthinkable and inescapable stasis, it becomes possible for students to imagine a new and different reality.

In order, however, to undertake this process, the oppressed must challenge their own internalization of the oppressor. The oppressed are accustomed to thinking of themselves as "less than." They have been conditioned to view as complete and human only the dominating practices of the oppressor, so that to fully become human means to simulate these practices. Against a "fear of freedom" that protects them from a cataclysmic reorganization of their being, the oppressed in dialogue engage in an existential process of dis-identifying with "the oppressor housed within." This dis-identification allows them to begin the process of imagining a new being and a new life as subjects of their own history.

Culture circle. The concrete basis for Freire's dialogical system of education is the *culture circle,* in which students and coordinator together discuss generative themes that have significance within the context of students' lives. These themes, which are related to nature, culture, work, and relationships, are discovered through the cooperative research of educators and students. They express, in an open rather than propagandistic fashion, the principle contradictions that confront the students in their world. These themes are then represented in the form of codifications (usually visual representations) that are taken as the basis for dialogue within the circle. As students decode these representations, they recognize them as situations in which they themselves are involved as subjects. The process of critical consciousness formation is initiated when students learn to read the codifications in their situationality, rather than simply experiencing them, and this makes possible the intervention by students in society. As the culture circle comes to recognize the need for print literacy, the visual codifications are accompanied by words to which they correspond. Students learn to read these words in the process of reading the aspects of the world with which they are linked.

Although this system of codifications has been very successful in promoting print literacy among adult students, Freire always emphasized that it should not be approached mechanically, but rather as a process of creation and awakening of consciousness. For Freire, it is a mistake to speak of reading as solely the decoding of text. Rather, reading is a process of apprehending power and causality in society and one's location in it. Awareness of the historicity of social life makes it possible for students to imagine its re-creation. Literacy is thus a "self-transformation producing a stance of intervention" (Freire 1988, p. 404). Literacy programs that appropriate parts of Freire's method while ignoring the essential politicization of the process of reading the world as a limit situation to be overcome distort and subvert the process of literacy education. For Freire, authentic education is always a "practice of freedom" rather than an alienating inculcation of skills.

Philosophy of Education

Freire's philosophy of education is not a simple method but rather an organic political consciousness. The domination of some by others must be overcome, in his view, so that the humanization of all can take place. Authoritarian forms of education, in serving to reinforce the oppressors' view of the world, and their material privilege in it, constitute an obstacle to the liberation of human beings. The means of this liberation is a *praxis,* or process of action and reflection, which simultaneously names reality and acts to change it. Freire criticized views that emphasized either the objective or subjective aspect of social transformation, and insisted that revolutionary change takes place precisely through the consistency of a critical commitment in both word and deed. This dialectical unity is expressed in his formulation, "To speak a true word is to transform the world" (Freire 1996, p. 68).

Freire's educational project was conceived in solidarity with anticapitalist and anti-imperialist movements throughout the world. It calls upon the more privileged educational and revolutionary leaders to commit "class suicide" and to struggle in partnership with the oppressed. Though this appeal is firmly grounded in a Marxist political analysis, which calls for the reconfiguring of systems of production and distribution, Freire rejected elitist and sectarian versions of socialism in favor of a vision of revolution from "below" based on the work of autonomous popular organizations. Not only does

Freire's project involve a material reorganization of society, but a cultural reorganization as well. Given the history of European imperialism, an emancipatory education of the oppressed involves a dismantling of colonial structures and ideologies. The literacy projects he undertook in former Portuguese colonies in Africa included an emphasis on the reaffirmation of the people's indigenous cultures against their negation by the legacy of the metropolitan invaders.

Freire's work constitutes a rejection of voluntarism and idealism as well as determinism and objectivism. The originality of Freire's thought consists in his synthesis of a number of philosophical and political traditions and his application of them to the pedagogical encounter. Thus, the Hegelian dialectic of master and slave informs his vision of liberation from authoritarian forms of education; the existentialism of Jean Paul Sartre and Martin Buber makes possible his description of the self-transformation of the oppressed into a space of radical intersubjectivity; the historical materialism of Karl Marx influences his conception of the historicity of social relations; his emphasis on love as a necessary precondition of authentic education has an affinity with radical Christian liberation theology; and the anti-imperialist revolutionism of Ernesto Che Guevara and Frantz Fanon undergird his notion of the "oppressor housed within" as well as his commitment to a praxis of militant anticolonialism.

Freire's pedagogy implies an important emphasis on the imagination, though this is not an aspect that has been emphasized enough in writings about him. The transformation of social conditions involves a rethinking of the world as a particular world, capable of being changed. But the reframing proposed here depends upon the power of the imagination to see outside, beyond, and against what is. More than a cognitive or emotional potential, the human imagination, in Freire's view, is capable of a radical and productive envisioning that exceeds the limits of the given. It is in this capacity that everyone's humanity consists, and for this reason it can never be the gift of the teacher to the student. Rather, educator-student and student-educator work together to mobilize the imagination in the service of creating a vision of a new society. It is here that Freire's notion of education as an ontological vocation for bringing about social justice becomes most clear. For Freire, this vocation is an endless struggle because critical awareness itself can only be a necessary precondition for it. Because liberation as a goal is always underburdened of a necessary assurance that critical awareness will propel the subject into the world of concrete praxis, the critical education must constantly be engaged in attempts to undress social structures and formations of oppression within the social universe of capital without a guarantee that such a struggle will bring about the desired results.

Criticism

Since its first enunciation, Freire's educational theory has been criticized from various quarters. Naturally, conservatives who are opposed to the political horizon of what is essentially a revolutionary project of emancipation have been quick to condemn him as demagogic and utopian. Freire has faced criticism from the left as well. Some Marxists have been suspicious of the Christian influences in his work and have accused him of idealism in his view of popular consciousness. Freire has also been criticized by feminists and others for failing to take into account the radical differences between forms of oppression, as well as their complex and contradictory instantiation in subjects. It has been pointed out that Freire's writing suffers from sexism in its language and from a patriarchal notion of revolution and subjecthood, as well as a lack of emphasis on domination based on race and ethnicity. Postmodernists have pointed to the contradiction between Freire's sense of the historicity and contingency of social formations versus his vision of liberation as a universal human vocation.

Freire was always responsive to critics, and in his later work undertook a process of self-criticism in regard to his own sexism. He also sought to develop a more nuanced view of oppression and subjectivity as relational and discursively as well as materially embedded. However, Freire was suspicious of postmodernists who felt that the Marxist legacy of class struggle was obsolete and whose antiracist and antisexist efforts at educational reform did little to alleviate—and often worked to exacerbate—existing divisions of labor based on social relations of capitalist exploitation. Freire's insights continue to be of crucial importance. In the very gesture of his turning from the vaults of official knowledge to the open space of humanity, history, and poetry—the potential space of dialogical problem-posing education—Freire points the way for teachers and others who would refuse their determination by the increasingly enveloping inhuman social order. To believe in that

space when it is persistently obscured, erased, or repudiated remains the duty of truly progressive educators. Freire's work continues to be indispensable for liberatory education, and his insights remain of value to all who are committed to the struggle against oppression.

See also: EDUCATION REFORM.

BIBLIOGRAPHY

DARDER, ANTONIA. 2002. *Reinventing Paulo Freire.* Boulder, CO: Westview Press.

FREIRE, PAULO. 1973. *Education for Critical Consciousness.* New York: Seabury.

FREIRE, PAULO. 1978. *Pedagogy in Process: The Letters to Guinea-Bisseau.* New York: Seabury.

FREIRE, PAULO. 1988. "The Adult Literacy Process as Cultural Action for Freedom and Education and Conscientizacao." In *Perspectives on Literacy,* ed. Eugene R. Kintgen, Barry M. Kroll, and Mike Rose, pp. 398–409. Carbondale, IL: Southern Illinois University Press.

FREIRE, PAULO. 1993. *Pedagogy of the City.* New York: Continuum.

FREIRE, PAULO. 1994. *Pedagogy of Hope.* New York: Continuum.

FREIRE, PAULO. 1996. *Pedagogy of the Oppressed* (1970). New York: Continuum.

HOOKS, BELL. 1994. *Teaching to Transgress.* New York: Routledge.

MAYO, PETER. 1999. *Gramsci, Freire, and Adult Education: Possibilities for Transformative Action.* London: Zed Books.

MCLAREN, PETER. 2000. *Che Guevara, Paulo Freire, and the Pedagogy of Revolution.* Oxford: Rowman and Littlefield.

PETER MCLAREN
NOAH DE LISSOVOY

FROEBEL, FRIEDRICH
(1782–1852)

The German educator Friedrich Froebel is significant for developing an Idealist philosophy of early childhood education and establishing the kindergarten, a school for four- and five-year-old children that is found worldwide.

Biography

Friedrich Wilhelm August Froebel was the youngest of five sons of Johann Jacob Froebel, a Lutheran pastor at Oberweissbach in the German principality of Schwarzburg-Rudolfstadt. Froebel's mother died when he was nine months old. When Friedrich was four years old, his father remarried. Feeling neglected by his stepmother and father, Froebel experienced a profoundly unhappy childhood. At his father's insistence, he attended the girls' primary school at Oberweissbach. From 1793 to 1798 he lived with his maternal uncle, Herr Hoffman, at Stadt-Ilm, where he attended the local town school. From the years 1798 to 1800 he was as an apprentice to a forester and surveyor in Neuhaus. From 1800 to 1802 Froebel attended the University of Jena.

In 1805 Froebel briefly studied architecture in Frankfurt. His studies provided him with a sense of artistic perspective and symmetry he later transferred to his design of the kindergarten's gifts and occupations. In 1805 Anton Gruener, headmaster of the Pestalozzian Frankfurt Model School, hired Froebel as a teacher. To prepare him as a teacher, Gruener arranged for Froebel, now twenty-four years old, to take a short course with Johann Henrich Pestalozzi at Yverdon. Froebel believed Pestalozzi's respect for the dignity of children and creation of a learning environment of emotional security were highly significant educational elements that he wanted to incorporate in his own teaching. He also was intrigued by Pestalozzi's form, number, and name lessons, which would form a basis for his later design of the kindergarten gifts. After his training with Pestalozzi, Froebel taught at Gruner's Model School until he returned to Yverdon in 1808 for two more years of study with Pestalozzi.

From 1810 to 1812 Froebel studied languages and science at the University of Göttingen. He hoped to identify linguistic structures that could be applied to language instruction. He became particularly interested in geology and mineralogy. From 1812 to 1816 Froebel studied mineralogy with Professor Christian Samuel Weiss (1780–1856) at the University of Berlin. Froebel believed the process of crystallization, moving from simple to complex, reflected a universal cosmic law that also governed human growth and development.

In 1816 Froebel established the Universal German Educational Institute at Griesheim. He moved the institute to Keilhau in 1817 where it functioned until 1829. In 1818 Froebel married Henrietta Wilhelmine Hoffmeister (1780–1839), who assisted him until her death. In 1831 Froebel established an institute at Wartensee on Lake Sempach in Switzerland and then relocated the school to Willisau. Froebel next operated an orphanage and boarding school at Burgdorf.

Froebel returned to Germany, where in 1837 he established a new type of early childhood school, a child's garden, or kindergarten, for three-and four-year-old children. Using play, songs, stories, and activities, the kindergarten was designed as an educational environment in which children, through their own self-activity, could develop in the right direction. The right direction meant that, in their development, children would follow the divinely established laws of human growth through their own activity. Froebel's reputation as an early childhood educator increased and kindergartens were established throughout the German states.

In 1851 Karl von Raumer, the Prussian minister of education, accused Froebel of undermining traditional values by spreading atheism and socialism. Despite Froebel's denial of these accusations, von Raumer banned kindergartens in Prussia. In 1852, in the midst of the controversy, Froebel died. Although kindergartens existed in the other German states, they were not reestablished in Prussia until 1860. By the end of the nineteenth century, kindergartens had been established throughout Europe and North America.

Froebel's Kindergarten Philosophy

Froebel shaped his educational philosophy during the high tide of German philosophical Idealism that was marked by the work of Johann Gottfried Herder (1744–1803), Immanuel Kant (1724–1804), and Georg Wilhelm Hegel (1770–1831). In the *Education of Man* (1826), Froebel articulated the following idealist themes: (1) all existence originates in and with God; (2) humans possess an inherent spiritual essence that is the vitalizing life force that causes development; (3) all beings and ideas are interconnected parts of a grand, ordered, and systematic universe. Froebel based his work on these principles, asserting that each child at birth has an internal spiritual essence—a life force—that seeks to be externalized through self-activity. Further, child development follows the doctrine of preformation, the unfolding of that which was present latently in the individual. The kindergarten is a special educational environment in which this self-active development occurs. The kindergarten's gifts, occupations, and social and cultural activities, especially play, promote this self-actualization.

Froebel was convinced that the kindergarten's primary focus should be on play—the process by which he believed children expressed their innermost thoughts, needs, and desires. Froebel's emphasis on play contrasted with the traditional view prevalent during the nineteenth century that play, a form of idleness and disorder, was an unworthy element of human life.

For Froebel, play facilitated children's process of cultural recapitulation, imitation of adult vocational activities, and socialization. He believed the human race, in its collective history, had gone through major epochs of cultural development that added to and refined its culture. According to Froebel's theory of cultural recapitulation, each individual human being repeated the general cultural epoch in his or her own development.

By playing, children socialize and imitate adult social and economic activities as they are gradually led into the larger world of group life. The kindergarten provided a milieu that encouraged children to interact with other children under the guidance of a loving teacher.

The Kindergarten Curriculum

Froebel developed a series of gifts and occupations for use in kindergartens. Representing what Froebel identified as fundamental forms, the gifts had both their actual physical appearance and also a hidden symbolic meaning. They were to stimulate the child to bring the fundamental concept that they represented to mental consciousness. Froebel's gifts were the following items.

- Six soft, colored balls
- A wooden sphere, cube, and cylinder
- A large cube divided into eight smaller cubes
- A large cube divided into eight oblong blocks
- A large cube divided into twenty-one whole, six half, and twelve quarter cubes
- A large cube divided into eighteen whole oblongs: three divided lengthwise; three divided breadthwise
- Quadrangular and triangular tablets used for arranging figures
- Sticks for outlining figures
- Whole and half wire rings for outlining figures
- Various materials for drawing, perforating, embroidering, paper cutting, weaving or braiding, paper folding, modeling, and interlacing

As a series, the gifts began with the simple undifferentiated sphere or circle and moved to more complex objects. Following the idealist principle of synthesis of opposites, Froebel's cylinders represented the integration of the sphere and the cube. The various cubes and their subdivisions were building blocks that children could use to create geometrical and architectural designs. Using the sticks and rings to trace designs on paper, children exercised the hand's small muscles, coordinated hand and eye movements, and took the first steps toward drawing and later writing.

The occupations were items such as paper, pencils, wood, sand, clay, straw, and sticks for use in constructive activities. Kindergarten activities included games, songs, and stories designed to assist in sensory and physical development and socialization. Froebel published *Mutter-und-Kose-lieder,* (Mother's songs, games, and stories), a collection of kindergarten songs, in 1843.

Diffusion of the Kindergarten

Kindergartens were established in Europe and North America. In the United Kingdom, Bertha Ronge, a pupil of Froebel's, established several kindergartens. In the United States, German immigrants introduced the kindergarten. In Watertown, Wisconsin, Margarethe Meyer Schurz established a kindergarten for German-speaking children in 1856. In New York, Matilda H. Kriege introduced and marketed kindergarten materials imported from Germany.

Henry Barnard, the first U.S. Commissioner of Education, popularized Froebel's philosophy in his *Common School Journal.* Elizabeth Palmer Peabody (1804–1894) established a kindergarten in Boston, translated several of Froebel's books into English, organized an educational organization called the Froebel Union, and established an institute to train kindergarten teachers.

Superintendent of Schools William Torrey Harris, (1835–1909) incorporated the kindergarten into the St. Louis, Missouri, public school system in 1873. Harris was assisted by his associate, Susan Elizabeth Blow (1843–1916), a dedicated Froebelian, who wrote *Letters to a Mother on the Philosophy of Froebel* in 1899 and *Kindergarten Education* in 1900.

In the early twenty-first century, kindergarten teachers continue to emphasize Froebel's ideas of developing the social side of a child's nature and a sense of readiness for learning. The important outcome for the kindergarten child is readiness for the intellectual learning that will come later in his educational career.

See also: EARLY CHILDHOOD EDUCATION; BLOW, SUSAN; EDUCATIONAL PSYCHOLOGY; PESTALOZZI, JOHANN.

BIBLIOGRAPHY

DOWNS, ROBERT B. 1978. *Friedrich Froebel.* Boston: Twayne.

FROEBEL, FRIEDRICH. 1889. *Autobiography,* trans. Emilie Michaelis and H. Keatley Moore. Syracuse, NY: Bardeen.

FROEBEL, FRIEDRICH. 1896. *The Education of Man,* trans. W. H. Hailman. New York: Appleton.

FROEBEL, FRIEDRICH. 1910. *Mother's Songs, Games, and Stories,* trans. Francis Lord and Emily Lord. London: Rice.

LAWRENCE, EVELYN, ed. 1969. *Froebel and English Education.* New York: Schocken.

LILLEY, IRENE M. 1967. *Friedrich Froebel: A Selection from His Writings.* Cambridge, Eng.: Cambridge University Press.

ROSS, ELIZABETH D. 1976. *The Kindergarten Crusade: The Establishment of Preschool Education in the United States.* Athens: Ohio University Press.

VANDEWALKER, NINA C. 1971. *The Kindergarten in American Education.* New York: Arno Press and New York Times.

WEBER, EVELYN. 1969. *The Kindergarten: Its Encounter with Educational Thought in America.* New York: Teachers College Press, Columbia University.

GERALD L. GUTEK

FULL-SERVICE SCHOOLS

According to David Tyack, writing in 1992, there is a long history in the United States of providing remediation services to children in a school setting. Early programs attempted to provide health and social services in the school setting. The intent of these early efforts was to assist immigrant children in adjusting to their new culture. Locating these services in the school changed the focus from serving the family to serving the individual child.

The following quote, from social reformer Robert Hunter, writing in 1904, is indicative of the environment in which full-service schools have evolved:

> The time has come for a new conception of the responsibilities of the school. The lives of youth are desperate, parents bring up their children in surroundings which make them in large numbers vicious and criminally dangerous. Some agency must take charge of the entire problem of child life and master it. (Kronick, p. 23)

In a similar vein, William Wort, the superintendent of schools in Gary, Indiana, in 1923 stated:

> The school should serve as a clearinghouse for children's activities so that all child welfare agencies may be working simultaneously and efficiently, thus creating a child's world within the city wherein all children may have a wholesome environment all of the day and everyday. (Kronick, p. 23)

The modern history of full-service schools must be traced to Joy Dryfoos. Her work is one of central importance for all who want to understand and implement full-service schools. Her 1994 book *Full-Service Schools: A Revolution in Health and Services for Children, Youth, and Families* is a landmark piece on the concept of full-service schools. She continues to write and advocate for full-service schools, and her writings and presentations are a critical force in the history and continued development of full-service community schools. According to Dryfoos, what is important in the historical evolvement of full-service schools is that many disparate groups were working toward the goal of creating such schools, but they did not know what each other was doing. These groups include the Charles Stewart Mott Foundation, the Children's Aid Society, Communities and Schools, and the Tennessee Consortium for the Development of Full Service Schools. The following definition of a full-service school evolved out of discourse between Dryfoos and those working with her to try to develop full-service schools.

A full-service school is a school that has broadened its mission and vision to meet the needs of all of its students. The school is where health, mental health, and other services are provided. The emphasis is on *prevention*. The full-service school is a new environment where a *systems* approach to change is used. It is not a school where human services are an add-on. Collaboration thus becomes a key process in the school. Input from the community determines what special services will be provided. By meeting the noncurricular needs of children and families, the full-service school ensures that learning will happen for all students in the school.

Community

Full-service schools have been around conceptually for quite some time. After all, the American philosopher and educator John Dewey (1859–1952) talked about the school as the community and the community as the school. Thus, community has been at the heart of full-service schools from the beginning. The concept of community is important to full-service schools in several ways. First, the school is a piece of real estate the community owns. This leads to the importance of building use after the end of the school day. The idea is that the sense of community increases as schools become better, and as schools improve the sense of community becomes stronger. At the same time each local community determines the needs for each school. Hence, the after-school needs may range from adult education to laundry services.

The importance of community is why full-service schools are often called full-service community schools. Other names include "lighted schools" and "beacons." The central idea, regardless of name, is that all children have the right to learn and the right to the best curriculum feasible. No learning will go on, however, if the children and their families' noncurricular needs are not met first. These needs might include alcohol and drug counseling, conflict resolution, general mental health issues, and many others. Research has found that the main need for the children and families is mental health care. It is impossible for children to learn when they come to school tired, hungry, and/or abused. Full-service schools support the notion that it is not whether the school will be a parent or not, but whether it will be a good parent.

Prevention

Along with community, prevention is another central tenet of full-service schools. Keeping students in school and learning is clearly a way of preventing them from going on welfare or becoming incarcerated in a correctional or mental health facility. In her 1994 book, Dryfoos asserted that one in four children in America drinks or does drugs, has early unprotected sex, and/or drops out of school. This statistic alone should make prevention a priority.

In many states corrections and mental health consume an undue amount of the state budget because not enough time, money, and effort has been spent on prevention. The best place for conducting prevention programs is in schools, because that is where the children and the families are. Full-service schools, by working to meet the ecological needs of children and families, begin prevention and intervention at an early age and seek to diminish the inequities that exist between the haves and the have-nots.

The philosophy of starting full-service schools is to begin where the need is the greatest. The thought is that if those who are on the bottom move up, all will benefit. The rising boat benefits all. In some schools, 90 percent of the students qualify for the free and reduced lunch program. The mobility of these students and their families is very high, resulting in a high turnover rate. Oftentimes the whereabouts of these people is unknown. More is known about migratory birds than is known about migratory people.

Collaboration

Dryfoos noted that a universal call has been issued for one-stop, unfragmented, health and social service systems that are consumer oriented, developmentally appropriate, and culturally relevant. Full-service schools can be seen as central institutions in the community to provide an important if not critical organizing focus for the coordination and integration of service.

Full-service schools are seamless organizations in which educators and human service workers work collaboratively. The goal is to meet the needs of the child. Collaborators must set aside their own agendas and work for the benefit of the child. Collaboration as a bare minimum requires communication, trust, and clear agreements. It is much more complicated than coordination or cooperation.

Systems Change

The full-service school is a new environment in which a systems approach to change is used. Full-service schools collaborate with human service agencies in a systems approach. Blaming the child for not being able to learn appropriately is replaced by a problem-solving approach that does not seek to push the child out of school. A focus on systems emphasizes the interconnection of health, welfare, and educational forces in the child's life. The full-service school program watches for and tries to prevent push-outs and dropouts. There is a definite difference between the two.

The focus on systems emphasizes the importance of education and human service collaboration. This focus strongly asserts that human services cannot be add-ons at the school. Add-ons ensure only failure. Tinkering with schools but not making thoroughgoing changes courts failure. The full-service school is thus about thoroughgoing change.

Controversies

Current controversies address the following issues: (1) Should the services be school based or school linked? (2) How should these services be integrated so that they are more than add-ons? (3) How can turfism be addressed? and (4) Do these support services water down academics?

School-based versus school-linked services. School-based or school-linked services are concerned with colocation of services as well as pay and the sources of pay. School-based services have the advantage of immediacy of response, collegiality, and teamwork. They have the disadvantage of being associated negatively with the school if the child and parent have a bad perception of the school. School-based services help deal with the problems of transportation and fragmentation of services.

Integration of the services. One of the strongest arguments for full-service schools is that they will cut down on the fragmentation of existing services. In one full-service school project, which was launched in 1999, this proved to be the case within three years of launching. Helping professionals and educators, who at most schools normally do not work with each another, are sharing and collaborating. This school's experiences with school-linked services is that they are nothing more than what currently exists. The coordinator of services has reduced fragmentation.

There must be collaboration between schools and human service personnel. School principals play a critical role in this process. Schools that operate in a human relations frame, where communication is

bottom up, horizontal, and top down, are more successful than those that are bureaucracies where communication is top down only. When people actually know each other they are more likely to trust one another.

Turfism. In dealing with a complex issue such as interprofessional collaboration, turfism arises as one of the thorniest issues to try to solve. The first problem here is responsibility. How do teachers and human service workers, who have historically not collaborated, work together harmoniously? This collaboration is well beyond the traditional working relationships between teachers and school social workers, school counselors, or school psychologists. The human service workers who are working in full-service schools are community personnel, and the collaboration with them is much more complex than those same professionals who are employed by school systems. Thus the second major issue of pay arises. Who is this worker actually working for, the school or the community agency? Is this worker a school system employee or a community service employee? This issue will be continually debated for quite some time. At the same time it is not an unsolvable problem.

Do these services water down academics? The final controversy is whether these services should be provided at the school, and if so, how will these services affect academics? Research answers the question in such a way that for a certain portion of school-age children, these support services must be offered for these children to have any chance at all for learning. To not provide these services yields the onerous option of the creation and continuation of a permanent underclass.

A related question, however, is what happens to the gifted child, in comparison to the average child? The money for education is fixed and not likely to expand. Thus the perennial question remains, can excellence and equity coexist? Excellence and education are not mutually exclusive. No, the idea is that full-service schools will not require education moving, but rather the moving of human service workers into school.

Evaluation

To those familiar with full-service schools it is not news that the evaluation process is lacking. Evaluation of the programs is essential in order to acquire funding, grants, and community support. Past attempts at documentation of success of the full-service school model have fallen drastically short of their goals because of poor planning and lack of data regarding the programs that constitute the school. Record-keeping may be the key to a successful school evaluation. This is a difficult task, especially so for the full-service school, because of the nature of the model. Because a full-service school consists of multiple components, such as a health clinic, after-school programs, adult education classes, and mental health services, an evaluation of the whole model must include all of the subcomponents. Turnover of students also affects the evaluation process. In many inner-city schools student turnover is upwards of 30 percent each school year. It is impossible to get an accurate reading of school improvement with such a loss of data.

Finally, time should be considered when evaluating a full-service school. These programs develop slowly and improve and change based on school and community needs. Therefore, it may take several years for the full effects on students and their families to become evident. Consequently a one- or two-year evaluation may not leave sufficient time for all the benefits to manifest. All these factors should be considered before an evaluation of a full-service school can take place.

One way to control many of the problems that will be encountered is for the evaluators to be involved from the conception of the program. Therefore they can establish the criteria for an evaluation and determine what data need to be tracked and for how long. Working intimately with the principal is essential to evaluation success. Also helpful is to employ an activities coordinator to oversee and keep documentation on all components of the school. This responsibility is too cumbersome for the principal to undertake and should not be pushed off onto already overworked teachers. Making good use of the position of activities coordinator will help the full-service school be seen as a unified institution, thereby making evaluation more effective.

The Future

In the early twenty-first century, democratic communities are needed more than ever. The schoolhouse can be the place for discourse on important international events that will affect the educational system for many years to come. The schoolhouse, as stated at the outset, belongs to the community. The full-service school has not been used a great deal in-

ternationally, but at the Community Schools Conference (March 2001, Kansas City, Missouri) there were architects from Japan present. Japan is very interested in learning how architects can help develop schools that can be used by students for both academic and nonacademic pursuits. Urban/city planners are also coming into the planning and development of full-service schools. Hence, nontraditional professionals are now entering the fray, trying to see that all children are educated, and the full-service school is certainly one way to do this.

See also: COMMUNITY EDUCATION; FAMILY, SCHOOL, AND COMMUNITY CONNECTIONS; FAMILY SUPPORT SERVICES; HEALTH SERVICES, *subentry on* SCHOOL.

BIBLIOGRAPHY

DRYFOOS, JOY. 1994. *Full-Service Schools: A Revolution in Health and Services for Children, Youth, and Families.* San Francisco: Jossey-Bass.

KRONICK, ROBERT F., ed. 2000. *Human Services and the Full Service School.* Springfield, IL: Charles C. Thomas.

MELAVILLE, ATELIA, and BLANK, MARTIN. 2000. "Trends and Issues in School-Community Interventions." In *Changing Results for Children and Families: Linking Collaborative Services with School Reform Efforts,* ed. Margaret Wang and William Boyd. Greenwich, CT: Information Age Publishing.

TYACK, DAVID. 1992. "Health and Social Services in Public Schools: Historical Perspectives." *Future of Children* 2:19–31.

ROBERT F. KRONICK

FUTURE FACULTY PREPARATION PROGRAMS

Future faculty preparation programs provide a smooth transition between graduate school and faculty positions by preparing graduate students to meet the demands and expectations they will face as faculty members in U.S. colleges and universities. By examining the multiple roles and responsibilities that faculty hold—including research, teaching, and service—these programs extend beyond the parameters of standard graduate education, which emphasizes research, and teaching assistant (TA) development or graduate teaching certification programs, which emphasize present or future teaching alone. Instead, future faculty preparation programs view graduate school as a time for professional development in all areas and emphasize the need for finding and maintaining balance among the wide range of roles future faculty will encounter. At core, these programs share a commitment to cooperatively supporting graduate education in a more holistic way, giving graduate students firsthand experience with appropriate mentoring. This process relies on cooperation and effective communication between diverse institutions, between institution and faculty, and between faculty and graduate students. Most importantly, future faculty preparation programs offer a new model of graduate student development—one not merely supplementary to existing graduate student education or TA development, but one that considers professional development as inherent to graduate schooling.

Impetus and Development

Future faculty preparation programs evolved from the TA training programs that proliferated between 1960 and 1990. Prior to the 1960s no formal training for teaching assistants existed; however, as colleges and universities began to depend on TAs more regularly to teach introductory courses, and as students, as well as the general public, began criticizing the resulting quality of their undergraduate educations, higher education institutions responded by organizing the first formal TA training programs. TA development programs were initially departmental in scope and designed to help TAs perform their graduate teaching tasks effectively, but they were not necessarily designed to equip students for their future roles as faculty members.

The 1986 National Consortium on Preparing Graduate Students as College Teachers initiated a public dialogue focusing on both the important role TAs played in undergraduate education and the lack of formal training to prepare them for faculty positions. This and subsequent biannual conferences provided a forum for new research on TAs' developmental stages and encouraged the proliferation of campus-wide, centralized training programs. By the mid-1990s, after legislators, public officials, and investigative reporters entered the conversation about TA training, the conference began to include broader issues of professional development for graduate students.

These conferences, together with Ernest Boyer's publication of *Scholarship Reconsidered: Priorities of the Professoriate* (1990), served as the real impetus for the development of future faculty preparation programs as entities distinct from TA training programs. The conferences prompted further inquiry into the state of TA training, and Boyer's book provoked discussion and debate about the meaning of scholarship and the relationship between teaching and learning. Both encouraged a deliberate focus on the issue of preparing graduate students to meet future professional challenges, "not as a by-product of TA development, but rather as an integral part of their doctoral studies" (Tice et al., p. 276). As this statement attests, although many future faculty programs developed out of TA training programs, they differ from them in their effort to prepare participants for the professoriate by exposing them to all aspects of their future occupations.

Future faculty preparation programs developed as an outgrowth of the public conversations about academic work introduced by Boyer and these TA conferences; this dialogue primarily addressed the frequently reported discrepancy between graduate training and the duties of junior faculty, particularly as many graduate students assumed jobs with very different responsibilities than those at the research university where they received their degree. By providing holistic professional development, early future faculty preparation programs also acknowledged that faculty at most institutions were increasingly expected to demonstrate both strong teaching skills as well as continued research. Growing dissatisfaction with the job readiness skills of doctoral students led to the recognition that graduate students were being trained for research but not for the multiple demands of teaching, research, and the administrative tasks accompanying academic jobs at various institutions. In 1996, for example, fewer than 10 percent of new Ph.D.s received faculty positions at research universities while the majority of the recipients of doctoral degrees took teaching jobs at institutions having very different combinations of mission, student populations, and expectations for faculty.

The launching of the Preparing Future Faculty (PFF) program in 1993 marked, according to its website, the first sustained "national initiative to transform doctoral education." The PFF program began as a collaboration between the Association of American Colleges and Universities (AACU), the

Council of Graduate Schools (GSC), and Pew Charitable Trusts. PFF programs bring "the *consumers* of Ph.D. programs into contact with the *producers* and provide opportunities for graduate students to gain personal experience with different types of institutions, faculty cultures, and student bodies" (Gaff and Pruitt, p. 1). PFF programs orchestrate this cooperation between the "consumer" (hiring institutions) and "producers" (doctoral degree–granting programs) by organizing partnerships, or *clusters,* between doctoral-granting institutions and diverse partner institutions or departments. These partners often include public and private four-year baccalaureate colleges, comprehensive state universities, and community colleges to give graduate students a sense of the different roles and responsibilities faculty have at these various institutions.

The explosion of future faculty preparation programs established in the late 1990s could only have happened because of the programs funded as part of PFF. The seventeen clusters of eighty-eight institutions funded in 1993 grew to seventy-six clusters at forty-six doctoral-granting institutions with more than 295 partner institutions by 2000. PFF programs funded between 1993 and 2002 developed in four distinct phases. The first two phases focused on developing model programs (1993–1996) and institutionalizing and spreading these as part of a national initiative (1997–2001). The next two phases shared an emphasis on discipline-specific future faculty preparation primarily through the provision of grants for disciplinary associations and professional groups to form departmentally based PFF programs. With support from the National Science Foundation and a private donor, AACU and GSC collaborated with disciplinary associations and professional groups to develop model programs in the sciences and mathematics (1998–2000) and in the humanities and social sciences (1999–2002).

Since 1993 many institutions have created future faculty preparation programs similar to the PFF model. These programs emphasize that graduate education should provide opportunities for graduate students to learn about and experience all aspects of faculty responsibilities: teaching, research, and service. As with the PFF model, which allows participating institutions to create their own programs to meet graduate student needs and relative stages of development, these programs attempt to anticipate changing faculty needs and expectations, to provide graduate students with training and professional development to help them meet these needs and expectations, and to heighten awareness among established faculty about the changing expectations for faculty and graduate students.

Characteristics of Programs

While they share a common mission, future faculty preparation programs vary in structure, as diverse models have arisen in response to differing participant needs and institutional climates. The impetus for developing the future faculty preparation program, whether as an outgrowth of a TA development program or an initiative to redefine graduate education, often dictates where the program is administered and how it is funded. Future faculty preparation programs are commonly developed and supported in one of three locations: graduate schools, academic departments, or TA development centers. On many campuses, these three units work in concert to offer a combination of centralized and departmentally based activities. Regardless of where they are housed, having a programmatic or financial connection to the graduate school or graduate dean generally fosters support among faculty on the home campus and helps to build collaborations with partner institutions. Many programs further expand their support base through advisory committees consisting of faculty and graduate students.

Where and how the future faculty preparation program is administered usually determines variables such as participant eligibility and length of time to complete activities. Some programs admit students only from certain participating departments, while others enroll participants from across the university. A few also include postdoctoral fellows. In some faculty preparation programs, students go through an application/selection process and participate in the program for a defined time period—often one to two semesters. Upon completion, they earn a graduate teaching certificate or some other honor. Other programs have structured activities that participants complete in stages as part of their graduate education and some allow participants to engage in various components of the program at any time during their graduate career. These latter models tend to have an open enrollment and do not selectively admit candidates to the program. Time commitments typically range from attendance at various short workshops to enrollment in a semester-long course or frequent travel to partner institutions.

While no generic faculty preparation program template exists, many programs offer some combination of the following components.

Courses, seminars, and workshops. These may last a few hours or a semester, with the longer ones often receiving course credit. Topics include comprehensive surveys of teaching techniques, specific pedagogical issues, academic job-market information, professional development tips, and issues in higher education. Some programs offer a cognate in college teaching, a master of science degree for teachers, or a graduate teaching certificate upon completion of certain courses or activities.

Development of materials. Materials for a teaching portfolio and/or web page showcasing their research and teaching are often required of participants. These materials usually include a curriculum vitae, cover letters, and other documents necessary for an academic job search, along with course syllabi, lesson plans, and various materials used to teach a course.

Collaborations with partner institutions. Collaborations are a key feature of many future faculty preparation programs, since they provide opportunities for participants to meet faculty at other institutions. Opportunities range from a one-day visit to shadowing a professor for a day, guest lecturing, or teaching a course at the partner institution. In some cases, participants can sit in on departmental and school committee meetings. These collaborations allow participants to experience the diversity of faculty roles and responsibilities that exist at different types of institutions.

Experiential activities. These provide opportunities for participants to get hands-on practical experience teaching, giving job talks, serving on committees, working with undergraduates, or networking with colleagues. These experiences take place on both the home campus and at the partner institutions.

Mentoring opportunities. These programs give graduate students the opportunity to work with a variety of mentors so that they learn about the varied duties of faculty. Mentors can include faculty and staff at the home campus and partner institution, recent alumni, and experienced future faculty preparation program participants.

Coverage of contemporary issues in higher education. Contemporary issues are often addressed through various activities and usually include a focus on the use of technology in teaching, increasing student diversity, university governance, or changing trends in higher education.

Future Trends

In general, faculty preparation programs encourage a more holistic approach to graduate education. Ideally, the mission and goals of these programs will eventually become part of the ethos of departments and institutions, particularly as the distinct activities and opportunities they provide become fundamental to the graduate curriculum, rendering separate faculty preparation programs obsolete. This transformation depends on the participation of all members of the academic community—from senior faculty and staff to undergraduates—as well as the strengthening of collaborations among diverse institutions so that hierarchical divisions fade away.

The development of future faculty preparation programs signals the beginning of a movement to re-examine, if not radically alter, graduate education. Program directors are beginning to think broadly about the set of skills that future faculty need in order to meet the changing demands of higher education institutions and to create opportunities for them to develop these skills and be leaders in this change. At the same time, many faculty preparation programs now realize that their responsibilities may lie outside the narrow scope of preparing graduate students to be faculty, and instead encompass a broader range of career options for graduate students, both within and outside of academia.

See also: COLLEGE TEACHING; GRADUATE SCHOOL TRAINING.

BIBLIOGRAPHY

ASSOCIATION OF AMERICAN COLLEGES AND UNIVERSITIES, COUNCIL OF GRADUATE SCHOOLS, and THE PEW CHARITABLE TRUSTS. 1997. *Preparing Future Faculty: A National Program.* Washington, DC: Association of American Colleges and Universities, Council of Graduate Schools, and the Pew Charitable Trusts.

BOYER, ERNEST L. 1990. *Scholarship Reconsidered: Priorities of the Professoriate.* Princeton, NJ: Carnegie Foundation for the Advancement of Teaching.

CHISM, NANCY VAN NOTE. 1998. "Preparing Graduate Students to Teach: Past, Present, and Future." In *The Professional Development of*

Graduate Teaching Assistants, ed. Michele Marincovich, Jack Prostko, and Frederic Stout. Bolton, MA: Anker.

GAFF, JERRY G., and LAMBERT, LEO M. 1996. "Socializing Future Faculty to the Values of Undergraduate Education." *Change* 28(4):38–45.

GAFF, JERRY G., and PRUITT, ANNE S. 1996. "Experiences of Graduate Students, Faculty Members, and Administrators in Preparing Future Faculty Programs: Year 1." *CGS Communicator* 29(1):1.

PRUITT-LOGAN, ANNE S.; GAFF, JERRY G.; and WEIBL, RICHARD A. 1998. "The Impact: Assessing Experiences of Participants in the Preparing Future Faculty Program 1994–1996." Washington, DC: Association of American Colleges and Universities.

TICE, STACEY LANE; GAFF, JERRY G.; and PRUITT-LOGAN, ANNE S. 1998. "Preparing Future Faculty Preparation Programs: Beyond TA Development." In *The Professional Development of Graduate Teaching Assistants,* ed. Michele Marincovich, Jack Prostko, and Frederic Stout. Bolton, MA: Anker.

INTERNET RESOURCES

GOLDE, CHRIS M., and DORE, TIMOTHY M. 2001. "At Cross Purposes: What the Experiences of Today's Doctoral Students Reveal About Doctoral Education." <www.phd-survey.org>.

PREPARING FUTURE FACULTY. 2002. <www. preparing-faculty.org>.

DEANDRA LITTLE
A. DARLENE PANVINI

G

GANGS

See: ADOLESCENT PEER CULTURE, *subentry on* GANGS.

GARY SCHOOLS

The Gary, Indiana, public schools, founded in 1906, were developed by Superintendent William A. Wirt from 1907 to 1938 and quickly expanded into an illustrious example of Progressive education through the 1920s. Born on a farm in eastern Indiana in 1874, Wirt attended nearby Bluffton High School, graduated from DePauw University, and returned to Bluffton as school superintendent in 1899. His school innovations, particularly a more diversified elementary curriculum and flexible schedule, as well as improved facilities, paved the way for his selection as Gary's first professional superintendent. Founded by U.S. Steel Corporation in 1906, Gary grew quickly and attracted a heterogeneous population. Heavily influenced by the ideas of the American philosopher and educator John Dewey, as well as his own rural, Protestant background, Wirt believed that public schools should provide salvation for the children as well as the community.

The Gary Plan, Work-Study-Play, or Platoon School Plan, as it was variously known, focused on establishing two central characteristics in the elementary grades. First, because of a concern for efficiency, Wirt believed in maximizing school facilities by constant use of all classrooms, including nights (for adults), weekends, and summers. Second, he expanded the curriculum to include manual training (numerous shops for the boys and cooking for the

girls, for example), recreation, nature study, daily auditorium activities (including public speaking, music lessons, and movies), and other subjects beyond traditional academic concerns. The plan theoretically organized students into two platoons. During the morning, Platoon A students occupied the specialized academic classrooms (mathematics, science, English, history, etc.), while Platoon B students were in the auditorium, shops, gardens, swimming pools, gym, or playground. They switched facilities during the afternoon. The students, busy every day, were supposed to develop their mental, social, cultural, and physical abilities. Gary's large schools, first Emerson, then Froebel, and a few others built in the 1920s and 1930s, were unique because they were unit schools including all grades, K–12, which allowed for a more efficient use of space and building funds. By the late 1920s about half of the system's 22,000 students were attending such schools, with the remainder in the smaller elementary buildings.

The Gary Plan, highly developed by World War I, quickly attracted national publicity because of its apparent efficiency and diversified curriculum. By 1929, now promoted by the National Association for the Study of the Platoon or Work-Study-Play School Organization, 202 cities had over 1,000 platoon schools. It also generated much controversy, with New York City, for example, rejecting it in 1917 after a three-year experiment. While the Gary schools, in many ways, captured the positive spirit of Progressive education, they also incorporated some troubling aspects. There was the perception in New York and elsewhere that the inclusion of manual training classes was designed to channel the working classes (the majority of Gary's students) into vocational trades; while the high school enrollment increased, most students did not graduate. The schools were also racially segregated, closely following the northern urban model. The 2,759 black children in 1930 mostly attended all-black elementary schools or the integrated (but internally segregated) Froebel School. The situation worsened as black enrollment increased to 6,700 by 1949 (34% of the student population), despite the school board's attempt in 1946 to promote building integration. By 1960, 97 percent of the 23,055 black pupils (over half of the 41,000 students) were in eighteen predominantly or exclusively black schools, with primarily black teachers and administrators, and the trend would continue as the black population increased and the white population decreased over the following decades.

The Gary work-study-play schools barely survived the depression years, when budgets were severely cut (and most platoon schools were abandoned throughout the country), and then Wirt's death came in 1938. Following an external study in 1940, which recommended dismantling the system, now considered old-fashioned and academically weak, the Gary schools began the slow process, not completed until the 1960s, of instituting the contained classroom, single-teacher model in the elementary grades (which were separate from the eight high schools by 1960). For the remainder of the century, with the mass exodus of whites, along with much of the business community, Gary's troubled schools managed to survive. They had long since lost their progressive luster, as the 25,000 African-American students (there were few others by 1990) from struggling families, an aging teacher corps, and shrinking federal dollars meant that the schools faced numerous problems into the foreseeable future.

See also: ELEMENTARY EDUCATION, *subentry on* HISTORY OF; INSTRUCTIONAL STRATEGIES; SECONDARY EDUCATION, *subentry on* HISTORY OF.

BIBLIOGRAPHY

CASE, ROSCOE D. 1931. *The Platoon School in America.* Stanford, CA: Stanford University Press.

COHEN, RONALD D. 1990. *Children of the Mill: Schooling and Society in Gary, Indiana, 1906–1960.* Bloomington: Indiana University Press.

COHEN, RONALD D., and MOHL, RAYMOND A. 1979. *The Paradox of Progressive Education: The Gary Plan and Urban Schooling.* Port Washington, NY: Kennikat Press.

RONALD D. COHEN

GAY AND LESBIAN STUDIES

Gay and lesbian studies are academic programs dedicated to the study of historical, cultural, social, and political issues of vital concern to lesbian, gay, and, increasingly, bisexual and transgendered individuals. The focus of such programs is on lesbian and gay lives and social institutions, as well as about homophobia and oppression related to sexual orientation. Gay and lesbians studies programs have encouraged many traditional disciplines to reassess their theoretical and political grounding and to consider sexuality and sexual diversity as critical facts determining social behaviors and political structures.

Goals

The goals of gay and lesbian studies programs are as varied as the programs themselves. The general goals include discovering and recovering the history and culture of homosexuality and bringing homosexuality to the forefront of academic studies, away from being an unspeakable or untouchable subject. The existence of gay and lesbian studies programs helps to challenge the invisibility of homosexuality in society and to expose students to gay and lesbian oppression as it has existed historically. Another goal of lesbian and gay studies is to explore the lives of lesbian and gay people through investigation of identity issues, experiences of oppression, and struggles for recognition. The programs seek to find a common understanding and language in which homosexuals and heterosexuals can better understand gay and lesbian lives. Many programs have an activist agenda that includes such goals as critiquing and transforming the social, political, cultural, economic, ethnic, and gender situations that continue to oppress gay and lesbian people.

In 2000 Jeffery Weeks, a professor of sociology at the University of London, identified five additional goals for gay and lesbian studies. The first is to find ways for society to learn to live with differences in sexual orientation and to provide a forum for discussing differences. The second is to adopt political and cultural stances that work toward sexual justice, which involves seeking fairness and equity in the treatment of all sexual orientations. The third goal is to challenge heterosexual norms that have been created throughout history. By addressing the second and third goals, homosexuality can be validated and affirmed while heterosexual norms are questioned so that equality of sexual orientations can be reached. The fourth goal is to question the existing body of knowledge related to sexual orientation, especially addressing who has the right to speak authoritatively on gay and lesbian issues. The fifth goal is to create spaces for debate, analysis, negotiations, disagreements, and finding common ground regarding issues of sexual orientation.

History

Gay and lesbian studies emerged from the civil rights movement, yet the roots of this discipline stretch back to the middle of the twentieth century. The Kinsey studies of human sexuality in the 1940s and 1950s challenged scientific assumptions related to sexuality and, by raising the visibility of homosexuality, provided a platform for gay and lesbian studies. Gay and lesbian studies, although taking place in academia, have been strongly influenced by the political and cultural development of gay and lesbian communities, especially in urban areas throughout the United States. As the political and cultural environment within society changed during the latter half of the twentieth century, so too did the frameworks in which gay and lesbian intellectuals and scholars worked. Specifically, during the 1950s and 1960s the homophile movement, combined with the gay liberation and lesbian feminism movements that began after the riots at the Stonewall Inn in 1969, helped to create the political climate that allowed for the development of the early stages of lesbian and gay studies in the 1970s. Additionally, the AIDS crisis in the 1980s added yet another layer that helped mature gay and lesbian studies. In 1991 the Center for Lesbian and Gay Studies (CLAGS) was founded at the City University of New York Graduate School. CLAGS is the first and only university-based research center in the United States dedicated to the study of historical, cultural, and political issues of concern to lesbian, gay, bisexual, and transgendered individuals.

Another way of understanding the historical development of gay and lesbian studies is to consider the focus of scholarly activity and its diversification during the last three decades of the twentieth centu-

ry. Jeffrey Escoffier, deputy director for policy and research of the Office of Gay and Lesbian Health in New York City, in 1992 identified several different interdisciplinary paradigms that arose during that period. The first, "Search for Authenticity, 1969–1976," was formed by the Stonewall generation as an effort to encourage research and writing from gay liberation and feminist perspectives. For example, during this period the Gay Academic Union was formed in New York City with the goal of confronting homophobia in academia. Although the union lasted only a short while, it did provide a forum for academics interested in issues related to sexual orientation and led to further organizing and eventually to program development.

"Social Construction of Identity, 1976–present" focuses on homosexual identity and how this identity is shaped and formed not only by homosexual behavior but also by cultural and societal action. "Essentialist Identity: Lesbian Existence and Gay Universals, 1975–present" is the complement to the socially constructed aspect of identity and concentrates on the structures and similarities in the gay and lesbian experience that span historical periods. "Difference and Race, 1979–present" addresses how culture, ethnicity, and race combine with homosexuality. One of its many concerns is that gay and lesbian studies and scholarship not remain focused on white culture, but rather emphasize the diversity of experience in gay and lesbian lives. The final paradigm, "The Pursuit of Signs: The Cultural Studies Paradigms, 1985–present," builds on the social construction of identity paradigm to include all forms of texts, cultural codes, signifying practices, and modes of discourse that form attitudes toward homosexuality.

Current Configurations

At the beginning of the twenty-first century, gay and lesbian studies programs vary widely in terms of focus, structure, and connections with other academic units. Most programs are at large institutions, both public and private, and most of these institutions are in urban areas. There are few programs at small, private, rural liberal arts colleges. Most programs are gay and lesbian specific while some also include the general categories of gender and sexuality. Others have expanded to include emphases on bisexuality, transgender issues, and queer theory. The majority of the lesbian and gay studies programs offer undergraduate minors or certificate programs.

Few institutions offer undergraduate majors or graduate degrees strictly in gay and lesbian studies. Some institutions offer undergraduate programs in which lesbian and gay studies can be combined with a traditional major (e.g., a major in history with a focus on gay and lesbian studies); others offer the opportunity to create degree programs through individualized learning or liberal studies programs; and some institutions offer dual or integrated graduate degree programs where lesbian and gay studies can be combined with programs in other disciplines.

Because lesbian and gay studies focuses on a group of subjects instead of a concept, it is difficult to place the field within a specific academic discipline. Therefore, virtually all programs are interdisciplinary in nature, working with other departments on campus covering a wide span of disciplines including biology, anthropology, anatomy, cultural anthropology, English, literature, film and video, history, art history, political science, psychology, religion, sociology, ethnic studies, and women's studies. Additionally, lesbian and gay studies programs are most often linked to or coupled with women's studies or gender studies.

The disadvantages of interdisciplinarity include diffused academic power and influence, constrained resources, and a lack of a disciplinary home. The advantage of interdisciplinarity is that once established, lesbian and gay studies programs are difficult to isolate and sequester. Interdisciplinary study then results in a change in how gay and lesbian lives, experiences, and reality are experienced, studied, and understood. It forces scholars to integrate the often-fragmented disciplines into which the academic experience has been sorted. Scholarship and study in separate disciplines makes it easier to ignore diversity and complexity and allows important questions to go unasked, a few chosen issues to be raised, select individuals to be studied, and leaves a large portion of the lesbian and gay population ignored. Interdisciplinarity reinforces the fact that no longer are there only the categories of heterosexual and homosexual, but that there are many variations in between. Interdisciplinary study encourages a constant questioning of the assumptions underlying theories that are being used and why they are being used.

Two growing areas under the rubric of lesbian and gay studies are lesbian studies as a self-contained unit and queer theory. There have been some efforts to separate lesbian studies from gay studies and women's studies because of concerns about sexism (in gay studies) and heterosexism and homophobia (in women's studies). The argument is that lesbian oppression has been ignored and needs to be investigated from the perspective of multiple disciplines separate from gay studies.

The category of queer theory first appeared in the early 1990s. Teresa de Lauretis is the theorist often credited with inaugurating the phrase. Queer theory expands the focus of lesbian and gay studies from socially constructed or essentialist identities to sexual practices and sexual representations. Queer theorists view sexuality along a continuum and question whether it is ever fixed at one point. Queer theory challenges all identity categories, such as heterosexual, homosexual, male, and female and analyzes the power imbalances that are inherent in them.

See also: SEXUAL ORIENTATION.

BIBLIOGRAPHY

CARROLL, LYNNE, and GILROY, PAULA J. 2001. "Teaching 'Outside the Box': Incorporating Queer Theory in Counselor Education." *Journal of Humanistic Counseling, Education, and Development* 40(1):49–57.

CORBER, ROBERT J. 1998. "Scholarship and Sexuality: Lesbian and Gay Studies in Today's Academy." *Academe* 84(5):46–49.

DE LAURETIS, TERESA. 1991. "Queer Theory: Lesbian and Gay Sexualities." *Differences: A Journal of Feminist Cultural Studies* 3(2):iii–xviii.

ESCOFFIER, JEFFREY. 1992. "Generations and Paradigms: Mainstreams in Lesbian and Gay Studies." In *Gay and Lesbian Studies,* ed. Henry L. Minton. Binghamton, NY: Harrington Park Press.

MINTON, HENRY L. 1992. "The Emergence of Gay and Lesbian Studies." In *Gay and Lesbian Studies,* ed. Henry L. Minton. Binghamton, NY: Harrington Park Press.

NAMASTE, KI. 1992. "Deconstruction, Lesbian and Gay Studies, and Interdisciplinary Work: Theoretical, Political, and Institutional Strategies." In *Gay and Lesbian Studies,* ed. Henry L. Minton. Binghamton, NY: Harrington Park Press.

SCHUYF, JUDITH, and SANDFORT, THEO. 2000. "Conclusion: Gay and Lesbian Studies at the Crossroads." In *Lesbian and Gay Studies: An Introductory, Interdisciplinary Approach,* ed. Theo Sandfort. Thousand Oaks, CA: Sage.

WEEKS, JEFFREY. 2000. "The Challenge of Lesbian and Gay Studies." In *Lesbian and Gay Studies: An Introductory, Interdisciplinary Approach,* ed. Theo Sandfort. Thousand Oaks, CA: Sage.

WILTON, TAMISIN. 1995. *Lesbian Studies: Setting the Agenda.* London: Routledge.

PATRICK LOVE

GENDER ISSUES, INTERNATIONAL

Many benefits accrue to investments in women's schooling, which range from social payoffs (such as lower fertility rates, improved children and women's health, greater life expectancy for women and men, and higher schooling attainment by new generations) to individual improvements (such as older age at marriage, reduced teen pregnancy, greater participation and productivity into the labor force, and a greater sense of independence in economic and political decisions). For education to have a positive effect, particularly in wages, it appears that women must reach a threshold of attainment between four years of primary-level schooling and completion of primary schooling.

Access to Schooling

Women's access to schooling is far from equal to that of men, with considerable variation among developing regions. Official statistics for enrollment tend to underestimate the dimension of this problem; nonetheless they indicate that there are between 120 million and 150 million children ages six to eleven out of school. This group is mostly poor, and about two-thirds are girls. In South Asia, the Arab region, and sub-Saharan Africa, about 600 million boys and girls attend school, but 42 million fewer girls than boys are enrolled at the primary level and 33 million fewer at the secondary school, as reported in 1999 by Shanti Conly and Nada Chaya. Due to low access to basic education when young, two-thirds of the 900 million illiterates are women. The literacy gender gap has been narrowing over time, except in South Asia.

If educating girls is such a win-win proposition, why are there not more girls in school? Cultural factors such as notions of a girl's proper age for marriage, anxiety about the sexuality and sexual safety of daughters, and the division of labor at home (with women in charge of domestic and childcare tasks) affect girls' enrollment and both primary and secondary school completion. In India and many sub-Saharan countries, where strong cultural norms require early marriage, parents often consider puberty as the cutoff for schooling.

Many countries in the developing world face heavy external debts, which forces governments to give priority to economic matters (industrial or manufactured production) over welfare or social justice. Across countries, completion of girls' schooling is at risk because poor parents are more willing to invest in boys since boys (when adults) will be expected to support parents while girls will follow their husbands' families. Another economic factor of importance is the immediate value of girls through their domestic work. Since parents tend to withdraw daughters from school when they do not perform well, girls are not allowed to repeat school as boys would, especially in sub-Saharan Africa. About 150 million of those currently enrolled in primary school will drop out before completing four years of education according to Kevin Watkins's 1999 study. The losses are greatest among girls who belong to poor families or marginalized ethnic groups. Finally, political factors also intervene when governments find it is easier to maintain the status quo than to risk antagonizing opposing groups.

What Is Learned in School

In developing countries some rural families are reluctant to send their daughters to school for fear they will learn new values, becoming less inclined to accept domestic work and more interested in joining salaried occupations. But formal education—both in developing and industrialized countries—tends to convey messages and experiences that reproduce traditional views of femininity and masculinity, with the consequence that girls do not acquire knowledge that makes them question the status quo and boys do not learn to appreciate girls' needs and conditions. The school curriculum in some subject areas avoids dealing with issues considered social taboos. Thus, sexual education does not consider the social relations of sexuality but emphasizes knowledge of reproductive organs and, now that AIDS has become an illness of major proportions, information about avoiding risky sexual practices, primarily via sexual abstinence. Discussion of sexual orientation, a major concern in adolescence, is especially avoided for fear of promoting homosexuality. Serious and widespread issues such as domestic violence and rape are usually sidestepped in the school curriculum.

Activism by the women's movement and some research about textbooks led to the improvement of content of many school materials. Most of the changes have dealt with incorporating a more inclusive language (referring not only to men but also to women), including more balanced roles between women and men, and displaying a greater presence of women as examples or significant historical actors. Yet, although studies of current textbooks are limited, evidence indicates that the changes do not question the existence of sexism in society, nor challenge girls and boys to confront everyday practices at home, school, and other institutions that sustain conventional gendered ways in which society is organized.

A major weakness in the efforts to make schools become venues for gender contestation has been the limited provision of teacher training (either in institutions that prepare new teachers or through in-service training) on issues of gender in society and education. As a result, teachers—many of whom are women—do not have a solid understanding of how gender operates in their lives and in the lives of others. Classroom behaviors by teachers favoring the intellectual development of boys and fostering the compliance of girls go unchecked. Outside the classroom, spaces where the reproduction of prejudicial gender beliefs and norms occurs, such as sports, the playground, and extracurricular activities, are seldom considered for examination and transformation.

Public Policies on Gender and Equity

Many governments have made public commitments to increasing the access of girls to schooling, reducing the gap in schooling between girls and boys, and reducing illiteracy, especially among women. Such commitments are seldom met. For example, the Education For All (EFA) initiative sought to provide universal education for all by the year 2000. By 2000 this goal had been deferred to 2015, with no firm promise that previous obstacles to policy implementation would be removed. Major international assistance agencies (notably the World Bank and the U.S. and Japanese bilateral development agencies) continue to justify support for girls' education for its value as an economic investment, downplaying reasons of social justice and individual autonomy. A

number of pilot studies attempted in several developing countries have demonstrated the power of interventions such as the provision of tuition subsidies or scholarships for girls to offset their economic value to families. Unfortunately, only a handful of countries have brought these interventions to nationwide application (scholarships for secondary schoolgirls in Bangladesh, family stipends to families with daughters in primary school in Guatemala, and subsidies to rural families in Mexico). Most governments are willing to uphold the importance of girls' and women's education, but fail to acknowledge the impact of ideological factors shaping definitions of masculinity and femininity, which in turn determine men's and women's unequal roles in society. When women shy away from male-dominated fields of study and occupations (particularly in science and technology), and as they give priority to family over professional or occupational responsibilities, their decisions are interpreted as entirely individual choices.

Schools throughout the world are undergoing major structural and substantive reforms. Efforts to decentralize the public school system and to foster the creation of private schools abound. It is not clear how community participation in the decentralized schools will favor gender equity if the parents themselves are not educated to understand the dynamics of gender reproduction and transformation. Privatization may further constrain girls' participation if the economic conditions of families do not improve. Substantive reforms of schools are focused on improving quality, but this objective is defined in narrow terms, emphasizing the preparation of future workers, rather than future citizens. Math and science are seen as the key curriculum subjects to the detriment of other disciplines. Evidence from Latin America indicates that current reforms express concern for issues of "productivity" and "competitiveness" but much less so for those of equity and social justice (Task Force on Education Reform in Central America, 2000). They seek to promote decentralization and nationwide assessments of student achievement to compare their performance within and across countries. They also seek differentiated pay for teachers on the basis of their performance, which will act as a mechanism to further concentrate on math and reading.

Concerned with the slow progress to improve education in general and the education of girls in particular, a number of nongovernmental organizations (NGOs) in developed countries have become active in advocating major financial resources for education in the Third World. It is estimated in Watkins's 1999 study that closing the gender gap by 2005 would require U.S. $9.5 billion in recurrent expenditures in the fifty-one countries with the largest gender differentials. As of the early twenty-first century, the quantity and content of girls' education is best described as being at an impasse, in which forces capable of implementing nationwide action are concentrating on the economic ends of schooling and seeing it as a gender-neutral institution, while forces for transformation, particularly those that could be carried by women's groups, are not receiving the support they need.

See also: INDIVIDUAL DIFFERENCES, *subentry on* GENDER STUDIES AND GENDER DEVELOPMENT; MODERNITY AND EDUCATION; POPULATION AND EDUCATION.

BIBLIOGRAPHY

KING, ELIZABETH, and HILL, ANNE, eds. 1993. *Women's Education in Developing Countries.* Washington, DC: The World Bank.

O'BRIEN, ROBERT; GOETZ, ANNE MARIE; SCHOLTE, JAN; and WILLIAMS, MARC. 2000. *Contesting Global Governance: Multilateral Economic Institutions and Global Social Movements.* Cambridge, Eng.: Cambridge University Press.

TASK FORCE ON EDUCATION REFORM IN CENTRAL AMERICA. 2000. *Tomorrow Is Too Late.* Washington, DC: Partnership for Educational Revitalization in the Americas.

UNITED NATIONS. 1995. *Women's Education and Fertility Behaviors: Recent Evidence from the Demographic and Health Surveys.* New York: United Nations.

UNITED NATIONS CHILDRENS' FUND (UNICEF). 2000. *Educating Girls: Transforming the Future.* New York: United Nations Childrens' Fund.

WATKINS, KEVIN. 1999. *Education Now: Breaking the Cycle of Poverty.* Oxford: Oxfam International.

INTERNET RESOURCE

CONLY, SHANTI R., and CHAYA, NADA. 1999. *Educating Girls—Gender Gaps and Gains.* Washington, DC: Population Action International.

<www.populationaction.org/resources/publications/educating_girls/index.htm>.

NELLY P. STROMQUIST

GENERAL EDUCATIONAL DEVELOPMENT TEST

The General Educational Development Test (GED) is a battery of tests designed to measure the educational level of people who did not formally complete high school. Candidates who successfully pass the five subject area tests are awarded a high school equivalency certificate recognized by state education departments. The American Council on Education (ACE) offers the GED and preparation guidance across the United Sates and worldwide. Other organizations, such as the National Institute for Literacy, also offer Adult Basic and Secondary Education programs designed to aid adults in completing the GED successfully. Developed during World War II to assist veterans who had left high school before graduation to enlist in the military, the GED test battery underwent revisions for 2002, which were designed to make the test comparable to standards-of-learning tests compulsory in most states since the mid-1990s.

History

After World War I, veterans who had left high school to enlist in the armed services were awarded diplomas in exchange for their service to the nation. After World War II, however, returning soldiers were required to pass a test before being given their high school equivalency certificates. The U.S. Armed Forces Institute examination staff first constructed the GED test in 1942. In 1945 ACE established the Veterans' Testing Service (VTS), and beginning in 1947 tests were distributed to civilian institutions where veterans were applying for employment or college admission. By 1959 more civilians than veterans were being given the GED test, and in 1963 the VTS changed its name to the General Educational Development Testing Service to reflect this shift in test-taking populations. Early tests were designed so that most veterans would pass, and more than 90 percent did. The test was revised in 1988 to include an essay section, and remained essentially unchanged until January 2002, when a series of revisions went into effect. At the turn of the twenty-first century, more than 860,000 people take the tests annually, and one in seven people who finish high school earns the credential by passing the GED test. High school graduation rates published by the U.S. Census Bureau include GED holders, and the certificate is seen as interchangeable with a high school diploma for most employers and colleges. Although researchers debate the success of the GED in helping individuals attain meaningful careers, it is clear that the GED is an important part of the American educational landscape.

Changes at the Start of the Twenty-First Century

The General Educational Development test questions and norms have been revised beginning in 2002 as a response to the standards movement in American secondary education. The overall impact of the revisions is to make the test more difficult. The previous test was structured to provide a failure rate of about one in three; however, revised cutoff scores are now designed so that 40 percent of high school seniors would not pass. The designers of the revised GED tests responded to complaints from colleges and employers about poorly educated GED holders by developing questions geared to identify and measure practical knowledge and life skills. Information sources such as product labels and legal documents are used to generate questions and answers. The revised GED tests are designed to be an improved measurement of a student's practical skills, dispositions, and abilities.

Test Description

Like other standardized tests, the GED is primarily a multiple-choice test in each content area. The General Educational Development questions fall into five test areas similar to those of public secondary standards-based assessments: writing skills, literature and arts, mathematics, social studies, and science. The writing test is divided into two sections: the first presents sentences that may or may not include errors that require correction. These questions are similar to those of the SAT Test of Standard Written English (as administered prior to 1994) and the Test of English as a Foreign Language (TOEFL). The second writing skills test is to construct an essay of about 200 words on one of several topics provided by the test makers.

Like the PSAT and SAT essays, the GED writing test is holistically scored on a scale from one to six. Graders emphasize clarity of composition, support for ideas, and sentence mechanics. The revised, two-part mathematics section tests skills in arithmetic operations, algebra, and geometry. Test takers respond to equations, word problems, and data displayed on charts and graphs. Sample questions provided by ACE emphasize real-world numeric texts, such as federal tax allocations, personal earnings, and nutritional values charts. All mathematics questions were formerly in the multiple-choice form; in 2002, 20 percent require fill-in responses and students are allowed to use calculators. The social studies section tests knowledge in economics, political science, geography, and the behavioral sciences (anthropology, psychology, sociology). Social studies questions are different in Canadian versions of GED tests than in the United States. Science questions are based on information typically taught in earth science, biology, physics, and chemistry. Students are asked to analyze charts, graphs, drawings, or questions, and identify the best solution to the practical problems presented. Sample GED science question topics include the principles of buoyancy, displacement, spectrum heat absorption comparison, and chart-reading skills. The literature and the arts section of the test once emphasized reading comprehension only in the areas of popular and classical poetry, fiction, nonfiction prose, and drama. The revised test includes passages from other real-world text sources such as tax documents and commentaries.

Resources

The American Council on Education provides test preparation materials and sample questions in each content area, as well as a comprehensive preparation guide. The GED Testing Center also includes a directory of adult education and GED prep classes. The GED tests are available in Spanish and French for qualified applicants, and special accommodations are available for candidates with disabilities. Accommodations include an audiocassette edition, large-print edition, braille edition, extended time, use of a scribe, talking calculators, private room use, one-on-one testing at a candidate's home, vision-enhancing technologies, video equipment, sign-language interpreter, or other accommodation in cases where circumstances warrant.

See also: DROPOUTS, SCHOOL; SECONDARY EDUCATION, *subentries on* CURRENT TRENDS, HISTORY OF.

BIBLIOGRAPHY

KLEINER, CAROLYN. 2001. "The GED's New Math." *U.S. News and World Report* December 17:42–43.

MURNANE, RICHARD J., and TYLER, JOHN H. 2000. "The Increasing Role of the GED in American Education." *Education Week* 19(34):64, 48.

INTERNET RESOURCES

AMERICAN COUNCIL ON EDUCATION. "General Educational Development Tests." 2002. <www.gedtest.org>.

NATIONAL INSTITUTE FOR LITERACY. "General Educational Development Tests." 2002. <www.literacydirectory.org>.

JAMES B. TUTTLE

GENERAL EDUCATION IN HIGHER EDUCATION

As American higher education moved from institutions that promoted learning for learning's sake to institutions that prepare individuals for work and careers, new approaches in college and university curriculum development became necessary. One significant evolution was the movement away from the classical, European model of liberal education to the development of a narrower, more selective model of liberal studies, that has become known in American colleges and universities as *general education.*

The Difference between Liberal Education and General Education

The original mission of American higher education was to provide a liberal education based on the European model of classical education. In the liberal education model, college students became well versed in classic literary works, philosophy, foreign languages, rhetoric, and logic. This model stressed the importance of a broad base of education that encouraged an appreciation of knowledge, an ability to think and solve problems, and a desire to improve society. American liberal arts colleges and universities most closely resemble this traditional model of liberal education.

In the late eighteenth century, however, social forces in American society began calling for a more utilitarian and practical education that would prepare students for work upon graduation. State normal schools emerged to prepare teachers for jobs in American schools. In addition, business schools and other vocational preparation programs became more popular. In 1862 the Morrill Act further pushed this utilitarian model by providing federal money to land-grant institutions chosen to develop agricultural and technical programs. By the late 1800s, students on many campuses had the ability to choose courses freely, without requirements, and could now choose a concentration, or major, in one particular field of study. By the late nineteenth and early twentieth centuries, many work-oriented fields such as teaching, business, engineering, and nursing had made their way into the four-year college and university curriculum. Vocational and practical education was now a major component of American higher education.

In the mid-twentieth century, a new movement for the revitalization of liberal education began. A great debate emerged between those in higher education who supported the movement toward specialized and vocational preparation and those who felt that this push to focus on a particular field was leading to overspecialized and narrow areas of study that would be of little use as careers and technology changed. Many supporters of liberal education also argued that specialized study did not contribute positively to the development of society. In 1947, as the debate became more heated, the President's Commission on Higher Education called for the development of a balance between "specialized training on the one hand, aiming at a thousand different careers" and a general curriculum that fosters "the transmission of a common cultural heritage toward common citizenship on the other" (p. 49).

Recognizing the importance of vocational training but still valuing the significance of classical education, many colleges and universities began to develop a series or set of courses that all students attending their institution would take prior to graduation. This set of courses became known as general education, sometimes referred to as a core curriculum. This model of curriculum has come to exist as a fundamental component of American higher education. According to Joan Stark and Lisa Lattuca, the American Council on Education found that in 1990 over 85 percent of American colleges and universities required all students to complete some sort of general education requirements.

The Goals of General Education

General education emerged in response to changing societal needs and the tension between classical liberal education and more practical or specialized education. The primary goal of general education is to provide a broad, yet focused, survey of courses that will promote critical thinking and increase students' awareness of the world around them. On many campuses, general education's purpose serves as a foundation for technical or vocational training, fostering in students the ability to think beyond their areas of specialization. Many faculty members and administrators on college and university campuses hope that requiring a set of specific courses will encourage students to make connections across disciplines and between formal course instruction and informal learning experiences outside the classroom.

General education requirements vary significantly from one institution to another. These expectations, however, often stem from the way in which different institutions answer the same guiding questions, such as: ideally, what knowledge, skills, values, and attitudes should graduates of the institution possess upon completion of their degree? And, how should the curriculum be designed to meet this goal? The variation in general education requirements stems from the broad array of institutional missions and goals and, accordingly, the many ways these broad questions are answered by the hundreds of American colleges and universities.

More important than specific requirements for general education is the time given by institutions to intentional thought, discussion, and development of general education curriculum. Ernest T. Pascarella and Patrick T. Terenzini (1991) affirmed this notion when they discovered that the greatest gains in students' ability to think critically were found at institutions with courses specifically designed to meet general education requirements. Even knowing this, however, extensive disagreement continues to exist among members of college and university communities regarding the identification of fundamental components and requirements of a general education curriculum. This continuing disagreement can lead to a tedious and lengthy debate, resulting in slow and difficult change on most campuses. The importance of general education was affirmed in a national study conducted by Ernest Boyer for the Carnegie Foundation for the Advancement of Teaching (1987). Boyer and his colleagues found that approximately 75 percent of undergraduates in American colleges and universities felt that general education courses "added to the enrichment of other courses" and "helped prepare [them] for lifelong learning" (p. 85).

A final goal, espoused by many supporters of general education, is that all students should have a common experience or be exposed to a particular set of knowledge. It is not uncommon in the early twenty-first century to find colleges and universities that provide required reading lists to all incoming students. These readings are often incorporated in the general education curriculum and provide a common foundation and experience for that cohort of students. These common learning experiences often emerge in discussions throughout students' experiences at that institution and continue into their lives beyond the collegiate experience. This approach to general education relates to the primary goal of general education stated earlier: to make connections between formal course instruction and informal learning experiences outside the classroom.

Typical Characteristics of General Education

Although specific requirements may vary among American colleges and universities, there are characteristics common to general education across institutions. Typically, general education does not emphasize practical knowledge or research skills. The emphasis of general education is to help students understand that they are not individuals who stand apart from society but rather one person living in community with others in a greater society. As Boyer eloquently wrote, general education "is significant when it shows us who we are as individuals and as citizens, and touches the hopes and fears that make each of us both unique beings and a part of corporate humanity" (p. 98). This level of understanding is often achieved through the weaving of courses across a variety of disciplines.

In order to foster this understanding of a broad picture of society and to lay a foundation upon which all else is built, general education requirements are often taken during the first few semesters of the college experience. Students on many campuses are given a set of courses from which they can choose specific classes that will fulfill specific requirements. Some general education requirements, however, become prerequisites for upper level courses so that students enter these classes with a common level of knowledge and understanding. An additional benefit of general education courses is that students tend to recognize others taking the same courses and establish friendships during those first few semesters that extend beyond the classroom and often last a lifetime.

With an increasing number of students attending two-year institutions and more students transferring to and among four-year colleges and universities, it has become more critical for colleges and universities to recognize and identify courses that fulfill general education requirements. Usually, courses such as English, mathematics, and foreign languages are transferable across institutions. Some courses directly align with and meet general education requirements, while other courses are accepted as electives but still count toward graduation credit. This change has made it easier and more financially possible for students to move among institutions without penalty. Many colleges and universities, however, do limit the total number of credits that they allow to transfer in order for students to receive the quality education desired by the institution.

Typical Requirements

A broad array of choices exist in general education across American colleges and universities. Some institutions follow a very prescribed and specific set of courses, whereas many others offer a broad spectrum of courses from which students select "some of these and some of those," a method often referred to as *cafeteria-style*.

One specific requirement that tends to remain constant across most institutions is a proficiency in English. Most colleges and universities agree that a fundamental component of being well educated is the ability to read and write. Thus, regardless of students' chosen fields, almost every college and university requires coursework in English literature and composition. Even professors of mathematics and engineering have stressed the importance of students being able to express themselves in the written and spoken word. Beyond this one component, requirements do vary with some overlapping expectations among colleges and universities.

According to Stark and Lattuca, by the mid-1980s most students in American colleges and universities (over 60%) were required to take courses in English and mathematics. Additionally, 45 percent of all institutions require courses in Western or world civilizations. Beyond these more common requirements, some institutions also require course-

work, at least at an introductory level, in laboratory sciences such as biology or chemistry, and in social sciences such as psychology, sociology, or political science. Some also require the study of a foreign language.

As noted earlier, over 85 percent of American colleges and universities have some sort of general education requirements for their undergraduate students. Stark and Lattuca noted that typical students at four-year institutions spend 33 to 40 percent of their studies meeting general education requirements. And, although debate continues regarding which courses should be considered critical in the development of educated graduates prepared for life beyond college, general education itself is firmly grounded in the modern American collegiate experience. Some colleges maintain a broad array of choices that satisfy general education requirements, whereas others are very specific with their curriculum. Many institutions have also been very successful at creating interdisciplinary courses that incorporate material and perspectives from a wide variety of disciplines; some of these courses have become quite popular and successful at institutions across the United States. Regardless of institutional choice, with such varying expectations from one institution to another, it is critical that students understand what is expected of them in order to develop a successful approach to their college studies.

See also: ACADEMIC MAJOR, THE; CURRICULUM, HIGHER EDUCATION, *subentry on* NATIONAL REPORTS ON THE UNDERGRADUATE CURRICULUM.

BIBLIOGRAPHY

BOYER, ERNEST. 1987. *College: The Undergraduate Experience in America.* Princeton, NJ: Carnegie Foundation for the Advancement of Teaching.

PASCARELLA, ERNEST T., and TERENZINI, PATRICK T. 1991. *How College Affects Students.* San Francisco: Jossey-Bass.

PRESIDENT'S COMMISSION ON HIGHER EDUCATION. 1948. *Higher Education for American Democracy.* New York: Harper and Row.

STARK, JOAN, and LATTUCA, LISA. 1997. *Shaping the College Curriculum: Academic Plans in Action.* Needham Heights, MA: Allyn and Bacon.

MOLLY BLACK DUESTERHAUS

GEOGRAPHY, TEACHING OF

Geography, like history, is not defined by the uniqueness of its content; rather, both gain their distinction by the way in which they organize and analyze the data they collect regarding particular aspects of the human experience. History compares and contrasts information within the framework of chronology, while geography organizes its information within the context of the spatial environment. Today, the focus of geographic inquiry is generally conceded to be on spatial interactions, that is, the geographer seeks to understand the significance of human activity within a spatial framework. Where historians report their findings primarily through written narratives, geographers present their data primarily through the construction of maps.

Until the advent of the Progressive movement in American life, beginning in the decades following the Civil War, geography was taught as a separate subject. Memorization of the names of important cities, physical features, and relational facts dominated instruction. Recognition of the temporary shelf life of that kind of information taught in rote fashion led Progressive educators to deemphasize the acquisition of facts and to instead emphasize the role of reasoning and problem solving in learning. Under this program, the traditional subjects of geography, history, and civics were fused. In this context the teaching of geography began to lose its identity as a unique area of study.

Effectiveness of Instruction

Whether taught as a separate subject or fused in some way with subject matter drawn from other fields of the natural and social sciences, there is a long history of ineffectiveness of instruction in the teaching of geography. From the first attempt to assess the effectiveness of instruction in geography, in the 1840s in Boston's public schools, to the most recent efforts, notably the National Assessment of Educational Progress (NAEP), there is a continuing record of what most consider to be substandard results. A much more sophisticated assessment tool than those of past years, the NAEP results have shown, for example, that secondary students learn more geographic information in history classes than in those classes devoted exclusively to the study of geography. Although one can decry such a seeming incongruity, the historical knowledge displayed by students on these tests was equally dismal.

How is it that geographic instruction appears to be so ineffective? One reason may be that teachers generally are not themselves geographically literate. One teaches what one knows, and today's teachers are as much a product of their schooling as anyone else. It might be hoped that professional geographers would be able to communicate the nature of geographic literacy and would be effective in educating teachers for the task of teaching geographic concepts. Unfortunately, the number of professional geographers is limited—hardly a drop in the bucket when compared to the number of professional historians, for example—so it is to be expected their ability to help teachers will also be limited. However, there are many geographers who are devoted to the task of teacher education and are actively involved in remediating this problem, which is coordinated to the extent possible through a professional organization, the National Council for Geographic Education.

A second reason that geographic instruction is not as effective as it might be is because not enough is known about how students acquire geographic concepts. There is, however, a body of information that is suggestive of that process. Swiss psychologist Jean Piaget (1896–1980) is the towering figure in the development of research techniques and in broadening understandings about the fashion in which spatial concepts develop. Rather than being interested in a child's ability to give a correct response to direct questions, he sought to understand the reasoning process that led children to give incorrect answers to the broader tasks he set before them to solve. As well, instead of attempting to secure answers in a third-person setting in which the correct answers were foretold—the paper-and-pencil test so familiar in American schools—he asked youngsters to talk their way through the solution to a particular spatial problem irrespective of "correctness."

Piaget's pioneering research, and that of many researchers who followed his lead in exploring the emergence of spatial concepts, tells us that the intellectual progression in the ability to comprehend spatial properties moves from perceived space to conceived space, from experiencing space only in the most direct sense to conceptions of space in which the child's thoughts, at first quite primitive, gradually become abstract and based on Euclidean (mathematical) conceptions. The development of a reasonably mature ability to comprehend spatial interactions appears not to be available to the student until early adolescence. If this is so, then the importance of providing direct environmental experience, especially in the elementary school, would be required for the development of the kind of thinking that is basic to the mature comprehending of spatial interactions. That school environments largely preclude direct experiencing of the spatial environment means that the development of geographic literacy faces some significant hurdles, and it also explains why the focus on "where-is-it," "what-is-it" kinds of questions persist in the school curriculum.

Maps and Spatial Concepts

Since the map provides the basic tool for reporting spatial interactions, the ability to read maps meaningfully is a primary objective of instruction. Map reading can be viewed as a more complex form of print reading—the reading of books, newspapers, and so forth— in which the number of symbols and their positions in relation to one another are both consistent and limited. Map reading, in contrast, requires the reader to develop meanings for a wide variety of symbols, some conventional print but others of varying degrees of abstraction, all arranged in a relational two-dimensional environment. The reading process, regardless of the symbol systems employed, requires the creation of meanings, which in turn are dependent upon the reader's conceptual base, that is, what the reader understands the symbols are intended to represent. There has long been controversy over how the reading process, regardless of the complexity of the symbol system involved, is initiated. Many believe that initial skills should be taught in a more or less arbitrary fashion and that the development of meanings follows. Others, and that is the argument here, believe that form follows function, that concepts, in this case of spatial relationships, are basic to the process of creating meanings in response to apprehending textual material.

As in learning to read conventional print, it is argued that the most constructive route to fluent reading involves much writing based on one's own experience. If map reading is, as it appears, similar to reading print in its more conventional form, but complicated by the presence of a variety of symbols representing different sets of meanings arranged in a two-dimensional plane (as well as an abstraction of the world's three-dimensional reality), then learning to read maps with some degree of sophistication must depend upon prior experiences in constructing maps out of one's personal experience. Taking this view, an important activity throughout the school curriculum for both elementary and secondary schools should entail an emphasis on a developmental sequence that takes the student from first creating maps directly out of one's own experience and going onward from there toward learning how the mathematics of map making results in the kind of representations seen in classrooms and the world at large.

Studies of children's conceptions of spatial interactions indicate the progression toward some degree of intellectual maturity in this regard is much slower than commonly perceived. For example, concepts of political entities (towns, states, nations, etc.), notions of boundary lines, slope, and elevation seem to commence their emergence late—in early adolescence at best. The argument that television and various forms of virtual reality, abstractions even at their best, have expanded student's views such that they are much more aware of the world they live in begs further examination. It is to be regretted in this regard that Piagetian research protocols have not been updated and applied to furthering our knowledge. The admittedly little evidence we do have suggests that we be cautious in coming to any conclusions about the efficacy of media, including the Internet, in promoting geographic understandings because the emergence of mature geographic understanding appears to be so highly dependent upon prior firsthand experiencing of the immediate environment.

Evaluating Geographic Learning

How, then, does one evaluate geographic learning? Geographers are not in agreement regarding the approach instruction should take and, consequently, how to judge whether significant learning has occurred. The major traditions of geographic inquiry, which might be used as the basic framework for making such judgments, have been defined as the *spatial tradition,* the *areas studies tradition,* the *man–land tradition,* and the *earth science tradition.* These are the traditional categories employed in developing college curricula. Geographers more interested in defining geography appropriate to elementary and secondary schools have argued for what they call the *five themes of geography*: location, place, relationships within places, movement over the earth, and regions.

Whichever set of criteria one uses for developing test items, and despite the popularity of paper-and-pencil multiple-choice questions, easily evaluated by mechanical means, it is now widely accepted that evaluation procedures, to be valid, must include questions requiring the student to demonstrate reasoning abilities for reaching a particular conclusion about spatial interrelationships. Evaluating responses that demonstrate reasoning powers along with knowledge of specifics requires more time than current test practice provides and will, therefore, not be widely used until there is a broader acceptance of in-depth analyses of knowledge as the better indicator of students' progress toward geographic literacy.

See also: CURRICULUM, SCHOOL; HISTORY, *subentry on* TEACHING OF; SOCIAL STUDIES EDUCATION.

BIBLIOGRAPHY

BROWN, LLOYD A. 1949. *The Story of Maps.* Boston: Little, Brown.

CALDWELL, OTIS W., and COURTIS, STUART A. 1925. *Then and Now in Education 1845–1923: A Message of Encouragement from the Past to the Present.* Highland Park, NJ: Gryphon Press.

DONALDSON, MARGARET. 1978. *Children's Minds.* New York: Norton.

DOUGLASS, MALCOLM P. 1998. *The History, Psychology, and Pedagogy of Geographic Literacy.* Westport, CT: Praeger.

GREENHOOD, DAVID. *Mapping.* Chicago: University of Chicago Press.

HALL, STEPHEN S. 1992. *Mapping the Next Millennium.* New York: Random House.

HANNA, PAUL R. 1987. *Assuring Quality for the Social Studies in Our Schools.* Stanford, CA: Hoover Institution Press.

MONMONIER, MARK. 1995. *Drawing the Line: Tales of Maps and Cartocontroversy.* New York: Henry Holt.

NABHAN, GARY PAUL, and TRIBLE, STEPHEN. 1994. *The Geography of Childhood: Why Children Need Wild Places.* Boston: Beacon Press.

NATIONAL ASSESSMENT OF EDUCATIONAL PROGRESS. 1990. *The Geography Learning of High School Seniors.* Princeton, NJ: Educational Testing Service.

NATIONAL GEOGRAPHIC EDUCATION STANDARDS PROJECT. 1994. *Geography for Life: National Geography Standards 1994.* Washington, DC: National Geographic Research and Exploration.

PIAGET, JEAN, and INHELDER, BÄRBEL. 1956. *The Child's Conception of Space,* trans. F. J. Langdon and J. L. Lunzer. London: Routledge and Kegan Paul.

SAXE, DAVID WARREN. 1991. *Social Studies in Schools: A History of the Early Years.* Albany: State University of New York Press.

U.S. DEPARTMENT OF EDUCATION. OFFICE OF EDUCATIONAL RESEARCH AND IMPROVEMENT. 1995. *NAEP 1994 Geography: A First Look: Findings from the National Assessment of Educational Progress.* Washington, DC: U.S. Department of Education.

U.S. OFFICE OF EDUCATION. NATIONAL ASSESSMENT OF EDUCATION PROGRESS. 1990. *The Geography Learning of High School Seniors.* Washington, DC: Office of Educational Research and Improvement, U.S. Office of Education.

UNWIN, TIM. 1992. *The Place of Geography.* Essex, Eng.: Longman.

MALCOLM P. DOUGLASS

G.I. BILL OF RIGHTS

On June 22, 1944, U.S. President Franklin D. Roosevelt signed into law the Servicemen's Readjustment Act of 1944, also known as the G.I. Bill of Rights. The purpose of the act was to help the nation reabsorb millions of veterans returning from overseas who had been fighting in World War II. During the decades since its enactment, the law and its amendments have made possible the investment of millions of dollars in education and training for a vast number of veterans. The nation has earned many times its investment in return, through increased tax revenues and a dramatically changed society.

A myriad of forces converged to bring about the successful passage of the G.I. Bill. The end of the war brought reduced demand for the production of wartime goods and fueled fears of the type of economic slowdown that followed previous wars. The influx of potential laborers created apprehension regarding job security and economic stability. The bill addressed these and other problems by providing six benefits, the first three of which were administered by the Veterans Administration (VA).

- Education and training
- Loan guarantees for a home, farm, or business
- Unemployment pay of $20 per week for up to fifty-two weeks

• Job-location assistance

• Building materials for VA hospitals as a priority

• Military review of dishonorable discharges

In enacting the legislation, lawmakers demonstrated that they had learned from the mistakes made by the United States government during the period following the World War I, when war veterans marched on the nation's capital in a crusade for increased compensation from the government. During the last years of World War II, the federal government began a period of activity designed to smooth the transition of society as a whole, and individual veterans in particular, to the postwar era. The economic stability provided by these federal efforts, the centerpiece of which was the G.I. Bill of Rights, boosted Americans' confidence and changed the way individuals lived, worked, and learned.

Initial expectations for the number of veterans who would utilize the educational benefits offered by the G.I. Bill were quite inaccurate. Projections of a total of several hundred thousand veterans were revised, as more than 1 million veterans were enrolled in higher education during each of 1946 and 1947, and well over 900,000 during 1948. Veterans represented between 40 and 50 percent of all higher education students during this period.

The increasing numbers of veterans in higher education created several changes on American college and university campuses. New facilities were constructed to accommodate the surging enrollments. New programs evolved, ones that were geared to the vocational and professional emphases that veterans sought from the classroom. The veteran was among the most successful of all college students academically, and this phenomenon generated a psychological shift for many within American society: no longer was the college campus seen as the exclusive preserve of elite sons and daughters. Once veterans were welcomed inside the college classroom, the irreversible trend began of more and more people, from all groups within society, being able to secure a stable and successful future through the pursuit of higher education and training.

Out of more than 15 million American veterans from World War II, more than 7,800,000 used the G.I. Bill to receive education in the years after the war. One primary reason for the program's success is the flexibility that it gave to veterans, who were able to spend their annual tuition stipend on a wide range of options, ranging from training in specific vocations to enrollment on Ivy League campuses.

This younger generation of Americans aspired to a way of life that was considerably different from that of their parents. Coupled with assistance for housing costs, the educational benefits of the G.I. Bill made possible a middle-class lifestyle that was characterized by white-collar work, home ownership, and life in the suburbs. War-weary citizens were finished with the sacrifices that had been necessary during both depression and wartime; the savings that had accumulated during the war could be spent without reservation, for the financial stability offered by the G.I. Bill's provisions allayed fears of postwar economic disruptions.

The empowerment of the individual veteran by the G.I. Bill helped to create the expectation that all Americans can and must have an opportunity to share in the dreams of a college education and a successful, middle-class lifestyle. In the decades following World War II, the federal government pursued initiatives designed to extend this opportunity to minorities, to women, and to the disabled within American society. The successes of the G.I. Bill encouraged legislators to create educational opportunities for individuals in these groups as a means of redressing past social and economic inequities.

This emphasis on advanced education and training for the masses has facilitated the development of America's knowledge-based economy and society. More than ever, Americans see knowledge and training as vital to each individual's future economic success and position within society. Though not entirely eradicated, barriers to accessing this knowledge and training have diminished in many areas of American society, due in large part to the efforts of the federal government. The G.I. Bill proved the ability of the federal government to promote social and economic advancement through educational attainment and training, and millions of veterans can attest to the importance in their own lives of the opportunities that welcomed them following the completion of their military service.

Subsequent legislation includes the following.

• The Veterans Readjustment Act of 1952, approved by President Truman on July 16, 1952, for those serving in the Korean War

• The Veterans Readjustment Benefits Act of 1966, signed into law by President Lyndon B. Johnson on March 3, 1966, for post–Korean War veterans and Vietnam-era veterans

• The Post–Vietnam Era Veterans' Educational Assistance program (VEAP) for individuals that entered active duty between December 31, 1976, and July 1, 1985

• The Montgomery G.I. Bill for individuals initially entering active duty after June 30, 1985

• The Montgomery G.I. Bill: Selected Reserve Educational Assistance Program for members of the Selected Reserve, including the national guard

• The Survivors' and Dependents' Educational Assistance Program, the only VA educational assistance program for spouses and children of living veterans

See also: FEDERAL FUNDS FOR HIGHER EDUCATION.

BIBLIOGRAPHY

BENNETT, MICHAEL J. 1994. "The Law That Worked." *Educational Record* (fall):7–14.

BENNETT, MICHAEL J. 1996. *When Dreams Came True.* Washington, DC: Brasseys.

CLARK, DANIEL A. 1998. "The Two Joes Meet: Joe College, Joe Veteran." *History of Education Quarterly* (summer):165–189.

OLSON, KEITH W. 1974. *The G.I. Bill, the Veterans, and the Colleges.* Lexington: University Press of Kentucky.

OLSON, KEITH W. 1994. "The Astonishing Story." *Educational Record* (fall):16–26.

URBAN, WAYNE J., and WAGONER, JENNINGS L., JR. 1996. *American Education: A History.* New York: McGraw-Hill.

INTERNET RESOURCE

U.S. DEPARTMENT OF VETERANS AFFAIRS, EDUCATION SERVICE. 2001. "The GI Bill: From Roosevelt To Montgomery." <www.gibill.va.gov/education/GI_Bill.htm>.

DEBORAH A. VERSTEGEN
CHRISTOPHER WILSON

GIFTED AND TALENTED EDUCATION

The term *gifted and talented* is often used in tandem to describe both a wide range of human exceptional performance, and people who display such high levels of competence in culturally valued domains or socially useful forms of expression. For children to be identified as gifted and talented, they need to demonstrate outstanding potential or promise rather than mature, expert performance. Thus different standards are used when the term is applied to children as opposed to adults. The term *gifted children* has a connotation that the outstanding potential they demonstrate is largely a natural endowment. However, the term *gifted* as used in educational contexts (e.g., gifted child or gifted performance) is descriptive rather than explanatory. Although efforts have been made to differentiate the two terms, with giftedness referring to natural (spontaneously demonstrated) abilities, and talents referring to systematically developed abilities, such differentiation proves difficult, if not impossible, in practice, as no reliable measures exist to tease apart the constitutional and acquired parts of individual differences in human abilities.

The Nature and Identification

The phenomenon of gifted and talented children is easier to describe than explain. Some scholars in the field attribute children's outstanding performance on IQ or culturally defined domains largely to their constitutional makeup (e.g., a neurological advantage), reminiscent of the position of Francis Galton (1822–1911), an early pioneer of behavioral genetics and intelligence testing. Other scholars are more cautious about bestowing the title of *gifted and talented* for some children by mere virtue of their test performance while treating the rest as nongifted. Rather, they emphasize the emergence of gifted and talented behaviors among children in more authentic contexts as a result of both genetic and environmental influences, involving motivational as well as cognitive processes. Still others point out that, to the extent that the phenomenon of the gifted and talented is subject to different interpretations and assessment strategies based on one's values and beliefs, consequently with different criteria and outcomes, it reflects a social construction rather than an objective reality.

One way of analyzing the research underlying conceptions of giftedness is to review existing definitions along a continuum ranging from conservative to liberal. Conservative and liberal are used here not in their political connotations, but rather according to the degree of restrictiveness that is used in determining who is eligible for special programs and services.

Restrictiveness can be expressed in two ways. First, a definition can limit the number of specific performance areas that are considered in determining eligibility for special programs. A conservative definition, for example, might limit eligibility to academic performance and exclude other areas such as music, art, drama, leadership, public speaking, social service, and creative writing. Second, a definition can limit the degree or level of excellence that one must attain by establishing extremely high cutoff points.

At the conservative end of the continuum is Lewis Terman's 1926 definition of giftedness as "the top 1 percent level in general intellectual ability as measured by the Stanford-Binet Intelligence Scale or a comparable instrument" (p. 43). In this definition, restrictiveness is present in terms of both the type of performance specified (i.e., how well one scores on an intelligence test) and the level of performance one must attain to be considered gifted (top 1 percent). At the other end of the continuum can be found more liberal definitions, such as the following one by Paul Witty in 1958: "There are children whose outstanding potentialities in art, in writing, or in social leadership can be recognized largely by their performance. Hence, we have recommended that the definition of giftedness be expanded and that we consider any child gifted whose performance, in a potentially valuable line of human activity, is consistently remarkable." (p. 62)

Although liberal definitions have the obvious advantage of expanding the conception of giftedness, they create two dilemmas. First, they introduce a values issue by forcing educators to delineate potentially valuable lines of human activity. Second, they introduce even greater subjectivity in the measurement and assessment of children's potentialities.

In recent years the values issue has been largely resolved. There are very few educators who cling tenaciously to a "straight IQ" or purely academic definition of giftedness. Multiple talents and multiple criteria are almost the byproduct words of the present-day gifted education movement, and most people would have little difficulty in accepting a definition that includes almost every socially useful form of human activity.

The problem of subjectivity in measurement and assessment is not as easily resolved. As the defi-

nition of giftedness is extended beyond those abilities that are clearly reflected in tests of intelligence, achievement, and academic aptitude, it becomes necessary to put less emphasis on precise estimates of performance and potential and more emphasis on the opinions of qualified judges in making decisions about admission to special programs. The crux of the issue boils down to a simple and yet very important question: How much are we willing to sacrifice purely objective criteria in order to allow recognition of a broader spectrum of human abilities? If some degree of subjectivity cannot be tolerated, then our definition of giftedness and the resulting programs will logically be limited to abilities that can be measured only by objective tests. A balance between the reliance on measurement technology and expert judgment seems to be the most reasonable course of action.

Goals and Purposes

Although Lewis Terman launched the first large-scale effort to identify gifted children in the United States, it was Leta Hollingworth in 1942 who shifted the focus of the gifted child movement to educational issues. However, a full-fledged gifted education movement was rather triggered by the launching of the satellite *Sputnik* by the Soviet Union in 1957 and the ensuing space race. The ensuing decline of targeted services in the second half of the twentieth century was closely related to political and economic circumstances and apparently inadequate educational conditions, as reflected in the reports by the National Commission on Excellence in Education 1983 (*A Nation at Risk*) and by the U.S. Department of Education in 1993 (*National Excellence: A Case for Developing America's Talent*). For example, by citing evidence of declined academic achievement and poor showing of American students compared to other industrialized nations, Joseph Renzulli and Sally Reis in 1991 proposed that a major goal of gifted education was to "provide the best possible education to our most promising students so that we can reassert American prominence in the intellectual, artistic, and moral leadership of the world" (p. 26). The general education curriculum, which is tailored to average students, is inadequate to provide such an education, thus necessitating special educational provisions for gifted and talented students.

Other educators and researchers of the gifted and talented have advanced an alternative argument for a special service for the gifted and talented. In line with Hollingworth, they emphasize the uniqueness of gifted and talented students' cognitive development, social-emotional experiences, and corresponding educational needs. Therefore, gifted and talented education is aimed not at advancing national or societal interests but at promoting individual gifted children's welfare, academically as well as socially and emotionally, not unlike special provisions for the mentally retarded or learning disabled.

A more recent approach to gifted and talented education focuses on talent development. This movement is largely a result of dissatisfaction with the notion of giftedness as unidimensional (i.e., high general intelligence) and the traditional gifted programs that are frequently short-term based, limited to school subjects, and typically do not address individual children's unique strengths, interests, and long-term development. The talent development approach, based on related psychological research that cumulated in the 1980s and 1990s, attempts to nurture talents among a more diverse group of children and address their unique needs with their long-term talent development in mind.

There are two main strategies to serve gifted children: acceleration and enrichment. With accelerated curriculum, gifted children can learn at a pace commensurate with their learning ability. This allows them to progress to high-level materials much faster for their age norms or grade levels. The constant challenges not only suit these advanced learners' intellectual levels, but also keep them motivated. Enrichment activities, on the other hand, provide gifted children with opportunities to explore topics and issues from (or beyond) regular curriculum in greater breadth and depth, to engage in independent or collaborative inquiry that cultivates their problem solving abilities, research skills, and creativity, and inspire their desire for excellence. Acceleration and enrichment, facilitated by various forms of grouping arrangement, constitute the core instructional adaptations to meet the educational needs of gifted and talented children. From a talent development perspective, both acceleration and enrichment can be used to provide individualized educational programs that aim at promoting long-term development and accomplishment in one's chosen area of human endeavor.

Programs and Their Effectiveness

Specific programs for the gifted and talented can be conceptualized as a continuum from activities that can be arranged in regular classrooms, sometimes with the participation of all students, to arrangements that are exclusively tailored to the needs of the gifted and talented. These programs encompass enrichment and acceleration services that take place (1) within regular classrooms or clusters from one or more grade levels; (2) during special grouping arrangements within classrooms, across grade levels, or in after-school and out-of-school programs; (3) in special schools such as magnet schools or high schools that focus on advanced learning opportunities in particular curricular areas; and (4) through arrangements made for individual students at colleges, summer programs, internship opportunities, or mentorship programs. Age and grade levels play a role in making decisions about special services. Students' abilities, interests, and learning styles tend to become more differentiated and more focused as they grow older. There is, therefore, more justification for interest and achievement level grouping as students progress through the grades. The nature of the subject matter and the degree to which classroom teachers can reasonably differentiate instruction also play a role in making decision about differentiation. For example, acceleration is a more viable option for subjects that are highly structured and linear-sequential in content (e.g., algebra, chemistry, physics). Within-class differentiation in literature is easier to accomplish at the elementary or middle school levels, but an advanced literature class is a more specialized option at the high school level.

With respect to the issue of effectiveness, gifted students in pull-out, separate class, and special school programs performed better than their gifted peers in the within-class arrangements or in schools without gifted programs. Academic gains from acceleration and various benefits regarding content, process and product aspects of objectives as well as positive affective and motivational effects are also reported for enrichment programs. Meta-analyses of the outcomes of these programs reveal quite compelling positive effects. Among other issues, concerns about social-emotional adjustment for students accelerated to higher grade levels or college, about the impact of the gifted label on social interaction, and about self-concept change when placed with equally competent peers, have also been addressed in research.

The effectiveness of gifted and talented programs is not easy to determine for many reasons. Difficulty in finding appropriate control groups, as well as in controlling extraneous variables, poses many threats to internal validity. Ceiling effects constitute another problem. In addition, some criteria (e.g., problem solving, creativity) for evaluating the effectiveness of gifted programs are not as amenable to reliable measurement as those typically used in general education. Because of these difficulties, there is a lack of high-quality research on the effectiveness of various gifted and talented programs. More systematic, methodic (instead of piecemeal) program evaluation is sorely needed.

Two issues about the effectiveness and equity of gifted programs remain controversial. The first one involves the argument that what is good for gifted students is good for most students. Such an argument is a double-edged sword. On the one hand, gifted education can be and has been a viable laboratory for educational experimentation. What is shown to be effective in gifted education may inform and facilitate reform in general education. On the other hand, however, it is preposterous to assume that only gifted children would benefit from such an education. Many critics who argue that gifted education is elitist hold such a view. Two responses have been advanced to address this concern. First, some components of gifted programs may indeed be applicable to general education, such as enrichment or inquiry-based learning, while other components are only suitable for gifted children, such as acceleration and some high-level curricular materials. Second, even though instructional principles and strategies appropriate for gifted learners may also be appropriate for other learners, there are differences in the pace and levels of learning and understanding that impose constraints on the effectiveness of implementation of these principles and strategies. In 1996 Carol A. Tomlinson identified nine dimensions along which to differentiate curriculum and instruction: foundational to transformational, concrete to abstract, simple to complex, few facets to multifacets, smaller leap to greater leap, more structured to more open, clearly defined or fuzzy, less independence to greater independence, slower to quicker.

The second issue is whether gifted education is nothing but "fluff," with fancy rhetoric but not much substance. This concern reflects the fact that the quality of gifted programs varies from school district to school district and that programs meet the needs of their constituents. There are many factors contributing to effectiveness or ineffectiveness of gifted programs, such as administrative support and

staff training. In general, gifted education needs to continue to develop and implement individualized programs rather than a one-size-fits-all gifted curriculum, integrating what students receive from regular classrooms and what they get from pull-out programs. Based on their extensive review of the literature, Bruce Shore and Marcia Delcourt in 1996 suggested that effective gifted programs (1) congregate gifted children at least part of the time; (2) address children at a high intellectual level; (3) use acceleration when warranted; (4) address real and challenging problems; (5) include well-supervised independent study; (6) place educational experiences in a life-span context for the learner; (7) build substantially upon opportunities for individualization; (8) include well-trained and experienced teachers; and (9) support the cognitive and affective needs of all gifted students.

Issues, Controversies, and Trends

Because the term *gifted and talented* is an umbrella concept meant to encompass various facets of excellence or potential for excellence, its meaning is an object of constant debate within and outside of the field. What is the basis for the phenomenon of gifted and talented performance: general mental power or highly specific abilities or talents, or both? Even though most experts in the field accept the notion of diverse expressions of excellence, they have their own leanings, ranging from the most traditional conception of giftedness as high general intelligence as indicated by IQ test scores, to the most pluralistic definition that defies any terms of psychometric measurement.

A related question is do gifted and talented manifestations reflect fundamental attributes of some children (hence gifted children) that set them apart from other children, or emergent developmental qualities of the child as a result of interaction with the environment? Is it a fixed or fluid condition? Major ideological differences exist in the field between those who believe that gifted children are a distinct group of exceptional children who share certain unique cognitive and social-emotional characteristics (i.e., being gifted made them different from the rest of children), and those who believe that gifted and talented performance or behavior should be understood in a more dynamic context in which it occurs, and can be attributed to contextual influences as much as personal characteristics. These differences have profound implications for identification. Should we develop a fixed formula for finding the right gifted child or should we instead focus on nurturing and facilitating the emergence of gifted behaviors among children, while holding flexible but "soft" identification criteria?

From an assessment perspective, the traditional approach, deeply rooted in the intelligence testing movement, focused on a set of static attributes or traits. On the other hand, a dynamic assessment approach affords a closer look at processes, strategies, insights, errors, and so on, and is thus more informative and explanatory. A contrast has been made between a static (trait) approach and a dynamic (process) approach that involves micro-level analysis and clinical insights regarding children's superior performance. This reinforces the issue of subjectivity in measurement and assessment. Time will tell whether a dynamic assessment will supplement, or even replace, the traditional way of identifying gifted and talented children. A better understanding of the nature and improved assessment of potential for talent development will also help address other derivative issues such as multipotentialities, multiple exceptionalities, and underachievement among highly able children.

Because of different understandings of the phenomenon in question and concerns about equity, some experts suggest that we abandon the term *gifted* altogether to avoid the arbitrary bifurcation of the gifted and nongifted, and that we should label services instead of labeling the child, whereas others view this movement as abandoning the very raison d'etre for gifted programs. The social-emotional impact of labeling aside, the issue is also that of restrictiveness discussed earlier: how inclusive and flexible gifted programs can be. On the one hand, programs such as Talent Search are highly selective in nature; some cutoffs (e.g., ninety-ninth percentile) are necessary to determine one's qualification, and intensive programs can be implemented with relatively high efficiency. On the other hand, various forms of enrichment and high-end learning can be open to a larger pool of able students, even to all students, and qualification can be determined in a flexible manner to maximize opportunities for participation, with gifted programs justified on the basis of needs (e.g., substituting regular curriculum with more advanced materials) rather than status (being identified as gifted), as is the case with the Revolving Door Identification Model.

As mentioned above, various forms of grouping are necessary to provide special services for gifted and talented children. It is not difficult to justify grouping as a way of providing an optimal educational environment for gifted and talented children. The challenge is justifying the services within the context of the whole educational system. Ability grouping practices are vulnerable to charges such as favoritism or elitism in a democratic society and egalitarian culture. The problem is exacerbated by the fact that ethnic minority (except Asian-American) students and students from families of low social economic status are underrepresented in gifted education programs in the United States. Until gifted education is well integrated into the whole education system, its identity and functions become better defined, and its pursuit of excellence is balanced with concerns over equity, it will continue to be the target of criticism.

On a positive note, gifted education has proven to be a vital force in American education. In many respects, programs for the gifted have been the true laboratories of our nation's schools because they have presented ideal opportunities for testing new ideas and experimenting with potential solutions to long-standing educational problems. Programs for high potential students have been an especially fertile place for experimentation because such programs usually are not encumbered by prescribed curriculum guides or traditional methods of instruction. It was within the context of these programs that the thinking skills movement first took hold in American education, and the pioneering work of notable theorists such as Benjamin Bloom, Howard Gardner, and Robert Sternberg first gained the attention of the education community in the 1980s. Other developments that had their origins in special programs are currently being examined for general practice. These developments include a focus on concept rather than skill learning, the use of interdisciplinary curriculum and theme-based studies, student portfolios, performance assessment, cross-grade grouping, alternative scheduling patterns, and perhaps most important, opportunities for students to exchange traditional roles as lesson-learners and doers-of-exercises for more challenging and demanding roles that require hands-on learning, first-hand investigations, and the application of knowledge and thinking skills to complex problems.

Research in a variety of gifted education programs has fostered the development of instructional procedures and programming alternatives that emphasize the need (1) to provide a broad range of advanced level enrichment experiences for all students, and (2) to use the many and varied ways that students respond to these experiences as stepping stones for relevant follow-up on the parts of individuals or small groups. These approaches are not viewed as new ways to identify who is or is not gifted. Rather, the process simply identifies how subsequent opportunities, resources, and encouragement can be provided to support continuous escalations of student involvement in both required and self-selected activities. This orientation has allowed many students opportunities to develop high levels of creative and productive accomplishments that otherwise would have been denied through traditional special program models. Practices that have been a mainstay of many special programs for the gifted are being absorbed into general education by reform models designed to upgrade the performance of all students. This integration of gifted program know-how is viewed as a favorable development, since the adoption of many special program practices is indicative of the viability and usefulness of both the know-how of special programs and the role gifted education can and should play in total school improvement. This broader and more flexible approach reflects a democratic ideal that accommodates the full range of individual differences in the entire student population, and it opens the door to programming models that develop the talent potentials of many at-risk students who traditionally have been excluded from anything but the most basic types of curricular experiences. This integration of gifted and talented education into the general education system is beginning to redefine the ways in which we develop the many and various potentials of the nation's youths.

See also: COUNCIL FOR EXCEPTIONAL CHILDREN; SPECIAL EDUCATION, *subentries on* CURRENT TRENDS, HISTORY OF.

BIBLIOGRAPHY

BLOOM, BENJAMIN S. 1985. *Developing Talent in Young People.* New York: Ballantine Books.

BORLAND, JAMES H. 1996. "Gifted Education and the Threat of Irrelevance." *Journal for the Education of the Gifted* 19:129–147.

CALLAHAN, CAROLYN M. 1996. "A Critical Self-Study of Gifted Education: Healthy Practice, Necessary Evil, or Sedition?" *Journal for the Education of the Gifted* 19:148–163.

GAGNE, FRANCOYS. 1999. "My Convictions about the Nature of Abilities, Gifts, and Talents." *Journal for the Education of the Gifted* 22:109–136.

HOLLINGWORTH, LETA S. 1942. *Children above 180 IQ (Stanford-Binet): Their Origin and Development.* Yonkers-on-Hudson, NY: Worldbook.

KULIK, JAMES A., and KULIK, CHEN-LIN C. 1997. "Ability Grouping." In *Handbook of Gifted Education,* 2nd edition, ed. Nicholas Colangelo and Gary A. Davis. Boston: Allyn and Bacon.

NATIONAL COMMISSION ON EXCELLENCE IN EDUCATION. 1983. *A Nation at Risk: The Imperative for Educational Reform.* Washington, DC: U.S. Government Printing Office.

RENZULLI, JOSEPH S. 1986. "The Three Ring Conception of Giftedness: A Developmental Model for Creative Productivity." In *Conceptions of Giftedness,* ed. Robert J. Sternberg and Janet E. Davidson. New York: Cambridge University Press.

RENZULLI, JOSEPH S., and REIS, SALLY. M. 1991. "The Reform Movement and the Quiet Crisis in Gifted Education." *Gifted Child Quarterly* 35:26–35.

RENZULLI, JOSEPH S., and REIS, SALLY M. 1997. *Schoolwide Enrichment Model: A How-To Guide for Educational Excellence.* Mansfield Center, CT: Creative Learning Press.

SHORE, BRUCE M., and DELCOURT, MARCIA A. B. 1996. "Effective Curricular and Program Practices in Gifted Education and the Interface with General Education." *Journal for the Education of the Gifted* 20:138–154.

STANLEY, JULIAN. 1997. "Varieties of Intellectual Talent." *Journal of Creative Behavior* 31:93–119.

STERNBERG, ROBERT J. 1985. *Beyond IQ: A Triarchic Theory of Human Intelligence.* Cambridge, Eng.: Cambridge University Press.

TANNENBAUM, ABRAHAM J. 1997. "The Meaning and Making of Giftedness." In *Handbook of Gifted Education,* 2nd edition, ed. Nicholas Colangelo and Gary A. Davis. Boston: Allyn and Bacon.

TERMAN, LEWIS M. 1926. *Genetic Studies of Genius: Mental and Physical Traits of a Thousand Gifted Children,* 2nd edition. Stanford, CA: Stanford University Press.

TOMLINSON, CAROL A. 1996. "Good Teaching for One and All: Does Gifted Education Have an Instructional Identity?" *Journal for the Education of the Gifted* 20:155–174.

VANTASSEL-BASKA, JOYCE. 1997. "What Matters in Curriculum for Gifted Learners: Reflections on Theory, Research, and Practice." In *Handbook of Gifted Education*, 2nd edition, ed. Nicholas Colangelo and Gary A. Davis. Boston: Allyn and Bacon.

WITTY, PAUL. A. 1958. "Who Are the Gifted?" In *Education of the Gifted*, ed. Nelson B. Henry. Chicago: University of Chicago Press.

JOSEPH S. RENZULLI

DAVID YUN DAI

GLOBALIZATION OF EDUCATION

In popular discourse, *globalization* is often synonymous with *internationalization*, referring to the growing interconnectedness and interdependence of people and institutions throughout the world. Although these terms have elements in common, they have taken on technical meanings that distinguish them from each other and from common usage. Internationalization is the less theorized term. Globalization, by contrast, has come to denote the complexities of interconnectedness, and scholars have produced a large body of literature to explain what appear to be ineluctable worldwide influences on local settings and responses to those influences.

Influences of a global scale touch aspects of everyday life. For example, structural adjustment policies and international trading charters, such as the North American Free Trade Association (NAFTA) and the Asia-Pacific Economic Cooperation (APEC), reduce barriers to commerce, ostensibly promote jobs, and reduce the price of goods to consumers across nations. Yet they also shift support from "old" industries to newer ones, creating dislocations and forcing some workers out of jobs, and have provoked large and even violent demonstrations in several countries. The spread of democracy, too, is part of globalization, giving more people access to the political processes that affect their lives, but also, in many places, concealing deeply rooted socioeconomic inequities as well as areas of policy

over which very few individuals have a voice. Even organized international terrorism bred by Islamic fanaticism may be viewed as an oppositional reaction—an effort at *deglobalization*—to the pervasiveness of Western capitalism and secularism associated with globalization. Influences of globalization are multi-dimensional, having large social, economic, and political implications.

A massive spread of education and of Western-oriented norms of learning at all levels in the twentieth century and the consequences of widely available schooling are a large part of the globalization process. With regard to the role of schools, globalization has become a major topic of study, especially in the field of comparative education, which applies historiographic and social scientific theories and methods to international issues of education.

Globalization Theory

Globalization is both a process and a theory. Roland Robertson, with whom globalization theory is most closely associated, views globalization as an accelerated compression of the contemporary world and the intensification of consciousness of the world as a singular entity. Compression makes the world a single place by virtue of the power of a set of globally diffused ideas that render the uniqueness of societal and ethnic identities and traditions irrelevant except within local contexts and in scholarly discourse.

The notion of the world community being transformed into a *global village*, as introduced in 1960 by Marshall McLuhan in an influential book about the newly shared experience of mass media, was likely the first expression of the contemporary concept of globalization. Despite its entry into the common lexicon in the 1960s, globalization was not recognized as a significant concept until the 1980s, when the complexity and multidimensionality of the process began to be examined. Prior to the 1980s, accounts of globalization focused on a professed tendency of societies to converge in becoming modern, described initially by Clark Kerr and colleagues as the emergence of *industrial man*.

Although the theory of globalization is relatively new, the process is not. History is witness to many globalizing tendencies involving grand alliances of nations and dynasties and the unification of previously sequestered territories under such empires as Rome, Austria-Hungary, and Britain, but also such events as the widespread acceptance of germ theory and heliocentricism, the rise of transnational agencies concerned with regulation and communication, and an increasingly unified conceptualization of human rights.

What makes globalization distinct in contemporary life is the broad reach and multidimensionality of interdependence, reflected initially in the monitored set of relations among nation-states that arose in the wake of World War I. It is a process that before the 1980s was akin to *modernization,* until modernization as a concept of linear progression from traditional to developing to developed—or from gemeinschaft to gesellschaft as expressed by Ferdinand Toennies—forms of society became viewed as too simplistic and unidimensional to explain contemporary changes. Modernization theory emphasized the functional significance of the Protestant ethic in the evolution of modern societies, as affected by such objectively measured attributes as education, occupation, and wealth in stimulating a disciplined orientation to work and political participation.

The main difficulty with modernization theory was its focus on changes within societies or nations and comparisons between them—with Western societies as their main reference points—to the neglect of the interconnectedness among them, and, indeed, their interdependence, and the role played by non-Western countries in the development of the West. Immanuel Wallerstein was among the earliest and most influential scholars to show the weaknesses of modernization theory. He developed *world system theory* to explain how the world had expanded through an ordered pattern of relationships among societies driven by a capitalistic system of economic exchange. Contrary to the emphasis on linear development in modernization theory, Wallerstein demonstrated how wealthy and poor societies were locked together within a world system, advancing their relative economic advantages and disadvantages that carried over into politics and culture. Although globalization theory is broader, more variegated in its emphasis on the transnational spread of knowledge, and generally less deterministic in regard to the role of economics, world system theory was critical in shaping its development.

The Role of Education

As the major formal agency for conveying knowledge, the school features prominently in the process and theory of globalization. Early examples of educational globalization include the spread of global religions, especially Islam and Christianity, and colonialism, which often disrupted and displaced indigenous forms of schooling throughout much of the nineteenth and twentieth centuries. Postcolonial globalizing influences of education have taken on more subtle shapes.

In globalization, it is not simply the ties of economic exchange and political agreement that bind nations and societies, but also the shared consciousness of being part of a global system. That consciousness is conveyed through ever larger transnational movements of people and an array of different media, but most systematically through formal education. The inexorable transformation of consciousness brought on by globalization alters the content and contours of education, as schools take on an increasingly important role in the process.

Structural adjustment policies. Much of the focus on the role of education in globalization has been in terms of the structural adjustment policies of the World Bank and other international lending organizations in low-income countries. These organizations push cuts in government expenditures, liberalization of trade practices, currency devaluations, reductions of price controls, shifts toward production for export, and user charges for and privatization of public services such as education. Consequently, change is increasingly driven largely by financial forces, government reliance on foreign capital to finance economic growth, and market ideology.

In regard to education, structural adjustment policies ostensibly reduce public bureaucracies that impede the delivery of more and better education. By reducing wasteful expenditures and increasing responsiveness to demand, these policies promote schooling more efficiently. However, as Joel Samoff noted in 1994, observers have reported that structural adjustment policies often encourage an emphasis on inappropriate skills and reproduce existing social and economic inequalities, leading actually to lowered enrollment rates, an erosion in the quality of education, and a misalignment between educational need and provision. As part of the impetus toward efficiency in the expenditure of resources, structural adjustment policies also encourage objective measures of school performance and have advanced the use of cross-national school effectiveness studies. Some have argued that these studies represent a new form of racism by apportioning blame for school failure on local cultures and contexts.

Democratization. As part of the globalization process, the spread of education is widely viewed as contributing to democratization throughout the world. Schools prepare people for participation in the economy and polity, giving them the knowledge to make responsible judgments, the motivation to make appropriate contributions to the well being of society, and a consciousness about the consequences of their behavior. National and international assistance organizations, such as the U. S. Agency for International Development and the United Nations Educational, Scientific and Cultural Organization (UNESCO), embrace these objectives. Along with mass provision of schools, technological advances have permitted distance education to convey Western concepts to the extreme margins of society, exposing new regions and populations to knowledge generated by culturally dominant groups and helping to absorb them into the consumer society.

A policy of using schools as part of the democratization process often accompanies structural adjustment measures. However, encouraging user fees to help finance schooling has meant a reduced ability of people in some impoverished areas of the world to buy books and school materials and even attend school, thus enlarging the gap between rich and poor and impeding democracy. Even in areas displaying a rise in educational participation, observers have reported a reduction in civic participation. Increased emphasis on formalism in schooling could plausibly contribute to this result. An expansion of school civics programs could, for example, draw energy and resources away from active engagement in political affairs by youths, whether within or outside of schools. Increased privatization of education in the name of capitalist democratization could invite greater participation of corporate entities, with the prospect of commercializing schools and reducing their service in behalf of the public interest.

Penetration of the periphery. Perhaps the most important question in understanding how education contributes to globalization is, what is the power of schools to penetrate the cultural periphery? Why do non-Western people surrender to the acculturative pressure of Western forms of education?

By mid-twentieth century, missionaries and colonialism had brought core Western ideas and practices to many parts of the world. With contemporary globalization, penetration of the world periphery by means of education has been accomplished mainly in other ways, especially as contingent on structural adjustment and democratization projects. Some scholars, including Howard R. Woodhouse, have claimed that people on the periphery are "mystified" by dominant ideologies, and willingly, even enthusiastically and without conscious awareness of implications, accept core Western learning and thereby subordinate themselves to the world system. By contrast, there is considerable research, including that of Thomas Clayton in 1998 and Douglas E. Foley in 1991, to suggest that people at the periphery develop a variety of strategies, from foot dragging to outright student rebellion, to resist the dominant ideology as conveyed in schools.

Evidence on the accommodation of people at the periphery to the dominant ideology embodied in Westernized schooling is thus not consistent. Erwin H. Epstein, based on data he collected in three societies, proposes a *filter-effect theory* that could explain the contradictory results reported by others. He found that children in impoverished areas attending schools more distant from the cultural mainstream had more favorable views of, and expressed stronger attachment to, national core symbols than children in schools closer to the mainstream. In all three societies he studied, globalization influences were abrupt and pervasive, but they were resisted most palpably not at the remote margins, but in the towns and places closer to the center, where the institutions representative of the mainstream—including law enforcement, employment and welfare agencies, medical facilities, and businesses—were newly prevalent and most powerfully challenged traditional community values.

Epstein explained these findings by reasoning that it is easier for children living in more remote areas to accept myths taught by schools regarding the cultural mainstream. By contrast, children living closer to the mainstream cultural center—the more acculturated pupils—are more exposed to the realities of the mainstream way of life and, being more worldly, are more inclined to resist such myths. Schools in different areas do not teach different content; in all three societies, schools, whether located at the mainstream center or periphery, taught an equivalent set of myths, allegiances to national symbols, and dominant core values. Rather, schools at the margin are more effective in inculcating intended political cultural values and attitudes because they operate in an environment with fewer competing contrary stimuli. Children living in more traditional, culturally homogeneous and isolated areas tend to be more naive about the outside world and lack the tools and experience to assess objectively the political content that schools convey. Children nearer the center, by contrast, having more actual exposure to the dominant culture, are better able to observe the disabilities of the dominant culture—its level of crime and corruption, its reduced family cohesion, and its heightened rates of drug and alcohol abuse, for example. That greater exposure counteracts the favorable images all schools convey about the cultural mainstream, and instead imbues realism—and cynicism—about the myths taught by schools.

In other words, schools perform as a filter to sanitize reality, but their effectiveness is differential; their capacity to filter is larger the farther they move out into the periphery. As extra-school knowledge progressively competes with school-produced myths, the ability and inclination to oppose the dominant ideology promoted by schools as part of the globalization process should become stronger. This filter-effect theory could clarify the impact of schools as an instrument of globalization and invites corroboration.

See also: INTERNATIONAL EDUCATION AGREEMENTS; INTERNATIONAL EDUCATION STATISTICS; RURAL EDUCATION, *subentry on* INTERNATIONAL CONTEXT.

BIBLIOGRAPHY

CLAYTON, THOMAS. 1998. "Beyond Mystification: Reconnecting World-System Theory for Comparative Education." *Comparative Education Review* 42:479–496.

DAUN, HOLGER. 2001. *Educational Restructuring in the Context of Globalization and National Policy.* New York: Garland.

EPSTEIN, ERWIN H. 1987. "The Peril of Paternalism: The Imposition of Education on Cuba by the United States." *American Journal of Education* 96:1–23.

EPSTEIN, ERWIN H. 1997. "National Identity among St. Lucian Schoolchildren." In *Ethnicity, Race and Nationality in the Caribbean,* ed. Juan Manuel Carrión. San Juan: Institute of Caribbean Studies, University of Puerto Rico.

FOLEY, DOUGLAS E. 1991. "Rethinking School Ethnographies of Colonial Settings: A Performance

Perspective of Reproduction and Resistance." *Comparative Education Review* 35:532–551.

GIDDENS, ANTHONY. 1987. *The Nation-State and Violence.* Berkeley: University of California Press.

HOOGVELT, ANKIE. 1997. *Globalisation and the Postcolonial World: The New Political Economy of Development.* Basingstoke, Eng.: Macmillan.

INKELES, ALEX, and SMITH, DAVID HORTON. 1974. *Becoming Modern: Individual Change in Six Developing Countries.* Cambridge, MA: Harvard University Press.

JARVIS, PETER. 2000. "Globalisation, the Learning Society and Comparative Education." *Comparative Education* 36:343–355.

KERR, CLARK, et al. 1960. *Industrialism and Industrial Man.* London: Heinemann.

McLUHAN, MARSHALL. 1960. *Explorations in Communication.* Boston: Beacon.

RAMIREZ, FRANCISCO O., and BOLI-BENNETT, JOHN. 1987. "The Political Construction of Mass Schooling: European Origins and World-wide Institutionalization." *Sociology of Education* 60:2–17.

ROBERTSON, ROLAND. 1987. "Globalization Theory and Civilizational Analysis." *Comparative Civilizations Review* 17.

SAMOFF, JOEL, ed. 1994. *Coping with Crisis: Austerity, Adjustment, and Human Resources.* London: Cassell.

SKLAIR, LESLIE. 1997. "Globalization: New Approaches to Social Change." In *Sociology: Issues and Debates,* ed. Steve Taylor. London: Macmillan.

TOENNIES, FERDINAND. 1957. *Community and Society.* New York: Harper and Row.

WALLERSTEIN, IMMANUEL. 1974. *The Modern World System.* New York: Academic Press.

WEBER, MAX. 1978. *Economy and Society.* Berkeley: University of California Press.

WELCH, ANTHONY R. 2001. "Globalisation, Postmodernity and the State: Comparative Education Facing the Third Millennium." *Comparative Education* 37:475–492.

WHITE, BOB W. 1996. "Talk about School: Education and the Colonial Project in French and British West Africa." *Comparative Education* 32:9–25.

WOODHOUSE, HOWARD R. 1987. "Knowledge, Power and the University in a Developing

Country: Nigeria and Cultural Dependency." *Compare* 17:121.

ERWIN H. EPSTEIN

GOALS 2000: EDUCATE AMERICA ACT

See: EDUCATION REFORM; SCHOOL REFORM; STANDARDS FOR STUDENT LEARNING; STANDARDS MOVEMENT IN AMERICAN EDUCATION.

GODDARD, HENRY H. (1866–1957)

Director of research at the New Jersey Home for the Education and Care of Feeble-Minded Children in Vineland, Henry H. Goddard used and elaborated Alfred Binet's intelligence tests for use with American students. Goddard made a number of important contributions in special education, including his guiding role in the establishment of the first state law mandating special education services. He is remembered, however, primarily for his work in popularizing Alfred Binet's approach to psychological testing in the United States and studying the hereditary roots of feeble-mindedness in his book, *The Kallikak Family: A Study in the Heredity of Feeble-Mindedness* (1912).

Background and Education

Goddard grew up in a devout Quaker family, and his initial educational experiences occurred at Haverford College, a Quaker institution in Pennsylvania. At various points during his education, he took teaching and administrative positions in Quaker schools. At one point, he lectured at the newly founded University of Southern California—where he held the distinction of being that university's first football coach. But Goddard's interests in psychology lured him to Clark University to study with G. Stanley Hall, where Goddard gained an appreciation for scientific approaches to studying human behavior.

Upon graduation with his doctorate, Goddard worked for several years at a teacher's college in Pennsylvania, where he became frustrated by the lack of emphasis on scientific psychology and peda-

gogy. As a result, in 1906 he accepted the position of director of research at the New Jersey Home for the Education and Care of Feeble-Minded Children in Vineland, a small town in the southern, rural part of the state. Although Goddard is best known for his work at the Vineland School, he also held two major positions in Ohio before his retirement.

Intelligence Testing

Early in the twentieth century, Goddard was concerned with separating, in his terms, the retarded—who suffered from poor health or environment and required remedial help—from the feeble-minded—who suffered from decreased mental capacity and required a special curriculum. Goddard believed that the Binet-Simon intelligence tests, recently developed in France, could aid in assessing the nature of this problem and began to advocate for the use of the scales in the United States.

About this time, American educators became concerned with the percentage of students who were older than would be expected given their grade. When the question of grade versus age became a major issue in American education, Goddard saw that the Binet scales with which he was already working could be used to study this issue. Goddard's advocacy for the Binet tests was enthusiastic and exhaustive. Well-connected in areas as diverse as medicine, education, psychology, and law, he championed the use of the tests in several venues. For example, he taught or organized courses for teachers on administration of the Binet tests at several institutions. These teachers proceeded to use the tests in educational settings throughout the United States. In addition, he advocated the value of test results as legal evidence. Goddard was also highly involved in the U.S. army psychological testing program during World War I, further legitimizing this particular approach to mental testing.

Goddard's advocacy of the Binet tests had two important outcomes. The mental testing approach gained popularity relative to the qualitatively different techniques used by Francis Galton and others who relied upon physical and physiological measures to estimate intelligence. Also, various forms of the Binet test, primarily revisions by Goddard and especially Lewis Terman, remain in use, and a majority of contemporary intelligence tests are based on similar methodologies. Without Goddard's influence, early-twenty-first century testing and related educational practices might look quite different.

The Kallikak Family Study

Goddard's other major contribution was his study of feeble-mindedness. Goddard's field-based research resulted in many publications, with the best known being *The Kallikak Family: A Study in the Heredity of Feeble-Mindedness.* Although Goddard and his assistants studied hundreds of families, the Kallikak family remains the most famous. The family was that of a Vineland student, Deborah. The name *Kallikak* is actually a pseudonym created from the Greek words *kallos* (beauty) and *kakos* (bad). The Kallikak family was divided into two branches—one "good" and one "bad,"—both of which originated from Deborah's great-great-great grandfather, Martin Kallikak. When Kallikak was a young soldier, he had a liaison with an "unnamed, feeble-minded tavern girl." This tryst resulted in the birth of an illegitimate son, Martin Kallikak Jr., from whom the bad branch of the family descended. Later in his life, Martin Kallikak Sr. married a Quaker woman from a good family. The good branch descended from this marriage.

Goddard's genealogical research revealed that the union with the feeble-minded girl resulted in generations plagued by feeble-mindedness, illegitimacy, prostitution, alcoholism, and lechery. The marriage of Martin Kallikak Sr. to the Quaker woman yielded generations of normal, accomplished offspring. Goddard believed that the remarkable difference separating the two branches of the family was due entirely to the different hereditary influences from the two women involved with the senior Kallikak.

Goddard's work had a powerful effect. Scholars were generally impressed by the magnitude of the study, and *The Kallikak Family* became very popular. Critical reaction in the popular press was positive, with more muted reaction within the scientific community. For example, James McKeen Cattell praised the contribution and conclusions but criticized the research design. The Kallikak study was a powerful ally to eugenicist movements, including that of the Nazi party, and contributed to the atmosphere in which compulsory sterilization laws were passed in many states.

Controversy

Controversy followed Goddard throughout his career. However, the Kallikak study and Goddard's eugenicism in the 1910s created the most serious problems. For example, Goddard concluded *The Kallikak Family* with recommendations of forced sterilization and segregation of the feeble-minded in isolated colonies. His work also had a strong anti-immigrant tone at a time when immigrants were seeking citizenship in record numbers. Goddard later admitted that many of his recommendations on social policy had been misguided, but his controversial role earlier in the twentieth century helped to place his work in low regard by the 1940s.

By the end of the twentieth century, Goddard's research once again came under fire. A photographic expert suggested that some of the Kallikak photographs—those of the bad branch of the family—were retouched. Critics charged that the modifications were made by Goddard to give a more disturbing appearance. However, several researchers have concluded that fraud appears to be unlikely. As Leila Zederland noted, a main thrust of Goddard's work was to show that feeble-minded people looked normal and were often quite attractive; he was advocating for mental testing, not visual inspection, to determine feeble-mindedness.

Contribution

Henry Goddard made substantial contributions to American education, including the popularizing of mental testing, compulsory special education, and gifted education. His research into the hereditary nature of feeble-mindedness and related eugenicist activities, however, has helped to paint the rather negative picture many people continue to hold of Goddard and his work.

See also: ASSESSMENT TOOLS, *subentry on* PSYCHOMETRIC AND STATISTICAL; BINET, ALFRED; INTELLIGENCE, *subentry on* MEASUREMENT; SPECIAL EDUCATION.

BIBLIOGRAPHY

FANCHER, RAYMOND E. 1987. "Henry Goddard and the Kallikak Family Photographs: 'Conscious Skullduggery' or 'Whig History'?" *American Psychologist* 42:585–590.

GODDARD, HENRY H. 1912. *The Kallikak Family: A Study in the Heredity of Feeble-Mindedness.* New York: Macmillan.

GODDARD, HENRY H. 1914. *Feeble-Mindedness: Its Causes and Consequences.* New York: Macmillan.

GODDARD, HENRY H. 1927. "Who Is a Moron?" *Scientific Monthly* 24:41–46.

GODDARD, HENRY H. 1942. "In Defense of the Kallikak Study." *Science* 95:574–576.

GOULD, STEPHEN J. 1981. *The Mismeasure of Man.* New York: Norton.

SMITH, JOHN D. 1985. *Minds Made Feeble: The Myth and Legacy of the Kallikaks.* Rockville, MD: Aspen.

ZENDERLAND, LEILA. 1998. *Measuring Minds: Henry Herbert Goddard and the Origins of American Intelligence Testing.* Cambridge, MA: Cambridge University Press.

JONATHAN A. PLUCKER
AMBER M. ESPING

GOODMAN, PAUL (1911–1972)

Social and educational critic Paul Goodman was referred to by his biographer, Taylor Stoehr, as a "prophet." Revered by the youth movement in the 1960s, his ideas on education and youth were extremely appealing to many people on the political left.

Goodman was born in New York, and raised amid the urban, Jewish intellectual community. He graduated from City College of New York in 1931. Goodman earned his Ph.D. at the University of Chicago, but moved back to New York and lived with his wife Sally until his death. His major works on education were *Growing Up Absurd, Community of Scholars,* and *Compulsory Mis-Education,* but he also wrote many articles that dealt with de-schooling, alternative education, mini-schools, and free universities.

The publishing of *Growing Up Absurd* in 1960 brought Goodman to the public as a social/educational critic. The book was rejected seventeen times before a publisher accepted it, after Norman Poderhotz serialized it in the then leftist *Commentary.* Goodman spent the last twelve years of his life teaching courses at universities in New York, speaking on campuses throughout the country, and as a visiting professor at San Francisco State University and the University of Hawaii. Goodman never held a tenure track appointment. *Growing Up Absurd* was adopted in education and sociology courses throughout the country. The book was read as a condemnation of the alienation and oppression in American society and schools, and was a forerunner to the educational criticism of John Holt, Herb Kohl, Jonathan Kozol, and Edgar Friedenberg. For sixties activists, as well as liberal educators, the book provided an analysis of the wrongs of American society and education.

Goodman published *Compulsory Mis-Education* and *Community of Scholars* as a single volume in 1962. The books were assigned reading in education courses and initiated thoughtful educational criticism. *Compulsory Mis-Education* became somewhat of a blueprint for de-schoolers as well as for the alternative school movement in the late 1960s and 1970s. Critical of education from kindergarten through the university, the work led seamlessly into *Community of Scholars,* which emphasized Goodman's endless quest for community while criticizing the status quo. Goodman spent much of his time in his final years bringing his philosophy on education to college campuses. He was actively antiwar, but he warned student activists of the danger in "action for the sake of action." He continued to write, mostly about educational criticism.

Decentralizing Power, Taylor Stoehr's biographical work on Goodman, is a collection of Goodman's writing on social and educational criticism. The general theme of the work is community life. Goodman's initial discussion of the issues and problems of youth analyzes the youth movement—both idealism and alienation—with the latter being predominant. He speaks of power-beating community, coining the phrase "school monks." The theme of community is also prevalent in his important essay on children's rights. Goodman laments the lack of community and gently criticizes both Maria Montessori and A. S. Neill for educational practices that ask children to become adults too quickly.

At the same time, he lauds Neill's school, Summerhill, for delaying socialization and protecting the wildness of childhood. Goodman discusses schools as therapeutic communities, where children can escape from bad homes and bad cities. Goodman also offers a plan to abolish high schools and to replace them with apprenticeships, academies, youth houses, and therapeutic free schools—in fact, it is a de-schooling plan that preceded Ivan Illich's book, *De-schooling Society.*

Although Goodman was philosophical, and asked searching questions about people's relationship with the world, his educational proposals were practical and simple. As a teacher, his classroom was an interactive laboratory. His proposals asked that education allow the same for young children, adolescents, and adults.

See also: ALTERNATIVE SCHOOLING; COMMUNITY EDUCATION; EDUCATION REFORM.

BIBLIOGRAPHY

GOODMAN, PAUL. 1960. *Growing Up Absurd: Problems of Youth in Organized Society.* New York: Vintage.

GOODMAN, PAUL. 1962. *Compulsory Mis-Education and the Community of Scholars.* New York: Vintage.

STOEHR, TAYLOR. 1994. *Decentralizing Power: Paul Goodman's Social Criticism.* New York: Black Rose Books.

ALAN WIEDER

GOSLIN, WILLARD E. (1899–1969)

A nationally acclaimed school superintendent, Willard E. Goslin became a symbol of the end of educational progressivism, when he was forced to resign from the Pasadena, California, schools in November 1950. Goslin's ouster was a victory for citizens' groups that deemed his support of racial understanding, outdoor education, child guidance, and mental health as evidence of subversive, un-American values.

Goslin was raised on a Missouri farm. He began teaching in the rural schools of Boone County, Missouri, in 1916. After receiving a B.S. degree from Northeast Missouri State Teachers College (later, Truman State University) in 1922, he was appointed principal (1922–1923) and superintendent (1923–1928) in Slater, Missouri. He earned an M.A. degree from the University of Missouri in 1928 and served as superintendent of Webster Groves, Missouri, from 1930 to 1944. In 1944 Goslin was named superintendent of Minneapolis schools. During his tenure there he was named one of the five outstanding public school administrators in the country. In 1948, while serving as Minneapolis's superintendent, he concurrently held the office of president of the American Association of School Administrators. That year he also accepted the superintendency of the Pasadena (California) Public Schools, a move

that was to bring him considerable fame as well as disappointment.

As a Progressive educator, he soon found himself the center of criticism from a vigorous and reactionary minority of Pasadena's residents, who criticized him not only for his advocacy of Progressive education, but also for his "ideological" support of the United Nations Educational, Scientific and Cultural Organization (UNESCO), his inclusion of sex education in the curriculum, his concern for African Americans, and his advocacy of racial integration of the schools.

In June 1950 Goslin and the Pasadena School Board proposed an increased tax levy, which was soundly defeated by a two-to-one vote. From then on, both the board and the superintendent experienced increasing difficulties. Goslin endeavored to prune the budget and carry on. The forces that, in the closing hours of the tax election campaign, had indulged in a number of misrepresentations and attacks on the superintendent, had created a rupture between the administration and the lay board. Early in November the board asked for his resignation. After a few weeks of discussion, private and public, which David Hulburd describes as "Turmoil in Pasadena," Mr. Goslin resigned from his position.

Although public criticism ultimately forced him to resign from his position, an action that stunned professional educators throughout the country, it was the lack of press support that became an important factor in his eventual ouster from the school board. Educators' interest in such an event is obvious, but the situation offered enough drama to stimulate a great deal of interest for the public as well. The forced resignation of Willard Goslin as superintendent of Pasadena schools had enough appeal to warrant prominent attention in the national press as in, for example, *Life* magazine.

At least two careful investigations found Goslin's dismissal to result largely from the demands of a comparatively small but very vocal group of critics. Goslin had received a warm welcome as the new superintendent. The end of the honeymoon period began with the defeat of a tax proposal to provide additional educational funds. The organization that had spearheaded the campaign to defeat the tax proposal went on to denounce as leftist and educationally unsound the "Progressive Education" that Goslin was alleged to represent. Among the charges hurled at Goslin by the Pasadena unit of Pro-

America and others were his association with W. H. Kilpatrick and the "Columbia [Teachers College] cult of progressive educators," and his support of a program alleged "to sell our children on the collapse of our way of life" (Hulburd, p. 89).

Despite untruths and what appears to be an absence of justice, the Goslin case involved events that transpired while he was superintendent. Not all attacks on schools of the day reached such a dramatic and pronounced climax, but even in more typical cases, where school personnel were not threatened to such an extent, intense assaults had widespread ramifications among school employees. For instance, a severe undermining of teachers' morale during the attack on Goslin took place in Pasadena. A 1955 survey conducted by the National Education Association's Defense Commission substantiated the effects of attacks on schools of the day. The study noted "various morale problems, and numerous resignations by teachers as well as by administrators" (p. 20).

Responding to criticisms of the public schools during this period, educators faced a familiar dilemma. On the one hand, the public schools belong to the people and should never be exempt from critical examination and appraisal by the people; nor should educators be unduly defensive or smug about claimed achievement for schools. On the other hand, the attacks on the schools were incited and supported by a minority and were often manifestly unfair and distorted.

Following the Pasadena crisis, Ernest O. Melby, dean of the School of Education at New York University, wrote *American Education under Fire: The Story of the 'Phony Three-R Fight.* Issued as one of the Freedom Pamphlets of the Anti-Defamation League of B'nai B'rith and sponsored by the American Education Fellowship, the John Dewey Society, and two constituent bodies of the National Education Association, this publication analyzed the methods used by the organizations that systematically attacked public schools of the day, particularly Allen Zoll's National Council for American Education. Over and above this Melby's discussion focused on identifying the characteristics of a "good education" and outlining procedures by which critics and criticism may be properly answered. His concluding section demonstrates how educators and interested citizens can cooperate to secure better schools.

In September 1951 Goslin became head of the Division of School Administration and Community

Development at George Peabody College for Teachers. The National Education Association gave him their American Education Award for 1952. In 1953 Goslin contributed a chapter to the Association for Supervision and Curriculum Development's 1953 yearbook, *Forces Affecting American Education.* His chapter, titled "The People and Their Schools," drove home the idea that the success with which public schools do their job depends upon the interest, support, and participation of all the citizens of every community and their understanding of educational principles and practices. In 1961, Seoul University awarded Goslin an honorary doctorate for his work as coordinator of a Korean teacher education project, hailing him as "the father of modern education in Korea" (*New York Times,* p. 27).

Goslin's work with Peabody College's "Multi-Year Project" in Korea was a capstone of his professional activities at Peabody. However, his seminars and regular classes were his true love. He specialized in teaching "foundations of education" and history of education, as well as teaching a colloquium on the superintendency each semester. It has been reported that his classes sometimes reached 80 to 100 students. Students and colleagues remember him as an excellent orator, having a "Will Rogers" kind of demeanor. He retired from teaching in 1966 at the age of sixty-seven, but remained actively involved with his students on a daily basis until his death in 1969.

BIBLIOGRAPHY

AXTELLE, GEORGE E. 1951. "Public Relations and Educational Statesmanship: Next Steps." *Progressive Education* 27–28 (May):214–216.

GOSLIN, WILLARD E. 1953. "The People and Their Schools," In *Forces Affecting American Education,* ed. William Van Til. Washington, DC: National Education Association.

HULBURD, DAVID. 1951. *This Happened in Pasadena.* New York: Macmillan.

Life. 1950. "Editorial." 29(24):95–96.

MELBY, ERNEST O. 1951. "American Education under Fire: The Story of the 'Phony Three-R Fight." *The New York Times Magazine* September 23:9, 57–60.

NATIONAL EDUCATION ASSOCIATION, COMMISSION FOR THE DEFENSE OF DEMOCRACY THROUGH EDUCATION. 1951. *State of the Nation in Regard to Attacks on the Schools and Problems of Concern to Teachers.* Washington, DC: National Education Association.

The New York Times. "Obituary." March 8, 1969, p. 7.

Who's Who in America. 1950–1951. Vol. 26. Chicago: Marquis.

ROBERT C. MORRIS

GOVERNANCE AND DECISION-MAKING IN COLLEGES AND UNIVERSITIES

There is no single or generally accepted definition of governance, as it has been described as structures, legal relationships, authority patterns, rights and responsibilities, and decision-making patterns. One commonly given definition of governance is the way that issues affecting the entire institution, or one or more components thereof, are decided. It includes the structure and processes, both formal and informal, of decision-making groups and the relationships between and among these groups and individuals. What distinguishes governance from administrative decisions is that governance tends to be early on in the process and establishes policies. Much of what happens later is administration.

Governance of higher education institutions around the world varies from nation to nation, ranging from direct and detailed control by the central government to laissez-faire, private profit-making enterprises, with many other arrangements in between. This entry will focus on governance patterns of colleges and universities that have emerged in the United States. One of the distinctive features of U.S. governance is the great diversity of forms that have emerged in contrast to other countries, which tend to have great uniformity. Each governance pattern reflects the unique history of the sector and the needs of those specific institutional types. There are several reasons for this diversity within the governance system, which include the absence of a centralized authority for education, strong public and private interests, a lay citizen governing board, and responsibilities that vary for trustees, presidents, and departments among institutions. The distinctive feature of governing boards has allowed for a decentralized system of governance where power and autonomy is distributed. Also, the U.S. governance

system has followed the general societal patterns for governance in a democracy—representative or collective decision-making often termed *shared governance.*

Shared Governance

The definition of shared governance has changed slightly over time, but the commonly accepted definition is from the 1966 Statement on Government of Colleges and Universities. It identified governance as the joint efforts in the internal operations of institutions, but also characterized certain decisions as falling into the realm of different groups. This statement was jointly formulated by the American Association of University Professors (AAUP), the American Council on Education (ACE), and the Association of Governing Boards of Universities and Colleges (AGB).

The statement, although not intended to serve as a blueprint for institutional decision-making, outlines roles for the president, faculty, administrators, and trustees in academic governance decisions. For example, it suggests that issues such as managing the endowment fall to the trustees, maintaining and creating new resources to the president, and developing the curriculum to the faculty. Not all decisions neatly fall into the domain of one of the three groups. It notes that much of governance is (or should be) conducted jointly. In other words, the statement argues that multiple members of the campus should have input on key decisions, a process termed *shared governance.* Questions over general education policy, the framing and execution of long-range plans, budgeting, and presidential selection should be decided jointly.

This open definition of shared governance is meant to respect the wide differences in history, size, and complexity of American higher education. For example, governance processes at liberal arts colleges are distinctive in that the whole faculty is often involved in governance; at larger institutions such as doctoral- and masters-granting institutions, governance tends to be a representative process through a faculty senate and joint committees. At community colleges, unions are also a key factor in the process. Although academic governance has changed over time, becoming highly participatory in the 1960s and more hierarchical in the 1980s, it has historically retained the notion of the importance of consultation and participation of campus constituents in major decision-making, reflecting democratic principles.

Governance Structure

The governance process is complex and includes many different layers (or groups). Each group differs in levels of responsibility by type of institution, culture of the campus, and historical evolution. Thus, there is no single organizing approach for governance. Trustees and boards have been delegated authority by college and university charters from the state legislature for oversight and decision-making. The legal requirements for boards are typically very loose; they need to assemble with a quorum periodically and oversee certain broad responsibilities. In the eighteenth and nineteenth centuries, boards dominated decision-making, and faculty had little involvement. However, as faculty professionalized in the late 1800s, there was a concerted effort among faculty to obtain greater authority within the decision-making process. As Robert Birnbaum notes, "the reality of governance today is much different than the strict legal interpretation would suggest" with boards having total authority (p. 4).

Even though governance is shared, trustees, governors, boards, or visitors play a significant role. Although holding different titles, these individuals maintain a similar function: to protect and ensure the interest and trust of the institution for the public or for a private group such as a church. The differing names reflect the different sectors and regional traditions. Trustees are more likely to play a custodial role over property and funds, being less involved with academic matters. Governors' roles tend to be more comprehensive and include academic matters. In general, board (this generic term will be used throughout the entry to designate these several different authority groups) responsibilities vary from clarifying mission, assessing president's performance, fund-raising, ensuring good management, and preserving institutional independence. Many boards have authority for ratifying institutional decisions, which can allow them to become involved in administrative details. Board authority varies by institution; thus to understand a particular campus it is necessary to obtain their charter and by-laws. Also, board members can be elected in public institutions or appointed in private institutions. Boards of private institutions tend to be larger than public ones.

Most boards report to another entity; for example, boards of trustees might report to a church while regents report to the legislature of a state. Today, most states have a system-wide coordinating board that campus governors or regents report to rather than directly to the legislature. Up until World War II, 70 percent of public colleges reported to their own board. However, when enrollments increased and there was major growth in the number of higher education institutions, state systems of governance developed. By the mid 1970s, only 30 percent of public colleges answered only to their governing boards.

Boards, trustees, and regents can be made up of very different types of individuals. Trustees are often alumni of the institution, whereas regents are often elected officials representing political party or district interests. Therefore, the perspective brought to the task of governing can vary greatly.

Another key player in governance is the president, who administers the policies set by the board. Presidents' and other administrators' role in governance is to make recommendations to the board and to implement policies. Faculty members, as noted above, became an integral part of governance around the turn of the twentieth century. In 1915 the American Association of University Professors developed a set of principles related to faculty rights, one of which is the right to offer input concerning institutional governance on matters related to academic decisions. Faculty members typically have input on decisions in such areas as employment, research, degrees and degree requirements, courses, evaluating programs, evaluation of faculty, admission, advising, and criteria for obtaining degrees.

Students' involvement in governance also varies by institution. Some boards have student membership. Some states, such as California, now have a law providing for student board membership. Also, most campuses have a student assembly or senate in which members are chosen by election. This body can operate as a governance body, providing recommendations to the president, administration and board. But it is rare for student assemblies to have any formal authority; rather, they are considered as part of the shared governance process.

Campus senates are the most common mechanism for faculty involvement in governance in a systematic way. Senators are elected to their positions from each college or school, making the campus senate a representative body. Most campus senates operate primarily through committees, and are only allowed to make recommendations to the president/administration and board about institutional matters. Several campuses have developed other formal governance structures in order to codify decision-making processes and input. Some campuses have developed joint committees of faculty, students, and administrators that develop recommendations for action on key institutional issues.

What are the areas in which governance decisions tend to be made? Policy setting areas tend to include mission, strategic direction, and selection processes for administrators, faculty, and staff; budgeting and expending funds; procedures related to construction of buildings; academic programs including degrees, course, admission, and graduation; promotion, tenure and salary increments; athletic programs; student matters; research, grants, and contracts; parking, security, and other services; and public relations.

External Influences

Although not formally part of campus governance, outside forces such as state governments, alumni, donors, federal government, accreditors, and associations often affect governance processes through funding, persuasion, policy, and guidelines. These other groups are important to acknowledge, even if their influence is infrequent and not formally defined by a charter, statement, or set of principles. Legislatures use budget allocation as a way to influence campus decision-making outside the formal governance processes. Individual donors might ask to have a say in certain institutional decisions in exchange for a monetary contribution to the institution. The federal government can establish rules and regulations that indirectly affect campus decision-making. For example, regulations about affirmative action have had an effect on campus admissions decisions and policies. Accreditors and associations probably have the least direct influence on campus governance. Accreditors, for example, can define requirements for a certain field of study. These requirements influence the decision-making processes at campuses that want to retain their accrediting status.

Trends in Governance

There are several trends in governance that are important to highlight: (1) the growth of external influ-

ences; (2) inability to respond to external challenges; (3) the lack of prominence and move away from shared governance; and (4) decreasing participation. These forces are related: The growth of external influences is coupled with institutions' trying to alter decision-making processes that were originally internally oriented to be more externally oriented. The lack of participation, among faculty in particular, is related to a move away from the tradition of shared governance.

Many commentators have noted that external agents are less reluctant to enter the decision-making process than in the past, even at the final stages. In addition, higher education is in the midst of a shift from its tradition of informal, consensual judgments to standardization, litigation, and centralization. Societal and legislative expectations have been altered, focusing more on accountability, quality, and efficiency. As Kenneth Mortimer and Thomas McConnell note, "the increased influence of state coordinating boards and system level administration in the last twenty years has moved decisions further away from campus based constituents." (p. 165). Boards and presidents now find themselves acting more as buffers to outside forces than in the past.

The intense environmental demands on higher education place great responsibility and strain on institutional leaders to make difficult decisions in a timely manner. The substance of academic governance has changed; traditional "maintenance" decisions, which include items such as the allocation of incremental budgets, modifications to the curriculum, and issues of faculty life, are being replaced with "strategic policy-making" decisions. These new decisions are high stakes challenges related to the changing nature of scholarship, prioritizing among programs, choosing among new opportunities, and reallocating either shrinking or unchanging (not growing) budgets. Current decision-making systems (e.g., academic senates) were not created to cope with these types of decisions and demands. These traditional academic governance structures are facing a cascade of criticism, describing them as being slow and ineffective. Campus senates and other joint administrative-faculty committees need to design processes to resolve unprecedented problems from the changing environment.

Although shared governance has been the norm for the last century, several commentators have noted that there are problems with shared governance that can no longer be ignored, including the following: (1) it does not actually represent or describe governance patterns in the majority of institutions; (2) it ignores the conflict of interests and adversarial decision-making practices inherent in a major new governance structure—collective bargaining; and (3) it takes in little account of the external forces. It is noted that shared authority only exists at a few elite institutions with powerful faculty, and that administrative authority is foremost at most institutions. Also, it is noted that there are few shared goals at most institutions, the principle that shared governance is built upon. Faculty and students are divided into different interest groups, making self-governance difficult with minimal consensus on issues. Thus, in practice, shared governance is usually not possible.

At the same time, academic governance is becoming less participatory, as fewer individuals care about or are involved in academic governance. Current trends work against widespread academic governance participation—fewer full-time faculty are employed, participation is not rewarded, other demands take precedence, and faculty allegiances favor disciplines rather than institutions. There is concern about institutional effectiveness, morale, and the quality of decision-making. Because of the complexity of institutional issues, well-considered decisions should be based on a high degree of input and thought, usually achieved through participation of multiple constituents. Institutions may jump to poor conclusions since decisions do not benefit from a thorough examination of the issues or multiple perspectives.

There are many challenges in governance that need to be resolved in the twenty-first century: perhaps new structures and governance forms will be applied to higher education, as developed in the last century, with the emergence of shared governance, campus senates, and state-wide coordinating boards.

See also: BOARD OF TRUSTEES, COLLEGE AND UNIVERSITY; COLLEGES AND UNIVERSITIES, ORGANIZATIONAL STRUCTURE OF; FACULTY SENATES, COLLEGE AND UNIVERSITY; PRESIDENCY, COLLEGE AND UNIVERSITY.

BIBLIOGRAPHY

AMERICAN ASSOCIATION OF UNIVERSITY PROFESSORS. 1995. *Statement on Government of Colleges and Universities.* Washington, DC: American Association of University Professors.

ASSOCIATION OF GOVERNING BOARDS OF UNIVERSITIES AND COLLEGES. 1996. *Renewing the Academic Presidency: Stronger Leadership for Tougher Times.* Washington, DC: Association of Governing Boards.

BERDAHL, ROBERT O. 1991. "Shared Academic Governance and External Constraints." In *Organization and Academic Governance in Higher Education,* 4th edition, ed. Marvin W. Peterson, Ellen E. Chaffee, and Theodore H. White. Needham Heights, MA: Ginn Press.

BIRNBAUM, ROBERT. 1991. *How Colleges Work: The Cybernetics of Academic Organization and Leadership.* San Francisco: Jossey-Bass.

CARNEGIE COMMISSION. 1973. *Governance in Higher Education: Six Priority Problems.* New York: McGraw-Hill.

DILL, DAVID D., and HELM, K. P. 1988. "Faculty Participation in Policy Making." In *Higher Education: Handbook of Theory and Research,* vol. 4, ed. John C. Smart. New York: Agathon.

DIMOND, JACK. 1991. "Faculty Participation in Institutional Budgeting." In *Faculty in Academic Governance: The Role of Senates and Joint Committees in Academic Decision Making,* ed. Robert Birnbaum. San Francisco: Jossey-Bass.

KELLER, GEORGE. 1983. Shaping an Academic Strategy. In *Academic Strategy: The Management Revolution in American Higher Education,* ed. George Keller. Baltimore: Johns Hopkins University Press.

LEE, BARBARA. 1991. *Campus Leaders and Campus Senates.* In *Faculty in Academic Governance: The Role of Senates and Joint Committees in Academic Decision Making,* ed. Robert Birnbaum. San Francisco: Jossey-Bass.

MORTIMER, KENNETH P., and McCONNELL, THOMAS RAYMOND. 1979. *Sharing Authority Effectively.* San Francisco: Jossey-Bass.

SCHUSTER, JACK H., and MILLER, LYNN H. 1989. *Governing Tomorrow's Campus: Perspectives and Agendas.* New York: American Council on Education/Macmillan.

SCHUSTER, JACK H.; SMITH, DARYL G.; CORAK, KATHLEEN A.; and YAMADA, MYRTLE M. 1994. *Strategic Governance: How to Make Big Decisions Better.* Phoenix, AZ: Oryx Press.

WESTMEYER, PAUL. 1990. *Principles of Governance and Administration in Higher Education.* Springfield, IL: Charles Thomas Publishers.

ADRIANNA KEZAR

GOVERNMENT AND EDUCATION, THE CHANGING ROLE OF

Since about 1990 the assumption that the public sector should be responsible for all aspects of education has been increasingly questioned, in both developed and developing countries, for four main reasons. First, there have been doubts about the effectiveness and efficiency of public education. Second, there are doubts about the equity and accountability of public education, which particularly affect the poor. Third, there is an increasing awareness of initiatives by educational entrepreneurs, and evidence to suggest that competitive pressures can lead to significant educational improvements. Fourth, there has been a need to restrain public expenditure in order to reduce budget deficits and external debts, and, consequently, a need to find alternative sources of educational funding.

About the fourth reason little more can be said, apart from the fact that this has motivated governments and international agencies to look to the possibility of an increasing private sector role. But potentially countering each of the other three reasons is the notion that education is a public good, and hence requires government intervention for its provision. Before reviewing relevant arguments, it is important to stress that the whole issue is controversial. Consequently, it is worth noting at the outset some recent overviews of the whole debate.

Largely unsympathetic to an increasing role for the private sector are philosopher Harry Brighouse, sociologists such as Stephen Ball, the Karl Mannheim professor of sociology of education at the University of London, and the journalist Alex Molnar. Brighouse, who is affiliated with both the American and the British reform movements, presents philosophical arguments against extending educational choice, particularly stressing how they will promote inequity. He is, however, sympathetic to some arguments about the way private sector could raise standards and be more efficient. Ball and his colleagues have explored the way market reforms have occurred in to England, and they suggest the evidence points to a deleterious impact on equality of opportunity. Finally, Molnar has explored the increasing commercialization of American schools, and he argues that the profit motive and education should not be allowed to mix.

For the alternative perspective, a good place to start is with the economic historian Edwin G. West's seminal work *Education and the State* (1994), followed by the work of Andrew Coulson and James Tooley. West suggests that before the government got involved in education in England and Wales and the United States, there was widespread private provision of education, which was crowded out by the intervening state. Coulson takes up the historical case in ancient Greece (among other places), and providing detailed economic and conceptual arguments to support the case for markets in education, and he challenges the idea that public education can promote social cohesion and equality of opportunity. Tooley takes up similar themes, conducting a thought experiment to explore historical, philosophical, and economic arguments that suggest the desirability for an increased role for the private sector in education—including addressing the objections to for-profit education.

Playwright George Bernard Shaw once quipped that the Americans and the British are divided by a common language. Nowhere is this more obvious than when we speak of the role of government in education. The British, for reasons buried in historical time, call their most elite private schools *public schools,* and other countries such as India followed this usage. To avoid confusion, this article will follow the more logical American usage, where *public* schools are those funded by government, and *private* schools are those that are not.

Education As a Public Good

It is often argued that education is a *public good,* and that this implies a particular role for government. Economists define a public good as satisfying up to three conditions: (1) indivisibility, (2) nonrivalry, and (3) nonexcludability. Indivisibility can be illustrated by the example of a bridge over a river, which can be used by anyone without extra costs being incurred. Nonrivalry is virtually the same, except that it is the benefits available to every member of the public that are not reduced, rather than the amount of the good. For example, the good of hiking in the

Grand Canyon could be, to a large extent, indivisible, in that many millions of people could do it without thereby hindering others also doing it. However, the greater the number of people who hike, the lower the enjoyment of those who wish to be in an empty wilderness—in which case the good is not nonrival. Finally, nonexcludability pertains when it is not feasible to exclude any individual members of the group from consuming the good. The classic economic example is of a lighthouse.

It would seem that education satisfies none of these conditions. It is clearly not nonexcludable, for a particular child can be excluded from a classroom or any other educational opportunity. The situation is similar for nonrivalry and indivisibility, for it is the case that if some children have the attention of an excellent teacher, then that teacher has less time for others, who therefore can obtain less benefit from the teacher. Indeed, it seems likely that it was precisely because of this nonrivalry or indivisibility that reformers wanted government to intervene in education—to alleviate this inequality of access.

However, if it is not a public good in this sense, education does seem likely to have *neighborhood effects,* or *externalities*—defined by economists as when an activity undertaken by one party directly effects another party's utility. That is, there are likely to be benefits to the community or society at large (if there are educational opportunities available) in terms of equality of opportunity, social cohesion, democratic benefits, law and order, economic growth, and so on. Crucially, these externalities are likely to exhibit a large degree of nonexclusion (it is costly to exclude people from these benefits or costs) and there are usually considerations relating to nonrivalry or indivisibility (the external benefits or costs are likely to be available to all with near zero marginal costs). For example, a society lacking in equality of opportunity could be a dissatisfied, lawless society. One could exclude oneself from the problems of such a society, but only at the expense of burglar alarms, bodyguards, high fences, or by restricting one's movements. It is in this sense that education could be referred to as a public good; and it is in this sense that it could legitimately be argued that education needs government intervention to ensure its provision and obtain these externalities.

From these considerations, the discussion would need to focus on the perceived effectiveness, efficiency, and equity of public education, and the presence, or lack, of private initiatives. These con-

cerns bring us squarely back to the major reasons adduced earlier for questioning the role of government in education. So, what of these reasons?

Standards and Efficiency

As far as the first reason is concerned, while doubts have arisen in many countries about standards in public schools, it is not until comparisons are made with private schools in the same countries that the role of government is significantly questioned. This comparative approach started with an 1982 American study by James Coleman, Thomas Hoffer, and Sally Kilgore, which predicted the score on a standardized test for an average public school student if he or she were to attend a private school. The study found that private schools were more effective at developing the cognitive abilities of students. After responding to criticisms that innate ability had not been controlled for, a follow-up study substantially confirmed the results.

Numerous studies since then have been carried out across a wide range of middle- and lower-income countries, all of which have found that private schools not only are more effective educationally (when controlled for socioeconomic factors), but are also more efficient. For instance, studies from the World Bank began by looking at achievement in verbal ability in Thailand, following up with studies of achievement in language and mathematics in Colombia, the Dominican Republic, the Philippines, Tanzania, and Thailand again. The studies explored the proportional gain in achievement score if a randomly selected student, with the characteristics of an average public school student, were to attend a private rather than a public school, holding constant the student's socioeconomic background. While there was a large range, the studies all showed the superiority of private education in terms of raising these cognitive abilities. In Colombia the results showed that private schools were 1.13 times more effective than public schools, averaging for verbal and mathematical achievement. In the Dominican Republic private schools were about one-and-a-half times more effective in raising achievement in mathematics; and in Thailand, again for mathematics, private schools were 2.63 times more effective than the public schools.

One obvious objection was that private schools can succeed where public schools cannot because of increased resources. However, when the same researchers probed this issue, they found the opposite to be the case. Comparing the cost per student in a private and a public school gave results ranging from a low of 39 percent in Thailand to a high of 83 percent in the Philippines. Combining these two sources of information, the researchers were then able to gain an answer to the question: "For the same per-pupil cost, how much more achievement would one get in private than in public schools?" The answer ranged from 1.2 times (Philippines) to a massive 6.74 times more achievement (Thailand) in the private than in the public schools.

Finally, Geeta Kingdon's evidence from India reveals similar findings. Kingdon controlled for twenty-one potentially confounding variables—including parental and family income, number of years of mother's education, number of books in the home, and student aptitude—for her study of a stratified random sample of schools in urban Lucknow, Uttar Pradesh. She found that the (unaided) private schools were 27 percent more effective at teaching mathematics, and slightly more effective at teaching language, than the public schools. But when per-pupil costs are brought into the equation, the results become quite striking. In the (unaided) private schools the per-pupil cost was less than half that in the public schools (38 rupees compared to 80 rupees).

Equity and Accountability

Doubts about public education that inform the debate about the role of government in education also focus on the fairness of public provision, although this is countered by doubts that privatization could be more equitable. In many countries, however, it has been observed that, despite public expansion of funding and provision, the expansion has not reached all members of society equally. Particularly acute is the wide gap in terms of educational provision offered to urban and rural populations. In Indonesia, for instance, only 3 percent of urban children of primary school age did not receive any schooling; while in the rural areas this figure rises to 10 percent. These comparison figures also obscure the fact that gender disparities in rural areas are even more severe. In Pakistan, for instance, while 73 percent of urban females age seven to fourteen have ever attended school, this figure plunges to 40 percent for rural females in the same age group.

In the poorest countries, it might be thought that spending on basic education would be a government priority, since these have yet to achieve universal primary-school enrolment. However, this often does not happen. In Africa, for instance, per-student spending on higher education is about forty-four times higher than on primary education. In most African nations, the poorest 20 percent of the population get significantly less than 20 percent of public education subsidy, while the richest 20 percent receive significantly greater than 20 percent. Most dramatically, in Nepal, the richest quintile gets almost half of total public spending on education.

Some of the most dramatic evidence of the inequity of public provision, which also raises the issue of accountability, comes from India. The PROBE Team's *Public Report on Basic Education in India* (1999) looked at primary education in four states, where it surveyed a random sample of villages in which there were a total of 195 government and 41 private schools. The report outlines some of the "malfunctioning" that is taking place in government schools for the poor in these four states. The schools suffer from poor physical facilities and high pupil-teacher ratios, but what is most disturbing is the low level of teaching activity taking place in them. When researchers called unannounced, only in 53 percent of the schools was there any teaching activity going on. In fully 33 percent, the head teacher was absent. The PROBE survey reported many instances of "plain negligence," including "irresponsible teachers keeping a school closed or non-functional for months at a time" and a school where "only one-sixth of the children enrolled were present" (p. 63). Significantly, the low level of teaching activity occurred even in those schools with relatively good infrastructure, teaching aids, and pupil-teacher ratios. Even in such schools, "teaching activity has been reduced to a minimum, in terms of both time and effort. And this pattern is not confined to a minority of irresponsible teachers—it has become a way of life in the profession" (p. 63).

These problems highlight the "deep lack of accountability" in the public schools, for these problems were not found in the private schools. The PROBE Team found a considerably higher level of teaching activity taking place in the private schools, even though the work environment is not better in these schools. For the researchers, this "brings out the key role of accountability in the schooling system. In a private school, the teachers are accountable to the manager (who can fire them), and, through him or her, to the parents (who can withdraw their children). In a government school, the chain of accountability is much weaker, as teachers have a permanent job with salaries and promotions unrelated to performance. This contrast is perceived with crystal clarity by the vast majority of parents" (p. 64).

All of this evidence is leading some governments and international agencies to wonder whether or not public education can reach the poorest in society, or whether some form of public-private partnership—perhaps with publicly funded vouchers being available for use at any school, public or private—would be a better role for government to play if reaching the poor is its aim.

Private Sector Alternatives

The existence of private schools for the poor in India might come as a surprise. In fact, this is a growing phenomenon throughout the developing world, and relates to the third major reason for the growing questioning of the role of government in education, the emergence of apparently viable private-sector alternatives. Schools for the poor are commonplace across a range of countries, including in India, where recent research has revealed a whole range of schools charging about $10 to $20 per year for each student, run on commercial principles and not dependent on any government subsidy or philanthropy. These fees are affordable by families headed by rickshaw pullers and market-stall traders. Even so, many of these schools also offer significant number of free places (up to 20 percent) for even poorer students, allocated on the basis of claims of need checked informally in the community. Similar schools have been reported in many African countries as well.

The emergence of private education alternatives is not only about the poor, of course. Recent research has uncovered a whole range of interesting examples of educational entrepreneurs who are creating innovative and effective private alternatives. The International Finance Corporation found for-profit education companies in developing countries that had created chains of schools and colleges, often operated on a franchise basis, with strict quality control procedures in place (including using the international standards of ISO 9000 series). These companies invest in research and development to explore new ideas in pedagogy and curriculum. Examples include Objetivo/UNIP in Brazil, which has over half a million students from kindergarten to university level across its 500 campuses around Brazil; and NIIT, based in New Delhi, which offers computer education and training in its forty owned

centers in the metropolitan areas, and about 1,000 franchised centers across India. It also has a global reach, with centers in the United States, Europe, Japan, Central Asia, Africa, and the Asia-Pacific region.

Notably, private entrepreneurs have harnessed information technology to the learning process. There has been a rapid growth of for-profit private-sector providers in education at all levels, creating e-learning opportunities in developing as well as developed countries. Many of these are in direct competition with traditional public-sector providers, such as the University of Phoenix, with 90,000 students across thirty-two campuses and seventy-one learning centers. However, many traditional universities have also responded to the challenge by either creating for-profit subsidiaries themselves—New York University, for instance, set up its NYOnline arm, and Columbia University created a for-profit arm, Fathom Knowledge Network Inc., in partnership with Cambridge University Press, the New York Public Library, and the University of Chicago. Other for-profit companies are emerging to provide e-learning for the K–12 market, including the appropriately named k12.com, led by William J. Bennett, the secretary of state for education during the Reagan administration.

The emergence and strength of these private-sector alternatives has impressed many governments looking to improve the quality and efficiency of public schooling. The British government is currently engaged in a process of contracting out failing schools and local education authorities to the private sector, trying to find best-value service wherever it can be found. But this process is not confined to developed countries. One notable example comes from India, where the Tamil Nadu state government wanted computer education in all high schools. Significantly, although allocating extra funds to this endeavor—about U.S. $22 million over five years—it didn't look to the public sector to provide this, but instead developed a model to contract out the delivery to private companies, who provide the software and hardware, while the government provides an electricity supply and the classroom. Significantly, companies that have won these contracts, such as NIIT, can also use the classroom as a franchised center, open to the school children and teachers during the day and open to the general public in the evenings and on weekends. The contracting out of curriculum areas such as this represents an important step forward in relationships between the public and private sectors, and provides an interesting model worth watching and emulating.

Conclusion

The debate will continue about the changing role of government in education, but there is considerable practical innovation and experimentation taking place globally that points to an acceptance of the changing role for government in educational delivery. Three types of reform can usefully be distinguished.

The first is the *contracting out* model, in which a state school has some or all of its educational functions contracted out to the private sector under accountability guidelines established by the local and/or central government. Education management companies such as Edison Schools in the United States and 3Es in England fit into this model, where all of the educational functions—pedagogy, curriculum, school management and improvement—are taken over by the private company.

Second, there is the *demand-side financing* model, which allows students to exit state schools—often when these are failing—and move to private schools through state-funded vouchers. Such schemes are found all around the world, including in the United States, Chile, Colombia, and the Ivory Coast, to name a few.

Third, there is the *state-funded private school* model, where either private schools are allowed to opt-in to state funding (as in Denmark and Holland), or new independent schools are specially created under government regulations to receive state funding, (as with charter schools in America, Canada, and China, and City Academies in England and Wales).

In Denmark for instance, the first private schools gained state subsidies in 1899. Now, any group of parents can claim the right to create a private school. Once established and running, the state guarantees to provide 80 to 85 percent of expenditures in the school. Some of these free schools are religious schools, but the majority are not: instead they are Rudolf Steiner schools, German minority schools, or simply independent academically-minded schools. Such private schools are becoming increasingly attractive to parents, with enrollments rising from 8 percent in 1982 to 12 percent in 1998.

See also: EDUCATION DEVELOPMENT PROJECTS; FEDERAL EDUCATIONAL ACTIVITIES; FEDERAL FUNDS FOR HIGHER EDUCATION; FEDERAL INTERAGENCY COMMITTEE ON EDUCATION; STATES AND EDUCATION.

BIBLIOGRAPHY

BRAY, MARK. 1996. *Privatisation of Secondary Education: Issues and Policy Implications.* Paris: United Nations Educational, Scientific and Cultural Organization.

BRIGHOUSE, HARRY. 2000. *School Choice and Social Justice.* Oxford: Oxford University Press.

COLEMAN, JAMES; HOFFER, THOMAS; and KILGORE, SALLY. 1982. "Cognitive Outcomes in Public and Private Schools." *Sociology of Education* 55:65–76.

COLEMAN, JAMES, and HOFFER, THOMAS 1987. *Public and Private High Schools: The Impact of Communities.* New York: Basic Books.

COMMONWEALTH OF LEARNING. 1999. *The Development of Virtual Education: A Global Perspective.* London: Commonwealth of Learning.

COULSON, ANDREW. 1999. *Market Education: The Unknown History.* London: Transaction Publishers.

GEWIRTZ, SHARON; BALL, STEPHEN J.; and BOWE, RICHARD. 1995. *Markets, Choice and Equity in Education.* Buckingham, Eng.: Open University Press.

GRACE, GERALD. 1989. "Education: Commodity or Public Good?" *British Journal of Educational Studies* 37:207–211.

JIMENEZ, EMMANUEL; LOCKHEED, MARLAINE E.; and PAQUEO, VICENTE. 1991. "The Relative Efficiency of Private and Public Schools in Developing Countries." *World Bank Research Observer* 6(2):205–218.

JIMENEZ, EMMANUEL; LOCKHEED, MARLAINE; and WATTANAWAHA, NONGNUCH. 1988. "The Relative Efficency of Private and Public Schools: the Case of Thailand." *The World Bank Economic Review* 2(2):139–164.

KITAEV, IGOR. 1999. *Private Education in Sub-Saharan Africa: A Re-examination of Theories and Concepts Related to Its Development and Finance.* Paris: International Institute for Educational Planning/United Nations Educational, Scientific and Cultural Organization.

KRASHINSKY, M. 1986. "Why Educational Vouchers May Be Bad Economics." *Teachers College Record* 88:139–151.

KINGDON, GEETA. 1996. "The Quality and Efficiency of Private and Public Education: A Case Study of Urban India." *Oxford Bulletin of Economics and Statistics* 58(1):57–81.

MOLNAR, ALEX. 1996. *Giving Kids the Business: The Commercialization of America's Schools.* Boulder, CO: Westview.

PATRINOS, HARRY ANTHONY, and LAKSHMANAN ARIASINGAM. 1997. *Decentralization of Education: Demand Side Financing.* Washington, DC: World Bank.

PROBE TEAM. 1999. *Public Report on Basic Education in India.* Oxford: Oxford University Press.

TILAK, JANDHYALA. 1997. "Lessons from Cost-Recovery in Education." In *Marketising Education and Health in Developing Countries—Miracle or Mirage,* ed. Christopher Colclough. London: Cassell.

TOOLEY, JAMES. 2000. *Reclaiming Education.* London: Cassell.

TOOLEY, JAMES. 2001. *The Global Education Industry,* 2nd edition. London: Institute of Economic Affairs.

WEISBROD, B. A. 1962. *External Benefits of Public Education* Princeton, NJ: Princeton University Press.

WEST, EDWIN G. 1994. *Education and the State,* 3rd edition. Indianapolis, IN: Liberty Fund

WEST, EDWIN G. 1997. "Education Vouchers in Practice and Principle: A Survey." *World Bank Research Observer* 12(1):83–104.

WORLD BANK. 1995. *Priorities and Strategies for Education. A World Bank Review.* Washington, DC: World Bank.

JAMES TOOLEY

GRADE RETENTION

See: SOCIAL PROMOTION.

GRADING SYSTEMS

SCHOOL
Thomas R. Guskey

HIGHER EDUCATION
Howard R. Pollio

SCHOOL

Few issues have created more controversy among educators than those associated with grading and reporting student learning. Despite the many debates and multitudes of studies, however, prescriptions for best practice remain elusive. Although teachers generally try to develop grading policies that are honest and fair, strong evidence shows that their practices vary widely, even among those who teach at the same grade level within the same school.

In essence, grading is an exercise in professional judgment on the part of teachers. It involves the collection and evaluation of evidence on students' achievement or performance over a specified period of time, such as nine weeks, an academic semester, or entire school year. Through this process, various types of descriptive information and measures of students' performance are converted into grades or marks that summarize students' accomplishments. Although some educators distinguish between *grades* and *marks,* most consider these terms synonymous. Both imply a set of symbols, words, or numbers that are used to designate different levels of achievement or performance. They might be letter grades such as *A, B, C, D,* and *F;* symbols such as $\sqrt{+}$, $\sqrt{}$, and $\sqrt{-}$; descriptive words such as *Exemplary, Satisfactory,* and *Needs Improvement;* or numerals such as *4, 3, 2,* and *1.* Reporting is the process by which these judgments are communicated to parents, students, or others.

A Brief History

Grading and reporting are relatively recent phenomena in education. In fact, prior to 1850, grading and reporting were virtually unknown in schools in the United States. Throughout much of the nineteenth century most schools grouped students of all ages and backgrounds together with one teacher in one-room schoolhouses, and few students went beyond elementary studies. The teacher reported students' learning progress orally to parents, usually during visits to students' homes.

As the number of students increased in the late 1800s, schools began to group students in grade levels according to their age, and new ideas about curriculum and teaching methods were tried. One of these new ideas was the use of formal progress evaluations of students' work, in which teachers wrote down the skills each student had mastered and those on which additional work was needed. This was done primarily for the students' benefit, since they were not permitted to move on to the next level until they demonstrated their mastery of the current one. It was also the earliest example of a narrative report card.

With the passage of compulsory attendance laws at the elementary level during the late nineteenth and early twentieth centuries, the number of students entering high schools increased rapidly. Between 1870 and 1910 the number of public high schools in the United States increased from 500 to 10,000. As a result, subject area instruction in high schools became increasingly specific and student populations became more diverse. While elementary teachers continued to use written descriptions and narrative reports to document student learning, high school teachers began using percentages and other similar markings to certify students' accomplishments in different subject areas. This was the beginning of the grading and reporting systems that exist today.

The shift to percentage grading was gradual, and few American educators questioned it. The practice seemed a natural by-product of the increased demands on high school teachers, who now faced classrooms with growing numbers of students. But in 1912 a study by two Wisconsin researchers seriously challenged the reliability of percentage grades as accurate indicators of students' achievement.

In their study, Daniel Starch and Edward Charles Elliott showed that high school English teachers in different schools assigned widely varied percentage grades to two identical papers from students. For the first paper the scores ranged from 64 to 98, and the second from 50 to 97. Some teachers focused on elements of grammar and style, neatness, spelling, and punctuation, while others considered only how well the message of the paper was communicated. The following year Starch and Elliot repeated their study using geometry papers submitted to math teachers and found even greater variation in math grades. Scores on one of the math papers ranged from 28 to 95—a 67-point difference. While some teachers deducted points only for a wrong answer, many others took neatness, form, and spelling into consideration.

These demonstrations of wide variation in grading practices led to a gradual move away from per-

centage scores to scales that had fewer and larger categories. One was a three-point scale that employed the categories of *Excellent, Average,* and *Poor.* Another was the familiar five-point scale of *Excellent, Good, Average, Poor,* and *Failing,* (or *A, B, C, D,* and *F*). This reduction in the number of score categories served to reduce the variation in grades, but it did not solve the problem of teacher subjectivity.

To ensure a fairer distribution of grades among teachers and to bring into check the subjective nature of scoring, the idea of grading based on the normal probability, bell-shaped curve became increasingly popular. By this method, students were simply rank-ordered according to some measure of their performance or proficiency. A top percentage was then assigned a grade of A, the next percentage a grade of B, and so on. Some advocates of this method even specified the precise percentages of students that should be assigned each grade, such as the 6-22-44-22-6 system.

Grading on the curve was considered appropriate at that time because it was well known that the distribution of students' intelligence test scores approximated a normal probability curve. Since innate intelligence and school achievement were thought to be directly related, such a procedure seemed both fair and equitable. Grading on the curve also relieved teachers of the difficult task of having to identify specific learning criteria. Fortunately, most educators of the early twenty-first century have a better understanding of the flawed premises behind this practice and of its many negative consequences.

In the years that followed, the debate over grading and reporting intensified. A number of schools abolished formal grades altogether, believing they were a distraction in teaching and learning. Some schools returned to using only verbal descriptions and narrative reports of student achievement. Others advocated *pass/fail* systems that distinguished only between acceptable and failing work. Still others advocated a *mastery* approach, in which the only important factor was whether or not the student had mastered the content or skill being taught. Once mastered, that student would move on to other areas of study.

At the beginning of the twenty-first century, lack of consensus about what works best has led to wide variation in teachers' grading and reporting practices, especially among those at the elementary level. Many elementary teachers continue to use traditional letter grades and record a single grade on the reporting form for each subject area studied. Others use numbers or descriptive categories as proxies for letter grades. They might, for example, record a 1, 2, 3, or 4, or they might describe students' achievement as *Beginning, Developing, Proficient,* or *Distinguished.* Some elementary schools have developed *standards-based* reporting forms that record students' learning progress on specific skills or learning goals. Most of these forms also include sections for teachers to evaluate students' work habits or behaviors, and many provide space for narrative comments.

Grading practices are generally more consistent and much more traditional at the secondary level, where letter grades still dominate reporting systems. Some schools attempt to enhance the discriminatory function of letter grades by adding plusses or minuses, or by pairing letter grades with percentage indicators. Because most secondary reporting forms allow only a single grade to be assigned for each course or subject area, however, most teachers combine a variety of diverse factors into that single symbol. In some secondary schools, teachers have begun to assign multiple grades for each course in order to separate achievement grades from marks related to learning skills, work habits, or effort, but such practices are not widespread.

Research Findings

Over the years, grading and reporting have remained favorite topics for researchers. A review of the Educational Resources Information Center (ERIC) system, for example, yields a reference list of more than 4,000 citations. Most of these references are essays about problems in grading and what should be done about them. The research studies consist mainly of teacher surveys. Although this literature is inconsistent both in the quality of studies and in results, several points of agreement exist. These points include the following:

Grading and reporting are not essential to the instructional process. Teachers do not need grades or reporting forms to teach well, and students can and do learn many things well without them. It must be recognized, therefore, that the primary purpose of grading and reporting is other than facilitation of teaching or learning.

At the same time, significant evidence shows that regularly checking on students' learning progress is an essential aspect of successful teaching—but checking is different from grading. Checking implies finding out how students are doing, what they have learned well, what problems or difficulties they might be experiencing, and what corrective measures may be necessary. The process is primarily a diagnostic and prescriptive interaction between teachers and students. Grading and reporting, however, typically involve judgment of the adequacy of students' performance at a particular point in time. As such, it is primarily evaluative and descriptive.

When teachers do both checking and grading, they must serve dual roles as both advocate and judge for students—roles that are not necessarily compatible. Ironically, this incompatibility is usually recognized when administrators are called on to evaluate teachers, but it is generally ignored when teachers are required to evaluate students. Finding a meaningful compromise between these dual roles is discomforting to many teachers, especially those with a child-centered orientation.

Grading and reporting serve a variety of purposes, but no one method serves all purposes well. Various grading and reporting methods are used to: (1) communicate the achievement status of students to their parents and other interested parties; (2) provide information to students for self-evaluation; (3) select, identify, or group students for certain educational paths or programs; (4) provide incentives for students to learn; and (5) document students' performance to evaluate the effectiveness of instructional programs. Unfortunately, many schools try to use a single method of grading and reporting to achieve all of these purposes and end up achieving none of them very well.

Letter grades, for example, offer parents and others a brief description of students' achievement and the adequacy of their performance. But using letter grades requires the abstraction of a great deal of information into a single symbol. In addition, the cut-offs between grades are always arbitrary and difficult to justify. Letter grades also lack the richness of other, more detailed reporting methods such as narratives or standards-based reports.

These more detailed methods also have their drawbacks, however. Narratives and standards-based reports offer specific information that is useful in documenting student achievement. But good narratives take time to prepare and as teachers complete more narratives, their comments become increasingly standardized. Standards-based reports are often too complicated for parents to understand and seldom communicate the appropriateness of student progress. Parents often are left wondering if their child's achievement is comparable with that of other children or in line with the teacher's expectations.

Because no single grading method adequately serves all purposes, schools must first identify their primary purpose for grading, and then select or develop the most appropriate approach. This process involves the difficult task of seeking consensus among diverse groups of stakeholders.

Grading and reporting require inherently subjective judgments. Grading is a process of professional judgment—and the more detailed and analytic the grading process, the more likely it is that subjectivity will influence results. This is why, for example, holistic scoring procedures tend to have greater reliability than analytic procedures. However, being subjective does not mean that grades lack credibility or are indefensible. Because teachers know their students, understand various dimensions of students' work, and have clear notions of the progress made, their subjective perceptions can yield very accurate descriptions of what students have learned.

Negative consequences result when subjectivity translates to bias. This occurs when factors apart from students' actual achievement or performance affect their grades. Studies have shown, for example, that cultural differences among students, as well as their appearance, family backgrounds, and lifestyles, can sometimes result in biased evaluations of their academic performance. Teachers' perceptions of students' behavior can also significantly influence their judgments of academic performance. Students with behavior problems often have no chance to receive a high grade because their infractions overshadow their performance. These effects are especially pronounced in judgments of boys. Even the neatness of students' handwriting can significantly affect teachers' judgments. Training programs help teachers identify and reduce these negative effects and can lead to greater consistency in judgments.

Grades have some value as rewards, but no value as punishments. Although educators would undoubtedly prefer that motivation to learn be entirely intrinsic, the existence of grades and other reporting methods are important factors in determining how much effort students put forth. Most students view high grades as positive recognition of their success, and some work hard to avoid the consequences of low grades.

At the same time, no studies support the use of low grades or marks as punishments. Instead of prompting greater effort, low grades usually cause students to withdraw from learning. To protect their self-image, many regard the low grade as irrelevant and meaningless. Other students may blame themselves for the low mark, but feel helpless to improve.

Grading and reporting should always be done in reference to learning criteria, never "on the curve." Although using the normal probability curve as a basis for assigning grades yields highly consistent grade distributions from one teacher to the next, there is strong evidence that it is detrimental to relationships among students and between teachers and students. Grading on the curve pits students against one another in a competition for the few rewards (high grades) distributed by the teacher. Under these conditions, students readily see that helping others threatens their own chances for success.

Modern research has also shown that the seemingly direct relationship between aptitude or intelligence and school achievement depends on instructional conditions. When the quality of instruction is high and well matched to students' learning needs, the magnitude of this relationship diminishes drastically and approaches zero. Moreover, the fairness and equity of grading on the curve is a myth.

Relating grading and reporting to learning criteria, however, provides a clearer picture of what students have learned. Students and teachers alike generally prefer this approach because they consider it fairer. The types of learning criteria teachers use for grading and reporting typically fall into three general categories:

1. *Product criteria* are favored by advocates of standards-based approaches to teaching and learning. These educators believe the primary purpose of grading and reporting is to communicate a summative evaluation of student achievement and performance. In other words, they focus on what students know and are able to do at a particular point in time. Teachers who use product criteria base grades exclusively on final examination scores, final products (reports or projects), overall assessments, and other culminating demonstrations of learning.

2. *Process criteria* are emphasized by educators who believe product criteria do not provide a complete picture of student learning. From this perspective, grading and reporting should reflect not just the final results but also how students got there. Teachers who consider effort or work habits when reporting on student learning are using process criteria. So are teachers who count regular classroom quizzes, homework, class participation, or attendance.

3. *Progress criteria,* often referred to as *improvement scoring, learning gain,* or *value-added grading,* consider how much students have gained from their learning experiences. Teachers who use progress criteria look at how far students have come over a particular period of time, rather than just where they are. As a result, grading criteria may be highly individualized. Most of the research evidence on progress criteria in grading and reporting comes from studies of differentially paced instructional programs and special education programs.

Teachers who base their grading and reporting procedures on learning criteria typically use some combination of these three types. Most also vary the criteria they employ from student to student, taking into account individual circumstances. Although usually done in an effort to be fair, the result is a "hodgepodge grade" that includes elements of achievement, effort, and improvement.

Researchers and measurement specialists generally recommend the use of product criteria exclusively in determining students' grades. They point out that the more process and progress criteria come into play, the more subjective and biased grades are likely to be. If these criteria are included at all, they recommend reporting them separately.

Conclusion

The issues of grading and reporting on student learning continue to challenge educators. However, more is known at the beginning of the twenty-first century than ever before about the complexities involved and how certain practices can influence teaching and learning. To develop grading and reporting practices that provide quality information about student learning requires clear thinking, careful planning, excellent communication skills, and an overriding concern for the well-being of students. Combining these skills with current knowledge on effective practice will surely result in more efficient and more effective grading and reporting practices.

See also: ASSESSMENT, *subentry on* CLASSROOM ASSESSMENT; ELEMENTARY EDUCATION, *subentries on* CURRENT TRENDS, HISTORY OF; SECONDARY EDUCATION, *subentries on* CURRENT TRENDS, HISTORY OF; SOCIAL ORGANIZATION OF SCHOOLS.

BIBLIOGRAPHY

AUSTIN, SUSAN, and MCCANN, RICHARD. 1992. "'Here's Another Arbitrary Grade for Your Collection': A Statewide Study of Grading Policies." Paper presented at the annual meeting of the American Educational Research Association, San Francisco, CA.

BAILEY, JANE, and MCTIGHE, JAY. 1996. "Reporting Achievement at the Secondary Level: What and How." In *Communicating Student Learning. 1996 Yearbook of the Association for Supervision and Curriculum Development,* ed. Thomas R. Guskey. Alexandria, VA: Association for Supervision and Curriculum Development.

BLOOM, BENJAMIN S.; MADAUS, GEORGE F.; and HASTINGS, J. THOMAS. 1981. *Evaluation to Improve Learning.* New York: McGraw-Hill.

BRACEY, GERALD W. 1994. "Grade Inflation?" *Phi Delta Kappan* 76(4):328–329.

BROOKHART, SUSAN M. 1991. "Grading Practices and Validity." *Educational Measurement: Issues and Practice* 10(1):35–36.

BROOKHART, SUSAN M. 1994. "Teachers' Grading: Practice and Theory. *Applied Measurement in Education* 7(4):279–301.

CAMERON, JUDY, and PIERCE, W. DAVID. 1994. "Reinforcement, Reward, and Intrinsic Motivation: A Meta-Analysis." *Review of Educational Research* 64(3):363–423.

CAMERON, JUDY, and PIERCE, W. DAVID. 1996. "The Debate about Rewards and Intrinsic Motivation: Protests and Accusations Do Not Alter the Results." *Review of Educational Research* 66(1):39–51.

CANGELOSI, JAMES S. 1990. "Grading and Reporting Student Achievement." In *Designing Tests for Evaluating Student Achievement.* New York: Longman.

CIZEK, GREGORY J.; FITZGERALD, SHAWN M.; and RACHOR, ROBERT E. 1996. "Teachers' Assessment Practices: Preparation, Isolation, and the Kitchen Sink." *Educational Assessment* 3(2):159–179.

CROSS, LAWRENCE H., and FRARY, ROBERT BARNES. 1996. "Hodgepodge Grading: Endorsed by Students and Teachers Alike." Paper presented at the annual meeting of the National Council on Measurement in Education, New York.

FRARY, ROBERT BARNES; CROSS, LAWRENCE H.; and WEBER, LARRY J. 1993. "Testing and Grading Practices and Opinions of Secondary Teachers of Academic Subjects: Implications for Instruction in Measurement." *Educational Measurement: Issues and Practice* 12(3):23–30.

FRISBIE, DAVID A., and WALTMAN, KRISTE K. 1992. "Developing a Personal Grading Plan." *Educational Measurement: Issues and Practices* 11(3):35–42.

GERSTEN, RUSSELL; VAUGHN, SHAWN; and BREN- GELMAN, SUSAN UNOK. 1996. "Grading and Academic Feedback for Special Education Students and Students with Learning Difficulties." In *Communicating Student Learning: 1996 Yearbook of the Association for Supervision and Curriculum and Development,* ed. Thomas R. Guskey. Alexandria, VA: Association for Supervision and Curriculum Development.

GUSKEY, THOMAS R. 2001. "Helping Standards Make the Grade." *Educational Leadership* 59(1):20–27.

GUSKEY, THOMAS R., and BAILEY, JANE M. 2001. *Developing Grading and Reporting Systems for Student Learning.* Thousand Oaks, CA: Corwin.

HALADYNA, THOMAS M. 1999. *A Complete Guide to Student Grading.* Boston: Allyn and Bacon.

KIRSCHENBAUM, HOWARD; SIMON, SIDNEY B.; and NAPIER, RODNEY W. 1971. *Wad-Ja-Get? The Grading Game in American Education.* New York: Hart.

LAKE, KATHY, and KAFKA, KENO. 1996. "Reporting Methods in Grades K–8." In *Communicating Student Learning. 1996 Yearbook of the Association for Supervision and Curriculum Development,* ed. Thomas R. Guskey. Alexandria, VA: Association for Supervision and Curriculum Development.

MCMILLAN, JAMES H. 2001. "Secondary Teachers' Classroom Assessment and Grading Practices."

Educational Measurement: Issues and Practice 20(1):20–32.

MCMILLAN, JAMES H.; WORKMAN, DARYL; and MYRAN, STEVE. 1999. "Elementary Teachers' Classroom Assessment and Grading Practices." Paper presented at the annual meeting of the American Educational Research Association, Montreal.

MILLION, JUNE. 1999. "Restaurants, Report Cards, and Reality." *NAESP Communicator* 22(8):5–7.

NAVA, FE JOSEFA G., and LOYD, BRENDA H. 1992. "An Investigation of Achievement and Nonachievement Criteria in Elementary and Secondary School Grading." Paper presented at the annual meeting of the American Educational Research Association, San Francisco, CA.

O'DONNELL, ANGELA, and WOOLFOLK, ANITA E. 1991. "Elementary and Secondary Teachers' Beliefs about Testing and Grading." Paper presented at the annual meeting of the American Psychological Association, San Francisco, CA.

ORNSTEIN, ALLAN C. 1994. "Grading Practices and Policies: An Overview and Some Suggestions." *NASSP Bulletin* 78(559):55–64.

STARCH, DANIEL, and ELLIOTT, EDWARD CHARLES. 1912. "Reliability of the Grading of High School Work in English." *School Review* 20:442–457.

STARCH, DANIEL, and ELLIOTT, EDWARD CHARLES. 1913. "Reliability of the Grading of High School Work in Mathematics." *School Review* 21:254–259.

STIGGINS, RICHARD J. 2001. "Report Cards." In *Student-Involved Classroom Assessment,* 3rd edition. Saddle River, NJ: Merrill Prentice Hall.

STIGGINS, RICHARD J.; FRISBIE, DAVID A.; and GRISWOLD, PHILIP A. 1989. "Inside High School Grading Practices: Building a Research Agenda." *Educational Measurement: Issues and Practice* 8(2):5–14.

TRUOG, ANTHONY L., and FRIEDMAN, STEPHEN. J. 1996. "Evaluating High School Teachers' Written Grading Policies from a Measurement Perspective." Paper presented at the annual meeting of the National Council on Measurement in Education, New York.

WOOD, LESLIE. A. 1994. "An Unintended Impact of One Grading Practice." *Urban Education* 29(2):188–201.

THOMAS R. GUSKEY

HIGHER EDUCATION

Over the course of an academic career the average student will be exposed to a variety of grading systems and procedures. Although some of these systems may be qualitative in nature, such as an annual or semiannual written narrative, the vast majority are quantitative and depend upon numerical or alphanumerical metrics. Perhaps the most familiar of these involves the letters "A" through "F," where "A" is usually given a value of 4.0 and is characterized in words as *outstanding* or *excellent* and "F" is given a value of 0.0 and is described as *unsatisfactory* or *failing*. The grades of A through F are usually derived from some more differentiated quantitative value such as test score, in which the specific nature of the relationship between grade and test score may take a variety of different forms: (e.g., an A is defined by a score of 90% or better or by a value that falls in the top 5–10% of scores independent of absolute value, and so on). Regardless of the specific translation of test performance into letter grade, the point to keep in mind is that the A–F scale defines the most frequent grading system used in higher education over the past half century or more.

Variations in the Grading System

Like all prototypes, the A–F system admits many variations. These often take the form of plusses and minuses, thereby producing a scale having the possibility of fifteen distinct units: A+, A, A–, B+, B . . . F–. In actual practice, the grade of A+ is scarcely ever used and the same is true for D+ and D– and F+ and F–, thereby yielding a scale of between eight to ten units. Generally speaking, the greater the number of units in the grading system the more precisely does it hope to quantify student performance. What is interesting in this regard are fluctuations in the actual number of units used in different historical eras. Without going too deeply into the relevant historical facts, it is clear that certain historical periods, such as the 1960s, reduced the grading system to two or so units—Pass, No Credit (P/NC)—whereas other periods, such as the 1980s, expanded it to ten, eleven or twelve units.

Variations in the breadth of the grading system would seem to have significant educational implications. At a minimum, these differences may be taken to imply that scales having a large number of units indicate a relative comfort in making precise distinctions, whereas those having fewer units suggest a relative discomfort in making such distinctions. In the case of more differentiated systems, distinctions and rankings are significant, and individual achievement is emphasized; in the case of less differentiated systems, distinctions and rankings are de-emphasized and interstudent competition is minimized. To some degree, it is possible to view fluctuations in American grading systems as reflecting a more general ambivalence the society has in regard to competition and cooperation, between individual recognition and social equity. Educational institutions sometimes emphasize strict evaluation, competition, and individual achievement, whereas at other times they emphasize less precise evaluation, cooperation, and sympathetic understanding for students of all achievement levels.

Another property of grading systems is that individual class grades often are combined to produce an overall metric called the grade point average or GPA. Unlike its constituent values, which usually are carried to only one (or no numerically significant places), the GPA presents a metric of 400 units yielding the possibility that a GPA of 3.00 will locate the student in the category of "good" whereas a value of 2.99 will exclude him or her from this category. In the same way, honors, admission to graduate school, preliminary selection for interviews by a desirable company, and so forth, may be defined by a single point difference on the GPA scale (e.g., 3.50 versus 3.49 for Phi Beta Kappa, etc.).

Because GPAs are significant in categorizing student performance, a number of evaluations have been made of their reliability and validity. One issue to be addressed here concerns field of study, where it is well documented that classes in the natural sciences and business produce lower overall grades than those in the humanities or social sciences. What this means is that it is unreasonable to equate grade values across disciplines. It also suggests that the GPA is composed of unequal components and that students may be able to secure a higher GPA by a judicious selection of courses.

Although other factors may be mentioned aside from academic discipline (such as SAT level of school, quality and nature of tests, etc.) the conclusion must be that the GPA is a poor measure and should not be used by itself in coming to significant decisions about the quality of student performance or differences between departments and/or educational institutions. The GPA is also a relatively poor basis on which to predict future performance, which perhaps explains why such attempts are never very impressive. In fact, a number of meta-analyses of this relationship, conducted every ten years or so since 1965, reveals that the median correlation between GPA and future performance is 0.18; a value that is neither very useful nor impressive. The strongest relationship between GPA and future achievement is usually found between undergraduate GPA and first-year performance in graduate or professional school.

Despite such difficulties in understanding the exact meanings of grades and the GPA, they remain important social metrics and sometimes yield heated discussions over issues such as grade inflation. Although grade inflation has many different meanings, it usually is defined by an increase in the absolute number of As and Bs over some period of years. The tacit assumption here seems to be that any continuing increase in the overall percentage of "good grades" or in the overall GPA implies a corresponding decline in academic standards. Although historically there have been periods in which the number of good grades decreased (so-called grade deflation), significant social concerns usually only accompany the grade inflation pattern. This one-sided emphasis suggests that grade inflation is as much a sociopolitical issue as an educational one and depends upon the dubious equating of grades with money. What really seems of concern here is a value issue, not a cogent analogy that reveals anything significant about grades or money.

How Grades Are Produced

Grading systems represent just one aspect of an interconnecting network of educational processes, and any attempt to describe grading systems without considering other aspects of this network must necessarily be incomplete. Perhaps the most important of these processes concerns the procedures used to produce grades in the first place, namely, the classroom test. Here, of course, are purely formal differences; for example, between multiple choice and essay tests, or between in-class and take-home tests or papers. Also to be included are the quality of test items themselves not only in terms of content but also in terms of the clarity of the question and, in the case of multiple choice tests, of the distractors.

One way to capture the complexity of possible ways in which grades are produced is to consider the set of implicit choices that lie behind an instructor's use of a specific testing and/or grading procedure.

Included here are such questions as: What evaluation procedure should I use? Term papers, classroom discussions, or in-class tests? If I choose tests, what kind(s)? Essay, true/false, fill-in-the-blank, matching, or multiple-choice? If I choose multiple-choice, what grading model should I use? Normal curve, percent-correct, improvement over preceding tests? If I choose percent-correct, how many tests should I give? Final only, two in-class tests and a final, one midterm and one final? How should I weight each test if I choose the midterm-final pattern? Midterm equals final, midterm is equivalent to twice the final exam grade, final equals twice the midterm grade? What grade report system should I use? P/F; A, B, C, D, F; or A+, A, A−, B+, . . . F? An examination of this collection of possible choices suggests that instructors have a large number of options as to how to go about testing and grading their students.

Any consideration of the ways in which testing and grading relate to one another must also deal with the ways in which one or both of these activities relate to learning and teaching. The relationship between learning and testing is a fairly direct (if neglected) one, especially if tests are used not only to evaluate student achievement but also to reinforce or promote learning itself. Thus it is easy to develop a classroom question or exercise that requires the student to read some material before being able to answer the question or complete the exercise. Teaching, on the other hand, would seem to be somewhat further removed from issues of testing and grading, although the specific testing and grading plan used by the instructor does inform the student as to what constitutes relevant knowledge as well as what attitude he or she holds toward precise evaluation and academic competition.

Students are not immune to testing and grade procedures, and educational researchers have made the distinction between students who are grade oriented and those who are learning oriented. Although this distinction is surely too one-dimensional, it does suggest that for some students the classroom is a place where they experience and enjoy learning for its own sake. For other students, however, the classroom is experienced as a crucible in which they are tested and in which the attainment of a good grade becomes more important than the learning itself. When students are asked how they became grade (or learning) oriented, they usually point to the actions of their teachers in emphasizing grades as a significant indicator of future success; alternatively, they describe instructors who are excited by promoting new learning in their classrooms. When college instructors are asked about the reason(s) for their emphasis on grades, they report that student behaviors—such as arguing over the scoring of a single question—make it necessary for them to maintain strict and well-defined grading standards in their classrooms. The ironic point is that both the student and the instructor see the "other" as emphasizing grades over learning, and neither sees this as a desirable state of affairs. What seems missing in this context is a clear recognition by both the instructor and the student that grades are best construed as a type of communication. When grades (and tests) are thought about in this way, they can be used to improve learning. As it now stands, however, the communicative purpose of grading is ordinarily submerged in their more ordinary use as a means of rating and sorting students for social and institutional purposes not directly tied to learning. Only when grades are integrated into a coherent teaching and learning strategy do they serve the purpose of providing useful and meaningful feedback not only to the larger culture but to the individual student as well.

See also: COLLEGE TEACHING.

BIBLIOGRAPHY

BAIRD, LEONARD L. 1985. "Do Tests and Grades Predict Adult Achievement?" *Research in Higher Education* 23:3–85.

CURRETON, LOUISE W. 1971. "The History of Grading Practices." *Measurement in Education* 2:1–9.

DUKE, J. D. 1983. "Disparities in Grading Practice: Some Resulting Inequities and a Proposed New Index of Academic Achievement." *Psychological Reports* 53:1023–1080.

GOLDMAN, ROY D.; SCHMIDT, DONALD, E.; HEWITT, BARBARA, N.; and FISHER, RONALD. 1974. "Grading Practices in Different Major Fields." *American Education Research Journal* 11:343–357.

MILTON, E. OHMER; POLLIO, HOWARD R.; and EISON, JAMES A. 1986. *Making Sense of College Grades.* San Francisco: Jossey-Bass.

POLLIO, HOWARD R.; and BECK, HALL P. 2000. "When the Tail Wags the Dog: Perceptions of Learning and Grade Orientation in and by Contemporary College Students and Faculty." *The Journal of Higher Education* 71:84–102.

HOWARD R. POLLIO

GRADUATE EDUCATION

See: BUSINESS EDUCATION; DENTISTRY EDUCATION; DIVINITY STUDIES; DOCTORAL DEGREE; ENGINEERING EDUCATION; GRADUATE SCHOOL TRAINING; GRADUATE STUDY; LAW EDUCATION; MEDICAL EDUCATION; NURSING EDUCATION; POSTDOCTORAL EDUCATION.

GRADUATE MANAGEMENT ADMISSION TEST

See: BUSINESS EDUCATION.

GRADUATE RECORD EXAMINATION

Every year, thousands of students prepare for, and take, the Graduate Record Examination (GRE)—a standardized test that measures the aptitude of promising graduate students. In 1998, 364,554 potential graduate students, a number that includes one-third of all bachelor degree recipients, took the GRE, according to the National Center for Education Statistics. Why does this test draw thousands of students? GRE scores are required for acceptance into most graduate programs. As a result, the exam, designed to assist graduate schools with their admissions decisions, also succeeds in sending would-be graduate students into a panic, raises questions of the efficacy of standardized testing, and funds a lucrative "test-prep" industry. Despite such side effects, it has proven useful to those it intends to serve—graduate schools. The GRE provides these institutions with a universal ruler against which applicants can be measured.

Administered by the Educational Testing Service (ETS), the GRE takes three basic forms: the General Test, Subject Tests, and the Writing Assessment. The General Test, most often referred to as the GRE, measures verbal, quantitative, and analytical reasoning skills. The Subject Tests measure achievement in eight disciplines. The Writing Assessment consists of two analytical writing tasks. Graduate institutions and departments independently determine which GRE test, or combination of tests, will be required for admission.

Genesis of the GRE General Test

Created in the early 1930s, the Graduate Record Examination General Test has been assessing college student aptitude for nearly seven decades. The Carnegie Foundation for the Advancement of Teaching funded the project, unaware of the vital part the test would soon play in graduate education. Widespread use of the GRE General Test began after World War II, when colleges and universities selected the test to help in the evaluation of the larger, more diverse pool of students applying to graduate programs. From this point forward, GRE test results have been used to evaluate students' capacity to succeed in graduate programs. Today, the Educational Testing Service and the GRE Board define the test as "a measure of knowledge and skills that members of the graduate community have identified as important for graduate study" (GRE 2001a, p. 2).

General Test

The Graduate Record Examination General Test's three parts—verbal, quantitative, and analytical—are designed to measure examinees' reading comprehension, mathematical, interpretative, and logical reasoning skills. Taken in a timed, proctored setting, the multiple-choice written test causes stress for many students. Though anxiety over the test has not changed, the format has. On April 11, 1999, the option to take the exam in written form was eliminated (except in developing countries). Today, the Computer Based Test (CBT), which replaces the pencil and paper version, is offered daily in centers around the world. Soon-to-be test-takers, and GRE test preparation companies, such as Kaplan Incorporated and The Princeton Review, have had to adjust to the features of the new design. In the past, paper-based GRE questions were identical: presented and weighted equally for all test-takers. Now, the "adaptive" CBT presents students with unique combinations of questions tailored to their skill level. Students complain about early questions on the computer-based test having greater bearing on their final scores and about the inability to answer questions out of sequence. Many agree, however, that the benefits of CBT, including instant scoring, continuous availability, and better data analysis capabilities,

far outweigh the disadvantages. Research indicates that scores from the paper-based tests are comparable to those of the computer-based test. Each section of the test yields a separate score ranging from 200 to 800. Scoring may change in October 2002 when one of the multiple-choice analytical sections will be replaced by a writing component.

Subject Tests

The GRE Subject Tests, offered in both paper and computer-based formats, are designed to help graduate school admission committees and fellowship sponsors assess applicants' preparation for graduate work in specific disciplines. The Subject Tests, offered in Biochemistry, Cell and Molecular Biology; Biology; Chemistry; Computer Science; Literature in English; Mathematics; Physics; and Psychology are required by select programs. Subject Test scores can range from 200 to 990.

The Writing Assessment Test

Launched in 1999, the Writing Assessment comprises two analytical writing tasks: one an opinion piece on an issue of the Educational Testing Service's choosing, the other a critique of a presented argument. The "tasks" are meant to complement each other, providing evidence of the examinees' ability to both make and analyze arguments. Like the Subject Test, this test can be taken on paper or electronically. Writing assessment scores range from 0 to 6.

Use of GRE Scores in Graduate Program Admissions Decisions

At every education level, controversy surrounds the use of standardized tests. According to the Business Council for Effective Literacy "objections [to standardized tests] tend to fall into two broad categories: their intrinsic defects and their misuse" (p. 6). At the turn of the twenty-first century national attention has turned to the Education Testing Service's GRE, with questions about GRE scores' assumed correlation with success in graduate school and issues of test fairness.

According to ETS, the Graduate Record Examinations measure general skills acquired over time. The scores have been validated for use in graduate admissions, fellowship selection, and other assessments related to graduate study. When interpreted and applied properly, GRE test scores can be helpful in admissions decisions. In the United States, master's and doctoral level admissions decisions are often based on a number of factors, including grade point averages (GPAs), transcripts from previously attended higher education institutions, GRE General Test scores, letters of recommendation, personal statements, self-reported information, and in some cases GRE Subject Tests, Writing Assessments, and personal portfolios. Problems arise when departments and colleges heavily rely on GRE scores, rather than considering all the information available on the student. As Judith Toyama states, "All too often, [GRE] scores, because they are numerical, [thus quantifiable], are given more importance" (p. 34). As a result of this pervasive misuse, the GRE is seen as a "gatekeeper" of minority and female—typically lower-scoring groups—access to graduate education. Many graduate schools use a combination of the verbal and quantitative section scores when considering applicants. How well does this composite predict academic success in graduate school? Peter Sacks, using data compiled by ETS, states, "Data from 1,000 graduate departments covering some 12,000 test-takers show that GRE scores could explain just 9 percent of the variation in grades of first year graduate students." Some studies have shown, however, that a combination of GRE scores and grade point averages can be indicative of student success.

Another controversial aspect of the GRE is that disparity in scores between ethnic groups points to the possibility of an intrinsic bias, or unfairness, in the General Test. Data analysis of GRE General Test scores reveals differences in the mean scores earned by racial, ethnic, and gender groups. According to the Graduate Record Examination Board, data from the 1999–2000 testing year shows the following: (1) white men scored at least 100 points higher, on average, than minority men and both minority and non-minority women; (2) self-classified whites, Asian/ Pacific Islanders, and "others" received higher scores on the verbal and analytical sections than other ethnic groups; and (3) within ethnic groups, men scored higher than women. In response to concerns over such performance gaps, the Educational Testing Service and the GRE Board instituted practices to reduce GRE test bias. Faculty have been included in the test design, review process, and analysis of differential item functioning (DIF) when the percentage of correct answers on the same test question differs between groups. Despite these efforts, differences still occur along ethnic and minority lines. ETS stresses, however, that differences

should be expected as "test results cannot be judged in isolation from the unequal outcomes produced by our educational, economic, and social systems" (2001a, p. 2).

Evaluation

Within our culturally, economically, and socially diverse population, no one measure could equitably evaluate individuals' promise. Even the GRE, a vetted, long-standing standardized test, has difficulty producing a fair measure of the diverse students that flock to test-taking centers each year. Moreover, when admissions committees make GRE scores the primary basis for their decisions, they overlook many characteristics and qualifications that are not measured on the test and are proven factors in student success, such as drive, passion, determination, and charisma. The use of GRE scores in the appraisal of students' ability in the tested areas is merited. The scores are inadequate, however, when applied as sole predictors of success. Students, scholars, and the ETS agree, the Graduate Record Examinations are valuable, as long as graduate school admissions committees exercise good judgment, and use the scores to supplement other admissions criteria.

See also: DOCTORAL DEGREE, THE; GRADUATE SCHOOL TRAINING; MASTERS DEGREE, THE.

BIBLIOGRAPHY

BUSINESS COUNCIL FOR EFFECTIVE LITERACY. 1990. Standardized Tests: Their Use and Misuse. *BCEL Newsletter for the Business Community* 22:6–9.

DAINOW, SUSANNAH. 2001. "Admission Exam for Graduate Schools Will Add a Writing Component." *The Chronicle of Higher Education* June 29.

GRADUATE RECORD EXAMINATIONS BOARD (GRE). 2001a. *Sex, Race, Ethnicity, and Performance on the GRE General Test 2001–2002.* Princeton, NJ: Educational Testing Service.

GRADUATE RECORD EXAMINATIONS BOARD (GRE). 2001b. *Guide to the Use of Scores 2001–2002.* Princeton, NJ: Educational Testing Service.

SACKS, PETER. 2001. "How Admissions Tests Hinder Access to Graduate and Professional Schools." *The Chronicle Review* June 8.

TOYAMA, JUDITH S. 1999. "What Will Be the Role of the GRE in Graduate Admissions Decisions in the 21st Century?" In *New Directions in Assessment for Higher Education: Fairness, Access, Multiculturalism, and Equity.* Princeton, NJ: The Graduate Record Examinations Board, Educational Testing Service.

INTERNET RESOURCES

COUNCIL OF GRADUATE SCHOOLS (CGS). 2001. "Changes to the GRE Test: An Interview with GRE Board Chair, Dr. Thach." <www.cgsnet.org/HotTopics/GREchanges.htm>.

NATIONAL CENTER FOR EDUCATION STATISTICS (NCES). 2001. "Table 315. Scores on Graduate Record Examination (GRE) and Subject Matter Tests: 1965 to 1999." *The Digest of Education Statistics.* <http://nces.ed.gov/pubs2002/digest 2001/table/dt315.asp>.

LORI J. CAVELL

GRADUATE SCHOOL TRAINING

Graduate and professional education is the continuation of academic study beyond the baccalaureate degree. Graduate education is distinguished from professional education in that the graduate student is preparing for a career in academia, the government, or other professions. Those continuing in professional education are in degree programs that will prepare them for work in law, medicine, or other professional fields. Both graduate and professional education have been well established in the United States for over 100 years; however it was only in the latter part of the twentieth century that the face of graduate education began to change as the higher educational system became more diversified through such developments as the proliferation of women and minority graduate students.

In the early nineteenth century, German universities were the leading force of graduate education. Leadership in this area passed to the United States in the twentieth century as American universities advanced their programs. Three universities—Harvard, Yale, and Johns Hopkins—are credited with the adaptation of post-baccalaureate education. While Harvard took the lead, in 1847 Yale developed a model that made the distinction between undergraduate and graduate education. Johns Hopkins University was the first institution to be founded primarily as a graduate education institution.

The Master's Degree

Graduate education is divided into two main areas: the master's degree and doctoral study. Obtaining a master's degree typically requires a minimum of thirty credit hours past the baccalaureate degree, although some programs may require more or less depending on the university and discipline requirements. At the completion of class work, either a comprehensive exam is administered or a written thesis is submitted, and either of these may be followed by an oral defense where the student is posed questions by the department faculty. This is the typical pattern of master's degree study, with most programs requiring two years of coursework. However, there are hundreds of different types of master's degrees offered in the United States and it is not unusual for each program to have unique characteristics and requirements.

The traditional master's degrees grounded in the arts and sciences curriculum are the master of arts (M.A.) and the master of science (M.S.). Examples of other master's degrees that have a more practical or professional approach are the master of business administration (M.B.A.), the master of education (M.Ed.), and the master of engineering (M.Eng.). While there are still a significant number of students who attend graduate school immediately following their undergraduate experience, more students are choosing to return for a master's degree several years after entering the work force. For these more mature students, the master's degree is considered a stepping-stone for career advancement. Many individuals have the added bonus that more businesses now make it possible for their employees to attend graduate school by offering tuition reimbursement and time off from work for educational purposes. At the same time, universities are offering more options for students who choose to remain employed while pursuing their master's degree. Examples include offering evening or weekend classes and conducting classes in the work environment rather than on the college campus.

Additionally, the proliferation of master's programs being offered by colleges and universities is increasing the options of those who choose to re-enter academia. Rather than graduate education being offered only at universities, liberal arts colleges are adding one or more master's programs to their curriculum. At the same time, they are targeting the more mature student as well as the student who would prefer the liberal arts college environment to the larger university. With the increased availability and visibility of master's education, the number of master's degrees awarded in the United States continues to grow each year.

The Doctoral Degree

A doctoral program is considered the basis for socialization into the professoriate. It has always been regarded as a beginning for developing skills, knowledge, and competencies associated with teaching and research. For this reason, there are some general requirements for doctoral degrees that apply to most institutions in the United States. While there are differences with course requirements and completion rates, the basic doctoral degree begins with one to two years of course work and ends with the oral defense of the dissertation. Some students, particularly those who enter a doctoral program without a master's degree, will earn their master's degree while pursuing the doctorate. In this case, course work could take more than two years to complete. In addition to these basic requirements, many doctoral students hold research or teaching assistantships in addition to taking classes. Likewise, faculty members are encouraged to and often include doctoral students in research projects. Both the assistantships and the mentor relationships with faculty are preparation not only for the dissertation but for the professorial role many will enter into upon completion of their degrees.

Allen R. Sanderson and Bernard Dugoni identified fifty-two different research doctorates in their 1997 summary report of doctoral recipients from United States universities. Traditionally, the non-professional doctoral degree most often awarded is the doctor of philosophy (Ph.D.), although other degrees such as the doctor of education (Ed.D.), doctor of arts (D.A.), and the doctor of science (D.Sc. or Sc.D.) are now being offered in greater numbers. Professional doctoral degrees such as the jurist doctorate (J.D.) and the medical doctorate (M.D.) also indicate that ending of advanced education but the requirements for these doctoral degrees differ from the Ph.D. and its equivalent.

Course work for a doctoral degree is most often individually tailored based on the student's background, interests, and professional goals. In addition to completing class work prior to the dissertation, doctoral students are required to take comprehensive exams. Depending on the program, a student may be required to take more than one comprehen-

sive exam throughout the course of study. Typically, a comprehensive exam is administered immediately following completion of course work and the exam itself may take various forms such as a day-long session where students answer questions based on knowledge obtained in their studies. In most circumstances this is a closed book exam and, after faculty members have had the opportunity to grade the exam, doctoral students must defend their responses orally before a faculty panel.

The dissertation is an original body of research conducted by a student in her final years as a doctoral student. A typical dissertation completed by a Ph.D. candidate will include five chapters: the first is a general introduction, the second chapter is a thorough literature review of the subject, the third chapter contains the methodology or how the research is to be conducted, the fourth chapter shows the findings from research, and the final chapter is a discussion of the findings with suggestions for possible future research.

Prior to conducting the dissertation research, the graduate student must defend his proposal to a dissertation committee which is generally made up of three to five members. The proposal is typically the first three chapters of the dissertation. After the proposal is approved the doctoral student may begin their research and move to completing the dissertation. After the research has been conducted and data analyzed, doctoral students must again orally defend the dissertation before their committee. Each Ph.D. candidate must show a thorough knowledge of the subject being studied along with the presentation of original research and findings that add to the body of knowledge for their discipline.

The Ph.D. (doctor of philosophy) is the typical doctoral degree awarded at universities although the areas of study range from the basic humanities to the sciences and education. Those receiving Ph.D.s have traditionally gone on to faculty positions at colleges or universities. It is not uncommon today, though, for Ph.D. recipients to go immediately into careers outside of academia. Not only do many choose to forego teaching or research opportunities, many are forced to look elsewhere for work due to the lack of available faculty positions. With the proliferation of doctoral recipients, it is natural to assume that not all Ph.D.s will find the ideal job at a college or university.

Other doctorates are available for those selecting a course of study that leads to careers outside academia. Some examples are the educational doctorate, which may be pursued by those with careers in K–12 classroom teaching or school administration, and the doctor of engineering, for candidates working in areas of technology or applied sciences. It is normal for these graduate students to focus their studies and dissertations on practical topics, rather than theoretical ones, that have immediate relevance to their field of work.

Professional Graduate Education

Professional doctoral education, as previously mentioned, is post-baccalaureate study in the professions. Two of the most established professional education fields are medicine and law. The requirements for obtaining an M.D. or J.D. are rigid and do not vary greatly at different universities, unlike programs for research doctoral programs, which offer more flexibility to students in their individual courses of study. Professional doctoral students enter their graduate program as a cohort, take the same classes as others who entered the program with them, and graduate within the recommended time period, unless serious circumstances delay their progress. The curriculum focuses on applied areas of study. Unlike a Ph.D., where the dissertation is the culmination of study, often after the professional doctoral education is completed, graduates are required to take state-regulated exams in order to practice their professions, as in medicine, law, or nursing.

See also: BUSINESS EDUCATION; DOCTORAL DEGREE, THE; FACULTY PERFORMANCE OF RESEARCH AND SCHOLARSHIP; FACULTY ROLES AND RESPONSIBILITIES; LAW EDUCATION; MASTER'S DEGREE, THE; MEDICAL EDUCATION.

BIBLIOGRAPHY

FOX, MARY F. 1996. "Publication, Performance and Reward in Science and Scholarship." In *Faculty and Faculty Issues in Colleges and Universities,* ed. Dorothy E. Finnegan, David Webster, and Zelda F. Gamson. Needham Heights, MA: Simon and Schuster.

SANDERSON, ALLEN R., and DUGONI, BERNARD. 1999. *Doctorate Recipients from United States Universities: Survey of Earned Doctorates.* Summary Report. Chicago: National Opinion Research Center.

PATRICIA A. HELLAND

GRADUATE STUDY IN EDUCATION

Graduate programs in the field of education are offered in U.S. colleges and universities at the master's, specialist, and doctoral levels. Like graduate programs in other disciplines and fields of study, graduate programs in education require baccalaureate degrees as a prerequisite. Degrees are typically awarded after students complete specified program requirements.

From 1997 to 1998 education was the most popular field of study at the master's and doctoral level. According to the U.S. Department of Education, slightly more than one-quarter (114,691) of the 430,164 master's degrees awarded in 1997 to 1998 were in the field of education, and at the doctoral level, approximately 15 percent (6,729) of the 46,010 doctoral degrees awarded were in education. Men earned slightly fewer than one-quarter of the master's degrees (24%) awarded in 1997 to 1998 and at the doctoral level men earned 37 percent of the degrees. Whites represented 77 percent of the master's degree recipients in 1997 to 1998, followed by black non-Hispanics (9%), Hispanics (4%), non-resident aliens (3%), Asian or Pacific Islanders (2%) and American Indian/Alaskan Natives (1%), with students who did not report their race/ethnicity representing 5 percent of master's degree recipients. At the doctoral level, whites earned 71 percent of the doctoral degrees, followed by black non-Hispanics (11%), nonresident aliens (8%), Hispanics (4%), Asian or Pacific Islanders (2%), American Indian/Alaskan Natives (1%) and students who did not report their race/ethnicity represented 3 percent.

Education Degrees

Similar to psychology and social work, but unlike many other graduate-level fields of study, students who enroll in education graduate programs choose between a research path and a professional practice path and in some cases, a path that combines research and practice. Traditionally, the research path is designed for people who want to examine and evaluate educational practices and research, with the goal of preparing students to become college faculty or researchers, while the professional path is designed for people who wish to practice in the field in positions such as school principal, school superintendent, chief financial officer within a primary or secondary school, a dean of admissions, or a dean of student affairs at a college or university. This difference between the applied and the research-oriented degree is reflected in the types of degrees. The master of education (Ed.M.), the specialist in education (Ed.S) a degree intended for teachers, counselors, and administrators who wish to pursue graduate study beyond the master's level, and the doctor of education (Ed.D.) programs prepare students to apply knowledge and scholarship toward addressing problems in educational settings. In contrast the master of arts (M.A.), the master of science (M.S.), the master of arts in teaching (M.A.T), the master of science in education (M.S.Ed.), the doctor of arts (D.A.), which is intended to develop pedagogical skills along with scholarly achievement and research excellence, and the doctor of philosophy (Ph.D.) programs prepare students to engage in research and scholarship on education to create knowledge.

Certificate programs are yet another post-baccalaureate educational option. Examples of some of the certificates include a post-baccalaureate certificate program (nondegree) and a Certificate of Advanced Graduate Study (CAGS). Most candidates for the CAGS have earned a master's degree. The CAGS often serves one of the following two purposes: (1) an end goal for individuals who seek advanced training without having the pressure or the time commitment of a doctoral degree program or (2) an intermediary step before students formally apply to a doctoral program.

Graduate education instructional programs cover the spectrum of the educational landscape from pre-kindergarten to adult education. The National Center for Education Statistics Classification of Instructional Programs has classified fifteen program of instruction areas in education:

- education, general
- bilingual, multilingual, and multicultural education
- curriculum and instruction
- educational administration and supervision
- educational/instructional media design
- educational assessment, evaluation, and research
- international and comparative education
- social and philosophical foundations of education
- special education and teaching
- student counseling and personnel services

- teacher education and professional development: specific levels and methods
- teacher education and professional development: specific subject areas
- teaching English or French as a second or foreign language
- teaching assistants/aides
- education, other

Within each of these sixteen categories are finer classifications of areas of instruction.

Admission to Education Graduate Programs

Unlike undergraduate admissions in which students apply to a college or university's central admissions office, which then reviews all students' application materials, admissions decisions at the graduate level are usually handled by a faculty committee at the education graduate school or the specific graduate program within the school (e.g. curriculum and instruction, or educational administration and planning). The typical application materials submitted for admission include the following: (1) academic transcripts from all prior colleges or universities attended; (2) an application for admissions; (3) an essay or statement of purpose and goals (4) an application fee; (5) letters of recommendation; and (6) admissions test scores.

There are three primary admissions tests accepted by graduate schools of education: Graduate Record Examination (GRE), Miller Analogies, and the Test of English as a Foreign Language (TOEFL). The GRE General Test has three parts: verbal, quantitative, and analytical. These parts are not related to any specific field of study, but rather are intended to assess the abilities of applicants to graduate school in mathematical reasoning, literacy, and analytical thinking. Scores for each section of the GRE General Test range from 200 to 800. A two-part writing assessment is also available to measure student abilities to articulate complex ideas clearly and effectively and to support their ideas with relevant reasons and examples. The writing assessment has one combined score. The GRE also includes eight subject area tests. Some graduate programs require students who are applying to educational psychology programs to take the GRE psychology test, which measures the extent of knowledge of psychology that would be acquired primarily in undergraduate psychology curricula. Subject test scores range from 200 to 990. The Miller Analogies Test consists of 100 partial analogies that are completed in fifty minutes. Miller Analogy score reports present three MAT Scores: a student's raw score (the number answered correctly), the percentile based on intended major, and the percentile based on the general population of MAT examinees. The TOEFL measures the ability of nonnative speakers of English to use and understand North American English.

Graduate school admission committees typically review several parts of an applicant's admission record:

- the reputation of their undergraduate institution
- undergraduate grade point average (UGPA), both overall and in some instances their GPA in their undergraduate major
- admission test scores
- personal statement
- work history if applicable
- letters of recommendation
- how student's research interests match faculty research interests.

The weight that each graduate program assigns to these components varies from program to program. Particularly at the doctoral level, admissions decisions may also be based on the amount of funds that are available to support students who are applying. Some programs do not admit more students than they anticipate being able to fully fund for the duration of their graduate career, while others seek to provide initial support to attract students, and assume that students will find a niche along with support after they are engaged in the process.

Students apply for financial aid for graduate school simultaneously with their application for admission. There are three primary types of financial assistance at the graduate level. The first is a fellowship. When a student receives a fellowship, she/he typically receives money without an obligation to perform any work in exchange for the money. Assistantships are the second form of financial assistance. There are three types of assistantships: teaching, research and administrative. Teaching assistantships usually require students to perform teaching duties in exchange for tuition and a stipend. Research assistantships usually require students to work with faculty on their research in exchange for tuition and a stipend. Administrative assistantships require students to work with administrative offices on programs or projects in exchange for tuition and a stipend. In both the cases of fellowships and assistantships, students may or may not receive health benefits. The third form of financial assistance is a loan. Loans require students to repay the money typically with interest. The exact terms of the loans vary depending upon the originating source of the loan. A less prevalent form of paying for graduate school is the use of employer tuition assistance plans. Graduate level financial aid awards may be made on the basis of academic credentials (e.g., test scores, undergraduate grades, if a an applicant's area of interest is related to one of the faculty's areas of interest), academic promise, or on the basis of financial need.

Degree Requirements

Students may be enrolled either full-time or part-time. Graduate programs may offer classes during the traditional academic year, during the summer, or in a two-day weekend format offered monthly throughout the calendar year. Graduate education programs are typically delivered in two formats. The traditional delivery method is in person where faculty meet students at the main campus or at a satellite campus location. Satellite locations may be either in-state or out-of-state. The other medium involves distance education technology.

Graduate degrees in education are typically awarded after students complete specified program requirements. Course work requirements are a basic degree requirement. Course requirements may include a set number of courses or credit hours as well as a distribution requirement. The distribution requirement may include courses within the education graduate program as well as courses in other related disciplines or fields of study offered at the institution. At the master's level students may be required to complete a culminating exercise ranging from creative projects to a master's thesis. Master's students may also be required to complete a field experience practicum.

At the doctoral level, students complete a qualifying or preliminary examination at the end of their course work. The structure of the exercise will vary from program to program and may be dependent upon whether the student is pursuing an Ed.D. or a Ph.D. After passing the qualifying or preliminary examination, the doctoral student is typically required to write and defend a dissertation. The requirements of the dissertation may vary depending upon the terminal degree. The Ed.D. dissertation may require doctoral students to examine an issue in education, while the Ph.D. dissertation requires the doctoral student to pursue original research.

See also: DOCTORAL DEGREE, THE; GRADUATE SCHOOL TRAINING; MASTER'S DEGREE, THE; TEACHER EDUCATION.

BIBLIOGRAPHY

U.S. DEPARTMENT OF EDUCATION. NATIONAL CENTER FOR EDUCATION STATISTICS. 2000a. *Classification of Instructional Programs—2000.* Washington, DC: Government Printing Office.

U.S. DEPARTMENT OF EDUCATION. NATIONAL CENTER FOR EDUCATION STATISTICS. 2000b. *Degrees and Other Awards Conferred by Title IV Participating, Degree-Granting Institutions: 1997–1998.* Report No. 2001–177. Washington, DC: Government Printing Office.

CATHERINE M. MILLETT

GRADUATION CEREMONY

See: COMMENCEMENT.

GRAY, WILLIAM SCOTT (1885–1960)

William S. Gray, as author of the popular "Dick and Jane" series, arguably helped to define the field of reading education in the United States. Gray received a bachelor's degree from the University of Chicago in 1913, a master's degree from Teachers College, Columbia University, in 1914, and a Ph.D. from the University of Chicago in 1916. He was associated with the University of Chicago from the time he became an instructor in 1915 to his retirement as professor emeritus in 1950. Always interested in the education of teachers, he was dean of the college of education from 1917 to 1930 and head of the university's teacher preparation committee from 1933 through 1945.

Conducting and analyzing research studies to improve reading instruction was Gray's passion, and his work impacted virtually every aspect of the field. During his lifetime he authored more than 500 publications that examined the characteristics of all ages of readers, from young children to adults, as well as teaching procedures appropriate for the characteristics. He also developed a standardized reading test in 1915, which continues to be used into the twenty-first century, and he pioneered the diagnostic/remedial approach to reading difficulties.

Influence of Reform Movements

The underpinnings of Gray's approach to research and practice were formed in the first two decades of the twentieth century when his work and education brought him into contact with the reform movements transforming American education. In 1908, to prepare to become a teacher, he entered the Illinois State Normal School, the center of the Herbartian movement in North America: Charles De Garmo and Frank and Charles McMurry were among those who had taught or studied there. Herbartianism at the turn of the century was a scientific approach to education based on principles of learning. Gray adopted Herbartian principles and had the opportunity to apply them when he became principal of the training school at Illinois Normal following his graduation in 1910. The experience led to Gray's first publications: twelve articles on the teaching of geography, based on the principles of Herbartianism, which appeared in *The School Century* from May 1911 through June 1912.

Gray's incipient interest in a scientific approach to education was nurtured at the University of Chicago, where he worked primarily with Charles Judd, head of the department of education. Judd was a psychologist as well as educator who utilized scientific methods and measurement techniques to study education. While at Teachers College Gray worked with Edward L. Thorndike, who, even more so than Judd, was applying scientific principles, measurement techniques, and statistical procedures to education. Gray's life-long interest in reading assessment began to focus at this time. Thorndike was developing achievement scales in various subject areas, and Gray, for his master's thesis, developed a scale for reading. The test, *Standardized Oral Reading Paragraphs, Grades 1–8,* was published in 1915. This test continued to be used with only minor revisions until 1963; in 2001 the fourth edition of the *Gray Oral Reading Test* was issued.

Gray returned to the University of Chicago to study for a Ph.D. and immediately began to work for Judd, who was participating in a survey of the Cleveland schools. The survey was a major reform effort to bring scientific principles to bear on school improvement, and Judd asked Gray to assess reading achievement in the Cleveland schools. The experience gave Gray the opportunity to observe reading instruction in many classrooms and to refine his skills in reading assessment. He received his Ph.D. degree with a dissertation entitled "Studies of Elementary School Reading through Standardized Tests." His dissertation was published in 1917 as the first number in the *Supplementary Educational Monographs of the University of Chicago.*

During the "Economy of Time" reform movement in the second decade of the twentieth century, Gray, by then dean of the college of education at the University of Chicago, used scientific methods to determine the most successful method of teaching reading. Gray identified the following components: (1) selecting content of interest and significance to students; (2) developing independent word-recognition skills by word study and phonetic analysis after the student has acquired a basic vocabulary through content reading; and (3) providing a system of phonics that will naturally lead to accurate analysis of longer words encountered past the second grade. Gray became an advocate of the sight method of teaching reading, and had the opportunity to directly impact classroom practice in 1930 when he became a coauthor, with William H. Elson, of a popular basal reading series titled the *Elson Basic Readers,* published by Scott, Foresman and Company. In 1936 these became the *Elson-Gray Basic Readers;* in 1940 he became first author of the renamed *Basic Readers.* These "Dick and Jane" readers became widely used throughout America.

Literacy Efforts

Gray's assessment experience made him aware of student reading difficulties and the necessity to fit instruction to the perceived weaknesses of students. In 1922 this led to an influential book titled *Remedial Cases in Reading: Their Diagnosis and Correction.* This book marked the beginning of a diagnostic/prescriptive approach to individual differences that remained in practice at the beginning of the twenty-first century.

Gray had a continuing interest in adult literacy, publishing *The Reading Interests and Habits of Adults* in 1929 and *Maturity in Reading: Its Nature and Appraisal* in 1956. He was also involved with literacy on an international level, working particularly with the United Nations Educational, Scientific and Cultural Organization (UNESCO). This led to *The Teaching of Reading and Writing: An International Survey,* first published in 1956. He was also a founder of the International Reading Association, serving as its first president in 1955–1956.

Biographical information and a complete list of Gray's publications are included in a 1985 publication of the International Reading Association: *William S. Gray: Teacher, Scholar, Leader,* edited by Jennifer A. Stevenson. This document is also available as ERIC No. ED255902.

See also: LITERACY AND READING; READING; THORNDIKE, EDWARD.

BIBLIOGRAPHY

GILSTAD, JUNE R. 1985. "William S. Gray (1885–1960): First IRA President." *Reading Research Quarterly* (summer):509–511.

GRAY, WILLIAM S. 1919. "Principles of Method in Teaching Reading, As Derived from Scientific Investigation." In *The Eighteenth Yearbook of the National Society for the Study of Education, Part II: Fourth Report of the Committee on Economy of Time in Education,* ed. Guy Montrose Whipple. Bloomington, IL: Public School Publishing.

GRAY, WILLIAM S. 1948. *On Their Own in Reading: How to Give Children Independence in Attacking New Words.* Chicago: Scott, Foresman.

GRAY, WILLIAM S., and ARBUTHNOT, MARY HILL. 1940–1948. *Basic Readers.* Chicago: Scott, Foresman.

STEVENSON, JENNIFER A., ed. 1985. *William S. Gray: Teacher, Scholar, Leader.* Newark, DE: International Reading Association.

GERALD W. JORGENSON

GROUPING PATTERNS AND PRACTICES

See: SOCIAL ORGANIZATION OF SCHOOLS.

GROUP PROCESSES IN THE CLASSROOM

Classrooms are social settings; teaching and learning occur through social interaction between teachers and students. As teaching and learning take place, they are complicated processes and are affected by peer-group relationships. The interactions and relationships between teachers and students, and among students, as they work side by side, constitute the group processes of the classroom.

Group processes are especially significant in twenty-first century schools. Group projects and cooperative teamwork are the foundations of effective teaching, creative curriculum, and positive classroom climate. Interpersonal skills, group work, and empathy are important ingredients of modern business, where employees must communicate well for their business to be productive and profitable. Group processes are also significant in modern global communities, where citizens must work together for a safe and secure world. Thus, along with teaching academic curriculum, teachers are expected to help students develop the attitudes, skills, and procedures of democratic community.

Classroom as Group

A group is a collection of interdependent, interacting individuals with reciprocal influence over one another. *Interdependent* means the participants mutually depend on one another to get work done; the teacher's part is to teach as the students strive to learn. *Reciprocal influence* refers to mutual effects exchanged and felt by the same people. In classrooms as few as two people can form groups, as long as the paired individuals have reciprocal influence through communication and mental contact. When the teacher engages the whole class in a learning activity common to all, then everyone forms into a single group, or as Herbert A. Thelen wrote, a "miniature society." Although the teacher and students of one class can be a whole group or from time to time many subgroups, groups are not simply people in proximity, such as a host of screaming students at a concert, or categories of individuals with something in common, such as the blondes and redheads of a school.

A group is also defined by its goals and structures. Goals are jointly held outcomes toward which group members work; structures are group roles taken regularly by members as they carry out the work. Groups seek to accomplish task or work goals and social-emotional or morale goals. Classroom groups become more successful as they pursue both task and social-emotional goals.

In most classrooms learning academic subject matter is a valued task goal, while developing a positive climate is a valued social-emotional goal. The class that accomplishes both is stronger than the class that reaches only one. In a parallel way group structures are made up of formal or official roles and informal or unofficial roles. Many classrooms have the formal roles of teacher, aide, student, administrative supporter, and parent helper along with the informal roles of leader, follower, friend, isolate, and rejectee. Classes with clear and understandable formal roles and nurturing and supportive informal roles are stronger than classes with just one or the other.

A Social-Psychological View

Social-psychological research helps one form an understanding of the place of group processes in the classroom. The students of a class form a miniature society with peers, teacher, and aides in which they experience interdependence, interaction, common striving for goals, and structure. Many subgroups in the class affect how the larger classroom society works and how individuals relate to one another. Students interact, formally and informally, with teachers, aides, and one another. The informal interactions usually are not discussed even though they can be very important to everyone. Students work on the curriculum in the physical presence of one another to grow intellectually, behaviorally, and emotionally. Their informal roles of friendship, leadership, prestige, and respect affect how they carry out formal aspects of the student role. The informal relationships among students can be charged with emotion; an interpersonal underworld of peer-group affect is virtually inevitable for all students.

While the class develops, informal relationships with peers increase in power and poignancy; the students' definitions and evaluations of themselves become more vulnerable to peer-group influence. Each student's self-concept is susceptible to change within the classroom society, where informal peer interactions can be either threatening or supportive. In particular, the social motives of affiliation, achievement, and power have to be partly satisfied for each student to feel comfortable and secure. The negative conditions of loneliness and rejection, incompetence and stupidity, powerlessness, and alienation arise when these three motives are frustrated. The more supportive peer relations are in satisfying these motives, the more likely students' learning and behavior will be enhanced. Having students work interdependently toward jointly established goals in supportive, cooperative learning groups can increase their compassion for one another, self-esteem, positive attitudes toward school, and academic learning.

Classroom Climate

Classroom climate refers to the emotional tones associated with students' interactions, their attitudinal reactions to the class, as well as to students' self-concept and their motivational satisfactions and frustrations. Climate is measured by observing physical movements, bodily gestures, seating patterns, and instances of verbal interaction. Do students stand close or far away from the teacher? Are students at ease or tense? How frequently is affective support communicated by smiles, winks, or pats on the back? Do students move quietly with measured steps to their desks, or do they stroll freely and easily, showing the class feels safe? Are students reluctant to ask the teacher questions? How do students relate to one another? Are they quiet, distant, and formal, or do they walk easily and laugh spontaneously? How often do students put a peer down or say something nice to one another? Do students harass or bully other students? How often does fighting erupt? How often does peacemaking occur? Are sessions run primarily by the teacher or do students also take the lead? Do seating patterns shift from time to time, or do they remain the same, regardless of the learning activity? Are students working together cooperatively?

A positive climate exists when the following are present: (1) leadership occurs as power-with rather than power-over; (2) communication is honest, open and transactional; (3) high levels of friendship are present among classmates; (4) expectations are high for the performance of others and oneself; (5) norms support getting academic work done well and for maximizing individuals' strengths; and (6) conflict is dealt with constructively and peacefully. Although each of these six properties of climate can be important by itself, positive climate is an ensemble of all of them. Climate describes how each property is integrated with the others. It summarizes group processes that a teacher develops when interacting with students and how the students themselves relate with one another. Climate is what the behavioral actions are in working toward curriculum goals; it is how curriculum materials are used through human exchange; and it is styles of relating among members

of the classroom group. In classrooms with positive climates we find students and teachers collaborating to accomplish common goals along with feelings of positive self-esteem, security, and warmth. We also find students influencing the teacher and their peers, high involvement in academic learning, and strong attraction for one's classmates, curriculum, and school.

Teaching Strategies

Ronald Lippitt and Ralph White, with guidance from Kurt Lewin, observed effects on youth of three leadership styles: autocratic, democratic, and laissez faire. Autocratic leaders made all decisions about group goals and work procedures. Democratic leaders specified group goals, but urged group members to decide among alternative ways of working. Laissez-faire leaders abdicated authority, permitting youth to work as they pleased. Groups with democratic leaders performed best with high quality work output and high morale. Autocratically lead groups had high quality work output, but low morale. Groups with laissez-faire leaders performed worst overall. Classroom research has shown that although autocratic teachers can get students to accomplish high amounts of academic work, they also create conformity, competition, dependency, and resentment. Students of democratic teachers accomplish both a great deal of excellent academic work, and establish positive social climates.

Effective communication is key in understanding differences between autocratic and democratic teachers. Autocratic teachers use one-way communication in persuading students to accept learning goals and procedures as well as rules for classroom behavior; such unilateral direction giving is often an ineffective way of transmitting information. Democratic teachers use two-way communication often to encourage students to participate in making decisions for themselves and in establishing group agreements for classroom procedures. By using transactional communication whereby students and teachers reciprocate in trying to understand one another, democratic teachers help build a climate that is participatory, relaxed, personal, and supportive. Attributes of democratic teachers who are effective transactional communicators are receptiveness to students' ideas, an egalitarian attitude, openness, warmth, respect for students' feelings, sensitivity to outcasts, a sense of humor, and a caring attitude.

Such participatory teachers understand that friendships in the classroom peer group cannot be separated from teaching and learning; friendly feelings are integral to instructional transactions between teachers and students and among students. Students who view themselves as disliked or ignored by their peers often have difficulty in performing up to their academic potential. They experience anxiety and reduced self-esteem, both of which interfere with their academic performance. As outcasts they might seek revenge, searching for ways to be aggressive toward teachers and peers. By watching their teacher interact with the class, students learn who gets left out and who gets encouragement and praise. Teachers can help rejected students obtain peer support by giving them an extra amount of encouragement and praise in front of their peers, and by assigning them to work cooperatively with popular classmates. Teachers with friendly classes see to it that they talk and attend to every student rather than focusing on a few, and often reward students with specific statements for helpful and successful behavior; they seek to control behavioral disturbances with general, group-oriented statements.

Also central to positive climate are the expectations that teacher and student hold for one another. Teachers' expectations for how each student might behave are particularly important because they affect how teachers behave toward that student. Thus, teachers should engage in introspection and reflection to diagnose their expectations, and obtain feedback from colleagues about how they are behaving toward particular students. Teachers should also use diverse information sources to understand what makes their students behave as they do. In particular, teachers should reflect on their expectations and attributions toward blacks and whites, girls and boys, students of different social classes and ethnic groups, and at-risk or students with disabilities. Teachers should deliberately seek new information about student strengths in order to free themselves of stereotypes.

Classroom norms form when most students hold the same expectations and attitudes about appropriate classroom behaviors. Although norms guide students' and the teacher's behavior, they are not the same as rules. Rules are regulations created by administrators or teachers to govern students' behavior; they might or might not become group norms. Student norms frequently are in opposition to teachers' goals, and can become counterproduc-tive to individual student development. Teachers should strive to help students create formal group agreements to transform preferred rules into student norms. In particular, cooperative peer-group norms enhance student self-concept and academic learning more than do norms in support of competition.

Conflict, natural and inevitable in all groups, exists when one activity blocks, interferes, or keeps another activity from occurring. Conflicts arise in classrooms over incompatible procedures, goals, concepts, or interpersonal relationships. The norms of cooperation and competition affect the management of conflict differently. With cooperative norms students believe they will obtain their self-interest when other students also achieve theirs. Teachers should strive, therefore, to build a spirit of teamwork and cooperation in their classes, so that students will feel that it is in their self-interest to cooperate with their peers. When a competitive spirit exists, particularly when students are pitted against each other to obtain scarce rewards, a student succeeds only when others lose. In the competitive classroom, interpersonal conflict will arise frequently between students.

For teachers to build and maintain successful classrooms with high student achievement and positive social climate, they should attend to their leadership style, communication skills, friendliness and warmth, expectations and stereotypes of students, tactics for establishing student group agreements, and their skills in managing conflict.

See also: ADOLESCENT PEER CULTURE; CLASSROOM MANAGEMENT.

BIBLIOGRAPHY

ARONSON, ELLIOT, and PATNOE, S. 1997. *Cooperation in the Classroom: The Jigsaw Method.* New York: Longman.

COHEN, ELIZABETH G. 1994. *Designing Groupwork: Strategies for the Heterogeneous Classroom,* 2nd edition. New York: Teachers College Press, Columbia University.

DEWEY, JOHN. 1916. *Democracy and Education.* New York: Macmillan.

GOOD, THOMAS, and BROPHY, JERE E. 1997. *Looking in Classrooms,* 7th edition. New York: Harper and Row.

JOHNSON, DAVID W., and JOHNSON, ROGER T. 1992. *Learning Together and Learning Alone,* 3rd edition. Englewood Cliffs, NJ: Prentice-Hall.

LEWIN, KURT. 1948. *Resolving Social Conflicts.* New York: Harper.

MILES, MATTHEW. 1981. *Learning to Work in Groups,* 2nd edition. New York: Teachers College Press.

SCHMUCK, RICHARD A., and SCHMUCK, PATRICIA A. 2001. *Group Processes in the Classroom,* 8th edition. New York: McGraw Hill.

THELEN, HERBERT A. 1981. *The Classroom Society.* New York: Wiley.

WHITE, RALPH K., and LIPPITT, RONALD O. 1960. *Autocracy and Democracy: An Experimental Inquiry.* New York: Harper.

RICHARD A. SCHMUCK
PATRICIA A. SCHMUCK

GUIDANCE AND COUNSELING, SCHOOL

School counselors help to make learning a positive experience for every student. They are sensitive to individual differences. They know that a classroom environment that is good for one child is not necessarily good for another. Counselors facilitate communication among teachers, parents, administrators, and students to adapt the school's environment in the best interests of each individual student. They help individual students make the most of their school experiences and prepare them for the future.

A Brief History of School Guidance and Counseling in the United States

The history of school counseling formally started at the turn of the twentieth century, although a case can be made for tracing the foundations of counseling and guidance principles to ancient Greece and Rome with the philosophical teachings of Plato and Aristotle. There is also evidence to argue that some of the techniques and skills of modern-day guidance counselors were practiced by Catholic priests in the Middle Ages, as can be seen by the dedication to the concept of confidentiality within the confessional. Near the end of the sixteenth century, one of the first texts about career options appeared: *The Universal Plaza of All the Professions of the World,* (1626) written by Tomaso Garzoni. Nevertheless, formal guidance programs using specialized textbooks did not start until the turn of the twentieth century.

The factors leading to the development of guidance and counseling in the United States began in the 1890s with the social reform movement. The difficulties of people living in urban slums and the widespread use of child labor outraged many. One of the consequences was the compulsory education movement and shortly thereafter the vocational guidance movement, which, in its early days, was concerned with guiding people into the workforce to become productive members of society. The social and political reformer Frank Parsons is often credited with being the father of the vocational guidance movement. His work with the Civic Service House led to the development of the Boston Vocation Bureau. In 1909 the Boston Vocation Bureau helped outline a system of vocational guidance in the Boston public schools. The work of the bureau influenced the need for and the use of vocational guidance both in the United States and other countries. By 1918 there were documented accounts of the bureau's influence as far away as Uruguay and China. Guidance and counseling in these early years were considered to be mostly vocational in nature, but as the profession advanced other personal concerns became part of the school counselor's agenda.

The United States' entry into World War I brought the need for assessment of large groups of draftees, in large part to select appropriate people for leadership positions. These early psychological assessments performed on large groups of people were quickly identified as being valuable tools to be used in the educational system, thus beginning the standardized testing movement that in the early twenty-first century is still a strong aspect of U.S. public education. At the same time, vocational guidance was spreading throughout the country, so that by 1918 more than 900 high schools had some type of vocational guidance system. In 1913 the National Vocational Guidance Association was formed and helped legitimize and increase the number of guidance counselors. Early vocational guidance counselors were often teachers appointed to assume the extra duties of the position in addition to their regular teaching responsibilities.

The 1920s and 1930s saw an expansion of counseling roles beyond working only with vocational concerns. Social, personal, and educational aspects of a student's life also needed attention. The Great Depression of the 1930s led to the restriction of funds for counseling programs. Not until 1938, after a recommendation from a presidential committee and the passage of the George Dean Act, which provided funds directly for the purposes of vocational guidance counseling, did guidance counselors start to see an increase in support for their work.

After World War II a strong trend away from testing appeared. One of the main persons indirectly responsible for this shift was the American psychologist Carl Rogers. Many in the counseling field adopted his emphasis on "nondirective" (later called "client-centered") counseling. Rogers published *Counseling and Psychotherapy* in 1942 and *Client-Centered Therapy* in 1951. These two works defined a new counseling theory in complete contrast to previous theories in psychology and counseling. This new theory minimized counselor advice-giving and stressed the creation of conditions that left the client more in control of the counseling content.

In 1958 the National Defense Education Act (NDEA) was enacted, providing aid to education in the United States at all levels, public and private. Instituted primarily to stimulate the advancement of education in science, mathematics, and modern foreign languages, NDEA also provided aid in other areas, including technical education, area studies, geography, English as a second language, counseling and guidance, school libraries, and educational media centers. Further support for school counseling was spurred by the Soviet Union's launching of *Sputnik* and fears that other countries were outperforming the United States in the fields of mathematics and science. Hence, by providing appropriate funding for education, including guidance and counseling, it was thought that more students would find their way into the sciences. Additionally, in the 1950s the American School Counselor Association (ASCA) was formed, furthering the professional identity of the school counselor.

The work of C. Gilbert Wrenn, including his 1962 book *The Counselor in a Changing World*, brought to light the need for more cultural sensitivity on the part of school counselors. The 1960s also brought many more counseling theories to the field, including Frederick Perl's gestalt therapy, William Glasser's reality therapy, Abraham Maslow and Rollo May's existential approach, and John Krumboltz's behavioral counseling approach. It was during this time that legislative support and an amendment to the NDEA provided funds for training and hiring school counselors with an elementary emphasis.

In the 1970s the school counselor was beginning to be defined as part of a larger program, as opposed to being the entire program. There was an emphasis on accountability of services provided by school counselors and the benefits that could be obtained with structured evaluations. This decade also gave rise to the special education movement. The educational and counseling needs of students with disabilities was addressed with the passage of the Education for All Handicapped Children Act in 1975.

The 1980s saw the development of training standards and criteria for school counseling. This was also a time of more intense evaluation of education as a whole and counseling programs in particular. In order for schools to provide adequate educational opportunities for individuals with disabilities, school counselors were trained to adapt the educational environment to student needs. The duties and roles of many counselors began to change considerably. Counselors started finding themselves as gatekeepers to Individualized Education Programs (IEP) and Student Study Teams (SST) as well as consultants to special education teachers, especially after passage of the Americans with Disabilities Act in 1990.

The development of national educational standards and the school reform movement of the 1990s ignored school counseling as an integral part of a student's educational development. The ASCA compensated partially with the development of national standards for school counseling programs. These standards clearly defined the roles and responsibilities of school counseling programs and showed the necessity of school counseling for the overall educational development of every student.

Major Roles and Functions for School Counselors

The roles of a school counselor are somewhat different at various grade levels.

Elementary school level. In elementary schools, counselors spend their time with children individually, in small groups, or in classrooms—thus having some connection with every student in the school. With the advent of systems thinking, the elementary school counselor now has a working relationship with students' families and with community social agencies. Although the roles of school counselors vary among settings, common tasks include individual counseling, small-group counseling, large-group or classroom presentations, involvement in schoolwide behavior plans for promoting positive and extinguishing negative behaviors, and consulting with teachers, parents, and the community. Additional duties might include developing classroom management plans or behavior plans for individual students, such as conducting SST and IEP meetings.

Middle and high school level. Like elementary school counselors, the roles of middle and high school counselors vary depending on the district and the school administrators. Counselors deal with a vast array of student problems—personal, academic, social, and career issues. Typically, these areas get blended together when working with a student on any one topic; hence, it is impossible to separate the duties of a counselor on the basis of a particular problem. Counselors in middle and high school have experience with all these areas and work with others in the school and community to find resources when a need arises. It is common for a school counselor to be the first person a student with a difficulty approaches. The school counselor then assesses the severity of the problem in order to provide appropriate support. School administrators sometimes assign counselors such responsibilities as class scheduling, discipline, and administration. These tasks can be integrated with the goals of school counseling but can also dilute the time available for helping individuals.

Training Requirements

The requirements for the credentialing (in some locations called certification, licensure, or endorsement) of professional school counselors vary from state to state. All states and the District of Columbia require a graduate education (i.e., completion of some graduate-level course work), with forty-five states and the District of Columbia requiring a master's degree in counseling and guidance or a related field. A majority of states also require that graduate work include a certain number of practicum hours, ranging from 200 to 700, in a school setting. Additionally, a majority of states require applicants to have previous teaching experience. Some of these states allow students to gain experience through the graduate program by means of internships.

Half of the states require standardized testing as part of the credentialing process. Many of these tests simply cover basic mathematics, writing, and reading skills, while some states require more specialized tests covering the field of guidance and counseling. Nineteen states require a minimum number of course credit hours specifically related to guidance and counseling. Fourteen states require students to take courses in other subject areas, such as education of children with disabilities, multicultural issues, substance abuse, state and federal laws and constitutions, applied technology, and identification and reporting of child abuse. Thirty-eight states recognize credentials from other states. Another thirty-eight states require applicants to undergo a criminal background check.

Major Trends, Issues, and Controversies

Among the many issues facing the school counseling profession are the following three: what the professional title should be, how counselors should be evaluated, and to what extent counselors should work on prevention instead of remediation.

Professional title. Some professionals in the field prefer to be called *guidance counselor,* while an increasing number prefer the term *school counselor.* The growing trend is for counselors to be seen as professionals in a large system, working fluidly with all aspects within the system. The expected duties are more extensive than those practiced by vocational guidance counselors of the past, hence the feeling of many school counselors that the name of the profession should reflect its expanded roles.

Evaluation. A major trend in education is the demand for accountability and evaluation. School counselors have not been immune to this demand. Since the early 1970s there has been a growing concern with this issue and numerous criteria have been developed to help school counselors evaluate their specific intervention techniques.

The National Standards for Professional School Counselors was adopted by ASCA in 1997. Similar to the academic standards used nationally by state departments of education, the counseling standards provide a blueprint of the tasks of and goals for school counselors. The standards have not been adopted by every state. The average state student–counselor ratio varies from a high of about 1,250 to a low of about 400, so the evaluation of counselor performance with different workloads is a difficult undertaking.

Prevention versus remediation. A growing trend in the field of counseling is the focus on prevention instead of remediation. In the past it was not uncommon for counselors to have interactions with students only after some crisis had occurred. There is now a shift for school counselors to intercede prior to any incidents and to become more proactive in developing and enacting schoolwide prevention plans. The schools, community, and families are requesting assistance in preventing students from being involved with many difficulties, such as participating in gangs, dropping out of school, becoming a teenage parent, using drugs, and participating in or becoming victims of acts of violence.

Gangs. Students as early as third grade are being taught gang-type activities. Students are more likely to end up in a gang if family members and peers are already involved in gang activity. It is difficult for children to leave a gang once they have been actively involved. Antigang resources are often focused on fourth and fifth graders—an age before most students join a gang. Counselors are in a position to ascertain whether a child is "at risk" of gang-type activity. The counselor can also be influential in working with the family to help the child avoid gang activity.

Dropouts. In many large metropolitan school districts, over 25 percent of students do not complete their high school education. Premature school termination is becoming an increasingly more difficult problem as more careers require education well beyond the high school level. Counselors are in a unique position to assist students with career guidance and help them establish meaningful goals including the completion of a basic education.

Teen pregnancy. Teen pregnancy continues to be a societal concern. Precipitating factors are visible prior to middle school. Counselors are often the liaison with community agencies that work to prevent student pregnancy and assist with students who do become pregnant.

Substance abuse. Drugs, including alcohol and tobacco, continue to be a serious problem for youth. Despite national efforts to eradicate these problems, many students still find their way to these mind-altering chemicals. Counselors are trained to understand the effects of different drugs and can assist with interventions or community referrals. The counselor is also essential in developing substance abuse prevention programs in a school.

School violence. School violence can range from bullying to gunfire. Counselors have training to assist teachers and students in cases of violence and to establish violence prevention programs. Counselor leadership in making teasing and bullying unaccept-

able school behaviors is a powerful way to provide a safer and more inclusive environment for students.

Diversity. Tolerance of diversity is an important goal in a multicultural society. School counselors help all students to be accepting of others regardless of sex, age, race, sexual orientation, culture, disability, or religious beliefs.

Child abuse. Many states have mandatory reporting laws concerning child abuse. Students in all grades are susceptible to abuse by others, and the counselor is often the first person to discover these deplorable acts and then report them to the proper authorities.

Terrorism. Terrorism is becoming an increasingly difficult problem in the world of the early twenty-first century. Children are affected, directly and indirectly, by both massive and small-scale acts of terrorism. Counselors are able to ascertain the extent to which a student or teacher may be adversely affected by terrorist acts. In these cases the counselor can either intervene or direct the person to more intensive interventions.

School Counseling around the World

How are other countries providing counseling? It is clear that school counseling has made significant progress in the United States. Political, social, and cultural factors are deeply embedded in the way a given country addresses the educational needs of its populace. Following are brief examples of how school counseling is practiced in some other countries.

In Japan, the goal of high school counseling is to "help every student develop abilities of self-understanding, decision-making, life planning, and action-taking to be able to adjust in the career options he or she decides to pursue" (Watanabe-Muraoka, Senzaki, and Herr, p. 101). In France, secondary school counseling was started in 1922 and by the late 1930s was adopted by the educational system and seen as a necessary part of the institution. School counselors assist students with vocational guidance.

In Thailand, school counseling often incorporates advice-giving by teachers. In Israel, school counselors devote one-third of their time to classroom instruction and the rest to personal and social counseling. Career counseling is somewhat curtailed because students are required to enlist with the armed services after high school. In Hong Kong, school counseling and guidance is becoming more of a service that is incorporated into the whole school with an emphasis on prevention. Turkey has a fifty-year history of counseling development. There is a professional association that publishes a journal and sponsors conferences. Many secondary schools have counseling services and receive support from the Ministry of National Education.

All countries benefit from professional dialogue and a continual exchange of information. In Europe the Transnational Network of National Resource Centres for Vocational Guidance was established to share information, include businesses and social agencies, and improve counseling methods and materials. The Internet is being used widely as a mechanism for disseminating information. Spain, Portugal, Denmark, Belgium, Finland, France, Italy, the Slovak Republic, and Norway are among many countries using the web to make career and counseling information available to guidance experts. As school counseling continues to define itself as a profession and to show its usefulness empirically, counseling services in schools are likely to expand worldwide in an effort to improve everyone's life satisfaction.

See also: ADOLESCENT PEER CULTURE, *subentry on* GANGS; PSYCHOLOGIST, SCHOOL; RISK BEHAVIORS; ROGERS, CARL; VIOLENCE, CHILDREN'S EXPOSURE TO.

BIBLIOGRAPHY

BEMAK, FRED. 2000. "Transforming the Role of the Counselor to Provide Leadership in Educational Reform through Collaboration." *Professional School Counseling* 3:323–331.

BREWER, JOHN M. 1918. *The Vocational Guidance Movement: Its Problems and Possibilities.* New York: Macmillan.

BURNHAM, JOY JONES, and JACKSON, C. MARIE. 2000. "School Counselor Roles: Discrepancies between Actual Practice and Existing Models." *Professional School Counseling* 4:41–49.

CAMPBELL, CHARI A., and DAHIR, CAROL A. 1997. *Sharing the Vision: The National Standards for School Counseling Programs.* Alexandria, VA: American School Counselor Association.

DAHIR, CAROL A. 2001. "The National Standards for School Counseling Programs: Development and Implementation." *Professional School Counseling* 4:320–327.

DOGAN, SULEYMAN. 1999. "The Historical Development of Counseling in Turkey." *International Journal for the Advancement of Counseling* 22:51–67.

FAUST, VERNE. 1968. *History of Elementary School Counseling: Overview and Critique.* Boston: Houghton Mifflin.

GIBSON, ROBERT L.; MITCHELL, MARIANNE H.; and HIGGINS, ROBERT E. 1983. *Development and Management of Counseling Programs and Guidance Services.* New York: Macmillan.

GINN, S. J. 1924. "Vocational Guidance in Boston Public Schools." *Vocational Guidance Magazine* 3:3–7.

GYSBERS, NORMAN C., and HENDERSON, PATRICIA. 1994. *Developing and Managing Your School Guidance Program,* 2nd edition. Alexandria, VA: American Counseling Association.

GYSBERS, NORMAN C., and HENDERSON, PATRICIA. 2001. "Comprehensive Guidance and Counseling Programs: A Rich History and a Bright Future." *Professional School Counseling* 4:246–256.

GYSBERS, NORMAN C.; LAPEN, RICHARD T.; and JONES, BRUCE ANTHONY. 2000. "School Board Policies for Guidance and Counseling: A Call to Action." *Professional School Counseling* 3:349–355.

HUI, EADAOIN K. P. 2000. "Guidance as a Whole School Approach in Hong Kong: From Remediation to Student Development." *International Journal for the Advancement of Counseling* 22:69–82.

ISAACS, MADELYN L.; GREENE, MARCI; and VALESKY, THOMAS. 1998. "Elementary Counselors and Inclusion: A Statewide Attitudinal Survey." *Professional School Counseling* 2:68–76.

KRUMBOLTZ, JOHN D. 1974. "An Accountability Model for Counselors." *Personnel and Guidance Journal* 52:639–646.

LUM, CHRISTIE. 2001. *A Guide to State Laws and Regulations on Professional School Counseling.* Alexandria, VA: American Counseling Association.

MALLET, PASCAL, and PATY, BENJAMIN. 1999. "How French Counselors Treat School Violence: An Adult-Centered Approach." *International Journal for the Advancement of Counseling* 21:279–300.

ROGERS, CARL D. 1942. *Counseling and Psychotherapy: New Concepts in Practice.* Boston: Houghton Mifflin.

ROGERS, CARL D. 1951. *Client-Centered Therapy: Its Current Practice, Implications, and Theory.* Boston: Houghton Mifflin.

SCHMIDT, JOHN J. 1996. *Counseling in Schools,* 2nd edition. Needham Heights, MA: Simon and Schuster.

SCORZELLI, JAMES F., and REINKE-SCORZELLI, MARY. 2001. "Cultural Sensitivity and Cognitive Therapy in Thailand." *Journal of Mental Health Counseling* 23(1):85–92.

TATAR, MOSHE. 2000. "Kind of Support Anticipated and Preferred during Counseling: The Perceptions of Israeli School Counselors." *Professional School Counseling* 4:140–147.

WATANABE-MURAOKA, A. MIEKO; SENZAKI, T.-A. T.; and HERR, EDWIN L. 2001. "Donald Super's Contribution to Career Guidance and Counseling in Japan." *International Journal for Educational and Vocational Guidance* 1:99–106.

WRENN, C. GILBERT. 1962. *The Counselor in a Changing World.* Washington, DC: American Personnel and Guidance Association.

JOHN D. KRUMBOLTZ
THIERRY G. KOLPIN

H

HAHN, KURT (1886–1974)

Progressive educator Kurt Hahn established a system of international schools and programs that even after his death are alive and expanding.

Hahn, a German of Jewish origin who subsequently became a Christian and naturalized English citizen, was born in Berlin as son of a wealthy industrialist. After graduation from the Royal Wilhelm gymnasium in Berlin (1904), he studied philosophy and the classics at Christ Church College, Oxford, and at the universities of Berlin, Heidelberg, Freiburg, and Göttingen with the firm intention of becoming an educator and school reformer in the tradition of Cecil Reddie and Hermann Lietz. In 1910, Hahn published a novel *Frau Elses Verheissung* (Mrs. Else's promise) in which he pondered his experiences as a schoolboy. Another book *Gedanken über Erziehung* (Ideas on education) drew heavily on Plato, Kant, and William James, but was never finished.

Unfit for military service, Hahn served during World War I as specialist for English affairs in the German foreign office and in the political office of the German High Command under General Ludendorff. He wrote commentaries, held lectures, attended international conferences to strive for the democratization of the German political system and for the termination of the unnecessary war at acceptable conditions for all. When Prince Max of Baden was appointed the first parliamentarian German prime minister, Hahn became his private secretary and closest political advisor. After the war, he initiated the "Heidelberger Vereinigung," an association of influential politicians, scientists, industrialists (among them Max Weber), to promote a "peace of justice and agreement." At the Peace Conference in Paris, Hahn served as secretary and ghost writer for the German minister of foreign affairs, Graf Brockdorff-Rantzau.

In 1919 Hahn moved to Salem castle near Lake Constance in order to realize his educational dream. Together with Prince Max, he founded a *landerziehungsheim* (boarding school), which soon became the largest and most prominent boarding school in Germany. Still politically active, Hahn supported the foundation of the German Institute of International Affairs (1923), wrote the main parts of the *Memoirs* of Prince Max of Baden (1927), and voiced his opposition to Hitler and the rising national socialism. When Hitler came to power, Hahn was imprisoned, but released through the intervention of influential British friends—among them Prime Minister Ramsay Macdonald. Nevertheless Hahn was dismissed as principal of Salem, banned from the state of Baden, and forced to emigrate to the United Kingdom. In 1934 he founded a new public school called British Salem Schools at Gordonstoun, near Elgin in Scotland, which flourished as quickly as its sister school had done. As political refugee Hahn wrote articles, memoranda, and letters to oppose the appeasement policy of the British government, publicize the horrors of the concentration camps, and organize support for the resistance movement in Germany. During World War II he served as translator and advisor for the British foreign office.

Hahn believed that young people are exposed to six declines: (1) the decline in fitness due to modern methods of locomotion; (2) the decline in initiative and enterprise due to the widespread disease of "spectatoritis"; (3) the decline in memory and imagination due to the confused restlessness of Western civilization; (4) the decline in skill and care due to the weakened tradition of craftsmanship; (5) the decline in self-discipline due to the ever present availability of stimulants and tranquilizers; and (6) the decline in compassion due to the unseemly speed with which modern life is conducted. To counter these social diseases, Hahn conceived a preventive cure called *Erlebnistherapie* (experience therapy) which offered listless and lawless adolescence the opportunity to discover healthy passions, like the zest for exploration and the love for art and music, that would absorb the child completely. Hahn's experiential education program consisted of four elements: (1) physical fitness—exercising the body and keeping free from cigarettes, alcohol, and drugs; (2) expedition—exploring the world by sea and land under difficult conditions, alone or in groups; (3) project work—planning and executing an enterprise in research, art, or construction; and, most important, and (4) social service—helping the injured, sick, old, and handicapped in hospitals, homes, and rescue stations.

Hahn wanted his educational program to develop active citizenship, social responsibility, and international understanding, and he wanted his experience therapy to be available for every boy and girl, whatever their age, social background, and national origin. Thus he provided for scholarships, initiated courses for short-term and long-term education, and founded institutions which are operating on all five continents. The schools and schemes Hahn originated can be arranged into four categories: (1) boarding schools (since 1920, united in the Round Square Conference, about twenty worldwide by 2002); (2) Outward Bound Schools (since 1941, short-term schools of three to four weeks for students and young workers; about thirty by 2002, many of them in the United States); (3) International Award for Young People (since 1956, the most well known is the Duke of Edinburgh Award, about 100,000 boys and girls of 14 to 25 years of age participate in more than 100 countries each year experiencing the fourfold program in their spare time); (4) United World Colleges (since 1962, international two-year colleges in England, Canada, the United States, Italy, Germany, Venezuela, Swaziland, Singapore, Hong Kong).

Hahn received many honors for his political and educational activities. After his death several prizes were instituted to his memory: the Kurt Hahn Award of the American Association for Experiential Education (since 1983); the Kurt Hahn Scholarships of the University of Cambridge (since 1986); and the Outward Bound Award of the University of Lüneburg (since 1990).

See also: PROGRESSIVE EDUCATION.

BIBLIOGRAPHY

HAHN, KURT. 1934. "A German Public School." *The Listener* January 17.

HAHN, KURT. 1934. "The Practical Child and the Bookworm." *The Listener* November 28.

HAHN, KURT. 1957. "Outward Bound." In *Year Book of Education,* ed. George Z. F. Bereday and Joseph A. Lauwerys. London: Evans Brothers.

HAHN, KURT. 1965. *The Young and the Outcome of the War.* London: Lindsay.

KNOLL, MICHAEL, ed. 1998. *Kurt Hahn: Reform mit Augenmass. Ausgewählte Schriften eines Politikers und Pädagogen.* Stuttgart: Klett-Cotta.

RÖHRS, HERMANN, and TUNSTALL-BEHRENS, HILARY, ed. 1970. *Kurt Hahn: A Life Span in Education and Politics.* London: Routledge and Kegan Paul.

SKIDELSKY, ROBERT. 1969. *English Progressive Schools.* Middlesex, Eng.: Penguin.

STEWART, W. A. C. 1968. *The Educational Innovators. Progressive Schools, 1881–1967.* London: Macmillan.

MICHAEL KNOLL

HALEY, MARGARET (1861–1939)

Margaret Angela Haley was the formative leader of America's first teacher union. In her forty years of leadership with the Chicago Teachers Federation, Haley advocated teachers' right to be involved in school decision-making, the promotion of Progressive educational practice, and the expansion of protective legislation for teachers.

Margaret Haley was born in Joliet, Illinois, of working-class Irish immigrant parents and she attended local rural schools. She developed an early interest in politics from her father, who was a labor activist in the Knights of Labor and the Farmers' Grange. At age sixteen, as she recalled in her autobiography, she was "catapulted" into teaching by her father's persistent financial troubles, and she began to teach at local country schools. She continued her education at local teacher training institutes where she learned principles of the "new education" that rejected old-fashioned rote memory learning and promoted problem solving and close analytical work.

Early Career

At the end of her fifth year of teaching, Haley made a further commitment to her education by registering for a four-week summer session at the Normal School at Illinois State University where she studied under leading proponents of Herbartian curriculum theory. But indicative of Haley's emerging interest in school politics, her favorite class at Illinois was not about pedagogy but about political economy. Her favorite teacher was Edmund Janes James, a scholar of education and economics whose research interests included the labor movement, tax reform, and school finance. In James's economics class, Haley read Henry George's recently published *Progress and Poverty* (1879), a book that was revolutionizing liberal American economic theory with its proposal for a single tax system that would allow a more egalitarian and benevolent operation of the capitalist system. George's theory, Haley recalled, opened up to her "a wide world" of economic restructuring for social improvement and helped her develop her own ideas about teachers' responsibility to engage in social change.

In 1883 Haley moved with her family to Chicago, and from 1884 to 1900 she taught sixth grade in an elementary school in the Stockyards district. During this time, she studied Progressive child-centered education under Francis Parker at the Cook County Normal School, where she paid particular attention to Parker's ideas about the role of the teacher. Along with his influential ideas about pedagogy, Parker believed that the individual classroom teacher needed to have the authority of a policymaker—a novel role for female elementary schoolteachers. In later years, Haley studied Progressive pedagogy again at the Buffalo School of Pedagogy in New York State, where she heard William James deliver his "Talks to Teachers on Psychology." In another summer, she attended a Catholic summer school in Wisconsin that was part of the liberal social movement of the American Catholic church designed to expose parochial and public school teachers to contemporary social problems and secular intellectual debates. From these varied educational experiences in different parts of the Progressive education movement, Haley learned about the importance of academic freedom, the professional role of the teacher, and the value of shaping the school as a community.

Contrasting with these ideals was Haley's experience as a teacher in one of Chicago's poorest school districts. For sixteen years, Haley taught sixth grade in the Hendricks school in the heart of the poverty-stricken meatpacking district of Chicago. Her students were the poorest of the city's immigrant children, and her classrooms were crowded, underserviced, and for most of her students, the last education they would ever experience. By her late thirties, Haley had merged her Progressive educational training with her readings in labor and political theory to develop a strong belief about teachers' right to shape and control their own workplace, and about the responsibility of the state to support public schools.

The Chicago Teachers Federation

In 1897 Haley joined the Chicago Teachers Federation, which was recently organized by a group of women elementary teachers to defend a legislative attack on a newly instituted pension law. She quickly rose to district vice president of the federation and began an investigation of the board of education's claim that a shortage of school funds necessitated a freeze on a promised salary increase for teachers. Haley found that the shortage was due to the tax underassessment of a number of Chicago's largest corporations, and she led a successful lawsuit in state courts to assess the corporations their full value and assure the promised salary increase. Haley's leadership of the tax equity battle gained national attention, drawing the praise of a wide variety of social, political, and educational reformers. The fight also spurred teacher membership to the federation so that by 1900 more than half of all Chicago elementary school teachers were members of the federation, making it the largest women's union in the country.

Haley quickly molded the federation into a powerful political force in Chicago politics. She shared the leadership with another Irish-American elementary teacher, Catharine Goggin, who balanced Haley's aggressive and legalistic mind with more politic organizing skills. Under their leadership, the federation developed a weekly news bulletin, teacher education programs, and a well-oiled political organization of teachers across the city. With the federation, Haley consistently advocated for a stable pension plan and tenure laws, arguing that the single women who made up the bulk of the elementary teaching staff were in particular need of job and pension security. She battled repeated attacks on federation authority in the state house, and directed a relentless publicity campaign that kept the federation in the public eye.

American Federation of Teachers

To strengthen the federation's authority, she negotiated an unprecedented affiliation with organized labor by joining the predominately female federation with the industrial Chicago Federation of Labor in 1902. In 1916 the federation became Local 1 of the newly formed American Federation of Teachers.

Haley also fought for women teachers' rights in the National Education Association (NEA), which she accused of being administratively biased, excluding the voice and interests of elementary teachers. In 1901 she became the first woman and first elementary school teacher to speak at a public forum of the NEA, and she promoted the reorganization of NEA elections to facilitate the election of candidates who were women classroom teachers. In her notorious 1904 speech before the NEA, "Why Teachers Should Organize," Haley laid out her reform proposals not only for the organization of protective unions for teachers, but also for an expanded notion of teacher professionalism that included the opportunity to develop progressive pedagogy, improve educational practice, and promote the democratic participation of teachers in school administration. In 1910 she orchestrated the election of Chicago school superintendent Ella Flagg Young as the first woman president of the NEA.

Politics

Haley's individual politics took her across a wide spectrum of the American Left. She supported women's suffrage, child labor laws, direct primaries, and tax reform, and was a member of the Women's Trade Union League. She lived and worked in a wide circle of women political leaders, including Ella Flagg Young, Jane Addams, and Catharine Goggin. A self-educated legal scholar and political tactician, Haley was a popular consultant to fledgling teachers' organizations and women's groups.

Yet Haley's persistent commitment to women teachers' rights kept her on the margins of other so-cial reform movements. She was excluded from much of middle-class Protestant women's reform because of her class and religious background, and because of her staunch affiliation to labor. Yet male-dominated labor groups also marginalized Haley and her teachers, holding them out as white collar feminized workers who threatened the solidarity of the industrial working class. Haley's refusal to align with more radical groups, including socialists, anarchists, and African Americans, also limited her power. Furthermore, Haley's strong identification of the federation as an elementary teachers' group for women kept her apart from newer organizations. As a broader teacher union movement grew in the 1920s, Haley was left behind by other groups that sought to include secondary teachers, male teachers, and teachers of color.

Haley's Contribution

Haley's federation was at its peak influence between 1909 and 1915 when federation friend Ella Flagg Young was superintendent of the Chicago schools. In 1915 a city law prohibiting teachers from joining labor unions forced Haley to withdraw the federation from the Chicago Federation of Labor. In 1916 her long-time colleague Catharine Goggin was killed in a traffic accident. Through the antilabor 1920s the federation declined in power, and Haley's influence faded through the 1930s as a new generation of teacher union leaders joined the American Federation of Teachers. Jealously guarding the authority of the federation, Haley refused to merge with the new groups. Her strong and opinionated character furthered her marginalization during the difficult economic years of the Great Depression, when she opposed the militant street tactics of the striking teachers in Chicago's American Federation of Teachers. To younger teachers, she may have appeared an outdated bossy spinster of a previous century.

Although Haley was a swaggering giant in Chicago and educational politics, in physical appearance she was a petite and stylishly attired woman. Haley could disarm her opponents by her quick wit and charm that she used to maneuver loyalties among city, labor, and education officials. Margaret Haley never married, and she left almost no personal records with which historians could describe her private life. Clearly, however, she led an intense and peripatetic life in which her professional life doubled as her private life. Throughout her career with the

Teachers Federation, she lived with various women federation members, including Goggin. Her few recorded words of personal affection are about her parents and her five younger brothers and sisters, with whom she felt a deep affection and almost mystical connection throughout her life. She died January 5, 1939, at age 77. She is buried next to her sister Eliza, a fellow teacher and federation member, in Joliet.

See also: AMERICAN FEDERATION OF TEACHERS; TEACHER UNIONS, *subentry on* HISTORY; URBAN EDUCATION; YOUNG, ELLA FLAGG.

BIBLIOGRAPHY

CREEL, GEORGE. 1915. "Why Chicago Teachers Unionized." *Harper's Weekly* June 19.

HARD, WILLIAM. 1906. "Chicago's Five Maiden Aunts." *American Magazine* September.

HOGAN, DAVID. 1985. *Class and Reform: School and Society in Chicago 1880–1930.* Philadelphia: University of Pennsylvania Press.

MURPHY, MARJORIE. 1990. *Blackboard Unions: The AFT and the NEA 1900–1980.* Ithaca, NY: Cornell University Press.

REID, ROBERT. 1982. *Battleground: The Autobiography of Margaret Haley.* Chicago: University of Illinois Press.

SANDBURG, CARL. 1915. "Margaret Haley." *Reedy's Mirror* December.

URBAN, WAYNE J. 1982. *Why Teachers Organized.* Detroit, MI: Wayne State University Press.

WRIGLEY, JULIA. 1982. *Class, Politics and Public Schools: Chicago 1900–1950.* New Brunswick, NJ: Rutgers University Press.

KATE ROUSMANIERE

HALL, G. STANLEY (1844–1924)

The "father of adolescence," G. Stanley Hall is best known for his prodigious scholarship that shaped adolescent themes in psychology, education, and popular culture. Granville Stanley Hall was born in a small farming village in western Massachusetts, and his upbringing was modest, conservative, and puritan. He began his scholarly work in theology, but traveled to Germany to study physical psychology. He would produce over 400 books and articles and become the first president of Clark University, in Worcester, Massachusetts, but his greatest achievement was his public speaking about child-centered research, education, and adolescence to a society in transition.

With the 1883 publication of "The Contents of Children's Minds," Hall established himself as the leader of the "child-study" movement, which aimed to utilize scientific findings on what children know and when they learn it as a way of understanding the history of and the means of progress in human life. Searching for a source of personal and social regeneration, Hall turned to the theory of evolution for a biologically based ideal of human development, the optimum condition of which was health. His pure and vigorous adolescent countered the fragmented, deadening, and routinized qualities of urban industrial life. Hall theorized adolescence as the beginning of a new life and welded this vision to a scientific claim that this new life could contribute to the evolution of the race, if properly administered.

Hall's work lent scientific support to the "muscular Christian" approach to education, an intersection of morals, physical health, and economic productivity that was popular among the reformers who started the Young Men's Christian Association (YMCA), Boy Scouts, and other character-building organizations. Central to this view of health attainment was a rational inventory and investment of limited energies in profitable activities. The reformers of boys were vigilant in their denunciation of masturbation as wasteful sexual activity. As president of Clark University, Hall sponsored Freud's visit to the United States in 1909 and likely accepted Freud's ideas about sexuality, motivation, and the problems of repression. However, Hall also believed that freely expressed sexuality would too often lead to debauchery, so the sexualized energies of boys needed to be promoted yet protected, managed, and channeled.

Fittingly, Hall recommended schooling that mixed Rousseau's emphasis on covert control of male pupils with a strict social efficiency attachment to education for future lives and roles. Hall's educational prescriptions for adolescents emphasized the following six areas:

• Differentiated curricula for students with different futures, that is, an efficient curriculum, including an education for girls that emphasized preparation for marriage and motherhood

- The development of manhood through close supervision of the body, emphasizing exercise and team sports and minimizing draining academic study

- An education that drew upon and utilized the expression of (boy-stage) emotions through emphases on loyalty, patriotism, and service

- A curriculum sequence informed by recapitulation theory or cultural epochs (i.e., study of the stages believed to have been key developmental points of the race. A cultural epochs curriculum focused upon "great scenes": sacred and profane myths and history, from folklore and fairy tales to Robinson Crusoe and bible studies, ending with St. Paul and Luther and the powerful stories of reformation and nationalization. Stories of great men would be used throughout to draw boys into the tales and to build on their natural interest.)

- A school program that kept boys as boys and discouraged precocity or assuming sexual adult roles at a young age

- An administrative gaze schooled to watch youthful bodies

Hall and other "boyologists" identified play as central to creating young men who had disciplined spirit and would obey superiors. Play was revered for making children and adolescents moral and strong via direct and efficient processes, unlike the passive, unfocused, and feminized school curriculum. Cognitive approaches to civilized behavior were deemed unsatisfactory. Play invoked muscles directly, and muscles were believed to be the location of automatic, instinctual morality. Muscles, if properly prepared, carried civilized morality, instantly accessible. Expertly organized play would promote discipline and control, qualities lacking in the immigrant children who were the play reformers' main targets. The play reformers, like the Boy Scouts, consciously nurtured peer relations to replace "unsatisfactory" families and extend expert influence by promoting boys watching over other boys.

At the beginning of the twentieth century, public schools, private philanthropic endeavors, Boy Scouts, Girl Guides, and juvenile courts participated in an enlarged and intensified discourse about adolescence. Modern facts of adolescence, produced by G. Stanley Hall and his colleagues and students,

emerged in a social context of worries over degeneracy and progress. Although adolescence had been demarcated before the late 1800s, the youth/adult boundary became sharper, more intently watched, and democratically applied to all youth. Hall emphasized adolescence as a new birth and the last chance for race improvement. Slow, careful development at adolescence must be vigilantly guarded; precocity had to be prevented. He and his colleagues issued "pedagogical imperatives," that is, disciplinary and instructional techniques that were essential for each stage of boyhood and adolescence. Thus, laissez-faire approaches to youth were deemed likely to lead to moral anarchy, and the administrative gaze of teachers, parents, psychologists, play reformers, scouting leaders, and juvenile justice workers was cultivated everywhere.

Hall's work has commonly been assessed as discredited and outdated, buried along with recapitulation theory by the 1930s. However, Hall's ideas and their applications in education, scouting, and team sports remain foundational. Hall's work defined adolescents in modern, scientific terms, that is, as natural and outside of social relations and history. The shapers of the modern, scientific adolescent made growing bodies and sexuality primary foci and the measures to prevent precocity enhanced youth's economic dependence. At a time when movie theaters, dance halls, and other new, urban pleasures beckoned, public focus on youth revolved around misuse of leisure time. Finally, Hall contributed to scientific knowledge about adolescents that catapulted youth ever more firmly into their peers' company (expertly guided by psychologists, social workers, and teachers). Hall's ideas continue to shape contemporary discussions of adolescent biology, growing bodies, peer-orientation, and problematic leisure time.

See also: ADOLESCENT PEER CULTURE; EDUCATIONAL PSYCHOLOGY.

BIBLIOGRAPHY

BEDERMAN, GAIL. 1995. *Manliness and Civilization: A Cultural History of Gender and Race in the United States, 1880–1917.* Chicago: University of Chicago Press.

HALL, G. STANLEY. 1883. "The Contents of Children's Minds." *Princeton Review* 2:249–272.

HALL, G. STANLEY. 1903. "Coeducation in the High School." *National Education Association Journal of Proceedings and Addresses* 42:442–455.

HALL, G. STANLEY. 1904. *Adolescence: Its Psychology and Its Relations to Physiology, Anthropology, Sociology, Sex, Crime, Religion, and Education,* 2 vols. New York: Appleton.

HALL, G. STANLEY. 1977. *Life and Confessions of a Psychologist* (1923). New York: Arno.

LESKO, NANCY. 2001. *Act Your Age! A Cultural Construction of Adolescence.* New York: Routledge Falmer.

ROSS, DOROTHY. 1972. *G. Stanley Hall: The Psychologist as Prophet.* Chicago: University of Chicago Press.

STRICKLAND, CHARLES, and BURGESS, C., eds. 1965. *Health, Growth, and Heredity: G. Stanley Hall on Natural Education.* New York: Teachers College Press, Columbia University.

NANCY LESKO

HANDWRITING, TEACHING OF

Since the advent of the typewriter, penmanship has been increasingly devalued, even ignored, in the curriculum. Despite the ubiquity of computers, handwriting is still an important means of note taking and communication. Bad handwriting, it has been shown, leads to lower grades in school. Bad handwriting skills may cause the writer physical pain and mental distress. An inappropriate grip on the writing instrument may lead to cramps and an inability to write with speed. This inability to keep up with one's thoughts leads to frustration, which may, in turn, inhibit a child's learning to compose. Illegible handwriting is a failed attempt at communication.

Qualities sought in penmanship are legibility, speed, ease, and individuality. Handwriting is a physical skill that is best learned early, and requires "a competent level of instruction in the components of the physical task." (Alston and Taylor, p. 2). Extra help given to those having trouble at an early stage can often prevent failure in later years. Unfortunately, modern teachers are not usually taught how to teach handwriting. Nor do they have enough class time to work with children individually, which is the proper way to diagnose individual problems and counter them.

Penmanship was, with the rising importance of commerce in the eighteenth century, and before typewriters, an essential job skill. The teaching of handwriting was a major task of education. It is helpful to look at the changes in styles, materials, and teaching methods over time to see the evolution of the current state of handwriting in American education.

The Eighteenth Century

Early colonists brought with them the hands and teaching methods of their native lands. A variety of hands were taught to be used in various occupations (e.g. law, accounting), or by different groups of people (e.g. university students, women, gentlemen, clerks). Instruction in reading came first; for many who came to the New World, the ability to read the Bible was necessary for all. The ability to write was required only of professionals, the well-born and their secretaries, and merchants and their clerks.

Teaching was accomplished by the rote copying of exemplars set for each student by the writing master. As demand for training increased with the burgeoning economy, a lack of skilled masters lead to the use of printed exemplars.

Late in the eighteenth century, a backwoods American teacher named John Jenkins revolutionized the teaching of handwriting by breaking all lower case letters down into six principal pen strokes, which were learned separately and then combined into letters. This method, plagiarized and modified, was used for decades, both in the United States and in Europe. The hand was still the basic English Round hand (often termed *copperplate*), used throughout Europe for commercial purposes since the mid-seventeenth century.

Jenkins's analytical system also required the student to memorize a dialogue about the principal strokes and the letters formed from them before actually writing letters with ink on paper. This memorization persisted through much of the nineteenth century; decades later, Platt Rogers Spencer would still require students to memorize an oral analysis of letters. Another of Jenkins's innovations was the inclusion in his writing manuals of detailed recommendations on teaching methods.

The Nineteenth Century

Copy slips, with each exemplar printed on a separate piece of paper, grew into copybooks, with blank lines below the text for the student to imitate the exemplar, thus requiring a new book for each student. By the 1870s there were graded series of books, with accompanying teacher's manuals, wall charts, and other teaching aids. Competition intensified in the nineteenth century, as city, town, or state school boards began selecting textbooks, including penmanship systems, for entire school systems.

An ever-increasing emphasis on speedy handwriting for commercial needs was met by modifications to the letterforms taught and the introduction of new methods of movement. Fewer hands were being taught by the beginning of the century. By 1805 beginners started with a large-sized Round hand, then moved into a *running hand,* similar to the Round hand but faster, because every letter within words was joined. Also offered was a miniaturized version of the cursive, thought suitable for girls.

The letterforms would degenerate throughout the century in two conflicting streams: the stronger current moving toward simpler, faster, more colorless letterforms; and a contradictory cross-current created by the exploration of the decorative possibilities inherent in the use of the flexible steel pen point. These pens, which replaced quills for general use in the 1830s, made possible the extreme thick-and-thin lines in mid-century letterforms. Spencer was the most famous exponent of these attenuated forms.

B. F. Foster introduced "muscular movement," derived from Joseph Carstairs in England, into the classroom in the 1830s. This technique depended on forearm movement, although finger movement was allowed after the student reached a certain level of proficiency. From this point, handwriting practice became more group-based, involving classroom drills.

The famous Spencerian handwriting and the similar system of Spencer's main competitors, Payson, Dunton, and Scribner, returned to the more logical combined use of arm, forearm, and hand movements. These systems still relied heavily on classroom drills and timed instruction.

All the eighteenth- and nineteenth-century systems were taught by copying and correction, so that each student would achieve an exact imitation of the style being taught. Teaching individual handwriting style was not an issue until the typewriter took over business writing and made handwriting newly personal.

Toward the end of the nineteenth century, doctors in Europe, concerned about what would now be called the ergonomics of writing, grew disturbed with the postures and methods of penmanship. A new style, Vertical Writing, unslanted and with simplified letterforms, was introduced to the United States from England and widely adopted by all the publishers of penmanship manuals, including the heirs of Spencer. The copybooks claimed that it was natural and more like print, and so it served as a foreshadowing of manuscript writing.

The Twentieth Century

The Palmer Method was the dominant system of the twentieth century. A. N. Palmer introduced his system in the 1880s; by 1928, three-quarters of all schoolchildren in the United States were being taught by the Palmer method. The simple, unshaded letterforms were built for speed, taught by drill to establish "kinesthetic memory," and written with a new technique based on arm movement alone (i.e., no finger movement). Unfortunately, while the students remembered the drills all their lives, their handwriting was not particularly successful. Tamara Thornton suggests that the penmanship drill was used especially in cities as lessons in conformity, to assimilate immigrants into mainstream citizenry.

Manuscript Writing and Other Systems

In 1913 the English calligrapher Edward Johnston gave a lecture at a teachers' conference in which he recommended that the student use a broad-nibbed pen and, starting from simple, rounded, Roman letterforms, achieve a formal italic hand, which would develop into a decent, useful, everyday handwriting. Inspired by the lecture, a group of educators developed *manuscript writing* (also known as *ball-and-stick* or *print-script*), simplified letterforms based on circles and straight lines. This system was, however, not quite what Johnston had in mind.

Until this time, it should be emphasized, children started writing a cursive script from the beginning. Marjorie Wise, an English educator, brought manuscript writing to the United States in 1922, where it was first adopted by progressive schools, and rapidly increased in popularity to the extent that manuscript writing was included in the Palmer company materials. A major advantage of the system was that children could start learning to write at a younger age, with less developed motor skills. With manuscript writing, reading and writing were taught in parallel for the first time. Also, the introduction of manuscript writing was associated with the idea that children want to learn to write to communicate, although creative writing would not be standard until the 1950s.

There is still controversy over manuscript writing in the early twenty-first century; advocates say it is closer to modern type styles and so easier for the beginner to learn; critics point out the difficulty of transition from print-script to cursive, or the disadvantages of never taking up cursive at all, a system which also has its advocates. There is a wide variety of manuscript writing programs and styles. The early ones had the disadvantage of pairing their geometric print-scripts with contemporary cursives (Palmer in the United States and Vere Foster in Britain), which were quite different. Schemes were developed with more developmental logic between print and cursive, including Marion Richardson's in the United Kingdom and Donald Neil Thurber's D'Nealian in the United States.

Some advocate starting with cursive, citing advantages for early writers in not needing to think where to start each letter, and a clearer division between words. This new idea (which is, of course, an old one) is the standard method in France and Germany. In France's carefully thought-out system, children start preparatory exercises at age three, and are surrounded by signs and texts in a nationally standardized script, all of which help the student learn handwriting earlier and with more success (but less individuality) than American practices.

Calligraphers and other historians of letterforms, including Alfred Fairbank in England, Paul Standard in New York, and Lloyd Reynolds in Oregon, have been advocating italic forms since the 1930s. Italic forms have the simplest transition from basic letterforms to mature cursive writing, and allow for considerable individualization.

Participants in the debate over handwriting education in the twentieth century included not only calligraphers and publishers of the educational materials, but also academics, including statisticians and psychologists. The scientists developed quantitative handwriting scales to evaluate handwriting starting in 1909, but their advice that handwriting required the use of not just Palmerian arm movements, but also the coordinated movements of finger, hand, and wrist, were ignored for decades.

Throughout the twentieth century, both publishers and researchers concentrated on reading rather than writing. Classroom teachers, often left with little official encouragement and training, pursued their own ways.

Contemporary handwriting research has focused on issues such as type of script, the use of evaluative scales, handedness, ergonomics (grip and posture), tools (writing instrument and paper), and, occasionally, teaching methods, including teacher training and use of pre-writing activities. While no one writing style or approach has been shown to be "the best," consistency of model through early grades does appear to be important, as long as the system is well thought-out.

Left-handedness is no longer disapproved of; instruction in this field concentrates on the different techniques needed to aid the left-handed writer, especially with appropriate grip and paper position. Some individual variation in grip is now considered appropriate for both right- and left-handed writers; however, it is important for the teacher to know which grips will lead to handwriting dysfunctionality, including cramps and lack of speed.

A variety of writing implements is also now considered appropriate, with the student and teacher choosing the one that feels best. Fat pencils used by early writers may lead to an inappropriate grip. Rubber or other pencil prosthetics may help students trying to overcome a bad grip.

Much work has centered on the use of lined versus unlined paper; there is some suggestion that first writers work best with unlined, but there are a variety of research results supporting other opinions.

A variety of pre-writing activities have been recommended, including drawing, painting, threading beads, building blocks, and play dough, aimed at encouraging better pencil hold, and helping to develop isolated finger movements, kinesthetic memory, and upper limb muscle tone. Montessori methods, including writing in sand, tracing letters on sandpaper, and other sensory techniques, have also proved useful.

Much attention has been paid to the handwriting training of dyslexic and learning disabled (LD) students, who need more early intervention to prevent formation of bad writing habits. It has been suggested that it might be easier for these students to start with cursive rather than manuscript writing, both because it is easier physically to write joined letters, and to forestall the switchover from print to cursive. Inconsistent models and teaching methods within a school make progress particularly difficult for less able children.

Handwriting continues to be an important skill, a building block for success in personal expression. Teaching the teacher to diagnose and remedy problems is vital. Individual attention to students, although often difficult or impossible given large classes, is necessary to achieve good results—pupils with writing that is legible, flowing, and individual.

See also: CURRICULUM, SCHOOL; ELEMENTARY EDUCATION, *subentries on* CURRENT TRENDS, HISTORY OF; LANGUAGE ARTS, TEACHING OF.

BIBLIOGRAPHY

ALSTON, JEAN, and TAYLOR, JANE. 1987. *Handwriting: Theory, Research and Practice.* London: Croom Helm.

EINHORN, KAMA. 2001. "Handwriting Success for All." *Instructor* 110(5):35–39.

GRAHAM, STEVE; HARRIS, KAREN R.; and FINK, BARBARA. 2000. "Extra Handwriting Instruction: Prevent Writing Difficulties Right from the Start." *Teaching Exceptional Children* 33(2):88–91.

GRAHAM, STEVEN. 1999. "Handwriting and Spelling Instruction for Students with Learning Disabilities: A Review." *Learning Disability Quarterly* 22(2):79–98.

KIMERER, KAREN LOUISE. 1986. *Five Decades of Research in Handwriting: Recommendations for Teaching.* Ed.D. diss, Arizona State University.

MONAGHAN, E. JENNIFER, and SAUL, E. WENDY. 1987. "The Reader, The Scribe, The Thinker: A Critical Look at the History of American Reading and Writing Instruction." In *The Formation of School Subjects,* ed. Thomas S. Popkewitz. New York: Falmer Press.

SASSOON, ROSEMARY. 1999. *Handwriting of the Twentieth Century.* London: Routledge.

SHEFFIELD, BETTY. 1996. "Handwriting: A Neglected Cornerstone of Literacy." *Annals of Dyslexia.* 46:21–35.

THORNTON, TAMARA. 1996. *Handwriting in America: A Cultural History.* New Haven, CT: Yale University Press.

VECITIS, RACHEL, and CUNNINGHAM, KASI. 2000. "Technology Resources for Enhancing Handwriting Skills." *Journal of Special Education Technology.* 15(3):54–57.

WILLIAMS, ROBERT. 2000. "Without a Borrowed Hand: The Beginnings of American Penmanship." *Society of Scribes Journal* (fall):3–11.

JANE RODGERS SIEGEL

HANNA, PAUL R. (1902–1988)

An educator initially trained in elementary education, Paul R. Hanna gained his greatest fame in both social studies and international education.

Hanna was born in Sioux City, Iowa, his father a Methodist minister and his mother the daughter of Swiss immigrants. He entered Hamline College (now Hamline University), and upon graduation in 1924 he enrolled at Teachers College, Columbia, from which he earned an M.A. in 1925 and a Ph.D. in 1929. He served as superintendent of schools in West Winfield, New York, from 1926 through 1927. On the faculty of Teachers College from 1929 through 1934, Hanna then joined the Stanford University School of Education, from whence he retired in 1967, having served a brief term as acting dean in 1963. After retiring he was a senior research associate at the Stanford-based Hoover Institution for War, Revolution and Peace and he continued his extensive work in international education, which he had begun while at Stanford.

Hanna was a pioneer in a number of areas of school curriculum. In the 1930s he explored the notion of the expanding environments model for elementary social studies, and beginning in the 1950s he popularized this model through his editing and writing of the Scott Foresman social studies textbook series. Hanna initiated a strong research component that focused on generalizations identified from the social sciences that could be used as a content base for the series. This was an issue first broached by the American Progressive educator Harold Rugg in the 1920s and reappears today in the demands for curricular standards in history and the various social sciences. He explored the notion of what is now called *service learning* for young people. With his wife, Jean, Hanna also produced some of the most popular spelling series for school use. These books were based on research that Paul and Jean Hanna did within and outside schools. Hanna's elementary social studies periodical series, Building America (coproduced and written with James Mendenhall), was revolutionary in its approach to topics, reflecting contemporary social concerns. These monthly picture magazines attempted to present what made such issues so important to Americans. Late in life Hanna returned to the social studies as the topic of his writing.

Hanna was also committed to and instrumental in developing international education. Hanna pursued understanding of international issues through education, serving in Latin America in 1940 through 1941 within the Coordinator of Inter-American Affairs Office. Following World War II he was one of a team of educational experts that served in Germany to advise the Office of Military Government for Germany on educational affairs. Hanna was appointed in 1948 as an elementary education and teacher education specialist with the United Nations Educational, Scientific and Cultural Organization's educational mission to the Philippines, ending his term in the summer of 1949. He returned in 1952 as a director of education for the Mutual Security Agency's mission to that country, serving to June of 1953. He also traveled on missions to Burma, the Canal Zone, and Yugoslavia, eventually becoming the founder of a degree program in international education in 1952. This later evolved into the Stanford International Development Education Center (SIDEC), which includes many of the world's educational leaders as alumni.

In his last years Paul Hanna became more active with the Hoover Institution, and he and his wife founded the Paul and Jean Hanna Collection on the Role of Education in the Twentieth Century with a large financial gift in the late 1970s. They continued to add to the gift, and Hanna traveled across the country soliciting materials for the collection. The collection publishes periodic guides and thus is accessible to scholars worldwide.

See also: SOCIAL STUDIES EDUCATION.

Bibliography

BASKERVILLE, ROGER, and SESOW, WILLIAM. 1976. "In Defense of Hanna and the 'Expanding Communities Approach to Social Studies.'" *Theory and Research in Social Education* 4(1):20–32.

GILL, MARTIN. 1974. "Paul R. Hanna: The Evolution of an Elementary Social Studies Textbook Series." Ph.D. diss., Northwestern University.

HANNA, PAUL. 1936. *Youth Serves the Community.* New York: Appleton-Century.

HANNA, PAUL. 1966. *Geography in the Teaching of Social Studies.* Boston: Houghton-Mifflin.

HANNA, PAUL. 1986. *Assuring Quality for the Social Studies in Our Schools.* Stanford, CA: Hoover Institution Press.

HANNA, PAUL, and HANNA, JEAN. 1956. *Building Spelling Power.* Chicago: Scott Foresman.

NEWMANN, ROBERT E., JR. 1961. "History of a Civic Education Project Implementing the Social-Problems Technique of Instruction." Ph.D. diss., Stanford University.

STALLONES, JARED R. 1999. "The Life and Work of Paul R. Hanna." Ph.D. diss., University of Texas at Austin.

MURRY NELSON

HARPER, WILLIAM RAINEY
(1856–1906)

The first president of the University of Chicago, William Rainey Harper was a leading figure in the development of the modern university in the United States. He was born in New Concord, Ohio, and was considered an academic prodigy, enrolling at age ten as a freshman at Muskingum College where he studied language and music. After graduation at age fourteen, he went to Yale and earned a Ph.D. in Philology in three years. While in graduate school he courted Ella Paul, daughter of the president of Muskingum College. They were married a few months after Harper completed his Ph.D.

Following his advanced studies at Yale, Harper was a teacher and principal in Tennessee and Ohio before accepting an instructorship in Hebrew Theology at the original University of Chicago. He became a full professor of divinity in 1880. In 1886 he was named president in the university's final year.

Upon the closing of the university he went to Yale as professor of Semitic languages in the graduate department and instructor in the divinity school. He taught Hebrew, Assyrian, Arabic, Aramaic, and Syrian. He continued to oversee his summer schools, journals, correspondence school, and printing office. Soon he branched out into lecturing, and began giving courses on the Bible to the public, finding a new means by which he could expound on its origins.

The University of Chicago

Harper's reputation as a prodigious scholar of religion, combined with his Baptist affiliation, attracted the attention of John D. Rockefeller, who was making plans and generous donations for the founding of a university. Harper accepted Rockefeller's invitation to be the first president of the new University of Chicago in 1891, and served fourteen years until his death in 1906 at the age of forty-nine.

Although Harper was impressive as a scholar, his enduring contribution to American higher education was as an organizational genius and innovative leader. He was gregarious, and worked well with civic leaders and donors in Chicago. Harper was unabashedly ambitious in his plans for the new University of Chicago, and transformed that zeal into successful and even ruthless recruitment of talented faculty, students, and administrators. He gained the envy and scorn of college presidents across the nation when he "raided" the faculty of Clark University in order to enhance the behavioral sciences and psychology departments at Chicago. In concert with Professor Albion Small of the sociology department, whom Harper named dean, the University of Chicago pioneered such innovations as an elaborate bureaucracy of academic departments and ranks. In sum, Harper housed a modern, innovative university in the historic motifs of a monumental Gothic Revival campus that was the pride of the city.

Harper was known as Chicago's "Young Man in a Hurry." As president of the University of Chicago, Harper understood and thrived in the setting of a complex, multipurpose institution. He added new features such as a two-year junior college and an extensive summer school. He planned and obtained generous funding for scientific laboratories, an observatory, a university press, a graduate school with numerous Ph.D. programs, research institutes, and a library. At the same time he also emphasized intercollegiate football with a magnificent stadium geared to a large spectator audience. His hiring of Yale's Amos Alonzo Stagg as football coach and athletic director was instrumental in making the University of Chicago Maroons the dominant champions of the Western (Big Ten) conference. And Stagg, with Harper's approval, created the prototype for the highly commercial athletic department that had direct access to the president and the board of trustees, with little accountability to faculty governance.

Although Harper was an historian of religion, as a campus leader he felt no deference to academic traditions, whether in admissions examinations or degree requirements. He endorsed the coeducation of men and women. He relied on advertising, billboards, and mass mailings to promote all facets of campus programs and activities. He was committed to systematic public relations and fund raising. He served on numerous boards and committees in the city and nation. The University of Chicago was to be a young, modern university that was central to a dynamic metropolitan area, and that created the national prototype for a truly great American university.

Contribution to Academia

In 1905 Harper's doctors discovered that he had cancer. In his final months he published a book about education; revised two scriptural articles; published a biblical text; and finished his greatest piece of scholarly work, his *Commentary on Amos and Hosea*. With his characteristic energy, Harper even on his death bed was busy making plans for his elaborate funeral procession, including detailed instructions for Chicago faculty to march wearing full academic regalia.

See also: HIGHER EDUCATION IN THE UNITED STATES, *subentry on* HISTORICAL DEVELOPMENT; UNIVERSITY OF CHICAGO.

BIBLIOGRAPHY

HARPER, WILLIAM RAINEY. 1883. *An Introductory New Testament Greek Method Together with a Manual, Containing Text and Vocabulary of the Gospel of John and Lists.* New York: Scribners.

HARPER, WILLIAM RAINEY. 1886. *Elements of Hebrew by an Inductive Method.* New York: Scribners.

HARPER, WILLIAM RAINEY. 1900. *The Prospects of the Small College.* Chicago: University of Chicago Press.

HARPER, WILLIAM RAINEY. 1905. *The Prophetic Element in the Old Testament: An Aid to Historical Study.* Chicago: University of Chicago Press.

MAYER, MILTON. 1941. *Young Man in a Hurry: The Story of William Rainey Harper, First President of the University of Chicago.* Chicago: University of Chicago Alumni Association.

SLOSSON, EDWIN E. 1910. *Great American Universities.* New York: Macmillan.

STORR, RICHARD J. 1966. *Harper's University: The Beginnings.* Chicago: University of Chicago Press.

VEYSEY, LAURENCE R. 1965. *The Emergence of the American University.* Chicago: University of Chicago Press.

JASON R. EDWARDS
JOHN R. THELIN

HARRIS, WILLIAM T. (1835–1909)

An important educational philosopher and statesman of the late nineteenth century, William Torrey Harris served as the chief administrator of the St. Louis Public Schools from 1868 to 1880 and as the United States Commissioner of Education from 1889 to 1906.

Beginning his career in 1857 as an elementary school teacher in the St. Louis public school system, Harris progressed through the ranks, becoming superintendent in 1868. During this same period, his life as a philosopher flourished. He founded the *Journal of Speculative Philosophy* in 1867, and became an important part of a small group of scholars and educators who studied the German philosopher Georg William Friedrich Hegel, a community that would become known as the St. Louis Philosophical movement.

Like Horace Mann, Harris was an advocate of the free common public school. He was an egalitarian who helped to extend the reach of the school, and provided a national model in St. Louis for the kindergarten in the school system. He believed in the separation of church and state in public schooling and reinvented the nature of school discipline by criticizing corporal punishment and favoring self-discipline that was based on internalized moral values. He made the library a normal feature of the school's infrastructure, expanded foreign language education in the curriculum, defended the importance of coeducation, was open minded about new pedagogical ideas (including Pestalozzi's object teaching), and emphasized the importance of perpetual self-education. He worked to universalize public education across class, gender, and racial lines, seeing the school as fundamentally a child-saving agency, and served under four different U.S. presidents during his seventeen-year tenure as Unit-

ed States Commissioner of Education. Many of his views on schooling can be discerned from the twelve annual reports he wrote for the St. Louis pubic schools during his time in the superintendent's office and from the various reports he authored as U.S. Commissioner of Education.

His philosophical life overlapped with his actions as a school leader. A dutiful follower of Hegel, Harris's philosophy of education elevated the importance of freedom and reason—and self-direction as it was guided by the institutions of civilization. Schooling was one of the processes that allowed youth to rise above their inborn savagery and to participate in a civilizing life. The school was supposed to bring students face-to-face with the accumulated wisdom of humanity and to teach them to find their place in the spiritual nature of all existence. The core philosophical tenets in Harris's life not only played a significant role in his handling of school matters, but also kept him quite busy with philosophical disquisitions, writing essays such as "Goethe's Theory of Colors," "The Phenomenology of Spirit," and "Aristotle's Teleology." These were certainly not typical writings for a professional school administrator. The *Journal of Speculative Philosophy,*which Harris founded and edited, produced a very real contribution to philosophical discourse, highlighting the work of various important thinkers over its twenty-one year run, including John Dewey, William James, Charles Pierce, Josiah Royce, G. Stanley Hall, and George S. Morris. It also featured much of Harris's most gritty philosophical essays, an output of more than 35 articles over the life of the journal. In 1879, Harris became a faculty member at A. Bronson Alcott's Concord School of Philosophy, where he taught primarily on the topic of Hegel. He stayed there until 1888, when the school closed because Alcott died.

Harris sided squarely with a subject-centered view of learning, believing that the wisdom of humanity resided in modern academic subjects and that, for democracy to flourish, public schools had to bring this civilizing insight to the experience of all American youth. This was a prejudice reflected in Harris's influence over the Committee of Ten and the Committee of Fifteen reports, which both helped to crystallize the subject curriculum in the school. Harris, in fact, established the foundational principle of bringing the common academic curriculum to the common school, not for preparation for college but for life in a self-governing democracy.

To Harris, the nature of course study in the public school was largely reducible to what he saw as the five great divisions in the life of civilization, which he labeled "the five windows of the soul." Two of the windows (or areas of inquiry), mathematics and geography, were committed to humanity's conquest and comprehension of nature. The other three, literature, grammar, and history, were more connected to human life: literature speaking to literary works of art; grammar, to the study and the use of language; and history, to a multifaceted understanding of the nation's institutions. Harris reflected these ideas in his various circles of influence. He was, for instance, the main author of the Committee of Fifteen 1895 report, which was designed to offer a course study blueprint for the American elementary school. Harris maneuvered against the American Herbartians, who sought to unify the course work in the elementary school around German philosopher Johann Herbart's idea of curriculum concentrations, where one subject, usually literature, is made the central core of the learning experience, and other subjects are organized around on the basis of their interrelations to the core's main features. Harris did not accept this idea of concentration, believing that the five windows of the soul would be weakened when made subordinate to one core area. Instead, he called for a kind of coordination, where each subject is given a definite place and equal attention. The Committee of Fifteen report bears the unmistakable stamp of Harris's five windows of the soul and is an early example of the kind of subject-centeredness that would mark Harris's ideas on the curriculum.

Harris's dedication to the common cultural canon eventually earned him the tag of conservative among some historians, a label that some modern-day scholars have found to be unnuanced and not nearly appreciative enough of the many progressive ideas that Harris also supported. Yet, Harris was undoubtedly among the most effective critics of educational progressivism in his day. He was especially critical of ideas that failed to capture what he believed to be the intellectual and civilizing qualities of the subject curriculum. Harris held in low regard the Progressive ideas embodied in the American child study movement, American Herbartianism, and the expansion of the curriculum into manual or vocational arts instruction. For him they were essentially anti-intellectual endeavors largely wasted on youth. In this sense, Harris became the subject-centered foil to the prevailing child-centered views favored by Progressives at the turn of the nineteenth century.

See also: ACADEMIC DISCIPLINES; COMMON SCHOOL MOVEMENT; MANN, HORACE; PHILOSOPHY OF EDUCATION.

BIBLIOGRAPHY

HARRIS, WILLIAM T., ed. 1867–1888. *The Journal of Speculative Philosophy.* St Louis, MO: Knapp.

HARRIS, WILLIAM T. 1868–1880. *Annual Reports.* St. Louis, MO: St. Louis Board of Education.

HARRIS, WILLIAM T. 1889. *Introduction to the Study of Philosophy.* New York: Appleton.

HARRIS, WILLIAM T., et al. 1895. *Report of the Committee of Fifteen.* Washington, DC: National Education Association.

HARRIS, WILLIAM T. 1970. *Hegel's Logic: A Book on the Genesis of the Categories of the Mind (1890).* New York: Kraus.

RESSE, WILLIAM J. 2000. "The Philosopher-King of St. Louis." In *Curriculum and Consequence: Herbert Kliebard and the Promise of Schooling,* ed. Barry M. Franklin. New York: Teachers College Press, Columbia University.

SCHAUB, EDWARD LEROY, ed. 1936. *William Torrey Harris 1835–1936: A Collection of Essays, Including Papers and Addresses Presented in Commemoration of Dr. Harris' Centennial at the St. Louis Meeting of the Western Division of the America Philosophical Society.* Chicago: Open Court.

PETER HLEBOWITSH

HARVARD UNIVERSITY

Harvard University, the oldest educational institution in the United States, was founded sixteen years after the arrival of the Pilgrims at Plymouth, Massachusetts. Established by the Massachusetts Bay Colony in 1636 and later chartered in 1650 in what is now the oldest corporation in the Western Hemisphere, Harvard University was named for its first benefactor, John Harvard of Charlestown, Massachusetts, who, on his death in 1638, left his library and a portion of his estate to the school. In 1640 Henry Dunster became the first president and also constituted the entire faculty. For more than fifty years Harvard remained the only college in America.

It has been said that "when Harvard speaks, the country listens," and throughout its history Harvard, as the country's premier university, shaped the direction of education in the United States. John Harvard's bequest was the first of the private gifts for education in America, and the act of the colony in 1636 marks the beginning of state aid to higher education in the United States. *New England's First Fruits,* an anonymous tract celebrating the establishment of higher education in the colonies, was published in London in 1643. Among the influential colonists were a number of Cambridge (hence Harvard's city name) and Oxford graduates who were eager to replicate the English college in the American frontier. During its early years, Harvard College offered a classic academic course based on the English university model merged with the prevailing Puritan philosophy of the early colonists. Harvard College was loosely affiliated with the Congregationalist church; not surprisingly most of its first graduates became ministers throughout New England, while other graduates entered government service or private business.

Curriculum

Harvard College's course of study was similar to the curricula of Cambridge and Oxford universities. Unlike the English model, Dunster first created a curriculum for Harvard that only lasted three years, but in 1652 a fourth year was added. The Harvard core curriculum became a model for American education institutions to follow, not only colleges but also grammar schools and academies that prepared students for higher learning and collegiate studies. The curriculum from its founding through the eighteenth century was theological; early nineteenth-century studies expanded the curriculum to include Latin, Greek, mathematics (including astronomy), English composition, philosophy, theology, natural philosophy, and either Hebrew or French. This prescribed course of study established a pattern for American liberal arts colleges. The most common forms of instruction were oral exercises—the lecture, the declamation, and the disputation.

Charles W. Eliot, who served as president from 1869 to 1909, transformed the college into a modern university, a feat accomplished primarily by transforming the curriculum. Although course electives existed at Harvard throughout the nineteenth century, Eliot became an unrelenting advocate of the elective system, which in turn permitted him to initiate

institutional reform where college studies could accommodate broader as well as more specialized interests of students. The elective system permitted Harvard to become more responsive to the many evolving democratic, technological, and vocational needs of society. By the turn of the twentieth century, Harvard's elective system was the freest in the country with no subject requirements for studies beyond the first year.

Faculty

With the expansion of the curriculum, Eliot increased the Harvard faculty from 60 to 600 members. During Eliot's administration Radcliffe College was established for women. Eliot and others refused to admit women to Harvard but were willing to create a coordinate college that would provide a similar education for women. In 1894 the Commonwealth of Massachusetts chartered Radcliffe College; Elizabeth Cary Agassiz served as this institution's first president. She was followed by LeBaron Russell Briggs, the former dean of students and a professor of rhetoric at Harvard.

President Abbott Lawrence Lowell, who served from 1909 to 1933, refocused the undergraduate course of study to ensure that a liberal education would include concentration on a single field as well as a distribution of course requirements among other disciplines. James Bryant Conant, who served as Harvard president from 1933 to 1953, initiated the examination of general education, which in turn served to redefine the concept of *core curriculum,* a course of study that delineated breadth in interdisciplinary fields outside the student's major field of study. Conant's General Education Committee, which released in 1945 the legendary Harvard Redbook, *General Education in a Free Society,* set the direction for American college and secondary curriculum for the later part of the twentieth century. Under Conant's leadership, in 1943 Harvard and Radcliffe agreed to enroll women students in Harvard classrooms for the first time. But women would not earn Harvard degrees until the 1970s.

Recent presidents Nathan M. Pusey, Derek Bok, and Neil L. Rudenstine have each contributed significantly toward strengthening the quality of undergraduate and graduate education at Harvard while at the same time maintaining the university's role as a preeminent research institution. "Harvard has shaped the world of higher education," said the late Ernest Boyer, president of the Carnegie Foundation for the Advancement of Teaching. "It's the cathedral that provides inspiration for all the others."

See also: ELIOT, CHARLES; GENERAL EDUCATION IN HIGHER EDUCATION; HIGHER EDUCATION IN THE UNITED STATES, *subentry on* HISTORICAL DEVELOPMENT.

BIBLIOGRAPHY

BAILYN, BERNARD, et al. 1986. *Glimpses of the Harvard Past.* Cambridge, MA: Harvard University Press.

KELLER, MORTON, and KELLER, PHYLLIS. 2001. *Making Harvard Modern: The Rise of America's University.* Oxford: Oxford University Press.

MORRISON, SAMUEL ELIOT. 1936. *Three Centuries of Harvard, 1636–1936.* Cambridge, MA: Harvard University Press

RUDOLPH, FREDERICK. 1977. *Curriculum: A History of the American Undergraduate Course of Study since 1636.* San Francisco: Jossey-Bass.

SOLLORS, WERNER; TITCOMB, CALDWELL; and UNDERWOOD, THOMAS A., eds. 1993. *Blacks at Harvard: A Documentary History of African-American Experience at Harvard and Radcliffe.* New York: New York University Press.

SYNNOTT, MARCIA G. 1979. *The Half-Opened Door: Discrimination and Admissions at Harvard, Yale, and Princeton, 1900–1970.* Westport, CT: Greenwood Press.

INTERNET RESOURCE

HARVARD UNIVERSITY. 2002. <www.harvard.edu>.

ROBERT A. SCHWARTZ
CRAIG KRIDEL

HAVIGHURST, ROBERT J.
(1900–1991)

Best known for his conceptualization of human development as mastery of a series of age-related cultural tasks, Robert J. Havighurst was an avid researcher, a prolific writer, and a civil rights activist. As a researcher, he conducted cross-sectional and longitudinal studies of the social, emotional, and moral development of children and adolescents in various American subcultures (including Native Americans) as well as in several other countries. To illustrate his writing proficiency, a student pushed a large wheelbarrow filled with Havighurst's publications into the banquet hall during a celebration of his sixty-fifth birthday. His 1964 survey of the Chicago public schools drew national attention for its far-sighted yet controversial plan for school and community integration. Many of the twenty-two recommendations offered by the committee concerned the need for organizational and structural changes in the Chicago public schools. A key recommendation called for extensive decentralization of authority; another, for the creation of the modern day equivalent of "schools-within-schools."

A member of a distinguished academic family, Robert J. Havighurst was born the son of Freeman Alfred Havighurst, who was on the faculty of Lawrence College, and Winifred Weter Havighurst, who had been on the faculty until her marriage. He was the oldest of five children—four boys and one girl—and attended public schools in college towns in Wisconsin and Illinois. Following high school he attended Ohio Wesleyan University, receiving his B.A. degree in 1921. He enrolled at Ohio State University, receiving his Ph.D. in chemistry in 1924. Following receipt of his Ph.D., he went to Harvard University as a postdoctoral fellow, studying the structure of the atom and publishing papers in journals of physics and chemistry. He then spent a year on the faculty of chemistry at Miami University.

In 1928, he accepted a position as assistant professor of physics at the University of Wisconsin. He also served as an adviser in the Experimental College there. Largely as a result of his experience with the Experimental College, his interest in the problems of adolescents grew, eventually surpassing his interest in teaching the natural sciences. He left the University of Wisconsin in 1932, taking a faculty position in education at the Ohio State University Laboratory School.

In 1934 he became the assistant director for programs in science education for the General Education Board of the Rockefeller Foundation. It was here, under the guidance of Lawrence Rank, that he became involved in the study of children and adolescents. Within three years, Havighurst became the director of the board. In that role he was instrumental in the funding of research programs in child development at major universities and research centers in the United States. He was also able to provide funds to enable refugee European scholars to resettle in the United States. Among those assisted were Bruno Bettleheim, Peter Blos, Erik Erikson, and Fritz Redl.

In 1941 Havighurst was appointed professor of education and executive secretary of the Committee of Human Development at the University of Chicago. For the next forty years, Havighurst conducted research and wrote on a variety of topics and issues.

From 1948 to 1953 he developed his highly influential theory of human development. The centerpiece of this theory was the developmental task. He defined a developmental task in the following manner:

> A development task is a task which arises at or about a certain period in the life of the individual, successful achievement of which leads to his happiness and to success with later tasks, while failure leads to unhappiness in the individual, disapproval by society, and difficulty with later tasks. (1953, p. 2)

As a concept development tasks were able to merge the relative influences of nature and nurture. As Havighurst wrote:

> Nature lays down wide possibilities in the developing of the human body, and which possibilities shall be realized depends on what the individual learns. This is true even of such crude biological realities as feeding habits and sexual relations, while the more highly social realities of language, economic behavior, and religion are almost completely the product of learning at the hands of society. (1953, p. 1)

To foster development, then, educators had to introduce students to these critical tasks at the "right time." This "right time" was described as the "teachable moment." "When the body is ripe, and society requires, and the self is ready to achieve a certain task, the teachable moment has come" (1953, p. 5).

In the 1950s and 1960s Havighurst directed a decade-long study of middle and old age. The results of this study, combined with his subsequent research, altered conventional wisdom about the aging process. His interest in life-span development continued throughout his life. He studied changes in the sex role behavior of men and women over fifty, the adaptation to the retirement process by male sociologists and psychologists, and alternative work schedules for older workers.

From 1967 through 1971, Havighurst directed the National Study of Indian Education, which was funded by the U.S. Office of Education. Native Americans were involved in planning the study as well as in the field work and data analysis. The results indicated that education for Indian youth across the United States varied widely according to numerous factors such as sources of funding, location, curriculum, faculty, degree of isolation, and cultural differences. Recommendations included finding ways for Indians to have an increased voice in their education and the establishment of a national Commission on Indian Education.

In the late 1960s and 1970s, Havighurst focused his attention on the problems of urban education. He conducted a study of public high schools in the forty-five largest cities in the United States, examining educational goals, school structure and organization, staff characteristics, curriculum, student activities, student activism, and school-community relations. He concluded that there was more and deeper segregation and separation of high school students of different socioeconomic and ethnic groups in 1969 to 1970 than there was ten or twenty years before. In 1977, at age seventy-seven, he coedited a book in which he developed a series of policies and practices for the improvement of big-city schools based on his research.

Havighurst continued to engage in research and writing well into his eighties, publishing six journal articles between 1980 and 1986. In his last published article, "The Challenge: 1985–2000," he argued that the challenge for the future of a democratic society is to develop educational programs that foster development in the areas of race and ethnic relations, civil rights, international relations, and gender role. At age eighty-six, there were still new developmental tasks. And, at age eighty-six, Havighurst was still looking toward the future.

See also: DEVELOPMENTAL THEORY; EDUCATIONAL PSYCHOLOGY; MORAL DEVELOPMENT; URBAN EDUCATION.

BIBLIOGRAPHY

FUCHS, ESTELLE, and HAVIGHURST, ROBERT J. 1973. *To Live on This Earth: American Indian Education.* Garden City, NY: Anchor Press/ Doubleday.

HAVIGHURST, ROBERT J. 1953. *Human Development and Education.* New York: McKay.

HAVIGHURST, ROBERT J. 1970. *A Profile of the Large-City High School.* Washington, DC: National Association of Secondary School Principals.

HAVIGHURST, ROBERT J. 1986. "The Challenge: 1985–2000." *Educational Forum* 50:307–308.

LEVINE, DANIEL U., and HAVIGHURST, ROBERT J., eds. 1977. *The Future of Big-City Schools: Desegregation Policies and Magnet Alternatives.* Berkeley, CA: McCutchan.

NUCCI, LARRY P. 1997. "Havighurst, Robert J." In *Biographical Dictionary of Psychology,* ed. Noel Sheehy, Anthony J. Chapman, and Wendy Conroy. New York: Routledge.

LORIN W. ANDERSON

HEAD START

See: COMPENSATORY EDUCATION, *subentry on* UNITED STATES.

HEALTH AND EDUCATION

The twentieth century saw extraordinary and dramatic improvements in human health. Life expectancy more than doubled, with most of the increase within the century's second fifty years. Improved income, higher levels of education, more and better food, better sanitation, public sewage systems, and new knowledge underpin these gains. This entry focuses on the effect of male and female education levels within the context of this broader range of determinants. The general discussion is illustrated with a more specific treatment of the child mortality rate across countries for the three decades from 1960 to 1990. Child mortality rate is defined as the number of deaths per 1,000 live births between birth and exact age five years; at the start of the twenty-first century the rate varies from less than 10 per thousand for high income countries to over 200 in some poor countries.

Education level has been constantly found to be related to the health status at the levels of individual, household, and country, usually with a stronger effect than that of income. Based on Jia Wang and Dean Jamison's 1997 estimations, one additional year of education for the female population can avert six deaths per thousand in child mortality rates. John Peabody and colleagues found that child mortality rates in 1993 and 1994 Bangladesh varied across the mothers' education level: 134 deaths per thousand for mothers with some primary education; 105 for mothers who completed primary education; and 90 for mothers with secondary or higher education.

In consequence, one way governments can improve health is to expand investment in schooling, particularly for girls. The World Bank's 1993 World Development Report concluded that education increases the opportunities for households, particularly for mothers, to seek access to information and to make better use of the financial resources to shape the diets, fertility, health care, and other lifestyle choices that have a crucial impact on the health of household members. Children's health is affected much more by the mother's education level than the father's. Educated mothers tend to marry and start families later, factors that diminish the child health risk associated with early pregnancies. Educated mothers are also more likely to use preventive care and delivery assistance, maintain better household hygiene, seek immunization more frequently, and have better use of medical services. According to the World Bank study, a 10 percent increase in female literacy rates in thirteen African countries in the period of 1975 through 1985 reduced child mortality rates by 10 percent, while a 10 percent increase in male literacy rates had little to no effect in decreasing child mortality (p. 42).

To give a sense of the methods and recent results of analyses of education's impact at the country level, it may be valuable to provide a brief illustration. Improved data sets now exist that include the following variables on individual countries at different points in time:

- Child mortality rates for all children, for girls, and for boys

- Real gross domestic product (GDP) per capita adjusted for purchasing power parity, expressed in 1985 U.S. dollars

- Education level for the female population and for the male population, calculated as the average number of years of education for the population aged 15 and over, according to Robert Barro and Jong-Wha Lee.

These variables are measured at a five-year interval for the period of 1960 though 1990 and they are available for 94 countries. The average years of education for the female and male population are 4 and

4.9 years for the period of 1960 to 1990. The mean child mortality rate is 75 deaths per 1,000 live births for boys, 69 deaths for girls, and 63 for both boys and girls. The income per capita has a mean of $2,368.

Education, income, and time (as a proxy for technical progress) are used by Anthony Bryk and Steve Raudenbusch as determinants of child mortality measures using hierarchical linear modeling (HLM). Jamison and Wang's 2001 study gives detailed information on data and methodology.

Three sets of analyses, with male education, female education, and both female and male education levels as the education measure, were done to assess gender differences in the effect of education on child mortality. Jamison and Wang found that an additional year of male education level is associated with a 3 to 4 percent reduction in child mortality. But the magnitude of the effect is statistically insignificant, whether it is child mortality for the whole population, for girls only, or for boys only. Female education level, on the other hand, has a statistically significant effect on all three measures of child mortality rates. The effect is about a 10 to 11 percent reduction in child mortality. Interestingly when the effect of time (or technical progress) is allowed to be country-specific the estimated effects of income and education on child mortality decline. That said, there is historical evidence to suggest that prior to major gains in medical science in the twentieth century, education had much less of an effect on mortality than today. The effects of new knowledge and of education appear to work together to contribute to the decline in child mortality.

This example confirms the existing literature on health and education in finding that higher education levels are associated with better health. A more careful look, however, finds that female education level has a much stronger effect in reducing child mortality rates than male education level, independent of whether it is the child mortality for boys only, for girls only, or for both.

See also: GENDER ISSUES, INTERNATIONAL; INTERNATIONAL DEVELOPMENT AGENCIES AND EDUCATION, *subentry on* UN AND INTERNATIONAL AGENCIES.

BIBLIOGRAPHY

BARRO, ROBERT, and LEE, JONG-WHA. 1996. "International Measures of School Years and School-

ing Quality." *American Economic Review: AER Papers and Proceedings* 86: 218–223.

BEHRMAN, JERE R. 1996. *Human Resources in Latin America and the Caribbean.* Baltimore, MD: Inter-American Development Bank/Johns Hopkins University Press.

BRYK, ANTHONY S., and RAUDENBUSH, STEVE W. 1992. *Hierarchical Linear Models.* Newbury Park, CA: Sage.

COCHRANE, SUSAN H.; LESLIE, JOANNE; and O'HARA, DONALD J. 1982. "Parental Education and Child Health, Intracountry Evidence." *Health Policy and Education* 2: 213–250.

ELO, IRMA, and PRESTON, SAMUEL H. 1996. "Educational Differences in Mortality: United States, 1979–1985." *Social Science and Medicine* 42: 47–57.

JAMISON, DEAN T., and WANG, JIA. 2001. "Education Inequity and Shortfalls in Female Life Expectancy." Paper presented at the 28th Global Health Council Conference, May 29 to June 1, Washington DC.

JAMISON, DEAN T.; WANG, JIA; HILL, KENNETH; and LONDONO, JUAN-LUIS. 1996. "Income, Mortality and Fertility in Latin America: Country-Level Performance, 1960–90." *Analisis Economico* 11(2):219–261.

PEABODY, JOHN, et al. 1997. *Policy and Health: Implications for Development in Asia.* Cambridge, Eng.: Cambridge University Press.

PRESTON, SAMUEL H., and HAINES, MICHAEL R. 1991. *Fatal Years: Child Mortality in Late-Nineteenth-Century America.* Princeton, NJ: Princeton University Press.

PRITCHETT, LANT, and SUMMERS, LAWRENCE H. 1996. "Wealthier Is Healthier." *Journal of Human Resources* 31(4): 841–868.

WANG, JIA; JAMISON, DEAN. T.; BOS, EDUARD; and VU, MY THI. 1997. "Poverty and Mortality among the Elderly: Measurements of Performance in Thirty-Three Countries, 1960–1992." *Tropical Medicine and International Health* 2(10):1001–1010.

WORLD BANK. 1993. *Investing in Health: World Development Report.* Washington, DC: Oxford University Press for The World Bank.

JIA WANG
DEAN T. JAMISON

HEALTH CARE AND CHILDREN

The United States has the most sophisticated and advanced medical care in the world, attracting people from around the globe for treatment of complex and difficult health conditions. The extent to which individuals living in this country benefit from this care, however, depends to a great degree on whether they have health insurance. Studies consistently show that persons without health insurance are far less likely to use health services than those with health insurance. In addition, the number of people without health insurance is on the rise, providing more cause for concern. More than 42 million Americans under the age of sixty-five were completely uninsured in 1999.

While children's access to care is a function of a wide range of factors, including family characteristics and the organization of the health system, financial barriers such as lack of health insurance play a significant role. Health insurance is by far the most important predictor of whether children will receive needed health care. Uninsured children receive fewer aggregate annual physician visits than their insured counterparts, and they are significantly less likely than publicly insured poor children to identify a usual source of routine care.

Despite the predominant role of health insurance in access to health care, sizable numbers of children in this country are uninsured. While no age group is immune from the threat of losing health insurance, children make up a significant proportion of the uninsured. In 1999, 10 million children, nearly 14 percent of all children in the United States, were uninsured.

The Importance of Access

Most children are healthy. Some may ask, therefore, why it is important for children to have access to health care. In fact, despite relatively good health, children do need access to regular health care, as well as access to special services when acute or chronic conditions occur. Moreover, children are distinct from other age groups in several important ways. For one thing, they are entirely dependent on their adult caregivers for health services. Children are incapable of making decisions about health care, purchasing services or insurance, or making judgments about the appropriateness of services. Children are also unable to voice preferences or to influence decisions made on their behalf. Thus, it is the responsi-

bility of adults to represent their interests and to ensure that their needs are met.

Children's health needs are also significantly different from those of adults. By nature, children grow and develop at rapid rates, placing them at special risk of being affected by illness and injury. If health problems are not identified and treated, they can affect a child's cognitive, physical, behavioral, and emotional development. It is therefore essential to identify and treat health conditions early to prevent or minimize the impact on overall growth and development.

Finally, the type, severity, and frequency of health conditions that children experience also differ from adults. Children generally experience a wider variety of health problems, but of less severity. Conversely, adults are more likely to have chronic degenerative conditions than children. But certain childhood conditions, though relatively mild in single instances, have the capacity to lead to long-term disabilities in children. For example, chronic otitis media (ear infections), if unchecked, can lead to hearing loss, and possibly learning disabilities. Other rare but severe conditions, such as spina bifida and sickle cell disease, manifest themselves early and require ongoing monitoring and expensive, tertiary care.

The Role of Insurance

The groups most at-risk of being uninsured are adolescents, minorities, children living with a single parent, and children in poor and near-poor families (especially working families living at the near-poverty level). Family income and ethnicity are the factors most associated with being uninsured. In 1990, Hispanic children were more than twice as likely to be uninsured as non-Hispanic white children. Similarly, children in poor and near-poor families were more than twice as likely to be uninsured as children in more advantaged families.

The percentage of children without health insurance grew sizably during the late 1970s and the 1980s. Between 1977 and 1987, the percentage of children without any form of health insurance rose by 40 percent. Since then, the overall percentage of uninsured children has remained relatively stable, though the distribution of children within various sources of insurance has dramatically shifted. Between 1987 and 1993, the proportion of children covered by private, employment-based insurance declined 12 percent, from 60.7 percent to 53.6 percent. Meanwhile, the proportion of children covered by Medicaid increased from 15.6 percent to 23.9 percent, and the number of children covered by Medicaid climbed from 10.0 million in 1988 to 20 million in 1999, reflecting a fundamental shift in the type of insurance children hold.

A number of factors account for this dramatic shift in the distribution of children's insurance coverage. A nationwide recession, in addition to the rising cost of medical care, affected the ability of insurance companies to provide increasingly expensive health insurance benefits. A rapid shift of jobs away from industries such as manufacturing, which typically have generous benefits, to service jobs industries, which typically offer few, if any, benefits, also contributed to changes in children's insurance status.

The large increase in the number of children covered by Medicaid is the result of legislative changes enacted by the Congress and the states in the middle and late 1980s, as well as the recession that pushed more families into poverty during the early 1990s. Following more than a decade of retrenchment in Medicaid eligibility at the state and federal levels, Congress enacted a series of Medicaid expansions between 1984 and 1990. These laws were designed to gradually cover additional low-income children and pregnant women, and to increase uniformity in income-eligibility levels across states. Virtually all poor children (with incomes below the federal poverty level) are eligible for Medicaid (with the exception of those who are undocumented).

These Medicaid expansions have produced important results. Numerous studies demonstrate that the availability of Medicaid has resulted in improved access to care among low-income children. Poor children with Medicaid were far more likely than poor uninsured children to have access to care, based on multiple dimensions of access, including the presence of a usual source of care, frequency of unmet health needs, and the use of medical services. Among adolescents, the impact of Medicaid has been even more dramatic. Although poor adolescents were 35 percent more likely than nonpoor adolescents to have waited two or more years between physician contacts, poor adolescents with Medicaid coverage used physician services at rates similar to nonpoor adolescents. The availability of Medicaid has also led to improvements among children in terms of the use of preventive services. A full year of

Medicaid increases the chances that a child will have a well-child visit by 17 percent, and also increases compliance with national guidelines from the American Academy of Pediatrics by 13 percent.

The State Children's Insurance Program (SCHIP), established in 1997, provides additional assistance to low-income children. This program is designed for uninsured children who are not eligible for Medicaid because their families' incomes are too high, but for whom private insurance is unaffordable. Close to 90 percent of these uninsured children have at least one parent who works, but for many of these families affordable health coverage is not offered through their employer. As of 2000, nearly 2 million children were enrolled in the program nationwide.

Unfortunately, both Medicaid and SCHIP suffer from under-enrollment. Of the 10 million uninsured children in the United States, more than half are likely eligible for either program. Studies show a variety of reasons for under-enrollment, including negative views about public insurance programs, confusion about eligibility, and complex enrollment processes. In addition, studies show that potential enrollees associate Medicaid with burdensome eligibility requirements, difficult enrollment processes, demeaning attitudes of eligibility workers, and inadequate services by health care providers. Other research has found that some immigrants fail to enroll in public programs because of their fear of potential ramifications for their immigration status. There may also be problems associated with communicating clear information about the programs. Research indicates that many low-income parents have not heard of SCHIP or are confused about their children's eligibility. Whatever the reasons, improvements in access to health care cannot be reasonably expected as long as eligible children are not enrolled in available programs.

The Limitations of Insurance

Extending health insurance to low-income children has a beneficial impact on access. However, simply providing insurance does not mean that children will necessarily have full access to health care, especially among low-income children. Indeed, insured low-income children use fewer services than more affluent, insured children. Moreover, poor children with insurance are less likely to go to a private physician's office and more likely to utilize community health centers, compared to nonpoor children with insurance. There are a number of reasons for these differences. The families of poor children with insurance face nonfinancial barriers to health care that insurance cannot address, such as lack of transportation, lack of child care, inconvenient location of services, and service hours that conflict with work. Children of immigrant families may face additional barriers, such as an inability to communicate in their primary language, fear of deportation, and cultural conflicts with Western medicine. For these reasons, providing insurance without developing a delivery system to serve the needs of low-income children does not produce the desired outcome of improved access to quality health care.

Conclusion

All children need health care, whether for regular check-ups, for episodic health problems such as ear infections, or for chronic conditions. Because health services are relatively expensive, children's access to care is largely dependent on whether or not they have health insurance. Unfortunately, far too many children are not covered and therefore, do not receive needed care. One solution is to assist eligible children to enroll in public programs like Medicaid and SCHIP. As indicated, approximately half of all uninsured children are eligible for these programs. To achieve this goal, the process by which children enroll must be simplified, eligibility rules clarified, and any negative stigma about public programs removed.

Other efforts will also be required for uninsured children who are not eligible for these programs. Many of these children are undocumented, which means that rules preventing them from participating in Medicaid and SCHIP would need to be revised, or special programs must be created for them.

See also: HEALTH AND EDUCATION; HEALTH EDUCATION, SCHOOL; HEALTH SERVICES, *subentry on* SCHOOL; MANAGED CARE AND CHILDREN.

BIBLIOGRAPHY

BILHEIMER, LINDA T., and COLBY, DAVID C. 2001. "Expanding Coverage: Reflections on Recent Efforts." *Health Affairs* 20(1):83–95.

ELLWOOD, MARILYN. 1999. *The Medicaid Eligibility Maze: Coverage Expands, but Enrollment Problems Persist: Findings from a Five-State Study.* Cambridge, MA: Mathematical Policy Research.

GUENDELMAN, SYLVIA, and PEARL, MICHELLE. 2001. "Access to Care for Children of the Working Poor." *Archives of Pediatric Adolescent Medicine* 155:651–658.

HALFON, NEAL; INKELAS, MOIRA; and WOOD, DAVID. 1995. "Non-Financial Barriers to Care for Children and Youth." *Annual Review of Public Health* 16:447–472.

HUGHES, DANA; CART, COURTNEY; MORENO, MELANIE; and NG, SANDY. 2000. *Barriers to Enrollment in Healthy Families and Medi-Cal: Differences by Race and Ethnicity.* San Francisco: Institute for Health Policy Studies, University of California.

HUGHES, DANA; CART, COURTNEY; VOGEL, SARAH; MORENO, MELANIE; and NG, SANDY. 2000. *Barriers to Enrollment in Healthy Families and Medi-Cal: Findings from Nine Focus Groups with Chinese, Korean, and Vietnamese Parents of Eligible Children.* San Francisco: Institute for Health Policy Studies, University of California.

KENNEY, GENEVIEVE; HALEY, JACK; and DUBAY, LISA. 2001. *How Familiar Are Low-Income Parents with Medicaid and SCHIP?* Washington DC: The Urban Institute.

LAVE, JUDITH R.; KEANE CHRISTOPHER R.; LIN, CHYONGCHIOU J.; et al. 1996. "Impact of a Children's Health Insurance Program on Newly Enrolled Children." *Journal of the American Medical Association* 279:1820–1825.

NEWACHECK, PAUL W. 1988. "Access to Ambulatory Care for Poor Persons." *Health Services Research* 23(3):401–419.

NEWACHECK, PAUL W. 1989. "Improving Access to Health Services for Adolescents from Economically Disadvantaged Families." *Pediatrics* 84(6):1056–1063.

NEWACHECK, PAUL W.; HUGHES, DANA C.; HUNG, YUNG-YI; et al. 2000. "The Unmet Health Needs of America's Children." *Pediatrics* 105:989–997.

NEWACHECK, PAUL W.; PEARL, MICHELLE; HUGHES, DANA C.; and HALFON, NEAL. 1998. "The Role of Medicaid in Ensuring Children's Access to Care." *Journal of the American Medical Association* 280:1789–1793.

NEWACHECK, PAUL W.; STODDARD, JEFFREY J.; HUGHES, DANA C.; and PEARL, MICHELLE. 1998. "Health Insurance and Access to Primary Care for Children." *New England Journal of Medicine* 338:513–519.

STARFIELD, BARBARA. 1997. "Social, Economic, and Medical Care Determinants of Children's Health." In *Health Care for Children: What's Right, What's Wrong, What's Next,* ed. Ruth Stein. New York: United Hospital Fund.

STODDARD, JEFFREY J.; ST. PETER, ROBERT F.; and NEWACHECK, PAUL W. 1994. "Health Insurance Status and Ambulatory Care for Children." *New England Journal of Medicine* 330:1421–1425.

WOOD, DAVID L.; HAYWARD, RODNEY.; COREY, CHRISTOPHER.; FREEMAN, HOWARD E.; and SHAPIRO, MARTIN F. 1990. "Access to Medical Care for Children and Adolescents in the United States." *Pediatrics* 86(5):666–673.

DANA HUGHES

HEALTH, CHILDREN'S PHYSICAL

See: HEALTH EDUCATION, SCHOOL; HEALTH SERVICES; IMMUNIZATION AND CHILDREN'S PHYSICAL HEALTH; NUTRITION AND CHILDREN'S PHYSICAL HEALTH; SLEEP AND CHILDREN'S PHYSICAL HEALTH.

HEALTH EDUCATION, SCHOOL

School health programs are said to be one of the most efficient strategies that a nation might use to prevent major health and social problems. Next to the family, schools are the major institution for providing the instruction and experiences that prepare young people for their roles as healthy, productive adults. Schools can—and invariably do—play a powerful role in influencing students' health-related behaviors. Elementary, middle, and secondary schools are therefore prime settings for public health programming: in 1999, nearly 99 percent of young people ages seven through thirteen and 96 percent of those between fourteen and seventeen were enrolled in school in the United States. Appropriate school interventions can foster effective education, prevent destructive behavior, and promote enduring health practices. For many young people in their formative years, school may, in fact, be the only nurturing and supportive place where they learn health information and have positive behavior consistently reinforced.

In addition, health and success in school are inextricably intertwined. Good health facilitates children's growth, development, and optimal learning, while education contributes to children's knowledge about being healthy. Studies of young people have found that health-risk behaviors negatively affect: (1) education outcomes, including graduation rates, class grades, and performance on standardized tests; (2) education behaviors, including attendance, dropout rates, behavioral problems, and degree of involvement in school activities such as homework and extracurricular pursuits; and (3) student attitudes, including aspirations for postsecondary education, feelings about safety at school, and positive personal attitudes.

Schools cannot achieve their primary mission of education if students and staff are not healthy and fit physically, mentally, and socially. Children who are sick, hungry, abused, using drugs, who feel that nobody cares, or who may be distracted by family problems are unlikely to learn well. One child's lack of progress can impede the learning of the other children in the classroom as well. Education reform efforts are bound to be of limited effectiveness unless health-related barriers to learning are directly addressed. As Harriet Tyson writes, "First among those barriers are poor physical and mental health conditions that prevent students from showing up for school, paying attention in class, restraining their anger, quieting their self-destructive impulses, and refraining from dropping out" (p. 2). When surveyed, most parents and members of the general public consistently rate health as an important topic that schools should address.

Although reliable data on the implementation of school health programs are lacking, there are indications that few schools operate comprehensive, co-ordinated programs designed to systematically address the nation's major health risks. For example, 71 percent of high school students surveyed in 1999 did not attend a daily physical education class, and 44 percent were not even enrolled in a physical education class. Only 72 percent of the nation's schools participated in the federal School Breakfast Program during the 1999–2000 school year, despite the well-documented health and educational benefits of doing so. In 1994 health education staff were involved in joint activities or projects with staff from other components of the school health program in only 65 percent of middle and high schools. Health services facilities were not available in 32 percent of all middle and high schools in 1994. During the 1998–1999 school year, 76 percent of public high schools and 55 percent of public middle schools operated vending machines, most of which were located in or near the cafeteria. The most common types of food offered in school vending machines are soft drinks, chips, desserts, and candy. Few schools are known to sponsor health promotion activities for staff.

Educators should work to ensure that every elementary, middle, and high school establishes and maintains comprehensive, well-coordinated school health programs. The American Public Health Association (APHA) supports the definition offered by the Institute of Medicine: "A comprehensive school health program is an integrated set of planned, sequential, school-affiliated strategies, activities, and services designed to promote the optimal physical, emotional, social, and educational development of students. The program involves and is supportive of families and is determined by the local community, based on community needs, resources, standards, and requirements. It is coordinated by a multidisciplinary team and accountable to the community for program quality and effectiveness . . . ." (p. 2). There is no single 'best' comprehensive school health program model that will work in every community. Programs must be designed locally, and collaboration among all stakeholders in the community is essential if programs are to be accepted and effective.

Characteristics of Effective Programs

There are eight elements that characterize high-quality school health programs. These elements are described below.

1. A focus on priority behaviors that affect health and learning. School health programs were initiated early in the twentieth century, in large part to address the numerous infectious diseases afflicting children. At the beginning of the twenty-first century, the etiology of health risks facing young people— and the adults they will become—are most often social or behavioral. The Division of Adolescent and School Health (DASH) of the Centers for Disease Control and Prevention (CDC) documents that six health-risk behaviors account for nearly two-thirds of the morbidity and mortality in adolescents. These behaviors are tobacco use; unhealthful dietary behaviors; inadequate physical activity; alcohol and other drug use; sexual behaviors that may result in HIV infection, other sexually transmitted diseases, or unintended pregnancy; and behaviors that may result in intentional injuries (i.e., violence and suicide) and unintentional injuries (e.g., motor vehicle crashes).

The leading causes of death among adults— including cardiovascular disease, cancer, and diabetes—are closely linked to these health-risk behaviors. In addition, these behaviors tend to co-occur, they tend to be established in youth, and they are preventable. Children and adolescents need to learn, and to practice, making health-enhancing choices before health-damaging behaviors are initiated or become ingrained.

CDC's Youth Risk Behavior Surveillance System provides reliable national data on the prevalence of specified behaviors. Most states, and some large cities, also conduct the Youth Risk Behavior Survey. Results from these state and city surveys, and other available state and local data from education and health agencies, can be used to plan school health program activities.

2. A foundation of support for every child and adolescent. Whether a student engages in health-debilitating or health-enhancing behaviors depends on the interplay of assets and deficits in the influential support systems surrounding the student, including friends, peers, family, community, and schools. Three protective factors have been found to frequently help young people overcome stress and adversity to become healthy competent adults with a sense of purpose: (1) caring and supportive relationships, (2) high expectations for success, and (3) active participation in school and community activities. For example, the ongoing National Longitudinal Study of Adolescent Health has found that students who feel "connected" to schools are more likely to adopt health-enhancing behaviors (respectful and caring teachers are among the factors related to students feeling connected). Applying a "positive youth development" approach, schools should aim to develop a full range of "life competencies" among students—not only academic and vocational competencies but also healthful living skills, personal and social skills, ethics, and citizenship.

3. A complete set of program components. Many national organizations and membership associations, as well as CDC's DASH, promote a school health program model consisting of eight mutually reinforcing components that communities can shape to fit their needs and circumstances. These eight basic components are health education; school health services; a healthy school environment; physical education; school nutrition services; counseling, psychological, and social services; health-promotion programs for staff; and family and community involvement.

Health education consists of a planned, sequential curriculum taught daily in every grade (prekindergarten through twelve) that addresses the physical, mental, emotional, social, and spiritual dimensions of health and is designed to motivate and help students maintain and improve their health, prevent disease, and avoid health-related risk behaviors. A quality curriculum allows students to develop and demonstrate increasingly sophisticated healthrelated knowledge, attitudes, skills, and practices while addressing a variety of topics, including personal health, family health, community health, consumer health, environmental health, sexuality education, mental and emotional health, injury prevention and safety, nutrition, prevention and control of disease, and substance use and abuse. The National Health Education Standards, jointly developed in 1995 by APHA, the American Cancer Society (ACS), the American School Health Association (ASHA), the American Association for Health Education (AAHE), and the Society of State Directors of Health, Physical Education and Recreation (SSDHPER), provide useful guidance for curriculum development, instruction, and assessment of student performance. Well-implemented health education has been shown to improve the adoption of health enhancing behaviors and school achievement.

School health services are provided for students and are designed to appraise, protect, and promote health. These services are designed to ensure access and/or referral to primary health care services, foster appropriate use of primary health care services, prevent and control communicable diseases and other health problems, provide emergency care for illness or injury, promote and provide optimum sanitary conditions for safe school facilities and environments, and provide educational and counseling opportunities for the promotion and maintenance of individual, family, and community health. Services should be provided by qualified professionals such as physicians, nurses, dentists, and other allied health personnel. Health services via school-based clinics that are linked with enhanced academic services have been associated with reduced absenteeism, improved academic achievement, and improved health status.

Although only 53 percent of states required schools to offer school nurse services in 1994, nearly every school had provisions for administering first aid (99%), administering medications (97%), and conducting vision, hearing, and height/weight screenings (89%). However, fewer schools provided less traditional services, such as mental health counseling (56%) or conducting health-risk appraisals to help students determine their lifestyle practices (36%). School-based or school-linked health centers are becoming more common, however, and many of these centers offer a wide range of physical and mental health services. A national survey identified a total of 1,157 school-based health centers that provided in-school care to children during the 1997–1998 school year. Thirty-seven percent were housed in high schools, 16 percent in middle schools, 34 percent in elementary schools, and the remainder were off-site.

A *healthy school environment* attends to the physical and aesthetic surroundings and to the school's psychosocial climate and culture, thus protecting the health and safety of students and staff and promoting health-enhancing behaviors. Physical environmental concerns include indoor and outdoor safety hazards, biological or chemical agents that might be detrimental to health, air temperature and quality, water quality, sanitation, precautions for infection control, lighting, noise levels, and access for persons with disabling conditions. The psychological environment includes the interrelated physical, emotional, and social conditions that affect the wellbeing and productivity of students and staff, including physical and psychological safety, positive interpersonal relationships, recognition of needs and successes of the individual, and support for building self-esteem in students and staff. In considering the school environment, there are things that both large and small schools can implement. In fact, a large body of research in the affective and social realms overwhelmingly affirms the superiority of schools with small enrollments.

Bullying and harassment can have damaging effects on students' health and well-being. Those who manage school environments also need to actively encourage health-enhancing behaviors by assuring that nutritious foods are available as an affordable option whenever food is served or sold, providing convenient and appealing opportunities for physical activity, enforcing tobacco-free policies, and conducting educational campaigns to promote positive health behaviors.

Physical education is a planned, sequential curriculum and program of physical activity taught daily in every grade. Cognitive content and learning experiences should be provided in a variety of activity areas, such as basic movement skills; physical fitness, rhythms and dance; games; team, dual, and individual sports; tumbling and gymnastics; and aquatics. Quality physical education should promote lifetime activities and sports that students can enjoy and pursue throughout their lives. The National Standards for Physical Education developed by the National Association for Sport and Physical Education (NASPE) provide useful guidance for curriculum development, instruction, and appropriate assessment of student performance.

Physical education needs to be taught by qualified teachers. Studies have found that well-prepared physical education specialists teach longer and higher-quality lessons than those not professionally prepared in physical education. Elementary schools also need to provide daily periods of supervised recess, and middle schools and high schools should provide multiple opportunities for all students to voluntarily participate in intramural programs, sports and recreation clubs, and interscholastic athletics. Links with community-based sports, recreation, and fitness programs should also be sought and fostered.

Studies among adolescents have demonstrated that physical activity is consistently related to higher self-esteem and to reduced levels of anxiety and stress. Conversely, low levels of physical activity are associated with high-risk behaviors such as cigarette smoking and marijuana use. Studies have found that students who participate in extracurricular programs tend to have higher grade point averages, better attendance records, lower dropout rates, and fewer discipline problems than students generally.

School nutrition services promote the health and education of students through access to a variety of nutritious and appealing meals, nutrition education, and a school environment that encourages students to make healthy food choices. The school food-service program can provide opportunities for students to practice healthful eating on a daily basis—more than half of the young people in the United States get one of their three major meals from school food programs, and 10 percent get two of their three main meals at school.

Sound school food-service programs reflect the current U.S. Dietary Guidelines for Americans (DGA) and other quality criteria necessary to achieve nutrition integrity. These programs provide pleasant eating areas for students and staff with adequate time for unhurried eating, offer opportunities for students to experience learning laboratories for classroom nutrition and health education, and serve as resources for linkages with nutrition-related community services.

Services should be provided by qualified child nutrition professionals. Studies have shown that chronically undernourished children attain lower scores on standardized achievement tests, especially tests of language ability. These children are also more likely than other children to become sick, to miss school, and to fall behind in class. Undernourished students are often irritable, have difficulty concentrating, and have low energy. School nutrition services have been associated with increases in learning, and studies of low-income elementary school students have shown that students who participate in the federal School Breakfast Program have greater improvements in standardized test scores and math grades, and reduced rates of absence, tardiness, and psychosocial problems, than children who qualify for the program but do not participate.

Counseling, psychological, and social services provide broad-based individual and group assessments, interventions, and referrals that attend to the mental, emotional, and social health of students in a range of school and community settings. Organizational assessment and consultation skills of counselors and psychologists contribute to the overall health of students, and to the health of the school environment. Services are provided by professionals, such as certified school counselors, psychologists, and social workers.

One in five visits to school-based health centers is related to mental health. In a 1999 report on mental health, the U.S. Surgeon General estimated that 21 percent of U.S. children ages nine through seventeen have a diagnosable mental or addictive disorder, yet studies indicate that approximately 70 percent of children and adolescents in need of treatment do not receive mental health services. Of those young people who do receive mental health services, about 70 percent receive services offered in school settings, compared to 40 percent using mental health specialists and 11 percent using the health sector (a young person might access more than one resource).

The report also acknowledges that private and public health insurance coverage for such services is often lacking. Schools can make efforts to enter into collaborative relationships with other service providers for help with the resource burden.

Some of the burdens students face include inadequate basic resources, such as food, clothing, housing; and a sense of security at home, at school, and in the neighborhood. Psychosocial problems include difficult relationships at home and at school; emotional upset; language problems; sexual, emotional, or physical abuse; substance abuse; delinquent or gang-related behavior; and psychopathology. Additional stressful situations, such as being unable to meet the demands made at school or at home, inadequate support systems, and hostile conditions at school or in the neighborhood, have also been identified. In addition, crises and emergencies such as the death of a classmate or relative, a shooting at school, or natural disasters such as earthquakes, floods, or tornadoes are becoming commonplace. Life transitions, such as the onset of puberty, entering a new school, and changes in life circumstances (moving, immigration, loss of a parent through divorce or death) also affect the health of the student.

Health promotion programs for staff are designed to promote the physical, emotional, and mental health of school employees through health assessments, health education, health-related fitness activities, and employee assistance programs. Evaluations have found that participation in staff health-promotion programs can increase morale, improve absenteeism rates, increase participation in vigorous activity, improve physical fitness, facilitate weight loss, lower blood pressure, and improve stress-management skills. Teachers who become interested in their own health have been found to take a greater interest in the health of their students and become more effective teachers of health.

Staff can influence student behaviors by being powerful role models for healthy lifestyles. Private industry has found that staff health-promotion programs can improve productivity, improve morale, reduce health insurance costs, and are usually well worth the cost: More than 81 percent of U.S. businesses with fifty or more employees have some form of health promotion program.

Family and community involvement promotes an integrated school, family, and community approach that establishes a dynamic partnership to enhance the health and well-being of students. Involving family members and the community has been linked with improvements in students' health knowledge and behaviors. Numerous studies link parent/family involvement to their children's achievement, academic standing, and decreased school failure and grade repetition, and a number of studies have shown that involving families enhances the effects of school health-promotion efforts. School health programs should be designed to actively solicit family involvement and assist and support families to effectively reinforce children's healthful habits and behaviors. The National PTA has developed the National Standards for Parent/Family Involvement Programs, which provide PTAs, schools, and communities with voluntary guidelines and quality indicators for effective parent/family involvement programs.

Schools should be encouraged to engage community resources and services to respond more effectively to the health-related needs of students. State and local government agencies, private businesses, youth-serving organizations, and other organizations in the community can be valuable additions to school health programs by serving as resources for student learning, offering opportunities for student service, coordinating community health-promotion efforts with school programs, raising funds to support specific activities, and providing expert advice and assistance to school health program planners. The *full-service school* model involves locating a variety of family and youth services at school to improve families' access to the services. New Jersey and Kentucky have pioneered statewide programs of linking schools with community agencies. Providing these kinds of services does not necessarily require an increase in the school's budget: typically, many of these services already exist, but in a fragmented manner that some families find difficult to use.

4. Multiple interventions. As the Carnegie Corporation has stated, "Given the complex influences on adolescents, the essential requirements for ensuring healthy development must be met through the joint efforts of a set of pivotal institutions that powerfully shape adolescents' experiences. These pivotal institutions must begin with the family and include schools, health care institutions, a wide array of neighborhood and community organizations, and the mass media" (p. 23).

Because the health problems facing students have a multifactorial etiology, a single health message delivered by one teacher during the year, particularly when there are so many competing messages from friends, family, and the media, is rarely sufficient to promote the adoption or maintenance of health-enhancing behaviors. Consistent and repeated messages delivered by several teachers, school staff, peers, and families are more effective.

A health promotion model that uses a variety of interventions in addition to instruction to promote the adoption of health-enhancing behaviors among children and youth is needed. Interventions that have been successful include policy mandates, environmental changes, direct interventions (screening, referral, and treatment), social support/role modeling, and media. The number of interventions necessary to address any one problem is unknown. Larry Green and Marshall Kreuter suggest that a minimum of three interventions be employed for each behavior that is targeted, and John Elder states that "true progress will be realized by using multicomponent packages which include multilevel and multiple-channel generalization efforts and appropriate evaluation criteria" (p. 31).

5. Program coordination and oversight. The value of a coordinated approach has been noted by numerous individuals. A variety of options have been proposed to implement and manage a coordinated school health program, including school health coordinators, school health advisory councils, interdisciplinary work committees and work teams, and interagency coordinating councils or networks. Health-program coordination can help reduce ambiguity about responsibilities and tasks, which often impedes program implementation, and can help ensure that the various program components are mutually reinforcing each other's efforts. School health advisory councils can involve a variety of health and education professionals, parents, and other community members who can mobilize community resources, represent the diverse interests within the community, provide school personnel and families with a sense of program ownership, and provide guidance to the school board. A 1994 national survey found that 33 percent of school districts and 19 percent of secondary schools had such councils.

Others advise that a more formalized structure, such as a coordinating council, is inherently more effective than an advisory group, as committed leadership has been found to be critical to the success of school-linked comprehensive services. In 2000 the American Cancer Society began conducting a national leadership program designed to train individuals to become school health coordinators, including the development of school health councils, and to replicate the training program in their respective regions of the nation. Responsibilities of a coordinating council can include assessing needs and resources, establishing program goals, developing a community plan, coordinating school programs with community programs and resources, providing leadership and assistance for local schools, and assuring continuous improvement through evaluation quality assurance mechanisms. The Institute of Medicine (IOM) recommends that a school health coordinator and a coordinating council are an integral part of the infrastructure needed to support a coordinated school health program.

6. Systematic program planning. Every organizational group that is part of the school health program (e.g., school work teams, school health committee, school-community coordinating council) needs to use a programming process to assure continuous improvements in programming. Included in the process is the need to involve all stakeholders, define the problem from a local perspective (a needs assessment), set realistic goals and objectives, identify priority strategies to be used in the action plan to attain goals and objectives, implement the plan, evaluate the results, and use the results to start the process over again. DASH has produced the *School Health Index for Physical Activity and Healthy Eating: A Self-Assessment and Planning Guide*, which schools can use to improve school health programs. Differences in health status among distinct regions and groups argue for the need to base policies on local data that might be available from public health departments. Planners should conduct needs assessments with community input; adapt activities to the interests and preferences of different ethnic, religious, and social groups; and foster effective school-community collaboration.

7. Ongoing staff development. To assure effective programming, there is a need for staff development programs. Many teachers received their training at a time when the problems and issues facing students were much different. Staff development increasingly is approached as the day-to-day fostering of continuous improvement in one's professional practice, and not as a workshop that occurs in isolation. Phyllis Gingiss has identified five concepts that those planning staff development need to consider:

- Teachers respond to innovations in developmental stages.

- A multiphase approach to staff development is necessary to assist teachers during each stage.

- Staff development requires opportunities for teacher collaboration.

- Approaches to staff development must fit the stage of teacher development.

- The organizational context for staff development is critical to its success.

Critical organizational and environmental factors that must be addressed before providing staff development programs include a positive school climate, administrative support, and supportive policies. Those schools that encourage teacher experimentation enhance the willingness of teachers to try new methods and programs. A meta-analysis of staff-development training revealed that the utilization of theory, demonstration, practice, and feedback produced meaningful differences in the faculty's acquisition attitudes, knowledge, and skills. However, for meaningful differences to occur in the transfer of training to the practitioners' practice in the classroom, peer coaching had to be added to the above mix of effective interventions. Without peer follow-up and peer coaching after training, transfer effects are negative to minimal.

The National Council for Accreditation of Teacher Education (NCATE) has developed various sets of standards for teacher preparation programs, in association with numerous professional organizations, including the American Association for Health Education (AAHE), the National Association for Sport and Physical Education (NASPE), and the National Association of School Psychologists (NASP). Many states and professional preparation programs have adopted or adapted the NCATE standards.

To ensure that students are taught by well-prepared and well-qualified teachers, health education and physical education professional associations suggest that state licensure agencies should: (1) establish separate teaching licenses for health education and physical education; (2) offer licenses for different levels (e.g., preschool and early elementary school, elementary school, middle school, high school); (3) require that all generalist teachers (preschool, elementary school, middle school) pass

courses or demonstrate their competence at applying the skills required to effectively teach health education; and (4) allow schools to assign teachers to courses they are not properly certified to teach only when a licensed teacher cannot be found and only on a temporary basis with the stipulation that such teachers receive the necessary training if they are to continue teaching the class.

8. Active student involvement. Peer instruction has proven effective in disseminating knowledge and changing behaviors. Students are more likely to turn to peers for advice, and change is more likely to occur, if someone similar to them recommends the change. In addition, peer instruction has been effective in improving decision-making and problem-solving skills, which may be prerequisites for implementing behavior change. Role modeling and peer support systems represent additional benefits of peer-education programs.

Peer involvement may occur in a variety of ways, such as peer counseling, peer instruction, peer theater, youth service, and cross-age mentoring. The elements of a successful peer program include positive interdependence, face-to-face interaction, individual accountability, training in social skills, time for group processing, heterogeneous composition, having each child be a helper, adequate duration, and involvement of participants in program implementation.

Conclusion

Because the health of students is inextricably linked to educational achievement, it is critical that schools promote health. Schools can provide the nurture and support needed to facilitate the adoption of health-enhancing behaviors. This helps assure that the educational gains achieved by a student will be maximized by a long and healthy life as an adult. A comprehensive, well-coordinated school health program can promote the optimal physical, emotional, social, and educational development of students.

See also: ELEMENTARY EDUCATION, *subentry on* CURRENT TRENDS; GUIDANCE AND COUNSELING, SCHOOL; HEALTH SERVICES, *subentry on* SCHOOL; PHYSICAL EDUCATION; SECONDARY EDUCATION, *subentry on* CURRENT TRENDS; RISK BEHAVIORS.

BIBLIOGRAPHY

ADELMAN, HAROLD. 1998. "School Counseling, Psychological, and Social Services." In *Health Is Ac-*

ademic: A Guide to Coordinated School Health Programs, ed. Eva Marx and Susan F. Wooley. New York: Teachers College Press.

ALLEGRANTE, JOHN P. 1988. "School-Site Health Promotion for Staff." In *Health Is Academic: A Guide to Coordinated School Health Programs,* ed. Eva Marx and Susan F. Wooley. New York: Teachers College Press.

ALLENSWORTH, DIANE D. 1987. "Building Community Support for Quality School Health Programs." *Health Education* 18(5):32–38.

ALLENSWORTH, DIANE D. 1997. "Improving the Health of Youth Through a Coordinated School Health Programme." *Health Promotion and Education* 4:42–47.

ALLENSWORTH, DIANE D., et al., eds. 1994. *Healthy Students 2000: An Agenda for Continuous Improvement in America's Schools.* Kent, OH: American School Health Association.

ALLENSWORTH, DIANE D., et al., eds. 1997. *Schools and Health: Our Nation's Investment.* Washington, DC: National Academy Press.

AMERICAN ASSOCIATION OF HEALTH EDUCATION. 1995. "NCATE Program Standards: Initial Programs in Health Education." Reston, VA: American Association of Health Education.

BERNARD, BONNIE. 1989. *Peer Programs: The Loadstone in Prevention. Prevention Plus II.* Rockville, MD: Office of Substance Abuse Prevention.

BERNARD, BONNIE. 1990. *The Case for Peers.* Portland, OR: Northwest Regional Educational Laboratory.

BLAIR, STEVE N., et al. 1984. "Health Promotion for Educators: Effect on Health Behaviors, Satisfaction, and General Well-Being." *American Journal of Public Health* 74:147–149.

BOGDEN, JIM. 2000. *Fit, Healthy, and Ready to Learn: A School Health Policy Guide.* Alexandria, VA: National Association of State Boards of Education.

BROOK, JUDITH; NOMURA, C.; and COHEN, P. 1990. "A Network of Influences on Adolescent Drug Involvement: Neighborhood, Social, Peer, and Family." *Genetic, Social, and General Psychology Monographs* 115:125–145.

BURGHARDT, JOHN, et al. 1993. *The School Nutrition Dietary Assessment Study.* Alexandria, VA: U.S. Department of Agriculture.

CARNEGIE CORPORATION OF NEW YORK. 1995. *Great Transitions: Preparing Adolescents for a New*

Century. New York: Carnegie Corporation of New York.

CENTERS FOR DISEASE CONTROL AND PREVENTION. 1997. "Guidelines for School and Community Programs to Promote Lifelong Physical Activity Among Young People." *Morbidity and Mortality Weekly Report.* 46:RR-6.

COLEMAN, JAMES. 1987. "Families and Schools." *Educational Researcher* 16(6):32–38.

COLLINS, JANET, et al. 1995. "School Health Education." *Journal of School Health* 65(8):306–307.

CONNELL, DAVID B.; TURNER, RALPH R.; and MASON, ELAINE F. 1985. "Summary of Findings of the School Health Education Evaluation: Health Promotion Effectiveness, Implementation, and Costs." *Journal of School Health* 55(8):316–384.

DORMAN, STEVE M., and FOULK, DAVID F. 1987. "Characteristics of School Health Education Advisory Councils." *Journal of School Health* 57(8):337–339.

DWYER, JOHANNA T. 1995. "The School Nutrition Dietary Assessment Study." *American Journal of Clinical Nutrition.* 161(supp.):173S–177S.

EDUCATION DEVELOPMENT CENTER. 1994. *Educating for Health: A Guide to Implementing a Comprehensive Approach to School Health Education.* Newton, MA: Education Development Center.

ELDER, JOHN P. 1991. "From Experimentation to Dissemination: Strategies for Maximizing the Impact and Speed of School Health Education." In *Youth Health Promotion: From Theory to Practice in School and Community,* ed. Don Nutbeam et al. London: Forbes Publication Ltd.

FELDMAN, RONALD A.; STIFFMAN, ARLENE; and JUNG, KENNETH, eds. 1987. *Children at Risk: In the Web of Parental Mental Illness.* New Brunswick, NJ: Rutgers University Press.

GINGISS, PHYLLIS L. 1992. "Enhancing Program Implementation and Maintenance through a Multi Phase Approach to Peer-Based Development." *Journal of School Health* 62(5):162–166.

GREEN, LARRY, and KREUTER, MARSH W. 1991. *Health Promotion Planning: An Educational and Environmental Approach.* Toronto: Mayfield Publishing.

HAWKINS, J. DAVID; CATALANO, RICHARD F.; KOSTERMAN, RICK; ABBOT, ROBERT; and HILL,

KARL G. 1999. "Preventing Adolescent Health-Risk Behaviors by Strengthening Protection During Childhood." *Archives of Pediatric Adolescent Medicine* 153:226–234.

JASON, LEONARD A., et al. 1987. "Toward a Multidisciplinary Approach to Prevention." In *Prevention: Toward a Multidisciplinary Approach,* ed. Leonard A. Jason. New York: Haworth Press.

KANE, WILLIAM M. 1994. "Planning for a Comprehensive School Health Program." In *The Comprehensive School Health Challenge,* ed. Peter Cortese and Kathleen Middleton. Santa Cruz, CA: Education, Training, and Research Associates.

KERR, DIANE L.; ALLENSWORTH, DIANE D.; and GAYLE, JACOB A. 1991. *School-Based HIV Prevention: A Multidisciplinary Approach.* Kent, OH: American School Health Association.

KILLIP, D. C.; LOVICK, SHARON R.; GOLDMAN L.; and ALLENSWORTH, DIANE D. 1987. "Integrated School and Community Programs." *Journal of School Health* 57(10):437–444.

KOLBE, LLOYD J. 1991. "An Epidemiological Surveillance System to Monitor the Prevalence of Youth Behaviors That Most Affect Health." *Health Education* 21(3):24–30.

KOLBE, LLOYD J.; COLLINS, JANET; and CORTESE, PETER. 1997. "Building the Capacity of Schools to Improve the Health of the Nation: A Call for Assistance from Psychologists." *American Psychologist* 52(3):1–10.

LEAVY SMALL, MEG, et al. 1995. "School Health Services." *Journal of School Health* 65(8):320.

MARSHALL, RAY, and TUCKER, MARCH. 1992. *Thinking for a Living: Work Skills and the Future of the American Economy.* New York. Basic Books.

MARX, EVA, and WOOLEY, SUSAN, eds. 1998. *Health Is Academic: A Guide to Coordinated School Health Programs.* New York: Teacher's College Press.

MARZANO, ROBERT, et al. 1999. *What Americans Believe Students Should Know: A Survey of U.S. Adults.* Aurora, CO: Mid-Continent Regional Educational Laboratory.

MELAVILLE, ATELIA I., and BLANK, MARTIN J. 1991. *What It Takes: Structuring Interagency Partnerships to Connect Children and Families with Comprehensive Services.* Washington, DC: Education and Human Services Consortium.

MEYERS, ALAN F., et al. 1989. "School Breakfast Program and School Performance." *American Journal of Diseases of Children* 143:1234–1239.

MEYERS, A.; SAMPSON, AMY E.; and WEITZMAN, MICHAEL. 1991. "Nutrition and Academic Performance in School Children." *Clinics in Applied Nutrition* 1(2):13–25.

MURPHY, J. MICHAEL, et al. 1998. "The Relationship of School Breakfast to Psychosocial and Academic Functioning." *Archives of Pediatric and Adolescent Medicine* 152:899–907.

MYRICK, ROBERT D., and BOWMAN, ROBERT P. 1983. "Peer Helpers and the Learning Process." *Elementary School Guidance and Counseling* 18(2):111–117.

NATIONAL ASSOCIATION OF STATE BOARDS OF EDUCATION. 1999. *The Future Is Now: Addressing Social Issues in Schools of the 21st Century.* Alexandria, VA: National Association of State Boards of Education.

NATIONAL CENTER FOR EDUCATION STATISTICS. 1996. "Parents' Reports of School Practices to Involve Families." In *Statistics in Brief.* Washington, DC: National Center for Education Statistics.

OFFICE OF ANALYSIS, NUTRITION, AND EVALUATION, U.S. DEPARTMENT OF AGRICULTURE. 2000. *School Nutrition Dietary Assessment Study II: Summary of Findings.* Alexandria, VA: U.S. Department of Agriculture Food and Nutrition Service.

PATE, RUSSELL, et al. 1996. "Associations Between Physical Activity and Other Health Behaviors in a Representative Sample of U.S. Adolescents." *American Journal of Public Health* 86:1577–1581.

PENFIELD, A. R., and SHANNON, T. A. 1991. *School Health: Helping Children Learn.* Alexandria VA: National School Boards Association.

PENTZ, MARY ANN. 1997. "The School-Community Interface in Comprehensive School Health Education." In *Schools and Health: Our Nation's Investment. Institute of Medicine,* ed. Diane Allensworth et al. Washington, DC: National Academy Press.

PITTMAN, KAREN, and CAHILL, MICHELLE. 1992. "Pushing the Boundaries of Education: The Implications of a Youth Development Approach to Education Policies, Structures, and Collaborations." In *Ensuring Student Success through Collaboration,* ed. Council of Chief State School Officers. Washington, DC: Council of Chief State School Officers.

POWELL, CHRISTINE A; WALKER, SUSAN P.; CHANG, SUSAN M; and GRANTHAM-MCGREGOR, SALLY M. 1998. "Nutrition and Education: A Randomized Trial of the Effects of Breakfast in Rural Primary School Children." *American Journal of Clinical Nutrition* 68(4):873–879.

RESNICK, MICHAEL, et al. 1997. "Protecting Adolescents from Harm: Findings from the National Longitudinal Study on Adolescent Health." *Journal of the American Medical Association* 278:823–832.

RESNICOW, KENNETH, and ALLENSWORTH, DIANE D. 1996. "Conducting a Comprehensive School Health Program." *Journal of School Health* 66(2):59–63.

ROGERS, EVERETT. 1973. *Communication Strategies for Family Planning.* New York: The Free Press.

TINDALL, JUDITH A., and GRAY, HAROLD DEAN. 1985. *Peer Counseling: In-Depth Look at Training Peer Helpers.* Muncie, IN: Accelerated Development Inc.

TOBLER, NANCY S. 1986. "Meta-Analysis of 143 Adolescent Drug Prevention Programs: Quantitative Outcome Results of Program Participants Compared to a Control or Comparison Group." *Journal of Drug Issues* 16:(4).

TYSON, HARRIET. 1999. "A Load off the Teachers' Backs: Coordinated School Health Programs." Kappan Special Report. *Phi Delta Kappan* January 1999.

U.S. GENERAL ACCOUNTING OFFICE. 1993. *School-Linked Human Services: A Comprehensive Strategy for Aiding Students at Risk for School Failure.* Washington, DC: U.S. General Accounting Office.

VINCENT, MURRAY L.; CLEARIE, A. F.; and SCHLUCHTER, M. D. 1989. "Reducing Adolescent Pregnancy through School and Community-Based Education." *Journal of the American Medical Association.* 18:304–321.

WOLFORD-SYMONS, CINDY, et al. 1997. "Bridging Student Health Risks and Academic Achievement through Comprehensive School Health Programs." *Journal of School Health* 67(6):220–227.

ZIMMERLI, WILLIAM H. 1981. "Organizing for School Health Education at the Local Level." *Health Education Quarterly* (8):39–42.

INTERNET RESOURCES

AMERICAN CANCER SOCIETY. 1995. *Health for Success: The National Health Education Standards, 1995.* <www.cancer.org>.

AMERICAN EDUCATION RESEARCH ASSOCIATION (AERA) and U.S. DEPARTMENT OF EDUCATION. 1995. *School-Linked Comprehensive Services for Children and Families: What We Know and What We Need to Know.* <www.ed.gov/pubs/Compre/index.html>.

CENTERS FOR DISEASE CONTROL AND PREVENTION, DIVISION OF ADOLESCENT AND SCHOOL HEALTH. 2000. "Assessing Health Risk Behaviors Among Young People: The Youth Risk Behavior Surveillance System At-a-Glance. <www.cdc.gov/nccdphp/dash/yrbs/yrbsaag.htm>.

THE ROBERT WOOD JOHNSON FOUNDATION. 1998. *1998 National Survey of State School-Based Health Centers Initiatives.* <www.healthinschools.org>.

U.S. DEPARTMENT OF HEALTH AND HUMAN SERVICES. 1999. *Mental Health: A Report of the Surgeon General.* <www.surgeongeneral.gov/library/mentalhealth/home>.

LARRY OLSEN
DIANE ALLENSWORTH

HEALTH SERVICES

SCHOOL
Kerry Redican
Charles Baffi
COLLEGES AND UNIVERSITIES
Molly Black Duesterhaus

SCHOOL

Provision of public school health services in the United States has been sporadic, reflecting the tenor of the times, and influenced by pressure groups, vested interests, and resistance to change by those in administrative positions.

The initial justification for provision of school-based health services was primarily to control communicable diseases in order to cut down on school absenteeism. At the turn of the twentieth century, physicians were appointed as public school health officers. The first school nurse was employed by the New York City Board of Education in 1902, for the express purpose of controlling communicable diseases, particularly infectious skin diseases. Even though the number of physicians who were employed by schools outnumbered the number of nurses employed by schools by approximately three to one, school nurses were the main providers of school health services. Because of prevailing social mores, hygiene instruction in the late 1800s and early 1900s centered on a physiological and anatomical study of the negative effects of alcohol, tea, coffee, and tobacco.

Administrative responsibility for health services was often assigned to a specifically established department within the school, which was often under the direction of a local physician who was accountable to a school superintendent. In other instances, the responsibility for this service was assumed by a community health agency under the direction of a local health officer. These remained accepted practices even into the twenty-first century.

As new scientific knowledge emerged, new movements for improved personal and community health became popular. Addressing health problems of children and youth required a multidimensional approach. School health services only focused on medical related services, not environment or education. It became clear that the school needed to be concerned about not only school health services but also about the school environment and health education. Further, school health services, provision of a healthful school environment, and health education needed to function in a coordinated context in order to be effective. This set the foundation for the development of the school health program.

The original school health program model consisted of school health services, healthful school living, and health education. The goal of the school health program was to provide opportunities for every child to reach their full potential as a student as well as a contributing member of society. The major objective of the school health program was the promotion of physical, mental, social, and emotional well being. This model prevailed for years.

School health services as a part of the overall school health program provided health and medical services to students. These services tended to be one of three types: basic, expanded, or comprehensive. Basic health services include such things as immunizations, hearing and vision screenings, scoliosis screening, sports physicals, health counseling, and nutritional screenings. Expanded health services included health promotion/disease prevention, mental health counseling, substance abuse counseling, family life/sex education, and care of special needs children. Finally, comprehensive health included reproductive health care, primary care, chronic illness management, and prenatal care.

CDC Model

The services, environment, instruction focused model of the school health program worked well but still was not inclusive or comprehensive enough to meet the needs and interests of students. A more comprehensive model was needed. The concept of the Centers for Disease Control and Prevention (CDC) comprehensive school health programs model was first proposed in a landmark work published by Diane Allensworth and Lloyd Kolbe in 1987. The model employed the use of eight components. These include the following:

1. Health education: classroom instruction addressing physical, mental, and social dimensions of health; developing health knowledge, attitudes, and skills; and tailored to each age level. Designed to motivate and assist students in maintaining and improving their health, prevent disease, and reduce the number of health-related problem behaviors they exhibit.

2. Physical education: planned, sequential instruction that promotes lifelong physical activity. Designed to develop basic movement skills, sports skills, and physical fitness as well as to enhance mental, social, and emotional abilities.

3. School health services: preventive services, education, emergency care, referral, and management of acute and chronic health conditions. Designed to promote the health of students, identify and prevent health problems and injuries, and ensure care for students.

4. School nutrition services: integration of nutritious, affordable, and appealing meals; nutrition education; and an environment that

promotes healthy eating behaviors for all children. Designed to maximize each child's education and health potential for a lifetime.

5. School counseling, psychological, and social services: activities that focus on cognitive, emotional, behavioral, and social needs of individuals, groups, and families. Designed to prevent and address problems, facilitate positive learning and healthy behavior, and enhance healthy development.

6. Healthy school environment: the physical, social, and emotional climate of the school. Designed to provide a safe physical plant, as well as a healthy and supportive environment that fosters learning.

7. School-site health promotion for staff: assessment, education, and fitness activities for school faculty and staff. Designed to maintain and improve the health and well-being of school staff, who serve as role models for students.

8. Family and community involvement in school health: partnerships among schools, families, community groups, and individuals. Designed to share and maximize resources and expertise in addressing the healthy development of children, youth, and their families.

Components to School Health Services

Every current comprehensive approach to school health includes at least the eight components of the CDC model. The School Health Services component is generally structured around preventive services, education, referral, emergency care, and management of acute and chronic conditions.

Preventive services. Activities typically included in preventive services are educating teachers on the signs and symptoms of health problems of students and health screenings. Teachers are in a unique position to observe health problems among students. They have an advantage in that they can compare students and notice differences that might indicate a potential health problem. Even parents do not have this strategic advantage. It requires that teachers be trained to identify health related issues that may be noticeable during their daily observations of students. This training is often included in a pre-professional course or through in-service instruction offered by the school or school district. The goal of teacher observation is not diagnosis but referral.

Preventive services also include health screenings of students. The most common health screenings conducted in schools include vision, hearing, growth and development, blood pressure, cholesterol, and dental health screenings. Often the school will establish a partnership with a local public health department. The health department's professional staff is responsible for conducting the screenings. The purpose of screening is not to diagnose but to identify a potential health problem and refer the student for a more complete evaluation.

Referral and follow-up represent the culmination of teacher observation and screening. The referral process is initiated in one of two ways: First, a teacher makes an observation that indicates a student might have a health problem, and refers the student to the school nurse or the person in the school responsible for health concerns. Second, if a student does not pass a particular health screening, the student is referred again to the school nurse or the person in the school responsible for health concerns. What follows is a series of conferences, such as teacher/nurse, nurse/parent, and student/nurse.

Emergency care. Unintentional injuries are the leading cause of death in children and youth ages one through twenty-one; for every childhood death caused by injury, there are approximately 34 hospitalizations, 1,000 emergency room visits, and many more visits to private physicians. Because of the magnitude of injuries to children and youth, and because many injuries occur in the school, it is important that schools as a part of health services address safety and emergency care.

Safety and emergency care is normally addressed in two ways: written policies including legal aspects and preparations for handling emergencies. All schools should have written policies, which reflect a sound philosophy of safety and emergency care and specific procedures for school personnel to follow in both prevention of accidents and the protocol in dealing with accidents and emergencies.

Management of acute and chronic conditions. School health services are concerned with both acute and chronic health conditions of students. Acute conditions are normally communicable diseases and chronic conditions are such things as diabetes, asthma, and juvenile arthritis.

It is extremely difficult if not impossible to prevent the spread of common communicable diseases in school settings. Such illnesses as colds and influenza will run their epidemiologic course. School health services must include policies on how to handle communicable diseases; in other words, when to allow students back in school or sending students home who are sick. Further, schools health services must have documentation that students are up-to-date on immunizations. Schools will typically partner with local public health departments to receive guidance in how to handle communicable disease in the school setting.

Education and universal precautions are two important pieces in the management of acute conditions. Spread of communicable disease can be prevented through sound health practices, even as simple as washing hands. Schools must educate both personnel and students on the importance of sound health practices.

At times, a student will have an injury, perhaps resulting in their bleeding or vomiting. Both blood and vomit, as well as other body fluids, can contain pathogens and disease can be transmitted. Blood can contain HIV and the viruses responsible for viral hepatitis. Following universal precautions will limit the likelihood of transmission of disease through exposure to body fluids. Universal precautions are those activities designed to deal with body fluids and include use of gloves, masks, and proper receptacles for placing materials used to clean up body fluids. School are required to have an exposure control plan and have materials readily available for use when dealing with body fluids.

Issues and Trends

Numerous health problems that were once largely family and community problems now impact the school. Violence, drug use, teen pregnancy, sexually transmitted diseases, and poverty all have tremendous implications for school health services, yet because of the political and economic environment, there is, in general, less funding for programs to deal with these issues. Further, the complexity of the health problems and issues makes citizens question what the exact role of the school is in trying to solve or manage problems that are a result of powerful cultural influences. There seem to be two major perspectives, both with political implications. One is that the role of the school is to teach basic skills, such as reading, writing, math, and history, and health-related issues are a family problem or at best a community problem. The opposite perspective is that the government and by extension the school should play

a major role with regard to student health problems and work closely with students in any way possible.

Perhaps the most controversial trend is the implementation of school-based health centers or clinics located in the school. School-based health centers were first established in the early 1970s. They were implemented as a response to health problems such as sexually transmitted diseases, unplanned teenage pregnancy, and substance abuse.

Funded by the federal government and private foundations, school-based health centers are located in forty-five states and the District of Columbia. As of 2000, approximately one-half of the health centers are located in high schools, one-quarter are located in elementary schools, and the remainder are located in other settings. The majority of the centers are located in poor urban and rural areas where coordinated medical and social services are lacking or where there are many uninsured children/parents, making access to services difficult.

Services provided by school-based health centers include but are not limited to primary care (diagnosis and treatment of simple illness), primary prevention (health education programs, vaccinations), and secondary prevention (early detection). These services range from diagnosing such maladies as colds, flu, and sexually transmitted diseases to substance abuse counseling. Services offered vary among communities and from community to community.

School-based health centers face an uncertain future primarily because they rely so heavily on external funding. As the nation grapples with the issue of providing access to health care for all Americans, school-based health centers need to be well positioned to meet the care and prevention needs of children and youth.

Given the political, cultural, and economic climate of the United States two future scenarios emerge. First, with the increasing emphasis on providing access to health care to all Americans it is possible that there will be a greater role for the school in providing health services to students, especially in medically underserved areas. Second, with the increasing shift to managed care it may prove more cost-effective for third-party payers to underwrite health services delivered in a school setting rather than in a community private sector setting.

See also: FAMILY AND CONSUMER SCIENCES EDUCATION; FULL-SERVICE SCHOOLS; GUIDANCE AND

COUNSELING, SCHOOL; HEALTH EDUCATION, SCHOOL; PHYSICAL EDUCATION; SCHOOL-LINKED SERVICES, *subentry on* TYPES OF SERVICES AND ORGANIZATIONAL FORMS; SEX EDUCATION.

BIBLIOGRAPHY

ALLENSWORTH, DIANE. 1994. "School Health Services: Issues and Challenges." In *The Comprehensive School Health Challenge,* ed. Peter Cortese and Kathleen Middleton. Santa Cruz, CA: ETR Associates.

ALLENSWORTH, DIANE, and KOLBE, LLOYD. 1987. "The Comprehensive School Health Program: Exploring an Expanded Concept." *Journal of School Health* 57(10):409–412.

NEWTON, JERRY; ADAMS, RICHARD; and MARCONTEL, MARILYN. 1997. *The New School Health Handbook,* 3rd edition. Paramus: Prentice-Hall.

SCHLITT, J. J. 1991. *Bring Health in School: Policy Implications for Southern States.* Washington, DC: Southern Center on Adolescent Pregnancy Prevention.

U.S. DEPARTMENT OF HEALTH AND HUMAN SERVICES. 1999. *School Health Programs: An Investment in Our Nation's Future.* Atlanta, GA: Centers for Disease Control and Prevention.

U.S. DEPARTMENT OF HEALTH AND HUMAN SERVICES. 2000. *Healthy People 2010.* Washington, DC: U.S. Department of Health and Human Services.

INTERNET RESOURCES

HURWITZ, NINA, and HURWITZ, SOL. 2000. "The Case for School-Based Health Centers." *American School Board Journal.* National School Boards Association website. <www.nsba.org>.

PORTER, MICHAEL, and KRAMER, MARK. 2000. "Determining a Policy Agenda to Sustain School-Based Health Centers." National Assembly on School-Based Health Care website. <www.nasbhc.org>.

KERRY REDICAN
CHARLES BAFFI

COLLEGES AND UNIVERSITIES

College health-service programs provide low-cost, primary medical care for students on college campuses. Kevin Patrick estimated in 1988 that 80 percent of America's more than fourteen million college students received primary health care from campus health programs. Just as modern medicine has changed, so too has the scope of services college health centers provide. Medical developments allow for most injuries and illnesses to be treated by ambulatory clinics, and this same trend is seen in most college health centers. These centers often provide care for acute illnesses and injuries on an outpatient basis, while also meeting the needs of students with continued and chronic illnesses and providing wellness education to the campus community.

In addition to meeting the basic and most common needs of the students they serve, campus health-service programs also act as referral agents for students to connect with medical providers, as needed, in the local community. College health services are continually evolving and changing in order to best provide treatment and education for the campuses they serve.

Staffing

College health-service staffs vary widely in the range and level of services they provide. Once directed mainly by full-time medical doctors, most college health centers are now lead by Licensed Nurse Practitioners (LPNs), Registered Nurses (RNs) or Physician Assistants (PAs). Some health centers continue to have full-time physicians on staff (particularly at larger universities and institutions with medical centers), while others maintain part-time relationships with local doctors to staff particular hours each week. Health centers with less comprehensive services (usually at smaller, private colleges) often act as a link to services in the immediate community.

Services

College health-service programs tend to have three primary areas of responsibility: physical, mental, and educational. Medical services range from basic care in the form of treatment for colds, viruses, and minor injuries at less comprehensive centers to thorough lab tests, X rays, specialists, and pharmacies at the most comprehensive centers. Many college health programs also provide counseling services. Some counseling services are limited to basic intervention and referral for long-term care, while others provide extensive and long-term psychotherapy.

The most common, and a primary focus of college health-service programs, is that of intervention and health, or wellness, education. Although all student health centers concern themselves with the immediate healing of ill students, most will also work to educate students about approaches to healthier lifestyles in order to prevent future illness or injury. Wellness themes exhibited on many college campuses are health and nutrition, stress management, eating disorder awareness, smoking cessation and prevention, time management, alcohol abuse prevention, strategies to avoid depression, and issues around sexually transmitted diseases and their prevention. Some colleges maintain twenty-four-hour care for students; however, most colleges maintain regular weekly hours during the academic year with a system for emergency assistance when needed.

Payment

Many college health centers are funded through fees students pay to the college or university and subsidized with institutional resources. Sometimes these fees are included within the tuition charges of a college or university, while other institutions may charge a separate student health fee in addition to the college tuition. Prepayment for student health services ensures that students have access to the treatment and services needed while at school. At many colleges, basic and most common services are offered to full-time students at little or no charge. Many college health centers will provide, as needed, over the counter medications free of charge; however, they will charge for, or send students to a pharmacy for, prescription medications. Students will usually incur charges for lab work, other diagnostic tests, and services provided by referrals made to outside physicians and specialists. Most colleges and universities require students to have and maintain health insurance. Although many students may continue on their parent's health insurance plans, other students may need to purchase individual health insurance, and can usually do so through programs offered at their college or university.

Requirements

Most, if not all, colleges and universities require that undergraduate students complete health history forms prior to their arrival on campus. This information assists health center staff to prepare for any special needs identified on the form and to have a recorded history in case information is needed to properly treat a student. In addition to the form, all students are required to have current immunizations per state law and institution policy. Documentation of these immunizations must be provided in order to attend the institution.

Confidentiality

Services provided by college health centers are deemed confidential. Health center staff work in partnership with students to get well, make good choices, and develop healthy living habits. The responsibility of informing parents falls to the student in most cases. Only when a condition warrants notification will health services staff break the confidence of the relationship, usually with the permission of the student unless there is concern about harm to self or others.

See also: DRUG AND ALCOHOL ABUSE, *subentry on* COLLEGE; PERSONAL AND PSYCHOLOGICAL COUNSELING AT COLLEGES AND UNIVERSITIES; PERSONAL AND PSYCHOLOGICAL PROBLEMS OF COLLEGE STUDENTS.

BIBLIOGRAPHY

Patrick, Kevin. 1988. "Student Health: Medical Care within Institutions of Higher Education." *Journal of the American Medical Association* 260:3301–3305.

INTERNET RESOURCE

American College Health Association. 2002. <www.acha.org>.

MOLLY BLACK DUESTERHAUS

HEARING IMPAIRMENT

SCHOOL PROGRAMS
Susan Dalebout
TEACHING METHODS
Elizabeth A. Martinez
Daniel P. Hallahan

SCHOOL PROGRAMS

Hearing loss occurs along a broad continuum ranging in degree from slight to profound. Individuals with severe and profound hearing loss generally are characterized as *deaf,* whereas individuals with lesser degrees of impairment, including those with unilateral hearing loss (i.e., involving only one ear), are characterized as *hard of hearing*. Childhood hearing loss of any type and degree, if unmanaged, is likely to have a negative impact on the development of spoken and receptive language, the ability to read and write, and academic achievement. For example, a 1998 study of 1,218 children with minimal hearing loss showed that 37 percent had failed a grade. Similarly, studies have shown that children with unilateral hearing loss are ten times more likely than normally hearing children to fail a grade. The vast majority (94–96%) of children with hearing loss are hard of hearing rather than deaf. For these children, speech may be *audible* (i.e., detectable) but not *intelligible* enough to allow them to hear one word as distinct from another.

There are approximately 50,000 school-age deaf children in the United States, a figure representing a dramatic decline since the early 1970s. An additional 5 million school-age children are permanently hard of hearing and at educational risk. An estimated 1.5 million more suffer from conductive, usually temporary, hearing loss. Inclusion of preschool children could put the total number of children with hearing loss close to 10 million.

Historical Overview

Historically, approaches to educating children who are deaf have been based on emotion and personal philosophy rather than positive outcome; in contrast, the education of children who are hard of hearing has largely been ignored. Educational practices in the United States can be linked directly to the teachings of European educators active during the eighteenth and nineteenth centuries. Of note, in 1770 French cleric Charles-Michel de l'Épée founded a school in which he emphasized the use of sign language and finger spelling (i.e., a *manual* approach). Around the same time, schools were established in England by members of the Braidwood family, who emphasized the use of spoken language and speechreading without sign language (i.e., an *oral* approach).

In the United States, the father of Alice Cogswell, who lost her hearing at an early age, commissioned Thomas Hopkins Gallaudet to travel to Europe and learn methods for teaching deaf children. Refused help by the Braidwoods, Gallaudet learned de l'Épée's manual method. In 1817 Gallaudet opened a school in the United States based on the manual approach (now the American School for the Deaf). Gallaudet's son became president of the first college for deaf students in the United States, now known as Gallaudet University.

Oralism took root years later when another young girl from a prominent family, Mabel Hubbard, lost her hearing. In 1867 her father helped establish an oral school. As an adult, Hubbard married Alexander Graham Bell, who became a passionate advocate for oralism. During the late nineteenth century, Bell and Gallaudet often engaged in debate about the merits of the oral and manual approaches. The debate would continue well into the twentieth century.

Education of and Services for Hearing-Impaired Children

Children in the United States who are deaf or hard of hearing are legally entitled to a free and appropriate education. Federal law requires a continuum of educational options, ranging from placement in a self-contained classroom with other children who are deaf to full-time placement in a regular education classroom with normally hearing peers. Most often, the placement involves a variation or a combination of the two extremes. An alternative placement is attendance at a residential school, in which the child can participate fully in the deaf culture.

Perhaps the most important educational decision is the communication method that will be used. The choice lies with the parents, and the best decision is specific to each child and family. Most children who are deaf use one or some combination of three communication modes: American Sign Language, a manual language that is distinctly different from English (i.e., a person does not sign and speak at the same time); a system of manually coded English (i.e., a signed version of English); or hearing and spoken language. A relatively smaller number of children use Cued Speech, a system in which hand gestures enhance speechreading.

Children with hearing loss require support services in order to benefit maximally from a free and appropriate education. For example, it is essential that they receive services from an audiologist, including management of their hearing aids, classroom listening devices, and listening environments. Poor listening conditions can render a hard of hearing child functionally deaf.

Trends and Research Findings

The education of children who are deaf will be revolutionized by two dramatic changes. First, legally mandated neonatal hearing-screening programs are changing the average age at identification from approximately three years to approximately three months. Research has shown that when appropriate hearing aids and early intervention are in place by six months of age, a child is likely to have age-normal language and learning milestones at kindergarten entry. In this light, the most important educational years are the child's very first years, when the family participates in parent–infant programming. Second, cochlear implants are being made available to increasingly younger children. These surgically implanted devices convert sound into electrical current, which then bypasses much of the hearing mechanism to stimulate surviving nerve elements directly. The coded electrical current creates sensations, which the brain, with considerable listening training, can learn to interpret as sound. Research suggests that children who use cochlear implants surpass children with similar degrees of hearing loss who use hearing aids in the areas of speech recognition, speech production, language content and form, and reading.

Children who benefit from early intervention and improved hearing technology, including cochlear implants, are likely to enter kindergarten ready for the educational mainstream. In the absence of additional disabilities, and with appropriate support services, it is possible that these children may never require special education placements and will choose to use sign language only if it is their cultural preference.

See also: HEARING IMPAIRMENT, *subentry on* TEACHING METHODS; SPECIAL EDUCATION, *subentries on* CURRENT TRENDS, HISTORY OF; SPEECH AND LANGUAGE IMPAIRMENT, EDUCATION OF INDIVIDUALS WITH.

BIBLIOGRAPHY

BESS, FRED H.; DODD-MURPHY, JEANNE; and PARKER, ROBERT A. 1998. "Children with Minimal Sensorineural Hearing Loss: Prevalence, Educational Performance, and Functional Status." *Ear and Hearing* 19(5):339–354.

BESS, FRED; KLEE, THOMAS; and CULBERTSON, JAN L. 1986. "Identification, Assessment, and Man-

agement of Children with Unilateral Sensorineural Hearing Loss." *Seminars in Hearing* 7(1):43–50.

ENGLISH, KRISTINA, and CHURCH, GERALD. 1999. "Unilateral Hearing Loss in Children: An Update for the 1990s." *Language, Speech, and Hearing Services in Schools* 30(1):26–31.

FLEXER, CAROL. 1999. *Facilitating Hearing and Listening in Young Children.* San Diego, CA: Singular.

MOELLER, MARY P. 2000. "Early Intervention and Language Outcomes in Children Who Are Deaf and Hard of Hearing." *Pediatrics* 106(3):1–9.

NATIONAL INSTITUTES OF HEALTH. 1993. *Early Identification of Hearing Impairment in Infants and Young Children: Program and Abstracts from the NIH Consensus Development Conference.* Bethesda, MD: National Institutes of Health.

NISKAR, AMANDA S.; KIESZAK, STEPHANIE M.; HOLMES, ALICE; ESTEBAN, EMILIO; RUBIN, CAROL; and BRODY, DEBRA. 1998. "Prevalence of Hearing Loss among Children Six to Nineteen Years of Age: The Third National Health and Nutrition Examination Survey." *Journal of the American Medical Association* 8:1071–1075.

SCHOW, RONALD L., and NERBONNE, MICHAEL A. 2002. *Introduction to Audiologic Rehabilitation,* 4th edition. Boston: Allyn and Bacon.

TYE-MURRAY, NANCY. 1998. *Foundations of Aural Rehabilitation.* San Diego, CA: Singular.

YOSHINAGA-ITANO, CHRISTINE; SEDLEY, ALLISON L.; COUTLER, DIANE A.; and MEHL, ALBERT L. 1998. "Language of Early and Later-Identified Children with Hearing Loss." *Pediatrics* 102:1168–1171.

SUSAN DALEBOUT

TEACHING METHODS

According to Lou Ann Walker, "the first real efforts to educate deaf people began around 1550 when Pedro Ponce de León, a monk from Spain, taught deaf children in a monastery in San Salvador" (p. 11). Seventy years later, Juan Pablo Bonet, a follower of Ponce de León, published the first book on the education of people who are deaf. In it he explained that he used a one-handed manual alphabet to build language. In 1700 Johann Ammons, a Swiss doctor, devised a method to teach speech and lipreading (now more accurately referred to as speechreading) to people who are deaf. In the mid-1700s, schools for deaf children were established in Scotland, Germany, and France. Teaching methods, according to Walker, focused, for the most part, on a combination of *oralism*—teaching students speech and speechreading—and *manualism*—teaching students a manual alphabet. Schools for the deaf did not reach the United States until 1817, when Thomas Hopkins Gallaudet, a divinity student, and Laurent Clerc, a deaf student of the National Institute of France, opened the American School for the Deaf (originally named the Connecticut Asylum for the Education and Instruction of Deaf and Dumb Persons) in Hartford, Connecticut. Many teachers trained at the American School, which focused on American Sign Language.

The controversy surrounding how to teach children with hearing impairment, sometimes referred to as the oralism-manualism debate, began centuries ago and continues into the twenty-first century. Opponents of oralism contend that denying children sign language is tantamount to denying them a language to communicate. However, children who can learn language orally are better prepared for a hearing world. Most educational programs at the turn of the twenty-first century involve a *total communication* approach—a blend of oral and manual techniques; however, some members of the deaf community contend that it is inadequate, and they prefer a bicultural-bilingual approach, whereby students learn about the history of deaf culture after learning American Sign Language and English. A controversial piece of this approach is the focus on American Sign Language—a true language that has evolved over generations but one that does not follow the same word order as spoken English. Proponents of American Sign Language contend that it is natural, fluent, and efficient, whereas signing English systems, which correspond with spoken English, are cumbersome and awkward. To date, however, few public schools use American Sign Language.

Regardless of teaching method, students with hearing impairment experience difficulties acquiring the language of the hearing society. Educators pay very close attention to the age of onset of the hearing impairment and the degree of hearing loss because each is closely associated with the severity of language delay. The earlier the hearing loss occurs and the more severe the hearing loss, the more severe the language delay. For many years, professionals believed that deficiencies in language among individuals with hearing impairment were related to deficiencies in intellectual ability; this is not the case. Unfortunately, results of research indicate that students with hearing impairment are behind their hearing peers in terms of academic achievement. Reading is the academic area most affected, wherein students with hearing impairment experience only one-third the reading growth of their hearing peers. They also lag behind their peers in mathematics. According to 1999 figures from the National Center for Health Statistics, "approximately 1.3 percent of all school-age students, ages six to twenty-one, who received special education services during the 1996–1997 school year were served under the disability category of hearing impairment" (Schirmer, p. 20). It is important to note, however, that estimates of the number of children with hearing impairment can differ markedly depending, for example, on definitions used, populations under investigation, and accuracy of testing.

Students with hearing impairment receive services in a variety of settings, from the general education classroom to residential schools. Parents and many professionals have not embraced the current controversial trend toward policies of inclusion (i.e., placing students with disabilities in general education classrooms for most or all of the school day). They caution that the general education classrooms are not necessarily the most appropriate placement for students with hearing impairment. However, some students with hearing impairment experience academic and social success in general education settings. This indicates that the preservation of the continuum of placements, whereby placement decisions can be made on individual bases, is in the best interest of students with hearing impairment.

See also: HEARING IMPAIRMENT, *subentry on* SCHOOL PROGRAMS; SPECIAL EDUCATION, *subentries on* CURRENT TRENDS, HISTORY OF.

BIBLIOGRAPHY

HALLAHAN, DANIEL P., and KAUFFMAN, JAMES M. 2000. *Exceptional Learners: Introduction to Special Education,* 8th edition. Boston: Allyn and Bacon.

SCHIRMER, BARBARA R. 2001. *Psychological, Social, and Educational Dimensions of Deafness.* Boston: Allyn and Bacon.

WALKER, LOU ANN. 1994. *Hand, Heart, and Mind: The Story of the Education of America's Deaf People.* New York: Dial Books.

ELIZABETH A. MARTINEZ
DANIEL P. HALLAHAN

HERBART, JOHANN (1776–1841)

German philosopher Johann Friedrich Herbart is the founder of the pedagogical theory that bears his name, which eventually laid the groundwork for teacher education as a university enterprise in the United States and elsewhere. Herbart was born in Oldenburg, Germany, the only child of a gifted and strong-willed mother and a father whose attention was devoted to his legal practice. Herbart was tutored at home until he entered the gymnasium at the age of twelve, from which he went on as valedictorian to the University of Jena at a time when such stellar German intellectuals as Johann Gottfried Herder, Johann Gottlieb Fichte, Johann Wolfgang von Goethe, and Friedrich von Schiller were associated with that institution. It was apparently Schiller's *Briefe über die ästhetische Erziehung des Menschen* (Letters concerning the aesthetic education of man), then in progress in 1795, that influenced Herbart to devote himself to philosophy and education.

Career

In 1797 and almost against his will Herbart was persuaded by his mother to accept a position as tutor to the sons of the regional governor of Interlaken in Switzerland. During his three years of work with these three very different boys, aged fourteen, ten, and eight when their relationship began, Herbart confronted in earnest the problems of teaching children, reporting monthly to their father on his methods and the results achieved. During his Swiss sojourn, he was also influenced by the thinking of Johann Heinrich Pestalozzi, whose school at Burgdorf he visited and whose ideas he systematized in 1802 in his *Pestalozzis Idee eines ABC der Anschauung untersucht und wissenschaftlich ausgeführt* (Pestalozzi's idea of an ABC of sense impression investigated and laid out scientifically).

Returning to Germany in 1800, Herbart completed his remaining doctoral work at the University of Göttingen, receiving his degree in 1802. He remained there as a lecturer in both philosophy and pedagogy until he received an appointment as professor of philosophy in 1805. Chief works related to education from his Göttingen period are *Über die ästhetische Darstellung der Welt als das Hauptgeschäft der Erziehung* (On the aesthetic representation of the world as the main concern of education), published in 1804, and *Allgemeine Pädagogik aus dem Zweck der Erziehung abgeleitet* (General pedagogy deduced from the aim of education), published in 1806. He also published on metaphysics and psychology.

In 1809 Herbart accepted the chair of pedagogy and philosophy at the University of Königsberg, formerly occupied by Immanuel Kant, and began a period of great productivity, ranging across the full spectrum of philosophical investigations. In the midst of work in metaphysics and psychology he also organized a pedagogical seminar for advanced students, attached to a demonstration school in which he and his students attempted to implement his pedagogical ideas, which were then critiqued and revised through the seminar discussions. This seminar, widely imitated by his later disciplines in Germany and elsewhere, was a first step toward trying to approach educational work scientifically.

Herbart left Königsberg in 1833, apparently because of disagreements with the Prussian government over his educational views in relation to state and church power. He returned to the University of Göttingen, where he remained for the last eight years of his life, producing his *Umriss von pädagogischen Vorlesungen* (Outlines of pedagogical lectures) in 1835, in which he attempted to connect more directly his early pedagogical theory and his later psychological work. He gave his last lecture two days before he died of a stroke on August 14, 1841.

Contribution

The legacy of Herbart to education was mediated through two major German disciples, Karl Volkmar Stoy and Tuiskon Ziller, who sought to implement his theories with varying degrees of alteration. Stoy was inspired by Herbart's early lectures in philosophy and pedagogy at the University of Göttingen and, upon qualifying as a lecturer at the University of Jena in 1842, took charge of a local private school that soon attracted students from all over Europe. In 1845 he was appointed professor at the university, then he moved in 1865 to the University of Heidelberg, establishing at nearby Bielitz a normal school based upon Herbartian principles. He returned to Jena in 1874 and established there the pedagogical seminar that would be taken over upon his death in 1885 by Wilhelm Rein, and brought to international renown by the end of the nineteenth century both for its practices and for its incorporation of teacher education into the university. It was there that the majority of Herbartians from other countries, including the United States, developed their ideas.

Rein had studied with the second major disciple of Herbart, Ziller, who had pursued a career in law, being appointed a lecturer at the University of Leipzig in 1853. Like Herbart, a period of teaching during his doctoral work led Ziller to investigate educational questions, and his first works, published in 1856 and 1857, were direct extensions and applications of Herbart's ideas. He established at the University of Leipzig a pedagogical seminar and practice school modeled after that of Herbart at Königsberg. Ziller was instrumental in founding the *Verein für wissenschaftliche Pädagogik* (Society for Scientific Pedagogy) in 1868, which published a quarterly that disseminated Herbartian ideas, and spread all over Germany as local clubs for the study of Herbartian approaches to educational problems. Ziller wrote *Grundlegung zur Lehre vom erziehenden Unterricht* (Basis of the doctrine of instruction as a moral force), published in 1865, and his *Vorlesungen über allgemeine Pädagogik* (Lectures on general pedagogy), published in 1876, five years before his death. These works provided the Herbartian legacy that Wilhelm Rein as a student of Ziller at Leipzig brought to his work when Rein resuscitated the pedagogical seminar at the University of Jena in 1886, a year after Stoy's death.

The German tradition of Herbartianism distinguishes between the Stoy and Ziller schools, the former being considered truer to Herbart's own ideas and the latter an extension of them more or less justified. Scholarship on both schools continues, centered at the University of Jena since its international conference, *Der Herbartianismus: die vergessene Wissenschaftsgeschichte* (Herbartianism: the forgotten history of a science), in 1997. The investigation of, or even attention to, the fine points of Herbartian theory, was notably lacking in American Herbartianism, although the central ideas remained intact. First and foremost was the development of moral character as the central aim of education. Second was the

adoption of Herbart's notion of apperception as the dynamic of learning: the ideas already configured in the mind are stimulated into activity by new information and either integrate that new information through meaningful connections or let it pass if such connections are not made. The essential unity of the ideas present in the mind is reflected in the theory of concentration as a principle for organizing the curriculum, which in relating several subjects to one another in the course of instruction also nurtures the many-faceted interest that is essential to full intellectual and thus spiritual development. Ziller added to these basic ideas the notion of the cultural-historical epochs as a curriculum principle that responds to the recapitulation in the individual of the psychic and cultural development of his group.

Rein and others developed a full eight-year course of study built upon this principle, which was translated and adapted to American use by Charles A. McMurry, one of the major disseminators of Herbartianism in the United States and a student with Rein. Charles DeGarmo, on the other hand, brought back to the United States the more conservative Herbartianism of Stoy, whose ideas were mirrored in the secondary schools of the *Franckische Stiftungen* in Halle established for orphans by August Hermann Francke in 1695 and under the directorship of Otto Frick during DeGarmo's doctoral study at the University of Halle. DeGarmo also provided for American readers the most thorough survey of the German Herbartians and Herbartian concepts in his *Herbart and the Herbartians,* published in 1895. It joined a substantial number of translations of work by Herbart and various German Herbartians made available in the 1890s.

American Herbartianism enjoyed a brief burst of national attention in the 1890s because of attempts by U.S. Commissioner of Education William Torrey Harris to stop its spread and the formation of the National Herbart Society in 1895 in response to those efforts. Within seven years the National Herbart Society had become the National Society for the Study of Education and its yearbooks had lost any obvious association with Herbartianism. Within that period at least eight universities were offering heavily Herbartian programs, and the demand for American Herbartian texts, particularly those of Charles McMurry, lasted until nearly 1930. Integrated curriculum, elementary school history teaching, and constructivist learning theory are part of the contemporary legacy of Herbartianism.

See also: EDUCATIONAL PSYCHOLOGY; INSTRUCTION-AL DESIGN; MCMURRY, CHARLES.

BIBLIOGRAPHY

DUNKEL, HAROLD B. 1967. "Herbart's Pedagogical Seminar." *History of Education Quarterly* 7:93–101.

DUNKEL, HAROLD B. 1969. *Herbart and Education.* New York: Random House.

DUNKEL, HAROLD B. 1969. "Herbartianism Comes to America," 2 parts. *History of Education Quarterly* 9:203–233; 376–390.

DUNKEL, HAROLD B. 1970. *Herbart and Herbartianism: An Educational Ghost Story.* Chicago: University of Chicago Press.

FELKIN, HENRY M., and FELKIN, EMMIE. 1898. *Letters and Lectures on Education.* London and Syracuse, NY: Sonnenschein, Bardeen.

FELKIN, HENRY M., and FELKIN, EMMIE. 1902. *The Science of Education.* Boston: Heath.

HERBART, JOHANN FRIEDRICH. 1964. *Sämtliche Werke in chronologischer Reihefolge,* (1887–1912), 19 vols., ed. Karl Kehrbach and Otto Flügel. Aalen, Germany: Scientia-Verlag.

LANG, OSSIAN H. 1894. *Outlines of Herbart's Pedagogics.* New York and Chicago: Kellogg.

KATHLEEN CRUIKSHANK

HIGHER EDUCATION CURRICULUM

See: CURRICULUM, HIGHER EDUCATION.

HIGHER EDUCATION IN CONTEXT

Universities are not ivory towers and never have been. They are subject to pressures and influences from external social forces of many kinds. This is not surprising, in light of the importance of universities to society, as well as the fact that institutions of higher education obtain their funds from external sources such as the government, students and their families, and donors. In the twenty-first century, universities are subject to the pressures of society more than ever, largely because of their importance to knowledge-based economies, and because more than half the college-age population attends postsecondary institutions.

Influences from external forces come from two basic directions. The first constitutes broad societal factors, such as economic trends and demographic factors, which affect the directions and realities of higher education. The second comes from the specific requirements of funding sources, government agencies, and others to account for, and sometimes control, the expenditure of funds, the nature and scope of research, and other university activities. This entry mainly discusses the broader external factors affecting higher education.

Economic Factors

Academic institutions, with few exceptions, constantly face financial challenges. All, even the most wealthy, depend on external elements for financial survival, including tuition payments provided by students and their families, funds from the government for operating expenses, research and training grants and contracts from a range of external agencies, charitable donations from alumni and foundations, and income-generating projects (including, for a few, intercollegiate athletics).

In the United States, 80 percent of postsecondary students attend public colleges and universities. For almost all public institutions, financial support from state governments is critical. Indeed, most postsecondary institutions depend on a combination of student tuition and direct support from the state for their financing. Federally backed student loans are also a central financial underpinning for higher education. These grants and loans are provided to individual students, who may use them at any accredited academic institution. Private universities and colleges depend to a much lesser extent on public support. Most are eligible for the student loan programs, and some states provide direct financial support to private institutions. Private institutions can also receive government research funding.

During the last decades of the twentieth century, there was a significant change in government policy concerning funding for postsecondary education. Previously, higher education was seen by most as a *public good*—an investment in human capital that, in the long run, benefited society as well as the individual, and is therefore worthy of public support. However, academic study is increasingly seen as a *private good*—something that mainly benefits the individual and should be paid for by the individual. Most states are less generous in their funding for higher education, and tuition charges have been raised. Nationally, students and their families are paying a higher proportion of the cost of higher education than was the case in the past. For many public universities, especially the nationally known public research institutions, less than one-third of income now comes from the states, with tuition, research grants, income generation, and donations constituting the majority of income.

Partly as a result of this change in philosophy, and partly because of competing state priorities and a general unwillingness to raise taxes, public higher education has faced financial problems, sometimes even during the boom years of the 1990s. External financial pressures also affect private colleges and universities. While the wealthiest institutions have endowments that provide a measure of financial stability, most private schools depend largely on tuition income. In the 1990s tuition increases were often higher than the level of inflation, and in the early twenty-first century there is resistance from students to high levels of tuition, and especially to rapid tuition increases. Private institutions have been forced to limit tuition increases, and this has had an impact on their financial viability in a competitive environment.

An Era of Competition

Competition has always been an element of academic life—for prestige, for the best students, and for donations, among other things—and competition has become one of the central driving forces in higher education. Competition for the best faculty, for students, for research grants, and for the ever more important rankings by *U.S. News and World Report* and other publications are all central to the contemporary academic enterprise. The most prestigious academic institutions see themselves in a race to provide better dormitories and sports facilities, faster access to computer networks, and improved campus services as part of a competitive struggle with their peers.

A central element of the new competitive environment is that students increasingly see themselves as "buyers" of a higher-education product. They demand that the academic institutions serve their specific needs in terms of curriculum, degree offerings, and facilities. This is an age of student consumerism,

where even the most prestigious and selective institutions must respond to student interests and concerns. Academic institutions have moved to provide flexible degree structures, new majors to meet student demand, and to supply, in many other ways, the educational "product" demanded by an increasingly sophisticated market.

Demographic Realities

This increased competition is partly a result of the changing demographic realities in American higher education. Dramatic changes have taken place that affect academic institutions. With the exception of a brief baby-boom *echo* for a few years at the beginning of the twenty-first century, the number of traditional college-age young people (18–21 year olds) has been modestly declining. Colleges and universities are thus competing for a declining number of potential students. Furthermore, the period of expansion in the proportion of college-age youth attending postsecondary education institutions has largely come to an end as well. The proportion of young people attending college increased from perhaps 20 percent in the period following World War II to more than 60 percent in the 1990s, but it did not increase between 1990 and 2000. Higher education in the United States has reached what sociologist Martin Trow has called "universal access."

A significant part of the numerical expansion of enrollments in the late twentieth century consisted of nontraditional students—people who are older then the usual college age and who begin or return to study mainly for vocational reasons. Another new population group consists of students who do not possess all of the skills needed for postsecondary study. These students often require remedial courses that colleges and universities must provide. As American higher education has become a mass phenomenon, the academic system has had to adjust to a more diverse student body and a wider array of student interests.

There have been other important changes in the student population that have affected academe. With 14 million students attending the nation's more than 3,000 colleges and universities, there is unprecedented diversity. Women constitute a majority of the student population, and racial and ethnic diversity has grown dramatically, with African Americans, Latinos, and especially Asian Americans present in large and growing numbers. Higher education is no longer a preserve of the white middle classes, and many working-class students are able to gain access. Higher education is seen as a passport to economic success, and statistics show that those with a bachelor's degree earn much more over their lifetimes than those without academic qualifications. A majority of students study part-time and the traditional model of a full-time traditional-age student living on campus is no longer valid.

The pressures of demography on the higher-education system have been immense. The dramatic expansion of the student population, increased diversity, and more variation by age, ability, and interest have all transformed the academic landscape.

Political, Governmental, and Legal Challenges

The higher-education system, as well as individual academic institutions, is affected by politics and government. The U. S. constitution stipulates that education is a responsibility of the states, and thus the fifty states have basic responsibility for higher education. As noted earlier, the states provide the bulk of funding for public higher education. They are also responsible for organizing and regulating public university systems, providing a legal structure for these systems, and in most cases providing charters and legal recognition for all higher-education institutions, both public and private. The state governments determine tuition charges, sponsor loan and grant programs, and in some cases determine admissions policy for the public colleges and universities. State authorities appoint governing boards (although in a few cases these boards are elected).

The policies of the fifty states are central to public higher education, though the states differ substantially in their approaches to higher education. Some states, especially in New England, where there is a strong tradition of private higher education, have provided limited support for public colleges and universities and tend to charge high tuition. In Massachusetts, for example, more than half the students attend private colleges—the highest proportion in the United States. In the Midwest and the West, however, states have been more supportive of large, and often excellent, public higher-education systems. California has the largest public higher-education system, and has been a model for shaping state higher education in an era of mass access. A combination of community colleges, four-year schools, and research universities has characterized the California system, and is common in other states. California has always had relatively low tu-

ition, while the New England states typically charge students more. The policies of the state governments concerning student tuition, financial support, access and accountability, and the size and shape of state systems of higher education are all crucial to public higher education. State policies also affect private universities and colleges. In some states, public funds are available for scholarships and other programs for private higher education, and in a few states, such as New York, the state has the power to approve degree programs and other initiatives in the private sector.

The federal government also has a significant impact on higher education. Indeed, the role of the federal government has increased dramatically in the period following World War II. The G.I. Bill, the major federally sponsored scholarship program following the war, enabled millions of returning veterans to attend college and resulted in a wave of expansion in higher education. Stimulated in part by the cold war, the federal government increased funding for research and became the major source of funding for scientific research. In the period of greatest expansion, during the 1960s, federal funds became available to build new facilities and expand libraries. Perhaps most important, the federal student loans programs and the Pell Grant system have become a major part of financing postsecondary education for millions of students.

The federal government regulates certain aspects of higher education, and these regulations reflect the external influences on American colleges and universities. Federal regulations affect such aspects of academic life as athletic programs, which are subject to regulations concerning gender equality and access, the use of human subjects in research, the treatment of animals in laboratories, and access to facilities through the Americans with Disabilities Act. Federal regulatory authority expanded during the 1980s and 1990s. Universities that receive federal funding, which means almost all American academic institutions, are subjects to regulations and reporting requirements. Statistics concerning the composition of the faculty and the student body, statistics on campus crime, and other aspects of academic life must all be submitted to the federal government to comply with regulatory requirements.

The legal system also affects higher education and constitutes an important external societal force for colleges and universities. Court decisions of all kinds directly affect higher education. Of considerable importance—and much controversy—have been court decisions concerning affirmative action for both students and faculty. The courts, for example, have limited, and in some cases even eliminated, considerations of race in university admissions and other programs, and they have ruled on faculty hiring and promotion. Courts occasionally intervene in university decisions concerning tenure and promotion if specific complaints are made, and academic decisions are sometimes overturned. Court decisions thus set precedents for academic policy.

Government, at all levels, is a central external force affecting colleges and universities. Because 80 percent of American postsecondary students attend public colleges and universities, governmental policy is especially important. The government provides the bulk of funding for public institutions, which are directly subject to government policy and direction. Although government funding supports a declining proportion of academic budgets, government influence and control remain strong. Higher education is subject to accountability at many levels, and the political, legal, and regulatory system of higher education has a strong influence on higher education at every level.

Religious Factors

Historically, religion has been a central force in American higher education. Most of the early colleges, including Harvard and Yale, were established by religious organizations with specifically religious purposes in mind. For almost two centuries, religion was one of the major motivations for the expansion of higher education, and a large majority of academic institutions were controlled by religious bodies. The curriculum was a combination of religious and secular subjects, with the religious elements gradually decreasing in importance. Regulations imposed by church sponsors governed extracurricular life, and had an impact on the faculty as well. By the end of the nineteenth century, with the expansion of public higher education, church-related institutions became a smaller part of the higher-education system.

By the end of the twentieth century, religious influences became much less pervasive. Religion plays no significant role in the public colleges and universities in the early twenty-first century. This reduced role is strengthened by the constitutional separation of church and state. Many of the private colleges and universities once sponsored by religious bodies have become secularized. Church groups no longer spon-

sor institutions such as Harvard, the University of Chicago, and Duke. At the same time, there are hundreds of religiously sponsored institutions—there are more than 200 Roman Catholic colleges and universities, and a large number of Protestant institutions. But these schools educate only a small part of the student population, and even they are, in general, less influenced by religious factors than was once the case. It is fair to say that religion is no longer a major factor in American higher education, and that its influence is limited to a small number of private religiously sponsored colleges and universities.

Societal Influences

Societal trends and developments uniquely influence American colleges and universities. Academe has always been attuned to demands for new curricula, new initiatives, and in general to the interests of external forces. This is in contrast to academe in many other parts of the world, which until recently were mostly elite institutions less influenced by society. Americans historically have established new institutions to meet perceived needs, from the desire of the Puritans to educate clergy, which led to the establishment of Harvard in 1636, to the growth of women's colleges in the nineteenth century to serve the needs of women seeking access to higher education, and to the inclusion of research in university curricula at the end of the nineteenth century to help meet the needs of a developing society.

Academic institutions have also moved quickly to expand and diversify the curriculum to meet new societal needs, whether it be the growth of medical education in the universities or the remarkable expansion of business schools in the post–World War II period. There is an inevitable tension between ideas of autonomy ingrained in academic institutions and pressures from society. In the twenty-first century, external pressures of all kinds—economic, political, and others—charcterize the higher-education system.

See also: Academic Freedom and Tenure; Curriculum, Higher Education; Federal Funding for Academic Research; Federal Funds for Higher Education; Higher Education in the United States.

BIBLIOGRAPHY

Altbach, Philip G.; Berdahl, Robert J.; and Gumport, Patricia J., eds. 1999. *American*

Higher Education in the Twenty-First Century: Social, Political, and Economic Challenges. Baltimore: Johns Hopkins University Press.

ALTBACH, PHILIP G.; GUMPORT, PATRICIA J.; and JOHNSTONE, D. BRUCE., eds. 2001. *In Defense of the American University.* Baltimore: Johns Hopkins University Press.

KERR, CLARK. 2001. *The Uses of the University.* Cambridge, MA: Harvard University Press.

LEVINE, ARTHUR. 1980. *When Dreams and Heroes Died: A Portrait of Today's College Students.* San Francisco: Jossey-Bass.

LEVINE, ARTHUR. 1993. *Higher Learning in America: 1980–2000.* Baltimore: Johns Hopkins University Press.

MARSDEN, GEORGE. 1994. *The Soul of the American University: From Protestant Establishment to Established Nonbelief.* New York: Oxford University Press.

SHILS, EDWARD. 1992. "Universities Since 1900." In *Encyclopedia of Higher Education,* ed. Burton R. Clark and Guy R. Neave. Oxford: Pergamon.

TROW, MARTIN. 1972. "The Expansion and Transformation of Higher Education." *International Review of Education* 18(1):61–83.

PHILIP G. ALTBACH

HIGHER EDUCATION, INTERNATIONAL ISSUES

Higher education has developed in numerous ways since the end of World War II. Throughout the world, issues such as autonomy and accountability, the impact of technology, the growing role of markets and the privatization of higher education, the role of research and teaching, various efforts toward curriculum reform, and the massive expansion that has characterized higher education systems in most countries have all played important roles in the development of higher education. Universities are international institutions, with common historical roots, and at the same time are embedded in national cultures and circumstances. It is worthwhile to examine the contemporary challenges to higher education in comparative perspective, as most issues affect academe everywhere.

Expansion: Hallmark of the Postwar Era

Postsecondary education has expanded since World War II in virtually every country in the world. The growth of postsecondary education has, in proportional terms, been more dramatic than that of primary and secondary education. Writing in 1975, Martin Trow spoke of the transition from *elite* to *mass* and then to *universal* higher education in the industrialized nations. While the United States enrolled some 30 percent of the relevant age cohort (18–21 year olds) in higher education in the immediate postwar period, European nations generally maintained an elite higher education system, with fewer than 5 percent of the population attending postsecondary institutions. By the 1960s many European nations educated 15 percent or more of this age group—Sweden for example, enrolled 24 percent in 1970, with France at 17 percent. At the same time, the United States increased its proportion to around 50 percent, approaching universal access. By the mid-1990s many European countries, including France, Germany, and the United Kingdom, enrolled around 50 percent of the relevant age group, and the proportion in the United States increased to three-quarters. While Europe and North America are now relatively stable, middle-income countries and countries in the developing world have continued to expand at a rapid rate.

In the Third World, expansion has been similarly dramatic. Building on tiny and extraordinarily elitist universities, higher education expanded rapidly in the immediate post-independence period. In India, enrollments grew from approximately 100,000 at the time of independence in 1947 to over 6.5 million in the 1990s—although India enrolls just 7 percent of the relevant age group. China enrolls a similar number, though this represents only 5 percent of its young people. China, especially, is engaged in a dramatic expansion program. Expansion in Africa has also been rapid, with the postsecondary student population growing from 21,000 in 1960 to 437,000 in 1983, but with growth stagnating in the 1990s as a result of the economic and political difficulties experienced by many sub-Saharan African countries. Recent economic difficulties in much of sub-Saharan Africa have meant that per-student expenditure has dropped, contributing to a marked deterioration in academic standards. Enrollment growth has also slowed.

Expansion is also a hallmark elsewhere in the non-Western countries. The situation is complex. In some countries, including the larger Latin American nations, the Philippines, and some others, enrollment rates have reached 30 percent or more. In most of the low-income nations, however, enrollments lag far behind. However, growth continues to be rapid in much of the Third World, with accompanying strains on budgets and facilities—and deterioration in standards. Expansion in the Third World has, in general, exceeded that in the industrialized nations, at least in proportional terms. It should be noted that there are significant variations among Third World nations—some countries maintain small and relatively elitist university systems, while others have expanded more rapidly. Among the highest rates of expansion, and now of participation, are in those newly industrialized countries such as South Korea and Taiwan.

There are many reasons for the expansion of higher education. A central cause has been the increasing complexity of modern societies and economies, which have demanded a more highly trained workforce. Almost without exception, postsecondary institutions have been called on to provide the required training. Indeed, training in many fields that had once been imparted on the job has become formalized in institutions of higher education. Whole new fields, such as computer science, have come into existence, and many of these rely on universities as a key source of research and training. Nations now developing scientific and industrial capacity, such as Korea and Taiwan, have depended on academic institutions to provide high-level training and research expertise to a greater extent than was the case during the first industrial revolution in Europe.

Not only do academic institutions provide training, they also test and provide certification for many roles and occupations in contemporary society. These roles have been central to universities from their origins in the medieval period, but have been vastly expanded in recent years. A university degree is a prerequisite for an increasing number of occupations in most societies. Indeed, it is fair to say that academic certification is necessary for most positions of power, authority, and prestige in modern societies. This places immense power in the hands of universities. Tests to gain admission to higher education are rites of passage in many societies and are important determinants of future success. Competition within academe varies from country to country, but in most cases an emphasis is also placed on high

academic performance and tests in the universities. There are often further examinations to permit entry into specific professions.

The role of the university as an examining body has grown for a number of reasons. As expansion has taken place, it has been necessary to provide ever more competitive sorting mechanisms to control access to high-prestige occupations. The universities are also seen as meritocratic institutions that can be trusted to provide fair and impartial tests to measure accomplishment honestly and, therefore, determine access. When such mechanisms break down—as they did in China during the Cultural Revolution—or where they are perceived to be subject to corrupt influences—as in India—the universities are significantly weakened. The older, more informal, and often more ascriptive means of controlling access to prestigious occupations are no longer able to provide the controls needed, nor are they perceived as fair. Entirely new fields have developed where no sorting mechanisms existed, and academic institutions have frequently been called upon to provide not only training but also examination and certification.

Expansion has also occurred because the growing segments of the population of modern societies demand it. The middle classes, seeing that academic qualifications are necessary for success, demand access to higher education. Governments generally respond by increasing enrollment. When governments do not move quickly enough, private initiatives frequently establish academic institutions in order to meet the demand. In countries like India, the Philippines, and Bangladesh, a majority of the students are educated in private colleges and universities. At present, there are powerful worldwide trends toward: (1) imposing user fees in the form of higher tuition charges, (2) increasingly stressing private higher education, and (3) defining education as a "private good" in economic terms. These changes are intended to reduce the cost of postsecondary education for governments, while maintaining access—although the long-term implications for the quality of, access to, and control over higher education remain unclear.

In most countries, higher education is heavily subsidized by the government, and most, if not all, academic institutions are in the public sector. While there is a growing trend toward private initiative and management sharing responsibility for education with public institutions, governments will likely con-

HIGHER EDUCATION, INTERNATIONAL ISSUES 1029

tinue to be central to funding postsecondary education, although the private sector is currently the major source of growth worldwide. The dramatic expansion of academic institutions in the postwar period has proved very expensive for governments and has led to a diversification of funding sources. Nonetheless, the demand for access has been an extraordinarily powerful one.

Change and Reform: Trends since the 1960s

The demands placed on institutions of higher education to accommodate larger numbers of students and to serve expanding functions has resulted in reforms in higher education in many countries. Much debate has taken place concerning higher education reform in the 1960s—and a significant amount of change did take place. It is possible to identify several important factors that contributed both to the debate and to the changes that took place. Without question, the unprecedented student unrest of the period contributed to a sense of disarray in higher education. The unrest was in part precipitated by deteriorating academic conditions that were the result of the rapid expansion. In a few instances, students demanded far-reaching reforms, although they did not always propose specific changes. Students frequently demanded an end to the rigidly hierarchical organization of the traditional European university, and major reforms were made in this respect. The *chair* system, which gave total power to small groups of senior professors, was modified or eliminated, and the responsibility for academic decision making was expanded in some countries to include students. At the same time, the walls of the traditional academic disciplines were broken down by various plans for interdisciplinary teaching and research.

In the 1990s the major trend in restructuring European universities has been on improving the administrative efficiency and accountability of the universities, and many of the reforms of the 1960s were modified or even eliminated. Students, for example, have less power now. In the Netherlands, a national restructuring has increased the power of administrators, reformed the governance system by reducing the power of the senior professors, greatly increased accountability, and shifted more of the financial responsibilities to the academic institutions themselves. Students have little authority in the new arrangements. While the Dutch have implemented the most dramatic reforms, similar trends can be seen in Germany, Sweden, and other countries.

In many industrialized nations structural change has been modest. In the United States, for example, despite considerable debate during the 1960s, there was very limited change in the structure or governance of higher education. Japan, which saw unrest that disrupted higher education and spawned a large number of reports on university reform, experienced virtually no basic change in its higher education system, although several *new model* interdisciplinary institutions were established—such as the science-oriented Tsukuba University near Tokyo. Britain, less affected by student protest and with an established plan for expansion in operation, also experienced few reforms during the 1960s, and some of the changes implemented in the 1960s have since been criticized or abandoned. In Germany, reforms in governance that gave students and junior staff a dominant position in some university functions were ruled unconstitutional by the German courts.

Many of the structural reforms of the 1960s were abandoned after a decade of experimentation, or they were replaced by administrative arrangements that emphasized accountability and efficiency. Outside authorities—including government, but in some cases business, industry, or labor organizations—have come to play a more important role in academic governance. The curricular innovations of the 1960s, as well as later decades, have proved more durable. Interdisciplinary programs and initiatives and the introduction of new fields such as gender studies have characterized changes in many countries.

Vocationalization has been an important trend in higher education change. Throughout the world there is a conviction that the university curriculum must provide relevant training for a variety of increasingly complex jobs. The traditional notion that higher education should consist of liberal, nonvocational studies for elites, or should provide a broad but unfocused curriculum, has been widely criticized for lacking "relevance." Students, worried about obtaining remunerative employment, have pressed the universities to be more focused. Employers have also demanded that the curriculum become more directly relevant to their needs. Enrollments in the social sciences and humanities, at least in the industrialized nations, have declined because these fields are not considered vocationally relevant.

Curricular vocationalism is linked to another key worldwide trend in higher education: the increasingly close relationship between universities and industry. Industrial firms have sought to ensure that the skills they need are incorporated into the curriculum. This trend also has implications for academic research, since many university-industry relationships are focused largely on research. Industries have established formal linkages and research partnerships with universities in order to obtain help with research in which they are interested. In some countries, such as Sweden, representatives of industry have been added to the governing councils of higher education institutions.

University-industry relations have become crucial for higher education in many countries. Technical arrangements with regard to patents, confidentiality of research findings, and other fiscal matters have become important. Critics have pointed out that the nature of research in higher education may be altered by these new relationships, as industrial firms are not generally interested in basic research. University-based research, which has traditionally been oriented toward basic research, may be increasingly skewed to applied and profit-making topics. There has also been some discussion of the orientation of research, particularly in fields like biotechnology, where broader public policy matters may conflict with the needs of corporations. Specific funding arrangements have also been questioned. Pressure to serve the immediate needs of society, and particularly the training and research requirements of industry, is currently a key concern for universities, one that has implications for the organization of the curriculum, the nature and scope of research, and the traditional relationship between the university and society.

Universities have traditionally claimed significant autonomy for themselves. The traditional idea of academic governance stresses autonomy, and universities have tried to insulate themselves from direct control by external agencies. However, as universities have expanded and become more expensive, there has been immense pressure by those providing funds for higher education (mainly governments) to expect accountability from universities. The conflict between autonomy and accountability has been one of the flashpoints of controversy in recent years. Without exception, autonomy has been limited, and new administrative structures have been put into place in such countries as Britain and the Netherlands to ensure greater accountability. The issue takes on different implications in different parts of

the world. In the Third World, for example, traditions of autonomy have not been strong, and demands for accountability, which include both political and economic elements, are especially troublesome. In the industrialized nations accountability pressures are more fiscal in nature.

The Twenty-First Century

The university in modern society is a durable institution. It has maintained key elements of the historical models from which it evolved over many centuries, while at the same time it has successfully evolved to serve the needs of societies during a period of tremendous social change. There has been a convergence of both ideas and institutional patterns and practices in higher education throughout the world. This has been due in part to the implantation of European-style universities in the developing areas during and after the colonial era, and in part to the fact universities have been crucial in the development and internationalization of science and scholarship.

Despite remarkable institutional stability over time, universities have changed and have been subjected to immense pressures in the post–World War II period. Many of the changes chronicled here are the result of great external pressure and were instituted despite opposition from within the institutions. Some have argued that the university has lost its soul. Others have claimed that the university is irresponsible because it uses public funds and does not always conform to the direct needs of industry and government. Pressure from governmental authorities, militant students, or external constituencies have all placed great strains on academic institutions.

The period since World War II has been one of unprecedented growth—the dominant trend worldwide has been toward mass higher education. The university is at the center of the postindustrial, knowledge-based society. The problems faced by higher education are, in part, related to growth and expansion. The following issues are among those that will be of concern in the coming decade and beyond.

Access and adaption. Although in a few countries access to postsecondary education has been provided to virtually all segments of the population, in most countries a continuing unmet demand exists for higher education. Progress toward broadening the social class base of higher education has slowed (and in many industrialized countries stopped in the 1970s). With the arrival of democratic governments in eastern Europe, the reemergence of demand in western Europe, and continuing pressure for expansion in the Third World, demand for access continues, fueling an expansion of enrollments in many countries. Often, limited funds and a desire for efficient allocation of scarce postsecondary resources come into direct conflict with demands for access. In addition, demands for access by previously disenfranchised groups will continue to place great pressure on higher education. In many countries, racial, ethnic, or religious minorities play a role in shaping higher education policy.

Administration, accountability, and governance. As academic institutions become larger and more complex, there is increasing pressure for a greater degree of professional administration. At the same time, the traditional forms of academic governance are increasingly criticized—not only because they are unwieldy, but also because in large and bureaucratic institutions they are inefficient. The administration of higher education will increasingly become a profession, much as it is in the United States. Academic institutions have become complex bureaucratic structures, requiring managerial expertise to administer. Demands for accountability are growing and will cause academic institutions considerable difficulty. As academic budgets expand, there are inevitable demands to monitor and control expenditures. The appropriate level of governmental supervision of higher education remains contested terrain. The challenge will be to ensure that the traditional—and valuable—patterns of faculty control over governance and the basic academic decisions in universities are maintained in a complex and bureaucratic environment.

Research and knowledge dissemination. Research is a central part of the mission of many universities, and of the academic system in general. Contemporary knowledge-based societies depend on research, both basic and applied, for their success, and universities have traditionally been key sources of research. Decisions concerning the control and funding of research, the relationship of research to the broader curriculum and teaching, the uses made of university-based research, and other related issues will all be in contention in future years. Current debates concerning the appropriate role of industry in sponsoring, and perhaps controlling, research, and about the control of knowledge products, will help to shape the future of academic research.

The system of knowledge dissemination, including journals, books, and computer-based data systems, is rapidly changing, and many questions remain unanswered. Who should control the new data networks? How will traditional means of communication, such as journals, survive in this new climate? How will the scientific system avoid being overwhelmed by the proliferation of data? Who will pay for the costs of knowledge dissemination? In addition, the needs of peripheral scientific systems, including both the Third World and smaller academic systems in the industrialized world, have been largely ignored, but are nonetheless important.

While the technological means for rapid knowledge dissemination are available, issues of control and ownership, the appropriate use of databases, problems of maintaining quality standards in databases, and other related questions are very important. It is possible that the new technologies will lead to increased centralization rather than to wider access. It is also possible that libraries and other users of knowledge will be overwhelmed, both by the cost of obtaining new material and by the flow of knowledge. At present, academic institutions in the United States and other English-speaking nations, along with publishers and the owners of the communications networks, stand to gain. The major Western knowledge producers currently constitute a kind of cartel of information, dominating not only the creation of knowledge but also most of the major channels of distribution. Simply increasing the amount of research and creating new databases will not ensure a more equal and accessible knowledge system.

The academic profession. In most countries, the professoriate has found itself under great pressure at the turn of the twenty-first century. Demands for accountability, increased bureaucratization of institutions, fiscal constraints in many countries, and an increasingly diverse student body have all challenged the professoriate. In most industrialized nations, a combination of fiscal problems and demographic factors have led to a stagnating profession. At the beginning of the twenty-first century, demographic factors and a modest upturn in enrollments are beginning to turn surpluses into shortages. In the newly industrializing countries (NICs), the professoriate has significantly improved its status, remuneration, and working conditions. In the poorer nations, however, the situation has, if anything, become more difficult with decreasing resources and ever-increasing enrollments. Overall, the professoriate will face severe problems as academic institutions change during the twenty-first century. Maintaining autonomy, academic freedom, and a commitment to the traditional goals of the university will be difficult.

In the West, it will be hard to lure the "best and brightest" into academe in a period when faculty positions are again relatively plentiful—in many fields, academic salaries have not kept pace with the private sector, and the traditional academic lifestyle has deteriorated. The pressure on the professoriate not only to teach and do research, but also to attract external grants, do consulting, and the like, is great. In Britain and Australia, for example, universities have become "cost centers," and accountability has been pushed to its logical extreme. British academics entering the profession after 1989 will no longer have tenure, but will, in the future, be periodically evaluated. In the NICs, the challenge will be to create a fully autonomous academic profession in a context in which traditions of research and academic freedom are only now developing. The difficulties faced by the poorer Third World countries are perhaps the greatest, as they struggle to maintain a viable academic culture under deteriorating conditions.

Private resources and public responsibility. In almost every country there has been a growing emphasis on increasing the role of the private sector in higher education. One of the most direct manifestations of this trend is the role of the private sector in funding and directing university research. In many countries private academic institutions have expanded, or new ones have been established. In addition, students are paying an increasing share of the cost of their education as a result of tuition and fee increases, and through loan programs.

Governments try to limit their expenditures on postsecondary education, while at the same time recognizing that the functions of universities are important. Privatization has been the primary means of achieving this broad policy goal. Inevitably, decisions concerning academic developments will move increasingly to the private sector, with the possibility that broader public goals may be ignored. Whether private interests will support the traditional functions of universities, including academic freedom, basic research, and a pattern of governance that leaves the professoriate in control, is unclear. Some of the most interesting developments in private higher education can be found in such countries as

Vietnam, China, and Hungary, where private institutions have recently been established. The growth of a new for-profit private sector in the United States and elsewhere creates an entirely new sector of higher education, and private initiatives in higher education will bring a change in values and orientations. It is not clear, however, that these values will be in the long-term best interests of the university.

Diversification and stratification. While diversification—the establishing of new postsecondary institutions to meet diverse needs—is by no means an entirely unprecedented phenomenon, it is a trend that has been of primary importance, and it will continue to reshape the academic system. In recent years, the establishment of research institutions, community colleges, polytechnics, and other academic institutions designed to meet specialized needs and serve specific populations has been a primary characteristic of growth. At the same time, the academic system has become more stratified, and individuals within one sector of the system are finding it difficult to move to a different sector. There is often a high correlation between social class (and other variables) and selection to a particular sector of the system.

To some extent, the reluctance of traditional universities to change is responsible for some of the diversification. Perhaps more important, however, has been the belief that it is efficient and less expensive to establish new limited-function institutions.

One element of diversification is the inclusion of larger numbers of women and other previously disenfranchised segments of the population. Women now constitute 40 percent of the postsecondary student population worldwide—and they are now a majority in U.S. institutions. In many countries, students from lower socioeconomic groups, and racial and ethnic minorities, are entering postsecondary institutions in significant numbers. This diversification will also present challenges in the coming decades.

Economic disparities. There are substantial inequalities among the world's universities—and these inequalities will likely grow. The major universities in the industrialized nations generally have the resources to play a leading role in scientific research—though it will be increasingly expensive to keep up with the expansion of knowledge. Universities in much of the Third World, however, simply cannot cope with the continuing pressure for increased enrollments, particularly when combined with budgetary constraints and, in some cases, fiscal disasters. For example, universities in much of sub-Saharan Africa have experienced dramatic budget cuts and find it difficult to function, not to mention to improve quality and compete in the international knowledge system. In the middle are academic institutions in the Asian NICs, where significant academic progress has taken place. Thus, the economic prospects for postsecondary education worldwide are mixed.

Conclusion

Universities share a common culture and reality. In many basic ways there is an international convergence of institutional models and norms. At the same time, there are significant national differences that will continue to affect the development of academic systems and institutions. It is unlikely that the basic structures of academic institutions will change dramatically; the traditional university will survive, although it will be changed by the forces discussed here. Open universities and other distance education institutions have emerged, and may provide new institutional arrangements. Efforts to save money may yield further organizational changes as well. Unanticipated change is also possible.

The circumstances facing universities in the first part of twenty-first century are not, in general, favorable. The realities of higher education as a "mature industry," with stable, rather than growing, resources in the industrialized countries, will affect not only the funds available for postsecondary education, but also practices within academic institutions. Accountability, the impact of technologies, and the other forces discussed here will all affect colleges and universities. Patterns will, of course, vary worldwide. Some academic systems, especially those in the newly industrializing countries, will continue to grow. In parts of the world affected by significant political and economic change, the coming decades will be ones of reconstruction. The coming period, therefore, holds many challenges for higher education.

See also: ACCREDITATION IN AN INTERNATIONAL CONTEXT, HIGHER EDUCATION; DISTANCE LEARNING IN HIGHER EDUCATION; HIGHER EDUCATION IN CONTEXT; RESEARCH UNIVERSITIES.

BIBLIOGRAPHY

ALTBACH, PHILIP G. 1987. *The Knowledge Context: Comparative Perspectives on the Distribution of Knowledge.* Albany: State University of New York Press.

ALTBACH, PHILIP G. 1998. *Comparative Higher Education: Knowledge, the University, and Development.* Greenwich, CT: Ablex.

ALTBACH, PHILIP G. 1999. *Private Prometheus: Private Higher Education and Development in the 21st Century.* Greenwich, CT: Greenwood.

ALTBACH, PHILIP G. 2001. "Academic Freedom: International Realities and Challenges." *Higher Education* 41:205–219.

ASTIN, ALEXANDER, et al. 1975. *The Power of Protest.* San Francisco: Jossey-Bass.

BEN-DAVID, JOSEPH, and ZLOCZOWER, AWRAHAM. 1962. "Universities and Academic Systems in Modern Societies." *European Journal of Sociology* 3:45–84.

BOWEN, HOWARD, and SCHUSTER, JACK. 1986. *American Professors: A National Resource Imperiled.* New York: Oxford University Press.

CLARK, BURTON R. 1998. *Creating Entrepreneurial Universities: Organizational Pathways of Transformation.* Oxford: Pergamon.

DAALDER, HANS, and SHILS, EDWARD, eds. 1982. *Universities, Politicians and Bureaucrats: Europe and the United States.* Cambridge, Eng.: Cambridge University Press.

GEIGER, ROGER L. 1986. *Private Sectors in Higher Education: Structure, Function and Change in Eight Countries.* Ann Arbor: University of Michigan Press.

GRAHAM, HUGH DAVIS, and DIAMOND, NANCY. 1997. *The Rise of American Research Universities: Elites and Challenges in the Postwar Era.* Baltimore, MD: Johns Hopkins University Press.

HUFNER, KLAUS. 1991. "Accountability." In *International Higher Education: An Encyclopedia*, ed. Philip G. Altbach. New York: Garland.

JOHNSTONE, D. BRUCE. 1986. *Sharing the Costs of Higher Education: Student Financial Assistance in the United Kingdom, the Federal Republic of Germany, France, Sweden, and the United States.* Washington, DC: The College Board.

KERR, CLARK. 2001. *The Uses of the University.* Cambridge, MA: Harvard University Press.

TASK FORCE ON HIGHER EDUCATION AND SOCIETY. 2000. *Higher Education in Developing Countries:*

Peril and Promise. Washington, DC: World Bank.

TROW, MARTIN. 1975. *Problems in the Transition from Elite to Mass Higher Education.* Paris: Organisation for Economic Co-operation and Development.

PHILIP G. ALTBACH

HIGHER EDUCATION IN THE UNITED STATES

HISTORICAL DEVELOPMENT
John R. Thelin
Jason R. Edwards
Eric Moyen
SYSTEM
Joseph B. Berger
Maria Vita Calkins

HISTORICAL DEVELOPMENT

At the start of the twenty-first century, higher education in the United States stands as a formidable enterprise. As an established "knowledge industry" it represents about 3 percent of the gross national product. Virtually every governor and legislature across the nation evokes colleges and universities as critical to a state's economic and cultural development. Its profile includes more than 4,000 accredited institutions that enroll over fifteen million students and confers in excess of two million degrees annually. Colleges and universities spend about $26 billion per year on research and development, of which $16 billion comes from federal agencies. The research universities' ability to attract expertise is recognized internationally.

This success story of growth and expansion began more than 300 years ago before the United States existed. Beginning in the seventeenth century, the idea of an American higher education grew to fruition throughout the ensuing centuries. At the same time, differences developed with each new era of collegiate growth, but the story has remained one of expanding access.

The Colonial Period

Imperial governments usually invested little in colonial colleges. The typical mercantile approach emphasized the exportation of agricultural products and raw materials from the provinces to the homeland. The British Empire, for instance, responded to Virginia's request for a seminary to save their souls, with "Souls?!? Damn your souls! Make tobacco." Despite such hostility, the American colonies generally enjoyed greater independence than the typical British territory. While a succession of kings and queens encouraged the cultivation and exportation of tobacco, rice, indigo, and cotton, colleges also flourished as an unlikely crop in America.

The colonists created institutions for higher education for several reasons. New England settlers included many alumni of the royally chartered British universities, Cambridge and Oxford, and therefore believed education was essential. In addition, the Puritans emphasized a learned clergy and an educated civil leadership. Their outlook generated Harvard College in 1636. Between Harvard's founding and the start of the American Revolution, the colonists chartered nine colleges and seminaries although only one in the South.

Religion provided an impetus for the creation of colonial colleges. As the First Great Awakening of the 1730s to 1770s initiated growth in a wider variety of Protestant churches, each denomination often desired its own seminary. Furthermore, each colony tended to favor a particular denomination and so the new colleges took on an importance for regional development as well. Presbyterians in New Jersey founded the College of New Jersey (later renamed Princeton). The College of William and Mary in Virginia maintained a strong Anglican orientation, reflecting that colony's settlement by landed gentry from England. The Baptists, who had been expelled from Massachusetts Bay Colony and settled in Rhode Island, established their own college but in an unusual move did not require religious tests for admission. Other dissenting religious groups, such as the Methodists and Quakers, became enthusiastic college builders after facing hostility in many colleges.

Small in size and limited in scope, colonial colleges rarely enrolled more than one hundred students and few completed their degrees. Yet the young men who attended these colonial colleges made historic and extraordinary contributions to both political thought and action. Also, colleges represented one of the few institutional ventures to receive royal and/or colonial government support and regulation during the eighteenth century. The college's multipurpose buildings were typically among the largest construction projects in the colony, matched only by a major church or a capitol.

Though colonial colleges were frontier institutions that expanded access to higher education, by contemporary standards the colonial period remained elite and exclusionary. Only white Christian males were allowed to matriculate. Women and African-Americans were denied participation by statute and custom, but colleges did serve Native Americans in a missionary capacity. The evangelism of the Protestant groups attracted donors, although in time the colonial colleges' devotion to such educational plans waned. In order to keep receiving financial support, however, the colleges argued that by educating young Christian men, missionaries would be available to preach Christianity to Native Americans.

Despite their limitations, the colonial colleges effectively educated a literate, articulate, and responsible American elite. Even though college education was not crucial for the professional and career advancement of sons of prosperous merchants and wealthy planters, the college alumni were disproportionately influential in politics and national affairs. Not only did they lead by action in revolutionary proclamations, but they followed through as military and political leaders. Due in part to a collegiate curriculum that drew from the advanced writings of Scottish and Enlightenment thinkers in political economy, the colonial college alumni designed a system of government destined to serve as a model for the world. The colonial colleges' legacy then was producing a generation of American leaders and thinkers whose combination of decisiveness and thoughtfulness literally turned the world "upside down."

Higher Education in the New United States

With the founding of the United States of America, governmental policies towards English-chartered colleges became unclear. Wary of centralized power, Americans maintained educational control close to home. Therefore, governance of colonial colleges became almost exclusively the jurisdiction of local and state governments. In actuality the schools enjoyed independence as the Supreme Court's famous *Dartmouth* decision in 1819 demonstrated that the new federal government would protect colleges from state intervention.

With the reputation of colleges remaining high, most state legislatures, particularly in the newer states west of the Allegheny and Appalachian mountain ranges, looked favorably on chartering colleges as long as the state did not have to provide financial support. Between 1800 and 1850, the United States experienced a "college building boom" in which more than two hundred degree-granting institutions were created. However, since most of these new colleges depended on student tuition payments and local donors, there was also a high closure rate and the schools that did survive typically struggled from year to year.

Although the classical languages and liberal studies of the bachelor of arts degree remained central to the character of American higher education in this era, several new fields gained a foothold in formal study. Engineering and science acquired a presence on the campus. Professional education for law and medicine usually also took place though in separate institutions. Nevertheless, few if any learned professions in the early nineteenth century required academic degrees or certification. Most states reserved the right to set requirements for professional practice, and these were for the most part meager.

Going to college early in the nineteenth century was not particularly expensive. The cost of potential lost opportunities presented a greater concern for students and parents. Employers seldom required college degrees, therefore college presidents faced the perpetual challenge of persuading young adults to delay pursuing their life's enterprises by spending four years on campus. Modest-income families decided whether or not a young man's potential contribution to family labor could be spared while he pursued higher education. The college experience and the college degree did confer prestige and often some professional advantages, but its perceived benefits did not always outweigh the costs.

The United States, for all its deserved acclaim of being a truly "new nation," remained faithful to many of the tenets of English common law. For example, in New England states, the small farms and principle of primogeniture forbade the division of a father's land among numerous sons, so families had to find useful work for those sons not inheriting land. Going to college provided an attractive alternative, especially in subsistence-farming regions. Affordable colleges in rural New England provided an important route to respect and employment in schools and churches. In fact, with the onset of the Second Great Awakening in the early nineteenth century, new denominations once again pushed for clergy educated in institutions dedicated to their particulars of faith. Their "missionary zeal" led to the founding of new schools and an increase in college attendance. In short, college became useful not just for the elite, but also for sons who had fewer prospects in the new nation. This development resulted in a host of small liberal arts colleges in the Northeast and later in Ohio, Kentucky, and Tennessee that served as an important incubator for a growing middle class.

Educational opportunities for young women followed a comparable pattern. Families often wondered how a young single woman could be self-supporting or contribute to the family welfare. A growing national demand for trained teachers due to the "common-school movement" of the 1830s provided one answer. Women could achieve financial independence and respectability within a rather rigid social structure by attending a normal school or female seminary that provided them with an education for employment as teachers in the ever-expanding nation.

The mid-nineteenth century. Variety and growth characterized college building during the mid-nineteenth century. In addition to the conspicuous church-related liberal arts colleges, various groups founded a range of other special interest institutions for advanced study. These included agricultural colleges, proprietary medical schools, freestanding law schools, engineering schools, and scientific colleges. Private philanthropy indicated a growing American interest in founding new institutions concentrated on advanced scientific, technical, and engineering education. Illustrative of this realm was the generous support for such colleges as Rensselaer, Drexel, Cooper Union, and the Massachusetts Institute of Technology.

One of the biggest shifts was the federal government becoming directly involved in higher education, which developed during the Civil War when southern congressmen who opposed the legislation were absent. The Morrill Act of 1862 set in motion an elaborate program whereby states received profits from the sale of an allotted portion of western lands if used to establish programs of agricultural, mechanical, and military sciences, along with liberal arts. The so-called land-grant act thereby stimulated numerous creative proposals and projects. In some cases, states attached their new engineering or agricultural programs to historic colleges. In others, they opted to create new state colleges. Between 1887 and

1914, the land-grant colleges gained support and collective political strength and expanded the definition and scope of university curricula. Legislation such as the Hatch Act and the "Second Morrill Act" of 1890 continued the expansion of federal involvement in education by bringing federal funding and projects to the new land-grant campuses.

Amidst this flurry of federal legislation, African Americans also received attention though the treatment tended to have mixed results. On the one hand, the Morrill Act of 1890 provided funding for African-American education, which led to the creation of Negro colleges in seventeen southern states—a substantial gain in educational opportunities. On the other hand, the guidelines meant that the U.S. government accepted and endorsed state and local practices of racial segregation. By increasing their role in funding higher education, the federal government helped shift the focus of many American colleges.

Higher education's gilded age: 1870 to 1910. Between 1870 and 1910 nearly all institutions of higher education enjoyed a surge in appeal both to prospective students and to benefactors. Some historians have called this period the "Age of the University." Although accurate, the image remains incomplete. The university ideal certainly took root and blossomed during this period, but the historic undergraduate college also enjoyed growth, support, and popularity. Because of an unprecedented era of commercial and industrial expansion, a new period of philanthropy made possible the founding of well-endowed universities. One enduring sign of this growth came in 1900 when the presidents of fourteen institutions created the Association of American Universities. Its charter members included Johns Hopkins, Columbia, Harvard, Cornell, Yale, Clark, Catholic University, Princeton, Stanford, and the Universities of Chicago, Pennsylvania, California, Michigan, and Wisconsin. Gradually, over the next decades, relatively young state universities in the Midwest, along with private institutions such as Brown, Northwestern, Massachusetts Institute of Technology, and Vanderbilt, would also gain recognition and "university" status for their acceptance into the Association of American Universities.

The creation of the Association of American Universities reinvigorated an ongoing and intense debate over the proper definition and role of a modern American university. Nevertheless, without any official consensus, some general patterns of practice and aspiration stood out. The new modern university emphasized graduate programs, including the study for and conferral of the doctor of philosophy degree or Ph.D. In fact, the proliferation of varied degree programs connected with professions illustrated a new era in higher education. Many undergraduate programs in agriculture, engineering, business, education, and home economics, along with military training, challenged the old definition of collegiate studies. Medicine, law, and theology, three traditional professions, developed varying relationships with universities and academic standards.

A lack of national academic standards, especially among secondary schools, colleges, and universities, gave rise to the entrance of private agencies into the higher education arena. Such organizations as the Carnegie Foundation for the Advancement of Teaching and the Rockefeller General Education Board adjudicated ratings among American universities. The foundation directors used a combination of coercion and incentives to prompt universities, including professional schools, to adhere to reasonable criteria of admissions, instruction, and certification. On balance, the foundations probably acknowledged and promoted those universities that were already reasonably strong and sound, and raised the floor for others.

Much to the chagrin of "serious scholars," students shaped the undergraduate world according to their own preferences. It was in the elaborate extracurricular experiences of intercollegiate sports, campus newspapers, collegiate drama, literary societies, alumni groups, and fraternities that students reveled. Student (and public) enthusiasm for these activities grew as the popular media glamorized the social activities rather than scholarly pursuits.

Although the new structure and ethos of the "university" gained attention for its innovation, equally important was the support for and interest in smaller liberal arts colleges. This rising tide for colleges included an extended boom for the founding of women's colleges. Mount Holyoke Seminary in western Massachusetts transformed itself into a bachelor's degree-granting institution. Other prominent women's colleges founded in this era were Smith, Wellesley, Radcliffe, Pembroke, Barnard, and Bryn Mawr. Women also gained access via new coeducational institutions such as the University of Chicago, Stanford University, and many state colleges and universities in the Midwest and the West.

Higher education between the world wars. Between 1914 and 1918 the American campus displayed some flexibility to accommodate special programs for the domestic effort during World War I. It included special training programs for military personnel and sporadic but important instances of faculty research leading to direct inventions and innovations in warfare. Projects such as future Harvard president James B. Conant's efforts to develop mustard gas foreshadowed even greater cooperation between the universities and federal government during World War II.

College enrollments and public enthusiasm surged after World War I. One indicator of this popularity was the proliferation of huge football stadiums—most of which were named "Memorial Field." Crowds exceeding 50,000 at campus games became standard at many universities. Although popular since the 1890s, intercollegiate athletics soared in commercial appeal during the 1920s. The absence of any substantive national voluntary self-regulation led the Carnegie Foundation for the Advancement of Teaching to publish a highly visible expose of college sports' excesses in 1929. Some university officials denied the report's findings, but the Carnegie Study was timely and accurate. The abuses in college sports underscored what Abraham Flexner of the Carnegie Foundation identified as the root source of problems in American higher education: a lack of consensus on clarity of mission and purpose. Unfortunately for Flexner and his colleagues, too many colleges and their constituencies were well served by the amorphous, unregulated nature of American higher education. What was intended as a marketplace of ideas became simply a marketplace, in which students were consumers and sports was the best-seller.

The onset of the Great Depression illustrated an interesting phenomenon: college enrollments increased during times of national financial hardship. While institutions reduced budgets, many worked to sustain American colleges in lean years. Some universities also demonstrated resourcefulness in seeking out business and industrial projects for their faculty in such fields as engineering and physics. These initiatives by such schools as Stanford, Massachusetts Institute of Technology, and California Institute of Technology laid the groundwork for external projects sponsored by both the private sector and the federal government that would come to fruition in the 1940s.

Higher education's golden age: 1945 to 1970. Between 1941 and 1945 American colleges and universities participated directly and effectively in a complex national war effort. This track record in times of duress brought long-term rewards and readjustments after the war. In 1947, the President's Commission on Higher Education in a Democracy concluded that federal funding of research should continue even in peacetime. In response to the "problem" of returning military personnel to the domestic economy and as a measure of gratitude, Congress passed the Servicemen's Readjustment Act (1944), popularly known as the "G.I. Bill." For at least a temporary period, this generous and flexible financial aid program enabled an unprecedented number of veterans to attend colleges, universities, and an array of "postsecondary" institutions. This legislation also gave energy to civil rights cases linked with educational access.

In addition to federal funding, growing states with enthusiastic governors and legislatures sought ways to work with their state's educational leaders to accommodate an impending enrollment boom. The rising birth rate and increased migration into selected states, along with a deliberate extension of college admissions, caused this dramatic growth. California led the way in statewide coordination with its Master Plan of 1960. This program aimed at accommodating mass access to affordable higher education by channeling students into tiered institutions.

Among the most conspicuous transformations was the emergence of a network of public junior colleges. Founded in the early 1900s, junior colleges experienced expansion in California during the 1930s. After World War II these institutions carried out two critical functions in mass postsecondary education. First, they developed a "transfer function" in which students could enter colleges or universities after two years of course work at the junior college. They also offered advanced, terminal degree instruction and certification in a range of professional and occupational fields. By the 1960s, the addition of a third function—readily accessible, low-priced continuing education for adults—led to a change in the name from *junior college* to *community college.*

The federal government participated in the expansion of sponsored research and development education during the 1950s and 1960s. Drawing from former MIT President Vannevar Bush's 1945 monograph, *Science: The Endless Frontier,* Congress and a succession of U.S. presidents endorsed federal sponsorship of high-level, peer-reviewed national research projects. Federal agencies that became most involved were those requiring applied technical research, specifically defense and agriculture. The behavioral sciences gradually adopted this model for large-scale psychological testing, and then various health care programs also sought funding. Agencies such as the National Institute of Health possessed a limited scope and a miniscule budget in the late 1940s, but acquired an increasing presence over the next four decades. In 1963, Clark Kerr's work *The Uses of the University* summarized this culmination of government patronage in research and development. According to Kerr, about fifty to one hundred institutions had positioned themselves to be "Federal Grant Universities": powerful incubators of advanced scholarship in the sciences possessing the ability to inspire confidence and funding in their research grant applications.

Both public and private universities benefited from governmental concerns about "cold war" defense and competition with the Soviet Union. Fears resulting from an extended definition of "national defense" led to funding for advanced studies in foreign languages, anthropology, and political science as well as the "hard" sciences of physics and chemistry. The transfer of these national programs to higher education institutions increased both the founding of new campuses and the construction of new buildings on older campuses. According to one study in 1986, about 75 percent of American campus buildings were constructed between 1960 and 1985, suggesting that the symbol for higher education during the cold war ought to be the building crane.

Enrollment also surged during the cold war era. Just prior to World War II the state universities with the largest enrollments—namely, the Ohio State University and the University of California at Berkeley—surged far ahead of other institutions with enrollments of around 19,000. Many major state universities prior to World War II had enrollments between 3,000 and 6,000. By 1970, however, the Ohio State University's main campus at Columbus enrolled more than 50,000—comparable to the University of Minnesota. The University of California had expanded its Berkeley campus enrollment to 26,000.

Some states responded to increasing enrollments with complex, multicampus systems. The University of California, for example, had ten campuses, with a total enrollment exceeding 150,000. At the same time, the network of California state colleges formed its own system, eventually enrolling about two hundred thousand students as well. In addition, California's community colleges further expanded the accessibility to higher education by forming more than one hundred campuses. In New York, education officials and legislators created an expanded system of more than sixty campuses, the State University of New York (SUNY). While individual states pursued some variation of this theme, public community college systems enjoyed the greatest gains in student enrollments and campus expansion. Especially in such populous states as California, Texas, and Florida, the community college systems served a larger and expanding portion of the state's population. Although relative enrollment in private (independent) colleges decreased from approximately 50 percent of college students in 1950 to about 30 percent, this change did not preclude substantial numerical growth. Rather, the construction of new institutions in the public sector was exceptionally brisk.

Prior to the 1970s, the federal government did not venture much into substantial student financial aid programs. Rather, state and local policies produced low tuition rates at public institutions. However, with the passage of the Education Amendments of 1972, the federal government increasingly promoted college access, affordability, and choice. The showcase of this government interest was a commitment to need-based, portable student financial aid. The Pell Grant, officially known as the Basic Educational Opportunity Grant (BEOG), provided entitlements to enrolled college students who demonstrated financial need. These initiatives fueled dramatic enrollment growth. Though initially popular, by 1978 the emphasis on student grants shifted increasingly to providing low-interest student loans.

Expanded access and growing national investment in the higher education infrastructure increased the need for administration and planning both inside and outside the campus. Hence, higher education in the United States underwent a "managerial revolution" in its decision-making and attempts at coordination. On another level this led to the proliferation of an increasingly complex academic bureaucracy. On a second level, it gave rise to a reliance on a prodigious testing industry. Although the College Entrance Examination Board (CEEB) had been in existence since the turn of the century, it gained great influence after World War II with the

development and diffusion of the Educational Testing Service's Scholastic Aptitude Test (SAT). The capacity of the SAT to make determinations about college admissions and projections on college academic performance coexisted with doubts and controversies about the equity and validity of such high stakes tests. The SAT expanded the nationwide search for academic talent, and enabled the historic institutions of New England and the Atlantic Coast to draw a large percentage of students from public high schools (rather than primarily from nearby private prep schools), while attracting students from a wide geographic base. Despite the promise of standardized exams, by the 1960s there would be intense debates over the ability of the SAT and other such tests to identify genuine aptitude without bias toward socioeconomic class or educational experiences.

Questions of social justice and the clash of national laws with local practices came to the fore in the decade following *Brown v. the Board of Education of Topeka, Kansas* (1954) decision. In numerous states where public universities were segregated by race, policies were challenged. The southern campus came to be a real and symbolic focus of civil rights in American life.

Tensions and transitions: 1970 to 1985. Although American campuses expanded in the late 1950s and 1960s, many students did not feel they were well served. Crowding, lack of dormitories, and reliance on large lecture halls created the "impersonality of the multiversity." This malaise over the relative lack of attention to undergraduate education, combined with political activism over free speech, the antiwar protests, and issues of civil rights and social justice, spawned unrest on many American campuses between 1968 and 1972. Whether at such conspicuous universities as Berkeley, Columbia, or Michigan, or at quieter campuses, a generation of campus presidents and deans were unprepared to deal with widespread student dissatisfaction. Furthermore, the nation was unprepared for the tragedies that occurred at Kent State and Jackson State in 1970.

What governors and state legislators perceived as administrative failure to keep a campus house in order ultimately led to a loss of public and government confidence in colleges and universities. This change in attitude, combined with a stressed national economy, signaled for the first time in decades a tapering in public support for higher education. Double-digit inflation and an energy crisis, combined with warnings of a decline in college matriculation, left most American colleges and universities in a troubled situation between 1975 and the early 1980s. Postsecondary institutions in the 1970s enrolled an increasingly diverse student body in areas of race, gender, and ethnicity. Less clear, however, was the question of whether the educational experiences within those institutional structures were effective and equitable, as American higher education faced criticisms for charges of tracking lower income students into particular subsets of institutions and courses of study.

The end of the twentieth century. A fifteen-year period beginning in 1985 was a financial roller coaster for higher education in the United States despite the underlying growth of the enterprise. By the mid-1980s virtually every gubernatorial candidate ran as an "education governor," testimony to the hope that states placed in their colleges and universities to stimulate economic development. Ambitious presidents seized the opportunity to "buy the best," whether it pertained to recruiting faculty, bright students, intense doctoral candidates, or, regrettably, even athletes. This period of opportunity, however, mortgaged institutions' futures—a situation that became clear to accountants and boards soon after declines in the stock market and state revenues. Between 1990 and 1993 overextension and uncertainty loomed.

Illustrative of the partial gains in equity and meritocracy was the changing profile of females in higher education, especially in graduate and professional students. Whereas in 1970 relatively few women pursued doctorates or degrees in law or medicine, by 2000 women constituted close to half the students entering law school and about forty percent of first-year medical students. Women even constituted a majority of the Ph.D. recipients in biology, literature, and the humanities. At the same time, however, they were substantially underrepresented in such graduate fields as engineering and the physical sciences.

Connecting past to present. One theme that pervades higher education in the United States in the second half of the twentieth century is that of a "managerial revolution." In response to the expanding definition of higher education, the ability to navigate institutions became a preoccupation. It extended to include the development of professional expertise in fund-raising, as colleges and universities acquired voracious appetites for resources while ex-

tending their mission into new fields and even into new roles. Higher education in the United States has succeeded in running its own operations while also considering new roles and constituencies. Its strength has ironically been its major source of weakness. In other words, the aspiration and ability of the American postsecondary institutions to accommodate some approximation of universal access has been its foremost characteristic. Institutions' shortfalls in completely achieving that aspiration have been the major source of criticism and debate within American higher education. It is the perpetual American dilemma of how achieve both equality and excellence.

Grappling with the questions of educational equality and access has taken on increased urgency for two reasons. First, the widespread embrace of higher education as a means to legitimacy, literacy, and respectability strikes a deep chord in all sectors of American society. Secondly, since higher education has acquired the strength and stability of being a "mature industry," it must then compete with numerous activities for a share of the public purse and private donations. Maintaining and bolstering widespread trust in postsecondary education will be the central determinant in present and future discussions about ways in which Americans support higher education.

See also: COMMUNITY COLLEGES; HISPANIC-SERVING COLLEGES AND UNIVERSITIES; HISTORICALLY BLACK COLLEGES AND UNIVERSITIES; LAND-GRANT COLLEGES AND UNIVERSITIES; LIBERAL ARTS COLLEGES; RESEARCH UNIVERSITIES; SINGLE-SEX INSTITUTIONS; TRIBAL COLLEGES AND UNIVERSITIES.

BIBLIOGRAPHY

BRINT, STEVEN, and KARABEL, JEROME. 1989. *The Diverted Dream: Community Colleges and the Promise of Educational Opportunity in America, 1900–1985.* Oxford and New York: Oxford University Press.

GOODCHILD, LESTER F., and WECHSLER, HAROLD S., eds. 1989. *ASHE Reader on The History of Higher Education.* Needham Heights, MA: Ginn Press for the Association for the Study of Higher Education.

HOROWITZ, HELEN LEFKOWITZ. 1987. *Campus Life: Undergraduate Cultures from the End of the 19th Century to the Present.* New York: Knopf.

JENCKS, CHRISTOPHER, and RIESMAN, DAVID. 1968. *The Academic Revolution.* Garden City, NY: Doubleday.

KERR, CLARK. 1963. *The Uses of the University.* Cambridge, MA: Harvard University Press.

LEMANN, NICHOLAS. 1999. *The Big Test: The Secret History of the American Meritocracy.* New York: Farrar, Straus, and Giroux.

RUDOLPH, FREDERICK. 1990. *The American College and University: A History,* 2nd edition. Athens: University of Georgia Press.

SOLOMON, BARBARA. 1985. *In the Company of Educated Women.* New Haven, CT: Yale University Press.

VEYSEY, LAURENCE. 1965. *The Emergence of the American University.* Chicago: University of Chicago Press.

JOHN R. THELIN
JASON R. EDWARDS
ERIC MOYEN

SYSTEM

The higher education system of the United States is not so much a formal system as it is an informal configuration of varied institutions. The development of the American system has been unique when compared with other national postsecondary educational systems around the world. Unlike most other countries, where higher education systems have largely developed outward from a central, government-supported university, the United States has never had such an institution. Instead, the evolution of the U.S. system has been shaped by many different influences, including state and local needs, demographics, religion, and changing social contexts. As a result, postsecondary institutions in the United States mirror the multifaceted complexities of the broader society in which they are embedded and the diversity of the people they serve. Moreover, American higher education is quite disorderly in structure and function in contrast to many national postsecondary systems and even in sharp contrast to the rationally organized American compulsory primary and secondary education system. Postsecondary institutions and the students they serve are diverse and not easily categorized. This disorder is characterized by a variety of individual institutional goals and missions, types of degrees offered, finance and governance structures, and even curricula, course contents, and instructional methodologies.

In order to understand how this informal and loosely structured "system" of diverse institutions serves the wide-ranging needs of American society, it is necessary to identify some of the main features that define the major types of institutions found in American higher education. In 1983 Robert Birnbaum noted that institutional diversity can be defined across several categories of institutional features. The most useful of these categories include defining differences in terms of the following dimensions of institutional diversity: systemic, structural, constituent, and reputational.

Systemic Diversity

Systemic diversity refers to differences in types of institutions with regard to their size and scope of mission. Starting in the 1970s, there have been many attempts to develop classification systems for categorizing postsecondary institutions in this manner. The best-known and most well-established classification system was developed by the Carnegie Foundation for the Advancement of Teaching and has come to be known as the "Carnegie Classification." Originally developed by Clark Kerr in 1970, this classification system was designed to serve the research analysis needs of the Carnegie Commission on Higher Education. The commission "sought to identify categories of colleges and universities that would be relatively homogeneous with respect to the functions of the institutions as well as with respect to characteristics of students and faculty members" (Carnegie Commission on Higher Education, p. v). The Carnegie Classification was originally published in 1973 and has been updated several times, most recently in 2000. It is the framework most often used in describing institutional diversity in the United States and is relied upon by researchers and educational leaders to ensure appropriate comparisons between and among colleges and universities.

The current classification divides institutions into six main categories: doctoral/research institutions, master's colleges and universities, baccalaureate colleges, associate's colleges, specialized institutions, and tribal colleges. Within most categories are subcategories. Doctoral/research institutions can be either extensive or intensive and offer a wide range of undergraduate degrees as well as master's and doctoral-level graduate degrees. Extensive doctoral/research institutions award more doctorates in a wider range of fields than do intensive institutions. Master's colleges and universities fall into one of two categories (master's I or II) and typically offer a wide range of undergraduate programs as well as graduate education through the master's degree. Category I master's institutions award more master's degrees in a wider range of disciplines than do their category II peers. Baccalaureate colleges primarily focus on undergraduate education and are divided into three categories: baccalaureate colleges–liberal arts, baccalaureate colleges–general, and baccalaureate/associate's colleges. Liberal arts colleges award at least half of their degrees in liberal arts fields, whereas general colleges award less than half of their degrees in liberal arts fields. Baccalaureate/associate's colleges award both associate and baccalaureate degrees. Colleges and universities identified as specialized institutions in the Carnegie Classification may award degrees ranging from bachelor's to the doctorate, but they award the majority of those degrees in a single field. There are several subcategories of specialized institutions, including theological seminaries and other specialized faith-related institutions, medical schools and centers, other health profession schools, schools of engineering and technology, schools of business and management, fine arts schools, schools of law, teachers colleges, military institutes, and other types of specialized institutions. Tribal colleges are generally tribally controlled and located on reservations.

While the Carnegie classification system is often used in making qualitative distinctions among institutions, the commission denies that this is the classification's purpose. In his foreword to the 1987 edition of the classification, Ernest Boyer emphasized that the classification "is *not* intended to establish a hierarchy among learning institutions. Rather, the aim is to group institutions according to their shared characteristics, and we oppose the use of the classification as a way of making qualitative distinctions among the separate sectors" (Carnegie Foundation, p. 2). Nevertheless, the process of "institutional drift," in which colleges strive to climb the hierarchy, is well documented in the literature. For example, junior colleges become baccalaureate-granting institutions by grafting another two years onto their programs, while doctoral/research-intensive universities increase funded research activities as they aspire to doctoral/research-extensive status. In the early twenty-first century, the Carnegie Foundation was in the process of reassessing the

classification system, rethinking how to characterize similarities and differences among institutions, and allowing multiple classifications of institutions. This work was expected to be concluded in 2005.

While the Carnegie Foundation's system is the most widely used typology in educational research, other classification schemes exist and are usually used for other purposes, such as providing information to prospective students and their families. For example, *U.S. News and World Report* classifies colleges and universities in several typologies. Institutions are divided into categories by whether they tend to serve a national or a regional population and then are rank-sorted into four "tiers." Schools are also ranked according to best departments for a particular major and best financial value.

Although such categorization schemes are useful in a system that includes tremendous institutional variety, such simplification hides the true complexity of the higher education system of the United States. For example, an institution categorized as a "research university" may also have its roots in land-grant legislation, or may be single-sex or religiously affiliated. Other key hidden aspects of institutional identity include the institution's historical roots—whether it began as a land-grant college, historically black college or university, Hispanic-serving college, tribal college, or religiously affiliated institution. Additionally, there are less apparent dimensions of institutional difference, such as ratios between part-time and full-time students or residential versus commuter students. Athletic division membership is an important facet of institutional identity, as is location (region, urban, rural, suburban). Hence, it is important to pay attention to other aspects of institutional diversity in order to truly understand the nature of the diverse system of American higher education.

Structural Diversity

Structural diversity focuses on the ways in which institutions are organized and controlled. Structural diversity is most often defined in terms of type of institutional control—public or private. Publicly controlled institutions are funded primarily by the government (usually by state governments) and are typically part of a larger state system. Private institutions are primarily funded by nongovernment sources and tend to be independent with their own private governing boards. There are many more private institutions in the United States than there are public colleges and universities, although public higher education has grown significantly since the 1960s.

While there is no national system of higher education, all states have developed some type of public postsecondary educational system. There are a number of ways in which these systems are structured and organized. Public colleges and universities differ both in the ways in which they are governed and in the ways in which they are coordinated as part of a larger state system. All states assign responsibility for operating public colleges and universities to governing boards, and there are three main types of governing board structures: consolidated governance systems, segmental systems, and single-institution boards. Consolidated boards are responsible for all public postsecondary institutions in a particular state, although in some states this may apply only to the four-year institutions. Segmental systems have different governing boards for different types of campuses; in some states this may mean that public research universities are governed by one board, comprehensive state colleges by another board, and community colleges by yet another board. States that use single-institution boards grant governance autonomy to each public campus by allowing each to have its own board. Public boards vary in the degree to which they have formal governance authority and the extent to which they merely coordinate activities across the state's public postsecondary educational sector without any substantive decision-making powers.

Public institutions within these systems tend to fall into one of three major categories: universities, state colleges, and community colleges. Public universities typically grant a full range of graduate degrees (master's and doctoral), tend to have a strong research emphasis, and typically have large student enrollments. State colleges are typically smaller, may serve a particular region of a state, and usually offer both bachelor's and master's degrees. Community colleges are two-year colleges that provide associate degrees, preparation for transfer to four-year institutions, vocational and technical education and training, and large numbers of continuing education offerings. Some public institutions have been identified as land-grant institutions. Land-grant institutions were first established by the Morrill Act of 1862, which provided federal funds for establishing universities that (1) were open to all types of students (including women, minorities, and low-

income students), (2) offered degrees in practical and applied fields such as engineering and agriculture, and (3) shared knowledge with citizens throughout their state.

Private institutions are less easily characterized than are their public counterparts. Private institutions cover the full range of missions and structures found in American higher education. The most prestigious and highly selective institutions, whether they be Ivy League research universities or smaller liberal arts colleges, are private; but so too are the least well-known institutions. In fact, Alexander Astin and Calvin Lee noted in 1972 that there are literally hundreds of small colleges scattered across the United States that can be thought of as "the invisible colleges." These are small, private institutions with limited resources. Some are affiliated with a particular religion; others began life as private junior colleges. One of the key distinctions among private colleges is whether they are religiously affiliated or not. Religious affiliation occurs in many forms. A religious denomination or order directly controls some institutions, whereas others have only nominal relationships with religious bodies or sponsors. There are also increasing numbers of proprietary institutions that tend to award specialized degrees or that engage in alternative modes of educational delivery, such as distance learning.

Constituent Diversity

Institutions also vary by the core constituencies they serve, particularly with regard to the particular types of students served. This type of constituent institutional diversity is manifested in many forms, but some of the most prominent institutions that serve particular types of students are those colleges and universities that provide education primarily for student groups that have been traditionally underserved by the majority of postsecondary institutions. These institutions include historically black colleges and universities (HBCUs), Hispanic-serving institutions (HSIs), tribal colleges, and women's institutions.

HBCUs primarily, although not exclusively, exist to provide postsecondary institutions that primarily serve African-American students. There are currently 109 HBCUs, almost half of which are public. They are concentrated in the southern region of the nation, with a few institutions located in the Northeast and Midwest. HBCUs enroll fewer than 20 percent of African-American undergraduates, yet produce one-third of all African-American bachelor's degrees. HSIs are institutions in which at least one-quarter of the undergraduates are Hispanic. Rapidly growing as a group, there are well more than 100 such institutions in the early twenty-first century. Tribal colleges tend to be controlled by Native American tribes. There are currently twenty of these institutions in the United States. Women's colleges are primarily private and provide postsecondary educational environments that cater specifically to female students. Although there were hundreds of these institutions at one time, that number has dwindled to approximately seventy-five. There are also a handful of male-only institutions scattered across the country. All of these institutions reflect the diversity found in American society and provide the informal system of American higher education with a means of better serving the diverse groups of individuals that constitute a multicultural society. The existence of such diverse institutions has been noted as a particular strength of the American higher education system.

Reputational Diversity

Another key feature of American higher education is reputational diversity. It has been noted that higher education institutions in the United States are extremely stratified. In 1956 David Riesman offered the classic characterization of the importance of hierarchy and stratification in American higher education when he described the system of higher education as a "snakelike" procession in which the tail (composed of institutions lower in the hierarchy) and the body (representing institutions in the middle of the hierarchy) of the snake continually try to move up and catch the head (those institutions at the top of the hierarchy that serve as a model for other institutions to follow). Reputation appears to depend on a complex set of factors, including undergraduate selectivity and peer evaluations of graduate programs.

Advantages of the U.S. System

While the lack of systemwide structure creates a somewhat incoherent system of higher education in the United States where widespread coordination is virtually impossible, there are many advantages to this noncentralized approach to a national higher education system. The large degree of institutional diversity that has arisen from the decentralized nature of American higher education has generated

benefits on three levels: institutional, societal, and systemic. At the institutional level, arguments center on serving students' needs. Diversity in this sense would include variety of student body, institutional size, programs offered, and academic standards. Higher education does not exist in isolation, however. Birnbaum stated that "higher education is intimately connected to, and therefore interacts with, other societal systems" (p. 116). Aside from education and research, institutions of higher education have also long served various political, economic, and social functions. Societal arguments for diversity thus center on issues of social mobility and political interests. From a systems theory perspective, higher education is viewed as an "open system," characterized by diverse inputs and outputs. For example, if colleges and universities in the United States admit students with high levels of racial diversity (input), then the impact on society (output) will be very different from what it would be if the U.S. college student population were more homogeneous. Additionally, diversity in higher education is important because "differentiation of component units . . . leads to stability that protects the system itself" (Birnbaum, p. 121). Such systems are able to sense and respond to environmental pressures more quickly and effectively simply because they encompass such extensive variety. In sum, the diverse system of postsecondary institutions in America reflects the diverse composition and needs of the society it serves.

See also: HISPANIC-SERVING COLLEGES; HISTORICALLY BLACK COLLEGES AND UNIVERSITIES; LAND-GRANT COLLEGES AND UNIVERSITIES; LIBERAL ARTS COLLEGES; MILITARY PROFESSIONAL EDUCATION SYSTEM; RESEARCH UNIVERSITIES; SINGLE-SEX INSTITUTIONS; TRIBAL COLLEGES AND UNIVERSITIES.

BIBLIOGRAPHY

ASTIN, ALEXANDER W., and LEE, CALVIN B. T. 1972. *The Invisible Colleges: A Profile of Small, Private Colleges with Limited Resources.* New York: McGraw-Hill.

BIRNBAUM, ROBERT. 1983. *Maintaining Diversity in Higher Education.* San Francisco: Jossey-Bass.

BRAZZELL, JOHNETTA C. 1996. "Diversification of Postsecondary Institutions." In *Student Services: A Handbook for the Profession,* 3rd edition, ed. Ursula Delworth and Gary R. Hanson. San Francisco: Jossey-Bass.

CARNEGIE COMMISSION ON HIGHER EDUCATION. 1973. *A Classification of Institutions of Higher Education*. Berkeley: Carnegie Commission on Higher Education.

CARNEGIE FOUNDATION FOR THE ADVANCEMENT OF TEACHING. 1987. *A Classification of Institutions of Higher Education*. Princeton, NJ: Carnegie Foundation for the Advancement of Teaching.

COHEN, ARTHUR M. 1996. "Orderly Thinking about a Chaotic System." In *Transfer and Articulation: Improving Policies to Meet New Needs,* ed. Tronie Rifkin. San Francisco: Jossey-Bass.

McGUINNESS, AIMES C. 1997. "The Changing Structure of State Higher Education Leadership." In *State Postsecondary Education Structures Handbook: State Coordinating and Governing Boards*. Washington, DC: Education Commission of the States.

RIESMAN, DAVID. 1956. *The Academic Procession: Constraint and Variety in American Higher Education*. Lincoln: University of Nebraska Press.

JOSEPH B. BERGER
MARIA VITA CALKINS

HIGH SCHOOL

See: SECONDARY EDUCATION.

HISPANIC-SERVING COLLEGES AND UNIVERSITIES

Hispanics constitute the fastest-growing minority population in the United States. According to the U.S. Census Bureau, Hispanics represented 12.5 percent of the national population of 281 million in 2000. This is also a fairly young population: 36 percent of Hispanics are under eighteen years of age, and only 5 percent are age sixty-five or older. Moreover, only slightly more than half of all Hispanics are high school graduates, and thus are employed more in service and unskilled occupations than are non-Hispanic whites. In light of these statistics, Hispanic-serving institutions (HSIs) have become important colleges and universities for increasing Hispanics' access to college and improving their economic opportunities.

HSIs are still largely unknown and little understood by most educators and policymakers in the United States. Although HSIs represent almost 6 percent of all postsecondary institutions, they enroll approximately half of all Hispanic students in college, granting more associate and baccalaureate degrees to Hispanic students than all other American colleges or universities combined. Despite these impressive outcomes, a federal definition for HSIs exists only in the Higher Education Act of 1965, under Title V, as amended in 1992 and 1998. The 1998 legislation defines HSIs as accredited, degree-granting, public or private, nonprofit colleges and universities with 25 percent or more total undergraduate, full-time equivalent, Hispanic student enrollment. HSIs with this enrollment must also meet an additional criterion to qualify for Title V funds, which stipulates that no less than 50 percent of its Hispanic students must be low-income individuals.

The recruitment and retention of Hispanics to college has been the subject of long-standing concern among educators, policymakers, and practitioners. Although still largely unknown, HSIs attract and retain Hispanics in larger numbers than all other postsecondary institutions. Specifically, HSIs educate over 1.4 million students in the United States, of which 50 percent are Hispanic and another 20 percent are students from other ethnic backgrounds. In fact, HSIs might also be called minority-serving institutions, in light of the high percentage of diverse student populations they routinely educate.

The History of HSIs

The vast majority of HSIs were not created to serve a specific population, as historically black colleges and universities (HBCUs) and tribal colleges were, but rather evolved, starting around 1970, due to their geographic proximity to Hispanic populations and to demographic shifts. With the exceptions of Hostos Community College and the four-year institutions of Boricua College and National Hispanic University, HSIs do not have charters or missions that address distinctive purposes and goals for Latinos. On the other hand, HBCUs, which were begun as early as the nineteenth century, and tribal colleges, which were founded after 1970, intentionally serve their target student populations in accordance with their declared mission statements. However, the incredibly rapid growth of Hispanic-serving colleges and universities since the 1970s has conferred on them an ad hoc mission to serve the Hispanic population, and they are recognized as such by Congress and the Higher Education Act.

The designation of HSIs, and the development of a national awareness of HSIs, is essentially due to the Hispanic Association of Colleges and Universities (HACU), which was founded in 1986. The concept of linking all colleges and universities serving high proportions of Hispanics into an association to gain national recognition and resources was the work of a group of prominent Hispanic educators. Working relationships with corporations, foundations, and federal government agencies were formed to increase funding and services to these institutions. These resources led to providing greater professional growth and development opportunities for Hispanic students, faculty, and administrators. In forming the HACU, a national office in San Antonio, Texas, and another in Washington, D.C., were established to parlay the organization into a national player in the educational, political, and policymaking arenas. As an advocate, HACU focuses on educating policymakers and national leaders about Hispanic educational needs and the resulting economic and political implications for a more democratic and just society.

The rise of HSIs has been rather rapid since these institutions were first recognized nationally. Their rapid growth stems primarily from three significant factors. First, the civil rights movement of the 1960s and college outreach efforts opened up educational opportunities to less traditional college-going populations, including Hispanics and others from diverse racial and ethnic backgrounds. This movement was accompanied by the development of federal and state financial aid that made it possible for more students to go to college. Second, Hispanic immigration to the United States has increased, especially in large urban areas and along the southwest border of the nation. Third, Hispanics are continuing to move into communities where other Hispanics already are established and that are geographically near higher education institutions. Migration patterns, however, also indicate that Hispanics are moving into regions of the country where they have not been before as they seek jobs and more affordable housing.

As a result of these factors, there were 195 HSIs in 2000 and 203 in 2001, according to the White House Initiative on Educational Excellence for Hispanic Americans. Of these, 156 are located in 12 states (Arizona, California, Colorado, Florida, Illinois, Kansas, Massachusetts, New Jersey, New Mexico, New York, Texas, and Washington) and 47 in Puerto Rico—geographic areas where large concentrations of Hispanics reside. California, with 57, has the most HSIs, followed by Puerto Rico with 47, and Texas with 32. In addition, Kansas, Massachusetts, and Washington each have one HSI. In terms of type and control, there are 96 four-year HSIs, of which 44 are public and 52 are private. Among the 107 two-year HSIs, 94 are public and 13 are private. Thus, the majority of HSIs are community colleges, and these institutions will most likely continue to increase their Hispanic student enrollments. It is not surprising that California has the highest number of HSIs in the nation. Nearly one out of every three residents of California is Hispanic and the state has a vast system of 108 community colleges, the largest in the United States. On the other hand, Florida's representation of only nine HSIs belies the fact that it is home to the largest community college in the nation: Miami-Dade Community College. This institution consists of five separate campuses, with a total combined enrollment of more than 50,000, and two-thirds of its students are Hispanic.

HSIs and Latino Educational Attainment

Hispanic-serving institutions continue to demonstrate remarkable progress in assisting Hispanics to achieve academic and career success by stimulating higher college-attendance rates and higher degree-attainment rates. For example, the national college-attendance rate of Hispanics was 36 percent in 1997, up nearly 8 percent since 1990. However, this relatively low rate continues to be of national concern to educators and policymakers. Nonetheless, comparative U.S. data for college degrees awarded to Hispanics in HSIs and non-HSIs are remarkable. In 1997 Hispanics earned approximately 46 percent of all associate degrees awarded in HSIs, compared to 7.6 in non-HSIs. They received 23 percent of all bachelor's degrees awarded in HSIs, compared to 5.3 percent in non-HSIs; 19.5 percent of all master's degrees, compared to 3.7 percent in non-HSIs; 4.4 percent of all first professional degrees, compared to 4.6 in non-HSIs; and 6.1 percent of all doctorates, compared to 3.7 in non-HSIs. These data offer evidence that HSIs are directly responsible for increasing the educational attainment of Hispanics.

Data suggest that HSIs may also be credited as producers of the highest number of Hispanics who go on to pursue advanced degrees. Two-year HSIs lead the way in producing the highest number of Hispanic transfer students and associate degree recipients. Research studies further reveal that four-year HSIs with high Hispanic baccalaureate graduation rates point directly back to community college HSIs as the source of a significant number of their transfer students. These studies also show that four-year HSIs are the highest producers of professional and graduate Hispanic students.

Although the term *Hispanic-serving institutions* was recognized by the Higher Education Act in 1992, HSIs are not listed as a distinct institutional type in the latest Carnegie Classification of Institutions of Higher Education, as are tribal colleges. Also, the federal definition of an HSI is the only one used formally, vis-à-vis Title V and by applicants for funds. The HACU promotes a less stringent definition. HACU members must only have a total of 25 percent Hispanic enrollment, and associate members need only a minimum of 1,000 students. Their publication, *The Voice*, their Internet site, and their annual conference all highlight members' activities and HACU's advocacy role in continuing to influence national policy and garnering corporate support. Yet as recently as March 2001, articles in *The Chronicle of Higher Education* still referred to HSIs as "so-called Hispanic-Serving Institutions" (Yachnin, p. A34), indicating that not everyone accepts this distinct designation thus far.

It is important, however, to consider not only what it is that these newcomers to the higher education lexicon are, but how they are successfully educating students in their institutions. Moreover, it is important to consider what lessons can be learned from them that may be applicable to diverse students in other collegiate environments. Public understanding about HSIs can undoubtedly affect their future in terms of educational policy decisions and funding allocations. Despite their large student enrollments and seemingly low resources, HSIs appear to buffer Hispanic students' socialization into college through culturally sensitive programs that facilitate student academic achievement and completion for these and other minority students. Outreach efforts into the local K–12 schools and surrounding communities where Hispanics reside also are part of the holistic approach many HSIs are taking to raising Hispanic educational attainment rates.

Conclusion

It is clear that HSIs will continue to increase in number nationally from within the identified 3,856 American public and private, two- and four-year institutions of higher education. They will continue to be important in the twenty-first century in educating Hispanics and other minorities, whose numbers will continue to rise (according to U.S. census projections). These institutions' unofficial, undeclared dual role will continue to be: to help increase Hispanic college participation and completion rates for this population; and to help narrow the educational and economic gaps for Hispanics. It may well be, as Lisa Wolf-Wendel notes in her 2000 study, that "differences in race, ethnicity, social class, and other experiences influence what students need from their campuses and how campuses should respond. While separate examinations of each institution's characteristics are illuminating, it is important to understand that their whole is greater than the sum of their parts . . . . Instead, it is the combination of characteristics—their ethos—that makes them unique, able to facilitate their students' success" (p. 342).

See also: HIGHER EDUCATION IN THE UNITED STATES, *subentries on* HISTORICAL DEVELOPMENT, SYSTEM; HISTORICALLY BLACK COLLEGES AND UNIVERSITIES; MULTICULTURALISM IN HIGHER EDUCATION; RACE, ETHNICITY, AND CULTURE, *subentry on* LATINO GROWTH; TRIBAL COLLEGES AND UNIVERSITIES.

BIBLIOGRAPHY

BASINGER, JAMES. 2000. "A New Way of Classifying Colleges Elates Some and Perturbs Others." *The Chronicle of Higher Education* 46(49):31–42.

BENÍTEZ, MARGARITA. 1998. "Hispanic-Serving Institutions: Challenges and Opportunities." In *Minority-Serving Institutions: Distinct Purposes, Common Goals,* ed. Jamie P. Merisotis and Colleen T. O'Brien. San Francisco: Jossey-Bass.

CARNEGIE FOUNDATION FOR THE ADVANCEMENT OF TEACHING. 2000. *The Carnegie Classification of Institutions of Higher Education.* Princeton, NJ: Carnegie Foundation for the Advancement of Teaching.

CARNEVALE, ANTHONY P. 1999. *Education = Success: Empowering Hispanic Youth and Adults.* Princeton, NJ: Educational Testing Service.

DE LOS SANTOS, ALFREDO, and RIGUAL, ANTONIO. 1994. "The Progress of Hispanics in American Higher Education." In *Minorities in Higher Education,* ed. Manuel J. Justiz, Reginald Wilson, and Lars G. Björk. Phoenix: Oryx Press.

LADEN, BERTA VIGIL. 1999. "Two-Year Hispanic-Serving Colleges." In *Two-Year Colleges for Women and Minorities: Enabling Access to the Baccalaureate* ed. Barbara K. Townsend. New York: Falmer Press.

LADEN, BERTA VIGIL. 2000. "Hispanic-Serving Two-Year Institutions: What Accounts for Their High Transfer Rates?" Paper presented at the annual meeting of the Association for the Study of Higher Education, San Antonio, TX.

MILES, MATTHEW B., and HUBERMAN, A. MICHAEL. 1994. *Qualitative Data Analysis.* Thousand Oaks, CA: Sage.

O'BRIEN, COLLEEN T., and ZUDAK, CATHERINE. 1998. "Minority-Serving Institutions: An Overview." In *Minority-Serving Institutions: Distinct Purposes, Common Goals,* ed. Jamie P. Merisotis and Colleen T. O'Brien. San Francisco: Jossey-Bass.

RUBIN, HERBERT J. and RUBIN, IRENE S. 1995. *Qualitative Interviewing: The Art of Hearing Data.* Thousand Oaks, CA: Sage.

SOLORZANO, DANIEL G. 1993. *The Road to the Doctorate for California's Chicanas and Chicanos: A Study of Ford Foundation Minority Fellows.* Berkeley: California Policy Seminar.

SOLORZANO, DANIEL G. 1995. "The Baccalaureate Origins of Chicana and Chicano Doctorates in the Social Sciences." *Hispanic Journal of Behavioral Sciences* 17(1):3–32.

WILDS, DEBORAH J. 2000. *Minorities in Higher Education 1999–2000. Seventeenth Annual Status Report.* Washington, DC: American Council on Education.

WOLF-WENDEL, LISA E. 2000. "Women-Friendly Campuses: What Five Institutions Are Doing Right." *The Review of Higher Education* 23(3):319–345.

YACHNIN, JANET. 2001. "Lawmakers Protest New Education Panels." *The Chronicle of Higher Education* A43.

YIN, ROBERT K. 1989. *Case Study Research: Design and Methods,* revised edition. Thousand Oaks, CA: Sage.

INTERNET RESOURCES

U.S. CENSUS BUREAU. 2000. <www.census.gov>.

WHITE HOUSE INITIATIVE ON EDUCATIONAL EXCELLENCE FOR HISPANIC AMERICANS. 1999. "What Are Hispanic-Serving Institutions?" <www.ed.gov/offices/OIIA/Hispanic>.

BERTA VIGIL LADEN

HISPANIC STUDENTS

See: AFFIRMATIVE ACTION COMPLIANCE IN HIGHER EDUCATION; HISPANIC-SERVING COLLEGES AND UNIVERSITIES; LITERACY AND CULTURE; INDIVIDUAL DIFFERENCES, *subentry on* ETHNICITY; MULTICULTURAL EDUCATION; MULTICULTURALISM IN HIGHER EDUCATION; RACE, ETHNICITY, AND CULTURE.

HISTORICALLY BLACK COLLEGES AND UNIVERSITIES

Historically black colleges and universities (HBCUs) are institutions that were established prior to 1964 with the mission to educate black Americans. Perhaps one of the greatest struggles faced by blacks in the United States has been the struggle to be educated. This struggle has been guided by the philosophies of black scholars who believed that without struggle there was no progress; black revolutionists who believed that education was the passport to the future; and black clergy who sermonized that without vision the people would perish. Education is now, and always has been, a vital weapon in the black arsenal. Essentially, black Americans used education as their primary source of ammunition in the fight against a segregated society, racism, illiteracy, and poverty. The steadfast desire of the black population to be educated influenced the development of HBCUs, and HBCUs have likewise contributed much to the advancement of the black population.

The Development of HBCUs

Since the establishment of the first HBCU, there has been a recurrent debate over the role of these institutions within the larger framework of higher education. During the years of strict and legal racial segregation in the United States, HBCUs served as "islands of hope" where blacks could learn to read and write without the fear of being retaliated against. The primary purpose of HBCUs was to educate black Americans, which they did almost exclusively from 1865 to the 1950s. The overwhelming majority of HBCUs opened after 1865 in response to the need to have institutions to educate newly freed slaves and to avoid admitting those newly freed slaves into the existing white institutions.

The first HBCUs were established in the North and were products of independent religious institutions or philanthropic Christian missionaries. The first two were Cheyney University (Pennsylvania), founded in 1837, and Wilberforce University (Ohio), founded in 1856. However, historically black colleges and universities cannot be examined without revisiting major legislations and court decisions that led to the birth of many and the death of a few. The First Morrill Act (also known as the National Land-Grant Colleges Act of 1862) made postsecondary education accessible to a broader population of American citizens. Ten years after this act was legislated, the Freedman's Bureau was established to provide support to a small number of HBCUs. The Second Morrill Act of 1890 led to the establishment of nineteen HBCUs. Although these three legislative acts provided an atmosphere for change, it was the segregation movement in the South that provided the impetus for black higher education, particularly with the 1896 Supreme Court decision in *Plessy v. Ferguson,* which ultimately established by law the right to set up *separate but equal* schools for blacks. This decision led to the expansion and growth of historically black colleges and universities.

Historically black colleges and universities increased from one in 1837 to more than 100 in 1973. Most of these colleges were founded after the *Plessy v. Ferguson* decision. According to Jacqueline Fleming, "the majority of black public colleges, then, evolved out of state desires to avoid admitting blacks to existing white institutions" (p. 5). On May 17, 1954, the Supreme Court ruled in *Brown v. Board of Education of Topeka, Kansas* that separate education for blacks in public schools was unconstitutional because separate facilities are inherently unequal. This decision, which ended de jure racial segregation in public schools, also impacted higher education, as states were required to dismantle dual systems of higher education. This required predominantly white institutions (PWIs) to open their doors to black students, who prior to this time could not attend these institutions.

Interestingly enough, the effects of a decision made in the mid-twentieth century still linger in higher education in the early twenty-first century,

for nowhere are the repercussions from the *Brown* decision more visible than in HBCUs. The dismantling of dual systems in higher education has resulted in mergers and closures of HBCUs because opponents of these institutions view them as segregated colleges and universities. This has led to a series of discussions, debates, and court rulings that underscore the fact that there not enough research has been done on this segment of higher education.

Academic and Social Experiences at HBCUs

The literature on higher education is scant in the area of HBCUs. These institutions did not become the subject of research studies until the early 1970s. However, researchers have learned a considerable amount about the academic and social experiences of students who attend HBCUs. In 1992, Walter Allen reported that black students who attend HBCUs have better academic performance, greater social involvement, and higher occupational aspirations than black students who attend PWIs. On black campuses students emphasize feelings of engagement, extensive support, acceptance, encouragement, and connection. Allen also found that HBCUs communicate to black students that it is safe to take the risks associated with intellectual growth and development.

Proponents of HBCUs argue that they have served black students with considerable effectiveness. Researchers contend that HBCUs provide assets for black students that are unavailable and unattainable in white institutions. Socially, Donald Smith found that they provide an accepting environment with emotional support. He also found that they serve as repositories for the black heritage. The environment at HBCUs is one of acceptance of students for who they are, and students do not experience social isolation, but rather integration into campus life and extracurricular offerings. HBCUs also foster healthy social relationships, and students form positive relationships with faculty members as well as their peers. It is not uncommon to find formal and informal mentoring relationships developing in this environment. In addition, HBCUs foster ethnic pride and self-esteem.

Academically, HBCUs offer programs designed to meet the unique needs of black students and the black community, and they educate many students with learning deficiencies. Although the facilities are generally modest and resources are limited, numerous studies indicate that HBCUs have done an outstanding job at educating their clientele. For an extensive period in American history, HBCUs were solely responsible for educating and preparing blacks to live as free people in the South. HBCUs accepted this responsibility and educated many black Americans with very little in the way of financial resources. The academic gains for black students attending HBCUs are high when compared to their counterparts at predominantly white schools. This is due in part to the nurturing campus environment and positive faculty relationships that motivate students to do well academically.

Historically black colleges and universities have been crucial in the development of black professionals. For more than 160 years, these institutions have educated a population that has lived under severe legal, education, economic, political, and social restrictions. Early HBCUs were established to train teachers, preachers, and other community members to remedy the despairs of slavery that scarred African Americans. First and foremost, HBCUs opened the door of educational opportunity for many blacks who were once legally denied an education. Secondly, they provided educational access to those who were educationally underprepared to enter predominantly white institutions. By 1950, HBCUs were responsible for serving 90 percent of black students in higher education. Moreover, HBCUs had produced 75 percent of all black Ph.D.'s, 75 percent of all black army officers, 80 percent of all black federal judges, and 85 percent of all black physicians. In 2001, HBCUs served 14 percent of all black students enrolled in college, but were annually responsible for 26 percent of black baccalaureate degrees.

Conclusion

It has been stated that HBCUs have a unique chapter in the history of American postsecondary education. Despite the tremendous obstacles that these institutions faced, there are 104 HBCUs as of 2002—approximately 3 percent of U.S. higher education institutions. While there was a period where HBCUs had fallen from the research literature, current research scholars have developed a renewed interest in these institutions. This renewed interest partly stems from the fact that these institutions still play a vital role in American higher education. While black students in the early twenty-first century can choose to attend any type of institution, many are electing to attend an HBCU. While these colleges and universities achieve tremendous success, it is important to

further investigate the unique identity and the diversity they bring to higher education. In 2001, Coaxum called for a separate classification of HBCUs, on in which the diversity of these institutions could be understood within the context of their institutional peers.

See also: HIGHER EDUCATION IN THE UNITED STATES.

BIBLIOGRAPHY

ALLEN, WALTER R. 1986. *Gender and Campus Race Differences in Black Student Academic Performance, Racial Attitudes, and College Satisfaction.* Atlanta, GA: Southern Education Foundation.

ALLEN, WALTER R. 1987. "Black Colleges vs. White Colleges." *Change* 30:28–39.

ALLEN, WALTER R. 1992. "The Color of Success: African-American College Student Outcomes at Predominantly White and Historically Black Colleges." *Harvard Educational Review* 6(2):26–44.

ALLEN, WALTER R.; EPP, EDGAR G.; and HANIFF, NESHA Z. 1991. *College in Black and White: African American Students in Predominantly White and Historically Black Public Colleges and Universities.* Albany: State University of New York Press.

BILLINGSLEY, ANDREW. 1982. "Building Strong Faculties in Black Colleges." *Journal of Negro Education* 50(1):4–15.

BROWN, M. CHRISTOPHER, II. 1999. *The Quest to Define Collegiate Desegregation: Black Colleges, Title VI Compliance, and Post-Adams Litigation.* Westport, CT: Bergin and Garvey.

BROWNING, J., and WILLIAMS, JOHN B. 1978. "History and Goals of Black Institutions of Higher Learning." In *Black Colleges in America: Challenge, Development, Survival,* ed. Charles V. Willie and Ronald R. Edmonds. New York: Teachers College Press.

COAXUM, JAMES, III. 2001. "The Misalignment between the Carnegie Classification and Black Colleges." *Urban Education* 36(5):572–583.

DAVIS, J. E. 1998. "Cultural Capital and the Role of Historically Black Colleges and Universities in Educational Reproduction." In *African American Culture and Heritage in Higher Education Research and Practice,* ed. Kassie Freeman. Westport, CT: Praeger.

FLEMING, JACQUELINE. 1984. *Blacks in College.* San Francisco: Jossey-Bass.

FRANKLIN, JOHN HOPE. 1980. *From Slavery to Freedom: A History of Negro Americans.* New York: Knopf.

FREEMAN, KASSIE. 1998. *African American Culture and Heritage in Higher Education Research and Practice.* Westport, CT: Praeger.

FREEMAN, KASSIE. 1999. "HBCs or PWIs? African American High School Students' Consideration of Higher Education Institution Types." *The Review of Higher Education* 23(1):91–106.

HILL, SUSAN. 1985. *Traditionally Black Institutions of Higher Education: Their Development and Status: 1860 to 1982.* Washington, DC: National Center for Education Statistics.

HOFFMAN, CHARLENE. 1996. *Historically Black Colleges and Universities: 1976–1994.* Washington, DC: National Center for Education Statistics.

JONES, BUTLER A. 1974. "The Tradition of Sociology Teaching in Black Colleges: The Unheralded Profession." In *Black Sociologists: Historical and Contemporary Perspectives,* ed. James E. Blackwell and Morris Janowitz. Chicago: University of Chicago Press.

LOMOTEY, KOFI, ed. 1989. *Going to School: The African American Experience.* Albany: State University of New York Press.

LOW, W. AUGUSTUS, and CLIFT, VIRGIL A. 1981. "Education: Colleges and Universities." In *Encyclopedia of Black America,* ed. W. Augustus Low and Virgil A. Clift. New York: McGraw-Hill.

LUCAS, CHRISTOPHER J. 1994. *American Higher Education: A History.* New York: St. Martin's.

ROEBUCK, JULIAN B., and MURTY, KOMANDURI S. 1993. *Historically Black Colleges and Universities: Their Places in American Higher Education.* Westport, CT: Praeger.

SMITH, DONALD H. 1981. *Admission and Retention Problems of Black Students at Seven Predominantly White Universities.* Washington, DC: National Advisory Committee on Black Higher Education and Black Colleges and Universities.

WILLIE, CHARLES V.; GRADY, MICHAEL K.; and HOPE, RICHARD O. 1991. *African-Americans and the Doctoral Experience: Implications for Policy.* New York: Teachers College Press.

JAMES COAXUM III

HISTORY

LEARNING

The learning of history is a complex undertaking. Cognitive research done since 1980, much of it in Great Britain and North America, has indicated that it is more difficult to learn and understand history than previously thought. Before the 1980s it was generally assumed that a gradual process of committing historical narratives—constructed around key events, details, names, and dates (substantive knowledge)—to memory would eventually result in a sturdy understanding of the past. The body of research compiled since 1980, however, demonstrates that learning history, if it is to lead to deeper understanding, involves not only the repeated study of such narratives, but also the acquisition and use of a set of domain-specific cognitive strategies (strategic knowledge). Applying these strategies serves as the means by which the past is learned and understood. Researchers and educators frequently refer to the application of these domain-specific strategies to the process of exploring and interpreting the past as historical thinking. Before examining in more detail the implications of this research for learning history, it is important to understand the nature of the domain that learners are attempting to comprehend.

History as a Subject Domain

History is a thoroughly interpretive discipline, closer in many ways to the humanities than to the social sciences. To understand the past, learners cannot conduct controlled experiments to recreate it and then study its effects. Nor can they travel back in time to witness events firsthand. And even if time travel were possible, learners would still be required to interpret the complex events that they were witnessing.

Access to the past is thus indirect, largely governed by artifacts and residue left behind by those who lived it. These include diaries, letters, journals, public records, newspapers, archeological artifacts, pictures, paintings, chroniclers' and historians' interpretations of past events, and the like. Those who make a living inquiring into the past divide the artifacts and historical residue into two types, primary and secondary sources. Primary sources include, among other things, diaries and personal journals compiled by people who actually witnessed or participated in an incident about which they report. Secondary sources include history textbooks or historical narratives written by someone not present at an event but who has studied and interpreted the primary sources that remain. Historical sources form a type of evidence chain or trail that must be painstakingly pieced together into carefully argued interpretations of past events. This piecing-together that learners and inquirers do as they make sense of the past's artifacts and residues has been a central subject of cognitive research studies.

Substantive Historical Knowledge and Understanding

Defining the nature of substantive historical knowledge is rife with debate. Largely, the debate turns on the matter of what constitutes historically significant events and occurrences. For roughly the first half the twentieth century, those who wrote American history, for example, seemed content to concentrate on political, military, and economic achievements in the United States. It was believed that those achievements were the most historically significant. During the 1960s, however, a new generation of historical scholars began to redefine significance in terms of what was often called "history from the bottom up." This generation (sometimes referred to as social historians) began inquiring into the influences on the American past of a variety of sociocultural groups that had often been rendered historically invisible by previous generations of scholars. These groups include antebellum slave communities, labor movements and their leaders, women, immigrants, and small, often marginalized, social organizations. The social historians maintained that these overlooked groups could be seen as powerful participants in, or resistors of, important changes and developments in American history, thus (at least in part) accounting for how change occurred as it did. To ignore such groups would be to misunderstand history. The work of social historians, with their proliferating foci and perspectives on events, has made constructing grand political-military-economic historical narratives less easy to accomplish.

This shifting terrain concerning issues of historical significance has raised difficult questions about what history students should learn. The late twentieth-century increase in the multiculturalization of the United States, for example, has only added to this concern by also raising questions about *whose* history children should learn. Some participants in the debate, such as Arthur Schlesinger Jr., believe that all U.S. children should acquire the same "common cultural" core of substantive historical knowledge. Schlesinger defines this core largely in terms of those political, military, and economic events that made the United States the most powerful nation on earth. Knowledge of these events would be delivered by traditional, uplifting narratives of American success stories. Current social historians, and those who champion a more multiculturalist portrait of America, consider such definitions of core substantive historical knowledge misleading at best, and dangerous at worst, because they risk characterizing the contributions of those groups of people thought to be less significant as meaningless.

This debate has continued into the twenty-first century. What, and whose, history students have opportunities to learn about in school vary depending on how school officials define what is historically significant. To the extent that they define it in traditional narrative terms, children's opportunities to learn substantive historical knowledge are often determined by the content of school history textbooks, which, for publishers, in their efforts to find a palatable middle ground to bolster sales, means opting in the direction of more traditional narrative treatments. To the extent that a more multiculturalized view of substantive knowledge is in play, students are more apt to study history from multiple sources, such as trade books, historical fiction accounts, and primary sources, that explore the lives of those not frequently included in the more voluminous textbook treatments.

Strategic Historical Knowledge

Much of the cognitive research done since 1980 has centered on the nature of expertise in historical thinking, and on how novices (e.g., grade school students, college undergraduates) differ from experts (e.g., historians). This research indicates that the process of thinking historically that enables deep historical understanding requires certain strategic-knowledge dispositions. These dispositions include the capacity to: (a) read, make sense, and judge the status of various of sources of evidence from the past; (b) corroborate that evidence by carefully comparing and contrasting it; (c) construct context-specific, evidenced-based interpretations; (d) assess an author's perspective or position in an account being studied; and (e) make decisions about what is historically significant. These capacities are exercised while taking into conscious account the way the learner is, by necessity, also imposing his or her own view on the evidence being interpreted.

Learning to think using these cognitive strategies is no small task. First, as historian David Lowenthal has observed, the past is a foreign country, difficult to penetrate from the locus of the present. Reconstructing historical context is troublesome because it often remains virtually impossible for "moderns" to get inside and understand the experiences of those "ancients." Second, evidence is often sparse, and thus so open to competing interpretations that understanding events by building context-sensitive, well-corroborated interpretations is tenuous at best. Third, any attempt to construct a history of events operates on a necessary connection between a past reality and present interpretations of that reality. This connection is, however, denied because there is no method for bringing that past reality back to life to establish the full accuracy of a contemporary interpretation. There are only chains of people's interpretations of the past, some more recent than others. Learning to use the strategies of thinking historically that enable an understanding of the past hinges on the cultivation of a number of such counterintuitive cognitive processes.

Development of Historical Thinking and Understanding

Most of the more recent North American research on learning history has focused on either expert-novice studies, as noted, or on the relationship between how teachers teach history and how students learn to think historically. Views on how the historical thinking and understanding develop have largely been extrapolated from the expert-novice research cited above, and from studies that show how teaching can influence development among novices. Educational researchers in Great Britain—who were initially influenced in the 1970s by Piagetian developmental theories, but later abandoned them for the most part—have done considerably more work in this area. One of the more promising lines of research is called Project Chata. *Chata* is an acronym for Concepts of History and Teaching Approaches. The goal of Project Chata is to "map changes in students' ideas about history between the ages of seven and fourteen years. The project focused on second-

order procedural understandings like *evidence* or *cause*" (Lee and Ashby, p. 201).

Preliminary results of the research on the progression of students' ideas about historical evidence and its relationship to the past indicate that naive views of history begin with the understanding that the past is simply a given. As students grow more sophisticated in their understanding, this simplistic view is abandoned, though history remains relatively inaccessible. They follow this with the belief that the past is determined by stories people tell about it. As sophistication grows, students note that reports on the past are more or less biased. This idea gives way to noting that the viewpoint or perspective of a reporter or storyteller becomes important. Finally, students develop an understanding that it is in the nature of accounts to differ, because varying reporting criteria are used by storytellers and chroniclers.

Project Chata researchers have also studied students' development of ideas about causal structure and historical explanations. They observe that: (1) students' ideas about explanation vary widely, with some younger children having more sophisticated ideas than older children; (2) students' ideas about causation in history and their rational explanations of causal structures do not necessarily develop in parallel; (3) student's ideas about causal structures and explanations in history may develop at different intervals, with some ideas occurring in big gains in younger children and others occurring later; and (4) progression in students' ideas about causation and explanation occurred most markedly in schools where history was an identifiable subject matter.

Some Pedagogical Implications

A tentative theory of how to teach learners to think and understand history can be fashioned from the current corpus of research studies. This results in certain propositions. First, learners construct deeper historical understandings when they have opportunities to consciously use their prior knowledge and assumptions about the past (regardless of how limited or naive) to investigate the past in depth. Second, as learners explore the past, attention must be paid not only to the products of historical investigation, but to the investigative process itself. Third, developing historical thinking and understanding necessitates opportunities for learners to work with various forms of evidence, deal with issues of interpretation, ask and address questions about the significance of events and the nature of evidence, wrestle with the issues of historical agency, and cultivate and use thoughtful, context-sensitive imagination to fill in gaps in the evidence chain when they appear.

Applying this theory in the classroom would mean approaching history effectively from the inside out. Teachers would structure learning opportunities by posing compelling historical questions that have occupied the attention of historical inquirers (e.g., Why did so many colonists starve at Jamestown in the winter of 1609–1610? How did antebellum slave communities construct oral cultures and to what effect?). Students would adopt investigative roles, obtaining and scouring evidence (much of it obtained off the Internet from rich archival sources now online); reading, analyzing, and corroborating that evidence; addressing perspective in accounts; dealing with questions of agency and significance; and building their own interpretations of events as they addressed the questions posed.

See also: Civics and Citizenship Education; History, *subentry on* Teaching of; Learning, *subentry on* Causal Reasoning; Literacy, *subentry on* Narrative Comprehension and Production; Technology in Education, *subentry on* Trends.

BIBLIOGRAPHY

Ashby, Rosalyn, and Lee, Peter. 1987. "Children's Concepts of Empathy and Understanding in History." in *The History Curriculum for Teachers,* ed. Christopher Portal. London: Falmer Press.

Greene, Stuart. 1993. "The Role of Task in the Development of Academic Thinking Through Reading and Writing in a College History Course." *Research in the Teaching of English* 27:46–75.

Holt, Thomas. 1990. *Thinking Historically: Narrative, Imagination, and Understanding.* New York: College Entrance Examination Board.

Lee, Peter, and Ashby, Rosalyn. 2000. "Progression in Historical Understanding Among Students Ages 7–14." In *Knowing, Teaching, and Learning History: National and International Perspectives,* ed. Peter N. Stearns, Peter Seixas, and Sam Wineburg. New York: New York University Press.

Leinhardt, Gaea, and Young, Kathleen M. 1996. "Two Texts, Three Readers: Distance and Expertise in Reading History." *Cognition and Instruction* 14:441–486.

Levine, Lawrence. 1993. *The Unpredictable Past: Explorations in American Cultural History.* Oxford: Oxford University Press.

Lowenthal, David. 1985. *The Past Is a Foreign Country.* Cambridge, Eng.: Cambridge University Press.

Novick, Peter. 1988. *That Noble Dream: The "Objectivity Question" and the American Historical Profession.* Cambridge, Eng.: Cambridge University Press.

Rouet, Jean-Francois; Favart, Monik; Britt, M. Anne; and Perfetti, Charles A. 1998. "Studying and Using Multiple Documents in History: Effects of Discipline Expertise." *Cognition and Instruction* 15:85–106.

Schlesinger, Arthur M., Jr. 1992. *The Disuniting of America: Reflections on a Multicultural Society.* New York: W.W. Norton.

Seixas, Peter. 1996. "Conceptualizing the Growth of Historical Understanding." In *The Handbook of Psychology in Education,* ed. David R. Olson and Nancy Torrance. Oxford: Blackwell.

Shemilt, Denis. 1984. "Beauty and the Philosopher: Empathy in History and Classroom." In *Learning History,* ed. Alaric Dickinson, Peter Lee, and Peter J. Rogers. London: Heinemann.

Sinatra, Gail; Beck, Isabel L.; and McKeown, Margaret. 1992. "A Longitudinal Characterization of Young Students Knowledge of Their Country's Government." *American Educational Research Journal* 29:633–662.

Stahl, Steven; Hynd, Cyndy; Britton, Bruce; McNish, Mary; and Bosquet, David. 1996. "What Happens When Students Read Multiple Source Documents in History?" *Reading Research Quarterly* 31:430–456.

Takaki, Ronald T. 1993. *A Different Mirror: A History of Multicultural America.* Boston: Little, Brown.

VanSledright, Bruce A. 2002. *In Search of America's Past: Learning to Read History in Elementary School.* New York: Teachers College Press.

Wilson, Suzanne. 1990. "Mastodons, Maps, and Michigan: Exploring Uncharted Territory While Teaching Elementary School Social Studies." *Elementary Subjects Center,* No. 24. East Lansing: Center for the Learning and Teaching of Elementary Subjects, Michigan State University.

Wineburg, Samuel. 1996. "The Psychology of Teaching and Learning History." In *Handbook of Educational Psychology,* ed. Robert C. Calfee and David C. Berliner. New York: Macmillan.

Wineburg, Samuel. 2001. *Historical Thinking and Other Unnatural Acts: Charting the Future of Teaching the Past.* Philadelphia: Temple University Press.

Bruce A. VanSledright

TEACHING OF

History has played a dominant role in the broader social studies curriculum in the United States and in other countries for at least the past 100 years. For example, in most school districts in the United States, state, national, or world history is taught in grades four through six, grade eight, and at several points in high school. In England, history forms the backbone of the social studies curriculum from primary through secondary schools. History is also a curriculum staple in continental European countries, among post-Soviet republics, in China, and in such places as post-apartheid South Africa.

History in the school curriculum has not been without a number of recurrent debates and controversies. Many of them stem from disputes over the goals and purposes school history should serve (e.g., political socialization and nationalist identity formation versus teaching historical habits of mind). Other issues arise in connection with questions about how, from the vastness of history itself, to define what constitutes historically significant events that should be taught. The proper role of integrating social science disciplines (e.g., geography, economics, political science) in the teaching of history is also a point of debate. Finally, various parties argue over maintaining a relative balance between transmitting historical knowledge derived from the work of historians and teaching students to learn to think and investigate the past the way historians do. Taking time to do both often creates time-use dilemmas within an already surfeited school curricula. Choosing between them repeatedly pits those who would use history for sociopolitical ends against those who see history's importance as a means of teaching critical reasoning and a fuller understanding of the past.

Political Socialization of Historical Thinking and Understanding

The interest in securing a firm place for history in the curriculum frequently stems from its sociopoliti-

cal uses. This is especially true in the teaching of national histories. As George Orwell reminded readers in his book, *1984,* control of the present (and the future) depends in good measure on control over the past. In many countries, a principal goal of teaching the nation's history is deeply linked to socializing future citizens, as defined by whomever controls the sociopolitical agenda at the time, conservatives, liberals, revolutionaries, or others. Perhaps no other school subject serves this political socialization purpose more than the study of history.

As political parties change or revolutions occur, new regimes attempt to rewrite history in general, and school history in particular, in order to cast themselves and their new politics and policies in a favorable light. Those disempowered by political change often resist such efforts to recast the past. Various groups use history in an effort to shape (or reshape) the nationalist identities of youth around whatever the prevailing view privileged by those in power is at any given time. In post-Soviet eastern European countries, for example, a major educational agenda has been to rewrite history textbooks and reconfigure the history curriculum since 1990.

Prior to the mid-1970s, little systematic research had been done on how history was taught in schools and what students learned from studying it. Since then, there has been a surge of interest in studying school history teaching and its learning outcomes, particularly among researchers in England and in North America. As a result, a sizable body of scholarship has emerged. Much of it challenges the practice of using school history to advance sociopolitical ends. In general, the research indicates that the sociopolitical use of history in schools warps students' views of what history is as a discipline and a subject matter, tends to turn history into a lifeless parade of someone else's facts, and otherwise drives away students' motivation to learn the subject. History education researchers have attempted to divert the teaching of history away from an exercise in socializing students to particular partisan views; instead suggesting the aim of history as an investigation of the past and the social world.

If one of the principal goals for teaching history is to socialize grade-school students to accept certain views of a nation's accomplishments as defined by those in power, thus shaping their nationalist identities, teaching history should take on a transmission approach. In other words, it is likely that in history classrooms teachers would lecture or tell stories about the past via lessons drawn from textbooks sanctioned by those in political control. Research bears out this image. For much of the past century, the teaching of history in schools in many places around the world has been dominated by textbook recitations and teacher lectures or storytelling. This has been especially true in the United States.

There have been moments of change is these traditional practices such as during the "New Social Studies" movement in the United States during the 1960s and early 1970s. During this period, historians and social scientists constructed curriculum units that were designed to assist students in learning more about how historical knowledge was constructed in the discipline. Teachers were to guide students in the process of investigating the past via study of primary sources, much the way historians do. However, such efforts to promote pedagogical and curricular change in history typically have not had lasting effects in the United States, and the traditional lecture-textbook-recitation-recall approach has remained dominant.

In England, the Schools Council History project had more lasting results. Educational and instructional changes there during the 1970s and 1980s in some ways mirrored the efforts of historians working under the auspices of the New Social Studies in the United States. The goal was for teachers to learn to teach students the reasoning process of historical investigators. Not only were students to study important ideas in English history, but also to learn how to read primary sources, judge their status relative to other sources, draw inferences about the past from them, and construct historical accounts of their own making. Research on the results of approaching history that way were generally favorable, indicating that students typically progressed in their capacity to learn to think historically as modeled by experts in the discipline itself. Data also indicated that students developed deeper understandings of English history. The project largely succeeded in changing the way teachers taught history because teacher educators and teachers along with education researchers were all involved in changing pedagogical and curricular practices.

In 1988 the Thatcher government attempted to reverse this trend. Alarmed that children in British schools, in their view, were not receiving adequate instruction in the stories of British national and international successes, the education establishment mandated significant changes in the British national history curriculum. Those changes called for more emphasis on teaching stories drawn, for example, from the days of the British empire. Less stress was to be placed on teaching historical-reasoning processes. The changes brought on by the Schools Council project and by the work of teacher educators and researchers however, had been institutionalized in many places. Reverting back to teaching history in lecture-textbook-recitation fashion became difficult. Many of Great Britain's history programs in schools therefore remain among the few in which history is taught more as a way of learning to think historically (as a way of knowing) than as a socialization exercise in memorization and recall of a nation's grand accomplishments and celebrations.

This debate continues. Cognitive scientists interested in history education and researchers in general who study how history is taught and to what result stress the importance of teaching history more closely aligned with the way in which history operates as a distinctive discipline. Researchers such as Peter Lee and Rosalyn Ashby point to gains in students' capacity to learn important thinking processes and habits of mind as they learn to understand the past more deeply. Those who are more interested in the power of using history to forge particular nationalist identities among youth remain skeptical of teaching history as an exercise in educating thinking processes and critical habits of mind. Generally, they prefer an approach that favors transmission of favored views of the past via lectures and textbook recitations, and a focus on stories that celebrate chosen accomplishments and historical successes.

Historical Significance

The debates about the purposes, goals, and uses of school history are exacerbated by the problem of choosing what constitutes historically significant events worth teaching. The very breadth and vastness of the past from which school history lessons must be chosen coupled with the finiteness of the school day and the press for curricular room by other subjects makes this issue difficult. It would be convenient if those who devise the history curriculum in the schools could turn to the discipline and to historians for help in addressing which events and historical actors of significance to choose. The debate within the discipline over what constitutes historical significance is perhaps even more intense than in school history. This has been especially true since about 1970 and advent of postmodernism with its deep skepticism about the veracity of Western knowledge-production projects rooted in the scientific method. The issue of historical significance has been further exacerbated by the multiculturalization of many Western societies, rendering questions about "whose" history to teach as important as "which" history.

The problem of defining historical significance leaves history teachers, curriculum designers, educational policymakers, and politicians without much firm ground upon which to anchor their decisions about which or whose history to teach. The inability to resolve this issue, however, gives history education researchers some support in their efforts to press the importance of teaching history primarily as an exercise in habits of mind.

Time in the Curriculum

Teaching history as both knowledge about a nation's history and its place in world history, and as an approach to learning a way of reasoning about the past requires more time than doing one or the other. Debates between advocates for the importance of subjects other than history can have the effect of reducing the time teaching history might otherwise have in the overall school curriculum. To the extent that politicians exercise greater control of textbooks and history curriculum and assessment approaches (e.g., in states, provinces, or countries where a centralized curriculum dominates), teaching history is often pressed into the service of socialization. History taught as historical reasoning and understanding tends to languish in the context of overabundant time pressures.

Interdisciplinarity

In some countries, educational policymakers and curriculum developers see the teaching of history as an opportunity to integrate the social science disciplines into history syllabi. Issues arise over the right mix and relationships of such disciplines as geography and political science to the teaching of history. Some express concern that such interdisciplinary approaches effectively water down the actual teaching of history, reduce its value for students, and contribute to confusion about how to conduct appropriate assessments of student learning. Others argue that history already draws from the social science disciplines; therefore, calling attention to its interdisciplinarity makes good sense, opening up learning opportunities for students. Much like the controver-

sies over historical significance, this issue of interdisciplinarity has not been resolved. The time factor also plays a role in this debate.

Assessments

The aforementioned issues and debates also intersect with questions about how to properly assess what students learn from being taught history. During the last quarter of the twentieth century, many Western countries moved closer to centralizing assessment practices in many school subjects including history. What consequences these tests hold vary from county to country. In the Unites States, a national test of history learning (the National Assessment of Educational Progress, or NAEP, which also tests other subject learning as well) was developed in the 1980s. It tests students' capacity to both recall elements of American history as well as construct short answer responses to written prompts. As of 2001 this test was voluntary and was considered to hold low stakes for participants. However, the U.S. Congress is engaged in a debate to make the NAEP a required national test, thus making it a high-stakes test with sanctions and resource allocations related to outcomes.

Between the late 1980s and 2001 the history portion of the NAEP was given three times. During the administrations of George Bush and Bill Clinton, the data suggested that students in grades four, eight, and twelve recalled low to moderate levels of historical knowledge about the United States. Some critics, such as Diane Ravitch and Chester Finn Jr., argued that this level of recall meant that students effectively knew very little about their country and thus required even heavier doses of American history to overcome the deficits in their knowledge. Based on the growing number of in-depth studies of teaching and learning history, educational researchers such as Linda Levstik countered with the claim that more history, particularly if taught as lecture and textbook recitation, would do little to solve the problem. Reminiscent of the debates described above, the U.S. researchers called for immersing students in a pattern of historical study characterized by investigating history using strategic knowledge borrowed from expertise displayed by historians as a means of developing more powerful substantive understandings about the American past.

This debate over the most productive pedagogical approach to teaching history (e.g., more drill in the substantive knowledge of history versus instruction into and exercise of historical thinking practices to foster deeper knowledge about history) continues largely unabated.

See also: ASSESSMENT, *subentry on* NATIONAL ASSESSMENT OF EDUCATIONAL PROGRESS; CURRICULUM, SCHOOL; ELEMENTARY EDUCATION; GEOGRAPHY, TEACHING OF; SECONDARY EDUCATION; SOCIAL STUDIES EDUCATION.

BIBLIOGRAPHY

AHONEN, SIRKKA. 1995. "Clio Throws Away the Uniform: History Education in Transition in Estonia and Eastern Germany 1989–1990." In *International Yearbook of History Education,* ed. Alaric Dickinson, Peter Gordon, Peter Lee, and John Slater. London: Woburn.

CARRETERO, MARIO, et al. 1994. "Historical Knowledge: Cognitive and Instructional Implications." In *Cognitive and Instructional Processes in History and the Social Sciences,* ed. Mario Carretero and James F. Voss. Hillsdale, NJ: Erlbaum.

CUBAN, LARRY. 1991. "History of Teaching in Social Studies." In *Handbook of Research on Social Studies Teaching and Learning,* ed. James P. Shaver. New York: Macmillan.

CUTHBERTSON, GREG, and GRUNDLINGH, ALBERT. 1995. "Distortions of Discourse: Some Problematical Issues in the Restructuring of History Education in South African Schools." In *International Yearbook of History Education,* ed. Alaric Dickinson, Peter Gordon, Peter Lee, and John Slater. London: Woburn.

DICKINSON, ALARIC; GORDON, PETER; LEE, PETER; and SLATER, JOHN, eds. 1995. *International Yearbook of History Education.* London: Woburn.

DOMINGUEZ, JESUS. 1995. "History Teaching in Spain: The Challenge of a New Curriculum." In *International Yearbook of History Education,* ed. Alaric Dickinson, Peter Gordon, Peter Lee, and John Slater. London: Woburn.

LEE, PETER. 1995. "History and the National Curriculum in England." In *International Yearbook of History Education,* ed. Alaric Dickinson, Peter Gordon, Peter Lee, and John Slater. London: Woburn.

LEE, PETER, and ASHBY, ROSALYN. 2000. "Progression in Historical Understanding Among Students Ages 7–14." In *Knowing, Teaching, and Learning History: National and International Perspectives,* ed. Peter N. Stearns, Peter Seixas, and Sam Wineburg. New York: New York University Press.

LEVSTIK, LINDA. 2000. "Articulating the Silences: Teachers' and Adolescents' Conceptions of Historical Significance." In *Knowing, Teaching, and Learning History: National and International Perspectives,* ed. Peter N. Stearns, Peter Seixas, and Sam Wineburg. New York: New York University Press.

LEVSTIK, LINDA, and BARTON, KEITH. 1997. *Doing History: Investigating with Children in Elementary and Middle Schools.* Mahwah, NJ: Erlbaum.

NOVICK, PETER. 1988. *That Noble Dream: The "Objectivity Question" and the American Historical Profession.* Cambridge: Cambridge University Press.

RAVITCH, DIANE, and FINN, CHESTER, JR. 1987. *What Do Our 17-Year-Olds Know? A Report on the First National Assessment of History and Literature.* New York: Harper and Row.

SHEMILT: DENIS. 1980. *History 13–16 Evaluation Study.* Edinburgh, Eng.: Holmes McDougall.

VANSLEDRIGHT, BRUCE A. 2002. *In Search of America's Past: Learning to Read History in Elementary School.* New York: Teachers College Press, Columbia University.

WERTSCH, JAMES. 2000. "Is It Possible to Teach Beliefs, as Well as Knowledge, About History?" In *Knowing, Teaching, and Learning History: National and International Perspectives,* ed. Peter N. Stearns, Peter Seixas, and Sam Wineburg. New York: New York University Press.

WINEBURG, SAMUEL. 2001. *Historical Thinking and Other Unnatural Acts: Charting the Future of Teaching the Past.* Philadelphia: Temple University Press.

BRUCE A. VANSLEDRIGHT

HIV/AIDS

See: RISK BEHAVIORS, *subentry on* HIV/AIDS AND ITS IMPACT ON ADOLESCENTS.

HOLT, JOHN (1923–1985)

John Caldwell Holt was a teacher, educational critic, and early spokesperson for the home-schooling movement. Born in Boston, Massachusetts, the son of well-to-do parents, he was formally educated in private schools in the United States and abroad. He described himself as a "good student in supposedly the best schools." At Yale University, Holt studied to be an industrial engineer, but found no intrinsic connections between his studies and the world around him. He soon left to join the navy at age twenty, serving for three years aboard the submarine U.S.S. Barbero during World War II. Holt later identified his time on this submarine as yielding the first genuine, purposeful educational experiences of his life.

In 1946, immediately following his tour of duty, John Holt found work in New York with the American Movement for World Government, and later with the United World Federalists—an organization devoted to stopping the proliferation of atomic weapons. Between 1952 and 1953 he traveled throughout Europe before settling briefly with his sister in Taos, New Mexico. Holt joined the faculty at the Colorado Rocky Mountain School in Carbondale, despite his complete lack of preparation for or formal knowledge of teaching. Years later Holt characterized himself while at this school as a "perfectly conventional schoolmaster" who flunked numerous students.

After four years of teaching school, John Holt had surmised that students did poorly because they learned to believe that schooling expected them to do poorly. Given this working hypothesis, in 1957 he returned to Massachusetts to teach younger students, hoping to influence them before they learned to expect such failure; he would teach elementary and secondary students for the next ten years.

John Holt found himself struck by the natural learning instincts of children. His perceptions and beliefs rested comfortably with those of earlier "child-centered" educators and philosophers like Johann Heinrich Pestalozzi (1746–1827), Friedrich Wilhelm August Froebel (1782–1852), Johann Friedrich Herbart (1776–1841), Herbert Spencer (1820–1903), and at times, the Progressive educator and pragmatist John Dewey (1859–1952). In his first book, *How Children Fail* (1964), Holt argued that schools maximized compliance and "good work" at the expense of traits like curiosity and creativity.

This position remained solid in *How Children Learn* (1967), in which he made a point of criticizing large class sizes as he believed that children learned best alone or in small groups.

Holt left classroom teaching in 1967 to pursue writing and lecturing. He was among a small but widely read group of neo- or contemporary "romantic" critics of schools (a group that included Jonathan Kozol, George Dennison, James Herndon, Herb Kohl, and later, Ivan Illich). After two years lecturing at Harvard University, the University of California at Berkeley, and elsewhere around the world (while continuing to write and publish about educational reform), Holt's perspective on both the purpose for and source of needed school reform began to shift. This shift is attributed, in no small part, to his decision to learn more about the thinking of Ivan Illich (who would soon publish his popular *Deschooling Society*) and his visit to Illich's Intercultural Center of Documentation during the late 1960s. In 1969 Holt became the president of John Holt Associates, Incorporated.

Holt continued to criticize American public schooling, though with the publication of *Freedom and Beyond* in 1972 he had abandoned any hope that teachers, school personnel, or parents and community members could enable such change. Still searching for ways to promote deeply personal, transformative teaching/learning situations like those he experienced in the military, Holt had decided that such encounters would and could never occur within schools as formal, social institutions. Holt returned to his original focus on the learner, ceasing his passionate critique of the social contract inherent in public schooling and calling, instead, for individual families to "teach your own." In 1977 Holt created a newsletter called "Growing Without Schooling" and published *Instead of Education,* in which he encouraged readers to forego efforts toward changing schools and to embrace his notion of "unschooling" (acknowledging, yet distinguishing himself from, Illich's "deschooling" concept).

Holt had turned a crucial corner as an educational critic. Consequently, his educational works represent the best and worst elements of child-centered Progressive ideals of the late twentieth century. By the late 1970s he had become a conservative libertarian, dismissing any relationship between the responsibilities of the state and the family with respect to young people's education. "Growing Without Schooling" became a support group by mail for the nation's pioneer home schoolers, and Holt became their leader. His longstanding respect for natural learners resonated with increasing numbers of parents who, with Holt's personal encouragement, support and published tales of unschooling success, became the core of the early-twenty-first century burgeoning home-schooling movement in the United States.

Criticized by his former circle of Progressive colleagues, Holt had little interest in such philosophical discussions, spending his remaining days encouraging and helping families through his publication *Teach Your Own* (1981). In his final years, Holt promoted home schooling in numerous popular print forums, including *Harper's, Life, Look, Mother Earth News, Ms., The Progressive, Psychology Today, Redbook, Saturday Evening Post, Time, USA Today,* and *The Wall Street Journal.* Begun before his death, Holt's final book, *Learning All the Time* (1989), was completed posthumously by members of its very audience—Holt's home-schooling colleagues.

See also: EDUCATION REFORM; HOME SCHOOLING.

BIBLIOGRAPHY

HOLT, JOHN C. 1964. *How Children Fail.* New York: Pitman.

HOLT, JOHN C. 1967. *How Children Learn.* New York: Pitman.

HOLT, JOHN C. 1972. *Freedom and Beyond.* New York: Elsevier North-Holland.

HOLT, JOHN C. 1974. *Escape from Childhood.* New York: Elsevier North-Holland.

HOLT, JOHN C. 1976. *Instead of Education.* New York: Delacorte.

HOLT, JOHN C. 1981. *Teach Your Own: A Hopeful Path for Education.* New York: Delacorte.

HOLT, JOHN C. 1989. *Learning All the Time.* Reading, MA: Addison-Wesley.

DEBRA M. FREEDMAN
J. DAN MARSHALL

HOME ECONOMICS

See: FAMILY AND CONSUMER SCIENCES EDUCATION.

HOME SCHOOLING

The term *home schooling* refers to the practice of parents educating a child at home, rather than in a conventional public or private school setting. These children would otherwise be enrolled in elementary or secondary school. The parent responsible for home schooling generally does not work and is rarely a trained teaching professional. Primary concerns for most home schoolers are strengthening family bonds and developing religious values. Technological innovations in the late twentieth century made home schooling an increasingly manageable proposition, as the availability of personal computers and the Internet permitted families to access computer-driven instruction, multimedia resources, and far-flung support networks. Families provide home schooling in many different ways, with tremendous variation in curricula, teaching methods, and technology, and in the amount of peer interaction that children experience. Some home-schooling parents bring their children together for group outings and field trips to provide enhanced socialization, while others have formed cooperative schools or charter schools to support their efforts.

The estimated number of home-schooled children is unreliable, due largely to uneven record-keeping. However, in a 1999 report, the U.S. Department of Education estimated that more than 850,000 children were home schooled in the United States, and scholars purport that the population is increasing at an annual rate of between 7 to 15 percent. Researchers suggest that home educators are generally married couples with one nonworking spouse and more than two children and that their median income is generally comparable to that of all families with school-age children. In approximately one-quarter of home-schooling families, at least one parent is a licensed teacher; however, this is rarely the parent who is specifically responsible for the home schooling. The small amount of existent data suggests that very few minority students are educated through home schooling, and that three-quarters of home-schooling families are primarily motivated by religious concerns.

History

From the colonial period through the mid-1800s, education was generally delivered through loosely-structured community schools. In the nineteenth century, in efforts that began in the northeast, reformers increasingly came to view public schools as a vital means of "Americanizing" the nation's growing immigrant population and as an opportunity to foster a common American culture. This effort gained momentum after Massachusetts became the first state to adopt a compulsory education law in 1852. The law required parents to send their children to the state's increasingly systematic public schools. In the early twentieth century, public schooling became an increasingly central component of American culture. Growing numbers of students attended public school and Progressive reformers promoted education as a means of social betterment. As formal public schooling expanded during the first half of the twentieth century, home education became virtually obsolete.

However, by the 1960s, some education critics had begun to voice concerns that public schools were preaching alien values, failing to adequately educate children, or were adopting unhealthy approaches to child development. As a result, a "deschooling movement" took root in the 1960s and 1970s. Critics of public schooling primarily voiced two distinct ideologies, both emphasizing child-centered learning. Liberal critics of public schooling believed that schools did not adequately respect children as individuals, while conservative critics argued that public schools undermined traditional values.

Starting in the early 1980s, increasing numbers of parents chose to educate their children at home as a growing number of states relaxed their compulsory attendance laws to permit home schooling. Previously, parents who home schooled their children were in violation of compulsory attendance and truancy laws, and were therefore subject to legal action. While Nevada (1956) and Utah (1957) were the only states with home-schooling legislation prior to 1982, thirty-four states passed enabling legislation between 1982 and 1993. By 1998, under the pressure of an increasingly active home-schooling movement, all fifty states had passed home-school laws specifying attendance, subject, teacher, testing, and record-keeping requirements for home educators.

In 2002 state laws regulating home schooling vary widely regarding such matters as teacher licensure, testing, compulsory curriculum, and required paperwork. Some states impose exacting regulations on home schooling, while others legislate few requirements. Nine states place no restrictions on parents' rights to home school, providing the legal option for any parent who is interested. Ten other states simply require parents to notify the state when a child is being home schooled. On the other hand, twenty states demand that parents provide test scores or professional assessment to monitor the student's progress. Finally, eleven states impose stringent requirements that mandate that parents provide the state with test scores or professional assessment to measure the student's achievement, in addition to other requirements such as regular home visits or professional training.

Legal Background

American courts have asserted that parents possess significant authority to direct the education of their children. *Meyer v. Nebraska* (1923) was the first case to protect parental educational authority against the incursion of state legislation, establishing a legal precedent when the U.S. Supreme Court found that states may not prohibit foreign language education if schools offer it and parents desire it. Parents' fundamental right "to direct the upbringing and education of children under their control" was etched more firmly in *Pierce v. Society of Seven Sisters* (1925). The *Pierce* decision stated that parents should be allowed to choose the type of school their children attend, public or private, as Oregon law could not require that parents send their children to public schools. In a 1972 ruling crucial to the home-schooling cause, the Supreme Court held in *Wisconsin v. Yoder* that parents had the right to supersede compulsory education laws if the laws unduly impeded religious freedom. The Court ruled that it was permissible for Amish parents to remove their children from school at age twelve to maintain their way of life and exercise their religious freedom.

Although the courts have protected the rights of parents, they have also defended the right of states to require and extensively regulate educational instruction. Courts have ruled that if a state exempts home schoolers from compulsory attendance laws it is entitled to regulate their activities. States have the right to impose "reasonable" standards on home schoolers. These may include regulations as invasive as administering achievement tests to monitor students' progress (*Murphy v. State of Arkansas*, 1988). While most state laws include such requirements, enforcement is often sporadic due to the decentralized nature of home schooling and the lack of established overseeing bodies.

Over the course of time, several states have refused to allow home instruction on the grounds that it would stunt the social development of children and would prevent them from living normal, productive lives. The courts have determined that states are within their rights to make such determinations (*Knox v. O'Brien,* 1950). States may mandate that children must attend school because of the interaction it provides with their peers and the exposure it provides to different types of people (*State v. Edgington,* 1983).

Legal Trends

In the late 1990s, the parents of home-schooled children began suing schools districts that denied requests for supplemental services, classes, extracurricular activities, and additional services such as lab science instruction that cannot be feasibly provided at home. However, the courts have not mandated that districts provide such additional services. In *Swanson v. Guthrie Independent School District* (1998), a U.S. Court of Appeals ruled that a school board may deny home-schooled children the right to attend public school part-time. Previously, the courts had held in *Bradstreet v. Sobol* (1996) that school districts could require students to be enrolled in public schools in order to be eligible to participate in interscholastic sports.

Effects

Although no randomized field trials have been conducted, some preliminary research suggests that children who are home schooled may outperform their counterparts in public or private schools. However, given the variety of home-school settings and the uneven nature of preliminary research, it is not yet possible to reach any meaningful conclusions regarding the effectiveness of home schooling. Families who practice home schooling are often different in significant ways than families who do not. These differences, including higher levels of education, larger family size, and divergent child-rearing practices, make comparisons problematic. Moreover, it is advocates of home schooling who conduct of the research on the subject; this raises questions as to the validity and reliability of findings. The largest and most comprehensive as of 2001, conducted by the National Home Education Research Institute, examined over five thousand home-schooled students' scores on national standardized achievement tests for the 1994 through 1995 school year, and found that children who were home schooled outperformed their peers on standardized assessments.

Future Implications

In the fall of 2000, Patrick Henry College in Purcellville, Virginia, became the first postsecondary institution intended primarily to serve students who had been schooled at home. Of the college's first class of ninety students, eighty had been home schooled. Patrick Henry College's curriculum has a moral focus comparable to many home schoolers' early education and values, and emphasizes traditional Christian values. The college is designed to address the typical challenges that many home schoolers face, as these students do not possess conventional educational records such as transcripts and may not be comfortable with their altered learning environment.

Home schooling poses a radical challenge to the centuries-long project of American public education. It raises important questions about how to balance the rights of family and community, of individual and state. There are no simple answers to these complex legal and ethical questions, and it is unclear the extent to which home schooling will transform educational practice in years to come.

See also: ALTERNATIVE SCHOOLING; ELEMENTARY EDUCATION, *subentry on* CURRENT TRENDS; SCHOOL REFORM; SECONDARY EDUCATION, *subentry on* CURRENT TRENDS.

BIBLIOGRAPHY

ALEXANDER, KERN, and ALEXANDER, DAVID M. 2001. *American Public School Law.* Stamford, CT: Wadsworth Group.

BRIGGS, DONALD, and PORTER, GERALD. 1994. "Parental Choice in the USA." In *Parental Choice and Education: Principles, Policy and Practice,* ed. J. Mark Halstead. Philadelphia: Kogan Page.

GREENE, JAY P. 1998. "Civic Values in Public and Private Schools." In *Learning from School Choice,* ed. Paul E. Peterson and Bryan C. Hassel. Washington, DC: Brookings Institution Press.

KILBORN, PETER T. 2000. "Learning at Home, Students Take the Lead." *New York Times* May 24.

KLICKA, CHRISTOPHER J. 1998. *The Right to Home School.* Durham, NC: Carolina Academic Press.

RAY, BRIAN. 1997. *Strengths of Their Own: Home Schoolers Across America: Academic Achievement, Family Characteristics, and Longitudinal Traits.* Salem, OR: National Home Education Research Institute.

Shepherd, Michael S. 1990. "Home Schooling: A Legal View." In *Schooling at Home,* ed. Anne Pederson and Peggy O'Mara. Santa Fe, NM: John Muir.

Stevens, Mitchell L. 2001. *Kingdom of Children: Culture and Controversy in the Homeschooling Movement.* Princeton, NJ: Princeton University Press.

Sugarman, Stephen D., and Kemerer, Frank R. 1999. *School Choice and Social Controversy: Politics, Policy, and Law.* Washington, DC: Brookings Institution Press.

Zirkel, Perry A. 1997. "Home/School Cooperation?" *Phi Delta Kappan* 78(9):727–729.

INTERNET RESOURCES

Home School Legal Defense Association. 2001. "The Home School Court Report." <www.hslda.org/courtreport/v17n1/v17N11.asp>.

National Home Education Research Institute. 2000. "Facts on Home Schooling by the NHERI." <www.nheri.org/add.html>.

Rudner, Lawrence M. 1999. "Scholastic Achievement and Demographic Characteristics of Home School Students in 1998." <http://epaa.asu.edu/epaa/v7n8/>.

Frederick M. Hess
Joleen R. Okun

HOMEWORK

Homework is defined as tasks assigned to students by school teachers that are intended to be carried out during nonschool hours. This definition excludes in-school guided study (although homework is often worked on during school), home-study courses, and extracurricular activities such as sports teams and clubs.

Purpose

The most common purpose of homework is to have students practice material already presented in class so as to reinforce learning and facilitate mastery of specific skills. Preparation assignments introduce the material that will be presented in future lessons. These assignments aim to help students obtain the maximum benefit when the new material is covered in class. Extension homework involves the transfer of previously learned skills to new situations. For example, students might learn in class about factors that led to the French Revolution and then be asked as homework to apply them to the American Revolution. Finally, integration homework requires the student to apply separately learned skills to produce a single product, such as book reports, science projects, or creative writing.

Homework also can serve purposes that do not relate directly to instruction. Homework can be used to (1) establish communication between parents and children; (2) fulfill directives from school administrators; (3) punish students; and (4) inform parents about what is going on in school. Most homework assignments have elements of several different purposes.

Public Attitudes toward Homework

Homework has been a part of student's lives since the beginning of formal schooling in the United States. However, the practice has been alternately accepted and rejected by educators and parents.

When the twentieth century began, the mind was viewed as a muscle that could be strengthened through mental exercise. Since this exercise could be done at home, homework was viewed favorably. During the 1940s, the emphasis in education shifted from drill to problem solving. Homework fell out of favor because it was closely associated with the repetition of material. The launch of the satellite *Sputnik* by the Soviet Union in the mid-1950s reversed this thinking. The American public worried that education lacked rigor and left children unprepared for complex technologies. Homework, it was believed, could accelerate knowledge acquisition.

The late 1960s witnessed yet another reversal. Educators and parents became concerned that homework was crowding out social experience, outdoor recreation, and creative activities. In the 1980s, homework once again leapt back into favor when *A Nation at Risk* (1983), the report by the National Commission on Excellence in Education, cited homework as a defense against the rising tide of mediocrity in American education. The push for more homework continued into the 1990s, fueled by increasingly rigorous state-mandated academic standards. As the century ended, a backlash against homework set in, led by parents concerned about too much stress on their children.

The Positive and Negative Effects of Homework

The most direct positive effect of homework is that it can improve retention and understanding. More indirectly, homework can improve students' study skills and attitudes toward school, and teach students that learning can take place anywhere, not just in school buildings. The nonacademic benefits of homework include fostering independence and responsibility. Finally, homework can involve parents in the school process, enhancing their appreciation of education, and allowing them to express positive attitudes toward the value of school success.

Conversely, educators and parents worry that students will grow bored if they are required to spend too much time on academic material. Homework can deny access to leisure time and community activities that also teach important life skills. Parent involvement in homework can turn into parent interference. For example, parents can confuse children if the instructional techniques they use differ from those used by teachers. Homework can actually lead to the acquisition of undesirable character traits if it promotes cheating, either through the copying of assignments or help with homework that goes beyond tutoring. Finally, homework could accentuate existing social inequities. Children from disadvantaged homes may have more difficulty completing assignments than their middle-class counterparts.

Extensiveness of Homework

In contrast to the shifts in public attitudes, surveys suggest that the amount of time students spend on homework has been relatively stable. Data from the National Assessment of Educational Progress suggests that in both 1984 and 1994, about one-third of nine-year-olds and one-quarter of thirteen- and seventeen-year-olds reported being assigned no homework at all, with an additional 5 percent to 10 percent admitting they did not do homework that was assigned. About one-half of nine-year-olds, one-third of thirteen-year-olds, and one-quarter of seventeen-year-olds said they did less than an hour of homework each night. In 1994 about 12 percent of nine-year-olds, 28 percent of thirteen-year-olds, and 26 percent of seventeen-year-olds said they did one to two hours of homework each night. These percentages were all within one point of the 1984 survey results.

A national survey of parents conducted by the polling agency Public Agenda, in October, 2000, revealed that 64 percent of parents felt their child was getting "about the right amount" of homework, 25 percent felt their child was getting "too little" homework, and only 10 percent felt "too much homework" was being assigned.

International comparisons often suggest that U.S. students spend less time on homework than students in other industrialized nations. However, direct comparisons across countries are difficult to interpret because of different definitions of homework and differences in the length of the school day and year.

Appropriate Amounts of Homework

Experts agree that the amount and type of homework should depend on the developmental level of the student. The National PTA and the National Education Association suggest that homework for children in grades K–2 is most effective when it does not exceed ten to twenty minutes each day. In grades three through six, children can benefit from thirty to sixty minutes daily. Junior high and high school students can benefit from more time on homework and the amount might vary from night to night. These recommendations are consistent with the conclusions reached by studies into the effectiveness of homework.

Research on Homework's Overall Effectiveness

Three types of studies have been used to examine the relationship between homework and academic achievement. One type compares students who receive homework with students who receive none. Generally, these studies reveal homework to be a positive influence on achievement. However, they also reveal a relationship between homework and achievement for high school students that is about twice as strong as for junior high students. The relationship at the elementary school level is only one-quarter that of the high school level.

Another type of study compares homework to in-class supervised study. Overall, the positive relationship is about half as strong as in the first type of study. These studies again reveal a strong grade-level effect. When homework and in-class study were compared in elementary schools, in-class study proved superior.

The third type of study correlates the amount of homework students say they complete with their achievement test scores. Again, these surveys show the relationship is influenced by the grade level of students. For students in primary grades, the correlation between time spent on homework and achievement is near zero. For students in middle and junior high school, the correlation suggests a positive but weak relationship. For high school students, the correlation suggests a moderate relationship between achievement and time spend on homework.

Research on Effective Homework Assignments

The subject matter shows no consistent relationship to the value of homework. It appears that shorter and more frequent assignments may be more effective than longer but fewer assignments. Assignments that involve review and preparation are more effective than homework that focuses only on material covered in class on the day of the assignments. It can be beneficial to involve parents in homework when young children are experiencing problems in school. Older students and students doing well in school have more to gain from homework when it promotes independent learning.

Homework can be an effective instructional device. However, the relationship between homework and achievement is influenced greatly by the students' developmental level. Expectations for homework's effects, especially in the short term and in earlier grades, must be modest. Further, homework can have both positive and negative effects. Educators and parents should not be concerned with which list of homework effects is correct. Rather, homework policies and practices should give individual schools and teachers flexibility to take into account the unique needs and circumstances of their students so as to maximize positive effects and minimize negative ones.

BIBLIOGRAPHY

CAMPBELL, JAY R.; REESE, CLYDE M.; O'SULLIVAN, CHRISTINE; and DOSSEY, JOHN A. 1996. *NAEP 1994 Trends in Academic Progress.* Washington, DC: U.S. Department of Education.

COOPER, HARRIS. 2001. *The Battle Over Homework: Common Ground for Administrators, Teachers, and Parents,* 2nd edition. Newbury Park, CA: Corwin Press.

COOPER, HARRIS, and VALENTINE, J. C., eds. 2001. "Homework: A Special Issue." *Educational Psychologist* 36(3).

INTERNET RESOURCES

HENDERSON, M. 1996. "Helping Your Student Get the Most Out of Homework." Chicago: National PTA and the National Education Association. <www.pta.org/Programs/edulibr/homework. htm>.

PUBLIC AGENDA. 2000. "Survey Finds Little Sign of Backlash Against Academic Standards or Standardized Tests." <www.publicagenda.org/ aboutpa/aboutpa3ee.htm>

HARRIS COOPER

HONOR SOCIETIES

ALPHA CHI
  Dennis M. Organ
ALPHA MU GAMMA
  Franklin I. Triplett
ALPHA OMEGA ALPHA
  Edward D. Harris Jr.
ASSOCIATION FOR WOMEN IN COMMUNICATIONS
  Mary Kay Switzer
ASSOCIATION OF COLLEGE HONOR SOCIETIES
  John W. Warren
BETA PHI MU
  Judith J. Culligan
DELTA KAPPA GAMMA SOCIETY
  Carolyn Guss
DELTA SIGMA RHO–TAU KAPPA ALPHA
  Herold T. Ross
KAPPA DELTA PI
  Michael P. Wolfe
KAPPA OMICRON NU
  Dorothy I. Mitstifer
LAMBDA IOTA TAU
  Bruce W. Hozeski
PHI BETA KAPPA
  Meaghan E. Mundy
PHI DELTA KAPPA INTERNATIONAL
  George Kersey Jr.
PI KAPPA LAMBDA
  George Howerton
PI SIGMA ALPHA
  James I. Lengle
RHO CHI
  Robert A. Buerki
SIGMA XI
  Meaghan E. Mundy
TAU BETA PI
  Meaghan E. Mundy

ALPHA CHI

A college honor scholarship society, Alpha Chi promotes academic excellence and exemplary character among college and university students and honors those who achieve such distinction. As a general honor society, Alpha Chi admits students from all academic disciplines. A member institution, which must be a regionally accredited, baccalaureate-degree-granting college or university, may invite to membership no more than the top ten percent of the junior and senior classes. Membership recognizes previous accomplishments and provides opportunity for continued growth and service. As the society's constitution states, Alpha Chi seeks to find ways to assist students in "making scholarship effective for good."

Founded on February 22, 1922, by five Texas institutions of higher learning, Alpha Chi was first called the Scholarship Societies of Texas, then the Scholarship Societies of the South (1927), and finally Alpha Chi (1934) when the decision was made to become a national society. By 1955 there were only thirty-six active chapters, all in the south except for two chapters in Nebraska and Massachusetts, but in the 1960s expansion was rapid. By the end of 1971, Alpha Chi had installed chapter number 120 and restructured itself under a new constitution. Growth was strong through the next three decades, with more than 300 active chapters in almost every state by 2000 and an organizational structure of seven geographic regions.

Alpha Chi, legally chartered by the state of Texas, is a 501(c)(3) nonprofit entity with headquarters in Searcy, Arkansas, on the campus of Harding University, one of its member institutions. Its paid staff includes a half-time executive director who is an academic and two full-time professionals overseeing day-to-day operations. The executive director is appointed by the society's governing board, the National Council, made up of twenty-two faculty and students elected by the general membership at regional and national conventions; eight council members are faculty elected at large; the remaining members are seven faculty and seven students elected by their respective regions. The council meets annually, as does the executive committee consisting of the council's president, vice president, and secretary and the executive director. The regions also elect an executive committee consisting of a president, vice president, secretary-treasurer, and student representative. Campus chapters are served by an official faculty sponsor, who is appointed by the institution's president, and by student officers elected by the local membership.

In addition to undergraduate members, who are nominated by the faculty of member institutions, Alpha Chi elects a limited number of honorary members annually. These typically are faculty and administrators of institutions with Alpha Chi chapters or other individuals with acceptable academic credentials who have given special support to Alpha Chi chapters, to the organization as a whole, or to the cause of scholarship in general. After members receive their baccalaureate degrees, they also may choose to maintain an ongoing relationship with the society by paying an annual fee for "active alumni" status. Such members receive invitations to the annual conventions and the society's publications. These publications are the *Recorder,* issued twice yearly (one issue authored by undergraduates and the other, by alumni and others associated with the society); and the *Newsletter,* a bulletin issued three times yearly. Undergraduate members receive these publications through chapter sponsors. The society also publishes a handbook for chapter operations. In 1997 Alpha Chi published *Scholarship and Character: Seventy-Five Years of Alpha Chi,* written by Robert W. Sledge, a long-time leader.

In addition to recognizing students for their academic achievement, Alpha Chi also offers numerous opportunities for their further growth. The society sponsors a competition for scholarships and fellowships totaling more than $50,000 yearly, mostly at the national level but also at the regional and local levels. Another program involves student scholarly and creative presentations at national and regional conventions. The 2001 national convention, which drew more than 500 students and faculty, featured the work of about 200 students from a wide range of fields. Many local chapters also sponsor programs on campus to promote scholarly activity, and engage in service projects benefiting the campus or the community, often with an academic focus, such as tutoring programs. Finally, students' involvement in leadership at all levels of the society's operation makes Alpha Chi distinctive among similar honor societies and provides excellent opportunities for members to develop their talents beyond the classroom.

BIBLIOGRAPHY

SLEDGE, ROBERT W. 1997. *Scholarship and Character: Seventy-Five Years of Alpha Chi.* Searcy, AK: Alpha Chi.

DENNIS M. ORGAN

ALPHA MU GAMMA

A national honor society for students of community colleges, four-year colleges, and universities, Alpha Mu Gamma honors achievement in the study of foreign languages. The society strongly believes that such recognition stimulates a desire for linguistic achievement; nurtures and promotes interest in the study of foreign languages, literatures, and civilizations; and fosters a sympathetic understanding of other peoples through the medium of languages.

Alpha Mu Gamma was founded in 1931 by members of the foreign language faculty at Los Angeles City College in Los Angeles, California. A semiannual publication, the *Scroll*, began production in 1933, and continues today as a newsletter. By 1938 there were chapters in five states: Arizona, California, Kansas, Missouri, and Minnesota. By 2001 there were 318 chapters in virtually every state.

The society annually awards scholarships for foreign language study and for study abroad to outstanding student members. Alpha Mu Gamma is registered in the state of California as a nonprofit educational organization. Its officers consist of a nationally elected president and vice president, regional vice presidents, a national executive secretary, a national treasurer, and an administrative assistant. The officers constitute the National Executive Council, which is responsible for the basic policies of the organization. The chapters must conform to the rules of the society concerning selection and initiation of members, and use of society regalia such as pins and cords; however, each chapter is completely autonomous is every other way.

Alpha Mu Gamma held its thirtieth biennial national convention at Fairfield University, Fairfield, Connecticut, in March 2001. The national convention of Alpha Mu Gamma is organized by member chapters to provide a forum where students and faculty can meet and make presentations related to foreign language teaching, study abroad, and the study of literature and culture. Often, scholars of national or international importance attend the conference as keynote speakers. The national convention also provides the society with an opportunity to honor its most distinguished student members and to install its nationally elected officers. The selection of a location for the convention is made by the National Executive Council based on proposals submitted by member chapters.

Alpha Mu Gamma derives its income primarily from student initiation fees and charter fees. It provides limited financial assistance to chapters involved in the organization of the national convention.

In January 1957, through the efforts of the eleventh national president, Sister Eloise-Therese of Sigma Chapter at Mount Saint Mary's College in Los Angeles, President Dwight D. Eisenhower proclaimed the third week of February as "National Foreign Language Week," now celebrated during the first full week of March. Every year since, the president of the United States and many of the nation's governors have continued to recognize this event. The National Executive Council annually commissions the design and publication of a poster, which is widely distributed among schools, colleges, and universities throughout the United States.

Alpha Mu Gamma not only provides a milieu for students to meet the high standards of achievement of a national honor society, but also offers students incentives to excel in foreign languages.

FRANKLIN I. TRIPLETT

ALPHA OMEGA ALPHA

The mission of Alpha Omega Alpha Honor Medical Society is to encourage high standards of scholarship among medical students, to enhance professionalism within medicine, and to encourage community and university service by all physicians and medical students.

Alpha Omega Alpha was founded in 1902 by a medical student, William Webster Root, and several of his classmates. (Root was also involved in the founding of the Association of College Honor Societies.) Steady growth of the society through the chartering of new chapters was facilitated by the encouragement of medical school faculties and deans. In 2000, Alpha Omega Alpha chapters in the United States, Canada, Puerto Rico, and at the American University of Beirut in Lebanon numbered 123.

Alpha Omega Alpha, a nonprofit society, is governed by a board of directors formed of twelve graduate members and three student members. Every chapter has a faculty councillor, secretary-treasurer, and a student president. The councillor is chosen by the dean. Chapters are organized into sixteen regions, each coordinated by a regional councillor.

Undergraduate medical students are elected by all members (residents, students, and faculty) at each institution. Students ranked academically in the top 25 percent of their graduating class are eligible for election, but only one-sixth of each class can be elected. The criteria, in addition to superior scholarship, include demonstration of collegiality, professionalism, service to the community, and promise for excellence as a practicing or academic physician. In addition to medical student members, each chapter may elect a limited number of faculty, alumni, and resident physicians at the institution. Honorary members may be nominated by any member of Alpha Omega Alpha; a number of those nominated are elected by the board. Honorary members are distinguished individuals not eligible for election by any other mechanism.

Upon payment of annual national dues, a member receives *The Pharos* (the Alpha Omega Alpha quarterly) and participates in supporting national programs. Lifetime membership is open to any member.

Each chapter is encouraged to sponsor service and educational projects within the medical school. The national office of Alpha Omega Alpha, located in Menlo Park, California, administers programs that include the following:

1. Alpha Omega Alpha Student Research Fellowships. These are awarded yearly for investigative and mentored activities for students in medical schools with active chapters.

2. The Alpha Omega Alpha Robert J. Glaser Distinguished Teacher Awards. As many as four outstanding teachers from American medical schools are chosen by committees representing Alpha Omega Alpha and the Association of American Medical Colleges (AAMC). The awards are presented each year at the annual meeting of the AAMC.

3. Alpha Omega Alpha Medical Student Service Project Awards. Any student or group of students at each medical school with an active chapter may apply for financial support for service projects at the school or in the surrounding community.

4. *The Pharos.* First published by Alpha Omega Alpha in 1938, *The Pharos* is the quarterly publication of Alpha Omega Alpha. Nonfiction, nontechnical articles, poetry, and photography relevant to medicine are reviewed by members of *The Pharos* editorial board.

5. Alpha Omega Alpha Helen H. Glaser Student Essay Award. Any student at a medical school with an active chapter may submit a nonfiction essay on a nontechnical medical subject. Judged by members of *The Pharos* editorial board, winners receive a cash award and the essay is published in the quarterly.

6. Leaders in American Medicine videotape series. Available for loan or purchase are more than 100 interviews of outstanding physicians in American medicine.

7. Alpha Omega Alpha Visiting Professorships. This program is available to all active chapters. A respected physician is invited to spend up to two full days at the medical school, interacting with students and residents on rounds, giving specialty lectures, and often giving a special Alpha Omega Alpha lecture.

The only national honor society for medicine (with chapters at all but five U.S. medical schools), Alpha Omega Alpha continues to play a significant role in providing leadership in academia and the practice of medicine. Membership in Alpha Omega Alpha enhances a medical student's curriculum vitae, a vital part of the application for residency in all specialties.

EDWARD D. HARRIS JR.

ASSOCIATION FOR WOMEN IN COMMUNICATIONS

In 1909 at the University of Washington in Seattle, seven female students who were enrolled in the country's second academically accredited journalism program decided to establish a women's journalism society. These students—Georgina MacDougall, Helen Ross, Blanche Brace, Rachel Marshall, Olive Mauermann, Helen Graves, and Irene Somerville—founded Theta Sigma Phi, which became the Association for Women in Communications in 1996, and also began the publication of a special women's edition of the university newspaper, *The Pacific Daily Wave.*

In 1918 Theta Sigma Phi held its first national convention at the University of Kansas. After the convention, alumnae started professional chapters in Kansas City, Des Moines, and Indianapolis.

Despite the fact that women gained the right to vote in 1920, many editors relegated women to composing society pages, not allowing them to cover "hard news." In a 1931 issue of the *Matrix,* the society's quarterly journal, Ruby Black, the Theta Sigma Phi national president and the first manager of an employment bureau for members, noted that female journalists could not get reporting jobs at the same pay as similarly qualified males.

Inaugurating the Headliner Awards in 1939, the society honored Eleanor Roosevelt for her efforts to aid female communicators by closing her news conferences to male reporters. Mrs. Roosevelt also contributed several articles to the *Matrix.* During the 1950s and 1960s there were over forty-seven campus chapters and twenty-nine professional chapters, with the national headquarters in Austin, Texas.

WICI and AWC

In 1973, during the national convention, Theta Sigma Phi delegates voted to change the name of the organization to Women in Communications, Inc. (WICI). Calling for institutions of higher learning to place more emphasis on affirmative action, to create more positions for female journalism professors, and to remove the discriminatory practices that impeded academic advancement, WICI members joined the national Equal Rights Amendment (ERA) coalition to fight the mounting opposition to the ERA. Accenting the need to promote professional excellence, WICI also created an awards program, which grew into the prestigious and highly competitive Clarion Awards.

In order to monitor legislation, national headquarters were moved closer to Washington, D.C. in 1988. Then, in the fall of 1996, the organization was again renamed—as the Association for Women in Communications (AWC). Increasing its influence on the professional growth of students in the communication fields, AWC moved into an alliance with the Accrediting Council on Education in Journalism and Mass Communications (ACEJMC). This resulted in AWC's participation in the development of

course offerings and requirements for institutions of higher learning.

Mission and Organization

The AWC mission is to "champion the advancement of women across all communications disciplines by recognizing excellence, promoting leadership, and positioning its members at the forefront of the evolving communications era." By 2001 AWC had fully developed an electronic communication network through the Internet. The AWC website includes several online services, including a membership directory, job bank, listserves, the monthly newsletter *Intercom,* the *Matrix,* and an interactive membership response survey system.

Approaching its hundredth birthday, AWC had a membership of about 10,000 in 2001. Its professional awards include the Clarion Award, the International Matrix Award, the Headliner Award, the Rising Star Award, the Georgina MacDougall Davis Award, the AWC Champion Award, the Chair's First Women in Communications Award, the Chapter Recognition Program, the Lifetime Achievement Award, and the Ruth Wyand Awards. Furthermore, AWC has affirmed its long-standing commitment to education with the Matrix Foundation, which provides scholarships and supports educational research and publications.

AWC members range in age from eighteen through ninety-plus. The average age is forty-one, with most members living in urban or suburban settings in the United States and abroad. About 95 percent are college graduates, with about 47 percent holding advanced graduate degrees or involved in graduate study. Disciplines represented within the AWC membership include print and broadcast journalism, television and radio production, film, advertising, public relations, marketing, graphic design, multi-media design, photography, and related areas. A national conference is held annually, with featured guests and honorees representing a range of professions.

INTERNET RESOURCE

ASSOCIATION FOR WOMEN IN COMMUNICATIONS. 2001. <www.womcom.org>.

MARY KAY SWITZER

ASSOCIATION OF COLLEGE HONOR SOCIETIES

The Association of College Honor Societies (ACHS) is a visibly cohesive community of national and international honor societies, individually and collaboratively exhibiting excellence in scholarship, service, programs, and governance. A coordinating agency for these societies in chartering chapters in accredited colleges and universities, the association sets a high priority on maintaining high standards, defining the honor society movement, and developing criteria for judging the credibility and legitimacy of honor societies.

History

During the first quarter of the twentieth century, higher education witnessed a sporadic evolution of honor societies, resulting in proliferation, duplication, and low standards. In October 1925, six credible honor societies, seeing the urgent need to define and enhance the honor society movement, organized the Association of College Honor Societies. Other legitimate societies soon affiliated, beginning an expanding membership that as of 2001 included sixty-seven societies.

More than seventy-five years of dedication to excellence have produced a highly respected professional organization that gives continuous attention to developing high standards and a process of assuring that members are in compliance with the association's bylaws. The Association of College Honor Societies is the nation's only certifying agency for college and university honor societies.

Membership

By certifying the quality of member societies, ACHS affirms that elections to honor society membership should represent superior academic achievement. Standards set by the association require membership participation in society governance in electing officers and board members, setting authority in organizational affairs, and keeping bylaws current. To provide guidelines for its diverse membership, the association has classified honor societies into distinctive groups and has set standards for societies in each group to follow in establishing their membership and induction requirements of scholarly achievement and leadership. For general honor societies, scholarship recognition represents the highest 20 percent of the college class no earlier than the fifth semester, or seventh quarter. For honoring leadership, these societies choose from the highest 35 percent, while specialized societies, representing particular fields, induct students who rank in the highest 35 percent of the college class and have completed three semesters, or five quarters. All these societies may elect superior graduate students.

Association members are academic honor societies, as opposed to college professional and social fraternities. Honor societies recognize superior scholarship and/or leadership achievement either in broad academic disciplines or in departmental fields, including undergraduate and/or graduate levels. According to ACHS bylaws, character and specified eligibility are the sole criteria for membership in an honor society. Membership recruitment is by written invitation and conducted by campus chapters—without applying social pressures such as solicitation or "rushing" to enlist initiates. Likewise, association societies must function without preferences to gender, race, or religion.

Programs

The association publishes the *ACHS Handbook*, which contains the association's bylaws, society profiles, a list of certified societies, and general information. Annual meetings offer opportunities to review standards, discuss issues of concern in higher education and the honors community, and provide guidance in society governance, operations, and campus activities. Information is available to all members through minutes, special studies, committee reports, or the ACHS website.

Recognition of the association at the national level is evident in the increasing collaboration with university administrators, faculty, educational associations, and other groups. Significant attention is seen in the use of the association's classification of honor societies in *Baird's Manual of American College Fraternities*, and in an action by the U.S. Civil Service Commission on April 13, 1973, stating that honor society membership meets one requirement for the civil service GS-7 level.

Organization

Meeting annually, a council of sixty-seven affiliate societies governs the association with one vote per society to be cast by each society's official representative. Between meetings, the executive committee conducts all business of the association and administers the policies, programs, and activities formulated by the council. The executive committee comprises the president, the vice president/president-elect, the secretary-treasurer, the immediate past president, and two members-at-large, elected from the council and representing general and specialized honor societies.

Annual dues from member societies provide the chief source of revenue, while other limited income may derive from vendor participation, annual meetings, and occasional grants.

BIBLIOGRAPHY

ANSON, JACK, and MARCHENASI, ROBERT, JR. 1991. *Baird's Manual of American College Fraternities,* 20th edition. Indianapolis, IN: Baird's Manual Foundation, Inc.

ASSOCIATION OF COLLEGE HONOR SOCIETIES. 2001. *ACHS Handbook 1998–2001.* East Lansing, MI: Association of College Honor Societies.

WARREN, JOHN W., and DOROTHY I. MITSTIFER. 2000. "Prelude to the New Millennium: Promoting Honor for Seventy-five Years." Speech given at ACHS 75th Anniversary Celebration. East Lansing, MI: Association of College Honor Societies.

INTERNET RESOURCE

ASSOCIATION OF COLLEGE HONOR SOCIETIES. 2002. <www.achsnatl.org>.

JOHN W. WARREN

BETA PHI MU

Beta Phi Mu is an international honor society that recognizes academic excellence and distinguished achievement in the field of library studies and information science. The society also sponsors and supports professional and scholarly projects, research, and publications related to librarianship, information science, and library studies.

Program

Every year Beta Phi Mu awards several grants, scholarships, and fellowships to students of library and information science. The Sarah Rebecca Reed Scholarship of $1,500 and the Blanche E. Woolls Scholarship of $1,000 are awarded to students who are just beginning graduate studies in information science.

The $1,000 Harold Lancour Scholarship for Foreign Study is awarded to a professional librarian or library student who wishes to study a foreign library or program, attend a foreign library school, or do research on library science in a foreign country. The $750 Frank B. Sessa Scholarship for Continuing Professional Education is given to a member of Beta Phi Mu who wants to augment his or her professional skills through additional study. The $1,500 Beta Phi Mu Doctoral Dissertation Scholarship and the $3,000 Eugene Garfield Doctoral Dissertation Fellowship are awarded to doctoral students in library and information science who are working on their dissertations. The Society usually awards several dissertation fellowships each year. Individual Beta Phi Mu chapters may also award scholarship, grants, and awards to their own members.

In 1998, in recognition of the society's fiftieth anniversary, Beta Phi Mu inaugurated an annual Distinguished Lecture Series. Each year an outstanding professional member of Beta Phi Mu is invited to present a lecture on a topic of interest to members of the library and information science field. The lecture is usually given during the annual national conference of the American Library Association.

Beta Phi Mu publishes a semiannual national newsletter, which is sent to all members. Some chapters also publish their own newsletters. In 1990, the society began publishing a series of monographs about the history of libraries and library science in America. Profits from monograph sales fund the Beta Phi Mu Distinguished Lecture Series. From 1952 to 1989 the society also published a series of chapbooks intended to provide exemplary examples of graphic artistry, typography, and book binding.

Organization

Beta Phi Mu is governed by an executive board consisting of a president, vice president, immediate past president, two directors-at-large, and six directors. Board officers are elected annually by mail ballot. Directors are selected by an assembly of representatives from each chapter. The executive board meets twice a year, usually in conjunction with the American Library Association's midwinter meeting and annual conference. An appointed executive director and treasurer carry out the administrative duties of the society. The president and board appoint members to both ad hoc and standing committees.

Membership. There are three categories of Beta Phi Mu membership: membership-at-large, membership with chapter affiliation, and honorary membership. Membership requirements include a scholastic average no lower than 3.75 and completion of all requirements leading to a master's degree from a library and information sciences school accredited by the American Library Association. Candidates for membership must also be recommended by the faculty of the school attended. Graduates from schools outside the United States and Canada may be accepted for membership upon the approval of the society's executive board.

The membership initiation fee is the primary source of funding for Beta Phi Mu activities. Members do not pay annual dues to the national society, but individual chapters may levy dues. Revenue is also derived from private donations, from the sale of the society's monograph series, and from the sale of society pins and other products.

History

Beta Phi Mu was founded in 1948 at an informal gathering of librarians and library school faculty at the University of Illinois. Twelve students from the University of Illinois Library School were invited to consider founding an honor society, with the faculty serving as sponsors. These students became the charter members of Beta Phi Mu, with Rolland Steven serving as the first Beta Phi Mu president and Harold Lancour as the first executive secretary. The founders chose the motto *Aliis inserviendo consumer* (Latin for "consumed in the service of others") as the Beta Phi Mu motto to express the professional librarian's ethic of dedicated service. The following year, thirty-four members of the graduating class of the University of Illinois Library School were initiated into the society. In 1969 Beta Phi Mu became a member of American Association of College Honor Societies. Beta Phi Mu became an affiliate of the American Library Association in 1997. By 2001 Beta Phi Mu had forty-three active chapters in the United States and Canada.

INTERNET RESOURCE

Beta Phi Mu: The International Library and Information Studies Honor Society. 2002. <www.beta-phi-mu.org>.

Judith J. Culligan

DELTA KAPPA GAMMA SOCIETY

The Delta Kappa Gamma Society is an international professional organization for women in education and closely allied fields. The largest organized group of women educators in the world, the society's purpose is to improve opportunities, to develop leadership qualities, and to advance the status of women educators employed at every level of education.

Program

The society annually awards more than twenty scholarships for advanced graduate study, numerous grants-in-aid to undergraduate women students interested in entering the teaching profession, and fellowships to women educators from other countries to pursue graduate study at universities in the United States or Canada. Each year the society sponsors several educational tours abroad. Delta Kappa Gamma also makes a biennial monetary award to the woman author whose educational publication is selected by a committee as the most significant contribution to education during the two-year period. Through conventions, conferences, committee meetings, and seminars, the society provides an outlet for the creativity of women educators and for the exchange of ideas of leaders in all fields of education.

Other Delta Kappa Gamma programs include the Golden Gift Fund, which provides travel grants and special stipends for education research and helps fund seminars and workshops; the Eunah Temple Holden Leadership Fund, which promotes leadership development projects; and the International Speakers Fund, which helps pay travel expenses for speakers invited to give addresses at Delta Kappa Gamma meetings and conferences.

One of the society's most important programs is the Educational Foundation, which encourages standards of excellence in education. It assists and cooperates with schools, colleges, universities, organizations, trusts, funds, or foundations to support, encourage, and improve education. The foundation has made grants to researchers and authors in the field of education, has supplemented the society's scholarship and world fellowship program, and has sponsored numerous study seminars. Delta Kappa Gamma has had continuing interest in fostering international understanding and providing educational services to underdeveloped areas or countries. Educational Foundation ambassadors have visited numerous countries, including Nicaragua, Costa

Rica, Ecuador, Peru, Chile, and Uruguay. Foundation ambassadors recommend and help implement teacher education programs in these countries, recruiting staff and planning courses and facilities.

The society publishes and distributes *The Delta Kappa Gamma Bulletin,* a quarterly professional journal containing articles of general educational interest, and *The Delta Kappa Gamma News,* published eight times a year. Numerous other intrasociety publications facilitate the work of committees and aid the implementation of special projects. Pamphlets and reports of general interest are available to nonmembers.

Organization

The Delta Kappa Gamma Society is made up of approximately 3,100 chapters in seventy-five state organizations in fourteen countries. The activities of the society are carried on by twenty standing committees and additional special committees working for teacher welfare, school support, graduate-study scholarships for women, educational research, development of leadership skills, service to children and youth, fellowship with women educators throughout the world, and recognition of women who have given distinctive service. Individuals hold membership in a chapter. Each state has a state organization of chapters within the state. The four regional units are composed of state organizations. The international society comprises the individual chapters and the state and regional units. Chapters meet six to eight times each year. State units usually meet annually, regions meet biennially, and the international society meets biennially.

Membership

Individuals make up the membership of the chapters and include rural and urban teachers who work at the kindergarten, elementary, high school, and college level. School librarians, administrators, and supervisors are also accepted as members. The requirements for membership include a minimum of five years of successful experience in educational work. Membership is by invitation; individuals are recommended by colleagues and are voted on by the chapters. Honorary membership on the chapter, state, and international levels is extended to women who are not professional educators but who have made significant contributions to education. In 2001 the society had more than 150,000 members.

History

The Delta Kappa Gamma Society was founded in May 1929 by Professor Annie Webb Blanton and eleven other women educators at the Faculty Women's Club of the University of Texas in Austin. Within its first year, the society was granted a charter and seventeen more chapters were formed. The international Delta Kappa Gamma office is located in Austin, Texas.

BIBLIOGRAPHY

HOLDEN, EUNAH TEMPLE. 1970. *Our Heritage in the Delta Kappa Gamma Society* (1960). Austin, TX: Delta Kappa Gamma Society.

CAROLYN GUSS
Revised by
JUDITH J. CULLIGAN

DELTA SIGMA RHO–TAU KAPPA ALPHA

Delta Sigma Rho–Tau Kappa Alpha is a collegiate honor society devoted to the promotion of public speaking (forensics). It is a member of the Association of College Honor Societies (ACHS), and it seeks to reward excellence and to foster respect for freedom of speech.

Program

The society maintains high standards for membership and for the establishment and conduct of its campus chapters. Faculty affiliated with the society are expected to supervise extracurricular debates and other public speaking activities in addition to teaching speech-related courses. In addition the society sponsors a variety of regional and national competitions in debate, prepared speech, and extemporaneous speech, and student members are expected to participate. The society publishes a journal, *Speaker and Gavel,* and has produced a textbook for use in public speaking courses: *Argumentation and Debate: Principles and Practices.* Written by David Potter under the auspices of Tau Kappa Alpha in 1954, it was revised and reissued in 1963.

The society seeks to attract promising candidates for membership well before they enter college. To this end the society provides a trophy to the winner of the annual National Forensics League tournament for high-school public speakers. It also awards a Student Speaker of the Year trophy to a college chapter member who is chosen for the honor by the vote of the entire national membership. Another Speaker of the Year trophy is awarded to a nonmember who, in the view of the society, epitomizes effective, intelligent, and responsible public speaking. Past honorees include LeRoy Collins, Reverend Billy Graham, J. William Fulbright, and Edward W. Brooks.

Organization and Funding

In 2002 the society had 195 active chapters serving 58,150 members. Campus chapters are organized into ten regions. Each region is administered by a governor chosen by active members of the regional chapters. A national council sets overall society policy, but local chapters enjoy a degree of autonomy in planning activities. The council officers are recruited from active or retired college speech faculty members. Society expenses are offset by an initiation fee charged to each new member and by subscriptions to the society journal. In addition fund-raising activities are held by campus chapters.

Membership

Eligibility for membership is based on active participation in college-level forensics or original speaking. A prospective member must demonstrate skill in these areas but must also show that he or she has the capability of achieving general academic excellence. Thus the student must have completed three semesters or five quarter terms of college-level study and must have attained a high level of scholastic achievement, demonstrated by a combination of high grade point average and class rank. Membership is for life, contingent on payment of annual dues. New members must pay an initiation fee, which entitles them to a two-year subscription to *Speaker and Gavel* along with the insignia of the society.

History

Delta Sigma Rho was founded in Chicago, Illinois, on April 13, 1906, by speech faculty from eight Midwestern colleges. Two years later, on May 13, 1908, Tau Kappa Alpha was founded by a similarly interested faculty at Butler University in Indianapolis, Indiana. Tau Kappa Alpha became a recognized member of the ACHS in 1937, and steadily gained chapters over the next two decades, achieving a total of ninety chapters by the fiftieth anniversary of its founding. Delta Sigma Rho, which had extremely rigid standards for prospective chapters, grew less quickly and was admitted to the ACHS in 1955. A year later it had eighty active campus chapters.

The two separate societies merged in Denver, Colorado, in 1963. The archives of both are maintained at Butler University, along with a research library for the use of scholars of American forensics. The society's official contact is through the Communications Department of the University of Alabama, Tuscaloosa.

HEROLD T. ROSS
Revised by
NANCY E. GRATTON

KAPPA DELTA PI

Kappa Delta Pi, an international honor society in education, was founded on March 8, 1911, at the University of Illinois. Selection as a member of Kappa Delta Pi is based on high academic achievement, a commitment to education as a career, and a professional attitude that assures steady growth in the profession. Kappa Delta Pi is an honor society of, about, and for educators. The society has 60,000 active members (as of 2001) that include outstanding leaders in the KDP Laureate Chapter, National and State Teacher of the Year winners, American Teacher Award winners, National Teacher Hall of Fame members, and Chicago Golden Apple Teachers. Membership in Kappa Delta Pi signifies more than a well-deserved line on a résumé: Members have the responsibility as a recognized honor student and honored educator to maintain the high ideals of the society and to extend the society's influence. Attending chapter meetings, performing service projects, serving as an officer, and modeling the behaviors and attitudes appropriate to the honor bestowed upon members are ways to contribute to the profession. Kappa Delta Pi supports member development through a multitude of member services. Because teaching is a lifelong process and a worthy profession and career, members are urged to renew their membership annually. The society's goal is to provide resources and services at each phase of members' careers.

The society as a whole prospers, and its influence is felt, to the degree that individuals in the chapters develop both personally and professionally. Membership in Kappa Delta Pi involves both privileges and responsibilities. Persons elected to membership remain members for life; however, active membership is maintained through the payment of annual dues. An active member is invited to attend the meetings of the chapter into which he or she was initiated and the meeting of any other chapter of Kappa Delta Pi. Attendance at conferences and the biennial Convocation is also open to active members. Each member's name is recorded permanently at society headquarters, located in Indianapolis, Indiana, with the name of the initiating chapter. However, any member may become affiliated with any other chapter of the Society and, upon payment of local dues, enjoy all the rights and privileges of membership in that chapter.

Mission

Kappa Delta Pi is dedicated to scholarship and excellence in education. The Society is a community of scholars dedicated to the following ideals:

- Scholarship and excellence in education
- Development and dissemination of worthy educational ideals and practices
- Continuous professional growth and leadership of its diverse membership
- Inquiry and reflection on significant educational issues
- A high degree of professional fellowship

Membership Opportunities

The Kappa Delta Pi Educational Foundation and local chapters award more than $80,000 in scholarship monies to members each year. Kappa Delta Pi sponsors—with the Association of Teacher Educators—the National Student Teacher/Intern of the Year Award Program. It also sponsors—with the American Education Research Association—the Outstanding Young Researcher Award. In addition, the society presents awards to counselors and chapters for outstanding achievements.

Publications. The *Kappa Delta Pi Record* is a quarterly journal for all members. It features articles with practical strategies for learning and teaching. The *New Teacher Advocate* is a quarterly newsletter, judged best among U.S. association newsletters by the American Educational Press Association. It features topics and practical strategies important to preservice and beginning teachers. *The Educational Forum* is an award-winning quarterly scholarly journal containing critical analyses of issues and practices that are of great importance to the improvement of education and educators.

Conferences. The Kappa Delta Pi Convocation is a biennial conference at which Society business is conducted and professional development workshops are presented. Regional Leadership Forums are daylong training conferences for members to learn leadership and chapter-management skills.

In addition, worldwide study tours and teacher exchanges are offered each summer. Members may access up-to-date information on society activities, job postings, and information on current issues in education at the society's website.

INTERNET RESOURCE

KAPPA DELTA PI. 2002. <www.kdp.org>.

MICHAEL P. WOLFE

KAPPA OMICRON NU

The Kappa Omicron Nu Honor Society is dedicated to empowering leaders through scholarship, research, and leadership development and to preparing scholars and researchers to be leaders in society. Kappa Omicron Nu aims to bring leadership to a sizable scholarly community in the human sciences and to emphasize the responsibility of scholars to the family and consumer sciences/human sciences professions and society. By enriching the intellectual environment through its local and national initiatives, Kappa Omicron Nu has provided leadership for collaboration among various organizations within the human sciences in leadership development, in strategic thinking about the future of the field in higher education, and in undergraduate research.

History

Kappa Omicron Nu was established on February 21, 1990, by the consolidation of Kappa Omicron Phi and Omicron Nu. Following a successful three-year collaboration as an Administrative Merger, Kappa Omicron Nu was structured to realize the synergistic benefits of the two organizations. Kappa Omicron Nu is headquartered in East Lansing, Michigan, close to the Michigan State University campus, which was the founding institution of Omicron Nu.

Omicron Nu was founded in 1912 at Michigan Agricultural College (now Michigan State University). Faculty members were familiar with other honor societies, so Dean Maude Gilchrist and the faculty decided to recognize home economics scholarship.

Promoting scholarship, research, and leadership motivated the expansion of Omicron Nu to campuses across the country.

Kappa Omicron Phi was formed in 1922 at Northwest Missouri State Teacher College, Maryville (now Northwest Missouri State University), with an emphasis on intellectual and scholastic excellence as well as personal development, including intellectual, spiritual, ethical, and aesthetic qualities.

Governance

Kappa Omicron Nu has adopted a governance model, by which the board of directors achieves its directives and avoids unacceptable circumstances and actions by stating what it will not accept. Policy categories include: (1) ends, (2) executive limitations, (3) board process, and (4) board-staff linkage. The effects of the model are clarity of values, a focus on results rather than administrative process, empowerment of executive authority, and an enhanced board-member relationship.

The Kappa Omicron Nu board includes the chair, chair-elect, vice chair for programs, vice chair for finance, secretary, and three student board members. The executive director is a nonvoting member of the board. The board is elected by active members, and the Biennial Conclave Assembly of Delegates sets authority for organizational affairs.

Membership

To be considered for membership, undergraduate students must have completed forty-five semester hours (or the equivalent), have a minimum grade point average of 3.0, and rank in the top 25 percent of their class. Graduate students shall have completed twelve semester hours of graduate work (or the equivalent) and have a minimum grade point average of 3.5. Professionals not previously initiated into the honor society and those with degrees outside the profession are also eligible.

Major Activities

Kappa Omicron Nu awards scholar program grants of between $150 and $500 to each chapter once each biennium. In total, fellowships and grants in excess of $30,000 are awarded each biennium. Chapter programming focuses on a national program theme and scholarly priorities, including undergraduate writing, ethics, mentoring, cultural diversity, leadership, and undergraduate research. The society's website is designed to support the development of a learning community. The Leadership Academy sponsors innovative programs and leadership development, including online courses. In collaboration with the Undergraduate Research Community for the Human Sciences, Kappa Omicron Nu sponsors an annual undergraduate research conference.

The society publishes *Kappa Omicron Nu FORUM*, a refereed, thematic scholarly journal, and *Kappa Omicron Nu Dialogue*, a substantive newsletter containing issue discussion, program themes, announcements, and awards. *FORUM* has featured a series titled "Legacies for the Future," which tells the stories of leaders who helped to develop the field of human sciences. Other stories have focused on the concepts of community, collaboration, empowerment, and leadership. *FORUM* is also available online, and an online newsletter, *Kappa Omicron Nu Spotlight*, serves as the annual report of Kappa Omicron Nu activities.

INTERNET RESOURCE

KAPPA OMICRON NU. 2002. <www.kon.org>.

DOROTHY I. MITSTIFER

LAMBDA IOTA TAU

An international honor society, Lambda Iota Tau recognizes and promotes excellence in the study of literature in all languages.

Lambda Iota Tau was founded at Michigan State University on December 3, 1953, and was incorporated in 1954 by representatives of chapters at Aquinas College, Baldwin-Wallace College, Eastern Michigan University, Marygrove College, Mercy College of Detroit, Purdue University, Sioux Falls College, and the University of Detroit. In 2001 the society had forty-seven active chapters with a total membership of approximately 40,000. The international office is located at Ball State University in Muncie, Indiana.

The society is a nonprofit organization. Elected officers of Lambda Iota Tau are the international executive secretary, the international assistant executive secretary, the treasurer, and the international board of chapter advisers. The international executive secretary conducts the affairs of the society, arranges for and presides over all international meetings, and consults with the international board in all actions affecting the society as a whole. The treasurer receives all dues and pays all financial obligations of the society. The international board of chapter advisers consists of five chapter advisers from five geographical areas. The board elects its own president, determines and initiates new policies within the constitutional limitations of the society, ratifies the appointments of the secretaries and treasurer, nominates candidates for all elective offices, corresponds with the chapters in their geographical areas, and determines the international dues.

Members are students majoring or minoring in literature, including literature written in foreign languages, who are in the upper 35 percent of their class in cumulative grade point average, have attained at least a full B average in at least twelve semester credit hours or eighteen term hours of literature and all prerequisites thereto, are enrolled in at least their fifth college semester or seventh college term, and have presented an initiation paper. The initiation paper is presented in such a manner as the local chapter requires, is of a quality certified by the chapter adviser, and is on a literary topic (research or critical) or of a creative nature (short story, essay, poem, drama). Graduate students must have completed one semester term with an A- average.

Members are initiated into local chapters established and maintained only at colleges or universities that grant the baccalaureate or higher degrees and that are accredited by the appropriate regional agency and certain appropriate professional accrediting agencies. The local chapters are approved by the administrations of their institutions. Lambda Iota Tau is a member of the Association of College Honor Societies and meets all of the high standards for member organizations.

Lambda Iota Tau publishes its annual journal *LIT,* which includes noteworthy poems, short stories, essays, and critical analyses written by its members. The best piece in each category of *LIT* is awarded a publication prize. The society also publishes a semiannual *Newsletter.* In addition, several scholarships are awarded to the membership each year.

Chapters are encouraged to hold regular meetings and to sponsor events and activities that will bring the study of literature to the attention of the campus at large. Chapters sponsor such projects as the appearance of outstanding speakers on their campuses, motion pictures based on works of litera-

ture, publications of student creative and critical writing, and library exhibits. They also hold book sales to foster more reading of literature. Some chapters volunteer for local Habitat for Humanity projects and various local literacy projects.

The international office has in the past sponsored lectures by famous individuals such as John Crowe Ransom, Robert Lowell, and Richard Eberhart. The society currently confers honorary memberships on individuals who have made worthy contributions to some area of literature, language, or linguistics, or who have demonstrated proficiency in teaching, scholarship, criticism, or creative writing. The society also bestows an honorary presidency on a literary figure who has achieved distinction in both critical and creative writing. Honorary presidents have included W. H. Auden, Archibald MacLeish, Daniel Hoffman, Robert Penn Warren, Richard Eberhart, Richard Marius, and Robert Pinsky.

BRUCE W. HOZESKI

PHI BETA KAPPA

Founded at the College of William and Mary in Williamsburg, Virginia, in 1776, Phi Beta Kappa is a college and university honor society established to recognize and promote intellectual scholarship and liberal arts education. Phi Beta Kappa is the oldest Greek-letter organization and national academic honor society. In addition to awarding membership to distinguished undergraduates, the Phi Beta Kappa Society also offers scholarships, awards, funding for visiting scholars, and high-school development programs.

Goals

For more than 200 years the Phi Beta Kappa Society has engaged its mission of promoting and recognizing excellence in the liberal arts and sciences. Phi Beta Kappa's purpose is to emphasize the importance of the literary and humane tradition by recognizing outstanding scholarship in those fields. At its inception, Phi Beta Kappa was distinguished by such characteristics as an oath of secrecy, a badge, mottoes in Latin and Greek, a code of laws, elaborate initiation rituals, a seal, and a special handshake. The society's distinctive emblem, a golden key, is widely recognized as a symbol of academic achievement. Though the original standards have been modified over time by such changes as omitting the secrecy clause and through the inclusion of women for membership, the focus on excellence in the liberal arts and scholarly achievement remain central tenets of Phi Beta Kappa's mission.

Programs and Activities

Programs are offered through the chapters and their community counterparts, the associations, both of which work in conjunction with the national office. The goal of the programs is to honor and champion liberal arts scholarship. Through its various programs and activities, Phi Beta Kappa provides support via scholarships and lectureships, book and essay awards, and funds for visiting scholars. More than one million dollars is raised and distributed each year to support these efforts and the students whom they benefit.

Scholarships are available from the national office, individual chapters, and associations. Individuals must apply for these scholarships and demonstrate merit for receipt of a scholarship. There is an application process, outlined by each respective organization, and committees that evaluate the applicants and confer the awards.

Sponsored by the Phi Beta Kappa Society, the Phi Beta Kappa book awards are granted annually to authors of exceptional scholarly books published in the United States in the fields of the humanities, the social sciences, the natural sciences, and mathematics. There are three book awards that each bestow a prize of $2,500 to recipients. The awards include the Christian Gauss Award in the field of literary scholarship or criticism; the Phi Beta Kappa Award in Science for contributions to the literature of science; and the Ralph Waldo Emerson Award for scholarship regarding the intellectual and cultural condition of humanity. In addition, the Phi Beta Kappa Poetry Award is presented annually for the best book of poems published in the United States within a given year. It carries a $10,000 one-time award.

The Visiting Scholar program affords chapters the opportunity to bring renowned scholars to their campuses to participate in lectures and seminars, meet with faculty and students, and address each institution's academic community over a two-day period. The objective of the program is to enhance the intellectual life of campuses by allowing an exchange among visiting scholars, faculty, and students. Twelve or more scholars participate each year.

To foster academic excellence and promote liberal learning at the secondary level, Phi Beta Kappa has built a partnership with the National Honor Society and the National Junior Honor Society. The partnership was initiated in 1994 and has as its central feature the participation of Phi Beta Kappa in the National Honor Society's annual meeting wherein the society provides the central academic program.

The society also circulates two main publications. *The American Scholar,* which has been in quarterly circulation since 1932, is a scholarly journal that provides articles and essays on various literary, artistic, and scientific subjects. *The Key Reporter* is distributed to all Phi Beta Kappa members and provides organizational information and news.

The Development of College and University Chapters

When Phi Beta Kappa was initially established, chapters were founded when a chartered Phi Beta Kappa organization on one campus granted a charter to another institution. This process details how the founding chapter at William and Mary awarded chapters to Yale, Harvard, and Dartmouth between 1776 and 1781. Then, in 1881, a national organization was created—the United Chapters of Phi Beta Kappa—to coordinate Phi Beta Kappa programs, activities, and membership. The United Chapters of Phi Beta Kappa evolved into what is known today as the Phi Beta Kappa Society.

The society's governing body, the Council, convenes every three years and brings together national representatives from every chapter and alumni association. This council sets general policies, elects officers and members to the twenty-four-member senate governing board, and decides on applications for new chapters. A Committee on Qualifications—a twelve-member elected body—receives all chapter applications, reviews them, and recommends to the Senate their opinions regarding applicants.

When a campus decides it would like to apply for membership, an informal group of faculty must organize to begin the process of applying for a charter. Since charters are granted to the Phi Beta Kappa members on the faculty rather than to an institution, adequate faculty representation is essential to the vitality and stability of organizing a new Phi Beta Kappa chapter. The appropriate faculty representatives communicate with Phi Beta Kappa headquarters to obtain an application and begin the documentation process. Because the Council only convenes every three years, timing is also critical. After submission of the application and the appropriate fee, the Committee on Qualifications considers applications and seeks reliable evidence that an applicant institution can meet the Phi Beta Kappa selection criteria.

Phi Beta Kappa sets very high standards not only for the students selected for membership but also for institutions desiring a campus Phi Beta Kappa chapter. Due to the vast differences among colleges and universities, no uniform, abstract standards exist for institutional membership and the awarding of Phi Beta Kappa chapters. Rather, institutions must provide valid evidence and submit to a rigorous assessment process based on individual campus distinctions. It is critical that institutions demonstrate their ability and willingness to uphold the Phi Beta Kappa ideals and standards in cultivating liberal learning. For example, the selection process gives careful consideration to the degree to which institutions possess standards that encourage excellence, a governance structure that fosters academic freedom and vitality, a scholarly faculty, a promising student body, sufficient resources (i.e., libraries and educational facilities), and adequate institutional income.

If institutions meet these standards and are deemed worthy candidates, a site visit is arranged. Phi Beta Kappa representatives conduct the site visits and reconvene to discuss their recommendations. These recommendations are forwarded to the Senate for discussion at the triennial Council meeting. A two-thirds vote by attending chapter and association delegations is required for approval of a new chapter. Upon approval, the charter for a new chapter is promptly granted and formal initiation procedures are arranged. In 2001 there were more than 250 chapters of Phi Beta Kappa in the United States.

BIBLIOGRAPHY

CURRENT, RICHARD N. 1990. *Phi Beta Kappa in American Life: The First Two Hundred Years.* New York: Oxford University Press.

VOORHEES, OSCAR M. 1945. *The History of Phi Beta Kappa.* New York: Crown.

INTERNET RESOURCE

PHI BETA KAPPA SOCIETY. 2002. <www.pbk.org>.

MEAGHAN E. MUNDY

PHI DELTA KAPPA INTERNATIONAL

Phi Delta Kappa International is a not-for-profit professional association of women and men in education. The purpose of the organization is to promote quality education—with particular emphasis on publicly supported and universally available education—as essential to the development and maintenance of a democratic way of life. This purpose is achieved through the genuine acceptance, continuing interpretation, and appropriate implementation of the ideals of leadership, service, and research.

History

Phi Delta Kappa was established in 1910 by representatives of three educational fraternities: Pi Kappa Mu at Indiana University (1906), Phi Delta Kappa of Columbia University (1908), and Nu Rho Beta at the University of Missouri (1909). Chapters were categorized as either *campus chapters* or *field chapters,* a practice that was abolished in 1973. The racial barrier for membership was stricken from the constitution of Phi Delta Kappa in 1938, but it was not until 1974 that the gender barrier was eliminated. The first international chapter was approved in 1955 at the University of Toronto, and in 1999 the constitution of Phi Delta Kappa was changed by chapter referendum to eliminate the use of the term *fraternity* and replace it with *association.*

Membership

Membership is open to professionals at all levels of education and to individuals in educationally related fields who have a baccalaureate degree and have academic standing sufficient for admission to graduate school. Student teachers are also eligible for membership. Membership is by election through the chapter structure; candidates for membership may be nominated by current members or through self-nomination. Membership is also available without affiliation with a Phi Delta Kappa chapter. Additionally, Phi Delta Kappa provides undergraduate student membership at half the amount of regular dues. Life, senior, and emeritus membership categories are also available.

Programs

Phi Delta Kappa International offers a variety of programs focused on members, local chapters of the association, the broader education profession, and local communities. Professional development activities are emphasized by the Center for Professional Development and Services (CPD&S), which offers seminars to school districts. CPD&S also houses the International Curriculum Management Audit Center. The Center for Evaluation, Development, and Research (CEDR) disseminates research information through publications and supports research activities through programs and services. The *Phi Delta Kappan*, the association's journal, is published ten times each year and confronts the most current issues facing K–12 schools and institutions of higher education.

Phi Delta Kappa International underwrites a number of scholarship programs for pre-service and in-service educators, as well as offering support to the Future Educators of America, which promotes teaching as a viable career option for young people. Through the International Travel Scholarship Program, Phi Delta Kappa also makes annual awards to members who wish to participate in educational travel tours sponsored by the association.

The association contributes to the national dialogue in the United States between the education community and U.S. citizens through its sponsorship of the Phi Delta Kappa/Gallup Poll of the Public's Attitudes Toward the Public Schools. The results of the poll are reported each September in the *Phi Delta Kappan*.

Organization and Governance

As of 2001, there were more than 600 Phi Delta Kappa chapters located in North America and approximately twenty others outside the United States and Canada. Chapters are grouped into areas, each under the direct administration of an elected area coordinator. Coordinators visit chapters, provide leadership training, and disseminate information about the international association. Areas are grouped into nine districts, each under the administration of an elected district representative who also serves on the international board of directors. The legislative council, meeting in odd-numbered years, sets association policy, elects international officers, and adopts the biennial budget. The international board of directors serves as the policymaking agent between meetings of the legislative council and employs the executive director who oversees a staff of approximately sixty persons. Financial support is derived through dues, the sale of publications, services, and grants.

INTERNET RESOURCE

PHI DELTA KAPPA. 2002. <www.pdkintl.org>.

GEORGE KERSEY JR.

PI KAPPA LAMBDA

Pi Kappa Lambda is a collegiate honor society dedicated "to the furtherance of music in education and education in music." Its goal is to honor outstanding academic and artistic achievement on the part of music majors working at the college or graduate-school level and to encourage students to continue to strive for excellence throughout their careers.

Program

The primary purpose of Pi Kappa Lambda is to recognize and encourage talented individuals working in the field of music by offering membership to qualified candidates. This honor is conferred by the election to membership itself, along with which the honoree is awarded an insignia of the organization (a symbolic key) and, on paying a nominal membership fee, is entitled to receive a copy of the society newsletter. In addition, the founding (Alpha) chapter at Northwestern University has underwritten several publications, most notably a series of monographs on American music. These monographs and similar studies have been published by Northwestern University Press.

Organization

Pi Kappa Lambda has enjoyed steady growth since its inception in 1916 and by 2002 enrolled 203 chapters, with 58,000 members, at colleges and universities throughout the United States and in Canada. A board of regents, elected from the official membership, oversees the business of the society during annual meetings. Every other year the society holds a national convention, to which local chapters may send delegates to express their concerns and interests. Every two years the regents commission a new composition.

Membership

Every year local chapters review the recommendations of their college's or university's school of music and choose from these candidates the students whose work, both artistic and academic, is judged to be outstanding. Students are eligible for consideration only if they meet certain stringent criteria:

They must be at an advanced stage in their studies—junior or senior undergraduates or graduate students. They must have elected music as their major course of study. In addition, they must have the support of their faculty, whose recommendations are carefully considered. Finally, they must meet or exceed certain academic standards. All candidates for membership must maintain a grade point average equivalent to the top 20 percent of the current graduating class, and juniors must be in the top 10 percent of their own class as well.

New members are required to pay a small fee, a portion of which covers the cost of their insignia and subscription to the society newsletter. The remainder of the fee goes to support the work of the national office. The society also earns revenues from its periodic publishing projects.

History

In 1916 several members of the alumni association of the School of Music at Northwestern University met to discuss ways in which they could help to encourage future students to strive for excellence in both their artistic and their academic lives. Of particular concern was the marriage of music and education, which these founding members felt was too often underappreciated. The group agreed to organize an honor society devoted to these issues. Among this group was Peter Christian Lutkin, whose enthusiasm for the project earned him the distinction of being the very first member of the newly organized honor society. Professor Lutkin contributed more than his enthusiasm, however. When deciding on the name for the new society, the founding group chose Professor Lutkin's initials (in their Greek form), thus, Pi Kappa Lambda.

The society, though still only local, grew quickly, and in 1918 it was officially granted a charter by the state of Illinois. Soon chapters were formed at other universities, and by the early 1970s it had grown to more than 13,000 members at seventy institutions of higher learning. The 1980s and 1990s were a time of dramatic growth, and during this period the society went international, with the first chapters forming in Canada.

The national office remains at Northwestern University where the first chapter was formed. Also at Northwestern are the society's archives, where the very first Pi Kappa Lambda key, issued to Professor Lutkin, is kept.

INTERNET RESOURCE

ASSOCIATION OF COLLEGE HONOR SOCIETIES. 2002. "Pi Kappa Lambda." <www.achsnatl.org/pkl.html>.

GEORGE HOWERTON
Revised by
NANCY E. GRATTON

PI SIGMA ALPHA

Pi Sigma Alpha is the national honor society in political science. Its purpose is to encourage, recognize, and reward academic and professional achievement in the study of politics and government. It pursues its objectives through awards, grants, scholarships, subsidies, meetings, and publications.

The honor society operates through a system of local chapters based in political science departments on the campuses of colleges and universities across the United States. Each chapter establishes and administers its own programs and activities to stimulate interest in politics and reward academic excellence. New chapters of the honor society are chartered by the national office. To qualify for a chapter, a political science department must meet a set of strict academic standards established by the rules of the honor society. These standards include official accreditation, autonomy over curriculum and faculty hiring, academic qualifications of faculty, number of majors, and size of the student body.

As a national honor society, Pi Sigma Alpha's primary responsibility is to oversee the annual induction into membership of students who have excelled both in their general academic course work and more specifically in their political science classes. Students are inducted into membership by local chapters based exclusively on academic performance. The national constitution establishes minimum academic standards for admission. These qualifications include a minimum grade point average, minimum number of semester hours completed in political science, and minimum class rank. Individual chapters may raise the eligibility standards, but they may not lower them. The honor society inducts approximately 6,000 new undergraduate and graduate student members each year. Since 1920 the society has inducted more than 160,000 members, and includes among its membership some of the nation's most distinguished and prominent politicians, civil servants, political consultants, journalists, and political scientists.

Pi Sigma Alpha promotes its objectives through a variety of programs. Some programs are directed toward student members and local chapters directly; others are directed more generally toward the broader community of political science scholars. Programs targeted directly at chapters and members include grants to local chapters to support noteworthy and worthwhile campus activities and programs, awards for best undergraduate student papers and theses and best graduate student papers, scholarships for first- and second-year graduate study in political science, awards for best chapters and chapter advisers, a biannual newsletter, and subsidies for student memberships in professional political science associations.

For the political science profession, the national society awards prizes for the best papers written and submitted by political scientists at national and regional political science association conventions; hosts lectures by prominent national politicians, policymakers, and journalists at national, regional, and state political science association conventions; and supports teaching awards for political scientists who distinguish themselves in the classroom.

Pi Sigma Alpha is governed by its biennial national convention. Each chapter may send one faculty delegate and one student to the convention. Representatives at the convention elect the officers and discuss and determine the policies of the society. Each chapter is entitled to one vote at the convention. Between conventions, the affairs of the society are directed by an executive council consisting of the president, president-elect, executive director, newsletter editor, the three most recent past presidents, and twelve council members elected by the membership. Council members serve four-year terms, with half of the council elected every two years.

The national office and the society's programs are funded by a national initiation fee paid by each new member inducted into the society. Individual chapters and their programs are supported by such additional local fees or dues as each chapter may determine.

Pi Sigma Alpha was founded in 1920 at the University of Texas. In 2001 there were more than 560 chapters of Pi Sigma Alpha throughout the United States. Pi Sigma Alpha has been a member of the Association of College Honor Societies since 1949.

INTERNET RESOURCE

THE NATIONAL POLITICAL SCIENCE HONOR SOCIETY. 2002. <www.pisigmaalpha.org>.

JAMES I. LENGLE

RHO CHI

Rho Chi is a collegiate and professional honor society devoted to the promotion of the pharmaceutical sciences. Induction into the society is a mark of recognized excellence in scholarship and professionalism. Goals of the society are to encourage teaching, scholastic achievement, and research and to encourage promising students to pursue graduate-level study in pharmaceutical studies.

Program

Like many other national honor societies, Rho Chi's primary mission is to recognize academic and professional excellence through induction into the society. Although membership brings the newcomer into association with others of professional caliber in the field of pharmacy, it is primarily the honor of recognition that membership endows on an initiate. However, the society is strongly committed to its mission of encouraging graduate-level study and to that end it cosponsors, with the American Association for Pharmaceutical Education, an annual first-year graduate fellowship to the most promising candidate embarking on a master's or doctoral program at an accredited institution.

In addition the society circulates an annual publication, *The Report*, which provides a forum for articles of professional, ethical, or educational importance written by its members. Each year the society honors the contributions of a distinguished member of the profession by presenting the Rho Chi Award, and it invites the recipient to deliver an address to the assembled members at a meeting held during the American Pharmaceutical Association's annual conference.

At the local chapter level, the most important event is the induction of new members into the society. The ritual for induction is prescribed by the national committee and is designed to be an occasion of dignified recognition of the inductees' proven excellence. Each initiate receives a copy of *The Rho Chi Society*, the official history of the organization; a copy of the *Constitution and Bylaws* of the society; and a key bearing the official insignia of the group.

At their graduation ceremony, following completion of their degree programs, they are entitled to wear the purple and white insignia of the society over their graduation gowns.

Membership

Undergraduate candidates for induction into the society must be enrolled in a program of pharmaceutical studies at an institution accredited by the American Council on Pharmaceutical Education (ACPE) and must have completed at least two years of the course work necessary for earning the degree. They must have demonstrated their commitment to scholastic excellence by earning a 3.0 grade point average (on a four-point scale) and ranking in the top twentieth percentile of their class. Finally, they must be certified as eligible by the dean of their degree program and must have no record of disciplinary problems.

Graduate students must meet similar standards of demonstrated excellence, but the grade point average is higher, at 3.5 on a four-point scale. Membership is also open to alumni of undergraduate or graduate programs, after they have entered the profession, and to faculty teaching pharmaceutical studies, if in the course of their professional work they have earned recognition by the society. Honorary memberships are also occasionally conferred.

New members pay an initiation fee that covers the cost of their key and insignia and entitles them to receive a copy of the annual publication. Annual dues are paid to the national board to support the society's activities.

Organization

Individual chapters must have a minimum of five members under the supervision of a faculty member appointed by the dean of the school of pharmacy at the institution. Local chapters are autonomous in planning activities and in electing their officers. The national organization is governed by an executive council, the members of which are elected for two-year terms. At the annual meeting each chapter is entitled to send one delegate and one alternate to represent the local organization.

History

The impetus for the formation of a national honor society in the field of pharmaceutical studies began at the University of Michigan, where the School of Pharmacy had established a local society in 1908. This group, known then as the Aristolochite Society, decided in 1917 to extend its message to other colleges and universities in the country and had succeeded in gaining the interest of pharmaceutical faculties at Oregon Agricultural College, which established a chapter in 1918. Also in 1917, the president of the national professional organization, the American Council of Pharmaceutical Faculties (ACPF, now the American Association of Colleges of Pharmacy) devoted a portion of his annual address to the membership to a call for the establishment of a national honor society, which would promote the council's principles and goals.

The ACPF found that the University of Michigan local organization shared its general philosophy and goals, and ACPE joined forces with them. By 1922 the Michigan organization had succeeded in founding a chapter at the University of Oklahoma and had changed its name to Rho Chi. In that same year it received a charter from the state of Michigan recognizing it as an official honor society.

The Rho Chi society grew slowly during the early years, with only ten chapters by 1932. By 1942, however, it had grown enough to earn recognition by and membership in the Association of College Honor Societies (ACHS), and as of 2002 it had seventy-seven chapters across the nation, serving 73,000 members.

INTERNET RESOURCE

RHO CHI. 2002. <www.rhochi.org>.

ROBERT A. BUERKI
Revised by
NANCY E. GRATTON

SIGMA XI

Sigma Xi, The Scientific Research Society was founded in 1886 at Cornell University in Ithaca, New York, as an honor society for science and engineering. It is an international, nonprofit membership society of more than 70,000 scientists and engineers elected because of their research achievements or potential.

Goals

Originally established to recognize the scholarly potential and accomplishments of young scientists and engineers, Sigma Xi also had the objective of bringing together scholars from a number of scientific disciplines so that they might communicate and collaborate. With these guiding principles, the main purpose of the Sigma Xi today is to honor scientific achievement and encourage research in science and technology through awareness, advocacy, and scholarly activities. Sigma Xi strives to promote an appreciation of the roles of science and research in society, and to foster worldwide interactions among science, technology, and society.

Programs and Activities

Sigma Xi sponsors numerous programs to support ethics and values in research; to improve science and education—and the public's understanding of science; and to promote the health of scientific research worldwide. Key programs include Distinguished Lectureships, the Forum Series of national and international conferences, and Grants-in-Aid of Research. The society also produces numerous publications.

The Distinguished Lectureship program provides an opportunity for society chapters to host visits from outstanding individuals who are at the leading edge of science. The lecturers are brought to campus to communicate their insights and excitement about science and technology to scholars, students, and to the community at large.

The Forum Series was initiated to provide national and international conferences on topics that concern the intersection of science and society. The conference and forum initiative was conceived at the society's centennial celebration in 1986 as part of its New Agenda for Science.

The Grants-in-Aid program awards stipends of $100 to $1,000 to support scientific investigation in any field. To be considered for a grant-in-aid, an individual must be an undergraduate or graduate student in a degree program. While membership in Sigma Xi is not a requirement for the program, the majority of the funds are designated for use by individuals whose primary advisers are Sigma Xi members or who are Sigma Xi student members themselves. Individuals are eligible to receive a total of two Grants-in-Aid from Sigma Xi headquarters in their lifetime. No citizenship restrictions apply, and international students and non-U.S. citizens are encouraged to apply. Upon the committee's receipt of an application for aid, notification occurs within twelve weeks of the application deadline.

American Scientist, a bimonthly magazine of science and technology, is the publication of Sigma Xi. Containing reviews of current research written by prominent scientists and engineers, it has been produced since 1913 and has received many awards for its exceptional quality.

Additionally, a number of new, smaller programs have also been developed to extend Sigma Xi's mission: The International Chapter Sponsorship Program promotes and assists the formation of new chapters worldwide; the Partnership Programs support joint initiatives sponsored by Sigma Xi and other organizations; and the Science, Math and Engineering Education Program that offers one-time grants of up to $1,000 to support science education projects. The basic policy is to provide seed money to initiate innovative programs, with special consideration given to those projects that are designed to stimulate young people's interest in science and mathematics.

The Development of College and University Chapters

Sigma Xi has more than 500 chapters at universities and colleges, government laboratories, and industry research centers worldwide. Having a chapter affords institutions the opportunity to honor individuals involved in science-related activities, supplies a vehicle for providing services (i.e. seminar series, awards, grants), and allows fellowship and interaction with colleagues across science, math, and engineering disciplines.

To receive approval for a chapter charter, Sigma Xi headquarters (in Research Triangle Park, North Carolina) must receive a letter of intent to petition for a charter that includes the signatures of at least eighteen active members in the area. With the letter and appropriate signatures, a description of the sponsoring institution is required, along with supporting recommendations from administrators, a proposed three-year schedule of activities, and member recruitment plans.

The review process is overseen by the Committee on Qualifications and Membership, and, upon their recommendation of approval of an application, the Sigma Xi Board of Directors gives final approval. For chapters to remain in good standing, regular communication with Sigma Xi headquarters is required, minimally providing officer names and an annual report each year. Representation at least once every three years at the Society's annual meeting is also mandatory. Activity within the chapter evidenced by new membership and programs is also critical to a chapter's good standing.

BIBLIOGRAPHY

WARD, HENRY BALDWIN, and ELLERY, EDWARD. 1936. *Sigma Xi: Half Century Record and History, 1886–1936.* Schenectady, NY: Union College.

INTERNET RESOURCE

SIGMA XI, THE SCIENTIFIC RESEARCH SOCIETY. 2002. <www.sigmaxi.org>.

MEAGHAN E. MUNDY

TAU BETA PI

Founded at Lehigh University in 1885 to recognize engineering students of distinguished scholarship and exemplary character, Tau Beta Pi is the only engineering honor society representing the entire engineering profession. The primary goals of Tau Beta Pi are to honor students and engineers who have demonstrated their abilities and shown an appreciation of high standards of character and ethics and to provide opportunities to students and engineers to further their scholarly activities and development in the field of engineering.

Programs and Activities

Tau Beta Pi offers a number of programs that assist the organization in carrying out its goals. These activities are implemented at both the local and national levels to generate interest and increase awareness among engineers, to recognize outstanding scholarship, and to emphasize civic responsibility. Key programs offered by Tau Beta Pi include the Engineering Futures program, the Fellowship Program, undergraduate scholarships, and chapter community service projects.

The Engineering Futures program teaches interpersonal skills to engineering students. This is accomplished by utilizing alumni who conduct on-campus training in people skills, team chartering, analytical problem solving, and group process. The Fellowship Program is Tau Beta Pi's single most important project for the advancement of engineering education and the profession. The purpose of the Fellowship Program is to finance a select group of

members chosen for merit and need, providing each of them a year of graduate studies at the college of his or her choice. Unlike many fellowships, a distinguishing feature of the Tau Beta Pi fellowship it that is it free of excessively binding restrictions. Tau Beta Pi fellows are free to do graduate work in any field that will enable them to contribute to the engineering profession. The only specific responsibility fellows must fulfill is to write a summary report at the completion of their fellowship year.

The Tau Beta Pi Association Scholarship Program was established in 1998 for undergraduates in their senior year of full-time engineering study. The amount of the scholarship awards is $2,000. Other gifts and endowments such as the Dodson Scholarship/Fellowship Fund, the Stabile Scholarship, and the Soderberg Awards, as well as gifts from such companies as Alabama Power Foundation and Merck and Co., also afford financial aid to undergraduate students. At the national level, Tau Beta Pi participates in the Society of Automotive Engineers scholarship program and the National Society of Professional Engineers educational program for first-year engineering students.

Another valuable service the Tau Beta Pi headquarters provides is employment resources for college students and alumni. Various jobs and internships in the engineering field are posted for Tau Beta Pi members through a contracted Internet server. Tau Beta Pi also offers a Recruiting Center at its Knoxville, Tennessee, headquarters, and many companies place recruitment advertisements in *The Bent,* the society's magazine. *The Bent* has been published since 1906 and is available quarterly with more than 94,000 copies circulated per issue. *The Bulletin of Tau Beta Pi,* published three times per year, disseminates news and information on the organization to collegiate chapters.

The Development of College and University Chapters

With approximately 429,000 total initiated members in Tau Beta Pi nationally, college chapters exist at more than 220 United States colleges and universities, and active alumnus chapters are available in sixteen regions across the nation. To establish a chapter at an institution of higher education, the recommended requirements are outlined in the Tau Beta Pi bylaws. These standards require that institutions have a specified number of engineering programs accredited by the Accreditation Board for

Engineering and Technology, at least forty engineering graduates per year, and a minimum of three faculty members who are also members of Tau Beta Pi.

To obtain a Tau Beta Pi chapter, an institution must first organize a local engineering honor society with members selected from the top fifth of the senior class or top eighth of the junior class. The chapter is open to all engineering students who fit these distinctions; technology students are ineligible. With the initial membership intact, this organization is expected to govern itself and elect members for two years in the exact ways a formal Tau Beta Pi chapter operates. After this two-year probationary period, a formal petition made to Tau Beta Pi headquarters can be accepted for consideration.

The formal petition and college catalogues are examined by the executive council of Tau Beta Pi, who, upon approval, direct a campus inspection visit. If the recommendations from the inspection group prove favorable, then the petitioners must prepare a formal request and send two representatives—a student and an adviser—to the next Tau Beta Pi National Convention. Based on convention approval, the new chapter would be formally instated and its first members initiated shortly thereafter. To ensure quality and commitment of new chapters, the lengthy process of developing a chapter typically takes about four years. Holding in high regard integrity and excellence in the field of engineering, Tau Beta Pi requires members, chapters, and alumni groups to meet the highest of standards of excellence in their roles as broadly based engineers in society.

INTERNET RESOURCE

Tau Beta Pi, The Engineering Honor Society. 2002. <www.tbp.org>

Meaghan E. Mundy

HONORS PROGRAMS IN HIGHER EDUCATION

Honors programs are housed in many different types of institutions of higher education. In general, honors education consists of "the total means by which a college or university seeks to meet the educational needs of its ablest and most highly motivated students" (Austin, p. 5). The goals of honors

programs usually include identifying and selecting highly able students; challenging those students academically and allowing them to exercise their potential; and, as the National Collegiate Honors Council website states, serving as a means by which to "raise the level of education . . . for all the students" by acting as an intellectual "laboratory." Institutional objectives for creating honors programs often include attracting and retaining students and faculty by displaying a "commitment to quality education," attracting funds, and "enhancing the public image of the institution as a place of superior scholarship" (Austin, p. 7). Not surprisingly, there are many different types of honors programs, often tailored to their specific types of institutions.

While Wesleyan University has had honors at graduation since 1873, and the University of Michigan (1873–1900), the University of Vermont (1888), Princeton (1905), Columbia (1920), and Harvard (1914) had some type of tutorial, exam, or thesis honors, fully developed honors education in America began in 1922 with the implementation of Frank Aydelotte's program at Swarthmore, which was modeled after the Oxford program of "pass/honors"—a system in which the only grades are pass, fail, or honors. In expectation of a student boom after World War II, Aydelotte felt that America's future depended on allowing gifted students to break out of the "academic lock step" through challenging courses of study that encouraged them to accept more freedom and responsibility and to develop their intellectual independence and initiative (Aydelotte, p. 15). Aydelotte's program allowed for greater student independence and specialization by replacing the traditional curriculum of the junior and senior years with unique "free-discussion" seminars with no attendance or hour requirements, culminating in a series of "less frequent, but more comprehensive" written and oral exams (Aydelotte, p. 37).

Subsequent to the success of the Swarthmore program, most universities developed honors programs—following either Swarthmore's plan of replacing the curriculum in its entirety, or using one of two other models: (1) honors work that replaced a specific number of courses, or (2) honors work as an extra activity beyond ordinary requirements for graduation. In 1928 Joseph W. Cohen, who developed an honors program for the University of Colorado, founded the Interuniversity Committee on Superior Students (ICSS). In 1966 the ICSS became the National Collegiate Honors Council (NCHC), which in the early twenty-first century has its own scholarly journal, numerous conventions, and publications, and also maintains a list of national and international honors programs, all available through their website.

At the beginning of the twenty-first century, there are almost as many different types of honors programs as there are institutions that create them. Still, as Clifford Adelman found in his 1985 study of postsecondary honors programs, there are "dominant models: the honors community, 'supply-side' honors, the 'exponential major' and general honors" (Adelman, p. 57). The *honors community* is a program that focuses on developing a "small select group of learners within an institution . . . tending to emphasize organization and support services over curriculum" (Adelman, p. 57). In *supply-side honors,* students are selected at different stages of their college careers and the emphasis lies on the programs—with variety viewed as the key to student demand and achievement. The *exponential major* is an honors version of a traditional major, and is usually open to students after their first year of college. It focuses on a coherent thematic or disciplinary program. The *general honors* model is an "interdisciplinary General Education program, confined to the first two years of college, and with a heavy emphasis on the traditional Liberal Arts" (Adelman, p. 57). In addition to these models, there are programs of independent study and mentor research participation, which involve close relationships with individual faculty members and often culminate in a senior honors thesis or creative project. Regardless of type, honors programs tend to emphasize selectivity and active student participation as customary characteristics, with many programs embracing the goal of producing "a knowledgeable and effective person" (Austin, p. 8).

While honors education has been plagued by accusations of elitism since its inception, this question became even more pressing with the spread of honors programs to community colleges in the early 1980s, particularly since community colleges have often been seen as serving diverse, and usually less-prepared, populations. Recent studies have found, however, that approximately 20 percent of community college students are "high-ability" students who are likely to benefit significantly from honors programs. In light of this, there has been growing recognition that honors programs play an important role in serving the diverse population of community colleges, which includes gifted students who are attending community college because of lower tuition, convenience, or for a variety of other reasons.

The goals of community college honors programs are very similar to those of four-year institutions. One role that honors programs serve in community colleges is facilitating students' transfer to first-rate baccalaureate programs, which helps to bolster the reputation of both community colleges and community college students. This is especially important in education systems such as the City University of New York (CUNY) that link community colleges and senior colleges.

Regardless of their design, most honors programs have at their core the goal of encouraging high levels of excellence in talented and motivated students. To support this goal, the NCHC urges all honors programs to have an articulated mission statement, to employ a director that reports to the chief academic officer of the institution, to occupy suitable quarters, to promote student liaisons with other committees, to offer special academic counseling, and to maintain continuous and critical program review.

See also: CAPSTONE COURSES IN HIGHER EDUCATION; COLLEGE SEMINARS FOR FIRST-YEAR STUDENTS; COMMUNITY COLLEGES; CURRICULUM, HIGHER EDUCATION, *subentry on* NATIONAL REPORTS ON THE UNDERGRADUATE CURRICULUM; GIFTED AND TALENTED, EDUCATION OF.

BIBLIOGRAPHY

ADELMAN, CLIFFORD. 1985. *Starting with Students: Promising Approaches in American Higher Education.* National Commission on Excellence in Education. National Institute of Education. Washington, DC: Government Printing Office.

AUSTIN, GREY C. 1986. "Orientation to Honors Education." In *Fostering Academic Excellence Through Honors Programs,* ed. Kenneth E. Eble. San Francisco: Jossey-Bass.

AYDELOTTE, FRANK. 1944. *Breaking the Lock Step: The Development of Honors Work in American Colleges and Universities.* New York: Harper.

BYRNE, JOSEPH P. 1988. *Honors Programs in Community Colleges: A Review of Recent Issues and Literature.* ERIC document ED417785.

INTERNET RESOURCE

NATIONAL COLLEGIATE HONORS COUNCIL. 1994. "Basic Characteristics of a Fully-Developed Honors Program." <www.runet.edu/~nchc/basic.htm>.

ANDREA S. POLSTER
JENNIFER GRANT HAWORTH
CLIFTON F. CONRAD

HOPKINS, L. THOMAS
(1889–1982)

Noted Progressive education theorist, consultant, and curriculum leader, L. Thomas Hopkins completed his major writings while a professor and laboratory school director at Teachers College, Columbia University.

Born in Truro, Massachusetts, Hopkins received his bachelor's and master's degrees from Tufts University in 1910 and 1911, respectively. Hopkins claimed that the central ideas of his philosophy of education derived principally from the influence of his mother, careful observation of nature, and interaction with students he taught.

In 1922 he completed the Ed.D. degree at Harvard University under the mentorship of professors Alexander Inglis and Walter Dearborn. Following his work at Harvard, Hopkins accepted an offer to become a tenured faculty member at the University of Colorado at Boulder. Through that post he began an extensive consulting career. One of his first major consultations was with the Denver Curriculum Revision Project, 1923 through 1925; its notoriety launched consultations with many other school districts across the country. His consulting and curriculum ideas are explicated in his *Curriculum Principles and Practices* (1929), which was built heuristically around a wide array of questions to guide curriculum leaders, school administrators, and teachers.

In 1929 Hopkins was invited to join the faculty of Teachers College, Columbia University, as professor of education; he remained there for twenty-five years. At Teachers College he also held the position of director of Lincoln School.

Following his retirement from Teachers College in 1954, Hopkins was a Fulbright scholar in Egypt (1956–1957). He surveyed Italian schools in 1957 and taught at Wheelock College in Boston and at the University of Maine in the 1960s. In 1960 he chaired the Committee on Schools and Moral Values for the White House Conference on Education. In 1971 he retired for a second time with his wife, Hester Hopkins, to Truro on Cape Cod. There, he continued to write, speak, complete his memoirs, and organize his papers until shortly before his death in 1982. His papers are located at the University of Colorado Library in Boulder, Colorado.

Hopkins's major ideas are outlined in three of his numerous books. In *Integration, Its Meaning and Application* (1937), he argued, contrary to many current interpretations of integrated curriculum, that integration is much more than merely combining subject matter areas around a common theme (i.e., the thematic unit). For Hopkins, integrating the curriculum meant integrating the person; thus, the organizing center for the integrated curriculum was not principally subject matter, but the individual. Drawing analogies from the study of physiology and embryology, Hopkins saw educative growth as moving through three phases: expansion, differentiation, and finally integration. He labeled these phases the normal learning process. In his view of integrated curriculum, subject matter and informal personal knowledge are to be acquired through inquiry that is expressly directed to build the self into a more diverse and integrated human being. An integrated person was, for Hopkins, one whose personal development incorporated the physical, social, mental, emotional, and spiritual aspects of the human organism into a functioning whole.

In *Interaction: The Democratic Process* (1941), Hopkins incorporated a social dynamic to expand the idea of the development of the individual or personal organism. Again, the process of the interacting forces of the normal learning process (expansion, differentiation, and integration) come into play in a social or political realm that argues for a democratic society as well as for the individual. Like John Dewey, Hopkins saw curriculum, writ large, as a dynamic interaction of school and society, experience and nature, and democracy and education. In the *Emerging Self in School and Home* (1954), Hopkins showed that education is not a function of schooling alone. In this book, he developed the image of an organic group, contrasting it with a mere aggregate group, to depict the integration of school, home, and community. Therein he argued that the needs and interests of the individual and those of the community and society are reciprocal. In fact, he argues for the home as a major site for education to take place, leading to speculation about the need to study other societal venues in which education takes place, which could include homes and families, nonschool organizations, mass media, peer groups, vocations and avocations, and more.

In the early twenty-first century, consistent interpretation of Hopkins's work can be seen in the writings of James A. Beane and in curriculum leadership. Hopkins condemned much that is fashionable in education (memorized knowledge, standardization, external control, extensive testing), calling it the "was curriculum" and characterizing it as useless. In contrast, he advocated the "is curriculum," which "celebrates the experiential . . . deals with the whole pupil who develops through internal control of the learnings that he or she self-selects . . . for personal growth." The is curriculum "is what each pupil can take from the teacher-pupil relationship to help him or her better understand and develop the self, for growth toward the highest possible maturity is the direction of all living organisms" (1970, p. 213).

See also: CURRICULUM, SCHOOL; ELEMENTARY EDUCATION, *subentry on* HISTORY OF; PROGRESSIVE EDUCATION.

BIBLIOGRAPHY

BEANE, JAMES. 1997. *Curriculum Integration: Designing a Core of Democratic Education.* New York: Teachers College Press, Columbia University.

HOPKINS, L. THOMAS. 1929. *Curriculum Principles and Practices.* New York: Sandborn.

HOPKINS, L. THOMAS, ed. 1937. *Integration, Its Meaning and Application.* New York: Appleton-Century.

HOPKINS, L. THOMAS. 1941. *Interaction: The Democratic Process.* Boston: Heath.

HOPKINS, L. THOMAS. 1970. *The Emerging Self in School and Home* (1954). Westport, CT: Greenwood.

SCHUBERT, WILLIAM H. 1995. "Toward Lives Worth Living and Sharing: Historical Perspective on Curriculum Coherence." In *Toward a Coherent Curriculum,* ed. James A. Beane. Alexandria, VA: Association for Supervision and Curriculum Development.

SCOTTEN, GREGORY. 1977. "A Study of the Formulation, Promulgation, and Defense of L. Thomas Hopkins's Position on the Curriculum." Ph.D. diss., State University of New York at Albany.

WOJCIK, JENNY T. 1992. *L. Thomas Hopkins (1889–1982): Profiles in Childhood Education.* Wheaton, MD: Association for Childhood Education International.

WILLIAM H. SCHUBERT
JENNY T. WOJCIK

HORTON, MYLES (1905–1990)

Activist and founder of the Highlander Folk School, Myles Falls Horton was born in a log cabin near Savannah, Tennessee, on July 9, 1905. His parents, Elsie Falls Horton and Perry Horton, had both been school teachers before Horton's birth, but had lost their jobs when the requirements for teachers were increased to include one year of high school, which neither had. After that, his parents supported their family (Horton was firstborn, followed by brothers Delmas and Daniel, and sister Elsie Pearl) by working in factories, as sharecroppers, and taking other jobs when they could find them. In his autobiography, Horton wrote, "We didn't think of ourselves as working-class, or poor, we just thought of ourselves as being conventional people who didn't have any money" (1990a, p. 1).

The Horton family was socially active; his mother shared scarce family resources with and organized classes for less well-off and often illiterate neighbors, and his father was a member of the Worker's Alliance, the union of the Worker's Progress Administration (WPA). "From my mother and father," Horton wrote, "I learned the idea of service and the value of education. They taught me by their actions that you are supposed to serve your fellow men, you're supposed to do something worthwhile with your life, and education is meant to help you do something for others" (1990a, p. 2).

Horton left home at fifteen to attend high school—his hometown had no secondary school—and he supported himself there by working first in a saw mill and then a box factory, where he said he learned about organizing and the strength of collective action. "When I heard people insulted by the factory owners, it hurt me personally," he wrote in his autobiography. "I guess I got as much help from the opposition in firming up my beliefs as I did from more positive sources" (1990a, p. 8). Later, with co-workers at a crate-building job, he formed a union that held a successful work slowdown for a wage increase.

Horton read widely, and was deeply influenced by the writings of social critics and Marxists. He felt he could learn from many sources, but that in the end he was responsible to himself and his own ideals. "I have to be the final arbiter of my beliefs and my actions," he said, "and I can't fall back and justify it by saying, I'm a Marxist, I'm a Christian, I'm a technological expert, I'm an educator" (1990a, p. 45). He worked with a wide range of people who shared a broad vision of a better world, but he remained a stubborn individualist who never joined a party. "I understood the need for organizations, but I was always afraid of what they did to people" (1990a, p. 49).

He attended Cumberland University, the University of Chicago, and the Union Theological Seminary, and sought out teachers who in many cases became lifelong supporters and friends; among these were Reinhold Neibuhr, John Dewey, Jane Addams, and George Counts. As a student in Chicago he heard about the Danish Folk School movement, a populist education experiment that had developed in opposition to the lifelessness of traditional schools and the detachment of academic schooling in Denmark. Danish Folk Schools encouraged students to broaden their experience by analyzing important questions and problems, and then actively participating in practical solutions. Horton resolved to go and see these schools himself.

In Denmark, Horton focused on a specific project: creating a school for life—a place where students and teachers could live together to pose and solve problems; an informal setting where experience could be the main teacher; a site for activists, organizers, and teachers for social justice. In his diary, Horton wrote, "The school will be for young men and women of the mountains and workers from the factories. Negroes would be among the students who will live in close personal contact with teachers. Out of their experiential learning through living, working, and studying together could come an understanding of how to take their place intelligently in the changing world" (1990a, p. 54). He worried that preparation to build his school might take forever, and although he felt inadequate to the task; he decided that the only way he could learn to embody his vision was to simply begin his project.

Horton opened the school, the Southern Mountains School, in 1932. A short time later, he and codirector Don West changed the name to the Highlander Folk School. At Highlander the purpose of education was to make people more powerful, and more capable in their work and their lives. Horton had what he called a "two-eye" approach to teaching: with one eye he tried to look at people as they were, while with the other he looked at what they might become. "My job as a gardener or educator is to know that the potential is there and that it will unfold. People have a potential for growth; it's inside, it's in the seed" (1990a, p. 33).

The school was a free space in an oppressive atmosphere—a place where labor organizers, civil rights activists, antipoverty workers, and others assembled to develop solutions. Through the 1930s Highlander was the education arm of the Congress of Industrial Organizations (CIO) in the South. Horton realized that labor would never be emancipated as long as racial segregation—turning workers against each other based on race privilege— remained intact, and he began organizing workshops designed to destroy racist social structures.

For many years Highlander was the only place in the South where white and African-American citizens lived and worked together, something that was illegal in that strictly segregated society. Highlander, Horton once claimed, held the record for sustained civil disobedience, breaking the Tennessee Jim Crow laws every day for over forty years, until the segregation laws were finally repealed.

The list of students at Highlander is a roll call of social activists: Rosa Parks, Eleanor Roosevelt, Pete Seeger, Woody Guthrie, Martin Luther King Jr., Andrew Young, Fanny Lou Hamer. People from the surrounding community used the school as well; all gathered there to give voice to the obstacles to their hopes and dreams, gather the conceptual, human, and material resources needed to continue, and to return home with a plan for forward progress. The school was under constant attack from white supremacists, antilabor groups, and the government.

Myles Horton died on January 19, 1990; his school, now known as the Highlander Research and Education Center, continues to be a catalyst for social change in the early twenty-first century.

See also: COMMUNITY-BASED ORGANIZATIONS, AGENCIES, AND GROUPS.

BIBLIOGRAPHY

BLEDSOE, THOMAS. 1969. *Or We'll All Hang Separately: The Highlander Idea.* Boston: Beacon Press.

GLEN, JOHN. 1988. *Highlander: No Ordinary School 1932–1962.* Lexington: University Press of Kentucky.

HORTON, AIMEE. 1989. *The Highlander Folk School: A History of Its Major Programs.* Brooklyn, NY: Carlson.

HORTON, MYLES. 1990a. *The Long Haul: An Autobiography,* with Judith Kohl and Herbert Kohl. New York: Doubleday Press.

HORTON, MYLES. 1990b. *We Make the Road by Walking: Conversations on Education and Social Change,* ed. Brenda Bell, John Gaventa, and John Peters. Philadelphia: Temple University Press.

BILL AYERS
THERESE QUINN

HUMAN SUBJECTS, PROTECTION OF

In 1974, after a long history of harmful research studies conducted on unwilling human subjects (such as the Tuskegee Syphilis Study initiated in the 1930s and a series of studies conducted in the 1960s at the Willowbrook State School, a New York institution for "mentally defective" children), the U.S. Congress established the National Commission for the Protection of Human Subjects of Biomedical and Behavioral Research. Four years later, this commission issued the *Belmont Report,* which is the cornerstone of the ethical principals guiding federal regulations for the protection of human subjects.

There are three fundamental ethical principles, as outlined in the *Belmont Report,* that guide research involving human subjects: (1) respect for persons, (2) beneficence, and (3) justice. By 1991, seventeen federal departments and agencies had adopted the federal regulations known as the *Common Rule* (Title 45 Code of Federal Regulations Part 46 [43CFR46]).

Research is defined as a systematic investigation (including development, testing, and evaluation of programs and methods) designed to discover or contribute to a body of generalizable knowledge. Not all scientific or scholarly activities qualify as research, nor does all research involve human participants. A *human subject* is a living individual about whom an investigator obtains either (1) data through interaction or intervention with the person, or (2) identifiable private information. Each investigator must decide if their study is to include human participants. If human participants are to be involved, the researcher is ethically obligated to become familiar with and adhere to the regulations governing the rights and safety of the human research participants.

Vulnerable Populations

Certain groups of human research participants—such as children, prisoners, individuals with questionable capacity to consent, students, or employees of the institution conducting the research—are considered to be either relatively or absolutely incapable of protecting their own interests. Because children have not legally attained an age where they can consent on their own to research or treatment, a parent or legal guardian may provide consent for a child to participate in a study. Above the age of seven, the child must also show willingness to participate by assenting to the study. Although many college students are below the age of twenty-one, they are generally treated as "emancipated adults" for the purpose of consenting to participate in research studies.

Institutional Review Boards

The National Research Act passed by Congress in 1974 that resulted in the Belmont Report also required the establishment of Institutional Review Boards (IRBs) to review all research involving human subjects funded by the Department of Health and Human Services. The regulations governing IRBs were revised in 1981.

Every institution in the United States receiving federal support for research with human subjects has to have its own IRB or access to an IRB. An IRB protects the rights, safety, and welfare of human research participants by: (1) reviewing research plans to ensure that, in its judgement, the research meets the criteria found in 45CFR46.111; (2) confirming that the research plans do not expose participants to unreasonable risks; (3) conducting continuing review of approved research at intervals commensurate with the degree of risk of the trial—but not less than once a year—to assure that human participant protections remain in force; and (4) assessing suspected or alleged protocol violations, complaints raised by research participants, or violations of institutional policies.

The IRB has the authority to approve, disapprove, or terminate all research activities that fall within its jurisdiction; require modifications in protocols, including previously approved research; require that information, in addition to that specifically mentioned in 45CFR46.116, be given to participants when the IRB deems that this information would add to the protection of their rights and welfare; and require documentation of informed consent or allow waiver of documentation, in accordance with 45CFR46.117.

IRBs must have at least five members with varied backgrounds who have no vested interest in the conduct or outcomes of the proposed research. At least one member of the IRB must not be affiliated with the institution, and the membership should be as diverse as possible. Most IRBs have many more than five members, and most are divided into subcommittees for the purpose of handling different types of studies, such as biomedical or behavioral studies.

In order to approve a research study, the IRB must assure that risks to participants are reasonable and minimized; that the selection of participants is equitable; that informed consent from each participant is sought and documented; and, when appropriate, that there are adequate provisions to protect the safety and privacy of the participants and the confidentiality of the data. Depending on the level of risk and the type of subject population, review may be done by the full IRB, or it may be expedited. Certain types of studies are exempted from IRB review and approval. Even in these exempt cases (many of which involve educational practices or tests), however, it is not the researcher but the IRB that makes this determination.

Informed Consent

Informed consent, as a legal, regulatory, and ethical concept, has become widely accepted as an integral part of research involving human subjects. A written consent document is a key part of the proposal submitted to an IRB. This is a document written to the proposed subject in a language understandable by the subject. All of the elements required by 45CFR46.116 must be included, plus any other information necessary for the prospective participant to make an informed decision. The required elements include a statement that the study involves research; an explanation of the purpose of the research, including why the individual was selected and the expected duration of the individual's participation; a description of all procedures to be followed; a description of any foreseeable risks, discomforts, and inconveniences (and what will be done to minimize or deal with them); a description of any anticipated benefits, both to the individual subject and to society; information about who to contact if there are additional questions; a statement that participation in the research is voluntary, that withdrawal may occur at any time, and that there is no penalty for withdrawal or refusal to participate; and, finally, an invitation for the participant to ask any questions about the proposed study before agreeing to participate.

In 2001 the National Cancer Institute of the National Institutes of Health introduced an online training program to educate research teams about human participant protections. This free access program available via the Internet elaborates greatly on all of the information contained in this article.

See also: ETHICS, *subentry on* HIGHER EDUCATION; FEDERAL FUNDING FOR ACADEMIC RESEARCH; RESEARCH METHODS.

BIBLIOGRAPHY

DEPARTMENT OF HEALTH AND HUMAN SERVICES. 1991. *Code of Federal Regulations: Title 45, Public Welfare; Part 46, Protection of Human Subjects.* Washington, DC: Department of Health and Human Services.

NATIONAL COMMISSION FOR THE PROTECTION OF HUMAN SUBJECTS OF BIOMEDICAL AND BEHAVIORAL RESEARCH. 1978. *Belmont Report: Ethical Principals and Guidelines for Research Involving Human Subjects.* Washington, DC: U.S. Government Printing Office.

ROTHMAN, D. J. 1982. "Were Tuskeegee and Willowbrook Studies in Nature?" Hastings Center Report 12(2):5–7.

NATIONAL INSTITUTES OF HEALTH. 2001. "Human Protection for Research Teams." <http://cme.nci.nih.gov>.

KENNETH A. WALLSTON

HUNTER, MADELINE CHEEK (1916–1994)

Madeline Cheek Hunter, professor of educational administration and teacher education, was the creator of the Instructional Theory Into Practice (ITIP) teaching model, an inservice/staff development program widely used during the 1970s and 1980s.

Hunter entered the University of California, Los Angeles (UCLA), at the age of sixteen and, over the course of her career, earned four degrees in psychology and education. In the early 1960s Hunter became principal of the University Elementary School, the laboratory school at UCLA, where she worked under John Goodlad. She left the school in 1982 amidst controversy over her methods, but continued at UCLA as a professor in administration and teacher education. She also continued to lecture and write, and by the time of her death at the age of seventy-eight, Hunter had written twelve books and over three hundred articles, and produced seventeen videotape collections.

Hunter's influence on American education came at a time when public schools were criticized widely for falling test scores, increasing dropout rates, and discipline problems. Hunter claimed that her teaching methods would transform classrooms into learning environments, allow the dissemination of more knowledge at a faster rate, and use positive reinforcement and discipline with dignity to greatly reduce disruptive behavior. Her seven-step model and related educational theories, outlined in her extensive writings, lectures, and videotape series, gave teachers strategies for controlling their classrooms and planning their lessons. Administrators used the model as a way to assess the effectiveness of their teachers.

Hunter defined teaching as a series of decisions that take place in three realms: content, learning behaviors of students, and teacher behaviors. Content refers to the specific information, skill, or process that is appropriate for students at a particular time.

Content decisions are based upon students' prior knowledge and how it relates to future instruction; simple understandings must precede more complex understandings. Decisions regarding learning behaviors indicate how a student will learn and show evidence of that learning. Because there is no best way for all students to learn, a variety of learning behaviors is usually more effective than one. Evidence of learning must be perceivable by the teacher to ensure that learning has occurred. The third area of decision-making, teacher behavior, refers to the use of principles of learning—validated by research—that enhance student achievement.

In order to successfully implement Hunter's methods, teachers undergo extensive professional development that conveys the types of decisions they must make. Training includes viewing videotapes that demonstrate effective decision-making in the classroom, and the Teaching Appraisal for Instructional Improvement Instrument (TAIII), administered by a trained observer or coach, which diagnoses and prescribes teacher behaviors to increase the likelihood of student learning.

Hunter's method of direct instruction, generally referred to as the *Madeline Hunter Method,* includes seven elements: objectives; standards; anticipatory set; teaching; guided practice; closure; and independent practice. Behavioral objectives are formulated before the lesson and clearly indicate what the student should be able to do when the lesson is accomplished. Standards of performance inform the student about the forthcoming instruction, what the student is expected to do, what procedures will be followed, and what knowledge or skills will be demonstrated. The anticipatory set is the hook that captures the student's attention. Teaching includes the acts of input, modeling, and checking for understanding. Input involves providing basic information in an organized way and in a variety of formats, including lecture, videos, or pictures. Modeling is used to exemplify critical attributes of the topic of study, and various techniques are used to determine if students understand the material before proceeding. The teacher then assists students through each step of the material with guided practice and gives appropriate feedback. Closure reviews and organizes the critical aspects of the lesson to help students incorporate information into their knowledge base. Independent practice, accomplished at various intervals, helps students retain information after initial instruction.

Although the Hunter Method was widely used during the last quarter of the twentieth century, it has not been without its critics. Based on behavioral psychological theory, some educators concluded that it is mechanistic and simplistic and is only useful—if at all—to teach the acquisition of information or basic skill mastery at the cost of stifling teacher and student creativity and independent thinking. Others deplore the use of the Hunter Method as a lockstep approach to instructional design. The *Hunterization* of teaching has even led some districts to require teachers to utilize the Hunter approach and base their teacher evaluation instruments on it. Hunter herself lamented this misuse of her methods and claimed that there was no such thing as a "Madeline Hunter-type" lesson. A significant body of criticism questions her claims that her method could enable students to learn more at a faster rate and improve student achievement. Several studies, most notably the Napa County, California, study, indicate little, if any, evidence to justify her claims.

Proponents point to Hunter's clear and systematic approach to mastery teaching. They argue that, rather than being prescriptive, Hunter provides a framework within which teachers can make decisions that are applicable to their own classrooms. Rather than being simplistic or superficial, Hunter's method is straightforward and uses a common language that classroom teachers can easily understand. Although Hunter's method may be easy to implement, it may also be complex in its application, depending upon the specific objectives of the teacher.

During the height of her popularity, Hunter's ITIP Model for mastery teaching was formally adopted in sixteen states and widely used by many others. Hunter is regarded by many as a "teacher's teacher" for her ability to translate educational and psychological theory into practical, easy-to-understand pedagogy, and her influence on classroom teaching techniques is still evident in the twenty-first century.

See also: TEACHER EDUCATION.

BIBLIOGRAPHY

GIBBONEY, RICHARD A. 1987. "A Critique of Madeline Hunter's Teaching Model from Dewey's Perspective." *Educational Leadership* 44(5):46–50.

HUNTER, MADELINE. 1967. *Teach More—Faster!* El Segundo, CA: TIP Publications.

HUNTER, MADELINE. 1979. "Teaching Is Decision Making." *Educational Leadership* 37(1):62–65.

HUNTER, MADELINE. 1982. *Mastery Teaching.* El Segundo, CA: TIP Publications.

ROBBINS, PAM, and WOLFE, PAT. 1987. "Reflections on a Hunter-Based Staff Development Project." *Educational Leadership* 44(5):56–61.

SLAVIN, ROBERT E. 1987. "The Hunterization of America's Schools." *Instructor* 96(8):56–60.

MARILYN HEATH

HUTCHINS, ROBERT (1899–1977)

A major voice for general education in American higher education, Robert Maynard Hutchins wrote, spoke about, and influenced public policy during his almost fifty years as teacher, educator, and administrator. Known in the educational world for his enthusiasm and dedication to liberal education with an emphasis on the Great Books and great ideas, he was also, during various times in his career, an ardent defender of academic freedom in the university and of democratic freedoms and principles in American society. He was known, too, for his style, wit, and sense of humor as he argued for what were often both iconoclastic and unpopular points of view.

Hutchins, born in Brooklyn, New York, moved at age eight to Oberlin, Ohio, where his father, a minister, taught at Oberlin College, an institution Hutchins attended from 1915 to 1917. He served in the ambulance service during World War I prior to attending and graduating from Yale University (1921) and the Yale Law School (1925). He was named dean of the Yale Law School in 1927 where he presided until 1930, when he became the youngest president ever of a major university, the University of Chicago. Upon leaving the University of Chicago in 1951, he spent four years with the Ford Foundation (1951–1954) and then the remainder of his career with the Ford Foundation-sponsored Fund for the Republic (1954–1977) and the Center for the Study of Democratic Institutions (1959–1973, 1975–1977).

While president of the University of Chicago (1930–1951), Hutchins was an eloquent spokesperson for a particular view of higher education. A liberal education was a moral endeavor to discover what was good and how to act on it. He believed that the university should nurture the life of the mind and be a community of scholars rather than an organization without a core, with specialization in the disciplines, and with increased vocationalism framing the curriculum. An expression of his approach was the Hutchins College of the University of Chicago, where young students who had not yet finished high school were admitted to study and acquired a liberal education and where, for example, successful completion of a degree was based on passing comprehensive examinations rather than accumulating course credits. The pedagogical model of choice was small discussion classes and the Socratic method, and the content for discussions included interacting with the Great Books.

Hutchins was a controversial administrator and no area of the university escaped his scrutiny. He continually engaged members of the University of Chicago faculty in attempts to make the university, from his point of view, more just and equitable. In the extracurricular arena, despite the fact that the University of Chicago dominated football in the Western Conference (later to become the Big Ten) and one of its players was the first Heisman trophy winner, Hutchins in 1939 convinced the university that it should drop intercollegiate football. He purportedly claimed, as the reason for dropping it, that it was possible to win 12 letters before learning to write one.

During his presidency at Chicago, Hutchins defended the university and its faculty in academic freedom issues. A staunch defender of free speech in both the academy and in a democratic society, his principled defenses prevailed. When the case of one faculty member accused of teaching communism was to be discussed by the board of trustees, a faculty colleague confronted Hutchins and said: "If the trustees fire [the faculty member], you will receive the resignations of 20 full professors tomorrow morning. Hutchins replied, "Oh, no, I won't. My successor will" (Mayer, p. xii).

During his tenure at the university Hutchins was involved in the publication of the *Great Books of the Western World* and the *Encyclopaedia Britannica*. These two enterprises both enhanced Chicago's reputation and brought additional monetary resources for use in the university. Despite his opposition to the pragmatists in the philosophy depart-

ment, Hutchins was a consummately successful fundraiser who had no difficulty spending money (he always exceeded the yearly university budget).

During World War II Hutchins committed the university to complete support of the war effort. The university was the site, or more precisely and perhaps ironically, a squash court under the football stands in Stagg Field was the site, of the first self-sustaining nuclear chain reaction. This theoretical advance, a part of the Manhattan project, led, of course, to the first atomic bomb and the beginning of the nuclear age. After the war Hutchins tried but failed to get nuclear physicists to not disseminate their knowledge and techniques and to discontinue such work.

Hutchins' strong beliefs in democratic values and his defense of fundamental freedoms continued during his tenure with Fund for the Republic, a Ford Foundation-sponsored organization. He led a number of projects that directly opposed the political machinations of the now infamous Joseph McCarthy, the House Un-American Activities Committee (HUAC) and other groups that perceived communist threats to the United States. Among the most devastating projects of the Fund for the Republic was one that produced a two-volume report of blacklisting in industry with an emphasis on television and the movies. Hutchins, however, did not emerge unscathed from this work and was attacked by the press and popular media for his views.

During its first few years the Fund for the Republic concentrated on projects that produced information and knowledge that could be widely disseminated. The major activity of the fund from the late 1950s until the mid-1970s, however, was support for the Center for the Study of Democratic Institutions. His last attempt to create a community of scholars, the Center in Santa Barbara, California, was a place for resident scholars and invited guests to discuss serious issues. Under Hutchins the Center hosted and supported numerous international conferences and a publishing enterprise that created an international presence for its deliberations.

See also: General Education in Higher Education; Liberal Arts Colleges; Philosophy of Education; University of Chicago.

BIBLIOGRAPHY

ASHMORE, HARRY S. 1989. *Unseasonable Truths: The Life of Robert Maynard Hutchins.* Boston: Little, Brown.

HUTCHINS, ROBERT MAYNARD. 1936. *The Higher Learning in America.* New Haven, CT: Yale University Press.

HUTCHINS, ROBERT MAYNARD. 1943. *Education for Freedom.* Baton Rouge: Louisiana State University.

HUTCHINS, ROBERT MAYNARD. 1968. *The Learning Society.* New York: Praeger.

MAYER, MILTON. 1993. *Robert Maynard Hutchins: A Memoir.* Berkeley: University of California Press.

EDWARD KIFER

ISBN 0-02-865597-4

90000

9 780028 655970